Lecture Notes of the Institute for Computer Sciences, Social Informatics and Telecommunications Engineering 411

More information about this series at https://link.springer.com/bookseries/8197

Mulatu Liyew Berihun (Ed.)

Advances of Science and Technology

9th EAI International Conference, ICAST 2021
Hybrid Event, Bahir Dar, Ethiopia, August 27–29, 2021
Proceedings, Part I

 Springer

Editor
Mulatu Liyew Berihun
Bahir Dar Institute of Technology, Faculty of Civil
and Water Resource Engineering
Bahir Dar University
Bahir Dar, Ethiopia

ISSN 1867-8211 ISSN 1867-822X (electronic)
Lecture Notes of the Institute for Computer Sciences, Social Informatics
and Telecommunications Engineering
ISBN 978-3-030-93708-9 ISBN 978-3-030-93709-6 (eBook)
https://doi.org/10.1007/978-3-030-93709-6

This Springer imprint is published by the registered company Springer Nature Switzerland AG
The registered company address is: Gewerbestrasse 11, 6330 Cham, Switzerland

Preface

We are delighted to introduce the proceedings of the ninth edition of the EAI International Conference on Advancements of Science and Technology (EAI ICAST 2021). EAI ICAST 2021 is an annual conference that takes place at Bahir Dar Institute of Technology, Bahir Dar University, Bahir Dar, Ethiopia. The conference covers topical science and technology issues and has brought together researchers, engineers, developers, practitioners, scholars, scientists, and academicians from around the world.

The technical program of EAI ICAST 2021 consisted of seven main tracks: Track 1, Chemical, Food and Bioprocess Engineering; Track 2, Electrical and Electronics Engineering; Track 3, ICT, Software and Hardware Engineering; Track 4, Civil, Water Resources, and Environmental Engineering; Track 5, Mechanical and Industrial Engineering; Track 6, Material Science and Engineering; and Track 7, Energy Science, Engineering and Policy. A total of 202 full papers were submitted, from which 102 papers were accepted in a peer reviewed process. Each paper was reviewed by on average three reviewers who are experts in the area. After a thorough evaluation process, the technical program consisted of 80 high quality full research papers in oral presentation sessions in the seven main conference tracks. The technical program of EAI ICAST 2021 also featured one invited talk, three keynote speeches, and seven session keynote speeches along with exhibitions and 12 poster presentations. The three keynote speakers were Timnit Gebru, the cofounder of Black in AI from the USA; Girma Gebresenbet from the Swedish University of Agricultural Science, Sweden; and Yilma Sileshi from the Addis Ababa Institute of Technology, Addis Ababa University, Ethiopia.

We sincerely appreciate the work of the Steering Committee chair and members, the Organizing Committee chair, Kibret Mekuanint, the Organizing Committee co-chairs, Mekuanint Agegnehu and Elias Wagari, and the Technical Program Committee (TPC) chair, Mulatu Liyew Berihun, for their constant support and guidance which ensured the success of the conference. It was also a great pleasure to work with such an excellent Organizing Committee team, we note that their hard work in organizing and supporting the conference. We are grateful to the Technical Program Committee led by our TPC chair, Aynadis Molla (Track 1), Hailu Desalegn (Track 2), Mekonnen Wagaw (Track 3), Mitiku Damtie (Track 4), Betsha Tizazu (Track 5), Misganaw Alemu (Track 6), and Muluken Temsgen (Track 7). They followed and completed the peer-review process for the technical papers and designed a high-quality technical program. We are also grateful to the conference manager, Viltare Platzner, for her support, and all the authors who submitted their papers to the EAI ICAST 2021 conference.

We strongly believe that the EAI ICAST 2021 conference provided a good forum for all scientific communities and a scientific body of knowledge we could use to discuss all science and technology aspects relevant to each track. We also expect that future EAI ICAST conferences will be as successful and stimulating, as indicated by the contributions presented in this volume.

Mulatu Liyew Berihun

Conference Organization

Steering Committee

Imrich Chlamtac   Bruno Kessler Professor, University of Trento, Italy

Seifu Admassu Tilahun   Bahir Dar Institute of Technology, Bahir Dar University, Ethiopia

Organizing Committee

General Chair

Kibret Mequanint   University of Western Ontario, Canada

General Co-chairs

Mekuanmt Agegnehu Bitew   Bahir Dar Institute of Technology, Bahir Dar University, Ethiopia

Elias Wagari Gabisa   Bahir Dar Institute of Technology, Bahir Dar University, Ethiopia

Solomon Workineh   Bahir Dar Institute of Technology, Bahir Dar University, Ethiopia

Technical Program Committee Chair

Mulatu Liyew Benhun   Bahir Dar Institute of Technology, Bahir Dar University, Ethiopia

Technical Program Committee

Aynaddis Molla   Bahir Dar Institute of Technology, Bahir Dar University, Ethiopia

Misganaw Alemu   Department of Materials Science and Engineering, Bahir Dar University, Ethiopia

Mitiku Damtie   Bahir Dar Institute of Technology, Bahir Dar University, Ethiopia

Betsha Tizazu   Bahir Dar Institute of Technology, Bahir Dar University, Ethiopia

Mokonnen Wagaw   Bahir Dar Institute of Technology, Bahir Dar University, Ethiopia

Muluken Temesgen   Bahir Dar Institute of Technology, Bahir Dar
                                    University, Ethiopia
Hailu Desalegn   Bahir Dar Institute of Technology, Bahir Dar
                                    University, Ethiopia

Sponsorship and Exhibits Chair

Bantelay Sintayehu   Bahir Dar Institute of Technology, Bahir Dar
                                    University, Ethiopia

Local Chair

Alganesh Ygzaw   Bahir Dar Institute of Technology, Bahir Dar
                                    University, Ethiopia

Workshops Chair

Bezawork Tilahun   Bahir Dar Institute of Technology, Bahir Dar
                                    University, Ethiopia

Publicity and Social Media Chair

Temesgen Getnet   Bahir Dar Institute of Technology, Bahir Dar
                                    University, Ethiopia
Bezawork Tilahun   Bahir Dar Institute of Technology, Bahir Dar
                                    University, Ethiopia

Publications Chair

Addisu Negash Ali   Bahir Dar Institute of Technology, Bahir Dar
                                    University, Ethiopia

Web Chair

Samuel Ashagirie   Bahir Dar Institute of Technology, Bahir Dar
                                    University, Ethiopia

Posters and PhD Track Chair

Fasikaw Atenaw   Bahir Dar Institute of Technology, Bahir Dar
                                    University, Ethiopia

Panels Chair

Dagnachew Aklog   Bahir Dar Institute of Technology, Bahir Dar
                                    University, Ethiopia

Demos Chair

Melkamu Binle   Bahir Dar Institute of Technology, Bahir Dar
                                 University, Ethiopia

Tutorials Chairs

Abreham Debasu   Bahir Dar Institute of Technology, Bahir Dar
                                 University, Ethiopia

Co-Technical Program Committee

Elefelious Getachew   School of Information Technology and Scientific
                                 Computing, Addis Ababa Institute of
                                 Technology, Ethiopia
Mesfin Abebe   School of Electrical Engineering & Computing,
                                 Adama Science and Technology,Ethiopia
Abdulkadir Aman   Addis Ababa Institute of Technology (AAiT),
                                 Addis Ababa University, Ethiopia
Sisay Addis   Debre Markos University, Ethiopia
Tadele Mamo   Mettu University, Ethiopia
Wuletawu Abera   International Center for Tropical Agriculture
                                 (CIAT), Zambia
Wubshet Mekonnen   Department of Chemistry, Wollo University,
                                 Ethiopia
Mulugeta Atlabachew   Jimma University, Ethiopia

Contents – Part I

Chemical, Food and Bioprocess Engineering

Synthesis, Optimization and Characterization of Pulp from Banana Pseudo
Stem for Paper Making via Soda Anthraquinone Pulping Process   3
  Tesfaye Kassaw Bedru and Beteley Tekola Meshesha

Effect of Toasting and Natural Fermentation on the Phytochemical
and Functional Properties of Oats Grown in Ethiopia   17
  Getaneh Firew Alemayehu, Sirawdink Fikreyesus Forsido,
  Yetenayet B. Tola, Minbale Adimas Teshager,
  Addisu Alemayehu Assegie, and Endale Amare

Correlation of UV Assisted Fenton Process and Fenton Process
for Removal of Reactive Red 2(RR2) Dye Color from Wastewater   33
  Gemechu Kassaye Abera, Fikiru Temesgen Hangarasa,
  and Nigus Gabbiye Habtu

Isolation and Characterization of Microcrystalline Cellulose
from Eragrostesis Teff Straw   44
  Ebise Getacho Bacha, Lema Deme Shumi,
  and Tsigab Tekleab Teklehaimanot

Process Revamping of H_2SO_4 Plant to Double Contact Double Absorption
(DCDA) Using ASPEN HYSYS to Reduce SO_2 Emission: Case of Awash
Melkassa Sulfuric Acid Factory   59
  Addis Lemessa, Melkamu Birlie, Metadel Kassahun, and Yared Mengistu

Effect of Blend Ratio on Physico-Mechanical Properties of Agro Stone
Composite Caulking Materials   73
  Tadelle Nigusu Mekonnen, Tewekel Mohammed Belay,
  Tinsae Tsega Beyene, Yenehun Gidyelem Andualem,
  Mulugeta Admasu Delele, Sissay Wondmagegn Molla,
  and Aregash Mamo Gizaw

Assessment of Nutrients and Heavy Metals in the Groundwater
and Surface Water in the Zeber Watershed: The Case of the Bahir - Dar
City Waste Disposal Site   87
  Dargie Haile and Nigus Gabbiye

Manufacturing of Tiles from Kieselguhr Sludge /Diatomaceous Earth/   106
  Dargie Haile

Electrical and Electronics Engineering

Optimal Transmit Antenna Selection for Massive MIMO Systems 117
Shenko Chura Aredo, Yalemzewd Negash, Yihenew Wondie,
Feyisa Debo, Rajaveerappa Devadas, and Abreham Fikadu

Design and Performance Analysis of Enhanced Directional MAC
Protocols for Cognitive Radio Wireless Mesh Networks 132
Mulugeta Atlabachew, Jordi Casademont, and Yalemzewd Negash

Performance Analysis of Hybrid Beamforming Techniques in Large MU
MIMO Systems 153
Fikreselam Gared Mengistu, Yosef Birhanu Malede,
and Amare Kassaw Yimer

Narrow-Linewidth Compound Ring Fiber Laser Using HBF as a Feedback
for Sensing and Communication Application 173
Hailu Dessalegn Ayalew

Design and Performance Analysis of 125 MW Floating Photovoltaic
Power Plant in Ethiopia: Metema vs Lake Tana 184
Tewodros G. Workineh, Biniyam Z. Taye, and Abraham H. Nebey

Efficiency Analysis of a Solar Photovoltaic DC and Existing AC
Distribution System for Bahirdar University Data Center 196
Tewodros G. Workineh, Tefera T. Yetayew, and Tesfaye B. Sisay

Design of Genetic Algorithm Based Robust LQG Controller for Active
Magnetic Bearing System 215
Enderias Alemayehu Workeye, Tamiru Getahun G/Meskel,
and Yakob Kiros T/Himanot

Pitch Angle Control for Optimal Power of Horizontal Axis Variable Speed
Wind Turbines Using Fuzzy Tuned PID Controller 237
Tamiru Getahun G/Meskel, Tefera Terefe Yetayew,
and Endrias Alemayehu Workeye

A Concise Evaluation of Auto-tuned PID and Fuzzy Logic Controllers
for Speed Control of a DC-Motor 256
Tefera T. Yetayew, Tamiru G. G/Meskel, and Dawit M. G/michael

Genetic Algorithm Tuned Super Twisted Sliding Mode Controller
(STSMC) for Self-balancing Control of a Two-Wheel Electric Scooter 269
Tefera T. Yetayew and Daniel G. Tesfaye

Artificial Neural Network Based Rotor Flux Estimation and Fuzzy-Logic
Sensorless Speed Control of an Induction Motor 288
    Tefera T. Yetayew and Rahel S. Sinta

Performance Analysis of Microstrip Antenna with Semi-eliptical Slotted
Patch and Defected Ground Structure at 28 GHz for 5G Communication
Systems 304
    Ayane Lebeta Goshu, Mulugeta Tegegn Gemeda, and Kinde Anlay Fante

Data-Driven Based Optimal Placement and Performance Evaluation
of FD-MIMO for Enhanced 4G Mobile Networks Under Realistic
Environment 318
    Seifu Girma Zeleke, Beneyam B. Haile, and Ephrem Teshale Bekele

Optimization of Dualband Microstrip mm-Wave Antenna with Improved
Directivity for Mobile Application Using Genetic Algorithm 331
    Arebu Dejen, Jeevani Jayasinghe, Murad Ridwan, and Jaume Anguera

ICT, Software and Hardware Engineering

N-Neuron Simulation Using Multiprocessor Cluster 343
    Derara Senay Shanka

A SVM Based Model for COVID Detection Using CXR Image 368
    *Sudhir Kumar Mohapatra, Beakal Gizachew Assefa,
    and Getamesay Belayneh*

Simultaneous Indoor Localization Based on Wi-Fi RSS Fingerprints 382
    Nooria Rafie and Bang Wang

Posture Prediction for Healthy Sitting Using a Smart Chair 401
    Tariku Adane Gelaw and Misgina Tsighe Hagos

Agricultural Domain-Specific Jargon Words Identification in Amharic Text 412
    Melaku Lake and Tesfa Tegegne

Design Event Extraction Model from Amharic Texts Using Deep Learning
Approach 424
    Amogne Andualem and Tesfa Tegegne

Identification of Nonfunctional Requirement Conflicts: Machine Learning
Approach 435
    Getasew Abeba and Esubalew Alemneh

A Survey of Stroke Image Analysis Techniques 446
Henok Yared Agizew and Asrat Mulatu Beyene

Amharic Fake News Detection on Social Media Using Feature Fusion 468
Menbere Hailu Worku and Michael Melese Woldeyohannis

Early Ginger Disease Detection Using Deep Learning Approach 480
Mesay Gemeda Yigezu, Michael Melese Woldeyohannis,
and Atnafu Lambebo Tonja

Towards Predicting the Risk of Cardiovascular Disease Using Machine
Learning Approach 489
Hanna Teshager Mekonnen and Michael Melese Woldeyohannis

Rainfall Prediction and Cropping Pattern Recommendation Using
Artificial Neural Network 500
Yohannes Biadgligne Ejigu and Haile Melkamu Nigatu

The Need for a Novel Approach to Design Derivation Lexicon for Semitic
Languages 517
Enchalew Y. Ayalew, Laure Vieu, and Million M. Beyene

A Branching Spatio-Spectral Dimensional Reduction Model
for Hyperspectral Image Classification and Change Detection 532
Menilk Sahlu Bayeh, Anteneh Tilaye Bogale, Yunkoo Chung,
Kirubel Abebe Senbeto, and Fetlewerk Kedir Abdu

Shared Syllables for Amharic Tigrigna Text to Speech Synthesis 550
Lemlem Hagos, Million Meshesha, Solomon Atnafu, and Solomon Teferra

OCR System for the Recognition of Ethiopic Real-Life Documents 559
Hagos Tesfahun Gebremichael, Tesfahunegn Minwuyelet Mengistu,
Million Mesheha Beyene, and Fikreselam Gared Mengistu

Efficient Architecture for a High Performance Authenticated Encryption
Algorithm on Reconfigurable Computing 575
Abiy Tadesse Abebe, Yalemzewd Negash Shiferaw,
and P. G. V. Suresh Kumar

Design and Development of an Autonomous Smart Stick Framework
for Assisting Visually Impaired People 586
Tesfahunegn Minwuyelet Mengistu, Ayalew Belay Habtie,
and Fikreselam Gared Mengistu

Multi-channel Convolutional Neural Network for Hate Speech Detection
in Social Media 603
    Zeleke Abebaw, Andreas Rauber, and Solomon Atnafu

Automatic Diagnosis of Breast Cancer from Histopathological Images
Using Deep Learning Technique 619
    Elbetel Taye Zewde and Gizeaddis Lamesgin Simegn

Author Index 635

Contents – Part II

Civil, Water Resources, and Environmental Engineering

Investigation of Properties of Concrete Containing Recycled Concrete
Coarse Aggregate and Waste Glass Powder 3
  Habtamu Melaku Dessie and Denamo Addissie Nuramo

Application of Potential Based Cohesive Model for Analysis of Concrete
Fracture 15
  Habtamu A. Tadesse, Temesgen Wondimu Aure,
  and Alemayehu Golla Gualu

Evaluations of Shallow Groundwater Recharges and Water Use Practices
at Robit Watershed 27
  Dagnew Y. Takele, Seifu A. Tilahun, Fasikaw A. Zimale, Petra Schmitter,
  Bayu G. Bihonegn, and Daniel G. Eshetie

Experimental Study of Recycled Aggregate Concrete Produced
from Recycled Fine Aggregate 49
  Wallelign Mulugeta Nebiyu, Denamo Addissie Nuramo,
  and Abel Fantahun Ketema

Prediction of Irrigation Water Supply Using Supervised Machine Learning
Models in Koga Irrigation Scheme, Ethiopia 68
  Menwagaw T. Damtie, Seifu A. Tilahun, Fasikaw A. Zimale,
  and Petra Schmitter

Numerical Investigation on the Effect of Reinforcement Shear Connectors
in Load Bearing Capacity of Partially Encased Composite Beams 82
  Tamirat Semu, Temesgen Wondimu, and Belay Worku

Lake Level Fluctuation Impact on River Morphology Change 99
  Sisay Mengistie Eshetie and Mengistie Abate Meshesha

Analyzing Seasonal Change of Water Quality Characteristics of Finote
Selam Town Drinking Water Sources, Amhara, Ethiopia 112
  Abayneh Agumass Amogne and Fasikaw Atanaw Zimale

Impact of Land Use Land Cover Dynamics on Stream Flow: A Case
of Borkena Watershed, Awash Basin, Ethiopia 128
  Metafet Asmare Abebe, Temesgen Enku, and Seid Endris Ahmed

Application of *in Situ* Thermal Imaging to Estimate Crop Water Stress
and Crop Water Requirements for Wheat in Koga Irrigation Scheme,
Ethiopia 144
  Tewodrose D. Meselaw, Fasikaw A. Zimale, Seifu A. Tilahun,
  and Petra Schmitter

Effect of Glass Fiber on Fracture Energy of Plain Concrete 160
  Samuel Demeke Shiferaw, Temesgen Wondimu Aure,
  and Alemayehu Golla Gualu

Assessment of Flood Hazard Areas Using Remote Sensing and Spatial
Information System in Bilate River Basin, Ethiopia 175
  Teshale Tadesse Danbara, Mulugeta Dadi Belete,
  and Ayele Getachew Tasew

Torsional Behavior of Steel Fiber Reinforced Concrete: A Review 195
  Esmael A. Asfaw, Temesgen W. Aure, and Alemayehu G. Gualu

Mechanical and Industrial Engineering

Performance Analysis of Cotton Seed Biodiesel in Diesel Vehicle
on Chassis Dynamometer 211
  Marta Zeleke and Ramesh Babu Nallamothu

Computational Fluid Dynamics Modeling of the Spray Process of Resin
Over a Laid Up Fiber Stack for the Purpose of Fiber Impregnation
and Composite Materials Manufacturing 226
  Amare Demelie Zegeye, Mulugeta Ademasu Delele,
  and Aart Willem Van Vuure

Performance Evaluation of Locally Fabricated Public Water Cooler 233
  Atrsaw Jejaw and Aschale Getnet

Recycled Polymer for FDM 3D Printing Filament Material: Circular
Economy for Sustainability of Additive Manufacturing 243
  Menberu Zeleke Shiferaw and Hailu Shimels Gebremedhen

Integrating Sustainability Measures and Practices in the Ethiopian
Industrial Parks: From Review to Conceptual Model 262
  Fitsum Getachew Bayu, Frank Ebinger, and Eshetie Berhan

Reducing Long-Run Average Planned Maintenance Cost Using Markov
Decision Modelling Based on Shifting Paradigm and Penalty Model 277
  Gedefaye Achamu Meretie, Eshetie Berhan Atanew,
  and Sisay Geremaw Gebeyehu

Development and Performance Testing of Rice Thresher for Fogera Hub
Farmers in Ethiopia 295
  Fetene Teshome Teferi, Eyob Messele Sefene,
  Sisay Geremew Gebeyehu, and Kishor Purushottam Kolhe

Metal Injection Molding (MIM) Process and Potential Remedies for Its
Defects: A Review 309
  Fetene Teshome Teferi and Assefa Asmare Tsegaw

The Advancement of Aluminum Metal Matrix Composite Reinforced
with Silicon Carbide Particles (Al-6061/SiC$_p$): A Review 326
  Fetene Teshome Teferi, Kishor Purushottam Kolhe,
  Assefa Asmare Tsegaw, Tafesse G. Borena, and Muralidhar Avvari

Material Science and Engineering

Modeling and Numerical Simulation of Ballistic Impact on Sandwich
Composite Materials 339
  Tibebu Merde Zelelew, Ermias Gebrekidan Koricho,
  and Addisu Negashe Ali

Investigate the Effects of Fiber Surface Chemical Treatment
on the Mechanical Properties of Bamboo Fiber Reinforced Polyester
Resin Composites 350
  Sewale Yasabu Enyew and Addisu Negash Ali

Investigation of Halide Ion Release Tunnels of Haloalcohol Dehalogenase
from Agrobacterium Radiobacter AD1; Computational Study 365
  Aweke Mulu Belachew and Tang Laxia

Effect of Annealing on the Photoluminescence Intensity of Gehlenite:Eu
Doped Phosphor Prepared in Different Gas Atmospheres 377
  Fetene Fufa Bakare, Abadi Hadush Tesfay, and Shao-Ju Shih

Energy Science, Engineering and Policy

Investigation of Solar Chimney Power Plant and Experimental Analysis
of Energy Yield from Small Size Draft Tube and Solar Collector 391
  Ashenafi Tesfaye Bicks, Solomon Tesfamariam Teferi,
  and Tewodros Walle Mekonnen

Design and Manufacturing of an Institutional Mirt Stove with Waste Heat
Recovery System 413
  Tesfaye Wondatir Mihretie and Nigusse Mulugeta

Experimental Investigation of Double Exposure Solar Cooker
with an Asymmetric Compound Parabolic Concentrator 425
  Lamesgin Addisu Getnet and Bimrew Tamrat Admassu

Exergy and Economic Analysis of Modified Mixed Mode Solar *Injera* Dryer ... 443
  Senay Teshome Sileshi, Abdulkadir Aman Hassen, and Kamil Dino Adem

Energy Management Control System for Hybrid Renewable Energy Power
Sources 464
  Sintayehu Alemnew Hailu, Getachew Biru Worku,
  and Minyamer Gelawe Wase

Comparison of Thermal and Emissions Performance on Three Stoves
for Distilling Areke, A Traditional Ethiopian Beverage 480
  Temesgen Assefa Minale and Kamil Dino Adem

Challenges and Prospects of Hydro-Pumps for Small Scale Irrigation 492
  Dessie Tarekegn Bantelay, Girma Gebresenbet,
  and Bimrew Tamerat Admassu

Numerical and Experimental Performance Investigation of Vertical-Axis
Hydrokinetic Turbine 506
  Muluken Temesgen Tigabu, D. H. Wood, and Bimrew Tamrat Admasu

Artificial Intelligence Based Security Constrained Economic Dispatch
of Ethiopian Renewable Energy Systems: A Comparative Study 522
  Shewit Tsegaye, Fekadu Shewarega, and Getachew Bekele

Facile Preparation and Electrochemical Investigations of Copper-Ion
Doped α-MnO_2 Nanoparticles 543
  Nigus Gabbiye Habtu, Ababay Ketema Worku, Delele Worku Ayele,
  Minbale Admas Teshager, and Zerihun Getahun Workineh

Performance and Stability of Halide Perovskite Solar Cells in Bahir Dar
Climatic Conditions 554
  Getnet M. Meheretu, Getasew A. Wubetu, Bart Roose, Amare Kassew,
  Hailu Shimels, Seifu A. Tilahun, Elizabeth M. Tennyson,
  and Samuel D. Stranks

Numerical Investigations of Variable Pitch Straight-Bladed H-Darrieus
VAWT 565
  Temesgen Abriham Miliket, Mesfin Belayneh Ageze,
  and Muluken Temesgen Tigabu

Author Index 585

Chemical, Food and Bioprocess Engineering

Synthesis, Optimization and Characterization of Pulp from Banana Pseudo Stem for Paper Making via Soda Anthraquinone Pulping Process

Tesfaye Kassaw Bedru[1(✉)] and Beteley Tekola Meshesha[2]

[1] Department of Chemical Engineering, Kombolcha Institute of Technology,
Wollo University, P.O. Box 208, Kombolcha, Ethiopia
tesfaye.kassaw@kiot.edu.et
[2] School of Chemical and Bio-Engineering, Addis Ababa Institute
of Technology, Addis Ababa University, P.O. Box 1176, Addis Ababa, Ethiopia
Beteley.tekola@aau.edu.et

Abstract. The need for pulp and paper currently in the whole world has become shooting up massively. The generation of the pulp, as well as paper from woody materials, has a challenge due to deforestation, huge chemical and energy consumptions. Now, another source for pulp and paper is lignocelluloses wastes materials, because of low cost, low energy, and chemical consumption. Among them, the pseudo stem was best for the input of pulp and paper production. This investigation was on the production and characterization of pulp from Banana Pseudo Stem for Paper Making via Soda Anthraquinone pulping process. The amount of cellulose (41.45%), ash (12.4%), hemicellulose (23.37%), extractive (12.72%), and lignin (10.46%) contents were obtained at the initial compositional evaluation of the pseudo stem. It has excellent fiber length (1.75 mm), fiber diameter (22.15 μm), an acceptable Runkle ratio (0.55), and flexibility coefficient (159.64). The effect of temperature (130, 140 and 150 °C), cooking time (45, 60, and 75 min), the concentration of soda (10, 12.5, and 15%), were examined. The maximum yield and kappa number of pulp was 36.7% and 22.8 respectively obtained at 10% of soda concentration, at 150 °C, and 63 min of cooking time from oven-dried raw material. The produced paper from the pseudo stem has a tensile index, tearing index, smoothness, and porosity were 78.75 Nm/g, 19.1 mN. m^2/g, 500–530 μm, and 50 s/100ml air respectively. This study indicates that high strength mechanical property and good surface properties paper can be produced from pseudo stem pulp with a more environmentally friendly pulping process.

Keywords: Banana pseudo stem · Fiber · Pulp · Paper · Temperature · Cooking time · Soda concentration

1 Introduction

The pulp and paper sector produces a great number of paper and other cellulose-based fiber products. The total quantities of cellulose products consumed every year worldwide exceed 400 million tons. Paper products are integrated into nearly every aspect of

M. L. Berihun (Ed.): ICAST 2021, LNICST 411, pp. 3–16, 2022.
https://doi.org/10.1007/978-3-030-93709-6_1

our daily lives. It is undeniably important to society [1]. In the pulp manufacturing sector, the scarcity of raw material is an issue in some regions in the world and is go with rising wood supply costs. Research on alternative fiber raw materials is well proceeding and new tree species annul plants and agricultural residual materials have been suggested for pulping and paper production [2]. Wood pays to about 90% of the conventional raw material used for pulp and paper production in the world. However, the reduction of forest resources to obtain wood had made an effect on the environment and humans. Several agricultural residues including rice husk, corn straw, wheat straw, corn stalk, plantain stalk, pineapple leaf, and corn husks which do not have abrupt beneficial applications in many communities have been suggested to prospective sources of pulp [3]. The production of the non-wood type of pulp has increased more rapidly than that of pulp from wood in the last two decades, by a factor of about two in Latin America and three in Africa and the Middle East [4]. Studies have shown that the production process of paper from non-wood fiber is significantly less expensive than wood fiber. Wood and non-wood resources are currently browbeaten for the manufacturing of pulp, paper, and soft boards [5]. Many non-wood fibers, such as bamboo, jute, straw, rice, and bagasse, are currently used in small commercial pulping operations. Other agricultural residues such as banana pseudo stem, wheat straw, cotton stalk pose a suitable characteristic for papermaking [6]. Ethiopia has an abundance of agro-waste material that has not been fully utilized to maximum production. Examples of such agro-waste materials are banana pseudo stem, coffee husk, wheat straw, rice straw, cotton stalks, corn stalks, etc. Among these agro-wastes, the banana pseudo stem holds a suitable characteristic for fiber sources suitable for textile, pulp and paper, packaging material, twines and ropes, and other industrial applications. Every year a massive amount of banana plant wastes remains leftover creating environmental pollution. For every 30–40 kg of banana sold in the market, 250 kg of waste is produced in the farm. The waste is then causing by the emission of toxic gases including CO_2 and also gives growth to the harmful fungi which attack remaining banana trees [7]. The banana plant is largely divided into three parts: pseudo stem, peduncle, and leaf. The pseudo stem possesses good physical strength properties. It consists of high cellulose, low lignin, and higher pentosane content together with gums and mucilage in the sheath of certain species of banana plant may be a suitable source for producing pulp and paper [8]. This study aimed to produce and characterization of pulp from the banana pseudo stem for paper making via the soda anthraquinone pulping process.

2   Materials and Methods

Materials: The banana (Musa Cavendish) pseudo stem was collected from Jimma agricultural site and the experiment was done in the school of Chemical and Bio-Engineering Laboratory, Addis Ababa University, Ethiopia. The 96% Sulfuric acid, 98% Toluene, 98% Ethanol, 96% Nitric acid, Safranin Solution, Sodium hydroxide, Anthraquinone, 42% Hydrogen peroxide and Potassium permanganate were used chemicals for experimental investigation.

Experimental Procedure: Fresh pseudo stem waste was obtained from Jimma agricultural site. The unwanted portions of the plant were discarded and only the needed portion; pseudo stem was used in the study. The sample was washed with water to remove all debris and unwanted particles. To measure fiber morphologic properties of the specimens, the pseudo stem was cut into the 0.5 mm thickness and 2 cm long in parallel to fiber [8]. To determine the chemical composition of the pseudo stem sample was first oven-dried and crushed to 60 meshes [9]. The ash content, moisture content, and extractive content was determined. For moisture content, the pseudo stem dried at 105 ± 3 °C for 24 h until getting a constant weight. After 24 h dried the yield was determined by using the TAPPI T 413 om-93 approach. The ash content of the pseudo stem sample was ignited at 525 °C for 4 h. After 4 h, the crucible was carefully withdrawn and cooled in a desiccator then weighed and the percentage was determined via TAPPI T 262 om-02. The content of extractive of the pseudo stem was done via Soxhlet extractor 200 mL of ethanol/toluene (1:2 (v/v)) used as a solvent for extraction for 8 h. After extraction, the sample was air-dried at 25 °C for few minutes and the percentage was determined via TAPPI T 204 cm-97. The content of cellulose was determined by using Kurschner–Hoffner approach and 5-g extractive free sample was cooking with 125 ml of alcoholic nitric acid solutions with a reflux during four cycles of 1 h. After each cycle, the alcoholic nitric acid solution is isolated and a fresh volume is added. The alcoholic nitric acid solution contained of mixing one volume of 65% (w/w) solution of nitric acid with four volumes of 96% purity ethanol [10]. At the termination of the four cycles, the cellulose was washed, dried, and weighed. The hemicellulose content was determined by taking 2 gr. of extracted dried biomass was transferred into a 250 mL Erlenmeyer flask. 150 mL of 500 mol/m^3 NaOH was added. The mixture was boiled for 3.5 h with distilled water [11]. The lignin content was determined by standard TAPPI procedure, 1.8 g of the dried extracted raw pseudo stem was weighted in glass test tubes and 18 mL of 72% H2SO4 was added. The sample was kept at 25 °C for 2 h with carefully shaking at 30 min intervals to allow for complete hydrolysis. After the first hydrolysis, 504 mL of distilled water was added. The next step of hydrolysis was made to occur in an autoclave for 1 h at 121 °C. The slurry was then cooled at 25 °C. Hydrolysates were filtered through a vacuum using a filtering crucible. The acid-insoluble lignin was determined by drying the residues at 105 °C. Then the pulping process was done using the autoclave. All the oven-dry pseudo stems were chipped into 2 cm × 1 cm size and pulped using the Soda anthraquinone (soda- AQ) method. The 40 g dried samples were cooked with 0.1% anthraquinone constantly and 10:1 liquor to sample ratio for each cycle. The concentration (10%, 12.5%, and 15%) and temperature values were 130 °C, 140 °C, and 150 °C and the time of cooking was 45 min, 60 min, and 75 min were evaluated. Next black liquor was removed after 20 min and wished with high distill water. The pulp yield and the residual lignin in the pulps were assessed by determining the kappa number.

Morphological property of banana pseudo stem: For fiber length and fiber diameter determination, the pseudo stem was macerated with 50% nitric acid. Match stick size samples were taken in test tubes, immersed completely in nitric acid solution, and kept in a water bath at 70 °C. The maceration process was taken for 5–6 h. to get many separated white-colored fibers. Then test tubes containing macerated fibers were removed from the water bath and allowed to cool at room temperature. After cooling, nitric acid was drained and macerated fibers were washed with distilled water and filtered using What Man Grade 1 filter paper for separation of fibers [12]. For slide, preparation fibers were stained with 20% safranin solution and again washed with distilled water for distaining of excess safranin and placed some amount of fiber suspension on a glass slide with the help of ink/medicine dropper and allowed for air drying and mounting by using Canada balsam [12]. Two slides were prepared per sample and images were taken with a total magnification of 40×s using a camera attached Motic BA210 compound stereo microscope. Finally, the length and width of 40 fibers were measured using Motic software.

Lumen diameter and cell wall thickness: The pseudo stem was soaked in warm water below 100 °C for one hour and sliced by 1520 µm using a Leica RM2255 automatic rotary sliding microtome. The first three slices were discarded to avoid cell deformation and the following slices were taken.

Then placed slice into safranin solution (1 gm of safranin adding to 100 ml of water) and immersed into 30%, 50%, 70%, 85%, and 97% alcohol and xylene for 1 min each respectively. In this process, safranin is used for staining, alcohol for dehydration of water, and xylene to enhance the contrast between cells. Finally, the specimen was put on a slide and one drop of Canada balsam was dropped and covered using cover slip and leaf the slide to dry. After making a permanent slide, good quality images were taken with a total magnification of 400×s by using a camera attached Motic BA210 compound stereo microscope.

FTIR Analysis: The Perkin-100 FTIR spectrometer mad of America was used for functional group assurance of the pseudo stem fiber proportionally using the technique of KBr pellet for recording the transmittances [13]. The pretreatment was carried out by tableting the mixture of each sample and KBr (where KBr has a proportion of 0.5 wt. %) into a film. The functional group peaks were noted from 4000 to 400 cm^{-1} with a resolution of 4 cm^{-1} in the spectrometer.

3 Results and Discussion

3.1 Proximate and Chemical Compositions Analysis

Table 1. Proximate and chemical compositions analysis

Raw Material	Cellulose [%]	Hemicellulose [%]	Lignin [%]	Extractive [%]	Moisture content [%]	Ash content [%]
Pseudo stem[a]	41.45	23.37	10.46	12.72	11.4	12.4
Wheat straw[b]	39.7	30.6	17.7	5.2	7.9	6.9
Bagasse[c]	55.75 ± 04	n.a	20.5 ± 1.7	3.25 ± 4.3	n.a	1.85 ± 3.7
Soft Wood[d]	40–45	25–35	25–35	n.a	n.a	n.a
Hard Wood[d]	40–55	24–40	18–25	n.a	n.a	n.a

[a][Current study], [b][14], [c][15], [d][16]

Based on Table 1 the cellulose amount of stem of pseudo banana (41.45%) is higher than that of straw of wheat (39.7%) and smaller than bagasse (54.3%). So, greater than 34% value of celluloses implies good promise for manufacturing of pulp and paper [17]. It corresponded directly with the yield of pulp and it provides stronger fiber [18]. The pulp swelling behavior depends on the quantity of hemicellulose, which implies to shoot up in burst index, tensile, and tearing resistance [19]. Additionally, the lignin content value of pseudo stem (10.46%) is lower than wheat straw (17.7%), bagasse, and below the hard and softwood materials content of lignin. A lower value of lignin means easily discard from the process of pulping and it requires less chemicals for pulping and produce quality paper [20]. The digesting of pulping and cooking process length depends on the amount of the lignin of materials. Indeed, less chemical consumption and bleaching will be easy and faster when the amount of lignin is very low [21]. The extractive of the pseudo stem was 12.72%, which is greater than that of straw wheat and bagasse. High extractive content cause high consumption of chemical during the extraction of pulp and bleaching implies pitch deposits.

3.2 Analyses of Pseudo Stem Fiber Morphology

The fiber properties (fiber length, cell wall thickness, lumen width, fiber diameter, and their second values) determination helps of lignocelluloses materials as feedstock for pulp and paper products and helps to justify their qualities [22]. According to the optical microscope, the fiber image of the pseudo stem is presented in Figs. 1 and 2.

Fig. 1. Fiber length images of banana pseudo stem obtained from Motic microscope 40× magnified.

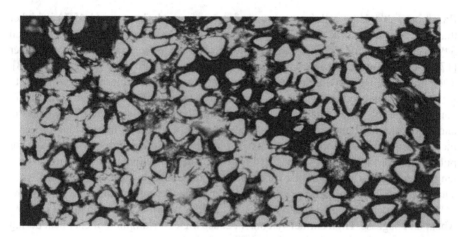

Fig. 2. Fiber diameter, lumen width, and cell wall thickness images of pseudo stem obtained from Motic microscope 100× magnified.

Table 2. Morphological characteristics of the pseudo stem and other plants

Parameter	Banana pseudo stem[a]	Wheat straw[b]	Eucalyptus Labill[c]	Enset Ventricosum stem[d]	Bagasse[e]
Fiber length [L] [mm]	1.75	1.14	0.98	1.66	1.7
Fiber diameter [D] [μm]	22.15	19.32	18.8	28.48	23
Lumen width [d] [μm]	35.361	10.54	n.a	25.87	19.55
Cell wall thickness [T] [μm]	9.7	4.39	4.9	2.88	4.77
Slenderness ratio [L/D]	79.01	0.83	n.a	58.48	73.4
Runkle ratio [2d/L]	0.55	59	n.a	0.22	0.49
Flexibility coefficient [D/L] * 100	159.64	54.55	n.a	90.83	85
Wall rigidity coefficient [d/D]	43.8	n.a	n.a	21.4	23.7

[a][Current study], [b][14], [c][15], [d][16]

Fiber Dimensions and Their Derived Values: The tear and paper machine run ability of paper strength depends on its fiber [23]. According to Table 2, the fiber average length (banana pseudo stem) is 1750 μm are with the range of non-woods, greater than of wheat straw (1140 μm), Enset Ventricosum stem (1660 μm), bagasse (1700 μm), and Eucalyptus labill (980 μm). Fiber classification is based on its length, so the stem of pseudo of banana grouped under long fiber (>1600) best to generate high tear resistance paper and classified as short below 1600 μm [18]. Still, the short and long fiber in length crucial for producing paper. More length of a fiber of wood or non-wood materials increase the formation of a matrix in the paper sheet causes great tensile strength, but shorter in the fiber of materials like grass and hardwood are essential for pulping extraction like printability, stiffness, and opacity [24]. The stem of pseudo banana thickness cell wall is 9.7 µm, which higher than of the straw of wheat (4.39 µm), Enset Ventricosum stem (2.88 µm), and bagasse (4.77 µm) eucalyptus labill (4.9 µm). The flexibility, collapsibility, and easy delignification are occurred due to thin cell walls of fiber materials during pulp generation. Whereas to produce high strengths, folding endurance and porosity of paper thick-walled materials of fiber are acceptable [29]. Accordingly, the cooking condition for the stem of pseudo banana needs higher than the others.

The beating of a paper also measured by its diameter of the fiber and lumen width, so the average diameter of the stem pseudo banana fiber was good (22.15 µm) conforms with coniferous and industrial pulping materials range as well as more than the set points (2.47–4.49 µm) of virgin raw materials [25]. Less flexibility of the fiber formed due to a small diameter of the fiber [26]. So, high strength paper easily made from the stem of banana pseudo. The conformity pulp, pulp yield, and paper are measured by the Runkle ratio (2 w/l) (typical value (=1)) [27]. Less value of the standard Runkle ratio (<1) is suitable for the properties of pulping strength. The Runkle ratio value of banana pseudo stem was 0.548, which was less than of straw of wheat (59). From this point of view, the fibers are suitable for papermaking. Less flexible, stiffer, and lower bonding properties causes due to high Runkle ratio compared to a low value (provides a large surface area and easily collapse) during the drying process [28, 29]. The bonding properties and good sheet forming characterized by the slenderness ratio (fiber length/fiber width). From Table 2 the cumulative value of slenderness ratio of the fiber (79.01) was higher than the value of 58.41 and 73.4 of Enset Ventricosum stem, and bagasse separately. Thus, the stem of pseudo banana has an approximately wonderful slenderness ratio, which indicates well for making of pulping and paper [30]. The paper during the drying and beating process can be characterized by the flexibility ratio of the fiber components. A large area and bonding form from the fiber collapsing properties implies high strength of tensile, bursting, and endurance of folding. It has higher flexibility ratio (159.64) of bagasse, straw of wheat, eucalyptus, and Enset Ventricosum stem fiber. Thus, it implies good bonding properties and the printing area also smooth [24]. The tear resistance, double-fold resistance, tensile, and burst of the paper were negatively affected by rigidity value [31, 32].

3.3 Pulp Yield and Kappa Number

The experimental values of pulp yield and kappa number obtained under different pulping conditions are presented in Table 3.

Table 3. The experimental values of pulp yield and kappa number obtained under different pulping conditions

Std.	Run	Con.NaOH (%)	Temperature (°C)	Time (min.)	Yield (%)	Kappa No
1	31	10	130	45	28.1	35.1
2	8	12.5	130	45	29.88	28.9
3	12	15	130	45	30.51	25.1
4	29	10	140	45	33.66	33.2
5	20	12.5	140	45	31.9	27.3
6	21	15	140	45	30.8	24.1
7	13	10	150	45	36.7	30.6
8	19	12.5	150	45	34.1	23.7
9	14	15	150	45	29.3	22.4
10	5	10	130	60	30.2	27.3
11	4	12.5	130	60	31.52	22.1
12	24	15	130	60	29.91	16.9
13	18	10	140	60	34.5	25.7
14	25	12.5	140	60	32.1	20.9
15	1	15	140	60	28.7	15.1
16	7	10	150	60	37.1	23.4
17	3	12.5	150	60	33.32	19.2
18	16	15	150	60	26.12	18.9
19	27	10	130	75	29.25	25.7
20	32	12.5	130	75	30.5	21.2
21	23	15	130	75	28.3	16.1
22	17	10	140	75	32.9	23.6
23	9	12.5	140	75	29.1	19.7
24	22	15	140	75	25.76	20.1
25	2	10	150	75	33.8	21.3
26	28	12.5	150	75	30.6	22.7
27	15	15	150	75	24.3	23.5
28	6	12.5	140	60	32.1	22.9
29	30	12.5	140	60	32.1	22.9
30	11	12.5	140	60	32.1	22.9
31	26	12.5	140	60	32.1	22.9
32	10	12.5	140	60	32	22.7

3.4 Process Parameters Investigation on Pulp Yield and Kappa Number

In Table 3 and Fig. 3 the soda concentration varied from 10 to 15%. In the absence of sodium hydroxide, pulping did not occur. Higher caustic soda amount causes simple delignification process and generates low lignin pulp. The increase value in the soda concentration decreased pulp yield, from 34.5% to 28.7%, and Kappa number of pulps from 25.7% to 17.9%. The pulp yield decreases due to the cellulosic fibers' degradation and solubilization of hemicelluloses in caustic soda and the kappa number decreases due to the positive effect of soda concentration on lignin delignification.

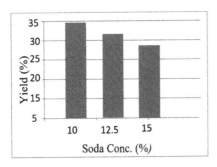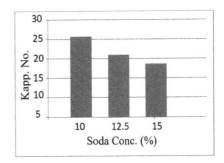

Fig. 3. Effects of soda concentration on pulp yield [a] and kappa number [b] at constant temperature [140 °C] and time [60 min.]

Choosing the appropriate temperature is avail to increase the pulp yield and decrease the kappa number. The lower temperature will make the lignin remove insufficiently, which results in a high kappa number. Higher temperature caused cellulose degradation and pulp yield decreased. Table 3 and Fig. 4 displays the influence of cooking temperature on yield and kappa number of the pulp. It is evident that the yield of pulp slightly increases from 31% to 33% with the increase in the cooking temperature this is possibly due to the bulky nature of the pseudo stem. The cooking temperature varied from 130 °C to 150 °C the kappa number decreases slightly. This shows that despite low lignin content, and the delignification of banana pseudo stems appears difficult.

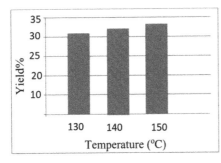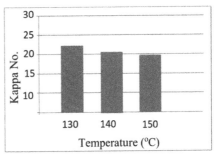

Fig. 4. Effects of temperature on pulp yield [c] and kappa number [d] at constant soda concentration [12.5%] and time [60 min.]

From Table 3 and Fig. 5 the cooking time varies from 45 to 75 min. The maximum yield was reached at 45 min, which is a short cooking time; for cooking times higher than 45 min the pulp yield decreases. According to Fig. 5 increasing the reaction time, reduced the Kappa numbers of the pulps, but at the same time encouraged polysaccharide degradation, as seen by the fall of the yield. This shows that cooking with a lesser time might offers pulps with better yield.

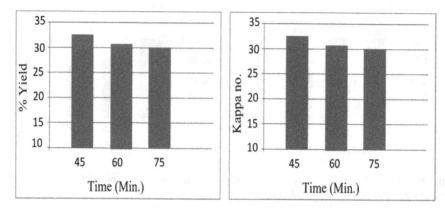

Fig. 5. Effects of time on pulp yield [e] and kappa number [f] at constant soda concentration [12.5%] and temperature [140 °C]

3.5   FTIR Analysis of Pseudo Stem and Pulp

Using the FITR the variation and clustering of the components of compounds of functional parts of materials at the micro-level can be determined. The major compositions of lignocellulosic fibers are cellulose, hemicelluloses, and lignin, while the minor constituents include minerals, pectin, waxes, and water-soluble components. To confirm the presence of functional groups and the removal of components present in the pseudo stem after the pulping process was carried FTIR analysis, illustrated in Fig. 6.

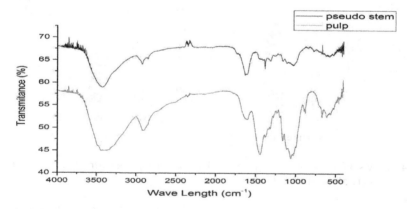

Fig. 6. FTIR spectra analysis of banana pseudo stem and pulp after the pulping process

The groups of hydroxyl and O–H functional groups fall a band between 3600–3100 cm^{-1} symbolized for holocellulose and lignin. The CH stretching bands (1500–1300 cm^{-1}) and a C–O stretching band at 1030 cm^{-1} are attributed to the presence of cellulosic structure. The pike at 1640 cm^{-1} indicates the derivatives of carboxylic acid and the functional group of carbon double bond oxygen(C=O). The aromatic groups of lignin fallen at the band of 1700–1500 cm^{-1} absorptions (1200–900 cm^{-1}) are predominantly dominated by a sequence of bands owing to C–O, C–C, C–OC, and C–O–P stretching vibrations of polysaccharides as well as CH3, CH2 rocking modes [33].

The most noticeable effect of pulping on the pseudo stem in FTIR spectra is the disappearance of the bands 1615 cm^{-1}, regarding the presence of the carbonyl (C=O), and 1247 cm^{-1}, associated with the carboxylic acid (COOH). It represents the components of lignin and hemicellulose structures. Comparing the spectra of the pulp and the in the pseudo stem, it is noticed the disappearance of the bands at 1615 cm^{-1} with the pulping process, attributed to vibrational modes of C=O and C–O groups present in lignin and hemicellulose, which were removed during the pulping process [34].

3.6 Sheet Making and Testing

After optimization of the cooking conditions of pseudo stem pulping, hand sheets were prepared from the pulp produced at the optimized pulping condition and tested for different physical properties like tensile strength, tear strength, tear factor, and tear index. The results obtained were presented in Table 4 and compared with wheat straw, eucalyptus and imported pulp paper.

Table 4. Result of paper characterization from pseudo stem pulp and comparison with others

Properties	Banana pseudo stem pulp sheet[a]	Corn sheath fibers[b]	Wheat straw[c]
Grammage [g/m^2]	60	66.052	60
Tensile strength [KN/m]	6.3	0.2576	n.a
Breaking length [m]	5250.0	n.a	n.a
Tensile index [Nm/g]	78.75	3.9	15.6–27.2
Tearing resistance [mN]	156	n.a	n.a
Tear factor [mNm^2/g]	195	95	n.a
Tear index [mN^2/g]	19.1	2.212	2.0–2.8

[a][Current study], [b][17], [c][35]

The mechanical and strength analysis of paper produced reflects the intrinsic chemistry, morphology, and structure of the individual fibers as well as the network structure of the paper. The result of paper characterization analysis done on the paper samples produced from pulp from pseudo stem pulp is presented in Table 4. The result shows that pseudo stem could be considered as a promising raw material for papermaking applications. The tear index of pseudo stem paper sample 19.1 mNm^2/g is greater than that of paper from wheat straw (2.0–2.8), and corn sheath fibers (2.212) respectively and it is good for average grades of writing and printing paper. The tear factor also higher than that of wheat straw sheet. This shows that pseudo stem has higher fiber length, flexibility, slenderness ratio, coefficient of rigidity than the others as shown in the raw material characterization because this property indicates a better formed, well bonded paper and good resistance of the paper to tear. The tensile index of the pseudo paper sample has a value of 78.75 Nm/g which was greater than of corn sheath fibers (15.6–27.2) and wheat straw sheet (3.9 Nm/g). Breaking length and tensile strength were also greater than that of imported pulp sheet and wheat straw. This is due to that the pseudo stem has a long fiber length and the Coefficient of flexibility gives the bonding strength of the individual fiber and by extension the tensile strength and bursting properties. The other properties like smoothness and porosity of the banana pseudo stem were 500–530 mμ and 50 s/100 ml air respectively and reasonable agreement with the imported pulp, so the banana pseudo stem pulp is suitable for good quality writing and printing paper.

4 Conclusions

This work was intended to study the morphological properties, the proximate and chemical composition analysis of the banana pseudo stem, the influence of pulping parameters: soda concentration, cooking temperature, and cooking time on the pulp yield and kappa number and characterization of paper sheets properties of banana pseudo stem pulp. Based on these results, the values of cellulose (41.45%), hemicellulose (23.37%), and lignin (10.46%) of the banana pseudo stem should be considered suitable for pulp and paper production. The fiber characteristics and morphological indices of the banana pseudo stem revealed that it contains long and thick-walled fiber, which gives a good Runkle ratio (0.55), and slenderness ratio (79.01), and high flexibility coefficient (159.64) indicating suitable for producing a high tear index and tensile index sheet which is suitable to produce different purpose papers. The optimized banana pseudo stem pulping conditions that have been considered high pulp yield, low kappa number, low chemical, and energy consumption with short pulping time has chosen using numerical optimization as a combination of 10% active alkali, 150 °C temperature, and 63 min, to obtain a good quality pulp (36.7% pulp yield and 22.8% kappa number). Using the optimized pulp, a hand sheet was made with the highest tensile index of 78.75 Nm/g and tear index of 19.1 mN × m²/g. Finally, the overall results showed that the banana pseudo stem has a promising potential to be used for the paper application alone or in combination with softwood or hardwood pulps in papermaking.

References

1. Rafiu, M.A.: Pulp and Paper Production from Nigerian Pineapple Leaves and Corn Straw as Substitute to Wood Source, pp. 1180–1188 (2015)
2. Pandita, S., Kaula, B., Passey, S.: Use of weeds and agro-based raw materials and their blends for handmade paper making. J. Undergraduate Res. Innovation 1(3), 169–179 (2015). http://journals.du.ac.in/ugresearch/pdfvol3/U17
3. Fahmy, Y., Fahmy, T.Y.A., Mobarak, F., El-sakhawy, M., Fadl, M.H.: Agricultural residues (wastes) for manufacture of paper, board, and miscellaneous products. Background Overview Future Prospects 10, 425–448 (2017)

4. Abd El-Sayed, E.S., El-Sakhawy, M., El-Sakhawy, M.A.M.: Non-wood fibers as raw material for pulp and paper industry. Nordic Pulp Paper Res. J. **35**, 215–230 (2020). https://doi.org/10.1515/npprj-2019-0064

5. Liu, Z., Wang, H., Hui, L.: Pulping and Papermaking of Non-Wood Fibers. In: Pulp and Paper Processing, pp. 3–32 (2018). https://doi.org/10.5772/intechopen.79017

6. Khan, M.Z.H., Sarkar, M.A.R., Ibne, F., Imam, A., Khan, M.Z.H., Malinen, R.O.: Paper making from banana pseudo- stem: characterization and comparison paper making from banana pseudo-stem. J. Nat. Fibers **11**, 199–211 (2014)

7. Hussain, I., Tarar, O.M.: Pulp and paper making by using waste banana stem. J. Modern Sci. Technol. **2**, 36–40 (2014). http://jmstpapers.com/static/documents/September/2014/4.Intizar.pdf

8. Kumar, A., Singh, B.P., Jain, R.K., Sharma, A.K.: Alternate Ligno-cellulosic raw materials banana (Musa sapientum) ankara (Calotropis procera) and pineapple (Ananas comosus) in handmade paper & their. Am. J. Eng. Res. **2**, 171–189 (2013)

9. Goswami, T., Kalita, D., Rao, P.G.: Greaseproof paper from Banana (Musa paradisica L) pulp fibre. Indian J. Chem. Technol. **15**, 457–461 (2008)

10. Browning, B.L.: Methods of Wood Chemistry, vol. 1 (1967)

11. Ayeni, A.O., Adeeyo, O.A., Oresegun, O.M., Oladimeji, E.: Compositional analysis of lignocellulosic materials: evaluation of an economically viable method suitable for woody and non-woody biomass. Am. J. Eng. Res. **4**, 14–19 (2015)

12. Ishiguro, F., et al.: Effects of radial growth rate on anatomical characteristics and wood properties of 10-year-old Dysoxylum mollissimum trees planted in Bengkulu, Indonesia. Tropics **25**, 23–31 (2016)

13. Poletto, M., Zattera, A.J., Santana, R.M.C.: Structural differences between wood species: Evidence from chemical composition, FTIR spectroscopy, and thermogravimetric analysis. J. Appl. Polym. Sci. **126**, 336–343 (2012)

14. Fatima, V., Gonzalez, Z., Rafael, S., Luis, J.: Cellulosic pulps of cereal straws as raw materials for the manufacture of ecological packaging. Bio-resource **7**, 4161–4170 (2012)

15. Hemmasi, A.H., Samariha, A., Tabei, A., Nemati, M., Khakifirooz, A.: Study of the morphological and chemical composition of fibers from Iranian sugarcane bagasse. Am. Eurasian J. Agric. Environ. Sci. **11**, 478–481 (2011)

16. Malherbe, S., Cloete, T.E.: Lignocellulose biodegradation: fundamentals and applications. Rev. Environ. Sci. Biotechnol. **1**, 105e114 (2002)

17. Alagbe, E.E, Bassey, E.S., Daniel, O.E., Shongwe, M.B., Ojewumi, M.E., Igwe, C.C.: Physical, chemical and mechanical properties of corn sheath as pulp and paper raw material. In: International Conference on Engineering for Sustainable World, pp. 1742–6596 (2019)

18. Jahan, M.S., Chowdhury, N., Ni, Y.: Effect of different locations on the morphological, chemical, pulping and papermaking properties of Trema orientalis (Nalita). Biores. Technol. **101**, 1892–1898 (2010)

19. Singh, S., Dutt, D., Tyagi, C.H.: Complete characterization of wheat straw (Triticum aestivum PBW-343 L. Emend. Fiori & Paul.) a renewable source of fibres for pulp and paper making. BioResources **6**, 154–177 (2011)

20. Hurter, R.W., Riccio, F.A.: Why CEOS don't want to hear about NON woods—or should they? In: TAPPI Proceedings, NON Wood Fiber Symposium, Atlanta, GA, USA, pp. 1–11 (1998)

21. Saikia, S.N., Goswanni, T., Ali, F.: Evaluation of pulp and paper making characteristics of certain fast growing plants. Wood Sci. Technol. **31**, 467–475 (1997)

22. Samariha, A., Kiaei, M., Talaeipour, M., Nemati, M.: Anatomical structural differences between branch and trunk in Ailanthus altissima wood. **4**(12), 1676–1678 (2011)

23. Mark, L.J., Martin, A.L.: Composting pulp and paper mill sludge- effect of temperature and nutrient addition method. Compost Sci. Utilization **5**, 74–81 (1997)
24. Fagbemigun, T.K., Fagbemi, O.D., Buhari, F., Mgbachiuzo, E., Igwe, C.C.: Fibre characteristics and strength properties of Nigerian pineapple leaf, banana peduncle and banana leaf – potential green resources for pulp and paper production. J. Sci. Res. Rep. **12**, 1–13 (2016). https://doi.org/10.9734/JSRR/2016/29248
25. Riki, J.T.B., Sotannde, O.A., Oluwadare, A.O.: Anatomical and chemical properties of wood and their practical implications in pulp and paper production: a review. J. Res. For. Wildl. Environ. **11**, ISSN 2141-1778 (2019)
26. Ogunjobi, K.M., Adetogun, A.C., Omole, A.O.: Assessment of variation in the fiber characteristics of the wood of vitex doniana sweet and its suitability for paper production. Bioresour. Technol. **6**(1), 141–1778 (2013)
27. Runkle, R.O.H.: Pulp from Tropical Woods. Bundesanstalt fur Forst und Holzwirtschaft, ReinbekBez. Hamburg, pp. 20–25 (1952)
28. Mostafizur Rahmana, M., Tohirul Islamb Jannatun Nayeema, M.: Variation of chemical properties of different parts of banana plant (Musa paradisica) and their effects on pulping. Int. J. Lignocellulosic Prod. **1**, 93–103 (2014)
29. Jahan, A.A.M.M.S.: Pulping and Papermaking Potential of Six Mangrove Species in Bangladesh. The Indian Academy of Wood Science, Bangladesh (2015)
30. Kumar, A., Sharma, A.K., Jain, R.K., Singh, B.P.: The use of banana and ankara (Calotropis procera) in the handmade paper industries. Am. J. Eng. Res. **2**, 269–280 (2013)
31. Akgül, M., Tozluo, A., Temp, M.: A comparison of soda and soda-AQ pulps from cotton stalks. Afr. J. Biotechnol. **8**(22), 6127–6133 (2009)
32. Hamzeha, Y., Ashorib, A., Khorasania, Z., Abdulkhania, A., Abyaza, A.: Pre-extraction of hemicelluloses from bagasse fibers: effects of dry-strength additives on paper properties. Ind. Crops Prod. **43**, 365–371 (2013)
33. Ghani, Z.A., Yusoff, M.S., Andas, J.: Development of Activated Carbon from Banana Pseudo- stem via Single Step of Chemical Activation (2017)
34. Gogoi, K., Phukan, M.M., Dutta, N., Singh, S.P., Sedai, P., Konwar, B.K., Maji, T.K.: Valorization and miscellaneous prospects of waste Musa Balbisiana Colla Pseudostem. J. Waste Manage. **8**, 1–8 (2014)
35. García, M.T., Alfaro, A., Garcia, J.C., Zamudio, M.A.M., Morales, A.B., López, F.: Obtainment of hemicelluloses derivatives and cellulose pulp from wheat straw following cold alkaline extraction. Cell. Chem. Technol. **51**(5–6), 465–475 (2015)

Effect of Toasting and Natural Fermentation on the Phytochemical and Functional Properties of Oats Grown in Ethiopia

Getaneh Firew Alemayehu[1,2]($\boxtimes$), Sirawdink Fikreyesus Forsido[1],
Yetenayet B. Tola[1], Minbale Adimas Teshager[2],
Addisu Alemayehu Assegie[2,3], and Endale Amare[4]

[1] Department of Post-Harvest Management, Jimma University, Jimma, Ethiopia
[2] Department of Chemistry, Debre Markos University, Debre Markos, Ethiopia
[3] Department of Material Science and Engineering, College of Science,
Bahir Dar University, Bahir Dar, Ethiopia
[4] Food Science and Nutrition Research Directorate, Ethiopian Public
Health Institute, Addis Ababa, Ethiopia

Abstract. Toasting and natural fermentation are traditional processing methods commonly practiced in Ethiopia. This study was carried out to examine the influence of these traditional processing methods on the phytochemicals and functional properties of oats. Oat grains were toasted for 3 h at 115 °C and milled into flour, and raw oats flour spontaneously fermented for 24 h and 48 h, while untreated oats flour served as a control. Results show that toasting caused a significant ($P < 0.05$) decrease in the bulk density, water solubility index, foaming capacity, and foaming stability in the range; (9.6–18.7%), (7.1–31.2%), (20–46%), & (14.4–38.5%), respectively, while it significantly ($P < 0.05$) increased the total phenolic contents, DPPH antioxidant activity, water absorption capacity, and oil absorption capacity in the range; (20.7–30.4%), (4.3–33%), (87.3–92.7%), (69.1–76%), respectively. Twenty-four hour and 48h fermentation of oats caused a significant ($P < 0.05$) decrease in the, bulk density, foaming capacity, and foaming stability in the range; (15.5–22.7%), (42.4–68%), & (4–74.2%), respectively, while it significantly ($P < 0.05$) increased the total phenolics, total flavonoids, DPPH scavenging capacity, oil absorption capacity, and water solubility index in the range; (18.6–52.2), (34.8–81.3%), (5.3–43.7%), (8–14.9%), (10.7–55.6%), respectively. Thus, the phytochemicals, and some functional properties of oats were amplified by these low-cost household traditional oat processing methods.

Keywords: Oats · Natural fermentation · Toasting · Functional properties · Total phenolic content · Total flavonoid content

1 Introduction

Oat (*Avena sativa*) is a cereal grain that belongs to the grass family *Poaceae*. Oat grain's nutritional composition makes it a valuable component of the human diet. Proteins, starches, essential fatty acids, vitamins, minerals, phytochemicals, and soluble

M. L. Berihun (Ed.): ICAST 2021, LNICST 411, pp. 17–32, 2022.
https://doi.org/10.1007/978-3-030-93709-6_2

dietary fibers are among the many nutrients abundant in oats (Rasane *et al.* 2015; Angelov *et al.* 2018; Jamil *et al.* 2016). Because of its high β-glucan, soluble dietary fiber, and avenathramide, an oats-specific antioxidant, oats have been known as a functional food (Van den Broeck *et al.* 2016).

Literature information indicated processing of oats had an impact on the oat matrix qualitatively and its composition quantitatively (Grundy *et al.* 2018). In the industry, kiln heating, extrusion cooking, microwave heating, superheated steam processing, and controlled fermentation are common methods used for boosting oats' nutrient content and functional properties (Nkhata *et al.* 2018; Franz *et al.* 2014; Freire *et al.* 2015; Marco *et al.* 2017). Processing improves nutrient digestibility and bioavailability by mixing up the food matrix. It can, however, affect food functionality by changing the structure of its components (Grundy *et al.* 2018; Ramashia *et al.* 2019). Finding the right balance between a high amount of food transformation and food processing is one of today's pressing challenges (Grundy *et al.* 2018). A distinction should be made on the degree of processing, which will aid in the acceptance of foods with the highest health importance.

In Ethiopia, oats are traditionally processed at the household level into a variety of foods such as *Injera, Kitta, Anebabiro*, gruel, porridge, *Enket,* and *tella.* All of these foods are subjected to thermal treatment (toasting), and some are subjected to natural fermentation. Toasting is a quick dry-heat treatment and it is a simple traditional experience that is mostly used to cook or pre-cook oats and is widely practiced in households and rural areas of the country. Natural fermentation has also been used traditionally to prolong the shelf life, improve the taste and flavor, and nutritional properties of oat-based food products. Their effects on these food product functionalities and phytochemical composition, however, have not yet been studied.

Processing changes the nutritional composition of foods in one way or the other before consumption. As a result, understanding the composition and food stability after processing is indispensable. Thus, cultural oat foods should be processed to keep them safe and acceptable for consumption, but not to the point where their nutritional value is compromised. Although some research findings on the impact of modern processing methods on the nutritional composition of oats are available, little is known about the effects of toasting and natural fermentation as practiced at the household level. The current study's goal is thus to investigate the impact of these traditional food processing methods on the phytochemicals and functional properties of two Ethiopian indigenous varieties and one improved variety of oats.

2   Materials and Methods

2.1   Sample Collection

Two Indigenous oat varieties (white and black–colored oats) were collected from the Gozamin district of northwest Ethiopia, and one improved oat variety (Goslin) was obtained from the Adet Agricultural Research Center (Fig. 1).

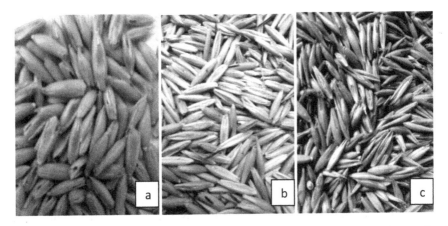

Fig. 1. Improved and local oat varieties (a) Goslin (improved variety) (b) white-oat (local variety) (c) black-oat (local variety)

2.2   Sample Preparation

All oat varieties were dehulled and winnowed to remove husks, ruptured and immature grains, and other unwanted materials. The grains were toasted in an oven (Blast Air Oven, DHG-9240A, China) for 3 h at 115 °C using the method described in (Sandhu *et al.* 2017). The raw and toasted oats grains were pulverized in an electric grinder (RRH-200, Zhejiang, China), and the flour was sieved through a 0.05 mm sieve. Natural fermentation of raw oat flour was conducted using the method described in (Ibrahim *et al.* 2005). Briefly, 250 g of oat flour was combined with 500 ml of deionized water and then fermented for 24 and 48 h at room temperature (22.2 °C). The blended flour sample was then placed on flat glass plates and dehydrated for 20 h in an oven (Blast Air Oven, DHG-9240A, China) at 45 °C, before being pulverized and sieved with a mesh size of 0.425 mm.

2.3   Determination of Phytochemicals

Extraction of Phytochemicals

A 0.5 g flour was shaken with a 10 ml methanol-water 80/20 (v/v) solution for 24 h. It was then centrifuged at 4000 rpm for 10 min before being purified with a filter paper (Whatman No. 1) (Azwanida 2015). This extract was used to determine the sample's DPPH percent inhibition, total phenolic, and total flavonoids.

Determination of Total Phenolic Contents (TPC)

The TPC was measured using the Singleton and Rossi (1999) method. In brief, 0.5 ml of the extract was mixed with 2.5 ml of Folin- Ciocalteu's reagent and 2.5 ml of 7.5% sodium bicarbonate, and then incubated for 30 min in a thermostat set to 45 °C. The color formed during the reaction was measured at 765 nm spectrophotometrically (JASCO V-630, Japan). The standard was gallic acid (0.0, 3.12, 6.25, 12.5, 25, 50, 100,

200 µg/ml, R^2 = 0.998). TPC of the sample was then measured in milligrams of gallic acid equivalent (GAE) per gram of dry matter.

Determination of Total Flavonoid Contents (TFC)

TFC was determined using the outlined method of (Xu and Chang 2007). The (+) - catechin was mixed with 0.25 ml of sample extract and 1.25 ml of deionized water before adding 75 µL of 5% sodium nitrite solution. Exactly 150 µL of a ten percent aluminum chloride solution was added after six min and then 0.5 ml of one molar sodium hydroxide solution was also added to the solution mixture after 5 min of standing. Deionized water was used to dilute the mixture to 2.5 ml and the absorbance was recorded immediately at 510 nm using a spectrometer (JASCO V-630, Japan). The obtained sample extract concentration was compared to the (+) - catachin calibration curve (0.0, 7.8, 15.2, 62.5, 125, 250, and 500 g/ml, R^2 = 0.996). TFC of the sample were quantified in milligrams of (+) - catachin equivalent (CE) per gram of dry matter.

Determination of DPPH Scavenging Activities

The current study employed DPPH (2, 2-diphenyl-1-picrylhydrazyl) scavenging activity to examine the antioxidant properties of oats. It offers valuable information on the antiradical activity of the sample. Oats extract directly react with and quench free radicals of the DPPH assay. The samples' DPPH percent inhibition was determined using the method outlined by (Kirby and Schmidt 1997). A stock solution of 500 ml DPPH (0.004%) was prepared in methanol. One ml of sample extract was mixed with 4 ml of DPPH solution and incubated for 30 min in the dark. The absorbance of this solution was measured using a spectrometer (JASCO V-630, Japan) at 517 nm. Among the various concentration of the sample extract (2−14 mg/ml), 8 mg/ml was chosen to assess the DPPH percent inhibition. The absorbance of the sample extract was compared to the absorbance of the standard L-ascorbic acids (8 mg/ml) and finally, the DPPH percent inhibition was computed using Eq. (1).

$$\text{Inhibition } (\%) = \frac{(\text{Absorbance of control} - \text{Absorbance of sample extract})}{\text{Absorbance of sample extract}} \times 100$$

$$(1)$$

2.4   Determination of Functional Properties

Bulk densities (BD) of the raw and processed (toasted and fermented) oats flour were determined following the described method in (Butt and Rizwana 2010). In a 25 ml measuring cylinder, 10 g of flour was transferred and tapped repeatedly until the constant volume was obtained. The BD was computed using Eq. (2).

$$\text{Bulk density } (g/ml) = \frac{\text{Weight of flour (g)}}{\text{Volume of flour after tapping (ml)}}$$

$$(2)$$

The Sosulski et al. (1976) method was used to assess the water absorption capacity (WAC), oil absorption capacities (OAC), and water solubility indexes (WSI). One g flour and 10 ml oil or deionized water was mixed in a 50 ml bottle. The solution mixture was shaken for 1 h and then centrifuged (Sigma 2-16KC, UK) at 3500 rpm for 30 min. The oil or water was drained with a pipette and hung on for 25 min (V_2) to finish dropping. The volume difference was considered as absorbed water or oil by the sample. Equation (3) was then used to determine the WAC and OAC of the sample.

$$\text{Water/oil absorption capacity (ml/g)} = \frac{(\text{Intial volume } (V_1) - \text{Decanted volume } (V_2))}{\text{Weight of sample flour}}$$

(3)

The supernatant collected from the WAC measurement is used to determine the WSI. This supernatant was heated in an oven (Blast Air Oven, DHG-9240A, China) at 105 °C for 12 h to evaporate the water (Sosulski et al. 1976). The soluble matter dried on the surface of the flat glass and then the WSI was calculated using Eq. (4).

$$\text{WSI } (\%) = \frac{\text{Supernatant weight after drying}}{\text{Sample weight}} \times 100$$

(4)

The method described in Narayana and Narasinga Rao (1982) was used to obtain the foaming capacity (FC) and foaming stability (FS) of the sample. In brief, 1.0 gof flour was mixed with 50 ml of deionized water in a glass measuring cylinder. The flour and deionized water were thoroughly shaken for 5 min, and the amount of foam produced was measured just after 30 s. The FC was then calculated using Eq. (5).

$$\text{Foaming capacity } (\%) = \frac{(\text{foam volume AS} - \text{foam volume BS})}{\text{foam volume BS}} \times 100$$

(5)

Where; AS - after shaking, BS - before shaking
The FS was calculated by measuring the amount of foam left after 1 h using Eq. (6).

$$\text{Foaming stability } (\%) = \frac{(\text{foam volume AS} - \text{foam volume after one hour})}{\text{Volume of foam AS}} \times 100$$

(6)

Where; AS - after shaking

2.5   Experimental Design and Statistical Analysis

This study employed a completely randomized design (CRD) with three replicates. The effects of processing were investigated using a one-way analysis of variance (ANOVA) to determine whether there were any significant differences in phytochemicals and functional properties among the three oat varieties. Means significant values were separated by Tukey's test and $p < 0.05$ values are considered statistically significant. Data were analyzed using Minitab®, Version 19.

3 Results and Discussion

3.1 Effect of Toasting and Fermentation on Phytochemicals

The effect of traditional processing methods (toasting and natural fermentation) on the total phenolics, total flavonoid, and total antioxidant content of oats is shown in Table 1. The phytochemicals of oats were significantly ($p < 0.05$) affected by the processing methods.

Phenolic compounds are affected by the temperature used during food processing (Cavalcante et al. 2017). The TPC of all oat varieties were significantly ($p < 0.05$) increased by the toasting. It increased by 20.7–30.4%, with Goslin oat having the highest increment. This increment might be linked with the release of phenolic compounds as a result of matrix fragmentation which occurs during heating (Kalam Azad et al. 2019). The current study is similar to the findings of Sandhu et al. (2017), a significant increment of the TPC of different oats varieties by 11.5–27.1% as a result of toasting. The rise in TPC as a result of heat treatment of cereals and legumes has also been stated by many other studies (Rasane et al. 2015; Chandrasekara and Shahidi 2011).

Natural fermentation also improved the TPC significantly ($p < 0.05$), in the range of 18.6–52.2%; the highest value was recorded for 24 h fermented flours. For 48 h fermented flours, increments in the TPC were observed in the first 24 h, and decrements in the second consecutive 24 h. This increase could be attributed to microorganisms degrading cereal grain matrices, resulting, previously attached polyphenols leaked during fermentation (Đorđević et al. 2010). For example, B. subtilis and L. plantarum both have an enzyme called β-glucosidase that breaks the glucoside bonds of polyphenols and reduced sugars, increasing phytoconstituents (Dueñas et al. 2005). Nkhata et al. (2018) and Martins et al. (2011) also reported phenolic compound enhancement could be because of the activity of enzymes like α-amylase, β-glucosidase, and lactase. As a result, natural flour fermentation is a low-cost traditional processing method for increasing phytochemicals and thus protecting the body from the potentially harmful effects of free radicals that may arise during body metabolism. Aside from the level of heat treatment and fermentation, storage conditions such as the amount of oxygen, exposure to sunlight, and the temperature of the room, all have an impact on a food product's phytochemical bioavailability (Cox et al. 2012). Toasting and natural fermentation would be commendable cultural food processing experiences for increasing the TPC of oat.

Table 1. Effect of traditional processing methods on TPC (mg GAE/g), TFC (mg CE/g), and DPPH percent inhibition (%) of white-colored, black-colored, and Goslin oat varieties

Oat varieties	Processing methods	TPC	TFC	DPPH percent inhibition
White	Raw (control)	1.75 ± 0.01^c	0.69 ± 0.02^c	13.4 ± 0.12^c
	Toasted	2.17 ± 0.08^b	0.60 ± 0.03^c	15.2 ± 0.06^b
	Fermented – 24 h	2.55 ± 0.04^a	1.14 ± 0.04^a	16.6 ± 0.16^a
	Fermented – 48 h	2.22 ± 0.05^b	0.93 ± 0.03^b	15.9 ± 0.20^b
	CV	14.17	26.77	8.1
Black	Raw (control)	1.88 ± 0.02^c	$0.75 \pm 0.02c$	18.16 ± 0.09^b
	Toasted	2.27 ± 0.06^b	$0.71 \pm 0.03c$	18.94 ± 0.04^b
	Fermented – 24 h	2.68 ± 0.07^a	1.36 ± 0.01^a	19.54 ± 0.05^a
	Fermented – 48 h	2.23 ± 0.06^b	$1.05 \pm 0.09b$	19.14 ± 0.04^a
	CV	13.57	29.2	2.8
Goslin	Raw (control)	1.61 ± 0.05^b	0.52 ± 0.02^b	11.2 ± 0.16^c
	Toasted	2.10 ± 0.18^{ab}	0.52 ± 0.08^b	14.9 ± 0.08^c
	Fermented – 24 h	2.45 ± 0.05^a	0.93 ± 0.03^a	16.1 ± 0.08^a
	Fermented – 48 h	1.98 ± 0.12^{ab}	0.82 ± 0.05^a	15.3 ± 0.12^b
	CV	17.61	29.49	13.7

The values represent the mean ± standard error (SE) of three replicates. Means with a different letter in the same row differ significantly.

In this study, total flavonoid decrement was observed by toasting even though statistically insignificant. According to Sandhu et al. (2017), the toasting of different oat cultivars led to a decrease in TFC by 23−40.1%. In buckwheat, toasting at 120 °C for 40 min caused a 33% decrease in flavonoids whereas, toasting at 160 °C for 30 min decreased total flavonoids by 15.9% (Qin et al. 2010; Zhang et al. 2012). The decrease in TFC after toasting could be attributed to the heat sensitivity of flavonoids compounds (Zhang et al. 2019). Most flavonoid compounds are thermally sensitive and may degrade (Mazumder et al. 2020). A significant ($p < 0.05$) increment of the total flavonoids was also observed which is in the range; 34.8–81.3% for all oat varieties. TFC increased in 24 h fermented flour, similar to that of TPC. TFC increment was indicated by Wang et al. (2014) in their study of fermentation effect on walnut, chestnut, and lotus seeds.

The DPPH percent inhibition of oats was used to determine their ability to quench reactive species. The antioxidant activities of all oat varieties were improved significantly ($p < 0.05$) upon toasting. It increased by 4.2–33%, with Goslin oat showing the highest increment. According to Sandhu et al. (2017), the toasting of oats at 115 °C for 3 h, increased the total antioxidant activity by 29.1−53.6% and Xu et al. (2009) reported increments of oats total antioxidant activity by 82.2% upon toasting. Maillard reaction products, which may result from the reaction of amino acids and reduced sugars when cereal products are heated, release compounds such as 5-hydroxymethyl-2 furaldehyde, which is known for its high antioxidant properties and could be one of the reasons for the increase in total antioxidant levels after toasting (Dueñas et al. 2006). Natural fermentation also improve significantly ($p < 0.05$) the antioxidant activity by

7.6−43.8% and 5.4−36.6% for 24 h and 48 h fermented flours, respectively. The higher DPPH percent inhibition values may be explained by oats' high antioxidant constituents and their cumulative synergistic action. The importance of antioxidants in human health is attributed to their ability to safeguard from oxidative damages such as atherosclerosis, diabetes, arthritis, cancer, and other aging diseases (Nambi et al. 2017; Ahn-Jarvis et al. 2019). Both raw and processed oats in this study showed a high antioxidant composition and it would further be amplified through the traditional processing methods.

3.2   Effect of Toasting and Fermentation on Functional Properties

Table 2 presents the functional properties of raw, toasted, and fermented oat flours and they exhibited a significant ($p < 0.05$) change upon the processing methods.

The results shown in Table 2 indicated toasting significantly ($p < 0.05$) reduced the bulk density (BD) by 9.6−18.7%, when heated, the link between macronutrients such as starches and proteins breaks, causing the food structure and configuration to deform. As a result, holes were created in its structure, causing it to expand in volume while retaining mass, resulting in a decrease in BD. It is an essential functional property of powders that has an immediate impact on packaging. It also specifies physical properties such as cohesion and porosity, which can have an impact on flow ability and storage stability. Because the BD of the toasted oats was low, they could easily be combined with other food flours to produce a nutritionally improved composite. The current study is in line with Sandhu et al. (2017) report, a decrease of BD of oats from 31 to 44% after toasting. For all varieties of oats, natural fermentation reduced the BD significantly ($p < 0.05$). Fermentation for 24 h reduced the BD by 16.4% for the white-colored oat, 20% for the black-colored oat, and 15.5% for the Goslin. Further decrements were shown by 48 h fermentation, 17.8% for the white-colored oat, 22.7% for the black-colored, and 22.5% for the Goslin. As shown in Table 2, the longer the fermentation period, the lesser the BD of the samples become. The current result was comparable to the outcomes of Oladeji et al. (2018) and Abd Elmoneim et al. (2005), who described a significant reduction in BD upon fermentation of quality protein maize flours and sorghum flour, respectively. Thus, natural fermentation of oats flour can be considered as a beneficial traditional processing method for preparing foods with low BD.

The water absorption capacities (WAC) of toasted oat flours were relatively high when compared to fermented and raw oat flours. WAC decreased 87.3−92.7% up on toasting. According to Sandhu et al. (2017), the toasting of oats led to an increase in WAC up to 51.4%. WAC increases due to structure deformity and the formation of holes in the matrix, which allows water to rise via capillary action (Wani et al. 2016). According to Abbey and Ibeh (1988), an increase in WAC is also linked to an increase in amylose leaching and a loss of crystalline starch structure. This effect could be caused by the weak interaction of amylose and amylopectin as a result of toasting (Iwe et al. 2016). The high WAC of toasted oat flours implies that they can be used to make sausage, dough, processed cheese, and bakery products (Butt and Rizwana 2010). Natural fermentation, on the other hand, reduced water absorption capacity though statistically insignificant ($p > 0.05$). The difference in WAC between raw and fermented flours could be credited to changes in protein content, the degree to which they interact with water, and their conformational structure induced during fermentation (McWatters *et al.* 2003). WAC is an essential parameter for flours used for the baking purpose (Awuchi *et al.* 2019). Because the added moisture slows the rate of staling, high water absorption is typically needed for baked products (Novie *et al.* 2018). A WAC of 1.25 ml/g or higher is a good indicator of bakery property (Giami and Alu 1994). As a result, all of the raw and processed oat flour analyzed in this study suggests oats could be an excellent functional ingredient in bakery products.

Oil absorption capacity (OAC) differs markedly among processing methods. For all oat varieties, toasted flours showed the highest increase (69.1−76%) in OAC, Similar to this study, heating increased the OAC of cowpea flour (Ma *et al.* 2011). The increase in OAC of the toasted sample could be attributed to the denaturation and detachment of protein components, exposing outside the nonpolar side of the protein molecule (Akaerue and Onwuka 2010). Different factors influence OAC, which include starch-protein-lipid bindings, polypeptide sequences, macromolecule conformational features, and the amount of nonpolar amino acids (Chandra and Samsher 2013). However, the main factor influencing OAC is a protein or amino acid that contains both hydrophilic and hydrophobic components. Through hydrophobic interactions, nonpolar amino acid side chains can interact with lipid hydrocarbon chains (Chandra and Samsher 2013). Because oil enhances tastiness, OAC is commonly used to predict product palatability Shah *et al.* (2016) and maintains flavor (Aremu *et al.* 2007). The OAC of raw oat flours was lower than that of toasted and fermented oat flours, which is preferred in the development of food products requiring minimal oil absorption. The higher OAC of processed oat flours would also be beneficial in the preparation of foods that requires high oil holding foods like cookies and bakery products.

After toasting, the water solubility index (WSI) reduced significantly ($p < 0.05$) for the two oat varieties, black-colored oat, and Goslin. It led to a decline of 7.1−31.2%. The WSI is proportional to the extent of soluble solids and is commonly taken as an indicator of starch molecule disintegration and dextrinization (Silva *et al.* 2009). However, natural fermentation significantly amplifies the WSI of the flours for all varieties of oats. It led to an increase by 10.7−48.8% through 24 h fermentation and by 24.7−55.6% via 48 h fermentation. High solubility indicates high leaching and a non-covalent bond between molecules within the flour (Onitilo *et al.* 2007). According to Onweluzo and Nwabugwu (2009), the likely cause of the increase in WSI by natural fermentation is the degradation of high molecular weight carbohydrates and proteins during fermentation to simpler and more soluble constituents.

Table 2. Effect of traditional processing methods on BD (g/ml), WAC (ml/g), OAC (ml/g), WSI (%), FC (%), and FS (%) of white-colored, black-colored and Goslin oat varieties

Oat variety	Processing methods	BD (g/ml)	WAC (ml/g)	OAC (ml/g)	WSI (%)	FC (%)	FS (%)
	Raw (control)	0.73 ± 0.02[a]	1.66 ± 0.03[b]	1.72 ± 0.02[c]	11.35 ± 0.27[c]	15.71 ± 0.46[a]	10.82 ± 0.46[a]
White	Toasted	0.66 ± 0.02[ab]	3.11 ± 0.04[a]	2.95 ± 0.03[a]	10.54 ± 0.04[c]	8.48 ± 0.34[b]	6.65 ± 0.34[b]
	Fermented – 24 h	0.61 ± 0.01[b]	1.62 ± 0.01[b]	1.86 ± 0.02[b]	12.56 ± 0.24[b]	7.30 ± 0.12[b]	6.38 ± 0.12[b]
	Fermented – 48 h	0.60 ± 0.03[b]	1.60 ± 0.03[b]	1.90 ± 0.01[b]	15.16 ± 0.14[a]	5.25 ± 0.02[c]	2.79 ± 0.02[c]
	CV	9.3	38.16	24.39	14.9	44.91	44.91
	Raw (control)	0.75 ± 0.01[a]	1.73 ± 0.01[b]	1.75 ± 0.04[c]	12.09 ± 0.28[c]	14.07 ± 0.10[a]	11.09 ± 0.25[a]
Black	Toasted	0.61 ± 0.01[b]	3.28 ± 0.05[a]	2.96 ± 0.01[a]	8.32 ± 0.11[d]	11.26 ± 0.22[b]	9.49 ± 0.17[b]
	Fermented – 24 h	0.60 ± 0.01[bc]	1.56 ± 0.03 [c]	1.89 ± 0.01[b]	13.60 ± 0.28[b]	8.11 ± 0.09[c]	5.68 ± 0.23[c]
	Fermented – 48 h	0.58 ± 0.00[c]	1.51 ± 0.01[c]	1.94 ± 0.02[b]	15.08 ± 0.08[a]	5.66 ± 0.23[d]	5.05 ± 0.10[c]
	CV	11.23	38.03	23.64	21.55	34.02	34.04
	Raw (control)	0.71 ± 0.01[a]	1.65 ± 0.01[b]	1.75 ± 0.04[c]	10.23 ± 0.21[b]	14.26 ± 0.21[a]	9.90 ± 0.07[a]
Goslin	Toasted	0.60 ± 0.01[b]	3.18 ± 0.07[a]	3.08 ± 0.07[a]	8.94 ± 0.22[c]	8.11 ± 0.07[b]	8.09 ± 0.07[b]
	Fermented – 24 h	0.60 ± 0.01[b]	1.64 ± 0.03[b]	1.91 ± 0.02[bc]	15.22 ± 0.23[a]	5.67 ± 0.21[c]	5.32 ± 0.06[c]
	Fermented – 48 h	0.55 ± 0.01[b]	1.55 ± 0.04[b]	2.01 ± 0.03[b]	15.92 ± 0.24[a]	4.57 ± 0.25[d]	4.35 ± 0.06[d]
	CV	10.11	35.57	25.32	25.34	48.24	33.30

The values represent the mean ± standard error (SE) of three replicates. Means with a different letter in the same row differ significantly.

The foaming capacity (FC) of oats flours has been shown in Table 2. It changes significantly (p < 0.05) for raw and processed oats. All processing methods used in this study reduced the FC. Toasting decreased by 20−46%, showing an extreme decrease in white-colored oat, and natural fermentation for 24 h decrease 42.4−60.2%, while fermentation for 48 h decreased the FC by 59.8−68%. Because of the soluble proteins on the surface, flours can produce foams (Adebowale and Lawal 2003). FC is primarily reliant on the availability of proteins to form an interfacial film by encapsulating surface tension, which upholds the gas pockets and the decelerating of the combination (Shah et al. 2016). The reduction in FC observed after toasting could be then due to the denaturation of the protein molecules during toasting (Jan et al. 2019). According to Kouakou et al. (2013), the native protein has a greater ability for foaming than the denatured one. Processing methods, pH, protein type, surface tension, and viscosity were the function variables to the FC (Lech 2016). Oat is the only grain with a higher concentration of avenalin (80%) as the primary storage protein (Ahmad et al. 2015). Where foaming is desired, i.e. for oat-based food products with a softer texture and lighter mouthfeel, raw oats flour could be a good alternative to toasted and naturally fermented flours.

The foaming stability (FS) of raw and processed oat flours differed significantly ($p < 0.05$). The raw oat flour had the highest foam stability, while the 48 h fermented flours had the lowest foaming stability. Toasting decreased the FS by 14.4−38.5%, while 24 h fermentation decreased FS by 41−48.8%, and 48 h fermentation decreased FS by 54.5−74.2%. A similar decrement in FS by heat processing has been reported by Khalid and Elhardallou (2015) for the cowpea flour. Toasted oats have a lower FS value because denatured proteins have a lower FS value than the native proteins (Kouakou et al. 2013). Because FS is dependent on thin-film-encapsulated gas bubbles remaining intact, only highly surface-active solutes can produce stable foams (Cherry and McWatters 2012). High-foaming flours create large air pockets surrounded by a protein film. The ability to create stable foam is essential when making sponge cakes, creamy condiments, and frozen desserts (Adelakun et al. 2012). When compared to raw oat flour, roasted and fermented oat flour may not be the best ingredient to use in such formulations. As a result, processed oat flours have a low likelihood of being used in foods that require stable foam formation.

3.3 Correlation Between Phytochemicals and DPPH Antioxidant Activity of Oats

As shown in Table 3, the correlation between DPPH antioxidant activities and phytochemicals contents (TPC and TFC) were evaluated for the raw, toasted, 24 h fermented, and 48 h fermented oats. The correlation coefficient varied from weak to very strong among the processing methods.

Table 3. Correlation coefficient for TPC vs. DPPH antioxidant activity, and TFC vs. DPPH antioxidant activity for the raw and processed oats

Oats	r-values for TPC vs. DPPH antioxidant activity	r-values for TFC vs. DPPH antioxidant activity
Raw	0.91	0.86
Toasted	0.31	0.67
Fermented – 24 h	0.77	0.88
Fermented – 48 h	0.47	0.67

Evans (1996) classified correlation strengths as "very weak," "weak," "moderate," "strong," and "very strong." The current study showed a highly significant positive correlation between TPCand DPPH antioxidant activity in raw oats ($r = 0.91$, $p < 0.05$). While the correlations between TPCand DPPH percent inhibition for toasted, 24 h fermented, and 48 h fermented samples were 0.31, 0.77, and 0.47, respectively, these values overlapped on the weak, strong, and moderate ranges of correlation. Sandhu et al. (2017) also reported a very strong positive correlation between TPCand DPPH percent inhibition ($r = 0.93$, $p < 0.05$) for all raw oat varieties. Similar outcomes were also found by (Lahouar et al. 2014) and (Keriene et al. 2015). Consequently, TPC and DPPH percent inhibition were found to be strongly correlated ($p < 0.01$).

The correlation between TFC and DPPH percent inhibition in raw oats was also significant and very strong ($r = 0.86$, $p < 0.05$). Correlation coefficients for processed oats were also classified as strong and very strong. According to Sandhu *et al.* (2017), TFC and antioxidant capacity of oats were positively correlated with an r-value of 0.71. The highest TPC and TFC were accompanied by the highest DPPH percent inhibition values. Hence, this result proposes the total phenolic and flavonoid compounds are the main sources of their antioxidant activities.

4 Conclusions

Toasting and natural fermentation brought a change in the phytochemicals and functional properties of oats. Toasting showed an increment of total phenolic content and a decrement of total flavonoids. It also modified the functionality of oats, particularly by increasing oil and water absorption capacities and reducing the bulk density and water solubility index. At the same time, natural fermentation enhanced the phytochemicals prominently. Fermented flours were found to have higher antioxidant capacity than unfermented flours. Optimal fermentation and thermal treatment should be established to maximize its nutritional benefits. Characterizations on the nutritional and phytochemical properties of indigenous and underutilized Ethiopian food crops should also be encouraged to diversify the food preference and diet of the community.

Acknowledgments. The authors would like to express their gratitude to the Adet Agricultural Research Centre for supplying the sample grains, and Jimma University College of Agriculture and Veterinary Medicine (JUCAVM) for their help with the nutrient analysis.

Funding Statement. This research was supported by the Ethiopian Ministry of Science and Higher Education.

Conflict of Interest. The authors declare that there is no conflict of interest.

References

Abbey, B.W., Ibeh, G.O.: Functional properties of raw and heat-processed cowpea (*Vigna unguiculata*, Walp) flour. J. Food Sci. **53**(6), 1775–1777 (1988)

Abd Elmoneim, O.E., Schiffler, B., Bernhardt, R.: Effect of fermentation on the functional properties of sorghum flour. Food Chem. **92**(1), 1–5 (2005)

Adebowale, K.O., Lawal, O.S.: Foaming, gelation, and electrophoretic characteristics of mucuna bean (*Mucuna pruriens*) protein concentrates. Food Chem. **83**(2), 237–246 (2003)

Adelakun, O.E., Ade-Omowaye, B.I.O., Adeyemi, I.A., Van de Venter, M.: Mineral composition and the functional attributes of Nigerian okra seed (*Abelmoschus esculentus* Moench) flour. Food Res. Int. **47**(2), 348–352 (2012)

Ahmad, M., Zaffar, G., Jehangir, I.A., Dar, R.A., Mehraj, U., Lone, A.A.: Oat grain production for human consumption: sustainable option under temperate climatic conditions of Kashmir valley. Int. J. Sci. Nat. **6**(4), 596–605 (2015)

Ahn-Jarvis, J.H., Parihar, A., Doseff, A.I.: Dietary flavonoids for immunoregulation and cancer: food design for targeting disease. Antioxidants **8**(7), 202 (2019)

Akaerue, B.I., Onwuka, G.I.: The functional properties of the dehulled and undehulled mung bean (*Vigna radiata* (l.) Wilczek) flours as influenced by processing treatments. Journal of Agricultural and Veterinary Science **2**, 1–28 (2010)

Alviola, J.N.A., Monterde, V.G.: Physicochemical and functional properties of wheat (*Triticum aestivum*) and selected local flours in the Philippines. Philippine J. Sci. **147**(3), 419–430 (2018)

Angelov, A., Yaneva-Marinova, T., Gotcheva, V.: Oats as a matrix of choice for developing fermented functional beverages. J. Food Sci. Technol. **55**(7), 2351–2360 (2018). https://doi.org/10.1007/s13197-018-3186-y

Aremo, M.O., Olaofe, O.: Functional properties of some Nigerian varieties of legume seed flours and flour concentration effect on foaming and gelation properties. J. Food Technol. **5**(2), 109–113 (2007)

Awuchi, C.G., Igwe, V.S., Echeta, C.K.: The functional properties of foods and flours. Int. J. Adv. Acad. Res. **5**(11), 139–160 (2019)

Azwanida, N.N.: A review on the extraction methods use in medicinal plants, principle, strength and limitation. Med. Aromat. Plants **4**(196), 21670412 (2015)

Butt, M.S., Rizwana, B.: Nutritional and functional properties of some promising legumes protein isolates. Pak. J. Nutr. **9**(4), 373–379 (2010)

Cavalcante, R.B., AraÚJo, M.A., Rocha, M.D., Moreira-Araújo, R.S.: Effect of thermal processing on chemical compositions, bioactive compounds, and antioxidant activities of cowpea cultivars. Revista Caatinga **30**(4), 1050–1058 (2017)

Chandra, S., Samsher,: Assessment of functional properties of different flours. Afr. J. Agric. Res. **8**(38), 4849–4852 (2013)

Chandrasekara, A., Shahidi, F.: Bioactivities and antiradical properties of millet grains and hulls. J. Agric. Food Chem. **59**(17), 9563–9571 (2011)

Cherry, J.P., McWatters, K.H.: Whippability and aeration role of proteins in foams. FAO, AGRIS (2012)

Cox, S., Abu-Ghannam, N., Gupta, S.: Effect of processing conditions on phytochemical constituents of edible Irish seaweed Himanthalia Elongata. J. Food Process. Preserv. **36**(4), 348–363 (2012)

Đorđević, T.M., Šiler-Marinković, S.S., Dimitrijević-Branković, S.I.: Effect of fermentation on antioxidant properties of some cereals and pseudo cereals. Food Chem. **119**(3), 957–963 (2010)

Dueñas, M., Fernández, D., Hernández, T., Estrella, I., Muñoz, R.: Bioactive phenolic compounds of cowpeas (Vigna sinensis L). Modifications by fermentation with natural microflora and with Lactobacillus plantarum ATCC 14917. J. Sci. Food Agric. **85**(2), 297–304 (2005)

Duenas, M., Hernandez, T., Estrella, I.: Assessment of in vitro antioxidant capacity of the seed coat and the cotyledon of legumes in relation to their phenolic contents. Food Chem. **98**(1), 95–103 (2006)

Evans, J.D.: Straight Forward Statistics for The Behavioral Sciences. Thomson Brooks/Cole Publishing Co., Pacific Grove, CA (1996)

Franz, C.M., et al.: African fermented foods and probiotics. Int. J. Food Microbiol. **190**, 84–96 (2014)

Freire, A.L., Ramos, C.L., Schwan, R.F.: Microbiological and chemical parameters during cassava based-substrate fermentation using potential starter cultures of lactic acid bacteria and yeast. Food Res. Int. **76**, 787–795 (2015)

Giami, S.Y., Alu, D.A.: Changes in composition and certain functional properties of ripening plantain (Musa spp., AAB group) pulp. Food Chem. **50**(2), 137–140 (1994)

Grundy, M.M.L., Fardet, A., Tosh, S.M., Rich, G.T., Wilde, P.J.: Processing of oat: the impact on oat's cholesterol lowering effect. Food Funct. **9**(3), 1328–1343 (2018)

Ibrahim, F.S., Babiker, E.E., Yousif, N.E., El Tinay, A.H.: Effect of fermentation on biochemical and sensory characteristics of sorghum flour supplemented with whey protein. Food Chem. **92**(2), 285–292 (2005)

Iwe, M.O., Onyeukwu, U., Agiriga, A.N.: Proximate, functional and pasting properties of FARO 44 rice, African yam bean and brown cowpea seeds composite flour. Cogent Food Agric. **2**(1), 1142409 (2016)

Jamil, M., et al.: A Review on multidimensional aspects of oat (*Avena sativa*) crop and its nutritional, medicinal and daily life importance. World Appl. Sci. J. **34**(10), 1269–1275 (2016)

Jan, K., Ahmad, M., Rehman, S., Gani, A., Khaqan, K.: Effect of roasting on physicochemical and antioxidant properties of kalonji (*Nigella sativa*) seed flour. J. Food Meas. Charact. **13**(2), 1364–1372 (2019)

Kalam Azad, M.O., Jeong, D.I., Adnan, M., Salitxay, T., Heo, J.W., Naznin, M.T., Park, C.H.: Effect of different processing methods on the accumulation of the phenolic compounds and antioxidant profile of broomcorn millet (Panicum miliaceum L.) Flour. Foods **8**(7), 230 (2019)

Kerienė, I., Mankevičienė, A., Bliznikas, S., Jablonskytė-Raščė, D., Maikšteniene, S., Cesnuleviciene, R.: Biologically active phenolic compounds in buckwheat, oats and winter spelt wheat. Zemdirbyste Agric. **102**(3), 289–296 (2015)

Khalid, I.I., Elhardallou, S.B.: The effect of pH on foaming properties of cowpea (Vigna ungiculata L. walp) flour and protein isolates. J. Nutr. Food Sci. **5**(4), 1000385 (2015)

Kirby, A.J., Schmidt, R.J.: The antioxidant activity of Chinese herbs for eczema and of placebo herbs-I. J. Ethnopharmacol. **56**(2), 103–108 (1997)

Kouakou, B., N'Da-Kouassi, A.M., Halbin, K.J., Tagro, G., N'Guessan, K.F., Dago, G.: Biochemical characterization and functional properties of weaning food made from cereals (millet, maize) and legumes (beans, soybeans). J. Food Chem. Nutr. **1**(1), 22–32 (2013)

Lahouar, L., et al.: Phytochemical content and antioxidant properties of diverse varieties of whole barley (*Hordeum vulgare* L.) grown in Tunisia. Food Chem. **145**, 578–583 (2014)

Lech, F.J.: Foam properties of proteins, low molecular weight surfactants and their complexes. Doctoral dissertation, Wageningen University (2016)

Ma, Z., Boye, J.I., Simpson, B.K., Prasher, S.O., Monpetit, D., Malcolmson, L.: Thermal processing effects on the functional properties and microstructure of lentil, chickpea, and pea flours. Food Res. Int. **44**(8), 2534–2544 (2011)

Marco, M.L., et al.: Health benefits of fermented foods: microbiota and beyond. Curr. Opin. Biotechnol. **44**, 94–102 (2017)

Martins, S., Mussatto, S.I., Martínez-Avila, G., Montañez-Saenz, J., Aguilar, C.N., Teixeira, J. A.: Bioactive phenolic compounds: production and extraction by solid-state fermentation. A review. Biotechnol. Adv. **29**(3), 365–373 (2011)

Mazumder, K., Nabila, A., Aktar, A., Farahnaky, A.: Bioactive variability and in vitro and in vivo antioxidant activity of unprocessed and processed flour of Nine cultivars of Australian lupin species: a comprehensive substantiation. Antioxidants **9**(4), 282 (2020)

McWatters, K.H., Ouedraogo, J.B., Resurreccion, A.V., Hung, Y.C., Phillips, R.D.: Physical and sensory characteristics of sugar cookies containing mixtures of wheat, fonio (*Digitaria exilis*) and cowpea (*Vigna unguiculata*) flours. Int. J. Food Sci. Technol. **38**(4), 403–410 (2003)

Nambi, V.E., Chandrasekar, V., Karthikeyan, S.: Value addition of grains using solid state fermentation. Nutr. Food Sci. Int. J. **3**(4), 6 (2017)

Narayana, K., Narasinga Rao, M.S.: Functional properties of raw and heat processed winged bean (*Psophocarpus tetragonolobus*) flour. J. Food Sci. **47**(5), 1534–1538 (1982)

Nkhata, S.G., Ayua, E., Kamau, E.H., Shingiro, J.B.: Fermentation and germination improve nutritional value of cereals and legumes through activation of endogenous enzymes. Food Sci. Nutr. **6**(8), 2446–2458 (2018)

Oladeji, B.S., Irinkoyenikan, O.A., Akanbi, C.T., Gbadamosi, S.O.: Effect of fermentation on the physicochemical properties, pasting profile and sensory scores of normal endosperm maize and quality protein maize flours. Int. Food Res. J. **25**(3), 1100–1108 (2018)

Onitilo, M.O., Sanni, L.O., Oyewole, O.B., Maziya-Dixon, B.: Physicochemical and functional properties of sour starches from different cassava varieties. Int. J. Food Prop. **10**(3), 607–620 (2007)

Onweluzo, J.C., Nwabugwu, C.C.: Fermentation of millet (*Pennisetum americanum*) and pigeon pea (*Cajanus cajan*) seeds for flour production: effects on composition and selected functional properties. Pak. J. Nutr. **8**(6), 737–744 (2009)

Qin, P., Wang, Q., Shan, F., Hou, Z., Ren, G.: Nutritional composition and flavonoids content of flour from different buckwheat cultivars. Int. J. Food Sci. Technol. **45**(5), 951–958 (2010)

Ramashia, S.E., Anyasi, T.A., Gwata, E.T., Meddows-Taylor, S., Jideani, A.I.O.: Processing, nutritional composition and health benefits of finger millet in sub-saharan Africa. Food Sci. Technol. **39**, 253–266 (2019)

Rasane, P., Jha, A., Sabikhi, L., Kumar, A., Unnikrishnan, V.S.: Nutritional advantages of oats and opportunities for its processing as value added foods-a review. J. Food Sci. Technol. **52**(2), 662–675 (2015)

Sandhu, K.S., Godara, P., Kaur, M., Punia, S.: Effect of toasting on physical, functional and antioxidant properties of flour from oat (Avena sativa L.) cultivars. J. Saudi Soc. Agric. Sci. **16**(2), 197–203 (2017)

Shah, A., Masoodi, F.A., Gani, A., Ashwar, B.A.: Geometrical, functional, thermal, and structural properties of oat varieties from temperate region of India. J. Food Sci. Technol. **53**(4), 1856–1866 (2016). https://doi.org/10.1007/s13197-015-2119-2

Silva, M.C.D., Carvalho, C.W.P.D., Andrade, C.T.: The effects of water and sucrose contents on the physicochemical properties of non-directly expanded rice flour extrudates. Food Sci. Technol. **29**, 661–666 (2009)

Singleton, V.I., Rossi, J.: Colorimetry of total phenolic with phosphomolybdic-phosphotungstic acid agents. Am. J. Enol. Vitic. **16**, 144–158 (1999)

Sosulski, F., Humbert, E.S., Bui, K., Jones, J.D.: Functional propreties of rapeseed flours, concentrates and isolate. J. Food Sci. **41**(6), 1349–1352 (1976)

Van den Broeck, H.C., Londono, D.M., Timmer, R., Smulders, M.J., Gilissen, L.J., Van der Meer, I.M.: Profiling of nutritional and health-related compounds in oat varieties. Foods **5**(1), 2 (2016)

Wang, C.Y., Wu, S.J., Shyu, Y.T.: Antioxidant properties of certain cereals as affected by food-grade bacteria fermentation. J. Biosci. Bioeng. **117**(4), 449–456 (2014)

Wani, I.A., Sogi, D.S., Sharma, P., Gill, B.S.: Physicochemical and pasting properties of unleavened wheat flat bread (Chapatti) as affected by addition of pulse flour. Cogent Food Agric. **2**(1), 1124486 (2016)

Xu, B.J., Chang, S.K.C.: A comparative study on phenolic profiles and antioxidant activities of legumes as affected by extraction solvents. J. Food Sci. **72**(2), S159–S166 (2007)

Xu, J.G., Tian, C.R., Hu, Q.P., Luo, J.Y., Wang, X.D., Tian, X.D.: Dynamic changes in phenolic compounds and antioxidant activity in oats (Avena nuda L.) during steeping and germination. J. Agric. Food Chem. **57**(21), 10392–10398 (2009)

Zhang, X., Wang, X., Wang, M., Cao, J., Xiao, J., Wang, Q.: Effects of different pretreatments on flavonoids and antioxidant activity of Dryopteris erythrosora leave. PloS one **14**(1), e0200174 (2019)

Zhang, Z.-L., et al.: Bioactive compounds in functional buckwheat food. Food Res. Int. **49**(1), 389–395 (2012)

Correlation of UV Assisted Fenton Process and Fenton Process for Removal of Reactive Red 2(RR2) Dye Color from Wastewater

Gemechu Kassaye Abera$^{(\boxtimes)}$, Fikiru Temesgen Hangarasa, and Nigus Gabbiye Habtu

Faculty of Chemical and Food Engineering, Bahir Dar Institute of Technology, Bahir Dar University, P.O. Box 26, Bahir Dar, Ethiopia

Abstract. Polluted effluents from the textile sector are dumped into the environment in massive quantities. As a result, this study was conducted to assess the efficacy of Fenton and photo-Fenton procedures in removing Reactive red 2 (RR 2) dye and to establish the best conditions for maximum removal. This research was done in laboratory scale. The effect of parameters, including Fe (II) concentration (0.1–0.15 mM), H_2O_2 concentration (0.1–1 mM), and dye concentration (0.06–0.1 mM) of dye removal were studied, and the best settings were found based on the maximum dye removal efficiency. The dye clearance rate rose as the Fe (II) concentration fell, according to the findings. Fe (II) concentration of 0.1 mM, H_2O_2 concentration of 1 mM, and starting dye concentration of 0.08 mM are the best conditions for RR 2 elimination from aqueous solution, at the reaction time of 45 min with 88.10% efficiency. Where, for the Fenton process the maximum decolorization efficiency (82.18%) of RR 2 dye was obtained at optimum concentrations values of 1 mM of H_2O_2, 0.1 mM of initial RR 2 dye and 0.1 mM of Fe^{+2} concentrations. The consequences of this investigation uncovered that the photo Fenton process was better than the removal of color contrasted with Fenton measure.

Keywords: Dye removal · Reactive red 2 · Fenton · Photo–Fenton

1 Introduction

Lately, wastewater treatments have been separate by the utilization of Advanced Oxidation Processes (AOPs), which proposition promising events to corrupt or even excavator alize defilements using smooth temperature and pressing factor conditions. A portion of the Advanced Oxidation Process that are usually applied incorporate ozonation, Fenton process, photocatalysis, wet air oxidation, microwave upgraded AOP, electrochemical oxidation, bright radiation, and hydrogen peroxide oxidation [1].

Among these AOPs, those including hydrogen peroxide, for example, the Fenton oxidation, and the photo-Fenton oxidation can produce profoundly receptive and no particular extremist species, similar to hydroxyl radical (HO•). H_2O_2/UV is the most every now and again used UV-AOP at large scale and has been explored at the lab and the pilot scales [2]. A lot of investigations have revealed the uses of photon assisted

© ICST Institute for Computer Sciences, Social Informatics and Telecommunications Engineering 2022
Published by Springer Nature Switzerland AG 2022. All Rights Reserved
M. L. Berihun (Ed.): ICAST 2021, LNICST 411, pp. 33–43, 2022.
https://doi.org/10.1007/978-3-030-93709-6_3

AOPS to weaken drugs, eliminate taste and smells, dispose of poisons and improve on the nature of cleaned water [2].

The greater part of the AOPs utilize a mix of solid oxidants, for example, ozone or hydrogen peroxide (H_2O_2) with either heterogeneous or homogeneous catalysts (generally transition metals and iron), semiconductor solids, radiation, or ultrasound to upgrade radical generation. On account of Fenton's reagent, it consolidates H_2O_2 and ferrous particles (Fe^{2+}) in an acidic medium, which prompts the arrangement of $^{\cdot}OH$ radicals through the oxidation of Fe^{2+} to Fe^{3+}. At the same time, Fe^{2+} is recovered by the reaction between Fe^{3+} and H_2O_2. The photo-Fenton measure joins Fenton's reagent with light energy, which quickens the debasement pace of organic pollutants.

Reductive metal particles can catalyze the hydrolysis of H_2O_2 to frame hydroxyl radicals. Fenton's reagent, a combination of ferrous particles and hydrogen peroxide, has been known as a ground-breaking oxidant for organic contaminants. Homogeneous Fenton measure process by iron has a characterized ideal pH of 3.0, which is restricted to a limited operational reach up to 4.0 because of the precipitation of iron hydroxides at higher pH esteems [3].

Late investigation centers around the utilization of AOPs for bioenergy creation [1]. The mix of AOPs can assist with further developing the general interaction execution by ensuring that more receptive radicals are delivered at low oxidant measurement.

1.1 Fenton Process

Fenton oxidation is an AOP whose customary application was in the treatment of recalcitrants in wastewater. H.J. Fenton was the first to report the popular Fenton reaction in 1894 and delineated the oxidation process using hydrogen peroxide as oxidant and iron (Fe) as a catalyst within the sight of acidic (H^+) medium.

The Fenton process can be arranged into two general classes—homogeneous and heterogeneous processes. In homogeneous cycles, iron species are in a similar stage as the reactants and there is no impediment for mass exchange. In heterogeneous catalysis, iron is supported inside the catalytic structure and can effectively invigorate the degradation of refractory materials without the development of ferric hydroxide sludge [4].

Generally accepted Fenton reaction mechanism utilizes hydrogen per oxides (H_2O_2) and ferrous iron to produce OH radicals (Eq. (1)) [5]:

$$Fe^{2+} + H_2O_2 \rightarrow Fe^{3+} + OH^- + OH^* \tag{1}$$

The breaking down of H_2O_2 to create OH revolutionaries is begun and catalyzed by ferrous particles. The OH radical framed assaults and oxidizes/mineralizes the waste. It in like manner oxidizes the organics by pondering of protons subsequently making natural revolutionaries (Eq. (2)). The revolutionary conveyed may respond with other natural substrates thus extending the chain.

$$RH + {}^*OH \rightarrow R^* + H_2O \tag{2}$$

In case of abundance impetus, the OH radicals are rummaged (Eq. (3)) subsequently diminishing the oxidation potential.

$$Fe^{2+} + OH^* \rightarrow Fe^{3+} + OH^- \tag{3}$$

The exemplary Fenton was the primary sort of Fenton oxidation where the oxidants are responded at pH 3 [6]. The cycle was confined by the huge costs of reagents and pH changes. The waste treatment by Fenton extends the biodegradability. It tends to be used for shading expulsion from the profluent before discharge. A part of the new progressions in the process fuses the usage of photograph Fenton where the energy from the sun or UV light is used to support the plan of revolutionaries from the reagents. This declines the use of engineered compounds and grows the viability of oxidation. Another headway is heterogeneous Fenton where the impetus or the corrosive gathering is embedded on a strong impetus. The interaction ensures that the catalysts are recovered for reuse and enable the action at higher pH regards [1]. [7] examined a combination of the Fenton process with CaO as a coagulant for the treatment of corrosive colors and found that the color of the dye solution was totally eliminated and up to 90% COD was taken out.

The Fenton process is utilized often for the degradation of a wide scope of synthetic substances, for example, anthraquinone, azo colors, phenol subordinates, feed additives, pharmaceutical drugs, sweet-smelling hydrocarbons, pesticides, and herbicides, just as in the treatment of landfill leachates and other modern effluents. The utilization of Fenton reagent for textile wastewater brought about a viable technique for decolorization, moderate COD, yet the moderate TOC evacuation and detoxification of textile wastewater and synthesized dye solutions. The inadequate mineralization of the organic matter has been accounted for with the Fenton framework [5].

1.2 Photo-Fenton and Related Processes

The improved type of the ordinary Fenton oxidation reaction within the sight of UV–visible light beneath 600 nm frequency is known as the photo-Fenton reaction [4]. In acid solution and in obscurity, the disintegration of H_2O_2 catalyzed by Fe^{2+} in leads prompts the creation of hydroxyl radicals, as indicated by the notable warm Fenton response [4]:

$$Fe^{2+} + H_2O_2 \rightarrow Fe^{3+} + HO^- + HO^\bullet \quad k = 76 \text{ M}^{-1}\text{s}^{-1} \tag{4}$$

The overall pace of the photo Fenton oxidation measure is compelled by the speed of the photolytic step that changes over Fe^{3+} back to Fe^{2+}, and the constant Fe(II)/Fe(III) reuse makes the association autocatalytic. The most standard use of the photo Fenton measure has been the treatment of industrial waters and lixivi-ates. Photograph Fenton cycles can utilize daylight rather than UV light with a minor de-wrinkle in the pace of debasement. This is a vital factor for the scale-up and business utilization of a PAOP, since the expenses of medicines will be considerably brought down in case daylight is utilized. The photo-Fenton process can benefit from the presence of constituents of real effluents such as iron or copper salts, avoiding the need for additional dosage, and oligocarboxylic acids such as oxalate or ethylenediaminetetraacetic acid (EDTA), which form photo-chemically active iron (III) complexes and improve the process. The iron salts should be chosen carefully, and the oxalate particulate should be used. The job of iron on the debasement of various natural mixtures, varying in their construction (aliphatic versus fragrant) and iron complex development limit, by traditional and photo Fenton process. These substance features have been shown to have an impact on the level of treatment in terms of COD (chemical oxygen demand) and TOC (total organic carbon) expulsions. While aromatic combinations showed a rapid and articulated drop in COD using the Fenton method, aliphatic mixtures required UV light to improve treatment results [8].

S.K. Petal [5] concluded that Photo Fenton combined with titanium dioxide (PF-TiO_2) for removal of TOC was more efficient than Photo-Fenton or combination with AC. Also, The Photo-Fenton process was reported as a comparatively efficient method for the degradation of various synthetic dyes [4].

Therefore, the objectives of this research were: 1) to determine low Fenton reagent concentrations suitable for the degradation of reactive red dye; 2) to compare the degradation of reactive red dye using the Fenton (H_2O_2/Fe^{2+}) process, and photo-Fenton ($UV/H_2O_2/Fe^{2+}$) processes.

2 Methodology

2.1 Chemicals and Equipment's

Equipment like jar test, beaker, test tubes, measuring cylinders, pipette, pH meter, electronic balance and UV/Vis spectrometer (PerkinElmer lambda 35) were frequently used to perform the experiment. Laboratory reagent like distilled water, powder of reactive red dye 2, powder of ferric sulphate hydrate ($Fe_2 (SO_4)_3 \times H_2O$), H_2O_2 (30% w/w) and sulfuric acid were also used in the experimentation process.

2.2 Preparation of Stock Solution

Reactive red 2 dye (RR 2 dye) was collected from Research Grade Laboratory, Bahir Dar Institute of Technology, Bahir Dar, Ethiopia. The physical state of RR2 dye is powder solid with a molecular formula of $C_{19}H_{10}C_{12}N_6Na_2O_7S_2$ and molecular weights of 615.34 g/mol. The stock solution (10 mM) of RR2 dye was prepared by dissolving 3.06 g of in 250 mL of distilled water. The maximum wavelength, λ_{max}, and absorbance of RR2 dye solution was scanned from 200 to 700 nm using UV/VIS spectrometer (PerkinElmer Lambda 35) and obtained at 539 nm. Dye absorbance values were determined at a maximum wavelength of 539 nm.

An amount of azo dye containing 0.06 mM is ready by dissolving the required amount in distilled water and leaving it in the dark. All volumetric flags are covered with aluminum foil to block light. All H_2O_2 working solutions were prepared from a commercial solution (H_2O_2, 30%) by dilution in distilled water to the required concentration. The estimation of the pH was carried out using a HACH pH meter

Table 1. Nomenclature and structure of reactive red dye 2

Parameter	Characteristic
Chemical name	Reactive red 2 dye
Molecular formula	C19H10Cl2N6Na2O7S2
Molecular weight	615.33 g/mol
UV absorption (maximum wavelength)	539 nm
Molecular structure	

calibrated with standard vials pH 4.01 and 7.00 at (25 °C), then the pH was adjusted to the ideal value by expanding a few drops of H_2SO_4 (0.1 M).

Adjust the pH value of the dye synthesis solution, the iron solution, and the H_2O_2 solution to the desired value. In the Fenton photographic test, Fe^{2+} particles are first added to the color array and homogenized for 15 min. Then add the H_2O_2 device at this time and the reaction will last 30 min. It is possible to notice that the Fe^{2+} particles are given by the arrangement of $Fe_2 (SO_4)_3 \times H_2O$ (1 mM).

When applying Fenton photo measurement, the pH value of all reagents is adjusted to 3. First add driving force to the color arrangement, homogenize the combination for 15 min, and then add H_2O_2 immediately. Turn on the light and the bleaching takes 30 min.

For all AOPs, logical examples of 5 ml were removed at known stretches and analyzed utilizing the UV–vis spectrophotometer. Color removal of Azo dye was monitored by estimating absorbance at a most extreme assimilation frequency of 539 nm. The decolorization productivity was controlled by Eq. 5:

$$\% Decolorization = \left(\frac{A_o - A_t}{A_o}\right) * 100 \qquad (5)$$

where A_0 is the underlying assimilation of azo color, and A_t is the retention of azo color at response time [2].

A Shellett UV lamp ZW30S19W (Y)-Z894 disinfection lamp 30W sterilizing lamp tube was placed horizontally in the reactor for the performance of the UV/Fenton process.

2.3   Experimental Design and Description

The experimental design was designed by response surface method as shown in (Table 1) below. The three factors i.e., initial RR 2 dye concentration, concentration of ferric sulphate and concentration of hydrogen peroxide were adjusted to determine the decolorization efficiency of RR 2 dye from aqueous solution. All experiments were conducted according to experimental design of initial concentration (0.06, 0.08 and 0.1 mg/mM), concentration of ferric sulphate (0.1, 0.125 and 0.15 mg/mM) and concentration of hydrogen peroxide (0.1, 0.55 and 1 mg/mM) at constant pH of 3, reaction time of 45 min and at room temperature. At the end of each experiment, small amount of the solutions was taken to determine the absorbance value for all experiments using UV/Vis spectrometer (PerkinElmer lambda 35) and the finial RR 2 dye concentration was calculated as per the calibration curve in Fig. 1 (Table 2).

Table 2. Variables and levels of factors used for optimization

Variable	Level		
	Low (−)	Middle (0)	High (+)
Dye conc. (mM)	0.06	0.08	0.1
$FeSO_4 \times H_2O$ conc. (mM)	0.1	0.125	0.15
H_2O_2 conc. (mM)	0.1	0.55	1

mM = millimolar

2.4   Preparation of Standard Solution

To calculate the final dye concentration from each run, a calibration curve first prepared by using the standard dye solution with known concentrations. Different concentrations were prepared and absorbance values were recorded at λ_{max} of the dye using UV/VIS spectrometer. Linear calibration curve of this data was served as the basis for determining the final dye concentration. Absorbance values have been presented in Table 3.

Table 3. Standard concentration and their absorbance values

Maximum wavelength (nm)	539				
Dye concentration (mM)	0.000	0.060	0.073	0.080	0.100
Absorbance value	0.000	0.697	0.874	0.911	1.911

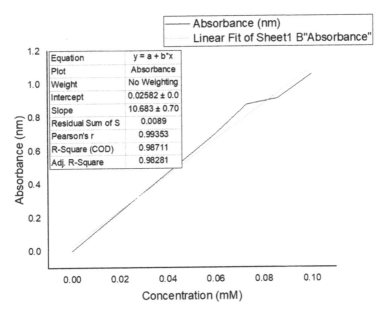

Fig. 1. Calibration curve of standard solution

3   Results and Discussions

3.1   Effect of H_2O_2 Concentration

The effect of H_2O_2 concentration on the decolorization of the aqueous solution containing RR 2 dye was investigated by ranging the values of H_2O_2 concentration from 0.1 to 1 mM. The experiments were done at pH 3 and at room temperature. As shown in Fig. 2 for Fenton process, the decolorization efficiency was increased from 59.08 to 72.12%, 61.9 to 79.01% and 64.72 to 82.18% for 0.06, 0.08 and 0.1 mM of initial dye concentration, respectively as concentration of H_2O_2 increased from 0.1 to 1 mM after 45 min and at optimum 0.1 of Fe^{+2} ion. For photo-Fenton process, the decolorization efficiency was increased from 76.5 to 79.05%, 60.9 to 88.1% and 67.6 to 85.8% for 0.06, 0.08 and 0.1 mM of initial dye concentration, respectively as concentration of H_2O_2 increased from 0.1 to 1 mM after 45 min and at optimum 0.125 of Fe^{+2} ion. In the Fenton process cases of initial dye concentrations i.e. 0.06, 0.08 and 0.1 mM the decolorization efficiency of dye increases as the concentration of H_2O_2 increases. However, for the photo-Fenton the maximum efficiency was seen at 0.08 mM dye concentration. The decrease of removal effeminacy at low concentrations of H_2O_2, it could not generate enough OH radicals, and the oxidation rate decreases.

Therefore, the addition of a higher H_2O_2 concentration does not improve the degradation with the simple Fenton process. The present circumstance was likewise revealed and clarified in [9]. The explanation of this may be the age of hydroperoxyl revolutionaries (HO_2) within the sight of an overabundance of H_2O_2. Although HO_2 advances revolutionary chain responses and is a successful oxidant itself, its oxidation potential is a lot of lower than that of hydroxyl extremist (■OH).

Dye concentration effect on decolorization

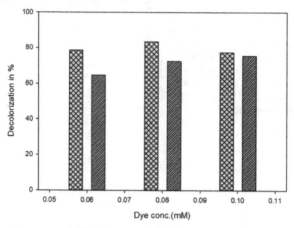

hydrogen per oxide effect on decolorization

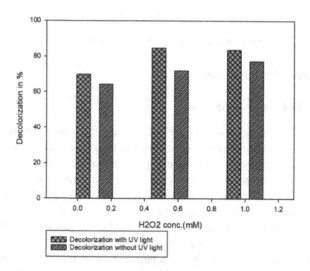

Fig. 2. Effect of H_2O_2 on decolorization of RR 2 dye from aqueous solution

3.2   Effect of Ferrous Ion (Fe^{+2}) Concentration

The effect of ferrous ion concentration on the decolorization of the aqueous solution containing RR 2 dye was investigated by ranging the values of ferrous ion concentration from 0.1 to 0.15 mM. As shown in Fig. 3, the decolorization efficiency was decreased from 66.27 to 54.12%, 75.98 to 70.98% and 82.18 to 78.22% for 0.06, 0.08 and 0.1 mM of initial dye concentration, respectively as concentration of ferrous ion increased from 0.1 to o.15 mM after 45 min and at optimum 1 mM of H_2O_2 concentration.

For UV/Fenton Process the decolorization efficiency was decreased from 80.35 to 75.20%, 87.40 to 78.60% and 78.25 to 75.15% for 0.06, 0.08 and 0.1 mM of initial dye concentration, respectively as concentration of ferrous ion increased from 0.1 to o.15 mM after 45 min and at optimum 1 mM of H_2O_2 concentration. Therefore, in both Fenton and photo-Fenton process, the dye reduction rate increased with Fe (II) concentration up to a specific level (0.1−0.125 mM) and then began to decrease (0.125−0.15 mM).

In light of this examination, the utilization of a lot higher Fe^{2+} impetus focus could prompt oneself rummaging of ■OH revolutionaries by Fe^{2+}. In addition, it likewise initiated a decrease in the degradation rate [9].

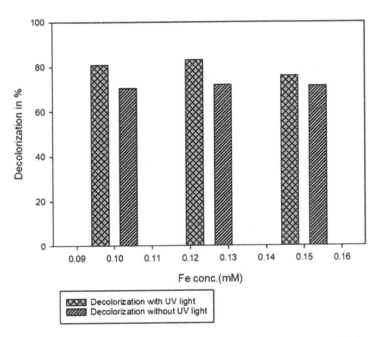

Iron concentration effect on decolorization

Fig. 3. Effect of ferrous ion (Fe (II)) on the removal of RR-2 by Fenton and photo–Fenton processes (pH = 3, initial dye concentration = 0.06 mM, reaction time = 45 min.)

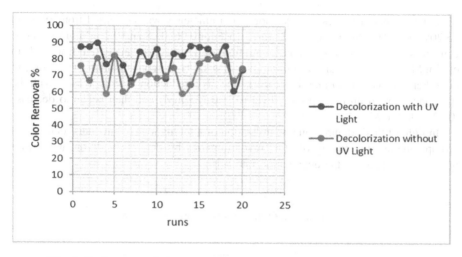

Fig. 4. Performance of photo-Fenton process over Fenton process for the run

3.3   Effect of RR2 Initial Concentration

The initial concentrations of RR–2 at three levels (0.06, 0.08 and 0.1 mM) had a considerable effect on the reduction rate of the dye in the aqueous phase. The effect of initial dye concentration on its removal efficiency is shown in Fig. 2. As the initial dye concentration increased from 0.06 to 0.08 mM, the removal efficiency was increased and shows decrease beyond that in the photo–Fenton process. Therefore, the maximum removal rate in the photo–Fenton process (88.10%) was observed at the concentration of 0.08 mM. However, in the Fenton process, an increase in the concentration of the dye from 0.06 to 0.1 mg/L had a significant increase in its removal rate. In the Fenton process, the maximum removal rate (82.18%) was observed at the RR–2 concentration of 0.1 mM.

Overall, as it can be seen on Fig. 4 above the photo Fenton process shows greater decolorization as compared to traditional Fenton process.

4   Conclusions and Recommendations

4.1   Conclusions

Fenton's and photo - Fenton process is a type of advanced oxidation processes which is an effective method for degradation of organic matter from wastewater. It is also the most effective to decolorize the dyes from aqueous solution. In this research work RR 2 dye has been taken as a modal pollutant in aqueous solution. Fenton's and photo - Fenton process has been applied to decolorize this dye from aqueous solution in comparison. Different types of operation factors such as H_2O_2, initial RR 2 dye and Fe^{2+} catalyst concentrations were investigated on decolorization efficiency of RR 2 dye at constant pH 3, reaction time of 45 min and at room temperature. The maximum degradation efficiency (82.18%) was obtained at 1 mM of H_2O_2, 0.1 mM of initial RR

2 dye and 0.1 mM of Fe^{2+} catalyst concentrations Fenton process. Whereas for photo Fenton, the maximum degradation efficiency (88.10%) was obtained at 1 mM of H_2O_2, 0.08 mM of initial RR 2 dye and 0.125 mM of Fe^{2+} catalyst concentrations. It was found out that the photo-Fenton process can be successfully applied for the decolorization of RR 2 in aqueous solution.

4.2 Recommendation

In this research work degradation and mineralization are not determined due to the limitations of some equipment and chemical reagents. Therefore, degradation and mineralization should be performed.

References

1. Arimi, M.M.M., Mecha, C.A., Kiprop, A.K., Ramkat, R.: Recent trends in applications of advanced oxidation processes (AOPs) in bioenergy production: review. Renew. Sustain. Energy Rev. **121**, 109669 (2020)
2. Laftani, Y., Boussaoud, A., Chatib, B., Hachkar, M., El Makhfouk, M., Khayar, M.: Comparison of advanced oxidation processes for degrading ponceau S dye: application of the photo-fenton process. Maced. J. Chem. Chem. Eng. **38**(2), 197–205 (2019)
3. Brillas, E., Garcia-segura, S.: Benchmarking recent advances and innovative technology approaches of Fenton, photo-Fenton, electro-Fenton, and related processes: a review on the relevance of phenol as model molecule. Sep. Purif. Technol. **237**(2019), 116337 (2020)
4. Javaid, R., Qazi, U.Y.: Catalytic oxidation process for the degradation of synthetic dyes: an overview. Int. J. Environ. Res. Public Health **16**(11), 1–27 (2019)
5. Patel, S.K.: Degradation of reactive dye in aqueous solution by Fenton, photo-Fenton process and combination process with activated charcoal and TiO_2. Proc. Natl. Acad. Sci. India Sect. A Phys. Sci. **90**(4), 579–591 (2019)
6. Zazo, J.A., Rodroguez, J.J., Bautista, P., Mohedano, A.F., Casas, J.A.: An overview of the application of Fenton oxidation to industrial wastewaters treatment. J. Chem. Technol. Biotechnol. **83**, 1323–1338 (2008)
7. Kulik, N., Panova, Y.: The Fenton chemistry and its combination with coagulation for treatment of dye solutions. Sep. Sci. Technol. **7**(42), 1521–1534 (2007)
8. Litter, M.I., Morgada, M.E., Bundschuh, J.: Possible treatments for arsenic removal in Latin American waters for human consumption. Environ. Pollut. **158**(5), 1105–1118 (2010)
9. Nurbas, M., Kutukcuoglu, S.B.: Investigation of water decolorization by Fenton oxidation process in batch and continuous systems. Desalin. Water Treat. **55**(13), 3731–3736 (2015)

Isolation and Characterization of Microcrystalline Cellulose from Eragrostesis Teff Straw

Ebise Getacho Bacha[✉], Lema Deme Shumi,
and Tsigab Tekleab Teklehaimanot

School of Chemical Engineering, Institute of Technology, Jimma University,
P. O. Box 378, Jimma, Ethiopia
ebise.bacha@ju.edu.et

Abstract. In this work, microcrystalline cellulose was isolated from Eragrostis teff straw through a chemical method using acidified sodium chlorite, alkali treatment, and acid hydrolysis and successively, various characterizations were conducted using different techniques. The ash, volatile matter, moisture, and fixed carbon contents were calculated and found to be 5.1%, 74.2%, 8.4%, and 15.6%, respectively. The extractives, lignin, hemicellulose, and cellulose content were found to be 6.4%, 15.6%, 29.5%, and 37.5%, respectively. The yield of the microcrystalline cellulose (MCC) extracted was 70.8% and the particle size was 156.4 μm. The pH, loss on drying, moisture sorption capacity, water-soluble substance, and hydration capacity of extracted MCC were found to be 6.7, 4.6%, 18.6%, 0.18%, and 3.7, respectively. The Fourier transformed infrared spectroscopy (FTIR) result of microcrystalline cellulose shows the removal of pectin, waxes, and lignin. The X-ray diffraction result shows that the crystallinity (CI%) of teff straw and microcrystalline cellulose was 47.7% and 72.8% respectively which reveals the removal and reduction of amorphous parts in the straw. A result of thermogravimetry analysis and differential thermo-gravimetry analysis (TGA/DTGA) reveals that microcrystalline cellulose shows better thermal stability over the untreated straw. The onset temperature of the straw was 255 °C and the maximum degradation temperature was 354 °C while the onset temperature for extracted microcrystalline cellulose was 315 °C and maximum degradation temperature was 363 °C.

Keywords: Microcrystalline cellulose · Alkali treatment · Acid hydrolysis

1 Introduction

Cellulose is a naturally available polysaccharide and has an attractive structure and unique properties. It contains hundreds to thousands of β $(1 \rightarrow 4)$ glucose units which are joined to form a straight linear structure and its chemical formula is $(C_6H_{10}O_5)$ n (Kumar et al. 2016). Mainly it is the constituent of numerous natural lignocellulosic materials like sugarcane bagasse, cotton, jute, hemp, wheat straw, teff straw, corn stalk, rice husk, and other biomass. It covers approximately one-third of plant tissues and is produced through photosynthesis. Each year around 1000 tons of this polymer is

© ICST Institute for Computer Sciences, Social Informatics and Telecommunications Engineering 2022
Published by Springer Nature Switzerland AG 2022. All Rights Reserved
M. L. Berihun (Ed.): ICAST 2021, LNICST 411, pp. 44–58, 2022.
https://doi.org/10.1007/978-3-030-93709-6_4

synthesized in the world (Mandal and Chakrabarty 2011). It has unique properties such as biocompatibility, biological degradability, and sustainability. Cellulose microcrystalline is the cellulose in a micrometer range. It is currently used in different application areas such as food, pharmaceuticals, cosmetics, paper, textile, adhesives, and composites (Moon and Schueneman 2016). The requirement of MCC in these application areas and industries results in the exploitation of naturally, easily, and locally available resources for its synthesis. It can be obtained from lignocellulosic materials by different methods such as mechanical methods, steam explosion, high-pressure homogenization, cyro-crushing, and chemical methods (Chakraborty et al. 2005). The chemical method is an effective way to get cellulose with high purity. A combination of acidified chlorite bleaching and hot alkali is the widely used technique for extracting cellulose and acid hydrolysis is known for the extraction of MCC and nanocellulose (NC).

Ethiopia is currently producing a large amount of teff annually in different areas. It is the widely cultivated cereal crop in Eritrea and Ethiopia for food. In recent years, different reports imply that 3.7 million tons of teff grain has been produced per year and above 2 million tons of its straw has been generated every year (Mottaleb and Rahut 2018). Teff straw has around 38% cellulose content, which makes it a competitive secondary source of cellulose with bagasse, wheat straw, rice husk, etc. (Chufo et al. 2015). In Ethiopia, it is produced on large scale and used for bedding, construction, and mulching. Nowadays, as the industry tries to reduce its reliance on non-renewable sources there is a growing necessity to explore additional environmentally pleasant materials which have improved properties and sustainable to replace the existing ones.

This study attempt was done to determine the proximate analysis of teff straw, its chemical composition, and to extract cellulose microcrystalline. In addition, the extracted microcrystalline cellulose was characterized by FTIR, TGA/DTGA, XRD, and the pH, loss on drying, particle size, moisture sorption capacity, water-soluble substance, and hydration capacity of the isolated MCC were determined and compared with the results of previously extracted cellulose microcrystalline from other lignocellulosic materials.

2 Materials and Methods

Sodium hydroxide (FINEM 97%) and sodium chlorite (HIMEDIA 80%) were purchased from the Ranchem industry and trading plc, Addis Ababa, Ethiopia. Ethanol (98%), sulfuric acid (UNICHEM, India 98%), Filter paper (90 mm) in diameter, distilled water, and glacial acetic acid (Neolab, 96%) were purchased from Alkane Plc, Addis Ababa, Ethiopia. Teff straw was collected from Agaro, Ethiopia.

2.1 Proximate and Chemical Composition Analysis of Raw Material

The moisture, ash, volatile matter, and fixed carbon content of the teff straw were determined according to procedures described in (Mustapha 2018).

The hemicellulose content was computed following the method ASTM D5896-96 (2012), the water and ethanol extractives were measured as the procedures described by (Vijayanand et al. 2016), the cellulose and lignin content of the straw was evaluated by using the procedures prepared by the institute of paper chemistry, Appleton, Wisconsin as described in (Halim 2014).

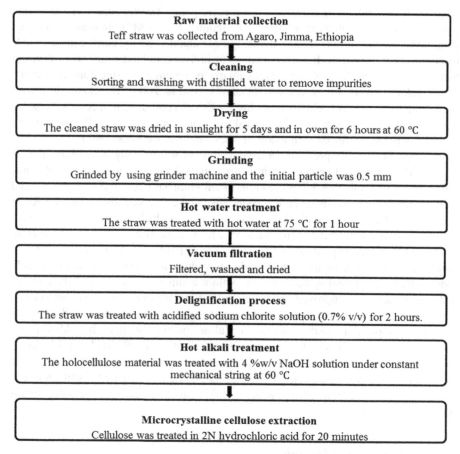

Fig. 1. Flow diagram representation for extraction of microcrystalline cellulose

2.2 Extraction of Cellulose

The first step is the delignification process in which lignin, wax, and other extractives in raw material were removed and this process was conducted according to the procedure described by (Mandal and Chakrabarty 2011) with some modification. The ground fiber was treated with hot distilled water before the delignification process to remove the water extractive substance. The fiber was treated at 75 °C when the ratio of fiber to water is 1:20 g/ml for an hour. Then, it was treated with acidified sodium chlorite solution 0.71% w/v at 75 °C in a water bath for 2 h under continuous mechanical stirring (400 rpm). The pH of sodium chlorite was adjusted to 4 by glacial acetic acid (5% v/v). The ratio of fiber to acidified sodium chlorite solution was 1:25 g/ml. This procedure was repeated five times till the color of the holo-cellulose was turned to white and the pH of a filtrate come to neutral then the residue was oven-dried for 24 h at 50 °C and kept for further process. Figure 1 shows the experimental setup for extraction of MCC.

The cellulose was extracted by an alkaline hydrolysis process using sodium hydroxide solution. This method was adopted per the procedures used by (Nasution et al. 2017). The dried holo-cellulose was treated with hot 4%w/v NaOH at 60 °C in a water bath for 1 h. The fiber to solution ratio was 1:20 g/ml with a constant mechanical string of 400 rpm. Then, the remained residue was vacuum filtered and washed until the pH of the filtrate becomes neutral.

2.3 Isolation of Microcrystalline Cellulose

A 34 g of extracted cellulose was hydrolyzed with 2N hydrochloric acid for 20 min in a hot water bath with a boiling temperature of 105 °C after that, 10 fold of excess cold water was added and the mixture was stirred vigorously by spoon and left to stand overnight. The microcrystalline cellulose extracted was washed until neutral, filtered, dried, and stored for further characterization. The procedures used were adopted from (Ohwoavworhua and Adelakun 2007) with slight modifications.

2.4 Characterization of Cellulose Microcrystalline

2.4.1 Yield Determination

The yield of MCC was determined according to the procedure described in (Ohwoavworhua and Adelakun 2007) and calculated by Eq. 1.

$$Yield = \frac{Final\,mass\,of\,MCC}{Initial\,mass\,of\,straw} \times 100\% \qquad (1)$$

2.4.2 PH Determination

The procedure used for pH determination was adopted from (Fong et al. 2018). A 1 g of the MCC powder was mixed with distilled water (50 ml) for 5 min and the pH of the mixture was measured by pH meter directly.

2.4.3 Particle Size Analysis

The particle size was analyzed by a sieve-shaker. This process was adopted from (Ohwoavworhua and Adelakun 2007) with a slight modification. The sieves used were arranged in descending order which ranges from 250 to 63 μm. A total of 30 g microcrystalline cellulose was measured and kept on top of the first sieve. After that, it was shaken for 5 min. The quantity of MCC retained on every sieve was measured and the average size was computed.

2.4.4 Determination of Water-Soluble Substance

The water-soluble substance was measured according to the procedures described in (Thoorens et al. 2015). 5 g of MCC powder was added to a conical flask containing 80 ml of distilled water and shaken for 10 min. Then, it was filtered through a filter paper into a cleaned and weighed beaker. After that, the filtrate in the beaker was evaporated on the hot plate and kept in the oven at 105 °C for 1 h. Finally it was computed by Eq. 2.

$$\%W_s = \frac{W_d - W_b}{W_i} \times 100 \tag{2}$$

Where W_s is a water-soluble substance, W_d is the weight of a beaker and filtrate after drying, W_b is the total weight of the empty beaker and W_i is the total weight of the sample taken initially.

2.4.5 Determination of Hydration Capacity

Water hydration capacity is the maximum amount of water that 1 g of material will absorb and hold under low-speed centrifugation. It was determined following the procedures adopted by (Maria et al. 2015). 1 g of the sample was placed in 15 ml plastic tubes and mixed with 10 ml distilled water and stoppered. The centrifuge tube was vigorously shaken manually for 2 min. The mixture was kept for 5 min and mixed by inverting three times. This step was repeated once and instantly centrifuged at 1000 rpm for 10 min. The residue was decanted and weighed. Then, it was calculated as a ratio of the residue to the mass of an initial sample. The hydration capacity was calculated by using Eq. 3.

$$H_c = \frac{W_s}{W_{ds}} \tag{3}$$

Where H_c is hydration capacity, W_s is a weight of sediment or residue and W_{ds} is a weight of a dried sample.

2.4.6 Moisture Sorption Capacity

2 g of the MCC was taken and uniformly dispersed on a Petri dish. The sample was kept in a desiccator which has distilled water in its tank (Relative humidity is 100%) at 25 °C for five days and the weight gained by the sample was noted then, the moisture sorption was computed by subtracting the final weight from the initial weight of a sample (Ohwoavworhua and Adelakun 2007).

2.4.7 Loss on Drying

5 g of microcrystalline cellulose was taken and kept in an oven at 105 °C until the mass of the sample becomes constant. Then the loss on drying was computed by Eq. 4.

$$\%LoD = \frac{W_2 - W_3}{W_2 - W_1} \times 100 \tag{4}$$

Where LOD is a loss on drying, W_1 is a weight of an empty dried bottle, W_2 is weight of the bottle and weight of MCC before drying and W_3 is weight of the bottle and dried sample (Ohwoavworhua and Adelakun 2007).

2.4.8 Functional Group Analysis

The functional groups of teff straw and microcrystalline cellulose were analyzed by using the Perkin Elmer FTIR spectrometer (Perkin Elmer, 65, USA) at Addis Ababa University, Department of Chemistry (Addis Ababa, Ethiopia). This was conducted to examine the changes that happened to the functional group of the straw after different steps of pretreatments and it was conducted with the range of 4000–400 cm^{-1}. KBr was used to make pellets for both teff straw and MCC analysis.

2.4.9 Crystallinity Analysis

The change in the crystallinity of the teff straw and MCC was evaluated by the X-ray diffractometer instrument. The XRD analysis was done at Jimma Institute of Technology, School of Materials Science and Engineering, Jimma as per the procedures adopted by (Vieyra et al. 2015). DW-XRD-Y7000 instrument was used with Cu Kα radiation. The scanning range was 2θ = 10 to 70 degrees at a scanning speed of 0.03°/s. To conduct the XRD analysis, the samples need to be dried in advance, which will affect the results as the structure changes upon drying. After that, CI was computed by Eq. 5 where CI is crystallinity index, A_c is an area of the crystalline peaks, and A_t is the total area of both crystalline and amorphous peaks.

$$CI\% = \frac{A_c}{A_t} \times 100\% \tag{5}$$

2.4.10 Thermogravimetry Analysis

Thermogravimetry analysis was done to study the thermal stability of the samples. It was done by TGA - 4000 Perkin Elmer Instrument at Jimma institute of technology, Jimma, Ethiopia. This was conducted for both teff straw and cellulose samples with nitrogen gas. It was conducted as the methods adopted by (Huntley et al. 2015) with minor modifications. A total of 5 g of a sample was used and the heating temperature was a range between 25 °C to 500 °C. The flow rate of nitrogen and heating rate was 20 ml/min and 10 °C/min respectively. The Derivative Thermogravimetry data also recorded.

3 Result and Discussion

3.1 Proximate and Chemical Composition Analysis

The study of proximate composition was conducted to investigate the moisture, ash, volatile, and fixed carbon content of the straw. It is important to understand the component of lignocellulosic materials before their application. The results obtained in this work are agreed with the previously stated works.

Table 1. Result of proximate analysis of teff straw

	MC	AC	VMC	FCC
(Bageru and Srivastava 2018)	7.3	4.0	74.7	14.0
(Chufo et al. 2015)	NA	NA	84.3	NA
(Gabriel et al. 2020)	NA	4.3	NA	NA
This work	8.4	5.1	74.2	15.6

[NB: the experiments were conducted on a dry basis and the average results were computed from triplicates for this work.] [MC: Moisture content, AC: Ash content, VMC: Volatile matter content, FCC: Fixed carbon content, NA: Not Available]

From Table 1, the moisture content of the raw material was 8.4% and it is in an agreement with the value reported by (Bageru and Srivastava 2018) which is 7.3%. The ash and volatile matter content determined were 5.1% and 74.2% respectively. The ash content determined by (Bageru and Srivastava 2018) and (Gabriel et al. 2020) was 4% and 4.3% respectively. The fixed carbon content was 15.6% and the previous value reported by (Bageru and Srivastava 2018) was 14%. The values of the proximate analysis determined in this work are in agreement with previously conducted researches.

The component analysis of lignocellulosic material is very important to understand the suitability of the material for the targeted application. This means it is necessary to know the component of the teff straw before the extraction of the cellulose. The cellulose, hemicellulose, and lignin component of the straw played a great role in the yield of the final product. The cellulose content of teff straw determined was 37.5% (Table 2).

Table 2. Result of the chemical composition of teff straw

	Extractives	Lignin	Hemicellulose	Cellulose
(Chufo et al. 2015)	NA	9.4	32.4	36.7
(Gabriel et al. 2020)	5.7	19.5	23.6	37.2
This work	6.4	15.6	29.5	37.5

[*NA: Not Available]

Extractives are responsible for the color and smell of lignocellulosic materials. The extractive amount of teff straw calculated was 6.4% based on a dry basis. The high amount of extractives produces a high amount of colors and it needs a repetitive treatment process to remove these extractives from raw material and to obtain a product with good purity.

Lignin is a rigid and stiffer part of the plant component and it can protect the cellulose and hemicellulose (Vijayanand et al. 2016). If a high amount of lignin is present in the raw material, it makes it rigid and difficult to decompose the plant to obtain cellulose products. Hemicellulose is the second part of plants that contains several types of sugar units such as galactose, mantose, and glucose. The high amount of hemicellulose and lignin may affect the crystallinity of the material, require a repetitive treatment process, and consume more chemicals than raw materials with lower hemicellulose and lignin content (Vijayanand et al. 2016). From the comparison in Table 3, teff straw has high cellulose content than that of previously used materials for cellulose extraction (water hyacinth, OPEFB, corn stover, rice husk).

Table 3. Comparison of the chemical composition of teff straw with other lignocellulosic materials

Biomass	Extractives	Lignin	Hemicellulose	Cellulose	Reference
Sugarcane bagasse	0.8	23.7	30.3	44.5	(Ferreira et al. 2018)
Rice husk	NA	13.5	32.6	26.5	(Ruan et al. 2016)
Corn stover	6.5	17.8	31.3	37.1	(Saha et al. 2017)
Water hyacinth	NA	8.6	34.1	24.5	(Ruan et al. 2016)
OPEFB	NA	18.6	35.8	36.7	(Ching and Ng 2014)
Teff straw	6.4	15.6	29.5	37.5	*This work*

[NA: Not Available, OPEFB: Oil Palm Empty Fruit Bunches]

The lignin content of teff straw is lower than that of OPEFB, corn stover, and sugarcane bagasse. The hemicellulose content of the teff straw is also lower than that of other materials presented in Table 3. These reasons make teff straw a suitable biomass for the extraction of cellulose because it reduces the consumption of high concentration chemicals and the retention time required for the extraction process.

3.2   Characterization of Cellulose Microcrystalline

The extracted MCC was white fine powder and odorless. The yield of extracted micro cellulose crystalline from teff straw by alkali hydrolysis was 70.8% based on a dry basis.

The alkalinity of cellulose microcrystalline affects its structure when stored for a long time. Therefore, pH should be near neutral to avoid the penetration of acid or base that remained on the surface of MCC since it causes the deterioration of its structure. In this work, the pH of the cellulose microcrystalline was found to be 6.7 (Table 4).

Table 4. Physicochemical properties of MCC

Parameters	(Ohwoavworhua and Adelakun 2007)	(Nkemakolam and Ifeanyi 2017)	This work
pH	7.6	6.58	6.7
Loss on drying (%)	7.2	8.88	4.6
Moisture sorption (%)	22.8	4.8	18.6
Water-soluble substance (%)	<0.2	NA	0.18
Hydration capacity	4.73	2.3	3.7
Mean particle size (μm)	113	166.6	156.4
Organoleptic properties	White powder taste and odorless,	NA	Odorless, white, fine powder

[NA: Not Available]

The result of the water-soluble substance of microcrystalline cellulose has been met the requirements prepared by British Pharmacopeia 2009 (Nasution et al. 2017) which is less than 0.25%. This value indicates the presence of the crystalline structure that existed in MCC and subsequently, the soluble substance was low and in an acceptable range.

Water holding capacity is the amount of water that 1 g of material can hold under low-speed centrifugation. The value computed was found to be 3.7 and it is in an acceptable range when compared to the commercial CMC (Ohwoavworhua and Adelakun 2007). The MCC extracted from a coconut tree reported on (Nkemakolam and Ifeanyi 2017) has a hydration capacity of 2.33.

The value of a loss on drying computed in this work is 4.6% and it is in an agreement with the standard value presented which is less than 6%. This low value indicates that the crystalline phase prevents the transmission of water in the material than the amorphous phase which results in low storage of water. (Ohwoavworhua and Adelakun 2007) reported the MCC with 7.2% of loss on drying which extracted from cotton.

The particle size determined using the sieve shaker was 156.4 μm. The value shows the reduction of the cellulose into small particles and this gives the MCC unique properties due to the large surface area. The particle size of MCC reported by (Nkemakolam and Ifeanyi 2017) and (Ohwoavworhua and Adelakun 2007) was 166.6 μm and 113 μm, respectively.

Moisture sorption capacity explains the stability of MCC during its storage and the variation in crystallinity may cause the change in moisture sorption. MCC may be stored alone or combined with different materials and knowing the moisture sorption capability of MCC helps to select an appropriate place to keep its quality (Roja et al. 2011). The moisture sorption capacity of MCC extracted in this work is 18.6%. Nkemakolam and Ifeanyi (2017) reported the MCC extracted from coconut has 4.8% of moisture sorption capacity.

3.2.1 Functional Group Analysis

The study of the functional group of the raw material and MCC was done by FTIR and the results were interpreted based on the peak observed at each functional group. As the spectra observed from the result shows there are different spectral bands.

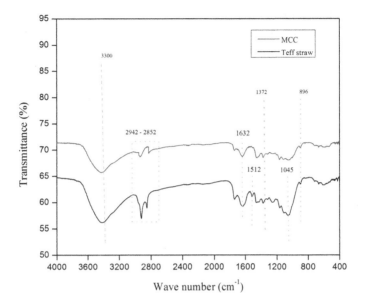

Fig. 2. Graph of FTIR spectra for both teff straw and MCC

The broad peak between 3344–3490 cm^{-1} shows the stretching of intramolecular hydrogen bonds of OH groups of cellulose and it became smaller after chemical treatments because of the reduction of the amorphous phase which is in agreement with (Hayati et al. 2017). The broadband between 2852 cm^{-1}–2942 cm^{-1} is related to C–H stretching of methyl and methylene groups which decreased after bleaching and NaOH treatments (Garcia de Rodriguez et al. 2006). The other peak observed at 1730 cm^{-1} implies a presence of acetyl and uronic ester groups in hemicellulose (Garcia de Rodriguez et al. 2006). This was reduced and disappeared gradually after the treatment process. The peak found around 1632 cm^{-1} is due to the water absorbed by teff straw (Liu et al. 2006). The other peak detected at 1512 cm^{-1} in the teff straw sample shows the presence of methoxyl groups of lignin, the C-H deformation of methyl, and aromatic C = C ring stretching. This peak disappeared in MCC which shows the absence or reduction of lignin and hemicelluloses after bleaching and alkali hydrolysis. The peaks observed at 1253 cm^{-1} and 1045 cm^{-1} in teff straw and disappeared in MCC were due to C-O out of plane stretching and C-O-C pyranose ring stretching respectively (Kallel et al. 2016). This shows the effectiveness of the chemical treatments to remove lignin, hemicellulose, and amorphous parts of lignocellulosic material. The spectral bands at 1155 cm^{-1} and 1118 cm^{-1} are from the C-C stretching in cellulose and C-OH skeletal vibration in lignin respectively (Kallel et al. 2016). The peak detected at 892 cm^{-1} shows the presence of β-glycosidic linkages in cellulose (Mzimela et al. 2018). The peaks at 1322 cm^{-1}, 1431 cm^{-1}, and 1372 cm^{-1} typical of pure cellulose. This FTIR result confirms the total removal of wax, lignin, other extractives, and partial removal of amorphous regions of the straw as indicated in Fig. 2.

3.2.2 Crystallinity Index Analysis

The crystallinity of cellulose plays a vital role in its chemical, physical and mechanical properties. Decreased crystallinity indicates that the presence of a higher amount of amorphous regions. This may result in increased moisture gain and chemical reactivity which affects the quality and application of cellulose microcrystalline.

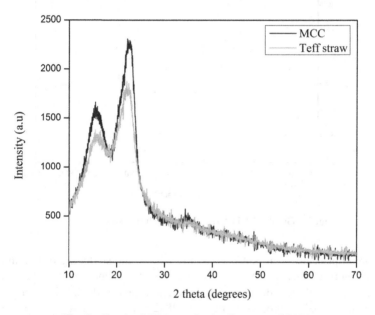

Fig. 3. Graph of XRD result of teff straw and MCC

The high crystallinity index shows the presence of a low amount of amorphous parts. The diffractometer peaks obtained from XRD analysis were scanned over 10 to 70 degrees with a step increment of 0.03 s^{-1}. It was done for teff straw and cellulose microcrystalline to observe the difference in their crystallinity after chemical treatments. As indicated in Fig. 3 there are two major peaks for both samples around 2θ of 15 degrees and 22 degrees.

The crystallinity index of MCC and teff straw was calculated by Eq. 9 and found to be 72.8% and 47.7% respectively. The CI of teff straw was 47.7% without any chemical treatment and it had the lowest CI compared to the chemical treated samples. The CI of microcrystalline cellulose was 72.8% which was increased by 25.1% after bleaching, alkali, and acid hydrolysis of teff straw which confirms the reduction of amorphous regions in straw (Sofla et al. 2016), extracted CMC from sugarcane bagasse with a crystallinity index of 68%. (Ching and Ng 2014) reported the crystallinity value of MCC with 58% that is extracted from OPEFB. So, the crystallinity index of MCC reported in this work is in a range with the value of previously reported on (Ching and Ng 2014) and (Sofla et al. 2016).

3.2.3 Thermogravimetry Analysis

Thermogravimetry analysis (TGA) is one of the well-known methods to examine the thermal stability of materials. Cellulose, hemicellulose, lignin, and other extractives in plant fiber decompose at various temperatures due to their different chemical structures.

Table 5. Thermal degradation of teff straw and MCC

Samples	TGA analysis		Weight of residue (%)
	T_{onset} (°C)	T_{peak} (°C)	
Teff straw	255	354	0.52
MCC	315	363	0.36

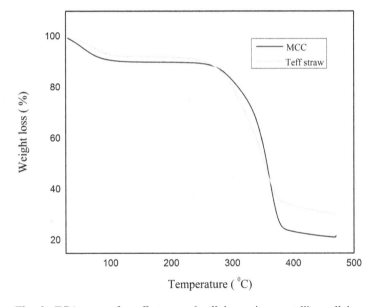

Fig. 4. TGA curves for teff straw and cellulose microcrystalline cellulose

As indicated in Table 5, the onset and maximum temperature of teff straw were 255 °C and 354 °C respectively. The onset and maximum temperature of MCC were 315 °C and 363 °C respectively. TGA curves (Fig. 4) of teff straw and MCC reveal three regions of mass loss. The first loss starts at lower temperatures around 25 °C −230 °C, due to moisture vaporization or low molecular weight degradation, the second is between 230 °C−375 °C and the third is above 376 °C which corresponds to char formation.

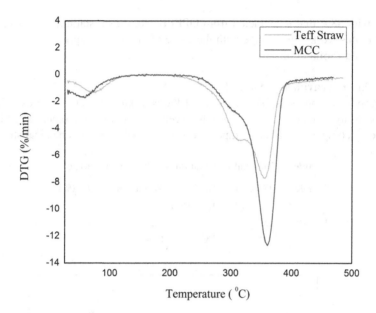

Fig. 5. DTGA curves for straw and MCC

From the DTGA curve in Fig. 5, the maximum peak reached 354 °C for teff straw and 363 °C for cellulose particles. This shows the untreated teff straw has lower thermal stability than MCC which is due to the presence of pectin, hemicellulose, and lignin. The extracted microcrystalline cellulose has better thermal stability than that of the untreated sample and it confirms the removal of other unnecessary amorphous parts which support the FTIR result. This illustrates the usefulness of chemical treatments used for the extraction of cellulose microcrystalline cellulose particles.

4   Conclusion

Cellulose microcrystalline has been successfully extracted from teff straw (Eragrostis Teff) by delignification, alkali treatment, and acid hydrolysis. The yield of MCC was 70.8% and it has 156.4 μm particle sizes. The cellulose content value determined in the chemical compositional analysis is 37.5% and this shows that the teff straw can be used as the source of cellulose like other cheap and locally available agricultural waste. The organoleptic and the value of other properties such as pH, loss on drying, moisture sorption, and water-soluble substance of microcrystalline extracted in this work were almost similar to that of commercial MCC. The functional group analysis, crystallinity index, and thermal stability of MCC reveals the presence of crystal structures in MCC and the total removal and partial degradation of wax, pectin, lignin, and amorphous regions of the straw. The properties are ideal and recommended for the application of MCC in the extraction of nanocellulose, pharmaceuticals, filler in polymer composites, and other applications.

References

Bageru, A.B., Srivastava, V.C.: Biosilica preparation from abundantly available African biomass Teff (Eragrostis tef) straw ash by sol-gel method and its characterization. Biomass Convers. Biorefinery **8**(4), 971–978 (2018). https://doi.org/10.1007/s13399-018-0335-5

Chakraborty, A., Sain, M., Kortschot, M.: Cellulose microfibrils: a novel method of preparation using high shear refining and cryocrushing. Holzforschung **59**(1), 102–107 (2005). https://doi.org/10.1515/HF.2005.016

Ching, Y.C., Ng, T.S.: Effect of preparation conditions on cellulose from oil. BioResources **9**(4), 6373–6385 (2014)

Chufo, A., Yuan, H., Zou, D., Pang, Y., Li, X.: Biomethane production and physicochemical characterization of anaerobically digested teff (Eragrostis tef) straw pretreated by sodium hydroxide. Biores. Technol. **181**(April), 214–219 (2015). https://doi.org/10.1016/j.biortech.2015.01.054

Ferreira, F.V., Mariano, M., Rabelo, S.C., Gouveia, R.F., Lona, L.M.F.: Isolation and surface modification of cellulose nanocrystals from sugarcane bagasse waste: from a micro- to a nano-scale view. Appl. Surf. Sci. **436**, 1113–1122 (2018). https://doi.org/10.1016/j.apsusc.2017.12.137

Fong, J.J.M., Ibrahim, A., Abdulah, M.F., Sam, S.T.: Optimizing yield of microcrystalline cellulose from empty fruit bunch via hydrolysis using ionic liquid. IOP Conf. Ser. Mater. Sci. Eng. **429**(1), 012060 (2018). https://doi.org/10.1088/1757-899X/429/1/012060

Gabriel, T., Belete, A., Syrowatka, F., Neubert, R.H.H., Gebre-Mariam, T.: Extraction and characterization of celluloses from various plant byproducts. Int. J. Biol. Macromol. **158**, 1248–1258 (2020). https://doi.org/10.1016/j.ijbiomac.2020.04.264

Garcia de Rodriguez, N.L., Thielemans, W., Dufresne, A.: Sisal cellulose whiskers reinforced polyvinyl acetate nanocomposites. Cellulose **13**(3), 261–270 (2006). https://doi.org/10.1007/s10570-005-9039-7

Halim, A.: Chemical modification of cellulose extracted from sugarcane bagasse: preparation of hydroxyethyl cellulose. Arab. J. Chem. **7**(3), 1–10 (2014). https://doi.org/10.1016/j.arabjc.2013.05.006

Hayati, N., Rahman, A., Chieng, B.W., Rahman, N.A.: Extraction and characterization of cellulose nanocrystals from tea leaf waste fibers. Polymers **9**(588), 1–11 (2017). https://doi.org/10.3390/polym9110588

Huntley, C.J., Crews, K.D., Abdalla, M.A., Russell, A.E., Curry, M.L.: Influence of strong acid hydrolysis processing on the thermal stability and crystallinity of cellulose isolated from wheat straw. Int. J. Chem. Eng. **1**(1–9), 2015 (2015). https://doi.org/10.1155/2015/658163

Kallel, F., Bettaieb, F., Khiari, R., García, A., Bras, J.: Isolation and structural characterization of cellulose nanocrystals extracted from garlic straw residues. Ind. Crops Prod. **87**, 287–296 (2016). https://doi.org/10.1016/j.indcrop.2016.04.060

Kumar, A., Negi, Y.S., Choudhary, V., Bhardwaj, N.K.: Sugarcane bagasse: a promising source for the production of nanocellulose. J. Polym. Compos. **2**(3), 1–6 (2016)

Liu, C.F., Ren, J.L., Xu, F., Liu, J.J., Sun, J.X., Sun, R.C.: Isolation and characterization of cellulose obtained from ultrasonic irradiated sugarcane bagasse. J. Agric. Food Chem. **54**(16), 5742–5748 (2006). https://doi.org/10.1021/jf060929o

Mandal, A., Chakrabarty, D.: Isolation of nanocellulose from waste sugarcane bagasse (SCB) and its characterization. Carbohyd. Polym. (2011). https://doi.org/10.1016/j.carbpol.2011.06.030

Maria, S., Grossa, P., Science, F., Maria, S.: Assessment of different methods for determining the capacity of water absorption of ingredients and additives used in the meat industry. Int. Food Res. J. **22**(1), 356–362 (2015)

Moon, R.J., Schueneman, G.T., Simonsen, J.: Overview of cellulose nanomaterials, their capabilities and applications. JOM **68**(9), 2383–2394 (2016). https://doi.org/10.1007/s11837-016-2018-7

Mottaleb, K.A., Rahut, D.B.: Household production and consumption patterns of Teff in Ethiopia. Agribusiness **34**(3), 668–684 (2018). https://doi.org/10.1002/agr.21550

Mustapha, D.I., Ahmed, S.I., Musa, A.M., Isah Yakub Mohammed, I.G.: Proximate and ultimate analyses of some selected lignocellulosic. BioResources **3**(6), 1–10 (2018). 322488094

Mzimela, Z.N.T., Linganiso, L.Z., Revaprasadu, N., Motaung, T.E.: Comparison of cellulose extraction from sugarcane bagasse through alkali. Mater. Res. **21**(6), 1–7 (2018). https://doi.org/10.1590/1980-5373-mr-2017-0750

Nasution, H., Yurnaliza, Y., Veronicha, Irmadani, Sitompul, S.: Physicochemical properties and characteristics of microcrystalline cellulose derived from the cellulose of oil palm empty fruit bunch. IOP Conf. Ser. Mater. Sci. Eng. **223**(1), 012056 (2017). https://doi.org/10.1088/1757-899X/223/1/012056

Nkemakolam, N., Ifeanyi, O.: Effect of drying methods on the powder and compaction properties of microcrystalline cellulose derived from Cocos nucifera. J. Pharm. Res. Int. **20**(2), 1–15 (2017). https://doi.org/10.9734/jpri/2017/37615

Ohwoavworhua, F.O., Adelakun, T.A.: Some physical characteristics of microcrystalline cellulose obtained from raw cotton of *Cochlospermum planchonii*. Trop. J. Pharm. Res. **4**(2), 501–507 (2007). https://doi.org/10.4314/tjpr.v4i2.14626

Roja, J., Moren, S., Lopez, A.: Assessment of the water sorption properties of several microcrystalline celluloses. J. Pharm. Sci. Res. **3**(7), 1302–1309 (2011)

Ruan, T., Zeng, R., Yin, X.-Y., Zhang, S.-X., Yang, Z.-H.: Water hyacinth (Eichhornia crassipes) biomass as a biofuel feedstock by enzymatic hydrolysis. BioResources **11**(1), 2372–2380 (2016). https://doi.org/10.15376/biores.11.1.2372-2380

Saha, B.C., Kennedy, G.J., Qureshi, N., Cotta, M.A.: Biological pretreatment of corn stover with Phlebia brevispora NRRL-13108 for enhanced enzymatic hydrolysis and efficient ethanol production. Biotechnol. Prog. **33**(2), 365–374 (2017). https://doi.org/10.1002/btpr.2420

Sofla, M.R.K., Brown, R.J., Tsuzuki, T., Rainey, T.J.: A comparison of cellulose nanocrystals and cellulose nanofibers extracted from bagasse using acid and ball milling methods. Adv. Nat. Sci. Nanosci. Nanotechnol. **7**(3), 035004 (2016)

Thoorens, G., Krier, F., Rozet, E., Carlin, B., Evrard, B.: Understanding the impact of microcrystalline cellulose physicochemical properties on tablet ability. Int. J. Pharm. **490**(1–2), 47–54 (2015). https://doi.org/10.1016/j.ijpharm.2015.05.026

Vieyra, H., Figueroa-López, U., Guevara-Morales, A., Vergara-Porras, B., San Martín-Martínez, E., Aguilar-Mendez, M.Á.: Optimized monitoring of production of cellulose nanowhiskers from opuntia ficus-indica (Nopal Cactus). Int. J. Polym. Sci. **2015**, 1–9 (2015). https://doi.org/10.1155/2015/871345

Vijayanand, C., Kamaraj, S., Karthikeyan, S., Sriramajayam, S.: Characterization of indigenous biomass. Int. J. Agric. Sci. **8**(50), 2124–2127 (2016)

Process Revamping of H_2SO_4 Plant to Double Contact Double Absorption (DCDA) Using ASPEN HYSYS to Reduce SO_2 Emission: Case of Awash Melkassa Sulfuric Acid Factory

Addis Lemessa[✉], Melkamu Birlie, Metadel Kassahun,
and Yared Mengistu

Bahir Dar Institute of Technology, Bahir Dar University, Bahir Dar, Ethiopia

Abstract. Sulfur dioxide (SO_2) is identified as among one of the major air pollutant gases in the globe. SO_2 cause severe adverse effects on the respiratory system of all living things and causes several difficulties in the environment such as acid rain and plant growth retardation. This work presents a virtual experimental investigation of the simulation of H_2SO_4 using Double contact double absorption (DCDA) to reduce the SO_2 emission. Awash Melkassa Aluminum Sulfate and Sulfuric Acid Share Company (AMASSASC) produce Sulfuric acid by using single contact single absorption (SCSA) which releases up to 3% SO_2 to the atmosphere. In this work, the simulation uses ASPEN HYSYS with Antoine based fluid package to predict several values. The major unit operation involved in the design includes four consecutive converters and absorption columns including the proposed intermediate absorber and secondary absorber. Different recycle setup configuration was considered to achieve the best possible SO_2 reduction. The effect of inlet temperature, split ratio of mass to the modeled absorber in response to the final SO_2 amount was studied. From the optimal design it was able to reduce SO_2 to 0.12 mol%. The trade-off between utility power consumption and SO_2 emission for different design options was also studied to obtain optimal design setup.

Keywords: SO_2 emission · H_2SO_4 · Aspen HYSYS · Simulation · SCSA · DCDA

1 Introduction

Sulfuric acid is one of the most widely produced chemical in the world and sulfuric acid production is a good indicator of a nation's industrial strength [1, 2]. It can be produced by different methods and it is very crucial chemical in process industries [3]. It has a vast application in different areas like fertilizer manufacture, mineral processing, oil refining, wastewater processing, chemical synthesis, domestic acidic drain cleaners, as an electrolyte in lead-acid batteries, and in various cleaning agents [4, 5]. Although the universal use of sulfuric acid has made it indispensable, its production process releases gaseous pollutants such as sulfur oxides (SO_x), nitrous oxides (NO_x) and acid mist (H_2SO_4) to the environment, which ecologically threaten the standard of living [6].

© ICST Institute for Computer Sciences, Social Informatics and Telecommunications Engineering 2022
Published by Springer Nature Switzerland AG 2022. All Rights Reserved
M. L. Berihun (Ed.): ICAST 2021, LNICST 411, pp. 59–72, 2022.
https://doi.org/10.1007/978-3-030-93709-6_5

The federal Clean Air Act (CAA) requires the United States Environmental Protection Agency (U.S. EPA) to set National Ambient Air Quality Standards (NAAQS) for six criteria pollutants that are considered harmful to public health and the environment in 1970. These pollutants are: particulate matter, carbon monoxide, ground-level ozone, nitrogen dioxide, SO_2, and lead. The NAAQS set limits for the criteria pollutants in the ambient air. Limits established to protect human health are referred to as primary standards while limits established to prevent the environmental damage are referred to as secondary standards. The primary NAAQS for SO_2 measured over a 1-h period is set at 75 parts per billion parts of air. A secondary NAAQS for SO_2 measured over a 3-h period is set at 0.5 parts per million parts of air. This standard cannot be exceeded more than once per year [7]. High level of sulfur dioxide emission is associated with various ecological damages and health problems. The major health issues due to the availability of sulfur dioxide in the atmosphere causes a series adverse effect on the respiratory system of all living beings [8, 9]. Short-term exposure to SO_2 may cause wheezing, chest tightness and shortness of breath. Longer-term exposure to sulfur dioxide causes series respiratory problems. The environmental effects of SO_2 are detrimental. SO_2 is dissolved in water and can be easily oxidized in to sulfurous acid and sulfuric acid in the water vapor in the air which will falls as an acid rain [10]. Therefore, SO_2 can be a major factor for the acid rain that is harmful for vegetation, agriculture and, corrosion of buildings and constructions [11].

Hence, strategies for mitigating these emissions become a major concern for sustainable development. Over the years, the design and modification of the sulfuric acid production process have received considerable attention to minimize air pollution. The lead chamber process was the earlier design employed for large scale production and this production process gradually outdated and replaced by single contact single absorption (SCSA) process [12, 13]. 97 to 98% of the SO_2 is oxidized to SO_3 in the SCSA process while the remaining 2 to 3% is vented to the environment [14]. To enhance the oxidation efficiency of SO_2 to SO_3 and to obtain a higher grade of sulfuric acid, the SCSA process was modified to the double contact double absorption (DCDA) process by Bayer in 1963 [14]. Currently, the DCDA process is the most preferable and widely used sulfuric acid production process. Basically, the operating principle of DCDA process is same as that of the lead chamber and SCSA processes [15]. The distinguished characteristics of the DCDA process over other types of production processes are the presence of double reactive-absorption towers and four or more converter beds in the catalytic reactor. These enhance the oxidation of SO_2 to about 99.5% or higher in the catalytic converters, and an acid concentration in the range of 98 to 99.9% in reactive-absorption towers [13]. The unreacted SO_2 and SO_3 from the process are emitted through the absorber exit gases to the environment and its emission should be below the permissible limit.

Several studies have been conducted by numerous researchers to reduce the emission of SO_2 to environment. Kiss et al. proposed a model to simulate a DCDA process with five converter-beds; air flow split to catalyst beds 3 and 4, and the burner. Their results showed that SO_x emissions are significantly reduced approximately by 40% by optimizing air flow rate to the burner or split fractions [16, 17]. Gomez-Garcia et al. also developed a rigorous heterogeneous model for the analysis of an industrial adiabatic multi-bed catalytic reactor for SO_2 oxidation based on the Maxwell-Stefan diffusion model. The implementation of the model in steady state simulation allows realistic prediction of each catalytic bed in terms of SO_2 oxidation, pressure and temperature profile, and the effectiveness factor variation along the reactor [18]. Many other studies were conducted and reported by different authors to reduce the emission of SO_2 to the atmosphere [19–23].

Awash Melkassa Aluminum Sulfate and Sulfuric Acid Share Company (AMAS-SASC) is the only sulfuric acid and aluminum sulfate factory in Ethiopia and it was established 1982 E.C. The annual production rate of the factory is 13,600 and 17,000 tons for aluminum sulfate with concentration of 17% and sulfuric acid with a concentration of 98.5%, respectively [24]. This factory produces sulfuric acid by using single contact single absorption (SCSA) process. Due to SCSA process, 2 to 3% SO_2 toxic gas is emitted into the environment and the release of this SO_2 emission into the environment has a tremendous impact on the health of all living things nearby. This study aimed at minimizing the emission of SO_2 gas from AMASSASC factory by improving the oxidation of sulfur dioxide to sulfur trioxide using double contact double absorption process through ASPEN HYSYS simulator.

This study mainly focuses on reducing the emission of SO_2 into the environment by increasing the oxidation of SO_2 to SO_3 and thereby improving the production of Sulphuric acid in AMASSASC. The specific objectives are to investigate the effect of recycle stream configuration to different converters on the final SO_2 amount, split ratio supplied to intermediate absorber on to the amount of SO_2 released to the environment and to study the tradeoff between percent emission reduction and utility consumption.

2 Methodology

2.1 Materials

Aspen HYSYS V10 was used to simulate the modified H_2SO_4 plant. Simulation data were obtained from the Awash Melkassa chemical factory.

Problem Definition: The process of sulfuric acid plant uses elemental sulfur (99.99%). The solid sulfur changes to liquid form in melting section. In this section the solid sulfur is fed into the feed hopper from the storage area and enters into the melting pit. As the coil is heated the solid sulfur become melted and change to black color liquid sulfur at a temperature between 135 °C–145 °C and at a pressure of 0.6 Mpa.

Molten sulfur is pumped by a screw pump to the burner through a jacketed pipe which used to prevent the solidification of molten sulfur inside the pipe. The liquefied Sulfur is oxidized in to SO_2 in burning section with temperature range between 700 °C to 1040 °C in the presence of dried air with temperature of 235 °C from directed from air drying tower. Then the molten sulfur is converted to SO_2 gas with 11% SO_2 gas according to reaction in Eq. 1.

$$S\ (l) + O_2\ (g) \Rightarrow SO_2\ (g) \tag{1}$$

The converter section has four fixed catalytic beds with its own heat exchangers. The gases with 11% SO_2 from the waste heat boiler is charged with a temperature of

425 °C at the top of the converter and the dried air from the drying tower also directed to the converter. Then the Sulfur dioxide gas is oxidized to sulfur trioxide in the presence of vanadium pent oxide (V_2O_5) catalyst according to the Eq. 2 shown below.

$$2 \, SO_2 \, (g) + O_2 \, (g) \Rightarrow 2 \, SO_3 \, (g) \tag{2}$$

All the reactions in the converter are exothermic and reversible in nature. The converters are operating in the temperature intervals of 400–600 °C and 1−2 atm.

First Bed: The gas with a temperature of 425 °C is directed to the 1st bed which is filled with the vanadium penta oxide catalyst and the first converter has a conversion of 63%. 1st converter bed with a temperature of 597 °C is sent to the gas-gas heat exchanger, where it's cooled down to a temperature of 440 °C.

Second Bed: The gas with the temperature of 440 °C is supplied to the 2nd bed where the unconverted gas further converted to SO_3. The conversion of 2nd bed is around 87% and gas lift from 2nd bed with the temperature of 505 °C sent to gas-water heat exchanger where it was cooled down to a temperature of 430 °C. SO_2 gas with the temperature of 430 °C was sent to 3rd bed converter.

Third Bed: The unconverted gas from 2nd bed converter is expected to be further converted to SO_3. The grade of conversion in the 3rd bed converter reaches to 96%. Gas leaving from 3rd bed with the temperature of 453 °C to 420 °C and sent to 4th bed converter.

Fourth Bed: The unconverted gas from 3rd bed further converted by mixing of the dried air with gas. Finally, the grade of conversion after 4th bed was 98%. Now the SO_3 gas with the temperature of 424 °C was sent to economizer (E501-3) or gas water heat exchanger where SO_3 gas cooled to a temperature of (180–200) °C. Finally, this SO_3 with temperature of 180–200 °C was sent to absorption tower.

Absorption Column: In an acid plant absorption tower, SO_3 gas was charged to the bottom of the tower from the converter and 10% concentrated sulfuric acid with 98.5% concentration from the circulation tank which is filled with 70% of concentrated sulfuric acid showers at the top of absorption tower by a circulating pump by reducing its temperature from 80 °C to 60 °C by acid cooler. The rate of absorption can be improved by rushing ring which maximizes surface contact area between gas and liquid while minimizing pressure drop. Sulfuric acid has the ability to absorb SO_3 gas. These acids contain 1.5% water which reacts with the SO_3 gas. Once SO_3 comes in contact with the acid, it is immediately absorbed by circulating acid and produces 99.1% concentrated sulfuric acid with a temperature of 89.3 °C. Here the top exit gas contains SO_2 is emitted to the environment at the concentration of 2–3%.

Dilution Tank: Finally, oleum enter into dilution tank to reduce the concentration from 99.1% to 98.5% by adding water or by an acid that return from drying tower with concentration of 98.3% according to Eq. 3. After mixing in the dilution tank the acid has concentration of 98.5%. Then enter into circulation tank with temperature of 80 °C. Figure 1 shows the overall Block flow diagram for the production of H$_2$SO$_4$ and revamped process synthesis.

$$SO_3 (g) + H_2O (l) \Rightarrow H_2SO_4 (l) \tag{3}$$

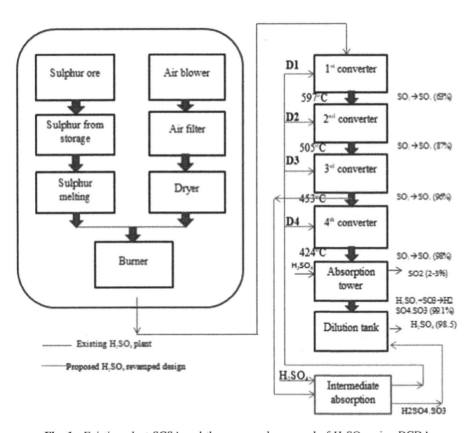

Fig. 1. Existing plant SCSA and the revamped proposed of H$_2$SO$_4$ using DCDA

2.2   The Proposed Intermediate Absorption

In this study some portion of the exit gas of the third converter will be taken to the proposed absorption column where H$_2$SO$_4$ is fed at the top of the column to react with SO$_3$ and leaving the column at the bottom as oleum (H$_2$SO$_4$.SO$_3$) increasing the sulphuric acid concentration then enters in to the dilution tank along with the oleum exiting the secondary absorption column (existing). The top stream of the absorption column containing SO_2 will be recycled to the subsequent converter to study the effect of the configuration. Figure 1 shows the existing and revamped process synthesis. There are three proposed configuration of the entrance of the exit unconverted SO_2 from intermediate absorption column. From figure these are designated as a, b and c that corresponds to that the exit gas SO_2 from the intermediate absorption column entering into 1st converter, 2nd converter and 4th converter respectively.

2.3   Reactions Package

Sulphuric acid is manufactured from elemental sulphur in a three-stage process. These stoichiometric were entered to the basic environment of the simulation. For the simulation modeling Conversion reactor model was selected for Eq. 4 and 5 that takes place in burner and converter 1 respectively. The reaction between SO_3 and H_2O was modeled using equilibrium reactor model using dilution tank according to the relation presented by Eq. 6.

$$S \ (l) + O_2 \ (g) \Rightarrow SO_2 \ (g) \tag{4}$$

$$2 \ SO_2 \ (g) + O_2 \ (g) \Rightarrow 2 \ SO_3 \ (g) \tag{5}$$

$$SO_3 \ (g) + H_2O \ (l) \Leftrightarrow H_2SO_4 \ (l) \tag{6}$$

2.4   Fluid Package

For the simulation of the modified design options, Antoine model was used. This model is applicable for low pressure systems that behave ideally. The equations are traditionally applied for heavier hydrocarbon fractionation systems and consequently provide a good means of comparison against rigorous models. They should not be considered for VLE predictions for systems operating at high pressures or systems with significant quantities of light hydrocarbons.

2.5   Simulation of Feed Conditions

For the implementation of the revamped H_2SO_4 plant simulation in ASPEN HYSYS, two feed streams were considered including sulfur and air having the process conditions and parameter specifications. The data were provided from Awash Melkasa sulfuric acid and aluminum sulfuric factory, Adama, Ethiopia. Table 1 presents process conditions and component composition considered for the simulation.

Table 1. Feed stream conditions

Stream name	Sulphur	Air
Vapour/phase fraction	0.00	1.00
Temperature [C]	25.00	25.00
Pressure [kPa]	1500.00	1500.00
Molar flow [kgmole/h]	27.12	51.99
Mass flow [kg/h]	869.5	1500.00
Std ideal liq vol flow [m^3/h]	0.48	1.73
Molar enthalpy [kJ/kgmole]	−77327.98	−94.07
Molar entropy [kJ/kgmole-C]	448.15	129.07
Heat flow [kJ/h]	−2096952.45	−4891.41
Major components (mole fraction)		
S	1	0
O_2	0	0.21
N_2	0	0.79
H_2O	0	0
H_2SO_4	0	0
SO_2	0	0
SO_3	0	0

3 Result and Discussion

3.1 Column Design Analysis

A SO_3 absorption column is a unit where gas flows up and liquid (H_2SO_4) flows down. SO_3 is transferred from the gas phase to the liquid phase where it reacts with the H_2SO_4 to form oleum ($H_2SO_4.SO_3$). The gas and liquid phases are made to get in contact by the help of column plates or random or structured packing. In this work plate type absorption column is selected for making ease of maintenance. The numbers of stages are 10 with 1.5 m internal diameter and tray spacing of 0.5 m. Figure 2(a) shows the temperature and pressure profiles of the intermediate absorber. Across the column from top to down arrangement, the pressure is 1 atmosphere however there is a slight rise in temperature in the first two stages from 156.9 to 159.9 °C. One of the most decisive considerations in designing gas absorption towers is to study whether or not temperatures in the trey along the height of the tower is varied. The solute solubility usually depends strongly on temperature. From stage 1 to stage 7 the temperature of the trays were isothermal at 159.4 °C. The equilibrium shows that the remaining stages including 7, 8, and 9 to 10 are at a high trey operating temperature with the corresponding values of 159.3, 159.4, 160 and 170 °C respectively. Figure 2 (b) and (c) presents the net liquid and vapor at every trey positions and the pictorial appearance of the intermediate absorption column.

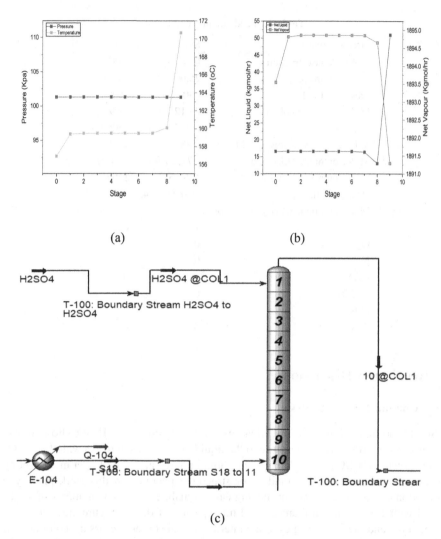

Fig. 2. Parameters profile for the intermediate against trey position (a) Temperature and pressure (b) net liquid and vapor (c) simulated unit block of absorption column

3.2   Effect of Inlet Temperature on SO₃ Absorption

An increase in gas and liquid inlet temperature leads to improve the absorption of SO_3 at equilibrium. Simulation results based on constant stage efficiency are shown in Fig. 3. As the temperature of the inlet gas stream is increasing from 80 °C to 300 °C, the column exhibits a significant absorption of SO_3 in the range of 0.0046 to 0.00016. In practice, a higher temperature gives a higher absorption and reaction rate [25]. The result obtained by the simulation sensitivity analysis on the inlet temperature against SO_3 removal proved similar trend.

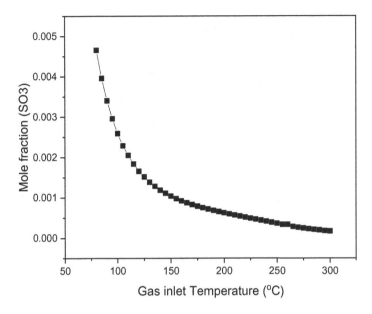

Fig. 3. Effect of inlet temperature on SO_3 removal in the absorption column

3.3 The Effect of Different Types of Recycles Setup

The top product from absorption column containing O_2, N_2 and SO_2 was recycled to in different design options. The first design option (Fig. 4 (a)) is building the recycle stream to the first converter. This configuration is by far results a higher removal of SO_2 which is 0.12%. The second design option (Fig. 4 (b)) fed the recycle stream directly to the second converter. These options dropped the removal capacity to 0.84%. Equal amount of removal of SO_2 was predicted by the third converter (Fig. 5 (c)). However the setting up the recycle to the last converter (Fig. 4 (d)), the removal of SO_2 was lower than the other subsequent converters that resulted a 1.08% SO_2 removal. High removal of SO_2 at the secondary absorber was noted because the unconverted SO_2 was subjected to a sequence of beds that increase the reaction time of SO_2 with excess O_2 at each bed. The recycled stream containing a large amount of SO_2 and other gases gas requires additional dosage of O_2. In every column, there is an excess O_2 supplied from air dryer to every converter to facilitate a complete conversion of SO_2 to SO_3 because according to Le Chatelier's Principle, Increasing the concentration of oxygen in the mixture causes the shifting of the equilibrium position towards the product side. Therefore the need of shifting the equilibrium position to the right side in order to produce the maximum possible amount of sulfur trioxide in the equilibrium mixture is the other design consideration (Table 2).

Table 2. Mole fractions results obtained at different recycle setup

Components	Design option 1	Design option 2	Design option 3	Design option 4
H_2O	0.0000	0.0000	0.0000	0.0000
SO_2	0.0012	0.0084	0.0084	0.0108
SO_3	0.0245	0.0142	0.0142	0.0183
H_2SO_4	0.0021	0.0012	0.0011	0.0036
Nitrogen	0.7942	0.7949	0.7949	0.7926
Oxygen	0.1779	0.1814	0.1814	0.1723
S_Liquid	0.0000	0.0000	0.0000	0.0025
Energy consumption				
Cooling duty (KJ/hr)	8.327E + 07	8.167E + 07	8.11E + 07	6.435E + 07
Heating duty (KJ/hr)	8.122E + 07	8.062E + 07	8.015E + 07	6.345E + 07
Total	1.6449E + 07	1.6229E + 07	1.6125E + 07	1.278E + 07

3.4   Effect of Split Ratio on the Amount of SO_2

Varying the split ratio of the 3rd converter product stream into intermediate absorption column and 4th column brought a significant change in the final concentration of the product. Figure 4 shows the variation of split ratio from 0.1 to 0.9 with respect to its corresponding calculated SO_2 mole fraction. Increasing the split ratio from 0.1 to 0.2% lifted the SO_2 amount from 1% to 1.6%. Further increased split ratio from 0.2 to 0.9 reduces the amount of the SO_2 amount to 0.002 (0.2%) which at the end give the optimal point of value set for split ratio. In overall perspective, the amount of SO_2 decreased significantly within the entire range of the split ratio. The Le Chatelier's principle states that equilibrium favor to forward side when removing the product SO_3 from catalytic converter.

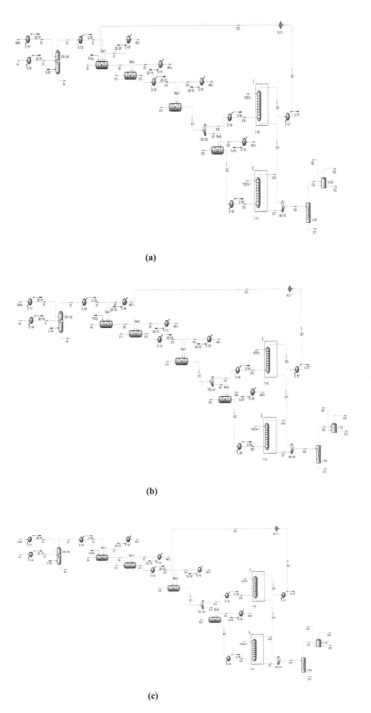

(a)

(b)

(c)

Fig. 4. Design options for H₂SO₄ production where unconverted SO₂ is recycled to (a) to 1st converter (b), to 2nd converter (c), to 3rd converter and (d) to 4th converter

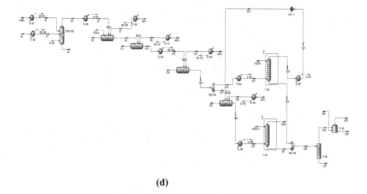

(d)

Fig. 4. (*continued*)

3.5 Trade-off Between Emission Reduction and Utility Consumption

Reduction of SO_2 emission to the environment is the first priority considering the fact that environment and profit should not be compromised. However, sophisticated designs can potentially increase the utility consumptions. Setting up the recycle stream according to the design option 1, reduce the emission significantly. In contrary, it requires higher power consumption. This is because of the large amount of recycle constituents passing through every converter which intern increase the flow rate of the material stream. This has a direct influence on the total utility usage (cooling and heating). The total utility consumption is reduced when reducing the exposure time (reactor bed) spent by the recycle stream. However the emission of SO_2 would be high compared to the other subsequent designs. This is well depicted by performing a preliminary optimization or trade-off study as shown in Fig. 5. The total utility consumption in terms of design option 1 is around 16,449,000 kJ/hr (4569.16 KW) and the corresponding amount of SO_2 is 0.12% mole. However, the optimal design according to Fig. 6 lies on design option 3 having optimal utility usage and SO_2 mole percentage of 15,500,000 kJ/hr (4305.55 KW) and 0.8% mole of SO_2 emission.

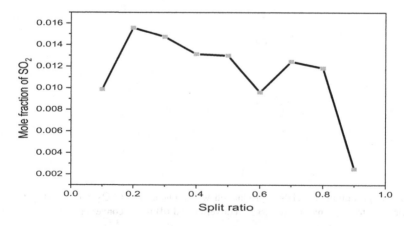

Fig. 5. Sensitivity analysis on the effect of split ratio on mole fraction of SO_2

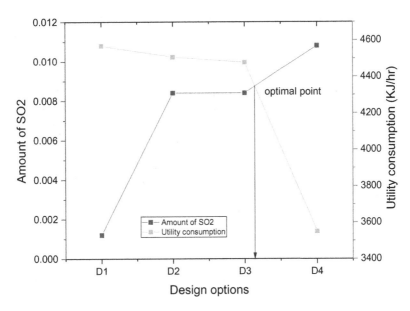

Fig. 6. Design options and their Trade-off between mole percentage of SO$_2$ amount and utility consumption

4   Conclusion

This research mainly emphasis on the reduction of SO$_2$ emission that contributes to the acid rain and substantially plant growth. The Antoine property package was used due to its compatibility with the actual process condition to handle the chemical reacting system and the separation process as well. It was proved that retrofitting the existing H$_2$SO$_4$ plant from SCSA to DCDA potentially has shown a promising result. Additionally, four different case studies were considered for setting up the recycle stream that contains SO$_2$ gas after concentrating SO$_3$ with H$_2$SO$_4$. Hence design option 1 (configuring gas effluent from the absorber to the 1st converter) that was able to drop the SO$_2$ amount to only 0.12% which is much lower that what is being released now a days using SCSA. The trade-off between power consumption and SO$_2$ emission reveled that setting up the recycle stream to directly the 3rd converter give an optimal power consumption and SO$_2$ emission. However, controversy between environment and cost should not be compromised for sustainability and a cleaner production.

References

1. Chenier, P.J.: Survey of Industrial Chemistry, pp. 45–57. Wiley, New York (1987). ISBN 978-0-471-01077-7
2. Lokkiluoto, A., et al.: Novel process concept for the production of H$_2$ and H$_2$SO$_4$ by SO$_2$-depolarized electrolysis. Environ. Dev. Sustain. **14**(4), 529–540 (2012)
3. Müller, H.: Sulfuric Acid and Sulfur Trioxide in Ullmann's Encyclopedia of Industrial Chemistry. Wiley-VCH, Weinheim (2000). https://doi.org/10.1002/14356007.a25_635

4. https://essentialchemicalindustry.org/chemicals/sulfuric-acid.html. Accessed 7 Mar 2021
5. Sulphuric Acid Drain Cleaner. https://www.dcs.supplies/datasheets/4910.pdf. Accessed 24 Feb 2021
6. Roy, P., Sardar, A.: SO_2 emission control and finding a way out to produce sulphuric acid from industrial SO_2 emission. J. Chem. Eng. Process Technol. 6(2), 230 (2015)
7. Indiana Department of Environmental Management Criteria Pollutants: Sulfur Dioxide (SO_2) Office of Air Quality - Air Programs Branch. (317) 232-0178, (800) 451-6027. https://www.in.gov/idem/files/factsheet_oaq_criteria_so2.pdf. Accessed 15 Feb 2021
8. Taieb, D., Brahim, A., Chimie, C.: Electrochemical method for sulphur dioxide removal from flue gases: application on sulphuric acid plant in Tunisia. C R Chim 16, 39–50 (2013)
9. Thanh, B.D., Lefevre, T.: Assessing health benefits of controlling air pollution from power generation: the case of a lignite-fired power plant in Thailand. Environ. Manage. 27(2), 303–317 (2001)
10. NLM: SO_2 Fact Sheet in Hazardous Substances Data Bank (HSDB) by U.S National Library of Medicine's (NLM), (1998). http://toxnet.nlm.nih.gov/cgi-bin/sis/search2/f?./temp/~YZ2g1Q:3. Accessed 19 Dec 2020
11. Ward, P.L.: Sulfur dioxide initiates global climate change in four ways. Thin Solid Films 517, 3188–3203 (2009)
12. Jones, E.M.: Chamber process manufacture of sulfuric acid. Ind. Eng. Chem. 42(11), 2208–2210 (1950)
13. Deanin, R., Mead, J.: Kent and Riegel's Handbook of Industrial Chemistry and Biotechnology, vol. 1. Springer Science & Business Media, NewYork, USA (2010)
14. Moeller, W., Winkler, K.: The double contact process for sulfuric acid production. J. Air Pollut. Control Assoc. 18(5), 324–325 (1968)
15. Müller, H.: Sulfuric acid and sulfur trioxide. In: Ullmann's Encyclopedia of Industrial Chemistry, vol. A25, 5th edn. Wiley-VCH, Weinheim (1994)
16. Kiss, A.A., Bildea, C.S., Verheijen, P.J.: Optimization studies in sulfuric acid production. In: 16th European Symposium on Computer Aided Process Engineering. Elsevier (2006)
17. Kiss, A.A., Bildea, C.S., Grievink, J.: Dynamic modeling and process optimization of an industrial sulfuric acid plant. Chem. Eng. J. 158(2), 241–249 (2010)
18. Gómez-García, M.-Á., Dobrosz-Gómez, I., GilPavas, E., Rynkowski, J.: Simulation of an industrial adiabatic multi-bed catalytic reactor for sulfur dioxide oxidation using the Maxwell-Stefan model. Chem. Eng. J. 282, 101–107 (2015)
19. Yildirim, Ö., Kiss, A., Hüser, N., Leßmann, K., Kenig, E.Y.: Reactive absorption in chemical process industry: a review on current activities. Chem. Eng. J. 213, 371–391 (2012)
20. Ibanez, J.G., Batten, C.F., Wentworth, W.E.: Simultaneous determination of SO_3 (g) and SO_2 (g) in a flowing gas. Ind. Eng. Chem. Res. 47(7), 2449–2454 (2008)
21. Van Nisselrooya, P., Lagasb, J.: Superclaus reduces SO_2, emission by the use of a new selective oxidation catalyst. Catal. Today 16(2), 263–271 (1993)
22. Urbanek, A., Trela, M.: Catalytic oxidation of sulfur dioxide. Catal. Rev. Sci. Eng. 21(1), 73–133 (1980)
23. Hudgins, R.R., Silveston, P.L.: Reduction of sulfur dioxide emissions from a sulfuric acid plant by means of feed modulation. Environ. Sci. Technol. 15(4), 419–422 (1981)
24. Tamrat, D.: Analysis Industrial Development, Market Performance and Competitiveness, Case Study On: Awash Melkassa Aluminum Sulfate Sulfuric Acid Share Company (AMASSASC), Thesis, pp.1–134 (2006)
25. Erik, L.: Aspen HYSYS simulation of CO_2 removal by amine absorption from a gas based power plant. In: The 48th Scandinavian Conference on Simulation and Modeling (SIMS 2007), 30–31 October 2007, Göteborg (Särö), no. 027, pp. 73–81. Linköping University Electronic Press (2007)

Effect of Blend Ratio on Physico-Mechanical Properties of Agro Stone Composite Caulking Materials

Tadelle Nigusu Mekonnen[1(✉)], Tewekel Mohammed Belay[2],
Tinsae Tsega Beyene[2], Yenehun Gidyelem Andualem[2],
Mulugeta Admasu Delele[2], Sissay Wondmagegn Molla[3],
and Aregash Mamo Gizaw[4]

[1] Departments of Chemical Engineering, Institute of Technology,
University of Gondar, Gondar, Ethiopia
[2] Faculty of Chemical and Food Engineering, Bahir Dar Institute of Technology,
Bahir Dar University, Bahir Dar, Ethiopia
[3] Schools of Chemical and Mechanical Engineering,
Woldia University, Woldia, Ethiopia
[4] Departments of Chemical Engineering, Samara University, Samara, Ethiopia

Abstract. This work aimed to study the effect of blend ratio on properties of Agro stone caulking materials. With the experiment, fixed ratio pumice filler and bagasse were used. Magnesia cement was used as binding material. Caulking were produced from different proportion of magnesium oxide and magnesium chloride brine solution (0.9:1, 0.95:1, 1:1, and 1.2:1, 1.32:1 kg per liter) with concentration of 28, 30, 33, 36 and 42 wt/wt % brine solution. The caulking materials were characterized by physical properties, mechanical properties, and free chlorine ions. After curing for 14 days and 28 days, the common mechanical properties tensile, compressive, and flexural bending strength was measured with the assistance of computerized testing machines according to testing procedures. The minimum and maximum water absorption capacities were 14 and 26.4% respectively. The optimum tensile, compressive and flexural bending strength of the experiments were 3.8 MPa, 25.8MPa, and 23.12MPa respectively with the ratio of caulking material 1:1 kg of MgO to a liter of MgCl2. The free chloride ion was reduced to 20% by adding 5%wt zeolite. The optimum mixing ratio was 1:1 with 36% of brine solution. The study shows the potential of high strength, and low corrosion biobased composite ecofriendly materials for the productions of agro stone composite caulking materials.

Keywords: Agro stone · Blend ratio · Bagasse · Brine solution · Caulking material · Water absorption

1 Introduction

The shelter is one of the three basic needs of a human being [1]. A wide range of construction facilities is required including in the area of residential, commercial, hospitals, schools, and transport infrastructure. Despite that, the construction industry is

© ICST Institute for Computer Sciences, Social Informatics and Telecommunications Engineering 2022
Published by Springer Nature Switzerland AG 2022. All Rights Reserved
M. L. Berihun (Ed.): ICAST 2021, LNICST 411, pp. 73–86, 2022.
https://doi.org/10.1007/978-3-030-93709-6_6

a major sector of the economy of most nations. However, this industry is a large consumer of factory-made building materials such as mineral-based materials ranging from aggregates, cement, bricks, and tiles to structural steel, glass, and ceramics. To overcome the common observed high construction cost, low-cost biobased composite materials are needed. Composite materials are made from two or more constituents with significantly different physical or chemical properties from each other. Biocomposites are materials in which one of their components is derived from biomass resources [2].

The major components of agro stone composite materials products are fillers such as (bagasse, pumice, wood, rubber [3], asbestos [2], fiberglass, and binder. Sorel s cement (SC) also known as magnesium oxychloride cement (MOC)was used as a binder for many years [4]. It is formed by a mixture of powdered magnesium oxide (MgO) and a brine solution of magnesium chloride ($MgCl_2$). Compared with Portland cement magnesium oxychloride cement has good resistance to oil, grease, superior mechanical properties, high fire resistance, fast hardening, low alkalinity, and high bonding ability [3]. The physical, mechanical, and chemical properties of the material which are made from Sorel s cement are significantly affected by the molar ratio of the reactants used in the formation process such as $MgO/MgCl_2$ or $H2O/MgCl_2$ [5]. The concentration of magnesium chloride significantly affects the strength, initial and final setting time. When the correct concentration of brine solution is not selected, this leads to the formation of magnesium oxide will react with water and form magnesium hydroxide, and also if its concentration beyond optimum the excess chloride ion cause corrosion problem [4].

The major commercial applications of magnesium oxychloride cement are industrial flooring, fire protection, grinding wheels, rendering wall insulation panels. Mostly it is limited for outdoor application this is because the prolonged contact with water results in leaching of $MgCl_2$, which leads to reduce the strength of the body. Most researchers devote themselves to improve the water resistance of magnesium oxychloride. It was found that some additives can greatly improve the water resistance of MOC cement, such as phosphoric acid and soluble phosphates, including the phosphates of alkali metals, alkali earth metals, iron, aluminum, and ammonia [6].

At present, Ethiopia has little experience within the utilization of various construction materials. The conventional materials are produced from mortar, gypsum, clay, limestone, and others excavated from the ground, however, it is unaffordable for everyone due to its high cost. Therefore it is important to focus on alternative building materials produced from raw materials like agro-industrial wastes, such as bagasse, wood rice husk. In recent years natural fibers have become the most interesting for reinforcement of composite material that Bagasse is cost-effective material used for the synthesis of agro stone composite materials. This is because it is a by-product of forestry and the agricultural industry. Compared with synthetic fiber natural fibers has an advantage such as widely available, good insulation properties, huge availability, cheaper and lightweight [7,8].

Nowadays Ethiopia uses composite materials for interior partition, ceilings, and exterior walls of building structures. Caulking materials formulated from MgO, $MgCl_2$ solution, and fillers are widely used as an economical joint binder for different partition and ceiling boards. Despite excellent properties associated with MOC-based caulks,

cracking at joints and corrosion have been common quality problems limiting customer s preferences. These characteristics quality is significantly sensitive to the
relative proportion of components listed above and admixtures used during processing.
Therefore the aims of this study were intended to determine the optimum mix design of
components responsible to produce caulk material with maximum strength, stability,
and corrosion resistance.

2   Materials and Method

2.1   Materials

The raw materials used in this study such as magnesium oxide (MgO) and magnesium
chloride (MgCl$_2$), pumice, and bagasse were collected from the Bahir Dar Agro stone
enterprise. Laboratory grade reagent such as hydrochloric acid, zeolite, nitric acid,
Potassium chromate, and silver nitrate was collected from Faculty of Chemical and
Food Engineering Bahir Dar Institute of Technology.

2.2   Fabrication of Mold

Metal molds were used in the production of the composite caulking samples. The mold
used for this process was made of mild steel material with a thickness of 10 mm. The
dimensions and shapes of cavities were made consistent with ASTM Standard D 63890
for tensile testing and ASTM Standard D 79097 for flexural (bending) testing (ASTM
E290, 1990). The molds which were used for this work have a dimension of
150 * 150 * 10 mm for compressive strength test, 400 * 50 * 10 mm dimension for
flexural strength test and 350 * 50 * 10 mm dimension for the tensile strength test.

2.3   Sample Preparation

Magnesium oxide powder and brine (magnesium oxychloride) were mixed according
to the experimental mix design shown in Table 1 the mixing ratio which is used by the
company was used as a reference. After the MOC was prepared the amount of filler,
bagasse and pumice was determined based on the working consistency by using British
standard as a reference. The size of bagasse filler that was used for this work was
reduced with the help of laboratory cutters to a small size and sieved with a 1.7 mm
laboratory sieve.

2.4   Setting Times Determination

The working consistency of the caulking sample was determined using the Vicat
apparatus. This was repeated for all mixing ratios initial and the final setting time of
paste was determined according to the following procedure.

2.4.1   1Initial Setting Time Determined by the Penetration Depth
The initial setting was determined by ASTM methods C 191 based on the principle of
penetration resistance according to [8]. A fresh paste of normal consistency was

prepared and filled into the Vicat mold. After 30 min the mold resting on a plate the needle was gently lowered and brought in contact with the surface of the paste and quickly released. Thirty seconds after releasing the needle the penetration was recorded. This was repeated every 15 min until penetration of 25 mm or less is obtained in thirty seconds.

Table 1. Experimental mix design

Code of sample	Brine ($MgCl_2$)[wt. %]	MgO powder/brine [Kg/Liter]
A1	28	0.9
A2	28	0.95
A3	28	1
A4	28	1.2
A5	28	1.3
B1	30	0.9
B2	30	0.95
B3	30	1
B4	30	1.2
B5	30	1.32
C1	33	0.9
C2	33	0.95
C3	33	1
C4	33	1.2
C5	33	1.32
D1	36	0.9
D2	36	0.95
D3	36	1
D4	36	1.2
D5	36	1.32
X1	42	0.9
X2	42	0.95
X2	42	1
X4	42	1.2
X5	42	1.32

2.4.2 Final Setting Time

For the determination of the final setting time the needle of the Vicat apparatus was replaced by Plunger. The paste was considered as finally set when the needle touches gently to the surface of the text block, only the needle makes an impression.

2.5 Water Absorption Test

The samples of the composite caulking material were dried by using an oven with a temperature of 105 ⸏ for 6 h and cooled to room temperature. The weight of this dry sample was weighed. The dried specimens were immersed completely in clean tap water at room temperature for 24 h. The samples were removed and the excess water was wiped out by using a cotton cloth. Finally, the wet sample was weighed. The water absorption capacity of the sample was determined by Eq. 1 according to [9,8].

$$W(\%) = \frac{M2 - M1}{M1} * 100 \tag{1}$$

Where; W is the percentage of water absorption [%], M1 is a mass of the dried sample before immersion in water [g], and M2 is a mass of the sample after immersion in water [g].

2.6 Specific Gravity

The specific gravity of the magnesium chloride solution was determined by using a pycnometer. Its values were determined by using the following formula.

$$SG = \frac{M1 - MO}{M2 - M1} \tag{2}$$

Where; Mo is the mass of the pycnometer[g], M1 is the mass pycnometer and brine solution[g], and M2 is the mass of the pycnometer and water[g].

2.7 Mechanical Properties

The time effect on the physic mechanical properties such as bending, tensile, and compression strength of the product produced was determined. All properties were tested After 14 days and 28 days according to [10,11].

2.7.1 Compressive Strength Test

The compressive strength of the caulking material with different blend ratios was carried out in a compressive test machine before this analysis was carried out the sample was dried by air. Cubic samples were adjusted so that the load was applied perpendicularly to the direction of molding. The stress continued until the destruction of the samples was carried out. The compressive strength was calculated by using the following formula.

$$P = \frac{F}{Ac} \tag{3}$$

Where; F is maximum destructive force [N], P is Compressive strength [pa], and Ac is the cross-sectional area of the sample [m^2].

2.7.2 Flexural Strength Test

Modulus of rupture or bend strength was determined According to ASTM C473 with the dimension of width 50 mm, length 400 mm, and 10 mm thickness. It was calculated by using Eq. 4.

$$\sigma = \frac{3FL}{2bd^2} \tag{4}$$

Where; F is load [N], L is the length of the support span [m], b is Width [m], and d is the thickness of the material[m].

2.7.3 Tensile Strength Test

The tensile strength of each sample was determined According to ASTM C473, with a sample size of 5 mm width, 300 mm length, and 10 mm thickness specimen with the help of a computerized automated tensile testing machine.

2.8   Determination of Free Chlorine

The excess chloride of caulking material was determined by using ASTM C1152 procedure. The prepared caulk material was crushed by using a laboratory disk mill and sieved with a 0.545 mm sieve and 5 gm of the sample was placed in 250 ml beakers. Then 10% of nitric acid was added. Then the mixture was stirred with the help of a magnetic agitator to enhance the mass transfer. Finally, the chloride content was determined by titration by using silver nitrate as a titrant agent and the free chloride ion was determined according to the Bohr titration method. It was calculated by using Eq. 5 according to [12].

$$C1, \% = 3.545[(V1 - V2)N] * W \tag{5}$$

Where; V_1 is volume of 0.05 N AgNO3 solutions used for sample titration [ml], V_2 is volume of 0.05 N $AgNO_3$ solution used for blank titration [ml], N is normality of 0.05 N $AgNO_3$ solution, and W is mass of sample [g].

3   Results and Discussion

3.1   Magnesium Chloride Solution Specific Gravity

As shown from Fig. 1 the density of prepared brine/magnesium chloride solution increases with increases in the concentration of brine. Saltwater is denser than regular water, which suggests there's more mass during a certain volume of saltwater than there's within the same volume of normal water. Magnesium chloride is a highly hygroscopic salt this is easily soluble in water. It dissociates into two ions: a cation of magnesium (Mg^{2+}) and two anions of chloride (Cl^-). There are two reasons for the density of brine increase. One is just that the $MgCl_2$ is far denser than water due to its ions have more mass than the oxygen and hydrogen atoms within the water molecules. And also the ions bind nicely with the water molecules. The density of sample D with a weight ratio of 36%wt salt within this experiment was bigger. However, the density of solution (×5) which is already used by Bahir Dar agro stone enterprise is 1.23. The density of the solution was increase with salt content.

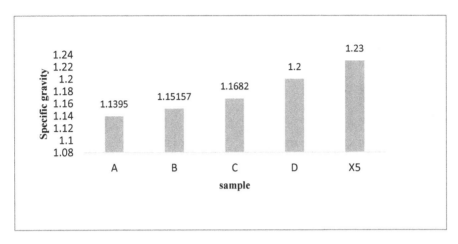

Fig. 1. The specific gravity of brine solution

3.2 Water Absorption

The water absorption test for oven-dried specimens was carried out for each caulking material in the different ratios of magnesium oxide to brine solution. As stated in the experimental design there are five ratios of magnesium oxide to magnesium chloride solution (0.9, 0.95, 1, 1.2 and 1.32, kg of MgO per liter of brine) and also the brine solution was between the ranges of 28 to 42% to make better magnesium oxy cement. As shown in Fig. 2 the water absorption of MgO caulking decreases from left to right which means the ratio of 0.9 to 1.32 is due to consumption of magnesium chloride increase. For all sample the water-resistance increase as a percentage of Sorel cement increase and by decreasing agro filler such as cellulose. The highest percentage of water absorption is observed in the A2 sample which means it is less reactive to admixture chemicals which help to impart the fiber hydrophilicity. And also it is highly porous. From the literature review, technical specifications and standards of Agro stone product's water absorption have to be less than 22% [13]. As shown in the result most of the sample's water absorption is below 22 it is good for water resistance. The water absorption ability of caulking material which is already used by the company was studied. The highest percentage of water absorption is observed on sample A2 with 26.4% which is above standard value. Since bagasse has a high amount of hemicelluloses. The water absorption capacity increase as the bagasse content increase in a caulking material. The structure of natural fibers and the chemical composition such as cellulose and hemicelluloses are responsible for hydrophilic behavior [8]. When the amount of pumice increases water absorption decreases this is due to the good interaction of pumice fillers with the binder makes better resistance to water than Bagasse filler. From the experiment sample, X5 has good water resistance (Fig. 3).

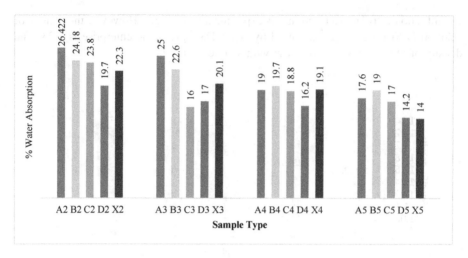

Fig. 2. Water absorption of magnesia cement composite caulking material

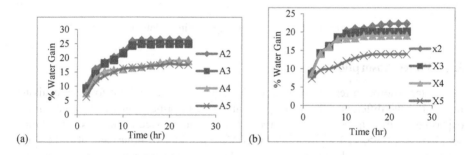

(a)   (b)

Fig. 3. Water gain of caulking materials a) 28% brine solution and b) 40% brine solution

3.3 Mechanical Properties

3.3.1 Compressive Strength

As shown in Fig. 4 different samples with different mix ratios of magnesium oxide to magnesium chloride with various brine concentrations in the range of 28 to 42 wt% have different compressive strengths. Sample D3 and X3 with a ratio of 1:1 magnesium oxide to magnesium chloride at brine concentrations of 36 and 42 wt % withstand greater loads as compared to others. For the production of MgO caulking material or board, the major raw materials to form magnesium oxychloride MOC cement are magnesium oxide and magnesium chloride. As shown from the results a ratio of 0.9:1, 0.95:1, 1.2:1, and 1:1.32 withstand a lower load than that of 1:1 kg of magnesium oxide to the liter brine solution. This is due to the reason that the former two ratio magnesium oxide are limiting reactant consumed before brine solution, therefore, there is unreacted brine this cause defect and decrease the ability to withstand load and also water resistance as depicted in Fig. 2. For the latter two ratios, the reason for decreasing compressive stress is brine solution is a limiting reactant has consumed before magnesium oxide this unreacted MgO causes a defect and leads to decrease compressive strength of the caulking materials. Therefore 1:1 ratio (with 36 wt/wt % of brine solution) is the optimum from this experiment to obtain good MOC. For all samples, compressive strength was increased from 7 days to 28 days. This is because as stated from literature reviews there is a different form of magnesium oxychloride but among

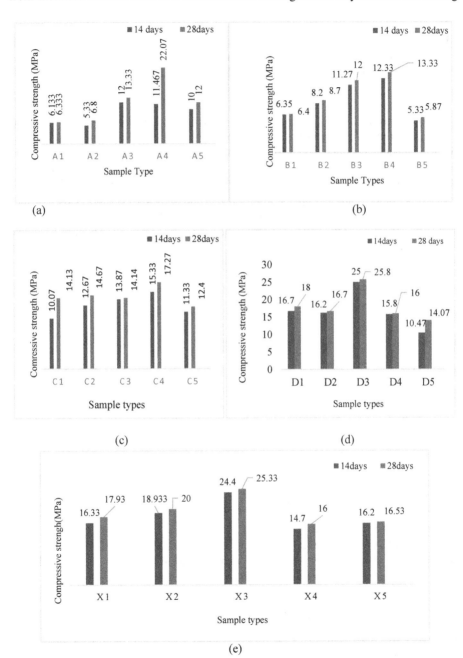

Fig. 4. Results of compressive strength of caulking material: a) 28%, b) 30%, c) 33%, d) 36% and, e) 42% by mass of brine solution

that 5-phase and 3-phase are stable at room temperature. 5-phase MOC withstands superior mechanical properties. As stated from literature kinetic experiments observed that the 5-phase is formed quickly, but the kinetics is not complete for several days this causes increasing in strength within an increasing day [4].

3.3.2 Flexural Strength

Figure 5 illustrates the different bending strength in X, D, C, B, and A specimen values due to varying the mixing ratio of the binder and the drying period of the sample. Therefore bending strength is found to be the highest in X5 followed by C5, D3, X1, D2, B5, D4, and from the rest of the other specimens. The bonding strength between the magnesium chloride and magnesium oxide is very strong in the X5 specimen which has a mixing ratio of 1.32 kg of magnesium oxide per liter of 42% magnesium chloride solution. It can be understood that specimen X5 has good resistance of the force applied due to proper magnesium chloride and magnesium oxide mixing ratio from the rest of the other specimens that leads to the maximum bending strength. In this particular case, defects are carefully minimized and the values seen can tell us that the maximum magnesium oxide and maximum magnesium chloride ratio as well as good MOC solution increase the ability to resist the downward force applied on the specimen which leads to maximum bending strength.

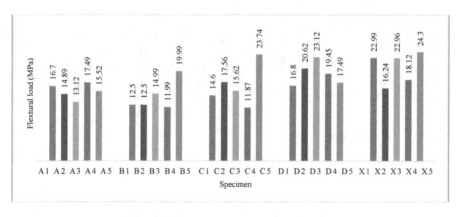

Fig. 5. Flexural stress result after 28 days

3.3.3 Tensile Strength Test

Figure 6 clearly shows that different samples that designated as A, B, C, D, and X with 28% 30% 33% 36% and 42% respectively of different magnesium chloride solution which has different tensile strength. As shown tensile strength increases with $MgCl_2$ solution from 28% to 42%. Compared with other samples D and X withstand greater tensile strength. From the ratio of the samples A to C, magnesium oxide is the limiting reactant and $MgCl_2$ solution in excess which will lead to absorb the moisture from the atmosphere that causes the surface of the cement to expand slightly or otherwise become irregular. Similarly, the amount of MgO of the samples D and X is excess and $MgCl_2$ solution is a limiting reactant especially for sample X there is unreacted MgO.

This will tend to combine with water and forms Mg (OH) $_2$, there will be excess water which must evaporate, slowing the curing time of cement and Mg (OH) $_2$ has no cement bonding properties with $MgCl_2$ and water. From the literature, the preferable range of specific gravity for the $MgCl_2$ solution is in the range from SG=1.179 to SG=1.218 which gives adequate strength. The specific gravity of samples D and X is SG=1.1682 and SG=1.2 respectively which is found in the acceptable range. Since compressive strength is the main parameter to be tested, which is sample X3 has the best compressive strength; as a result, sample D at 36% of $MgCl_2$ solution with a tensile strength of 3.8 MPa is preferable to the other.

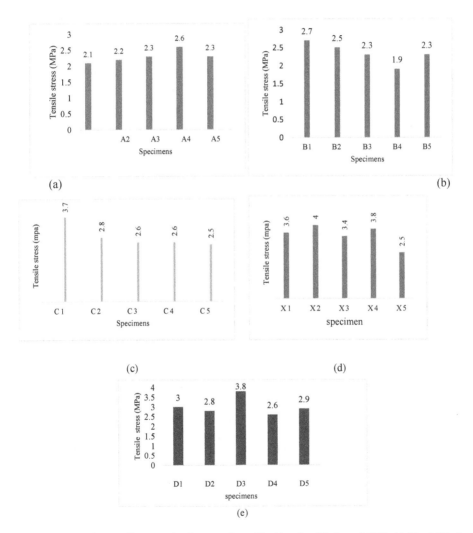

Fig. 6. Results for tensile strength of magnesium chloride after 28 days a) 28%, b) 30, c) 33, d) 42%, and e) 36%

3.4   Results of Free Chloride in Caulking Material

As shown in results from Fig. 7 when the ratio of magnesium oxide to magnesium chloride increases the free chloride decrease this is due to the excess reactant of MgO. At the ratio of 0.9:1 kg of MgO to a liter of $MgCl_2$, the free chloride ion is higher in both D1 and X1 because MgO is a limiting reactant. Chloride that causes corrosion was reduced by adding a corrosion resistance agent of 5% zeolite [14]. It reduced a free chloride ion of 20% with a ratio of 1:1. Zeolite can be added to 15% but it harms strength and water resistance. The Free Chloride ion of sample X is higher than sample D with the same ratio since the concentration of brine is higher.

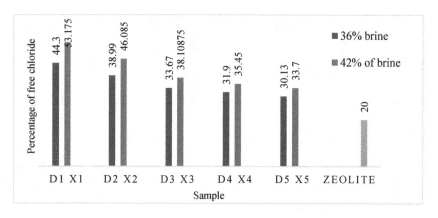

Fig. 7. Results of free chloride ion that cause corrosion

4   Conclusion

It can be concluded that the production of construction material from composite material is important. Magnesium oxide board is a composite material that acquired a significant role owing to fire resistance. Magnesium oxide is found to form a good and compatible formula in the production of composite material for partition boards and ceilings. Despite the strength and good fire resistance of magnesium boards, the caulking material used to join boards faces problems like cracking and corrosion. This study focused on the analysis of this problem. The physical properties (water absorption), mechanical properties (tensile stress, bending strength, and compressive strength), and the free chloride ion that causes corrosion of caulking material were studied. The water absorption of caulking material decreases as the ratio of magnesium oxide to brine solution increases this is due to the consumption of magnesium chloride increase. A mixing ratio of 1:1 magnesium oxide to magnesium chloride (magnesium oxychloride) at brine concentration of 36 and 42% wt withstand greater loads as compared to others. Therefore 1:1 ratio is the optimum for this experiment to obtain good MOC. The corrosion problem of caulking material was reduced to 20% by incorporated zeolite admixture.

5   Recommendation

- Further researches have to be done to analyze fire resistively, and sound insulation, of the caulking material.
- To improve water tightness and corrosion resistance of agro stone caulking materials further research have to be done by incorporating additive for instance various alkali metal phosphates; such as Magnesium mono or dihydrogen phosphate, Magnesium Stearate Aluminum Sulfate or Magnesium Sulfate for water resistance and nitrites, and other novel additives for corrosion resistance.
- The effect of weather conditions or season on caulking material should be investigated.
- The structure of the product should be analyzed with the help of a scanning electron microscope and also the porosity with the help of BET machines.

Acknowledgment. The authors wish to thank both Bahir Dar Agro stone enterprise company and Bahir Dar Institution of Technology.

References

1. Ali, M.M.: Design and development of cost-efficient houses the challenges and prospects of affordability. In: Technical Report of the Housing Development & Management, Lund University, pp. 120 (2009)
2. Hasmadi, M., Noorfarahzilah, M., Noraidah, H., Zainol, M.K., Jahurul, M.H.A.: Functional properties of composite flour: a review. Food Res. **4**(6), 18201831 (2020). https://doi.org/10.26656/fr.2017.4(6).419
3. Jin, F.: Magnesium oxychloride cement. Magnesia Cem., 2974 (2020). https://doi.org/10.1016/b978-0-12-391925-0.00009-1
4. Karimi, Y., Monshi, A.: Effect of magnesium chloride concentrations on the properties of magnesium oxychloride cement for nano SiC composite purposes. Ceram. Int. **37**(7), 24052410 (2011). https://doi.org/10.1016/j.ceramint.2011.05.082
5. Malinowski, S., Jaroszyńska-Wolińska, J.: The physical and mechanical properties of magnesium oxychloride cement-based materials. Bud. I Archit. **14**(4), 089098 (2015). https://doi.org/10.35784/bud-arch.1539
6. Kandeel, A.M., El-Mahllawy, M.S., Hassan, H.A., Sufe, W.H., Zeedan, S.R.: Effect of type of mixing water and sand on the physicomechanical properties of magnesia cement masonry units. HBRC J. **8**(1), 813 (2012). https://doi.org/10.1016/j.hbrcj.2012.08.002
7. Ita-Nagy, D., et al.: Life cycle assessment of bagasse fiber-reinforced biocomposites. Sci. Total Environ. **720**, 137586 (2020). https://doi.org/10.1016/j.scitotenv.2020.137586
8. Sahu, P., Gupta, M.K.: Lowering in water absorption capacity and mechanical degradation of sisal/epoxy composite by sodium bicarbonate treatment and PLA coating. Polym. Compos. **41**(2), 668681 (2020). https://doi.org/10.1002/pc.25397
9. Gbadeyan, O.J., Adali, S., Bright, G., Sithole, B., Awogbemi, O.: Studies on the mechanical and absorption properties of achatina fulica snail and eggshells reinforced composite materials. Comp. Struct. **239**, 112043 (2020). https://doi.org/10.1016/j.compstruct.2020.112043

10. Uddin, M.A., Jameel, M., Sobuz, H.R., Hasan, N.M.S., Islam, M.S., Amanat, K.M.: The effect of curing time on compressive strength of composite cement concrete. Appl. Mech. Mater. **204208**(October), 41054109 (2012). https://doi.org/10.4028/www.scientific.net/AMM.204-208.4105

11. Pivák, A., et al.: Foam glass lightened sorel s cement composites doped with coal fly ash. Materials (Basel) **14**(5), 116 (2021). https://doi.org/10.3390/ma14051103

12. ASTM International. ASTM C1115/C1152M Standard test method for acid-soluble chloride in mortar and concrete, vol. i, pp. 700703 (2004)

13. Taffese, W.Z.: Low-cost eco-friendly building material: a case study in Ethiopia. Int. J. Civil Environ. Struct. Constr. Archit. Eng. **6**(2), 183187 (2012)

14. For, C.: (12) United States Patent Primary Examiner Paul Marcantoni, **2**(12) (2013)

Assessment of Nutrients and Heavy Metals in the Groundwater and Surface Water in the Zeber Watershed: The Case of the Bahir - Dar City Waste Disposal Site

Dargie Haile[1(✉)] and Nigus Gabbiye[2]

[1] Lecturer of Chemical Engineering (Master's Degree in Environmental Engineering), Department of Chemical Engineering, Institute of Technology Woldia University, Woldia, Ethiopia

[2] Chemical Engineering, Environmental and Process Engineering Coordinator for the PHL - IL Project Feed the Future Innovation Lab, Department of Chemical Engineering, Bahir-Dar Institute of Technology Bahir-Dar University, Bahir Dar, Ethiopia
Nigus.gabiye@bdu.edu.et

Abstract. Surface water and groundwater have been experiencing increasing risks of contamination in recent years because of the poor management of the immense amounts of waste created by different human activities. Inappropriate dump sites have served for many years as marginal disposal sites for a wide range of wastes, including solid waste, fresh sewage and hazardous waste, in developing nations such as Ethiopia. Physical, anthropogenic and organic procedures continuously interact to degrade the waste. One of the results of these practices is artificially contaminated leachate, which is potentially hazardous waste from disposal sites. If not managed appropriately, dumping sites can contaminate groundwater (through leachates) and surface water (through contaminant transport by flooding and groundwater movement). Along these lines, this study focuses on the spatial and temporal variations in the ground and surface water quality caused by the waste disposal site of Bahir Dar city within the Zeber watershed during the dry and wet seasons. Water testing was performed on 5 samples of surface water and 6 samples of groundwater in each month from the 30th of March (dry season) to the 20th of August (wet season). Water quality parameters, for example, total coliforms, NO_3^-, PO_4^{3-}, Cr, Mn, and Pb concentrations were examined in both ground and surface water. It was discovered that the NO_3^-, Mn and Pb contents were within established limits for both ground and surface water, while the remaining parameters varied depending upon the sampling period. The water quality study results show that spatial and temporal variations have strong impacts on the changes in microbial, heavy metal and nutrient parameters throughout the watershed.

Keywords: Groundwater · Seasonal variation · Waste disposal site · Surface water

© ICST Institute for Computer Sciences, Social Informatics and Telecommunications Engineering 2022
Published by Springer Nature Switzerland AG 2022. All Rights Reserved
M. L. Berihun (Ed.): ICAST 2021, LNICST 411, pp. 87–105, 2022.
https://doi.org/10.1007/978-3-030-93709-6_7

1 Introduction

1.1 A Subsection Sample

Water is the most plentiful asset on earth, yet just 3% is available for human activities, while the remainder is available in the sea as salt water [1]. Water may be accessible in different forms and amounts, yet its utilization for different purposes is the source of its value. Of all the ecological problems that developing nations face, the absence of sufficient and clean water remains the most important issue [2]. When contaminated, groundwater will remain contaminated in the absence of remediation or treatment. Diseases may be spread through water contamination, particularly groundwater contamination, and quickly overwhelm human abilities to control their spread [3]. Wastes of various kinds, for the most part solid waste, make up a significant proportion of dump sites/landfills. Hydrological studies of groundwater show that it flows from areas of higher elevation towards areas of lower elevation. Along these lines, we assessed the degradable materials that make up leachate and taint the groundwater in the study area. Unfortunately, groundwater is not visible and is therefore considered irrelevant; however, it requires substantial consideration. Groundwater is not disconnected from water supplies or streams; it typically becomes surface water through springs and enters waterways, and it is frequently significant for supporting wetlands and their biological systems. The expulsion or impoundment of groundwater can influence the total flow. A decrease in either the nature or the amount of released groundwater can fundamentally impact surface water quality and the fulfillment of water quality goals. Surface water and groundwater are intricately connected with the water cycle, with numerous recurrent patterns. In the event that groundwater becomes contaminated, it is challenging, though certainly feasible, to restore this water. The moderate pace of groundwater flow and the low microbiological movement limit self-filtration. In developing nations, open and inappropriate dumping destinations have served as final removal sites for a wide range of wastes over many years; these wastes include city solid waste, raw sewage and hazardous wastes [4]. Physical, synthetic and natural procedures interact, resulting in breakdown of the waste. One of the side effects of these practices is artificially contaminated leachate, which is possibly unsafe waste from waste removal destinations. If legitimate waste administration is not performed, such dumping sites can contaminate groundwater (as a result of leachates) and surface water (through contaminant transport by flooding, wind and groundwater from open dump sites). The Bahir-Dar city open landfill is one such open dump site and is situated in a location close to human settlements. The people who live close to the removal site (both below and above the point source) utilize contaminated ground and surface water in their everyday activities. This poses a great deal of danger to those communities with respect to water quality. Along these lines, the focal point of this study was to survey and assess the water quality in that watershed, especially close to the waste disposal site, to assess its impact on ground and surface water quality.

2 Methodology

2.1 Descriptions of the Study Area

The Eriamecharia municipal waste disposal site is 5 km from Bahir Dar city, Ethiopia, near the expressway to Addis Ababa and the Tis Abay waterfall. It forms part of the Sebatamit provincial network. According to the Central Statistics Agency of Ethiopia (CSA 2007 G. C), approximately 6,401 people, 3,053 females and 3,348 males, live around the dump site. Its geographical location is as follows: latitude, 11.54; longitude, 37.38; altitude, 1803 m at 3°; and elevation above sea level, 1801 m. The length and width of this removal site are 384 m and 174 m, respectively. This site was not equipped with liners or a leachate sorting system until ten years ago and was not efficiently planned before being utilized for waste removal/dumping. In addition, no environmental impact assessment was performed before this location was established as a waste disposal site. Trucks and other vehicles from various parts of the city collect the waste, carry it to this site and dump it in a disorganized manner. The waste is dumped as-is without isolation. The base amount of solid waste that is generated from the city and dumped at the site is as follows: private waste 12,610 kg/day, business waste 4,202 kg/day, service provider waste 98 kg/day, municipal waste 1,044 kg/day, and overall waste 22,774 kg/day (Source: Solid Waste Portrayal and Evaluation from the Bahir Dar city report, 2007). Currently, the average amount of waste dumped at the site is estimated to be 31,321 kg/day.

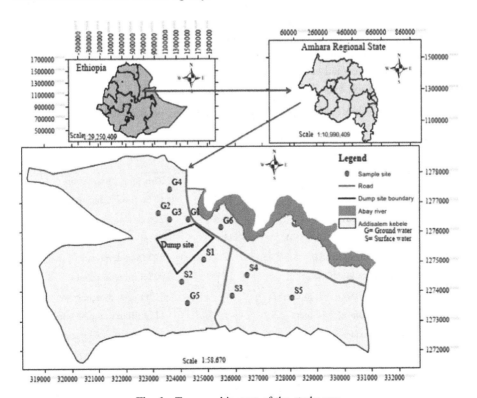

Fig. 1. Topographic map of the study area.

2.2   Sample Collection, Preservation and Laboratory Analyses

Water samples were collected from the selected test areas close to the dump site, which are locally called Abohoy manekia and Tikkurit. The samples were taken to the research Centre for the investigation. The eleven testing sites were selected based on their availability (not being dried throughout the year) and vicinity (distance from the waste disposal site) to contamination sources, for example, accessibility and lodging. A worldwide positioning system device (GPS etrex VISTA HCX) was utilized to identify the actual locations of the study sites, and the sites were geo-referenced to guarantee consistency in the testing sites during the subsequent test periods. The test sites were deliberately chosen to incorporate below and above the waste disposal site, as shown in Fig. 1. Sampling began during the dry season starting in March and proceeded through the wet season in August at all eleven study sites below and above the dump site. Groundwater samples (existing boreholes) were taken from depths of 5–12 m above and below the waste disposal site using borer drills to obtain a 3 L maximum sample with a straightforward core approach that allowed the study of groundwater samples at different borehole depths. To evaluate the water quality, the water samples were kept in 1 L polyethylene plastic containers that had been cleaned with a cleanser that did not contain metals, flushed with deionized water, treated with 10% corrosive nitric acid for 24 h, and finally washed with ultra-pure water. All water samples were stored in a cooler and were transported to the laboratory at [5] approximately the same time. All samples were kept at a consistent temperature of 4 °C to prevent deterioration due to light until the analysis was performed at the research Centre [6]. The total coliform analysis utilized the film channel technique, and the heavy metal (Cr, Pb, and Mn), phosphate (PO_4^{3-}) and nitrate (NO_3^-) contents were determined using a Palintest spectrophotometer (WAGTECH 8000). All analysis procedures were performed according to the Standard Methods for the Examination of Water and Wastewater [7].

Table 1. Types of water source and distance of sampling point from the dump site.

Sample number	Type of water source	Depth (m)	Distance from dump site
1	Shallow well(GSS$_1$)	8m	87m from dumping site
2	Shallow well (GSS$_2$)	5m	187m from dump site
3	Shallow well(GSS$_3$)	10m	229 m from dump site
4	Shallow well(GSS$_4$)	11	501m from dumping site
5	Spring (GSS$_5$)		927 from dump site
6	Shallow (GSS$_6$)	12	908m from dump site
7	Surface(river source,SS$_1$)	-	317m from dumping site
8	Surface(river source SS$_2$)	-	115m from dumping site
9	Surface(river source SS$_3$)	-	3km from dumping site
10	Surface(river source SS$_4$)	-	3 km from dumping site
11	Surface(river source SS$_5$)	-	6km from dumping site

3   Results and Discussions

3.1   Spatial and Temporal Variations in the Nutrients and Microbiological Parameters of Surface Water

The results for the spatial and temporal variation in surface water concentrations of nutrients and microbiological parameters measured are presented in Table 2.

Table 2. Spatial and temporal variations in the concentrations of nutrients and microbiological parameters of surface water in the Zeber watershed.

Sampling sites (SS)	NO_3^- (Mg/L)		PO_4^{3-} (Mg/L)		TC (CFU/100 ml)	
	Dry Season	Wet Season	Dry season	Wet Season	Dry Season	Wet Season
SS_1	0.303 ±0.23	0.42 ±0.11	0.153 ±0.031	0.253 ±0.055	11±2	19.33 ±3.055
SS_2	0.0664 ±0.0023	0.903 ±0.083	0.13 ±0.02	0.6233 ±0.051	22±4	34.333 ±3.512
SS_3	0.0593 ±0.0021	0.7633 ±0.106	0.21333 ±0.0153	0.27 ±0.0361	16 ±2.65	20.667 ±3.512
SS_4	0.225 ±0.11	0.607 ±0.021	0.245±0.033	0.363 ±0.050	21.67 ±2.082	30.66 ±3.512
SS_5	0.050 ±0.002	0.316 ±0.056	0.127 ±0.012	0.58 ±0.046	13.67 ±2.082	24 ±3.61

Dynamics of nitrate in the surface water: The nitrate levels in the surface water samples varied from 0.050 ± 0.002 to 0.303 ± 0.23 mg/L with a mean value of 0.141 ± 0.068 mg/L. In the wet season, the levels ranged from 0.316 ± 0.056 to 0.903 ± 0.083 mg/L (Table 2) with a mean value of 0.601 ± 0.074 mg/L. In the two seasons, the levels of nitrate at all testing sites were well below the EPA limit of 10 mg/L. This is most likely because of the absence of DO in the water samples; the lower levels of nitrate may be due to the higher levels of ammonia as a result of the disintegration of nutrient waste and different sources of protein. As indicated by Weiner et al. (2003), the sources of nitrates in water include rotting plant or animal materials, horticultural compost, excrement, human or animal waste, and household sewage. The most notable nitrate levels were observed at SS2 ($0.903 \pm .083$ mg/L), SS3 (0.7633 ± 0.106 mg/L) and SS4 (0.607 ± 0.021 mg/L) during the wet season because of evaporation. NO_3^- leaches from several sources, for example, rotting plant and animal materials, farm compost and residential sewage, excessive use of manure, and high levels of natural waste originating from point and non-point sources. The lowest levels of nitrate in the water samples of the study region were recorded during the dry season at SS2 (0.0664 ± 0.0023 mg/L), SS3 (0.0593 ± 0.0021 mg/L) and SS6 (0.050 ± 0.002 mg/L); these values were much lower than those measured in the wet season. As indicated by the WHO water quality threshold of 10 mg/L, the water in the study region should be prevented from contaminating the surrounding water bodies with nitrate. This contamination could be expected due to nitrifying microscopic organisms fixing the free nitrogen in the air into nitrate, making it usable for photosynthetic plants in the study zone. Excessive levels of nitrate can negatively impact water quality and can accelerate eutrophication.

Dynamics of phosphate in the surface water: The levels of phosphate, measured as PO_4^{3-}, in all samples in the dry season ranged from 0.127 ± 0.012 to 0.245 ± 0.033 mg/L with a mean level of 0.174 ± 0.023 mg/L. In the wet season, the level of phosphate ranged from 0.253 ± 0.055 to 0.6233 ± 0.051 mg/L (Table 2), with a mean value of 0.42 ± 0.048 mg/L. The research facility results demonstrated that PO_4^{3-} fixation in all samples of surface water in the dry and wet seasons was frequently much higher than the recommended threshold of 0.1 mg/L for drinking water set by the EPA/WHO. This is likely due to the waste disposal site, which contains diverse forms of metropolitan waste such as human waste, shampoos, food waste and beautifying agents. This is in accordance with a study conducted by Tjandraatmadja [8] who found that phosphate levels increase because of an increase in the use of phosphate-generating products, for example, cleaning products (cleansers), beautifying agents, relaxer shampoos, food items, wastewater with high phosphate levels from the surrounding communities, spill-over containing soil-bound phosphates, yard waste, overflow from animal feedlots, storm water, and other sources including human waste (faeces and urine). High levels of phosphate indicate the severity of contamination and are, to a great extent, responsible for eutrophic conditions. Phosphate is fundamental for the development of vegetation and other natural living beings. Tjandraatmadja [8], found that unlawful methods of waste disposal into a zone used for surfing brought about excessive algae growth, eutrophication and oxygen consumption in water bodies. In light of this study, the Bahir Dar city waste disposal site is a case study for waste disposal sites, and it represents the seriousness of this issue. Despite the fact that phosphate levels were very high compared with the baseline phosphate levels, the highest levels of phosphate were found in the wet season at test sites SS2, SS5 and SS4; the lowest levels were found in the dry season at test sites SS5, SS2, and SS1 (Table 2). Overall, phosphate fixation was highest at SS2 during the rainy season (0.6233 ± 0.051 mg/L) followed by the highest value recorded during the dry season (0.245 ± 0.033 mg/L) at SS4. This could be ascribed to the increased flooding during the wet season at the dump site (household waste) and the upstream rural contributions to the water test sites, especially those containing cleaning products and compost overflow from dump locales and other sources. The low levels recorded in the dry season may have been caused by evaporation. The water sources in the study region are likely not safe for drinking and residential purposes due to the phosphate levels. This is in accordance with the findings of a few specialists. For instance, Akpan [9] demonstrated that phosphate fixation in water was higher than the level recommended by the

World Health Organization (WHO). Abundant phosphate in water promotes algal blooms and the growth of toxic algae that harm the neurological system and lead to oxygen consumption in the water [9]. From the ANOVA results, there was a significant difference in phosphate fixation between the wet season and the dry season. This indicates that the season is one of the principal factors determining the level of phosphate in the water.

Total Coliform in the Surface Water: The motivation behind measuring the total coliform content in the water bodies was to assess the quantity of coliform bacteria in the water samples as an indication of the extent of natural contamination. The total coliform content of the surface water samples in the dry season ranged from 11 ± 2 to 22 ± 4 CFU/100 ml, while in the wet season, it ranged from 19.33 ± 3.055 to 34.333 ± 3.512 CFU/100 ml. Table 1 above shows that the highest level of total coliforms was measured at SS2 (34.333 ± 3.512 CFU/100 ml) in the wet season, while SS1 (19.33 ± 3.055 CFU/100 ml) recorded the lowest total coliforms in the same season. During the dry season, the highest level of total coliforms was recorded at SS2 (22 ± 4 CFU/100 ml), while SS1 (11 ± 2 CFU/100 ml) had the lowest total coliform count in the same season. These results show that in the study area, total coliform levels were low in the dry season and high in the wet season. This is because of the movement of effluent from pit toilets, residential sewage, city waste and rotting natural materials from the waste disposal site to the surface water test sites. In addition to the increased water temperature and the decrease in decomposition, oxygen may contribute to critical levels of total coliform pollution in water bodies in the study area [10]. As indicated by the WHO allowable limit, the total coliform levels recorded in the two seasons in the study area were much higher than the recommended value. Consequently, based on this parameter, the water is unacceptable for use. The high total coliform value during the wet season (at the same sampling point as in the dry season) was in accordance with Venkatesharaju [11] who researched the physicochemical and bacteriological parameters of water at Cauvery College in Karnataka. Their study revealed that the wet season had higher coliform values than the dry season. This high coliform level during the wet season was attributed to the release of residential waste containing faecal matter to the water body and open defecation at the edges of the stream bank. Overall, the ANOVA results from SPSS show that the total coliform level was temporally critical but not spatially critical during the study time frame. This implies that season has a more important role than location because of ecological conditions such as precipitation, moisture, and temperature.

3.2   Spatial and Temporal Variations in the Levels of Heavy Metals in Surface Water

The spatial and temporal concentrations of heavy metals in surface water estimated at each of the five test sites throughout the study period are presented in Table 3.

Table 3. Spatial and temporal variation of heavy metals in surface water.

Sampling sites (SS)	Cr (mg/L)		Mn (mg/L)		Pb (mg/L)	
	Dry season	Wet season	Dry season	Wet season	Dry season	Wet season
SS$_1$	0.0066 ±0.0001	0.063 ±0.0086	0.0046 ±0.0034	0.023 ±0.0057	0.0017 ±0.000252	0.009133 ±0.0112
SS$_2$	0.0677 ±0.0015	0.29 ±0.053	0.0029 ±0.0037	0.00933 ±0.0112	0.002233 ±0.00038	0.00293 ±0.000252
SS$_3$	0.0241 ±0.0311	0.04 ±0.001	0.0026 ±0.0034	0.0072 ±0.0094	0.001967 ±0.0032	0.00267 ±0.00031
SS$_4$	0.064 ±0.00153	0.2467 ±0.057	0.00202 ±0.0026	0.0053 ±0.0067	0.002067 ±0.00032	0.0074 ±0.00922
SS$_5$	0.056 ±0.0034	0.25 ±0.0361	0.00251 ±0.0033	0.0133 ±0.0171	0.00167 ±0.000322	0.00467 ±0.0055

Manganese: - The concentration of manganese in all samples of surface water during the dry season ranged from 0.00202 ± 0.0026 mg/L to 0.0029 ± 0. 0037 mg/L (Table 2) with a mean value of 0.00291 ± 0.00326 mg/L, while in the wet season, it ranged from 0.0053 ± 0. 0067 to 0.023 ± 0.0057 mg/L with a mean value of 0.012 ± 0.01014 mg/L. Based on the results in both the dry and wet seasons, the levels of manganese were well below the EPA/WHO/January 2004 standard value (0.5 mg/L).

Chromium: - From the study, levels of chromium in all samples of surface water during the dry season ranged from 0.0066 ± 0.0001 to 0.068 ± 0.0015 mg/L (Table 3) with a mean value of 0.044 ± 0.18 mg/L. In the wet season, the levels of chromium ranged from 0.04 ± 0.001 to 0.29 ± 0.053 mg/L with a mean value of 0.178 ± 0.0311 mg/L. The most extreme levels of chromium during the dry season were recorded at SS2, SS4 and SS5, with the lowest level at SS1. During the wet season, nearly all qualities increased to above the WHO (January 2004) standard value (0.05 mg/L). Chromium may have reached the sampling sites through the movement of leachate because of precipitation at the dump site. Therefore, the water in the study area should not be used by residents due to its chromium levels, since chromium is one of the most lethal metals due to its influence on the nervous system and effects on the brain and kidneys. Infants and children who drink water containing chromium levels higher than the recommended level could encounter delays in their physical or mental advancement. Children can experience shortfalls in their capacity to focus and learn, while adults who drink this water could conceivably develop kidney issues or hypertension [12].

Lead: - The concentrations of lead in all samples of surface water during the dry season ranged from 0.00167 ± 0.000322 mg/L to 0.002233 ± 0.00038 mg/L (Table 3) with a mean value of 0.00192 ± 0.00032 mg/L, while in the wet season, it ranged from 0.00267 ± 0.00031 to 0.009133 ± 0.0112 mg/L with a mean value of

0.0054 ± 0.0053 mg/L. As is clear from the results in both the dry and wet seasons, the concentrations of lead were lower than the EPA/WHO/January 2004 standard value (0.01 mg/L). This may be because of the lack of disposal of lead-corrosive batteries, paint, fuel and colourants at the waste disposal site that could flow to the surface water sampling sites. It appears that the waste disposal site did not contribute fundamentally to increasing lead levels over the standard values. Despite the fact that all values were low, the concentration of lead that was measured during the study time frame fluctuated from site to site and season to season. The most extreme concentrations of lead were recorded at SS1, SS4 and SS5, with the lowest level at SS3 during the wet season. During the dry season, the highest levels were recorded at SS2 and SS4, with the lowest level at SS5. At the beginning of the period, the most extreme mean value, 0.0054 ± 0.0053 mg/L, was obtained in the wet season, though the lowest value, 0.00192 ± 0.00032 mg/L, was obtained in the dry season due to the impact of precipitation forcing the contamination to spill out of its source into the surface water test sites.

3.3   Spatial and Temporal Variation in the Estimations of Nutrients and Microbiological Parameters of Groundwater Quality

The results for the spatial and temporal variation in groundwater concentrations of nutrients and microbiological parameters measured are presented in Table 4.

Table 4. Spatial and Temporal Variations in the Nutrients and Microbiological Parameters of Groundwater.

Sampling sites	NO_3^- (mg/L)		PO_4^{3-} (mg/L)		TC (CFU/100ml)	
	Dry season	Wet season	Dry season	Wet season	Dry season	Wet season
SS1	0.071±0.0011	0.53±0.056	0.0058±0.003	0.0018±0.001	8.33±0.1.53	13±3
SS2	0.72±0.023	0.66±0.053	0.0088±0.0029	0.031±0.023	6.33±1.53	13.67±5.132
SS3	0.09±0.003	0.94±0.056	0.048±0.0023	0.0072±0.005	7.33±3.51	18.33±4.51
SS4	0.73±0.01	0.51±0.02	0.039±0.003	0.05±0.0075	5±1	16±1
SS5	0.073±0.0021	0.52±0.16	0.064±0.0042	0.264±0.34	11.67±2.52	23±6
SS6	0.08±0.0021	0.55±0.06	0.098±0.001	0.262±0.87	9±2	20±4.583

Dynamics of nitrate in groundwater: From the investigation, the levels of nitrate during the dry season ranged between 0.071 ± 0.0011 and 0.08 ± 0.0021 mg/L with a mean value of 0.34 ± 0.006 mg/L, while in the wet season, it ranged from 0.51 ± 0.02 to 0.94 ± 0.056 mg/L with a mean value of 0.62 ± 0.07 mg/L (Fig. 2). Figure 2 shows that all values in the dry and wet seasons were well lower than the WHO standard value of 50 mg/L nitrate for groundwater. This is likely because of the total absence of DO in the wastewater; the low level of nitrate is the result of ammonification from the decomposition of food waste and different sources of protein. Generally, the factors that influence the occurrence of nitrate in groundwater boreholes are subsurface mud focal points and land use practices. The findings of low levels of nitrate (below the WHO standard) during the assessment time period were similar to those of Akale, Moges et al. and Tilahun [13], who evaluated nitrate in wells and springs in northern Ethiopian regions and discovered values lower than the WHO standard threshold throughout the study time frame. Despite the fact that all values were below this threshold, the mean concentrations of nitrate obtained during the wet season were higher than the concentrations in the dry season (Fig. 2).

Dynamics of Nitrate in Groundwater: The high levels of nitrate in the wet season during the study time frame were similar to those in the study of Akale and Adugnaw [14] who examined groundwater quality in an upland farming watershed in sub-humid Ethiopian regions and discovered higher levels of nitrate during the wet season than during the dry season. The high nitrate level in the wet season may have been due to an expanded flush of nitrate-containing substances (blended sources, for example, rotting plant or animal materials, farming compost, fertilizer, manure, human or animal wastes and household sewage) from the waste disposal site, and storm events may have brought nitrate from the site to the surrounding areas; the high nitrate level may also have been due to freshwater inflow and surface run-off during the wet season [15]. Another conceivable method for nitrate removal is through the oxidation of the alkaline type of nitrogen into nitrite [16]. For the most part, during the wet season, groundwater is refreshed by precipitation due to permeation, prompting a general increase in the water level. This makes groundwater exceptionally vulnerable to contamination and overflow activities, as the components in soils and rocks are readily discharged into the water. The fundamental source of nitrate in these groundwater samples could be the utilization of compound composts on ranches that generate releases and overflow from animal feedlots, which have been distinguished as some of the primary drivers of nitrate in groundwater. In addition, the ill-advised disposal of human and animal wastes on open lands filters lingering nitrate, resulting in high nitrate fixation in groundwater in the wet season. In most cases, the use of synthetic composts, the ill-advised disposal of human and animal waste and the impact of seasons are the principal factors influencing the sources of nitrogen that is converted to nitrate in the soil. The lowest mean value was recorded during the dry season due to the low freshwater inflow and high salinity [17] and [18]. In terms of spatial variance, the highest value was obtained at ground water sampling site four (GSS4) and the lowest was obtained at ground water sampling site one (GSS1) during the dry season. In the wet season, the highest value occurred at GSS3, and the lowest occurred at GSS1 (Fig. 2). The high values may have been caused by rotting plants, fertilizer, manure and spill over since ground water sampling site three (GSS3) and ground water sampling site four (GSS4) are located near grooming areas and plant nurseries. For the low values, the opposite is true. Based on the ANOVA results, there was no significant difference between the test sites or between the seasons that could have brought the nitrate levels over the WHO threshold.

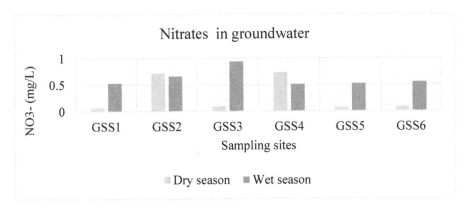

Fig. 2. Seasonal variation in the nitrate level in groundwater in the study area.

Dynamics of phosphate in groundwater: The level of phosphate in the groundwater samples ranged from 0.0088 ± 0.0029 to 0.098 ± 0.001 mg/L in the dry season and 0.002 ± 0.001 to $0.264 \pm 0.0.34$ mg/L in the wet season (Fig. 3). The findings of the study show that higher levels of phosphate were found during the wet season than in the dry seasons in all the groundwater samples except GSS3 (Fig. 3). This difference can be attributed to high moisture levels in the soil of the waste disposal site, which contains human waste, relaxer shampoos, food waste and beautifying agents that can leach phosphate into the groundwater. For the most part, the level of phosphate during the wet season may increase because of the contribution of phosphates from external sources, ill-advised solid waste disposal, overflow from the excessive utilization of mixed manures and the decay of rocks and minerals that contain phosphates. Phosphates are generally very well adsorbed into the soil and can be transported into the surrounding catchments. The water bodies receive runoff from rainstorms, explaining the high phosphate levels in nearby water bodies. The lowest level of phosphate was measured during the dry season, which may have occurred because of the low solvency of local phosphate minerals and the capacity of soils to retain phosphate. This is in accordance with the findings of Gadhia and Ansari [19], who studied regular variations in the physical attributes of an estuary in the Hazira industrial region and measured a higher level of phosphate during the wet season than during the dry season. With respect to the spatial variation, the most noteworthy concentrations of phosphate were recorded at ground water sampling site five (GSS5) followed by ground water sampling site six (GSS6) during the wet season, with the lowest level measured at GSS1. In the dry season, the highest level was measured at GSS6, and the lowest at GSS2 (Fig. 3). This was because of the location (being below and above the point source) of the boreholes at the chosen waste disposal site. According to the results (Fig. 3), aside from GSS5 and GSS6, the concentration of PO_4^{3-} in both the dry and wet seasons was below the WHO limit ($PO_4^{3-} = 0.1$ mg/L). In accordance with this, the statistical (ANOVA) result demonstrates that there was no significant difference in the mean phosphate levels among test sites or seasons during the study time frame ($p < 0.05$).

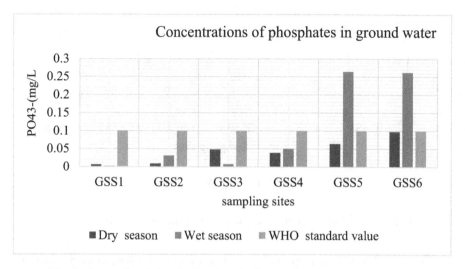

Fig. 3. Seasonal variation in phosphate in the groundwater in the study area.

Total Coliforms: The results of the bacteriological study of borehole water samples showed that the total coliform level during the dry season ranged from 5 ± 1 to 11.67 ± 2.52 CFU/100 ml with a mean value of 7.9 ± 2.01 CFU/100 ml, while in the wet season, total coliforms ranged from 13 ± 3 to 23 ± 6 CFU/100 ml, with a mean value of 17.3 ± 4.04 CFU/100 ml (Fig. 4). This result shows that the bacterial values exceeded the WHO threshold of 0 CFU/100 ml for drinking purposes. This indicates that the groundwater samples were contaminated with coliform bacteria. This is likely due to waste, especially human waste that is shipped from Bahir Dar city and released directly to the open landfill (at the open waste disposal site). It can thus be construed that the samples were, for the most part, contaminated by the channels flowing out from the waste site that release their substances directly, without any land barriers. The mean value of total coliforms measured during the wet season was higher than that measured during the dry season. This may be because the released human waste or faecal matter was flushed/washed away by precipitation from its source to the various water bodies. At that point during its flow, the waste joins surface waters and open wells and also drains into groundwater through permeation and invasion. The uncovered soil is contaminated with faeces as a result of rainstorms and drainage into open wells due to surface spill over, and this could likewise have been responsible for the higher bacterial load during the wet season than during the dry season. The test sites that are closest downstream of the disposal site, GSS5 and GSS6, showed increasing levels of total coliform. The test sites situated across the dump site were suddenly contaminated with coliform bacteria. This may have been because of excrement and different waste from anthropogenic sources (open field defecation along ditches by people and the different animals that eat near the groundwater sites) located in brambles near the drilled holes. This area was eventually flushed with water as spill over; the waste then spilled into the groundwater and was mixed in the open wells and spring water by means of surface streams. The highest values of total coliform among the six groundwater samples were found at GSS5,

GSS6, GSS1 and GSS3, with the lowest value at GSS4 during the dry season. In the wet season, the highest levels were measured at GSS5, GSS6, GSS3 and GSS4 with the lowest level measured at GSS1. The mean total coliform values in the water at the six testing sites in the study area during the dry and wet seasons are shown in Fig. 4.

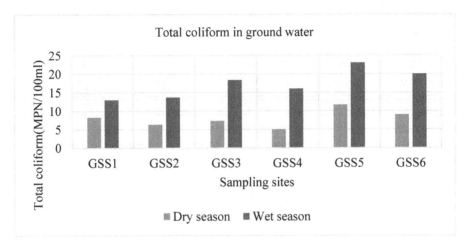

Fig. 4. Seasonal variation in total coliforms in groundwater in the study area.

3.4   Concentrations of Heavy Metals in Groundwater

Table 5. Spatial and temporal variation of heavy metals in Groundwater.

Sampling sites	Cr (mg/L)		Mn (mg/L)		Pb(mg/L)	
	Dry season	Wet season	Dry season	Wet season	Dry season	Wet season
SS1	0.0225 ±0.017	0.039 ±0.0285	0.0018 ±0.00053	0.034 ±0.0047	0.00051 ±0.0007	0.00073 ±0.001
SS2	0.011 ±0.0146	0.0203 ±0.026	0.0024 ±0.0001	0.036 ±0.0056	0.00098 ±0.0007	0.00088 ±0.0012
SS3	0.0164 ±0.0124	0.0242 ±0.0174	0.00224 ±0.0017	0.043 ±0.00473	0.00019 ±0.0001	0.00024 ±0.00018
SS4	0.0056 ±0.00021	0.0063 ±0.00082	0.00144 ±0.0019	0.0183 ±0.0042	0.0008 ±0.00061	0.0019 ±0.0009
SS5	0.055 ±0.0049	0.064 ±0.004	0.00196 ±0.00255	0.0166 ±0.023	0.0014 ±0.002	0.00203 ±0.0032
SS6	0.032 ±0.001	0.046 ±0.00551	0.0025 ±0.0032	0.00267 ±0.00065	0.0012 ±0.0015	0.0018 ±0.0026

Chromium: The findings of the study demonstrate that the chromium concentrations of the groundwater samples ranged from 0.0056 ± 0.00021 mg/L to 0.055 ± 0.0049 mg/L during the dry season with a mean value of 0.024 ± 0.0083 mg/L (Fig. 5). However, during the wet season, the concentrations of chromium ranged from 0.0063 ± 0.00082 mg/L to 0.064 ± 0.004 mg/L with a mean value of 0.033 ± 0.014 mg/L. The measured values show that the concentrations of chromium throughout the study time frame were lower than the WHO admissible limit of 0.05 mg/L for both the dry and wet seasons, with the exception of GSS5 (Fig. 5). The reason for the slight increase at GSS5 was because the fluid waste moving from the dump site passed through the channels that were closer to this borehole sample than to the others. Consequently, there was a higher likelihood of waste draining into this borehole than the other boreholes. This has, in accordance with the possibility of the separation by depth of boreholes from the source of leachate, a stronger effect on the degree of contamination of groundwater. The groundwater samples close to the dump site contained a higher number of particles and cations than those far from the dump site, and the shallow wells in the vicinity of the waste dumping site had higher concentrations of particles, cations, and organic compounds than those farther away from the dump site [20]. Overall, the highest and lowest values were observed at GSS5 and GSS4, respectively, in both the dry and wet seasons because of their location and distance from the waste disposal site. From the ANOVA results, there was a potential significant difference among the testing sites but not between the seasons.

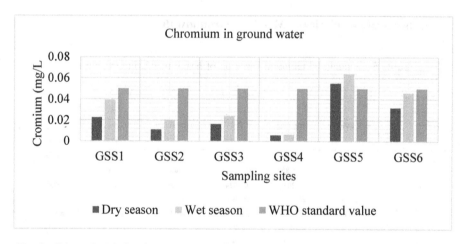

Fig. 5. Seasonal variation in the chromium concentration of groundwater in the study area.

Manganese: As Fig. 6 shows, the concentrations of manganese ranged from 0.0018 ± 0.00053 mg/L at GSS1 and 0.0025 ± 0.0032 mg/L at GSS6 with a mean value of 0.00205 ± 0.0017 mg/L in the dry season and from 0.0166 ± 0.023 mg/L at GSS5 to 0.043 ± 0.00473 mg/L at GSS3 with a mean value of 0.02499 ± 0.0071 mg/L in the wet season. The results (Fig. 6) show that the concentrations of manganese in nearly all groundwater samples were considerably lower than the WHO allowable level of 0.5 mg/L. This implies that the investigated groundwater samples acquired from the region of the dump site did not obviously indicate that the water quality was influenced by manganese leached from the dump site. Overall, the slightly higher values of heavy metals measured during the wet season (Fig. 6) firmly indicate the impact of precipitation on leachate movement to the groundwater test sites. Another reason for the low values of manganese throughout the study region may have been the absence of natural soils and the stratigraphy of the soil at the selected waste disposal site, which are responsible for the maintenance and assimilation of manganese. Overall, manganese is normally found in groundwater, can vary occasionally in concentration, and changes with the depth and purpose of the well in addition to the geography of the region. Manganese in groundwater is likewise normal in zones where the groundwater flow is moderate and in regions where groundwater is contaminated with natural contaminants. The harmful impacts of manganese intake by humans include neuro-toxicity causing ataxia, motor difficulties, anxiety, dementia and autonomic conditions such as Parkinson's disease.

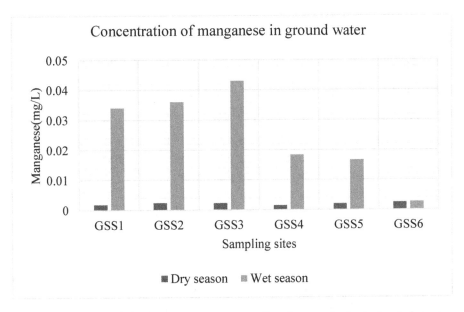

Fig. 6. Seasonal variation in manganese concentrations in groundwater in the study area.

Lead: The levels of lead in the study region ranged from 0.00019 ± 0.0001 to 0.014 ± 0.002 mg/L with a mean value of 0.004 ± 0.002 mg/L in the dry season period, while in the wet season, the levels ranged from 0.00024 ± 0.00018 to 0.0203 ± 0.0032 mg/L with a mean value of 0.0008 ± 0.0002 mg/L (Fig. 6). From Fig. 6, the profile of each study site throughout the study region shows that the mean values of lead in both the wet and dry seasons were lower than the WHO standard limit of 0.01 mg/L. This could be because of the absence of critical garage and painting activities in the community close to the study area or because solid waste, for example, scrap metal, batteries and electronic waste found at the waste disposal site, which are sources of heavy metals, did not contribute substantially to the lead levels. During the wet season, the levels of lead did not increase, similar to those of Cr and Mn, which may have been because of the extremely low penetration of lead in spring water. This is in accordance with the suggestion of Ohwoghere-Asuma [21] that the extremely low concentrations of heavy metals during the wet season recorded at the waste disposal site indicate the roles played by the occurrence of natural soils and clayey soils below the site. Heavy metals will, in general, be fixed in the waste or waste-stone interface because of redox-controlled responses. These results suggest that the groundwater is not contaminated with lead. Water soaks through the layers of solid waste at the waste removal site. The compounds and the organic and physical procedures cause hazardous synthetic substances from different waste materials to form a dangerous leachate. The risk level of the toxins depends upon the soil type and porosity, the permeability and geophysical attributes of the subsurface, the water table depth and the flow of groundwater.

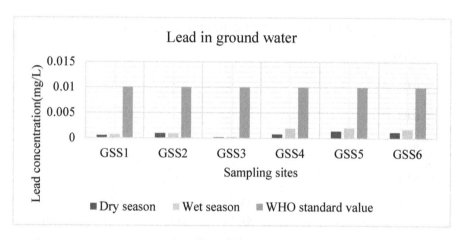

Fig. 7. Seasonal variation in the lead concentration of groundwater in the study area.

4   A Comparison of the Effect of the Open Dump Site on Surface Water and Groundwater Quality in the Zeber Watershed

A general water quality evaluation (ground and surface water) of the Zeber watershed was performed. The results are presented in Fig. 7. As shown in Fig. 7, the average standardized values of the surface water quality parameters were higher than the average standardized values of the groundwater quality parameters. Along these lines, it may be possible to state that the surface water quality was more impacted by the dumping site leachate than the groundwater quality. For most study sites, this was observed through the parameter's phosphate and chromium. Surface water was more influenced than groundwater because surface water is more readily exposed to toxins released by anthropogenic activity. Each anthropogenic activity takes place at the surface, and consequently, its impacts first influence the surface water. Groundwater is less susceptible to unexpected contamination than surface water given that the soil and rock screen out most of the toxins through groundwater flow. This does not mean that groundwater is safe from tainting, since readily soluble synthetic compounds represent a strong potential to contaminate groundwater. This is similar to the findings of Trivedi, Bajpai, and Thareja, 2008, who discovered that surface water was more strongly influenced than groundwater by outside impact.

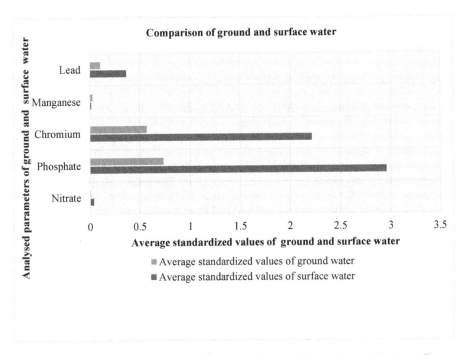

Fig. 8. Comparisons of the effect of the dump site on surface and groundwater quality.

5   Conclusion

The global and spatial fluctuations in the ground and surface water characteristics of the Zeber watershed were evaluated in terms of the WHO water quality parameters. The study of the concentrations of heavy metals and nutrients showed that NO3-, Mn and Pb in both ground and surface water were within the limits during the study period, while the remaining characteristics changed with the seasons.

The findings of the study showed that the sampling sites downstream of the dump site were more strongly influenced by the dump site than the sampling sites upstream of the dump site.

The total coliform levels measured were much higher than the limits for drinking water at all sampling sites. This suggests the importance of more careful consideration of household pollution, natural sanitation control and awareness of water pollution since the open waste disposal site and the practice of open defecation have greatly affected the watershed of the study zone.

The results of the statistical analysis (one-way ANOVA) performed on the surface water Cr, Mn, Pb, nitrate, phosphate and total coliform data suggest that all measured.

parameters essentially shifted between the seasons during the study period (P-value < 0.05).

Acknowledgments. The authors would like to thank Bahir Dar University, Bahir Dar institute of technology for financial supports of this project.

References

1. Love, J., Luchsinger, V.: Sustainability and water resources. J. Sustain. Green Bus. **2**, 1–12 (2014)
2. Markandya, A.: Water quality issues in developing countries. In: López, R., Toman, M.A. (eds.) Economic Development and Environmental Sustainability: New Policy Options, pp. 307–344 (2006)
3. Afolayan, O., Ogundele, F., Odewumi, S.: Hydrological implication of solid waste disposal on groundwater quality in urbanized area of Lagos state, Nigeria. Int. J. Appl. **2** (2012)
4. Nathanson, J.: Solid-waste management. Encyclopaedia Britannica (2015)
5. Hamad, O.H.M.: Occupational and Environmental Hazards among Workers in Petroleum Stations, Khartoum State, Sudan (2013–2015). University of Gezira (2018)
6. Clesceri, L., Greenberg, A., Eaton, A.: Standard methods for the examination of water and wastewater, 20th edn. American Public Health Association, Washington, DC (1998)
7. Apha Awwa, W.: Standard methods for the examination of water and wastewater 20th edition. American Public Health Association, American Water Work Association, Water Environment Federation, Washington, DC (1998)
8. Tjandraatmadja, G., Pollard, C., Sheedy, C., Gozukara, Y.: Sources of contaminants in domestic wastewater: nutrients and additional elements from household products. CSIRO, Water for a Healthy Country Flagship Report (2010)
9. Akpan, A.E., Ugbaja, A.N., George, N.J.: Integrated geophysical, geochemical and hydrogeological investigation of shallow groundwater resources in parts of the Ikom-Mamfe Embayment and the adjoining areas in Cross River State, Nigeria. Environ. Earth Sci. **70**(3), 1435–1456 (2013). https://doi.org/10.1007/s12665-013-2232-3
10. Kale, V.S.: Consequence of temperature, pH, turbidity and dissolved oxygen water quality parameters. Int. Adv. Res. J. Sci. Eng. Technol. **3**, 186–190 (2016)
11. Venkatesharaju, K., Ravikumar, P., Somashekar, R., Prakash, K.: Physico-chemical and bacteriological investigation on the river Cauvery of Kollegal stretch in Karnataka. Kathmandu Univ. J. Sci. Eng. Technol. **6**, 50–59 (2010)
12. Water, D.: State of Florida Department of Environmental Protection (2000)
13. Akale, A., Moges, M., Dagnew, D., Tilahun, S., Steenhuis, T.: Assessment of nitrate in wells and springs in the north central Ethiopian highlands. Water **10**, 476 (2018)
14. Akale, A.T., et al.: Groundwater quality in an upland agricultural watershed in the sub-humid Ethiopian highlands. J. Water Resour. Prot. **9**, 1199 (2017)
15. Karuppasamy, P., Perumal, P.: Biodiversity of zooplankton at Pichavaram mangroves, South India. Adv. Biosci **19**, 23–32 (2000)
16. Rajasegar, M.: Physico-chemical characteristics of the Vellar estuary in relation to shrimp farming. J. Environ. Biol. **24**, 95–101 (2003)

17. Krishnamurthy, K., Mani, P.: Variation of phytoplankton in a tropical estuary (Vellar estuary, Bay of Bengal, India). Internationale Revue der gesamten Hydrobiologie und Hydrographie **74**, 109–115 (1989)

18. Murugan, A., Ayyakkannu, K.: Ecology of uppanar backwaters, Cuddalore: 2. nutrients. Mahasagar **24**, 103–108 (1991)

19. Gadhia, M., Surana, R., Ansari, E.: Seasonal variations in physico-chemical characterstics of Tapi estuary in Hazira industrial area. Our Nature **10**, 249–257 (2012)

20. Zhang, X., Qian, H., Chen, J., Qiao, L.: Assessment of groundwater chemistry and status in a heavily used semi-arid region with multivariate statistical analysis. Water **6**, 2212–2232 (2014)

21. Ohwoghere-Asuma, O., Aweto, K., Akpoborie, I.: Investigations of groundwater quality and evolution in an estuary environment: a case study of Burutu Island, Western Niger Delta. Nigeria. Environ. Hydrol **22**, 1–14 (2012)

Manufacturing of Tiles from Kieselguhr Sludge /Diatomaceous Earth/

Dargie Haile[(✉)]

Lecturer of Chemical Engineering (Master s Degree in Environmental Engineering), Department of Chemical Engineering, Institute of Technology, Woldia University, Woldia, Ethiopia

Abstract. Diatomaceous earth sludge this has a negative impact on the ecosystem because kieselguhr has some heavy metals which poison the environment and it has cementing behavior that cause desertification. But kieselguhr is able to produce the simplest unit of tiles and becomes beneficial for the process economy of the factories. The objective of this project was to prepared floor tiles from the brewery filtration by product so-called kieselguhr. The primary one was pretreatment of the brewery by product by the help of bases (NaOH) in order to make it neutralize. The next task was mixing of the raw materials (kieselguhr, sand, fifty percent cement water and aggregate) using their standard ratio. After this molding and drying of bricks has done. The required tiles must be with the require shape, so in this project the task of molding was done to give the shape for the bricks. Later, the tiles were dried using sun light from 1428 days to remove its moisture. The parameters which were checked during this project work were Compression strength, percentage water absorption, moisture content and density. The experimental result showed that it was not as expected to produce floor tiles from pure 100%kieselguhr in the replacement of cement, but by mixing through the percentage ratio of 50% of kieselguhr with the remaining percentage of cement was used to produce floor tiles. As the result showed the compression strength and the percentage water absorption mainly depends on the porosity.

Keywords: Aggregate · Cement · Floor tiles · Kieselguhr · Manufacturing · Sand · Tiles · Water

1 Introduction

The brewing spent kieselguhr is an industrial by product, in the sludge form, that is mainly composed by diatom frustules, yeast (fungi) and other organic matter (hop and malt) restrained in the filtration phase of the beer production process [2]. Kieselguhr also called diatomaceous earth or diatomite, is a non-metallic, soft, friable, fine grained and siliceous sedimentary rock that can be easily crumbled in to a white to off-white powder [3]. This powder shows a granular feel, and it is very light due to its high porosity [4]. Diatomaceous deposits are formed by sedimentation from silica bearing waters of unicellular algae called diatoms, [5] whose skeletons are made of cryptocrystalline silica associated to clay minerals and quartz as accessory components. Diatoms have quite complex structure showing numerous fine pores, cavities and

© ICST Institute for Computer Sciences, Social Informatics and Telecommunications Engineering 2022
Published by Springer Nature Switzerland AG 2022. All Rights Reserved
M. L. Berihun (Ed.): ICAST 2021, LNICST 411, pp. 106–114, 2022.
https://doi.org/10.1007/978-3-030-93709-6_8

channels, reason why this material has low specific weight, low heat conduction, high specific surface area and high adsorption capacity [2]. As a filer medium, kieselguhr is currently used to separate very fine particles that otherwise pass or clog the filter net. This geometrical can be used as filter medium for water, juice wine, sprits, syrups, gelatin, sugar and several chemical substances [6]. Recently diatomite powder was sinterized around 1000% to manufacture ceramic monoliths with bimodal porosity and high strength. Scientists have studied the use of diatomaceous earth mixed with lime and gypsum to make autoclaved light weight bricks [2]. The beer industry has to find sustainable solution to prevent the environmental impact of kieselguhr waste deposition which carries sanitary and economic implication. The current eliminations of this by product is either its deposition on land fill or its spread over agricultural fields [7]. The procedures referred are not satisfactory with regard to sustainable development and environmental care. This study aims to manufacture floor tiles with recycled brewing spent kieselguhr in order to achieve a sustainable solution for the Environment and or for the byproduct incorporation without significant impact on the physico-mechanical properties of the floor tile material.

2 Methodology

Treatment of kieselguhr sludge: -For determining pretreatment of kieselguhr sludge 1.5 kg of kieselguhr sludge was mixed with 1000 mL of the NaOH under heating system in order to neutralize with holding time of 30 min and maximum cross pending temperature of 62.5° centigrade (boiling condition), the alkaline activation is carrying out on a stirrer. Afterward the sample solution is filtered and washed sequentially with deionized water five times to remove the salt ions and other residues. The resulting solid which is separated by the process of settling is finally dried at 105° centigrade for 24 h (Fig. 1).

Fig. 1. Treated kieselguhr powder after it discharges

Mixing process:- The washed and screend through three milimeter sand, agrregate, 50%kieselghure and cement togother were mixed in a vessel folowed the standard values of C25 2:3:1 respectively (where C stands for compression). The mixing mechanisim was electricaly and it was processed at the standard values of temprature and pressure for 15minutes in the precence of slowly adding 2 liters of water.Genarally the mixing time and the amount of water to be used is depend on on the size of the part taken.

Molding and Drying: molding oftiles isthe mechanisims of giving shape for the tiles by letting the time from 24 to 72 h after puting the mixed ingrdients on the molding box and then vibrating 26 min. Water was added durin mixing to incease wokablity of the mixture and also after molding to sterngthn or to decrease its porosity by creating the hydrogen bond initially. So to remove this water drying mehanisim with 1428 days at the standard temprature and presure was recomended up to the calculated moisture content will be 10%. Then in this study the tiles had dried using sun light for 21 days (weight of tile at the end of the third week) at which the moisture content of the tiles was less than 10%.

$$\text{percentage moisture content} = \frac{W1 - W2}{W1} * 100 \tag{1}$$

Weight Composition of the Produced Tiles:- was the percentage composition of the raw materials which existed in the final produced tiles. This can be calculated using the following formula.

$$\text{Weight percentage composition} = \frac{\text{Component mas of each raw material}}{\text{Total mas of produced tiles}} * 100 \ldots \tag{2}$$

Compression Strength test for Floor Tiles:- the mandatory strength for floor tile is compression strength. This is the resistance of the tiles to the compression force which was applied by compression mechanism, until the first cracking occurs. This was determined by putting the sample on the compression machine and reading the values (Fig. 2).

Fig. 2. Compression strength test

Density of Tiles:- was determined by dividing the weight of the sample to equivalent weight of water or volume of the sample. Then the dispersed volume of water due to the sample was 698 ml or 0.000698 m^3.

$$\text{Density of the tile} = \frac{\text{mass of tile}}{\text{volume of tile}} \tag{3}$$

Determining Water Percentage Absorption Capacity of Tiles:- The produced tiles were dried in oven for 48 h at a temperature of 112° centigrade and cooling for 4 h at a room temperature and pressure in order to weigh (W1 of it).Then after it was immersed in clean water at a water bath with a temperature of 25° centigrade for 24 h. Finally it was removed from the water bath and the moisture was swept by clean cloth then and weighed in three minutes (W1). The percentage water absorption capacity of tiles was calculated by using the following formula (Fig. 3).

$$Water\ percentage\ absorption = \left(\frac{W2 - W1}{W1}\right) * 100 \tag{4}$$

Fig. 3. Water absorption and weighting balance of the tile.

3   Characterizations of the Produced Floor Tiles

Table 1. Characterizations of the produced tiles

	Checked parameter	Obtained value	Recommended values
Ratio of kieselguhr (50% over cement)	Compression strength	4653.19 N	10005000 N
	% water absorption	5%	<20%
	Density	2177.7 kg/m^3	20002300 kg/m^3

The above Table 1 indicates that all the parameters were within the range of the standard values. Therefore, the floor tiles made up of this waste was acceptable in the aspect of those parameters.

Generally the methods that followed to produce the tiles from the byproduct of the brewery filtration so called kieselguhr sludge was as follows (Fig. 4).

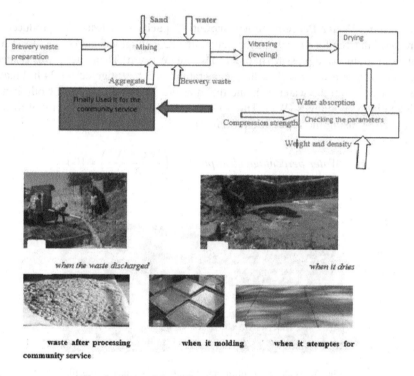

Fig. 4. General flow diagram of the entire process

4   Results and Discussion

The %moisture content of the produced tiles with respect to time was as follows.

W_1 (weight of tile at the beginning of the first week) = 1845 g
W_2 (weight of tile at the end of the second week) = 1652 g
W_3 (weight of tile at the end of the third week) = 1520 g
W_4 (weight of tile at the end of the fourth week) = 1416 g

Then the drying time at which the moisture content is less than 10% was calculated by using Eq. (1) (Fig. 5).

$$\text{Percentage moisture content (W2)} = \frac{1845\ g - 1652\ g}{1845\ g} * 100 = 10.46\%$$

$$\text{Percentage moisture content (W3)} = \frac{1652\ g - 1520\ g}{1652\ g} * 100 = 7.99\%$$

$$\text{Percentage moisture content (W4)} = \frac{1520 - 1416}{1520} = 6.8\%$$

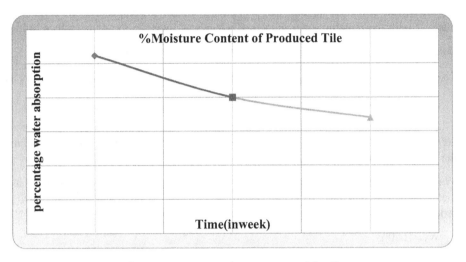

Fig. 5. Percentage moisture content of the tile

As it was seen from the graph when the time increased, the moisture content of the floor tile was decrease. This was due to the drying temperatures of sun light which makes to vaporize the water content. on the other hand, the weight of the tiles also observed to have inversely proportional with the drying time. This means when the drying time increases from week one to week four the weight of he produced tiles were decreasing from 1845 g to 1416 g.

Weight Composition of the Produced Tiles:- The dried tile had the following composition of sand, cement, kieselguhr and aggregate when the produced tile weight was 1.52 kg. The following calculated result was obtained through applying Eq. (2) (Table 2).

Table 2. Weight percentage compositions of the produced tile.

Ratio of kieselguhr sludge (%)	Raw materials	Mass of raw materials (k.g)	Mass of produced tiles	% weight composition
50	Sand	0.433	1.52	28.5
50	Aggregate	0.575	1.52	37.8
50	Kieselguhr	0.175	1.52	11.5
50	Cement	0.175	1.52	11.5

From this one can see that the percentage weight a composition of each raw material with the remaining percentage of water was found in the unit produced tile.

Density of Tile: The unit density of the produced tile was found using Eq. (3)

$$\text{Density of tile} = \frac{1.52 \text{ kg}}{0.000698 \text{ m}^3} = 2177.7 \text{ kg/m}^3$$

The obtained density was within the range the recommended values of tiles which is 2002300 kg/m^3. Then in the aspect of this parameter the tiles which is produced from the kieselguhr sludge was acceptable.

Water Percentage Absorption Capacity of the Produced Tile: by following its method which is stated in methodology part the water absorption capacity of the newly produced tile was found to be 4.73% by using the equation of (4).

$W_1 = 1620$ g.
$W_2 = 1696.6$ g

$$\text{Water\% absorption of tile} = \left(\frac{1696.6 - 1620}{1620}\right) * 100 = 4.73\%$$

This result sows the absorbing capacity of the tile 4.73% was much less than the recommended value (20%). This lower value of water absorption indicates the porosity of the produced tile was decreasing and then the compression strength increase.

Compression Strength:- During the compression strength test the first cracking of the produced sample was occurred at the 3952.6 Newton at the end of the week one and continue linearly up to week four (Fig. 6).

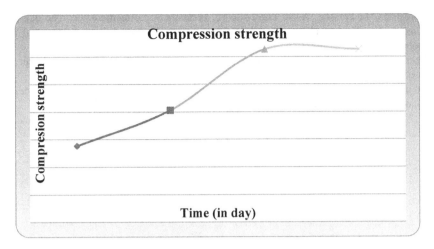

Fig. 6. Compression strength of the produced tile

As it was seen from the graph when the drying time becomes longer the compression strength also increased. this indicates that the porosity of the produced sample narrowed as the hydration bond or the particle were compacted.

5   Conclusion

Generally, the experimental result shows that it is possible to produce tiles from 50%/ kieselguhr over cement and use it for different services like walkways, compounds as a floor tiles.

Compression strength and percentage water absorption mainly dependent on porosity. Means the lower the porosity and %water absorption the higher the strength.

Manufacturing of tiles from brewery sludge (diatomaceous earth) can make the environment safe, increase the income of the company, create the work opportunity and minimize the cost of cement.

Acknowledgments. The author would like to thank Bahir Dar University, Bahir Dar institute of technology for financial supports of this project.

References

1. ECHA: Assessment report, peracetic acid, regulation (EU) no 528/2012 concerning the making available on the market and use of biocidal products, evaluation of active substances. European Chemicals Agency Finland (2015)
2. Ferraz, E., Coroado, J., Silva, J., Gomes, C., Rocha, F.: Manufacture of ceramic bricks using recycled brewing spent Kieselguhr. Mater. Manuf. Processes **26**(10), 13191329 (2011)
3. Quarles, W.: Diatomaceous earth for pest control. IPM practitioner **14**(5/6), 111 (1992)

4. Nordström, J., Persson, A.-S., Lazorova, L., Frenning, G., Alderborn, G.: The degree of compression of spherical granular solids controls the evolution of microstructure and bond probability during compaction. Int. J. Pharm. **442**(12), 312 (2013)
5. Bakr, H.: Diatomite: its characterization, modifications and applications. Asian J. Mater. Sci. **2**(3), 121136 (2010)
6. Brennan, J.G., Grandison, A.S., Lewis, M.J.: Separations in food processing. Food processing handbook, p. 429 (2006)
7. B. Association: Solid Waste Reduction Manual, Brewers Association A Passionate Voice for Craft Brewers (2013)

Electrical and Electronics Engineering

Optimal Transmit Antenna Selection for Massive MIMO Systems

Shenko Chura Aredo[1](✉), Yalemzewd Negash[2], Yihenew Wondie[2], Feyisa Debo[3], Rajaveerappa Devadas[3], and Abreham Fikadu[4]

[1] Institute of Technology, Hawassa University, Hawassa, Ethiopia
[2] Addis Ababa Institute of Technology, Addis Ababa University, Addis Ababa, Ethiopia
[3] Adama Science and Technology University, Adama, Ethiopia
[4] Alexanderia, VA, USA

Abstract. Antenna selection in Multiple input Multiple Output (MIMO) is a signal processing method in which the elements of Radio Frequency (RF) chain are switched to their corresponding subset of antennas. Due to the large number of RF transceivers, antenna selection resolves the complexity and power consumption. In this paper, a suboptimal antenna selection algorithm that combines two selection techniques is proposed. The algorithm leverages the use of minimum signal to noise ratio (SNR) at the cell edge and dynamic channel condition due to mobility. To apply fractional transmit power re-allocation at sub 6 GHz and mmWave frequencies, the same number of RF components are set to be active and the rest to sleep mode after adaptive selection. As a result, the branch in the array with the best signal quality is chosen and applied in iteration until the desired value is reached however re-selection boosts EE at the expense of total rate. In comparison to complete array consumption and random selection, the results show that the algorithm outperforms random selection and achieves higher energy efficiency. Furthermore, capacity loss due to selection is offset by using nonlinear precoding at the expense of complexity.

Keywords: Antenna selection · Energy efficiency · Massive MIMO · mmWave · Precoding

1 Introduction

Massive MIMO (mMIMO) is a large-scale MIMO device that is becoming more common in wireless communications. It potentially scales up traditional MIMO by orders of magnitude. Itconsiders multi-user MIMO, in which a base station has hundreds of thousands of antennas supporting multiple single-antenna users in the same time-frequency resource [1,2]. A device with a large number of base sta- tion antennas will increase connection reliability, spectral quality, and radiated energy efficiency [3]. Each antenna element is linked to a single RF

M. L. Berihun (Ed.): ICAST 2021, LNICST 411, pp. 117–131, 2022.
https://doi.org/10.1007/978-3-030-93709-6_9

chain at the base station, which comprises an amplifier, an analog-to-digital converter (ADC), and mixers. RF chains are generally expensive and power-hungry as a result of these characteristics. Furthermore, because of the high power consumption, increasing the number of antennas at the base station will result in physical restrictions, complexity, and expense. RF chains, in particular, are responsible for 50–80% of total transceiver power consumption [4]. As a result, antenna selection could be a viable option for ad- dressing the inherent hardware complexities of massive MIMO while still taking advantage of the increased degrees of freedom provided by the base station's antenna excesses.

For the classic MIMO, a variety of antenna selection standards and algorithms have been investigated over the last few decades. In [5], basic selection algorithms for realistic detectors were used to investigate error-rate directed antenna selection. Many studies promoted capacity-oriented selection criteria like the greedy algorithm and convex optimization [6–8]. The author of [9] presented an antenna selection technique (AS) with a minimal level of complexity that picks antennas that minimize constructive user interference. When used in conjunction with a simple matched filter (MF) precoder at the transmitter, the suggested AS algorithm outperformed systems that used a more complicated channel inversion method (CI). The work in [10,11] aimed to remove the destructive portion of interference, which was established by the connection between the sub streams of a modulated MIMO PSK transmission.

The authors in [12] presented a distance based selection algorithm with spatial modulation in the process of optimization. The algorithm uses a singular value decomposition in order to minimize complexity and symbol error rate compared to the exhaustive search. In this article, the down-link massive MIMO system's transmit antenna selection is considered. The procedure is divided into three parts: first, the EE of a full array device is evaluated at the cell edge using an equivalent power allocation technique, and then an optimal number of BS antennas that retains the optimal value is calculated. Second, minimum threshold SNR is cal- culated using the optimum number of antennas (M*) as a benchmark to further reduce M*. For each mobile terminal, free space path-loss (FSPL) and Close-In (CI) path-loss (PL) models are used, with adaptive power allocation based on PL and minimum obtained power at the edge. Finally, after re-identifying M*, the antenna elements with best gains are employed, and EE is assessed at various frequency ranges using spatial selectivity. The rest of the work is structured as follows: A system model for mMIMO antenna selection is defined in section two. In sections three and four, the proposed technique's sum rate and EE are tested, and the effects are then illustrated in Sect. 5. In Sect. 6, the overall work is summarized and conclusions are drawn.

2 System Description

There are two sections of the system description. A signal model for a downlink large MIMO device is presented with antenna selection. Then the mathematical formulations for the selection is analyzed and simulated with different scenarios.

2.1   System Model

This channel model uses only free space LoS transmission between the BS and user terminals. The BS has a ULA with a λ spaced M antennas, where λ is the signal wavelength and the mutual resonance effect between antenna element is ignored. Inside the cell, there are K single-antenna devices that transmit data to the BS at the same time using the same time-frequency resources. Furthermore, it is believed that all of the K devices served by the BS are located at different angles on the antenna array's far-field and experience large and small scale fading. The downlink For a single- cell massive MIMO structure, Mo RF chains associated with $K(K \leq MoM^o)$ are considered.

2.2   Mobile Location Positioning

In today's cellular networks, identifying a mobile position is a critical problem. Angle of Arrival (AoA), Time of Arrival (ToA), and GPS are among the techniques used. In general, there are three methods for determining the location of a mobile terminal: satellite positioning, cellular network-based positioning, and indoor positioning. The trilateration method is used to calculate a mobile's location using the relative position of a base station (BS). Unlike the triangulation process, which requires the angle of each user for position tracking, only the distance between the BS and each user is needed in this case.

2.3   Close-In(CI) Path Loss Model

The CI model is based on Friis and Bullington's fundamental radio propagation concepts, wherein the PLE gives insight into route loss dependant on environment. Previous UHF models applied 1–100 m as CI reference distance since BS tower was tall and inter-site distances for certain frequency bands were many kilometers [14]. The CI 1m reference distance, as proposed in [15], is a suitable recommended norm that relates the real path loss to a practical CI distance of 1m. Standardization to a 1m reference distance simplifies dimension and model comparisons, provides a consistent description for the PLE, and allows for simple and quick route loss estimates without the need of a calculator. In a given situation, the CIPL model is a generic frequency model that explains large scale transmission path loss at all relevant frequencies. The equation for the CI model is as follows: simpler, gives a consistent description for the PLE, and allows for intuitive and quick path loss computation without the need of another computations. There will be few users within a few meters of the base station antenna in emerging mmWave mobile systems, and close-in users in the near field will have strong signals or be power-controlled compared to typical users much farther from the transmitter and so that any path loss error in the near field will be much smaller than the dynamic range of signals. The general formula for CIPL according to [14] is given by

$$PL_{dB}^{CI} = FSPL_{dB} + 10nlog_{10}(d) + \chi_a^{CI} \tag{1}$$

where $n = \dfrac{\sum(DA)}{\sum(D^2)}$, $A = PL^{CI}(f,d)_{dB} - FSPL(f,1m)$, $10log_{10}d$ indicates the single model criterion, the path loss exponent (PLE), with 10n defining path loss in dB in terms of decades of distances starting at 1m (making power over distance very easy to compute and the loss model for free space is stated as

$$FSPL_{dB} = 20log10(4\pi/\lambda) \tag{2}$$

This is worth noting as the CI model is described on the basis of an inherent frequency dependent path loss contained into 1 m FSPL as a single parameter to optimize opposed to the ABG model. Table 1 shows the frequency ranges to be used in CI pathloss model in urban micro for street canyon (UMi-SC) and open space (UMi-OS) at line of sight (LOS) and non line-of-sight (NLOS) environments respectively [15]. As shown in the table, the CI model provides path loss exponent (PLE) of 2.0 and 1.9 in LOS, which approaches the FSPL.

Table 1. Parameters for CI path loss model [41].

Scenarios	Frequency (GHz)	Distance (m)	PLE/α	σ_{dB}^{CI}
UMi-SC LOS	2–73.5	5–121	2.0	2.9
UMi-SC NLOS	2–73.5	19–272	3.1	8.0
UMi-OS LOS	2–60	5–88	19	4.7
UMi-OS NLOS	2–73.5	8–235	2.8	8.3
UMa LOS	2–73.5	58–930	2.0	4.6
UMa NLOS	2–73.5	45–1429	2.7	10.0

2.4   Trilateration Based Antenna Selection

The number of antennas to be chosen is determined by adjusting an appropriate amount of transmit power to be radiated by only the selected number of antennas during the selection process. Trilateration is used to pinpoint a user's position so that the main beam can focus only on the target region, reducing leakage. The transmit power adapts when the user's location changes as a function ofdistance due to user mobility. In this case, instead of using all arrays and wasting resources, the number of transmit antennas can be decreased adaptively as the consumer gets closer to the center of the BS, using the minimum SNR at the cell edge as a threshold value. In comparison, when allocating maximum transmit power based on edge distance, the BS only allocates power proportional to the reduced distance, resulting in only a few antennas being activated, as described in (3). After that, using factorial permutations as $\binom{M}{N} = \dfrac{M!}{N!(M-N)!}$, the antennas with the best channel gains are chosen from the list.

$$N = (\frac{M * \sum_{i=1}^{K} p_t/K}{P_T}) \tag{3}$$

where p_t is the transmit power adjusted for each user based on path loss, P_T is the total transmit power and $N = M^o$ is the number of RF chain components. The selection process for the whole system is stated in a sub optimal algorithm I below.

Algorithm I: Sub Optimal Algorithm

---

1. Initialize: R, M, K, $Cap_i \leftarrow 0$, γ P_t, B, p_{amp}, p_{bb}, p_{syn}, p_{dac}, p_{mix}, p_{filt}
2. **For** l = 1 : length (M) **do**
3. $p_{tot} \leftarrow p_{amp} + (p_{bb} + p_{syn}) + (\ell * (p_{dac} + p_{mix} + p_{filt}))$
4. $H \leftarrow (randn(K, \ell) + j * randn(K, \ell))$
5. $R(\ell) = log_2(real(det(I + (\frac{\gamma_{sel}}{\ell}) * HH')))$
6. $EE \leftarrow \dfrac{R(\ell)}{P_{total}(\ell)}$
7. End **for**
8. $M^* \leftarrow \ell(find(EE == max(EE)))$
9. Find r of k_x using trilateration and $\Gamma(R)$ for cell edge user
10. $P_{rmin} \leftarrow P_{tmax}/\Gamma(R)$
11. $Pt_r \leftarrow \Gamma_r * Pr_{min}$
12. $M_1^o = \dfrac{M * \sum_{i=1}^{K} P_t/K}{P_T}$
13. $M_2^o \leftarrow round(\sum(\Gamma(r))/K) * M/\Gamma(R)$
14. **If** $M^o \neq M^o$ **goto** 9
15. Else $M^o \leftarrow M_1^o$; Selecting M^o best branches among M.
16. **For** $\gamma = 1 : M^o$ **do**
17. $H = (rand(K; M) + j * rand(K, M))/\sqrt{M^o}$);
18. **For** $M_i^o = 1 : M^o$
19. $H_c = [H :; [MoiM - i]]$.... Select column with maximum capacity.
20. $C(m) = log_2(real(det(I + \gamma * H_c * H_c')))$
21. End **for**
22. $C_{max} = max(C(m))$; Calculating maximum Capacity.
23. $M_i^o \leftarrow find(C = Cmax)$
24. End **for**
25. $C(\gamma) \leftarrow C$
26. End **if**

In the algorithm, $\Gamma(r)$, $\Gamma(r)$ and is SNR in dB at cell edge and at reduced distance respectively..

3   Sum Rate Evaluation

There are M antennas on the base station, and each antenna has its own transceiver chain. The N matching transceivers are turned on when N antennas are selected, while the other $M - N$ are turned off. In the same time-frequency resources, this base station with N operational antennas and transceivers supports K single-antenna users. With massive MIMO, $M \gg K$ and N should be within the range of K to M. Where N, K is the number of antennas to be selected and the total number of single antenna user terminals. The received signal at the BS can be stated as

$$\hat{y}_l = \sqrt{\rho K} H_l^{(N)} \hat{z}_l + \hat{n}_l \tag{4}$$

where H_l^N is a KxN channel vector at carrier ℓ and the superscript N shows that antennas are selected such that H_l^N are chosen from the KxM full vector or matrix H_l. The components of $H(N)l$ are normalized such that they have the same size, same energy across all sub-carriers, antennas, and K user terminals. The Nx1 transmit vector over the N chosen antennas is thus z_l, which satisfies $\mathbb{E}\{||z_l||^2\} = 1$. The transmit power is represented by the factor ρ_K. The transmit power per user is managed using the rules in [16]. As a result, the overall transmission power rises with uplink terminals and unaffected by N. The normalized transmit SNR per user is represented by the parameter ρ. The average per-user received SNR with random antenna selection is ρN and enhances the number of chosen antenna elements N owing to higher branch gains. If only a limited number of RF chains are activated and the number of users K changes, the average peruser received SNR stays unchanged, as does the average peruser rate (ignoring interference).

Because the "best" antennas are picked, the resulting SNRs should be greater with smart antenna selection than with random antenna selection. To prevent favoring users with a sufficient average gain, normalization of the array matrix is utilized to combat the impacts of pathloss and large scale obstructions [15]. Normalization is conducted when users are both far and close to the base station. However, since channel differences among antennas are crucial for selection scenario, they should never be put on an equal basis.

3.1   Dirty Paper Coding Sum Capacity(C_{DPC})

The down-link sum capacity for DPC is [7]:

$$C_{DPC_l} = \max_{P_l} \log_2 det\left(I + \rho K (H_l^{(N)})^H P_l H_l^{(N)} \right) \tag{5}$$

which is achieved using dirty-paper coding (DPC) [9]. The diagonal optimal control matrix Pl, i in (5) has Pl, i I = 1, 2,...K. The optimization is also done with the total power restriction $sum i = 1KPl, i = 1$ in mind. This convex optimization issue may be addressed with iterative water filling technique to sum power. In practice, DPC is quite difficult to execute. However, there are inferior linear precoding methods that are significantly less complicated and work rather well for large MIMO, such as zero-forcing (ZF) precoding.

3.2   Zero Forcing Sum Capacity(C_{ZF})

For ZF linear precoder, the total rate is given by [16]

$$\hat{C}_{ZF,l} = \max_{\hat{Q}_l} \sum_{i=1}^{K} log_2(1 + \rho K \hat{Q}_{l,i}), \tag{6}$$

The received signal of various user terminals are represented by $\hat{Q}_l, i$, and the maximizing is done under the total power restriction.

$$\sum_{i=1}^{K} \hat{Q}_{l,i}\left[\left(H_l^{(N)}\left(H_l^{(N)}\right)^H\right)^{-1}\right] = 1 \tag{7}$$

$\hat{Q}_l$ is a diagonal matrix with i=1, 2,...,K, as illustrated in (6) and (7) and the diagonal, with $[.]i,i$ denoting the ith diagonal elements $\left(H_l^{(N)}\left(H_l^{(N)}\right)^H\right)^{-1}$ which represent the power penalty of removing the interferences.

The detected SNRs at users are influenced by the precoding method and channel condition in general. The received SNR in the single-user scenario, for example, is ρN. In the multi-user case with zero-forcing precoding, the peruser received SNR is $\rho N/Tr\left(H_l^{(N)}\left(H_l^{(N)}\right)^H\right)^{-1}$, where Tr{.} represents the trace of a matrix. When the user channels are orthogonal, $H_l^{(N)}\left(H_l^{(N)}\right)^H$ is diagonal, and the average per-user received SNR reaches the upper bound given by the single-user case, i.e., ρN. When the number of base station antennas increases under "favorable" situations or contexts, the user channels get orthogonal, and the average received SNR approaches this absolute limit.

The DPC sum-capacity is used as the foundation for antenna selection algorithms. However, in relevant circumstances, the performance of the resultant selection will also be assessed in terms of ZF sum-rate. On various subcarriers, different antenna configurations may be optimum. Though in a real MIMO systems, all subcarriers should use the same antennas. As a result, the DPC throughput will be enhanced through selecting the antennas only with better gains after iteration over all possible combinations. In selection process of those columns from full array of H_l, $M * M$ matrix Δ with binary diagonal element has been introduced.

$$\Delta_i = \begin{cases} 1, & Select \\ 0, & \text{otherwise} \end{cases} \tag{8}$$

showing whether the ith element is chosen, and achieving $\sum_{i=1}^{L} = N$. According to Sylvester's identity, det (I+UJ) = det (I+JU), DPC total rate can be rewritten as in (5) as

$$C_{DPC_l} = \max_{P_l} \ log_2 \ det(1 + \rho K P_l H_l \Delta(H_l)^H) \tag{9}$$

where $\sum_{i=1}^{K} P_{l,i} = 1$. The desired Δ is discovered by increasing the average DPC sum rate,

$$\mho opt = \underset{\mho}{\mathrm{argmax}} \ \frac{1}{L} \sum_{l=1}^{L} log_2 \ det \left(I + \rho K P_l H_l \mho (H_l)^H \right) \qquad (10)$$

The corresponding sum rate of ZF after selection is

$$C_{ZF,l} = \underset{Q_l}{\max} \sum_{i=1}^{K} log_2 (1 + \rho K Q_{l,i}), \qquad (11)$$

subject to

$$\sum_{i=1}^{K} Q_{l,i} \left[\left(H_l^{(N)} \left(H_l^{(N)} \right)^H \right)^{-1} \right]_{i,i} = 1 \qquad (12)$$

Despite $\mho_{opt}$ could not be optimal for ZF, using a more realistic precoding scheme than DPC helps in achieving efficient antenna selection. Conversely, if the throughput is to be more affected due to minimized number of antennas, DPC compensates by leveraging the loss in capacity. Moreover, although an extensive search of all available permutations of N antennas would definitely produce the optimal $\mho$, as described above, such a search is very complicated and infeasible for massive MIMO. From (11) and (12), it can be seen that in ZF, zeroing the upper and lower matrix elements consumes more power, but it is still easier to process than DPC, which has no additional power penalty but is more complex.

4   Energy Efficiency Evaluation

The total energy efficiency of the system can be evaluated as [16]

$$EE = \frac{\sum_{k=1}^{K} \left(E\{R_k^{ul}\} + E\{R_k^{dl}\} \right)}{P_{Tx}^{dl} + P_{Tx}^{ul} + P_{CP} + P_{fix}} \qquad (13)$$

where $P_{total} = P_{amp} + P_{CP}$, $P_{CP} = P_{bb} + P_{syn} + M^o(P_{dac} + P_{mix} + P_{filt})$ and P_{CP} accounts for the circuit power consumption. The amount of power provided by various analog components and other digital processors is referred to as P_{amp}. Baseband signal processing (P_{bb}) and synchronization (P_{syn}) are unaffected by the number of BS antennas in P_{CP}, while digital to analogue conversion power (P_{dac}), mixing (P_{mix}), and filtering (P_{filt}) power linearly increase with the number of BS antennas. Table 2 lists the parameters that will be used for simulation in the evaluation of EE in accordance with (13).

Table 2. Simulation parameters.

Parameter	Value	Description
P_{tx}	5 mW	Transmission power
P_{mix}	0.033	Mixing consumption
P_{fil}	0.02	Filtering consumption
P_{bb}	0.03	Base band signal processing power
P_{syn}	0.05	Synchronization power
P_{dac}	0.015	Digital to analogue conversion power
$P_{amp} = \dfrac{p_{tx}}{\eta}$	$\eta = 0.01$	Amplier powerr
f_s	2.5 GHz	Sub 6 Ghz frequency
f_m	37 GHz	mmWave band

5 Results and Discussion

Figure 1 depicts the ergodic capacity of various MIMO configurations for the iid (independent identically distributed) channel. The capacity of massive MIMO

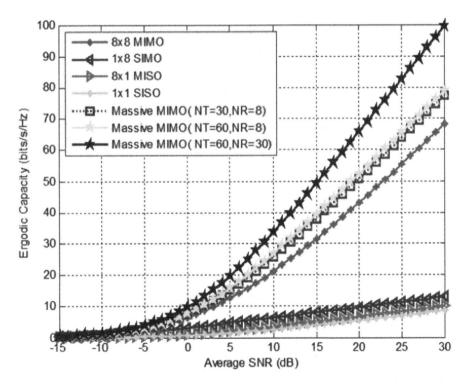

Fig. 1. Ergodic capacity for i.i.d. Rayleigh fast fading channel in different MIMO congurations.

systems with different number of antenna configurations is higher than classical MIMO systems as shown in the figure. Nevertheless, the difference is much smaller at lower SNR levels and can be ignored. However, as the number of BS antennas grows, so does the SNR, indicating that the system's power grows as well.

The effect of randomly selected transmit antennas on system energy efficiency is depicted in Fig. 2. The energy efficiency rises with the number of transmit antennas (M) at first, then drops abruptly after reaching an optimal point. This is because an increase in BS antennas is directly proportional to an increase in the corresponding radio frequency chain elements, which account for the majority of the system's power consumption. The optimal number of antennas ($M^* = M^o$) is also dependent on the number of user terminals (K), as shown in the diagram. For K = 5, 10, 15 and 20, M^* = 5, 7, 8 and 9 respectively. This is the point at which the increase in the system's total power consumption exceeds the increase in the total rate. As a result, the number of antennas chosen should not surpass this point in order to preserve EE; however, due to processing difficulty, finding the optimal point presents its own set of challenges.

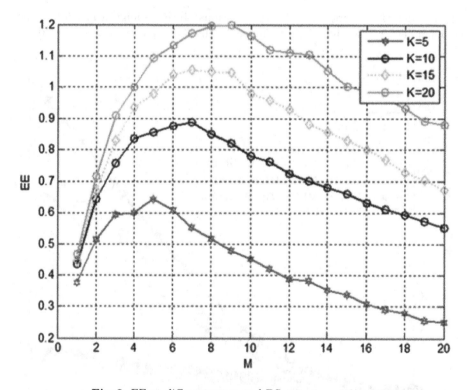

Fig. 2. EE at different users and BS antenna settings.

Figure 3 depicts the relationship between energy efficiency, K, and M in a massive MIMO system with statistical and instantaneous SNR values. For cell edge users in LoS conditions, the outcome is evaluated using procedures 1 to 9 of algorithm I. While the energy efficiency increases with the increase of M at first, it begins to decline at some point as M continues to increase, according to the simulation.

Furthermore, when comparing statistical and instantaneous or fixed SNR for the same K, it has been demonstrated that fixed SNR outperforms for small M and underperforms for large M. It has also been shown that EE increases as the number of user terminals increases, and that due to random channel conditions, EE exhibits different optimal points. Figure 3 depicts the optimal number of antennas (M^o) and maximum total power for the mmwave band at statistical, instantaneous, or fixed SNR.

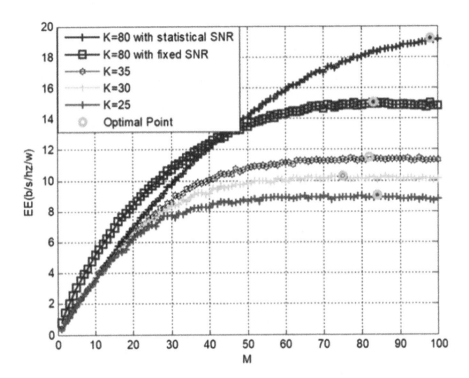

Fig. 3. EE for statistical and xed SNR at sub 6 Ghz.

In Fig. 4, the effect of channel variation on total power and optimal number of antennas to be selected is shown. When statistical channel variation is considered, the SNR varies and therefore both total power and M* grow large to combat small scale fading by adaptively allocating desired amount of power. With fixed SNR, smaller number of antennas can achieve optimal level than statistical SNR. From the figure, evaluation with statistical SNR accounts for more total power consumption than instantaneous SNR assumption which is 20 mW and nearly 19 mW for statistical and fixed SNR respectively.

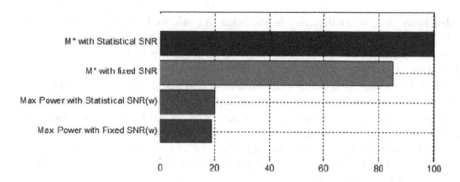

Fig. 4. Optimal number of antennas and maximum power for statistical and xed SNR.

Figure 5 depicts minimum SNR based antenna selection using linear and nonlinear precoders and also compares with EE at full array implementation with no any precoders. After finding an optimal number of antennas as figure5, it applies (3) to recalculate a new optimal point which depends on the current position or distance of the users and adaptive reduction of M instead of transmit power. In this case the optimal M^* which was found in full array implementation

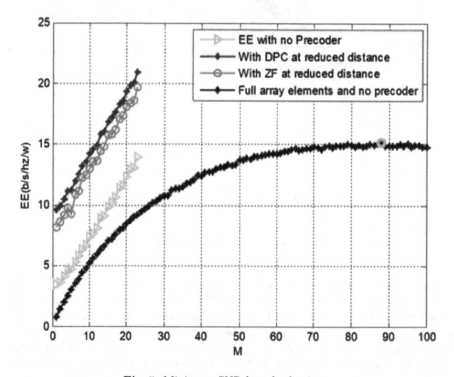

Fig. 5. Minimum SNR based selection.

is used as M to re-searching new optimal value M^o as in (3). Despite reduction in total rate when the number of antennas reduced, the reduction in total power consumption compensates in maintaining EE. Finally applying precoders in general and nonlinear DPC in particular boost total rate of the system and EE as well. It is observed that EE of a proposed selection is larger even without any precoders compared to full RF implementation at fixed SNR.

Figure 6 presents the results according to the proposed algorithm by combining the three scenarios and compares the performance of each at CI and FSPL using mmWave and sub 6 Ghz frequency ranges. The first scenario is finding M^* from full array at indoor cell edge, finding M^o according to (3) and finally selecting M^* and M^o data rate values by factorial combination $^{M}P_{M^*}$ and $^{M}P_{M^o}$.

Accordingly, it has been observed that after finding M^o using minimum SNR scenario at mmWave range, EE becomes higher than all with the same number of BS antennas. Due to the fact that mmWave reduces the range of communication and wave length, it leads to either the adaptive reduction of branch's transmit power or M^o BS antennas. In this case, the minimum received power is maintained to a threshold which is the minimum received power at the cell edge and other parameters are varied. Furthermore, adaptive EE in mmWave using DPC according to (9) and found to be better than that of at sub 6 GHz at the same environment.

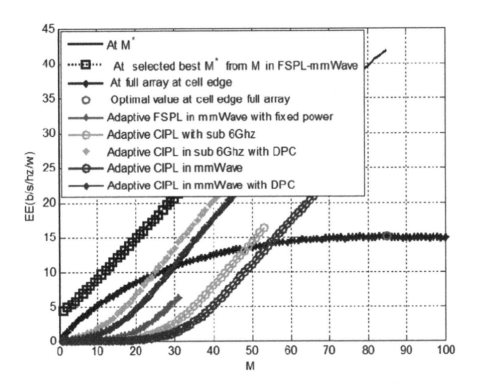

Fig. 6. Antenna Selection with the proposed algorithm at k = 35, pt = 5 mw and R = 0.5 km.

6 Conclusions

This work has focused on the problem of massive MIMO system's energy effi ciency due large number of antenna elements to be installed on a single BS in the upcoming wireless communication era. Adaptive antenna selection technique has been proposed as a novel strategy in resolving substantial amount of power consumption and complexity as a result of power-hungry RF elements which grow with antenna elements. The selection has been done for cell edge users with full array at fixed power allocation and minimum SNR based selection for cell center users. Both cases are used to achieve optimal number of antennas at which EE becomes maximum. The key idea of the proposed algorithm is to minimize the number of RF chains and performance evaluation has been done at several scenarios by applying precoders at different frequency ranges. The numerical results show that the proposed antenna selection algorithm performs better than full utilization of the array while finding some computational com plexity when applying nonlinear precoders to compensate the total rate whilst selection gets negative effects.

References

1. Larsson, E.G., Tufvesson, F., Edfors, O., Marzetta, T.L.: Massive MIMO for next generation wireless systems, CoRR, vol. abs/1304.6690 (2013)
2. Auer, G., Van der Perre, L.: Challenges and enabling technologies for energy aware mobile radio networks. IEEE Commun. Mag. **48**(11), 6672 (2010)
3. Heath, R.W., Sandhu, S., Paulraj, A.: Antenna selection for spatial multiplexing systems with linear receivers. IEEE Commun. Lett. **5**(4), 142–144 (2001)
4. Correia, L., et al.: Challenges and enabling technologies for energy aware mobile radio networks. IEEE Commun. Mag. **48**(11), 66–72 (2010)
5. Gharavi-Alkhansari, M., Gershman, A.B.: Fast antenna subset selection in MIMO systems. IEEE Trans. Signal Process. **52**(2), 339–347 (2004)
6. Dua, A., Medepalli, K., Paulraj, A.J.: Receive antenna selection in MIMO systems using convex optimization. IEEE Trans. Wireless Commun. **5**(9), 2353–2357 (2006)
7. Wang, B., Hui, T., Leong, M.S.: Global and fast receiver antenna selection for IMO systems. IEEE Trans. Common. **58**(9), 2505–2510 (2006)
8. Xu, Z., Sfar, S., Blum, R.S.: Analysis of MIMO systems with receive antenna selec tion in spatially correlated Rayleigh fading channels. IEEE Trans. Veh. Technol. **58**(1), 251–262 (2009)
9. Masouros, C., Alsusa, E.: Dynamic linear precoding for the exploitation of known interference in MIMO broadcast systems. IEEE Trans. Wireless Commun. **8**(3), 1396–1404 (2009)
10. Gesbert, M.: Soft linear precoding for the downlink of DS/CDMA communication systems. IEEE Trans. Veh. Technol. **59**(1), 203–215 (2010)
11. Xiang, G., Edfors, O., Liu, J., Tufvesson, F.: Antenna selection in measured massive MIMO channels using convex optimization. In: IEEE GLOBECOM Workshop, Atlanta, Georgia, United States (2013)
12. Gao, X., Edfors, O., Rusek, F., Tufvesson, F.: Massive MIMO performance evalua tion based on measured propagation data. IEEE Trans. Wireless Commun. **14**(7), 3899–3911 (2015)

13. Rappaport, T.: Wireless Communications: Principles and Practice, 2nd ed, Prentice Hall, Upper Saddle River (2002)
14. Molisch, A.F., Win, M.Z., Winters, J.H.: Capacity of MIMO systems with antenna selection. IEEE Trans. Wireless Commun. 4(4), 1759–1772 (2005)
15. Rappaport, T.: Wideband millimeter-wave propagation measurements and channel models for future wireless communication system design. IEEE Trans. Commun. 63(9), 3029–3056 (2015)
16. Guthy, C., Utschick, W., Honig, M.: Large system analysis of sum capacity in the gaussian MIMO broadcast channel. IEEE J. Sel. Areas Commun. 31(2), 149–159 (2013)

Design and Performance Analysis of Enhanced Directional MAC Protocols for Cognitive Radio Wireless Mesh Networks

Mulugeta Atlabachew[1]([✉]), Jordi Casademont[2],
and Yalemzewd Negash[3]

[1] Jimma University, Jimma Institute of Technology, Jimma, Ethiopia
mulugeta.atlabachew@ju.edu.et
[2] UPC, BarcelonaTech, Barcelona, Spain
jordi.casademont@entel.upc.edu
[3] Addis Ababa University, AAiT, Addis Ababa, Ethiopia
yalemzewd.negash@aait.edu.et

Abstract. This paper presents the design and analysis of directional random access MAC protocols for cognitive radio wireless mesh network (CRWMN). We have proposed three directional random access MAC protocols for CRWMNs using three different access mechanisms called Directional CSMA/CA MAC protocols for Cognitive Radio (DCR-MAC). An event driven simulator is used to make performance comparison for the three MAC protocols. Moreover, the performances of the DCR-MAC protocol for the three access mechanisms are also compared with an omni-directional CRMAC protocol in terms of average throughput and average packet delay. The performances of the proposed directional protocols show better performance for CRWMN.

Keywords: Cognitive radio wireless mesh network (CRWMN) · MAC protocol · Random access mechanisms · Directional MAC

1 Introduction

Directional antennas have many advantages over omni-directional antenna system in wireless networks like improving network capacity, reducing interference, increasing coverage area, improving spectrum usage, improving energy efficiency, and so forth [1–4].

In spite of the major benefits of directional antenna to the wireless domain, it has introduced new challenges to the MAC layer. The most popular MAC protocol in the wireless networks particularly in the wireless LAN and multi-hop wireless networks is the Carrier Sense Multiple Access with Collision Avoidance (CSMA/CA). The CSMA/CA MAC protocol might not be used with directional antenna without modification, because of the newly emerged challenges such as deafness, New Hidden Terminal Problem (NHT), Head-of-Line Blocking, Communication Range Under-Utilization, Neighbors Location Discovery, and MAC-Layer-Capture [5–7].

2 Directional MAC Protocol for CRWMNs

In this section we are going to present our works which is the design of directional random access MAC protocol for cognitive radio networks (CRNs) in general and to CRWMNs in particular. WMN has either a chain or grid types of networking topology. In the WMNs the nodes are connected in such a way that traffic is generated in to or away from the mesh gateways (MGs). The mesh routers (MRs) located in the proximity of the MG are more congested than those which are located far away from the MRs.

We are proposing a CRWMN where the MRs and the MGs are equipped with multiple antenna systems. The MRs and the MGs are empowered by cognitive radio (CR) capabilities. The MRs and the MGs performs spectrum sensing using the multiple antenna systems so as to decrease the spectrum sensing time, and improves the PUs detection probability and decrease the probability of false alarm. By using beam-forming techniques it is possible to improve the spectrum utilization efficiency of the opportunistically available spectrum, and the network capacity by allowing concurrent transmission [8, 9].

More importantly, to manage the traffic congestion created due to the mesh networking topology, it could be possible to assume MRs which are more closer to the MG to be equipped with more number of antenna in relative to the MRs which are located far away from the MG(s) to reduce the system complexity. It could also be possible to equip the MGs with Massive MIMO systems so as to communicate concurrently with more than one MR at time.

Due to limited mobility, the locations of the MRs or MGs are known as a result it is possible to use MAC-MU-MIMO for the signaling phase to broadcast the signaling to all the remaining mesh nodes. This operation will help to reduce the effect of new hidden terminal problem which is seen in directional communication.

Consider a CRN which has uniformly distributed N number of secondary users (SUs) in a square area and each one of them are equipped with multiple antennas. Let U be an arbitrary SU, where the transmission and interference area of U with range d covers M number of SUs when it operates in omni-directional modes. Let ρ be the node density, therefore the number of nodes for a coverage range of d is given by

$$M = \pi d^2 \rho \tag{1}$$

For a directional antenna with beam width of θ, the number of nodes which is going to be covered by the beam produced by any arbitrary node U is given by

$$M_b = (\theta/2\pi)\pi d^2 \rho = (\theta/2)d^2 \rho \tag{2}$$

The maximum number of concurrent transmissions becomes

$$N_c = M/M_b = \left(\pi d^2 \rho\right) / \left(\frac{\theta}{2}d^2 \rho\right) = 2\pi/\theta \tag{3}$$

Analytically it is possible to drive the average number of links that could be established among the M SUs which is presented below.

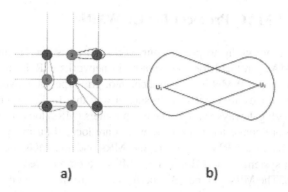

Fig. 1. (a) directional grid type mesh networking, (b) Pictorial representation of directional link between any arbitrary SUs

In Fig. 1(b) a directional communication link is presented between two SUs U1 and U2. When U1 establish link with U2, the area covered by the directional link is given by

$$A_{link} = \theta r^2 - (r^2/2)\tan(\theta/2) \qquad (4)$$

The ratio of area of the surface covered by the directional communication to the disc surface area becomes /

$$A_{ratio}^L = (\theta r^2 - (r^2/2)\tan(\theta/2))/\pi r^2 = \left(\theta - \frac{1}{2}\tan\left(\frac{\theta}{2}\right)\right)/\pi \qquad (5)$$

Then the maximum possible number of link that can be directionally established is given by

$$L_{max} = \pi / \left(\theta - \frac{1}{2}\tan\left(\frac{\theta}{2}\right)\right) \qquad (6)$$

Then, the average number of nodes covered with this directional communication given that a tagged node covers M nodes (uniformly distributed) in omnidirectional communication is given by

$$M' = MA_{ratio}^L = M\left(\theta - \frac{1}{2}\tan\left(\frac{\theta}{2}\right)\right)/\pi \qquad (7)$$

Having this link successful, the remaining number of nodes which are eligible for establishing another concurrent successful communication is given by

$$M_1 = M - M^{'} = M\left(1 - \left(\theta - \frac{1}{2}\tan\left(\frac{\theta}{2}\right)\right)/\pi\right) \tag{8}$$

Out of these M_1 nodes, the probability a node establishes a successful link without disturbing the initial communicating nodes is given by $\frac{M_1}{M}$. The remaining number of nodes which are eligible for establishing the next concurrent successful transmission is given by

$$M_2 = M - 2M^{'} \tag{9}$$

Therefore, the minimum number of nodes which are eligible for establishing the last possible link is given by

$$\begin{aligned} M_{Lmax} &= M_{Lmax-1} - M^{'} \\ M_{Lmax} &= M - L_{max}M^{'} \\ M_{Lmax} &= M\left(1 - L_{max}\left(M\left(\theta - \tfrac{1}{2}\tan\left(\tfrac{\theta}{2}\right)\right)/\pi\right)\right) \end{aligned} \tag{10}$$

The probability of establishing the first link among any arbitrary pair of nodes from the M nodes domain is given by $\frac{M_0}{M}$, where $M_0 = M - 1$, for large number of nodes we can approximate $M_0 \cong M$. The probability of establishing a link with the remaining number of nodes without creating interference to the nodes of previously established link, is given by $\frac{M_i}{M}$, where $1 \leq i \leq L_{max}$, and M_i is the remaining number of nodes. The average number of concurrent directional link can be calculated as follows

$$L_{avg} = \sum_{i=0}^{L_{maz}} M_i/M \tag{11}$$

Equation 3 shows that the maximum number of concurrent transmission is not dependent on the number of nodes, rather it is dependent on the radiation pattern (beamwidth) of the multiple antenna which is dependent on number of antenna elements, distance of separation between antenna elements and the excitation phase (it is analyzed in chapter three).

The proposed directional MAC protocols for CR system (DCR-MAC) are contention based protocols which are analyzed for the three access mechanisms, namely basic, RTS/CTS, and M-CTS mechanisms. Every transmission is performed directionally and reception is performed Omni-directionally between two SUs (SUs).

The DCR-MAC protocol operates as follows. DCR-MAC protocol operates in time slot bases. The time axis is divided in to time slots denoted by δ. An SU with a packet to transmit must performs carrier sensing, if it detects a signal from PU or SU, it will defer its transmission and continue its carrier sensing operation at the beginning of every time slots. A SU that detects no carrier will send a directional prepare to sense frame (DPTS) to the direction of the intended secondary receiver since it is assumed that every SU has location information of their neighbor SUs. Following the DPTS frame both of the users perform spectrum sensing to detect the presence of PU in their corresponding vicinity. The spectrum sensing outcomes might be either one of the following as presented in tabular form below (Table 1).

Table 1. Spectrum sensing outcomes of an arbitrary SU operating in sensing mode

S.No.	Transmitter Spectrum Sensing (SS) Outcome	Receiver Spectrum Sensing (SS) Outcome	Result
1.	PU Detection	PU Detection	No transmission following SS (Transmitter Blocking)
2.	PU Detection	No PU Detection	No transmission following SS (Transmitter Blocking)
3.	No PU detection	PU Detection	There shall be transmission but the receiver does not respond (SU and PU Collision)
4.	No PU detection	No PU detection	There shall be at least one transmission (successful transmission or collision between SUs transmissions)

Following the spectrum sensing operation outcomes, three contentions based medium access mechanisms for the directional CRN MAC protocol are proposed which essentially use multiple antenna technology. These access mechanisms are directional basic access mechanism, directional RTs/CTS mechanisms, and directional M-CTS access mechanism, which are shown in Figs. 2, 3 and 4. The basic operation principle of directional basic access and directional RTS/CTS access mechanisms is similar to the conventional IEEE 802.11 DCF protocols except its customization so as to suit the directional antenna and CRN behaviors.

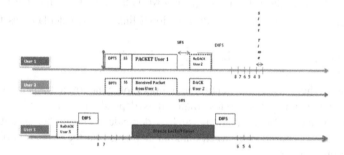

Fig. 2. Directional basic access mechanism for CRN

In the directional M-CTS access mechanism, a SU that wants to transmit make carrier sensing and if it does not detect any signal it sends PTS frame to the intended SU so as to reserve the coming slot for spectrum sensing and both of them perform spectrum sensing to detect the PU. The intended SU respond with RTS frame to the transmitting SU, following the RTS frame the transmitting SU transmit the data packet and if it is successfully received by the intended SU, the receiving SU will send an acknowledgment frame.

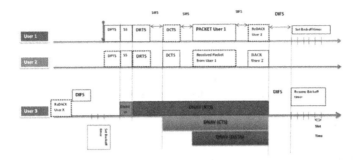

Fig. 3. Directional RTS/CTS access mechanism for CRN

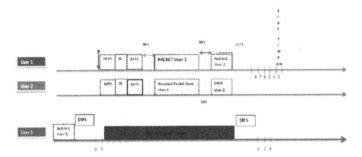

Fig. 4. Directional M-CTS access mechanism for CRN

The directional M-CTS access mechanism reduces one CTS frame and one SIFS compared to the directional RTS/CTS access mechanism, and compared to the directional basic access mechanism it introduces one RTS frame and one SIFS during a successful transmission process. When collision is detected on the channel, the amount of time an overhearing SU freezes its backoff timer will be smaller for the directional M-CTS access mechanism than the other two types. With respect to directional basic access, the hybrid access mechanism freezing time during collision is less than by the amount of time used to transmit a DATA packet, whereas with respect to directional RTS/CTS access mechanism the freezing time during collision is less than by the amount of time used to transmit an RTS frame.

3 Design and Performance Analysis of Directional CSMA/CA MAC Protocol for CRN (DCR-MAC)

In this section the design and analysis of directional CSMA/CA MAC protocols for CRNs are presented. The following assumptions are considered in the design and analysis of DC-RMAC. There is no SUs' mobility, every SUs knows the location of its neighbors, both transmission and reception are done in directional mode, the SUs always have packet to transmit (Saturated Condition), and there are M number of SUs under the omini-directional coverage of any arbitrary SU. The performance of DCR-

MAC for the three access mechanisms including the one that is proposed and analyzed in the previous chapter is presented. The proposed M-CTS access mechanism also shows better performance in the directional MAC protocol for the CRN. We have used different literatures for this work [11–23].

The packet transmission at each SU can be modeled as a single server queue system. Based on DCR-MAC, there exist five possible events occurring in directional packet transmission attempt between two arbitrary SUs. These are, Transmitter Blocking (E1), Collision between SUs' directional transmission to the direction of the same SU (E2), Collision between SU and PU transmission (E3), Receiver in Communication (E4), and Successful Directional Transmission (E5).

Now let's compute the probability and respective transmission period for each one of these events. First let's define two hypotheses on the status of neighboring PUs to an arbitrary SU. H0 represents the hypothesis that the neighboring PUs of a SU are not active, and H1 represents the hypothesis that the neighboring PUs of a SU are active. Let P_{H0} denotes the occurrence probability of event H0, and P_{H1} denotes the occurrence probability of event H1. Let's define additional variable V to denotes the probability a SU can access the channel, which can be expressed in terms of probability of false alarm (p_f), and probability of detection (p_d).

A SU can access the channel under two conditions; the first one is when the channel is idle and sensed idle by the SU, and the second one is when the channel is busy (it is being used by the PU(s)) but sensed idle by the SU. Therefore, the probability an arbitrary SU can access the channel is given by

$$V_k = \left(1 - p_{f,k}\right)P_{H0,k} + \left(1 - p_{d,k}\right)P_{H1,k} \qquad (12)$$

Where k = 1, 2, 3, ..., M

3.1 Transmitter Blocking (E1)

When a SU has a packet to transmit, first it performs carrier sensing. In the carrier sensing time if it doesn't detect any signal then it transmits prepare to sense (PTS) frame directionally to the intended secondary receiver. During the spectrum sensing period the transmitting SU may detect PUs and discontinue the communication, this is called transmitter blocking. The probability of this event considering an arbitrary SU, U1 as a transmitter is given by

$$P_{E1}^D = (1 - V_1) \qquad (13)$$

The period of transmission failure due to event 1 for the three access mechanisms is given by

$$T_{E1}^{Dbas} = T_{E1}^{Drts} = T_{E1}^{Dmcts} = DPTS + SS + DIFS \qquad (14)$$

When transmitter blocking occurs, the transmitting SU will defer its transmission for additional predefined blocking time (TB) but those SUs covered by the transmitting beam may attempt transmission after an additional time of DIFS if the channel is sensed idle at the beginning of the time slot.

3.2 Directional Transmission Collision Between SUs (E2)

DRTS failure occurs when more than one DRTS are sent to the direction of the intended receiver at the same time slot. At this time, the intended receiver fails to respond to the DRTS due to collision. Let us consider U2 as the receiver and U1 as the transmitter, and drive an expression for the probability of directional collision.

$$P_{DRTS} = prob.\{RTS \text{ transmission to } U_2's \text{ direction at any time slot}\}$$
$$= prob.\{a \text{ SUcan access the channel at any time slot}\}x$$
$$prob.\{packet \text{ transmission by a SU at any time slot}\}x$$
$$prob.\{packet \text{ transmission to the direction of } U_2\}$$

$$P_{DRTS,k} = V_k \tau_k \beta / 2\pi c(\beta)$$

$$P'_{DRTS,k} = prob.\{a \text{ SU do not transmit DRTS in the direction of } U_2 \text{ at any time slot}\}$$

$$P'_{DRTS,k} = 1 - P_{DRTS,k}$$

$$P'_{DRTS,k} = 1 - (V_k \tau_k \beta / 2\pi)c(\beta)$$

$$P = prob.\{\text{none of the SUs among}$$
$$(M - 2) \text{ transmit DRTS in the direction of } U_2 \text{ at any time slot}\}$$

$$P = \prod_{k=1}^{M-2} \left(1 - P_{DRTS,k}\right)$$

$$P = \prod_{k=1}^{M-2} (1 - (V_k \tau_k \beta / 2\pi)c(\beta))$$

$$P = prob.\{\text{at least one SU among}$$
$$(M - 2) \text{ transmit DRTS in the direction of } U_2 \text{ at any time slot}\} = 1 - P$$

$$P = 1 - \prod_{k=1}^{M-2} (1 - (V_k \tau_k \beta / 2\pi)c(\beta))$$

The probability of DRTS failure is given by

$$P_{E2}^D = V_1 P = V_1 \left\{1 - \sum_{k=2}^{M} (1 - (V_k \tau_k \beta / 2\pi)c(\beta))\right\} \qquad (15)$$

Where K = 3, 4, ..., M.

Due to collision there is transmission failure, and the period of this transmission failure for the three access mechanism is given by

$$T_{E2}^{Dbas} = DPTS + SS + DDATA + SIFS + DACK + DIFS \tag{16a}$$

$$T_{E2}^{Drts} = DPTS + SS + DRTS + SIFS + DCTS + DIFS \tag{16b}$$

$$T_{E2}^{Dmcts} = DPTS + SS + DCTS + DIFS \tag{16c}$$

3.3   Collision of SU's Directional RTS with PU Transmission (Receiver Blocking) - (E3)

During the spectrum sensing time if the intended secondary receiver (U2) detects the presence of PU(s), it will fail to respond to the DRTS frame sent from the intended secondary transmitter (U1). This is called receiver blocking only when there is only one SU (U1) transmitting to the direction of the intended secondary receiver.

$$P_{E3}^D = V_1(1 - V_2) \sum\nolimits_{k=3}^{M} (1 - (V_k \tau_k \beta / 2\pi) c(\beta)) \tag{17}$$

The period of transmission failure due to receiver blocking is given by

$$T_{E3}^{Dbas} = DPTS + SS + DDATA + SIFS + DACK + DIFS \tag{18a}$$

$$T_{E3}^{Drts} = DPTS + SS + DRTS + SIFS + DCTS + DIFS \tag{18b}$$

$$T_{E4}^{Dmcts} = DPTS + SS + DCTS + DIFS \tag{18c}$$

3.4   Receiver Already in Communication (E4)

This is event happens when the intended SU (U2) is already in communication with another SU which is not in the direction of the intended secondary transmitter (U1). The case when the U2 is acting as transmitter and receiver are different. At this time the intended secondary transmitter cannot respond to the DPTS/DRTS sent by the intended Secondary receiver (U2), which is the unique case that we experience due to beam-forming. When it is acting as a receiver collision will occur and it is considered in case 2. Our interest is when U2 is acting as a transmitter in the direction other than U1, the probability is given by

$$P_{E4}^D = prob.\{U_2 \text{ transmit to another SU not in the direction of } U_1$$
$$\text{at the time slot when } U_1 \text{ is sending DRTS to the direction of } U_2\}$$

$$P_{E4}^D = \underbrace{V_1 V_2 \tau_2 \left(1 - (\beta/2\pi)c(\beta)\right)}_{\text{1}} \underbrace{\prod_{k=3}^{M}\left(1 - (V_k \tau_k \beta/2\pi)\, c(\beta)\right)}_{\text{2}} \quad (19)$$

Where 1 and 2 represent probability of U2 transmission other than U1 direction and the probability the remaining (M-22) SUs do not transmit in the direction of U2.

The period of transmission failure due to this event for the three access mechanism is given by

$$T_{E4}^{Dbas} = DPTS + SS + DDATA + SIFS + DACK + DIFS \quad (20a)$$

$$T_{E4}^{Drts} = DPTS + SS + DRTS + SIFS + DCTS + DIFS \quad (20b)$$

$$T_{E4}^{Dmcts} = DPTS + SS + DCTS + DIFS \quad (20c)$$

3.5   Successful Directional Transmission (E5)

Successful directional transmission between the intended secondary transmitter (U1) and the intended secondary receiver (U2) is accomplished when both of them detects no PU, and U2 is not communicating with another SU (U2 is not transmitting) and U1 is the only transmitter in the direction of U2 at that time slot. The probability of successful directional transmission is given by

$$P_{E5}^D = V_1 V_2 (1 - \tau_2) \prod_{k=3}^{M} \left(1 - (V_k \tau_k \beta/2\pi)c(\beta)\right) \quad (21)$$

The period of successful transmission for the three access mechanisms is given by

$$T_{E5}^{Dbas} = DPTS + SS + DDATA + SIFS + DACK + DIFS \quad (22a)$$

$$T_{E5}^{Drts} = DPTS + SS + DRTS + SIFS + DCTS + SIFS + DDATA + SIFS + DACK + DIFS \quad (22b)$$

$$T_{E5}^{Dmcts} = DPTS + SS + DCTS + SIFS + DDATA + SIFS + DACK + DIFS \quad (22c)$$

Then, for an arbitrary SU which is in transmission mode the sum of the probabilities of the following expression holds true

$$P_{E5}^D = 1 - \left(P_{E1}^D + P_{E2}^D + P_{E3}^D + P_{E4}^D\right)$$

$$P_{E5}^D = 1 - P_{Dtf} \quad (23)$$

Where $P_{Dtf} = P_{E1}^D + P_{E2}^D + P_{E3}^D + P_{E4}^D$

The following possible events could be detected when an arbitrary SU (U1) is in listening mode (backoff state). An arbitrary SU who is in listening mode could detect the channel idle (no PU and SU transmission), or it detects PU signal only, or it may detects both SU and PU signals (PU-SU collision detection). Generally, we can classify the detection output as idle channel or busy channel detection. Now let's derive expression for the occurrence probability of these events and the corresponding time length that U1 will defer. By the time when the backoff timer become zero and finds the channel idle, the node will start transmitting.

3.6   Idle Channel Detection (E6)

This event occurs when the arbitrary SU which is in listening state detects no transmission from both the PUs and SUs at the time slot. The arbitrary SU may detect the channel idle for either one of the following scenarios: when all the SUs detects the channel idle but there is no transmission to the direction of the detecting SU, or when all the M-1 SUs detects the channel busy due to false alarm and defer their transmission, or when some of the SUs detects the channel idle but do not transmit to the direction of the detecting SU and the remaining SUs detect the channel busy due to false alarm and defer their transmission, or when all the M-1 SUs detect the channel idle but they do not transmit (in back off state). The probability of idle channel detection expression for an arbitrary SU can be derived as follows.

The probability all of the SUs detects the channel idle but there is no directional transmission to the direction of the detecting SU is given by

$$P_{ID1}^D = PH_0(1 - p_f) \prod_{k=1}^{M-1} (1 - (V_k \tau_k \beta / 2\pi) c(\beta))$$

The probability all of the M-1 SUs detects the channel busy due to false alarm and defer their transmission is given by

$$P_{ID2}^D = PH_0(p_f)$$

Therefore, the probability of idle channel detection by an arbitrary SU is given by

$$P_{E6}^D = \left(P_{ID1}^D + P_{ID2}^D \right)$$

$$P_{E6}^D = PH_0(1 - p_f) \sum_{k=1}^{M-1} (1 - (V_k \tau_k \beta / 2\pi) c(\beta)) + PH_0(p_f) \tag{24}$$

At this time U1 will decrement its back off timer by 1 at the end of the current time slot.

Now let's analyze the probability of busy channel detection by an arbitrary SU in terms of PU signal detection only, SU signal detection only, and in terms of both PU and SU signal detection.

3.7   Only PU's Signal Detection (E7)

An arbitrary SU may detect PU signal only when one of the following events occurs; when all of the SUs detect the channel busy and defer their transmission, or when all of the M-1 SUs detect the channel idle but do not want to transmit to the direction of the detecting SU, or when some of the SUs detect the channel idle and transmit to the direction other than the detecting SU and the remaining SUs may detect the channel busy and defer transmission or the remaining SUs may detect the channel idle but do not want to transmit (may be in back off state). The probability expression of only PU signal detection by an arbitrary SU is given by the sum of the following probabilities.

The probability all of the SUs detect the channel busy and defer their transmission is given by

$$P_{PU1}^D = PH_1 p_d$$

The probability all of the M-1 SUs detect the channel idle but do not transmit to the direction of the detecting SU is given by

$$P_{PU2}^D = PH_1 (1 - p_d) \prod_{k=1}^{M-1} (1 - (V_k \tau_k \beta / 2\pi) c(\beta))$$

Therefore, the probability of PU signal detection by an arbitrary SU is given by

$$P_{PU}^D = P_{PU1}^D + P_{PU2}^D$$

$$P_{E7}^D = PH_1 (1 - p_d) \prod_{k=1}^{M-1} (1 - (V_k \tau_k \beta / 2\pi) c(\beta)) + PH_1 p_d \tag{25}$$

At this time the detecting SU will freeze its backoff timer for some time duration depending on the access mechanisms (for our case it freezes for a time length of T_{E1}^D).

3.8   Only SU's Signal Detection (E8)

An arbitrary SU detects only SU(s) signal when one of the following conditions are satisfied. When all the SUs detect the channel idle and only one SU transmit to the direction of the detecting SU and the receiving SU can communicate with the transmitting SU (at this time the SU detects a successful transmission), or when all the SUs detect the channel idle and more than two SUs transmit in the direction of the detecting SU (at this time the SU detects collision), or all the SUs detects the channel idle and only one SU transmit in the direction of the detecting SU but the intended receiver might already been in communication with other SU not in the direction of the detecting SU, or when some of the SUs detect the channel busy due to false alarm and defer transmission but when the remaining SUs transmit to the direction of the detecting SU (at this time collision of SUs transmission is detected by the detecting SU). The expression for the probability of detecting PU signal only is derived below.

The probability all of the SUs detect the channel idle and only one SU transmit to the direction of the detecting SU and the receiving SU can communicate with the transmitting SU (at this time the SU detects a successful transmission) is given by

$$P_{ST}^D = PH_0(1 - p_f)\binom{M-1}{1}((V_x\tau_x\beta/2\pi)c(\beta))V_y(1 - \tau_y)\prod_{k=1}^{M-2}(1 - (V_k\tau_k\beta/2\pi)c(\beta))$$

The detecting SU shall defer its transmission for a period of T_{E5}^D which is given by Eq. (22).

The probability all of the SUs detect the channel idle and more than two SUs transmit in the direction of the detecting SU (at this time the SU detects collision) is given by

$$P_{SSC}^D = PH_0(1 - p_f)\sum_{k=1}^{M-1}\binom{M-1}{k}\{\prod_{y=1}^{k}\left(V_y\tau_y\frac{\beta}{2\pi}c(\beta)\right)\prod_{x=k+1}^{M-1}((1 - (V_k\tau_k\beta/2\pi)c(\beta))\}$$

At this stage, the listening node defer its transmission for a period of T_C^D which is given by

$$T_C^{Dbas} = PTS + SS + DATA + DIFS \qquad (26a)$$

$$T_C^{Drts} = PTS + SS + RTS + DIFS \qquad (26b)$$

$$T_C^{Dmcts} = PTS + SS + DIFS \qquad (26c)$$

The probability all the SUs detects the channel idle and only one SU transmit in the direction of the detecting SU but the intended receiver might initiate communication with other SU which is not in the direction of the detecting SU at the same time slot is given by

$$P_{SDC}^D = PH_0(1 - p_f)\binom{M-1}{1}(V_x\tau_x(\beta/2\pi)c(\beta))V_y\tau_y(1 - (\beta/2\pi)c(\beta))\prod_{k=3}^{M-1}(1 - (V_k\tau_k\beta/2\pi)c(\beta))$$

At this time the detecting node defer its transmission for a period of T_{E4}^D.

The probability all of the (M-2) SUs detects the channel idle and only one SU transmission is detected but this communication might be interrupted due to the invisible directional communication to the detector. The invisible directional communications may happen in one of the following conditions. The first condition is when the intended SU receiver receives more than one request in different direction at the same time slot (for example more than one RTS frames or DATA packet), at this time the intended receiver fail to respond to any of the SUs, as a result of which communication failure could be detected by the detecting SU (we may call this event as collision at the intended SU receiver). The second condition is observed when there is at least one transmission to the direction of the intended transmitter and the intended transmitter may receive more than one acknowledgments (for example more than one CTS or ACK frames) at the same time slot which results in communication failure detection at the detecting SU (we may call this event as collision at the intended SU transmitter.

The probability of detecting communication failure by an arbitrary detecting SU due to a collision observed at the intended SU receiver is given by

$$P^D_{TFRC} = PH_0(1 - p_f)\binom{M-1}{1}(V_x\tau_x(\beta/2\pi)c(\beta))V_y(1 - \tau_y)$$

$$\sum_{k=1}^{M-3}\binom{M-3}{k}\{\prod_{z=1}^{k}(V_z\tau_z(\beta/2\pi)c(\beta))\prod_{x=k+1}^{M-3}((1 - V_k\tau_k(\beta/2\pi)c(\beta))\}$$

Since every user start transmission at the beginning of a time frame, the time period the detecting SU defer its transmission for this event is given by T^D_{E4}.

The probability of detecting communication failure by an arbitrary detecting SU due to a collision observed at the intended SU transmitter is given by

$$P^D_{TFTC} = PH_0(1 - p_f)\binom{M-1}{1}(V_x\tau_x(\beta/2\pi)c(\beta))V_y(1 - \tau_y)$$

$$\sum_{k=1}^{M-3}\binom{M-3}{k}\{\prod_{z=1}^{k}(V_z\tau_z(\beta/2\pi)c(\beta))\prod_{x=k+1}^{M-3}((1 - V_k\tau_k(\beta/2\pi)c(\beta))\}$$

The time period the detecting SU defer its transmission for this event is given by T^D_{E4}.

Therefore, the probability of only SU signal detection is given by

$$P^D_{E8} = P^D_{ST} + P^D_{SSC} + P^D_{SDC} + P^D_{TFRC} + P^D_{TFTC} \tag{27}$$

3.9   Detection of Both PU and SU Signal (E9)

An arbitrary SU detects both the PU and SU signal when one of the following conditions occurs. An arbitrary SU detects both the SU and PU signals when the PU is present and all the M-1 SUs miss detect the presence of PU and at least one among these SUs transmit in the direction of the detecting SU, or when the PU is present and some of the SUs detect the presence of PU and defer transmission and the remaining SUs miss detect the PU presence and start transmitting to the direction of the detecting SU. The expression for probability of detecting both PU and Su signal simultaneously is derived below.

The probability all the M-1 SUs miss detect the presence of PU and at least one among these SUs transmit in the direction of the detecting SU is given by

$$P_{PS}^D = PH_1(1 - p_d) \sum_{k=1}^{M-1} \binom{M-1}{k} \{\prod_{y=1}^{k}(V_y\tau_y(\beta/2\pi)c(\beta)) \prod_{x=k+1}^{M-1}(1 - V_x\tau_x(\beta/2\pi)c(\beta))\}$$

Therefore, the probability of detecting both SU and PU signal is given by

$$P_{E9}^D = P_{PS}^D$$

$$P_{E9}^D = PH_1(1 - p_d) \sum_{k=1}^{M-1} \binom{M-1}{k} \{\prod_{y=1}^{k}(V_y\tau_y(\beta/2\pi)c(\beta)) \prod_{x=k+1}^{M-1}(1 - V_x\tau_x(\beta/2\pi)c(\beta))\}$$

$$(28)$$

For this event the detecting node defer its transmission for a period of T_{E3}^D.

4 Throughput for DCR-MAC Protocol

Therefore, the total average throughput of directionally CR MAC protocol can be expressed by

$$U^D = \frac{E[\text{Payload Information transmitted in a slot time}]}{E[\text{length of a slot time}]} \qquad (29)$$

$$E[slot]^{Dbas} = P_{E6}^D\delta + P_{E7}^D T_{E1}^{Dbas} + P_{ST}^D T_{E5}^{Dbas} + P_{SSC}^D T_{C}^{Dbas} + P_{SDC}^D T_{E4}^{Dbas} + P_{TFRC}^D T_{E4}^{Dbas} + P_{TFTC}^D T_{E4}^{Dbas} + P_{E9}^D T_{E3}^{Dbas}$$

$$(30a)$$

$$E[slot]^{Drts} = P_{E6}^D\delta + P_{E7}^D T_{E1}^{Drts} + P_{ST}^D T_{E5}^{Drts} + P_{SSC}^D T_{C}^{Drts} + P_{SDC}^D T_{E4}^{Drts} + P_{TFRC}^D T_{E4}^{Drts} + P_{TFTC}^D T_{E4}^{Drts} + P_{E9}^D T_{E3}^{Drts}$$

$$(30b)$$

$$E[slot]^{Dmcts} = P_{E6}^D\delta + P_{E7}^D T_{E1}^{Dmcts} + P_{ST}^D T_{E5}^{Dmcts} + P_{SSC}^D T_{C}^{Dmcts} + P_{SDC}^D T_{E4}^{Dmcts} + P_{TFRC}^D T_{E4}^{Dmcts} + P_{TFTC}^D T_{E4}^{Dmcts} + P_{E9}^D T_{E3}^{Dmcts}$$

$$(30c)$$

$$U^D = L_{avg}P_{ST}^D E[L]/E[slot]^D \qquad (31)$$

The maximum throughput of a directional MAC protocol is given by

$$U_{max}^D = L_{max}P_{ST}^D E[L]/E[slot]^D \qquad (32)$$

5 Simulation and Discussion

In this section different simulation works are presented to show the performance advantage of directional CR MAC protocol (DCR-MAC) in terms of throughput and packet delay.

The simulator used is an event driven MATLAB simulator (MATLAB R2013b). We choose MATLAB because it is a powerful simulator to work with analytical and more of physical layer dominated tasks. To perform the simulation we have used the following parameters which are presented in a tabular form below.

Table 2. DCR-MAC protocol simulation parameters

Simulation parameters used	
Channel bit rate	1 Mbit/sec
Slot time	20 μsec
Spectrum sensing time	0.5 ms
SIFS	10 μsec
DIFS	50 μsec
Initial contention window size (W)	32
Maximum backoff stage (m)	5
PHY header	192 bits
MAC header	272 bits
Packet payload	8000 bits
DPTS	112 bits + PHY Header
DRTS	160 bits + PHY Header
DCTS	112 bits + PHY Header
DACK	112 bits + PHY Header

The throughput performance of DCR-MAC protocol for the three accessing mechanisms namely Basic, RTS/CTS, and M-CTS are presented in Fig. 5 and Fig. 6 below. For our simulations the throughput is measured in bit per second. The simulations are carried out based on the simulation parameters given in Table 2. Besides, the following parameters are used in the simulations, probability of false alarm (Pf = 0.01), probability of detection (Pd = 0.9), and probability of vacant channel availability (PH0 = 0.9) unless otherwise.

Simulation in Fig. 5(a) shows the throughput performance of the three access mechanisms. The simulation is carried out for transmission probability of 0.1, and beamwidth of 300. We used a multiple antenna to produce the required beamwidth (radiation pattern). The simulation result shows that the M-CTS access mechanism outperforms the remaining two access methods. As the number of SUs increases the average throughput of the three access mechanisms increases linearly and equally for almost number of users less than fifteen which was true for the conventional wireless communication system, but as the number of SUs keeps increasing the performance of the three access mechanisms becomes different. The performance of the Basic access mechanism keeps increasing with the increase of number of SUs only up to twenty SUs then the performance starts to decline. For the remaining two access mechanisms the performance increases with the increasing number of SUs but with the slow rate. The performance of RTS/CTS mechanism becomes almost constant after forty SUs and starts to decline after nearly sixty SUs. The performance of M-CTS access mechanism keeps increasing up to sixty SUs and becomes constant and starts to decrease its performance after eighty five SUs. As compared to the omni-directional CR-MAC protocol proposed in the previous chapter, all the three prosed directional CR-MAC protocols outperform the throughput performance by nearly four folds, this is due to the concurrent transmission capability of directional communication. The performance gain of the newly proposed access mechanism, M-CTS, brings an additional throughput gain of nearly 0.8 Mbits/sec.

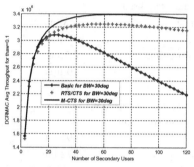

a) Average throughput Vs number of SUs for Basic,
RTS/CTS, and M-CTS access Mechanisms

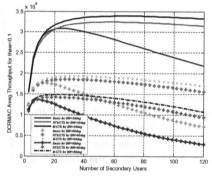

b) Average throughput comparison for Basic, RTS/CTS, and M-CTS
access Mechanisms for different Beamwidth Vs number of SUs

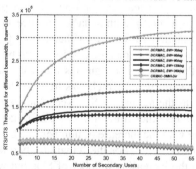

c) Average throughput comparison for different beamwidth Vs
CRMAC-OMNI-Dir based on RTS/CTS access mechanism

Fig. 5. Impact of number of SUs on the performance DCR-MAC throughput

Simulation in Fig. 5(b) shows as the size of the antenna beam becomes wider and wider, the average throughput performance of the DCR-MAC protocol continuous decreasing. This is because as the antenna beamwidth increase the average number of concurrent transmissions decreases, in a single link much of the area will be covered which means much of the SUs will defer their transmission, and as a result it reduces the spectrum utilization efficiency and reduce the average throughput of the protocol. Therefore, narrower beamforming antenna is very fundamental.

Simulation in Fig. 5(c) shows a simulation carried out for RTS/CTS access mechanism for DCR-MAC and CRMAC (OMNI-Directional) for constant probability of transmission and different antenna beamwidth for the case of DCR-MAC protocol. In the simulation it is shown that the average throughput performance of DCR-MAC protocol with a radiation beamwidth of 3600 becomes almost the same as to the throughput performance of CRMAC which operates in omni directional mode. Generally, increasing the number of SUs improves the performance of average throughput of DCR-MAC protocol in a much meaning full way than the CRMAC protocol.

The simulation in Fig. 6 presents the impact of probability of transmission on the performance of average throughput of DCR-MAC protocol. In Fig. 6(a) the simulation shows that DCR-MAC protocol results better average throughput for lower probability of transmission particularly as the number of SUs becomes larger and larger. As the number of SUs and the probability of packet transmission becomes larger, greater number of the SUs attempt transmission and there will be a higher probability of collision which degrades the average throughput of the DCR-MAC protocol. Whereas, as the number of SUs becomes smaller and smaller and the average throughput decline very faster as the probability of transmission increases because due to high probability of transmission the probability of collision increases which results lower spectrum utilization efficiency. Figure 6(b) shows that the average throughput of DCR-MAC protocol for a beamwidth of 300 become maximum around 0.1 probability of transmission for the three access mechanisms especially as the number of SUs becomes large. The graph shows the chopped section of the simulation.

Simulation in Fig. 6(c) shows the throughput performance comparison between DCR-MAC and CRMAC protocols for RTS/CTS access mechanisms which holds true for both basic and M-CTS access mechanisms. The maximum average throughput of DCR-MAC protocol for a beamwidth of 300 is at least three times higher than the maximum throughput of CRMAC protocol. As the number of SUs becomes smaller the CRMAC protocol shows better performance gain (in terms of throughput) in relative to the DCR-MAC protocol this is due to poor spectrum utilization efficiency.

Simulation in Fig. 6(d) compare the throughput of a single link DCR-MAC protocol and the throughput of CRMAC protocols for different number of SUs and different values of probability of transmission. Until now the performance of DCR-MAC and CRMAC has been compared in terms of average throughput. As can be observed from the simulation, a node may enjoy the maximum throughput in CRMAC protocol than in DCR-MAC protocol. This is because the link in directional communication could fail due to hidden communication to the transmitter or receiver which decreases the maximum throughput but DCR-MAC shows remarkable performance for all probability of transmission in relative to CRMAC.

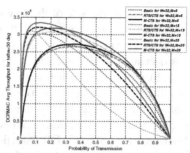

a) Throughput performance comparison of DCR-MAC protocol for different number of SUs Vs probability of transmission

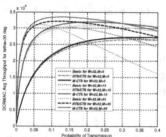

b) Throughput performance comparison of DCR-MAC protocol for different number of SUs Vs probability of transmission to clearly observe the optimum average throughput for beamwidth of 30⁰.

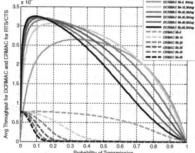

c) Throughput performance comparison of DCR-MAC and CRMAC protocols for different number of SUs Vs probability of transmission for beamwidth of 30⁰.

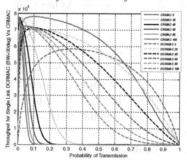

d) Single link throughput performance comparison of DCR-MAC and CRMAC protocols for different number of SUs Vs probability of transmission for the RTS/CTS access mechanism.

Fig. 6. Impact of probability of transmission on the throughput of DCR-MAC protocol.

6   Conclusion

In this paper, we have designed MAC protocols for CRN in general and to CRWMN in particular using multiple antenna systems. DCR-MAC protocol is a random access MAC protocols proposed for CRWMNs using multiple antenna systems. In the design of DCR-MAC protocol, directional communication is the corner stone of our finding. Assuming directional communication we have proposed a directional random access MAC protocol using the three access mechanisms. In relative to the omni-directional CR MAC protocols, all the directional CR MAC protocols show better performance. Especially, the newly proposed DCR-MAC protocol which uses the M-CTS access mechanism shows a motivating performance improvement in terms of average throughput and average packet delay.

References

1. Ersin S., Enis A., Ender, A.: Diversity analysis of single and multiple beamforming. In: Proceeding of the IEEE VTC, Spring 05, Stockholm, Sweden, pp. 1293–1296 (May 2005)
2. Andrea, G., Syed, A.J., Nihar, J., Sriram, V.: Capacity limits of MIMO channels. IEEE J. Select. Areas Commun. 21(5), 684–702 (2003)
3. Enis, A., Ersin, S., Ender, A.: Performance analysis of beamforming for MIMO OFDM with BICM. In: Proceeding of the IEEE ICC 05, Seoul, Korea, pp. 613–617 (May 2005)
4. Mulugeta, A., Jordi, C., Yalemzewid, N.: Multiple antenna (MA) for cognitive radio based wireless mesh networks (CRWMNs): spectrum sensing (SS). In: Mekuria, F., Nigussie, E.E., Dargie, W., Edward, M., Tegegne, T. (eds.) Information and Communication Technology for Development for Africa. Lecture Notes of the Institute for Computer Sciences, Social Informatics and Telecommunications Engineering, vol. 244, pp. 182–192. Springer, Cham (2018). https://doi.org/10.1007/978-3-319-95153-9_17
5. Romit, C., Xue, Y., Ram, R., Nitin, V.: Using directional antennas for medium access control in ad hoc networks. In: ACM International Conference on Mobile Computing and Networking (Mobicom), Atalanta, Georgia, pp. 59–70 (September 2002)
6. Young, K., Shankarkumar, V., Nitin, V.: Medium access control protocols using directional antennas in ad hoc networks. In: IEEE International Conference on Computer Communications (INFOCOM), Tel Aviv, Israel, pp. 13–21, (March 2000)
7. Hrishikesh, G., Carlos, C., Dave, C., Dharma, P.A.: The deafness problems and solutions in wireless ad hoc networks using directional antennas. In: IEEE Global Telecommunications Conference (GLOBECOM) Workshops, pp. 108–114 (November 2004)
8. Tao, C., Honggang, Z., Gian, M., Imrich, C.: CogMesh: A cluster-based cognitive radio network. In: 2nd IEEE International Symposium on New Frontiers in Dynamic Spectrum Access Networks. IEEE, Dublin, Ireland (2007)
9. Anusha, M., Vemuru, S.: Enhancement of wireless mesh network using cognitive radio's. Eur. J. Appl. Sci. 7(3), 108–113 (2015)
10. Al-mefleh, H.: Design and analysis of MAC protocols for wireless networks. Ph.D. Dissertation, Iowa State University, USA (2009)
11. Giuseppe, B.: Performance analysis of the IEEE 802.11 distributed coordination function. IEEE J. Select. Areas Commun. 18(3), 535–547 (2000)

12. Qian, C., Wai-Choong, W., Motani, M., Ying-Chang, L.: MAC protocol design and performance analysis for random access cognitive radio networks. IEEE J. Select. Areas Commun. **31**(11), 2289–2300 (2013)

13. Kaushik, R.C., Ian, F.A.: Cognitive wireless mesh networks with dynamic spectrum access. IEEE J. Select. Areas Commun. **26**(1), 168–181 (2008)

14. Nazir, B., Brent, I., Raouf, B.: Performance of cognitive radio-based wireless mesh networks. IEEE Trans. Mobile Comput. **10**(1), 122–135 (2011)

15. Mehdi, M., Luong, D., Dung, M.H., Zbigniew, D.: A scalable decentralized mac scheduling for cognitive wireless mesh network. In: The 7th Advanced International Conference on Telecommunications AICT (2011)

16. Yang, X., Jon, R.: Throughput and delay limits of IEEE 802.11. IEEE Commun. Lett. **6**(8), 355–357 (2002)

17. Periklis, C., Vasileios, V., Anthony, C.B.: Throughput and delay analysis of IEEE 802.11 protocol. In: Proceeding of the IEEE IWNA, Liverpool, UK, pp. 168–174 (2002)

18. Yong, S.L., Arek, D., Jayasuriya, A.: Performance analysis of IEEE 802.11 DCF under limited load. In: Proceeding of the IEEE Asian-Pacific Conference on Communications, Perth, pp. 759–763 (October 2005)

19. Juki, W.T., Chuan, H.F., Adel, B.M.: Throughput and delay analysis of the IEEE 802.11e EDCA saturation. In: The Proceeding of the IEEE ICC (2005)

20. Shao-Cheng, W., Ahmed, H.: Performance limits and analysis of contention-based IEEE 802.11 MAC. In: 31st IEEE Conference on Local Computer Networks, pp. 418–425. IEEE (2006)

21. Periklis, C., Anthony, C.B., Vasileios, V.: IEEE 802.11 packet delay-a finite retry limit analysis. In: Proceeding of the IEEE GLOBECOM, pp. 950–954 (2003)

22. Hai, L.V., Taka, S.: Accurate delay distribution for IEEE 802.11 DCF. IEEE Commun. Lett. **10**(4), 317–319 (2006)

23. Mulugeta, A., Jordi, C.S., Yalemzewid, N.: MAC protocols design for multiple antenna based cognitive radio wireless mesh network. Ph.D. Dissertation, AAU, IT Doctoral Program, Addis Ababa, Ethiopia (2018)

Performance Analysis of Hybrid Beamforming Techniques in Large MU MIMO Systems

Fikreselam Gared Mengistu[1(✉)], Yosef Birhanu Malede[2],
and Amare Kassaw Yimer[1]

[1] Bahir Dar University, Bahir Dar, Ethiopia
[2] Debretabor University, Debra Tabor, Ethiopia

Abstract. Massive multiple input multiple output (MIMO) at mmWave frequency is one of the primary suggestions for next-generation networks in order to support this large mobile data load. The large number of antennas at the base station (BS) allows multiple users (MU) to share the same time-frequency resources and concentrate energy in a smaller area. As a result, massive MIMO can significantly enhance spectrum and energy efficiency. However, because of the needed number of RF chains per antenna element, fully digital beamforming is undesirable when the number of antennas at the BS becomes very large, resulting in excessive complexity and high power consumption. In this work, we evaluate the performances of hybrid beamforming techniques in downlink MU mmWave large MIMO systems. Specifically, we consider, hierarchical singular value decomposition (SVD) and two-stage iterative MU hybrid beamforming algorithms to alleviate the optimization complexity on finding optimal analog and digital precoding matrices. First, based on the mmWave system and channel model, we formulate the spectral efficiency expression and theoretical analysis is done. Then, the proposed hybrid beamforming algorithms are formulated and numerical simulation are done to evaluate the spectral efficiency and computational complexity of the algorithms. The results reveal that fully-connected hybrid beamforming techniques outperform partially-connected hybrid beamforming techniques in terms of spectrum efficiency.

Keywords: Energy efficiency · Hybrid beamforming techniques · Large MIMO · mmWave · Spectral efficiency

1 Introduction

According to information theory, there are three main techniques to increase the capacity of a wireless communication system: ultra-densification of networks, operating at mmWave bands, and using numerous antennas at the base station. [1,2]. Ultra-dense networks (UDNs) deployment reduces the pathloss due

© ICST Institute for Computer Sciences, Social Informatics and Telecommunications Engineering 2022
Published by Springer Nature Switzerland AG 2022. All Rights Reserved
M. L. Berihun (Ed.): ICAST 2021, LNICST 411, pp. 153–172, 2022.
https://doi.org/10.1007/978-3-030-93709-6_11

to shorter line of sight path but the interference is high when the access point is closer. Increasing the operating spectrum to mmWave bands (i.e. frequencies of 30–300 GHz) provides significant improvement on network capacity. mmWave frequencies, in example, can be used for outside point-to-point backhaul or indoor high-speed wireless applications. Most notably, because mmWave frequencies have exceptionally short wavelengths, a huge number of antenna elements may be packed into a tiny area, allowing for enormous multiple input multiple output (MIMO) at the base station and consumers. The third method for increasing wireless communication capacity is to use a high number of antennas, known as massive MIMO, at the base station and users to improve the system's spectral efficiency. Massive MIMO improves the system's overall performance, especially the possible sum rate, because the BS can communicate with several users at the same time using the same time-frequency resources. Furthermore, huge MIMO increases energy efficiency, reduces signal processing complexity, and generates channel hardening, allowing small scale fading and random noise to be averaged out. To ensure sufficient received signal power in mmWave systems, massive antenna arrays must be deployed at both the BS and the consumers. mmWave large MIMO systems are the result of this nomenclature. This method is predicted to result in a wireless platform made up of small cells with a high capacity. Although mmWave bands have the aforementioned benefits due to their higher frequency, they are unable to pass through buildings and other impediments and are absorbed by plants and rain. As a result, it has a significant propagation loss and a short symbol time, necessitating the use of complex equalization algorithms. Multipath from practically co-incident signals can also produce significant small-scale alterations in the channel's frequency response.

At mmWave bands, the wave length reduces by a factor of 10 to 20 times. Small wavelength enables thousands of antennas to be packed in a small space to focus the power along one direction. Within a very small dimension, it is possible to encompass very large number of antenna elements there by enabling massive MIMO. Besides, in mmWave bands the number of cluster which provides the angle of arrival for different rays are also significantly less compared to sub $6GHz$ band and this helps to make the beam more directional [3, 4]. As a result, mmWave massive MIMO with beamforming technology may properly assess directions of arrival, alter beam patterns to reduce interference, and capture the desired signal. However, to drive the growing number of antennas, a high number of RF chains are necessary, considerably increasing system complexity, power consumption, and hardware cost. A viable solution to solve this problem is to offload part of the precoding/processing to the analog domain via analog precoding or combining.

Beamforming techniques with large antenna array makes the propagation between BS and users more directional [5, 6]. Beamforming with a larger antenna results in reduced interference and lower energy usage, allowing for higher capacity. Fully - connected and partially connected structures are the two most common hybrid beamforming techniques. Before transmission through the antenna, the beamformer in fully connected hybrid beamforming integrates all of the antennas and RF signals from the RF chains. Signal attenuation and power losses can occur when using additional components to combine RF signals. Separate antenna arrays are used for RF beamforming of each RF chain in partially-connected hybrid beamforming. This leads to wide beam-width, less directivity and strong interference from other chains [7–9]. In this work, we study and evaluate the performances of full-connected and partially-connected hybrid beamforming techniques for downlink MU mmWave massive MIMO systems. Two novel hybrid beamforming algorithms such as hierarchical singular value decomposition (SVD) and two-stage iterative MU hybrid beamforming algorithms are proposed to alleviate the optimization complexity on finding optimal analog and digital precoding matrices. We evaluate the spectra efficiency, energy efficiency of computational complexity of these algorithms.

The rest of the paper is organized as follows. In Sect. 2, review of related work is stated. The system and channel model for downlink mmWave massive MIMO is presented in Sect. 3. Hybrid precoding algorithm for MU mmWave massive MIMO systems is formulated in Sect. 4. Numerical results are discussed in Sect. 5 and conclusions are drawn in Sect. 6.

Notations: Vectors and matrices are expressed in lower and upper case boldface letters, accordingly. $\mathbf{A}^{H}$, $\mathbf{A}^{T}$, $\mathbf{A}^{*}$ and $\mathbf{A}^{-1}$ to represent conjugate transposition , transpose, conjugate and inverse of matrix $\mathbf{A}$, respectively. $\text{Tr}(\mathbf{A})$ denotes the trace of a square matrix $\mathbf{A}$. $\mathbf{x} \sim \mathcal{CN}(\mu, \sigma^2 \mathbf{I})$ represents circular symmetric complex Gaussian distributed random variable $\mathbf{x}$ with mean μ and variance σ^2. $\mathbb{E}\{.\}$ is the expectation operator and $\|.\|$ is the Euclidean norm.

2   Related Works

Hybrid beamforming has been studied in the last decades for single user (SU) and multiuser (MU) massive MIMO systems. The authors in [10] proposed beamforming and multi-stream precoding in SU systems with large mmWave antenna arrays at both transmitter and receiver. The beamforming algorithm is constructed by explicitly accounting for the features of large antenna arrays in settings with little dispersion. The authors in [11] proposed hybrid beamforming for fully connected SU-MIMO systems. The mathematical formulas based on the input parallel data streams are used to construct the best beamforming methods. They show that hybrid beamforming approach significantly reduces the complexity of the systems. In [12] for SU mmWave vast MIMO systems with partially-connected hybrid precoding structures, the author developed a sequential interference cancellation (SIC). They break down the non-convex attainable rate optimization problem into a succession of simple sum-rate optimization problems, each with only one sub-antenna array to consider. This method attempted to maximize the possible sum-rate of each antenna array until the last antenna array was analyzed. The sumrate optimization issue aids in obtaining a precoding vector that is sufficiently close to the ideal unconstrained solution. This approach minimizes the computational complexity by eliminating the need for single SVD and matrix inversion.

Xiaoyong Wu et al. in [8] optimized the beamforming matrices for hybrid analog and digital precoding architectures. In MU large MIMO systems, they presented two-stage iterative methods for fully coupled hybrid beamforming structures. Maximizing the capacity of the baseband channel with proper analog precoding/combining is done in the first analog stage, which aids in achieving optimal capacity in the next step. A sum-rate maximization is performed in the second digital step. Due to the reduced gap between its performance and that of the capacity-reaching strategy, the suggested scheme is better suited to Rayleigh channels than mmWave channels. The authors in [13] proposed a joint design of analog and digital beamformers based on matching pursuit for fully-connected hybrid beamforming techniques that rely on the sparse nature of mmWave channels in the angular domain. By evenly sampling the beam steering space, the recommended precoders may be efficiently quantized, and the precoding method is well-suited for restricted feedback systems. Kilian Roth et al. in [14] compared the spectral and energy efficiency of hybrid beamforming and digital beamforming structures under practical system constraints like effects of channel estimation, transmitter impairments and multiple simultaneous users for mmWave channel.The impacts of transmitter impairments, channel estimate errors, and mixed analog to digital converter (ADC) resolutions are also taken into account. The findings reveal that for MU scenarios, digital beamforming systems with low resolution ADC are more energy efficient and yield a greater attainable rate than hybrid beamforming systems. The authors in [15] proposed a coordinated hybrid beamforming scheme for fully connected structure supporting multiple-stream transmissions for downlink MU massive MIMO systems at mmWave frequencies.They used the generalized low rank approximation of matrices (GLRAM) algorithm to divide the beamforming design into two pieces. The authors next suggest an efficient modified GLRAM algorithm that has no dimensionality constraint, converges in three or four iterations, and takes use of BS and user collaboration. They use the block diagonalization technique to take advantage of the multiplexing gain. The proposed system outperforms equal gain transmission and is nearly as good as the completely digital beamforming technology, according to the author.

In [16,17] fully-connected hybrid structure at the BS and analog-only combining at the MS is proposed for MU large MIMO systems at mmWave bands. The goal is to increase the system's attainable pace with minimal training and feedback. To obtain the analog precoder and combiner, a two-stage iterative technique based on a codebook is provided. To minimize the error between the preamble transmitted by the BS and the estimated received data at the MS, they use a zero forcing (ZF) and Kalman filter based baseband precoder. The authors in [7] For fully connected and partially connected hybrid approaches, analyze the spectral and power efficiency of downlink mmWave large MIMO systems. To facilitate multi-stream transmission, they explore hybrid beamforming at the BS and entirely digital beamforming at the MS. They use a phase shifter with a power amplifier in the analog precoder to regulate the amplitude and phase of the signal at the same time. The proposed model results in a significant overhead associated with the information exchange alignment of the BS and MS beams. The beam-width is limited when high gain is required, making hardware limitations, channel gathering, and continuous alignment of the best beams in a dynamic environment challenging. The authors in [18] study downlink mmWave system with hybrid beamforming at the BS and analog-only combining at the MS. By decoupling analog and digital beamformers at each connection, the effort hopes to reduce complexity and overhead. They demonstrate that the proposed technique works for both partially and fully-connected structures. When channel station information is excellent at the BS, the results show that fully connected design outperforms partially connected architecture. According to the preceding assessment, there are only a few studies that discuss both fully-connected and partially connected hybrid beamforming structures in MU mmWave big MIMO systems. As a result, the goal of this paper is to investigate and assess the performance of these hybrid beamforming algorithms in downlink MU mmWave large MIMO systems. The suggested hybrid beamforming techniques' performance is assessed by looking at their spectral efficiency, energy efficiency, and computational complexity.

3 The System and Channel Model for mmWave Massive MIMO Systems

3.1 the mmWave Large MIMO System Model

We consider a single cell downlink MU mmWave massive MIMO system shown in Fig. 1 where the BS adopts hybrid precoding to support U active users at the MS that deploy only analog combining receiver architectures. The BS is equipped with A_{BS} number of antennas and each user is equipped with A_{MS} number of antennas. The number of concurrent users served at MS is thought to be equal to the total number of data streams, allowing the BS to communicate with all users in the cell using a single data stream. In the same way, the number of RF chains in the BS must be more than or equal to the number of beams in order for the BS to communicate with the MS via multiple beams. Therefore, the number of RF chain in the BS is equal with the number of users in MS as $B_{\mathrm{RF}} = U$ [7]. Let the input data stream to hybrid precoding at the BS be $\mathbf{s} = [s_1, s_2, s_3, \cdots, s_U]^T \in \mathbb{C}^{U \times 1}$ with $\mathbb{E}\{\mathbf{s}\mathbf{s}^T\} = \frac{P}{U}\mathbf{I}_U$ where P is the average total transmitted power and $\mathbf{I}_U$ is a $U \times U$ identity matrix. At the BS, the precoder is composed of analog precoder and baseband digital precoder. The BS first performs a $U \times U$ baseband digital precoding that apply to all B_{RF} chains. The baseband digital precoding matrix is expressed as [7]

$$\mathbf{P}_{\mathrm{BB}} = [\mathbf{p}_1^{\mathrm{BB}}, \mathbf{p}_2^{\mathrm{BB}}, \mathbf{p}_3^{\mathrm{BB}}, \cdots, \mathbf{p}_U^{\mathrm{BB}}] \in \mathbb{C}^{U \times U} \qquad (1)$$

For fully connected hybrid precoding technique, the analogue precoding is performed over A_{BS} path per RF chain and added together before being transmitted at each antenna element. Thus, in fully connected hybrid precoding techniques, the analogue precoding matrix P_{RF} is expressed as

$$\mathbf{P}_{\mathrm{RF}} = [\mathbf{p}_1^{\mathrm{RF}}, \mathbf{p}_2^{\mathrm{RF}}, \mathbf{p}_3^{\mathrm{RF}}, \cdots, \mathbf{p}_U^{\mathrm{RF}}] \in \mathbb{C}^{A_{\mathrm{BS}} \times U}. \qquad (2)$$

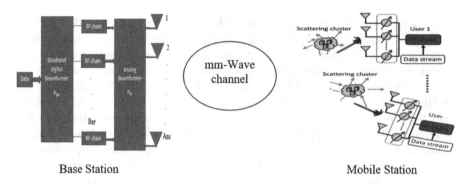

Fig. 1. Hybrid beamforming architecture for MU mmWave large MIMO systems.

It is noteworthy that in fully connected hybrid precoding techniques, RF precoder has full beamforming matrix and its entries are constant modulus with normalized non-zero elements that satisfy $|\mathbf{p}_u^{\mathrm{RF}}(m)|^2 = \frac{1}{A_{\mathrm{BS}}}$ [18]. Each vector contains $\mathbf{p}_u^{\mathrm{RF}} \in \mathbb{C}^{A_{\mathrm{BS}} \times 1}$ where $\mathbf{p}_u^{\mathrm{RF}}$ is the analog weighting vector for the mth array antenna and whose element have the same amplitude but different phase as the RF precoder is realized as analog phase shifter.

For partially connected hybrid precoder techniques, all antenna arrays are divided into $A_{\mathrm{BS}}/B_{\mathrm{RF}}$ number of subarrays and each subarray of antenna is connected to a single RF chain via a phase shifter. The RF precoding is performed over $A_{\mathrm{BS}}/B_{\mathrm{RF}}$ RF paths in each RF chain. Hence, the RF precoder vector consists of a block diagonal beamforming matrix $P_{\mathrm{RF}} \in \frac{A_{\mathrm{BS}}}{B_{\mathrm{RF}}} \times U$ which is expressed as [7, 18, 19]

$$\mathbf{P}_{\mathrm{RF}} = \begin{bmatrix} \mathbf{p}_1^{\mathrm{RF}} & 0 & \cdots & 0 \\ 0 & \mathbf{p}_2^{\mathrm{RF}} & \cdots & 0 \\ \vdots & \vdots & \ddots & \vdots \\ 0 & 0 & \cdots & \mathbf{p}_U^{\mathrm{RF}} \end{bmatrix} \tag{3}$$

where $\mathbf{p}_u^{RF} \in \mathbb{C}^{\frac{A_{\mathrm{BS}}}{B_{\mathrm{RF}}} \times 1}$ is the analog weighting vector for the mth subarray antenna and whose element have the same amplitude but different phase. Due to the constraint at the analog phase shifters, the entries of each RF precoder has constant modulus that normalize to satisfy $|\mathbf{p}_u^{\mathrm{RF}}(m)|^2 = \frac{1}{A_{\mathrm{BS}}/B_{\mathrm{RF}}}$. To simplify our analysis, we assume equal power allocation among users for both hybrid precoding techniques. As a result, normalization is used to enforce the total power constraint. P_{BB} such that $\|\mathbf{P}_{\mathrm{BB}}\mathbf{P}_{\mathrm{RF}}\|_F^2 = U$.

3.2 The mmWave Massive MIMO Channel Model

Diffraction, reflection, and scattering affect the gain of the wireless channel as the signal transmitted from the BS approaches the MS. In mmWave communication, the number of clusters which provide the angle-of-arrival (AOA) for different rays are significantly less as compared to sub 6 GHz bands in the same propagation environment. To build the limited number of clusters in mmWave bands, geometric-based stochastic channel models are used. Every electromagnetic ray that is emitted from the BS to the MS is taken into consideration by the geometrically based stochastic channel model. Individual ray gain will be a function of the BS antenna gain, the mmWave channel gain, and the MS antenna gain, which will be modeled using electromagnetic wave propagation fundamental equations. Thus, by using the geometric based sparse channel model, the mmWave channel model between the BS and MS is expressed as [20,21]

$$\mathbf{H}_u = \sqrt{\frac{A_{BS}A_{MS}}{P_u}} \sum_{p=1}^{L_u} \alpha_{u,p} a_{MS}(\theta_{u,p}^{MS}, \phi_{u,p}^{MS}) a_{BS}^*(\theta_{u,p}^{BS}, \phi_{u,p}^{BS}) \quad (4)$$

where L_u is the number of effective channel paths corresponding to the number of multipath channel, $\alpha_{u,p}$ is the pth path complex gain including pathloss of the wireless channel between the BS and MS. The variable $(\theta_{u,p}^{MS}, \phi_{u,p}^{MS}) \in [0, 2\pi]$ is the pth path's AoA of emanating from the MS and $(\theta_{u,p}^{BS}, \phi_{u,p}^{BS}) \in [0, 2\pi]$ is the pth path's angle-of-departure (AoD) launched in BS. $a_{MS}(\theta_{u,p}^{MS}, \phi_{u,p}^{MS})$ and $a_{BS}(\theta_{u,p}^{BS}, \phi_{u,p}^{BS})$ are the antenna array response gain at each user and the BS, respectively.

The array response vectors for transmit and receive antennas depends on the structure of antenna arrays (such as uniform linear array(ULA) or uniform plannar array(UPA)) rather than the antenna element properties. In mmWave large MIMO systems, UPA geometry has a number of advantages over ULA. We assumed that the MS is aware of the antenna array geometry for the purposes of evaluation and analysis. The directional spread or angular spread of signals arriving at the MS would be substantially less in mmWave bands because to the lower number of clusters compared to other scenarios. For each multipath channel, the gain associated with the BS and MS becomes a complex number with Gaussian distributions for the real and imaginary components. As a result, this complex number's amplitude repose has a Rayleigh distribution. The Rayleigh distance, which separates the near- and far-field portions of an antenna array, can be calculated as a function of the antenna array's maximum physical dimension and wavelength. λ.

By using the precoding matrices in (2) and (3), and the channel model in (4), the received signal at the uth user is given by

$$r_u = \mathbf{H}_u \mathbf{P}_{RF} \mathbf{p}_{BB}^u s_u + \mathbf{H}_u \sum_{n \neq u}^{U} \mathbf{P}_{RF} \mathbf{p}_{BB}^n s_n + n_u \quad (5)$$

where $\mathbf{P}_{BB}^u$ is the uth column of $\mathbf{P}_{BB}$, s_n is the nth element of $\mathbf{s}$ and n_u is the noise at user u with zero mean and variance σ^2. Since the MS employ only analog combining $c_{RF}^u = c_u$, after the combining process, the estimated symbol of the uth MS can be expressed as

$$\tilde{s}_u = c_u^* \mathbf{H}_u \mathbf{P}_{RF} \mathbf{p}_{BB}^u s_u + c_u^* \mathbf{H}_u \sum_{n \neq u}^{U} \mathbf{P}_{RF} \mathbf{p}_{BB}^n s_n + c_u^* n_u. \tag{6}$$

Thus, the achievable rate of the uth user is given by [7,17,18]

$$R_u = \log_2 \left(1 + \frac{\frac{P}{U} \|c_u^* \mathbf{H}_u \mathbf{P}_{RF} \mathbf{p}_{BB}^n\|^2}{\frac{P}{U} \sum_{n \neq u} \|c_u^* \mathbf{H}_u \mathbf{P}_{RF} \mathbf{p}_{BB}^n\|^2 + \sigma^2} \right). \tag{7}$$

Finally, the achievable sum rate of the proposed MU mmWave large MIMO system is expressed as

$$R_s = \sum_{u=1}^{U} \log_2(1 + R_u) \tag{8}$$

4 Hybrid Precoding Algorithms for MU mmWave Large MIMO Systems

The main aim here is to find the optimal baseband precoder matrix $\mathbf{P}_{BB}$, analog precoder matrix $\mathbf{P}_{RF}$ at the BS and analog combiner $\mathbf{C}_{RF}$ at the MS that maximize the achievable rate of each user with affordable hardware and signal processing complexity while providing near-optimal performance. In this paper, we apply hierarchical decomposition and two-stage iterative MU hybrid beamforming methods to solve the proposed system's generic optimization problems. In a two-stage iterative technique, optimization is accomplished by separating the precoder's computation into two parts. This method eliminates the need for explicit channel estimation. Whereas for hierarchical decomposition approach, each of the optimal baseband precoder $\mathbf{P}_{BB}$, analog precoder $\mathbf{P}_{RF}$ and analog combiner $\mathbf{C}_{RF}$ can be determined independently using singular value decomposition (SVD). This method necessitates a thorough understanding of each user's channel. In two-stage iterative based hybrid beamforming algorithm, we can compute the optimal analog combining vector,c_u for each MS and hybrid analog and baseband precoding matrices, $\mathbf{P}_{RF}$ and $\mathbf{P}_{BB}$ at the BS iteratively for both fully and partially connected architectures. The details of this approach is shown in Algorithm 1 [17]. In hierarchical decomposition hybrid beamforming algorithm, we compute the analog combining vector, c_u for each MS and the hybrid analog and digital precoding matrices, P_{RF} and P_{BB} at the BS by using singular value decomposition. The details of this approach is shown in Algorithm 2 [18].

5 Simulation Results and Analysis

The proposed hybrid beamforming techniques for single cell downlink MU mmWave big MIMO systems are evaluated in this section. First, we use the

Algorithm 1. Two-stage iterative based hybrid beamforming algorithms for fully and partially connected MU mmWave large MIMO systems.

Stage 1: Optimal RF precoder and combiner design

1. For each user, compute analog precoder $\mathbf{P}_{RF}$ and analog combiner $\mathbf{c}_u$ jointly.
2. Choose the appropriate beam-steering path that maximizes the effective channel gain as
$$\{\mathbf{o}_u^*, \mathbf{b}_u^*\} = \underset{o_u \in \mathbf{W}, b_u \in \mathbf{F}}{\arg\max} \ \|o_u \mathbf{H}_u \mathbf{b}_u\|.$$
3. Set $\mathbf{c}_u = \mathbf{o}_u^*$ for each users at MS.
4. For fully connected hybrid structure, set the full matrix $\mathbf{P}_{RF} = [\mathbf{b}_1^*, \mathbf{b}_2^*, \cdots, \mathbf{b}_U^*]$ at the BS.
5. For partially connected hybrid structure, set the diagonal matrix

$$\begin{pmatrix} \mathbf{b}_1^* & 0 & \dots & 0 \\ 0 & \mathbf{b}_2^* & \dots & 0 \\ \vdots & \vdots & \ddots & \vdots \\ 0 & 0 & \dots & \mathbf{b}_U^* \end{pmatrix}$$

at the BS.

Stage 2: MU optimal baseband precoder design

1. Estimate the effective channel $\mathbf{H}_u^{eff} = \mathbf{c}_u^* \mathbf{H}_u \mathbf{P}_{RF}$ for each user at MS.
2. Quantize $\mathbf{H}_u^{eff}$ using a codebook $\mathbf{H}_{qua}$ for all users at MS.
3. Calculate and sends back the quantized channel matrix, $\mathbf{H}_u^{quindx} = \arg\max \|\mathbf{H}_u^{eff*} \mathbf{H}_u^{quindx}\|$ to BS.
4. Estimate $\mathbf{P}_{BB}$ at the BS by using Zero-Forcing (ZF), Minimum Mean Square Error (MMSE) and Maximum Ratio Transmitter (MRT) based baseband precoder.
5. Normalize $\mathbf{P}_{BB}$ to ensure the power constraint

Output: $\mathbf{P}_{RF}^*, \mathbf{P}_{BB}, \mathbf{c}_u^*$

SNR to assess the algorithms' attainable rate. The effects of the number of BS and users on the spectral efficiency are then analyzed. In addition, a comparison of the performance of hybrid beamforming algorithms with digital beamforming methods is shown.

5.1 Simulation Parameters

For the simulation, we assume single cell downlink system that the users are distributed uniformly in a circular cell of radius $r_c = 500$ m except for an exclusion zone ($r_h \leq 35$ m) near the BS. We use Matlab with the optimization solver to simulate the system. The simulation is run for 1000 Monte-Carlo realizations where in each snapshot, the users are distributed randomly in the cell. Part of the simulation parameters used for the performance analysis is shown in Table 1.

Algorithm 2. Hierarchical decomposition based hybrid beamforming algorithms for fully and partially connected MU mmWave large MIMO systems.

---

1. Express the SVD of the channel matrix as $\mathbf{H}_u = \mathbf{U\Sigma V}^H$
2. Each c_u sets as the normalized singular vector which corresponds to the largest singular value as $c_u = \dfrac{1}{\sqrt{A_{MS}}}e^{ju_m}$ where $m \in A_{MS}$ and u_m is the phase of the A_{MS}^{th} element in u

3. For each MS u, denote $t_u = c_u^H \mathbf{H}_u$.
4. For fully connected hybrid structure, with an element-wise normalization, the BS sets the full matrix
   $\mathbf{P}_{RF} = \dfrac{1}{\sqrt{A_{BS}}}e^{j(\,a_m^t\,)}$, where $m \in A_{BS}$ and a_m is the phase of the mth element in the vector t_u.
5. For partially-connected hybrid structure, with an element-wise normalization the BS sets block-diagonal matrix
   $\mathbf{p}_{RF} = \dfrac{1}{\sqrt{\frac{A_{BS}}{B_{RF}}}}e^{j(a_n^t)}$, where $n = (\,u-1)\dfrac{A_{BS}}{B_{RF}}+m$, $m \in \dfrac{A_{BS}}{B_{RF}}$ and a_n is the phase of the nth element in the vector t_u.
6. Obtain the effective channel $\mathbf{H}_{\text{eff}} = \mathbf{C}_{RF}^H \mathbf{H} \mathbf{P}_{RF}$.

7. At the BS, design the baseband precoder based on $\mathbf{H}_{\text{eff}}$ and by using ZF, MMSE and MRT baseband precoder.
8. Normalize $\mathbf{P}_{BB}$ to ensure the power constraint.

Output: $\mathbf{P}_{RF}^*$, $\mathbf{P}_{BB}$, $\mathbf{c}_u^*$.

5.2   Analysis of the Achievable Rate of the Proposed Algorithms

Here, we analyze the spectral efficiency of downlink massive MU-MIMO system in mmWave channel model and linear precoding techniques. Figure 2 shows the spectral efficiency of hybrid beamforming with two-stage iterative algorithm. The results suggest that boosting the SNR improves the system's spectral efficiency. In addition, the results reveal that fully connected hybrid beamforming with MMSE precoding outperforms other linear precoding strategies.

However, when it comes to partially connected hybrid beamforming, ZF precoding performs the worst. The rationale for this is that the MMSE technique is superior to the ZF and MRT techniques in terms of noise reduction, as MMSE considers both noise and signal variance, ensuring that noise is not magnified as in the ZF technique. At low SNR, MRT performs similarly to MMSE, but at high SNR, it lags behind. For all linear precoding approaches, we observe

Table 1. Part of the simulation parameters

Parameters	Values and assumptions
Number of cell	Single cell
Maximum distance between user and BS	$\geq 400\,\mathrm{m}$
System deployment	Hybrid precoder at the BS and analog only combining at the MS.
Number of data stream	Equal to the number of RF chain of the BS.
Number of RF chain at the BS	Equal to the number of users: $B_{\mathrm{RF}} = U$.
Channel model	Geometric based stochastic channel model
Hybrid precoder techniques	Fully-connected and partially-connected hybrid beamforming structure.
Channel State Information	BS has perfect effective channel knowledge and MS perfectly knows its channel H_u.
Propagation scenario	Limited multipath channel
Antenna array geometry	Uniform planar array (UPA)
RF beam-steering vectors P_{RF} and P_{RF}	Takes continuous value
Azimuth (AoAs, AoDs)	Emanating in $\in [0, 2\pi]$
Elevation (AoAs, AoDs)	Emanating in $\in [\frac{-\pi}{2}, \frac{\pi}{2}]$
Propagation scenarios	Based on Rayleigh criterion non-line of sight paths
Number of Monte-Carlo realizations	1000

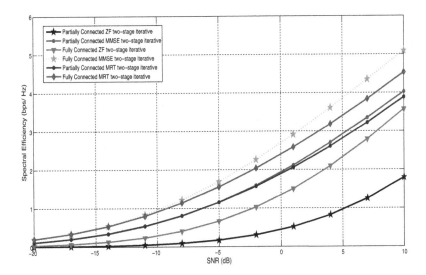

Fig. 2. Spectral efficiency of fully connected and partially connected hybrid beamforming with two-stage iterative algorithms. We assume $A_{\mathrm{BS}} = 64$, $U = 8$, $A_{\mathrm{MS}} = 4$, and $P = 5$.

that partially connected hybrid beamforming schemes perform worse than fully connected hybrid beamforming schemes. We also plot the spectral efficiency of hierarchical decomposition based hybrid beamforming as shown in Fig. 3. The SNR for ZF and MMSE precoding methods is used to show the spectral efficiency of completely and partially linked hybrid beamforming algorithms.

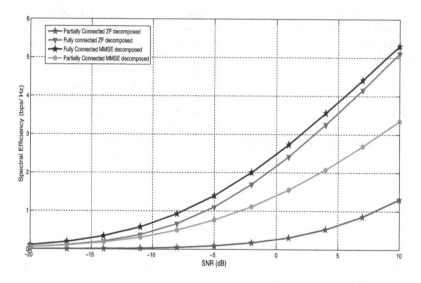

Fig. 3. Spectral efficiency of fully connected and partially connected hybrid beamforming with hierarchical decomposition algorithm. We assume $A_{\mathrm{BS}} = 64$, $U = 8$, $A_{\mathrm{MS}} = 4$, and $P = 5$.

Joint analog combiner and RF precoder design are used in a two-stage iterative based hybrid beamforming technique to jointly select the normalized eigenvectors and analog precoders that maximize the effective analog channel gains with limited feedback and information exchange. The analog combiner and the RF precoders are designed separately for hierarchical decomposed SVD based hybrid beamforming approaches. As can be seen from Fig. 2 and Fig. 3, When compared to hierarchical decomposed methods, the two-stage iterative based hybrid beamforming algorithm performs better since to enhance the effective channel gain, the RF precoder and RF convolution are intended to work together, whereas hierarchical decomposed algorithms employ separate designs.

5.3   Impact of Number of BS Antennas on Spectral Efficiency

Figure 4 and Fig. 5 present the impact of number of BS for fixed number of users ($u = 4$), number of channel path ($P = 5$), and SNR value ($SNR = 5dB$)

for iterative two-stages and hierarchical decomposed algorithm respectively. One can observe from Fig. 4 that the achievable rates of MMSE, ZF, and MRT are increased by increasing the number of antennas. Specially, in down-link large MIMO systems where the number of antennas at the BS is large the performance increases dramatically. As A_{BS} goes to very large, the channel becomes more or less deterministic, means the diagonal element in the effective analog channel gain all having the same power, and the rest of the non-diagonal elements are zero so that do not be affect by channel variability. Thus, by increasing the number of antenna elements in the BS, the capacity increases linearly, and the appropriate spectral efficiency can be achieved. A_{BS}.

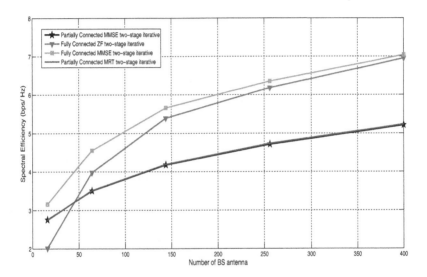

Fig. 4. Impact of varying the number of antenna at the BS for two-stage iterative algorithms $SNR = 5\text{dB}$, $u = 4$, $A_{MS} = 4$, and $P = 5$

Fully connected MMSE and MRT deliver full beamforming advantages compared to partially connected hybrid beamforming approaches when the number of antennas at the BS increases to a very large value. A large number of antenna elements at the BS, in general, improves spectral efficiency performance.

The performance loss induced by partially connected hybrid beamforming techniques can be compensated by increasing the number of antenna elements at the BS. At SNR of 7 dB with 64 antenna element in partially MMSE hierarchical decomposed hybrid beamforming algorithm there is 2.6 bps/Hz achievable rate but by fixing and reducing the SNR value to 5dB and increasing the number of antenna elements at the BS to 144 we can get 4.135 bps/Hz achievable rate . The performance gap for fully connected MMSE hierarchical decomposed is grater than 2.064 compared with partially connected MMSE decomposed techniques at $A_{BS} = 400$. When the number of antennas at the BS grows to between 256

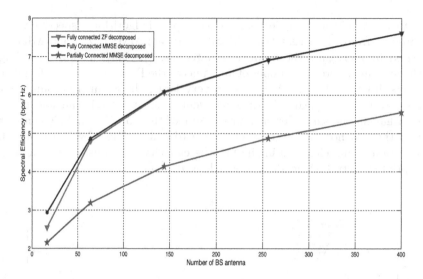

Fig. 5. Impact of varying the number of antenna at the BS for hierarchical decomposed hybrid beamforming algorithms $SNR = 5$dB, $u = 4$, $A_{MS} = 4$, and $P = 5$

and 400, the hierarchical decomposed based hybrid beamforming algorithm outperforms the iterative two-stage based hybrid beamforming algorithm in terms of spectral efficiency.

From the spectral efficiency versus number of BS antenna shown in Fig. 4 and Fig. 5, we can observe that in hierarchical decomposed SVD based hybrid beamforming algorithm the analog precoder matrices P_{RF} is matched with the channel. Then, the arbitrary beams are created based on the particular cluster realization of the channel. As a result, exact matching precoder matrices can be obtained from the channel. In the iterative two-stage codebook-based hybrid beamforming algorithm, there are predetermined matrices from which one is chosen as the best for a given realization. As the number of antenna elements at the BS approaches 256, we can have much more control over the types of beams we can form and match more closely to the channel with the SVD decomposed algorithm, whereas with the iterative codebook based two-stage hybrid beamforming algorithm, we have much more options to choose from the predefined codebook that will match very closely to the channel.

5.4 Spectral Efficiency for Various Number of Users

In this section, we evaluate the impact of the number of users in the MS on the proposed system's performance. We assumed that the number of users at the MS is similar to the number of data streams to be transferred and the number of RF chains at the BS in the proposed system model. ($S = B_{RF} = U$).

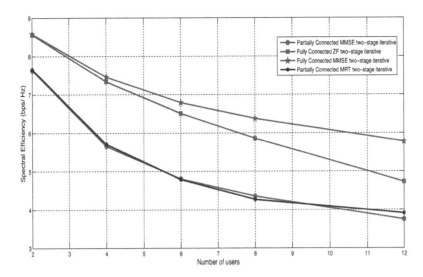

Fig. 6. Impact of varying the number of users at the MS for two-stage iterative algorithms $SNR = 5$dB, $A_{BS} = 144$, $A_{MS} = 4$, and $P = 5$

The performance of two-stages iterative hybrid beamforming algorithms and the hierarchical decomposed hybrid beamforming algorithm are respectively shown and evaluated in Fig. 6 and Fig. 7 by varying the number of users. One can observe from the results that varying the number of users in the range of 2 to 12 while the number of antenna elements, number of channel path, and the transmitting power are fixed enhance the achievable rate performance because of increased number of independent data streams. The partially connected MRT and MMSE hybrid precoder presents almost the same performance gap until the number of user reaches beyond 10 as shown in Fig. 7.

When the number of users is larger than 10, however, the performance of the MRT partly connected precoder improves. MRT is ideal for high SNR regions because it maximizes SNR at the MS. When the number of users is increased, the ZF fully connected precoder performs the worst. This is because the ZF precoder is unable to eliminate the growing interference caused by a rise in the number of users, resulting in a limited beamforming gain. In general, Co-channel interference, which is introduced by improper cross-correlation features of random spreading sequences across users, causes a reduction in spectral efficiency when the number of users drastically increases.

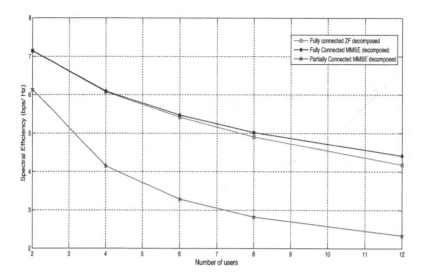

Fig. 7. Impact of varying the number of users at the MS for hierarchical decomposed algorithms $SNR = 5$dB, $A_{BS} = 144$, $A_{MS} = 4$, and $P = 5$

5.5   Spectral Efficiency for Hybrid Beamforming with Digital and Analog Beamforming Approaches

The spectral efficiency by varying SNR with eight number of users, and five number of channel paths for hierarchical decomposed hybrid beamforming algorithms is shown in Fig. 8 and The outcome is compared to SU and merely analog beamsteering. The fact that numerous users can communicate over the same spectrum at the same time improves the system's performance. MU-MIMO networks, on the other hand, are subject to significant inter-user interference, which is not the case with single-user MIMO. For partially and fully connected Hybrid Beamforming systems, ZF and MMSE precoder algorithms are used to overcome the problem of interference in MU-MIMO systems.

A single RF chain is used to transmit a single data stream and generate a single signal beam in analog beamforming. When SNR is low, analog beamforming outperforms partially connected ZF hybrid precoding, and when SNR is 4dB, partially connected ZF precoding performs approximately identically to analog beamforming. In comparison to analog only beamforming, partially ZF precoding achieves the maximum spectral efficiency when SNR is more than 4 dB. To achieve the multiplexing advantage, the ZF precoder requires a high SNR. The performance of the MMSE precoder is close to optimal. As a result,

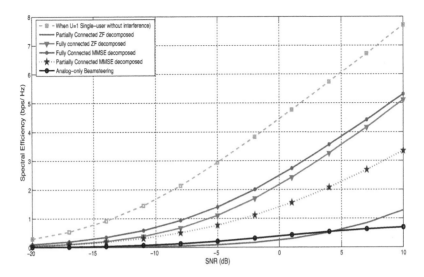

Fig. 8. Hybrid beamforming techniques compared with Analog only beamforming and single user by varying SNR $P = 5$, $A_{BS} = 64$, $A_{MS} = 16$, and $U = 8$

in multi-user hybrid precoding scenarios, an interference management system is required. In addition, we evaluate the performance of fully digital beamforming techniques along with partially and fully connected two-stages iterative hybrid beamforming algorithms by varying the SNR values as shown in Fig. 9.

The fully digital bemforming with ZF and MMSE precoding schemes in the digital baseband yields better spectral efficiency due to the RF chain B_{RF} is behind each antenna element at the BS compared to the fully and partially connected hybrid beamforming techniques. The fully connected MMSE iterative technique near fully digital beamforming capability from –20dB to –5dB SNR region. Beyond –5dB SNR range it can be seen that a small performance gab between fully digital and fully connected hybrid beamforming techniques occurred. One can look at also the performance of both hybrid techniques are inferior to that of the fully digital one, but fully connected based on iterative two-stages algorithm is optimal compared with partially connected hybrid beamforming techniques.

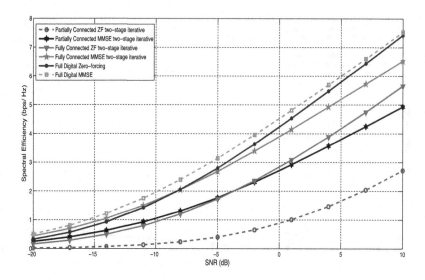

Fig. 9. Hybrid beamforming techniques compared with full digital beamforming techniques by varying SNR $P = 5$, $A_{BS} = 64$, $A_{MS} = 16$, and $U = 8$

6   Conclusion

The work's general conclusion is that, in response to the growing demand for increased data rates and dependability in wireless communication systems, hybrid beamforming for large MIMO systems in the mm-Wave scenario has emerged and attracted a lot of study attention. The performance of MU hybrid beamforming algorithms in mm-Wave large MIMO systems was evaluated in this paper, and hybrid beamforming was compared to fully digital and analog beamforming in terms of spectral efficiency. As discussed from the obtained results fully digital beamforming requires number of RF chains which is equal to the number of transmit antennas, which incur a significant increase in the power consumption, especially when the number of antenna element array in the BS goes to very large.

Hybrid beamforming techniques are an emerging technique for large MIMO systems because they can achieve the performance of traditional fully digital beamforming schemes with far less hardware implementation complexity and power consumption due to the use of a small number of RF chains in hybrid beamforming techniques. With much less RF chains, the fully-connected MMSE hybrid precoder approach can reach spectral efficiency close to that of the ideal fully-digital solution. With more hardware and computational complexity, fully digital beamforming provides improved performance. Analog beamforming, on the other hand, is a simple and cost-effective approach with limited versatility. In addition it is observed that iterative two-stages based on codebooks and hierarchical SVD based decomposition algorithms achieve near optimal solutions to the generic non-convex optimization problem. Because just the codebook indices of the selected array propagation vectors must be provided to the MS in the proposed multi-user downlink system, the complexity and feedback overhead of the iterative based two-stages technique is lower than that of hierarchical SVD based decomposition.

References

1. Ehab Ali, E., Ismail, M., Nordin, R., Abdulah, N.F.: Beamforming techniques for massive MIMO systems in 5G: overview, classification, and trends for future research. Front. Inf. Technol. Electron. Eng. **18**(6), 753–772 (2017)
2. Rappaport, T.S.: Wireless Communications: Principles and Practice. Prentice-Hall PTR, New Jersey, vol. 2 (1996)
3. Molisch, A.F., et al.: Hybrid beamforming for massive MIMO: a survey. IEEE Commun. Mag. **55**(9), 134–141 (2017)
4. Ngo, H.Q.: Massive MIMO: Fundamentals and system designs. Linköping University Electronic Press, Linköping, vol. 1642 (2015)
5. Mumtaz, S., Rodriguez, J., Dai, L.: MmWave Massive MIMO: A Paradigm for 5G. Academic Press, Cambridge (2016)
6. Marzetta, T.L.: Non-cooperative cellular wireless with unlimited numbers of base station antennas. IEEE Trans. Wirel. Commun. **9**(11), 3590–3600 (2010)
7. Song, X., Kuhne, T., Caire, G.: Fully-connected vs. sub-connected hybrid precoding architectures for mmWave MU-MIMO. In: ICC 2019 IEEE International Conference on Communications (ICC), pp. 1–7 (2019)
8. Xiaoyong, W., Liu, D., Yin, F.: Hybrid beamforming for MU massive MIMO systems. IEEE Trans. Commun. **66**(9), 3879–3891 (2018)
9. Li, N., Wei, Z., Yang, H., Zhang, X., Yang, D.: Hybrid precoding for mmWave massive MIMO systems with partially connected structure. IEEE Access **5**, 15142–15151 (2017)
10. El Ayach, O., Heath, R.W., Abu-Surra, S., Rajagopal, S., Pi, Z.: The capacity optimality of beam steering in large millimeter wave MIMO systems. In: IEEE 13th International Workshop on Signal Processing Advances in Wireless Communications (SPAWC), pp. 100–104 (2012)
11. Molu, M.M., Xiao, P., Khalily, M., Cumanan, K., Zhang, L., Tafazolli, R.: Low-complexity and robust hybrid beamforming design for multi-antenna communication systems. IEEE Trans. Wirel. Commun. **17**(3), 1445–1459 (2017)
12. Gao, X., Dai, L., Han, S., Chih-Lin, I., Heath, R.W.: Energy-efficient hybrid analog and digital precoding for mmWave MIMO systems with large antenna arrays. IEEE J. Sel. Areas Commun. **34**(4), 998–1009 (2016)
13. El Ayach, O., Rajagopal, S., Abu-Surra, S., Pi, Z., Heath, R.W.: Spatially sparse precoding in millimeter wave MIMO systems. IEEE Trans. Wirel. Commun. **13**(3), 1499–1513 (2014)
14. Roth, K., Pirzadeh, H., Swindlehurst, A.L., Nossek, J.A.: A comparison of hybrid beamforming and digital beamforming with low-resolution ADC for multiple users and imperfect CSI. IEEE J. Sel. Top. Sign. Proces. **12**(3), 484–498 (2018)
15. Song, N., Sun, H., Yang, T.: Coordinated hybrid beamforming for millimeter wave multi-user massive MIMO systems. In: 2016 IEEE Global Communications Conference (GLOBECOM), pp. 1–6 (2016)
16. Vizziello, A., Savazzi, P., Chowdhury, K.R.: A Kalman based hybrid precoding for multi-user millimeter wave MIMO systems. IEEE Access **6**, 5712–5722 (2018)

17. Alkhateeb, A., Leus, G., Heath, R.W.: Limited feedback hybrid precoding for multi-user millimeter wave systems. IEEE Trans. Wirel. Commun. **14**(11), 6481–6494 (2015)
18. Li, A., Masouros, C.: Hybrid precoding and combining design for millimeter-wave multi-user MIMO based on SVD. In: 2017 IEEE International Conference on Communications (ICC), pp. 1–6 (2017)
19. Geng, S., Kivinen, J., Zhao, X., Vainikainen, P.: Millimeter wave propagation channel characterization for short-range wireless communications. IEEE Trans. Veh. Technol. **58**(1), 3–13 (2008)
20. Hemadeh, I.A., Satyanarayana, K., El-Hajjar, M., Hanzo, L.: Millimeter-wave communications: Physical channel models, design considerations, antenna constructions, and link-budget. IEEE Commun. Surv. Tutorials **20**(2), 870–913 (2017)
21. Bogale, T.E., Le, L.B.: Beamforming for MU massive MIMO systems: digital versus hybrid analog-digital. In: 2014 IEEE Global Communications Conference, pp. 4066–4071 (2014)

Narrow-Linewidth Compound Ring Fiber Laser Using HBF as a Feedback for Sensing and Communication Application

Hailu Dessalegn Ayalew[✉]

Bahir Dar University (BDU), Bahir Dar Institute of Technology (BiT), Bahir Dar, Ethiopia

Abstract. Narrow-linewidth compound ring fiber laser using high birefringence fiber(HBF) as feedback is newly proposed to generate highly stable narrowband fiber laser and enhance the free spectral range. The laser is basically structured on a Compound ring resonator with end reflector by inserting a piece gain mediam EDF in the main cavity, it has two rings: a primary ring that serves as a resonator, and a secondary ring that serves as a filter. When an Er^{3+}-doped fiber is properly pumped, linear polarizer is located at the input port, effective free spectral range (FSR) of the reflected linearly polarized light is dramatically enhanced in compound ring setup due to the vernier effect between the traveling orthogonally polarized lights along the fast and slow axes of the HBF as well as between the primary and secondary rings. What's more, it alleviates the cavity-length problem. To sum up, these special properties Compound ring resonator with high birefringence fiber in one arm is used in our configuration. Theoretical and simulation results are presented. The optimum design relationships are obtained.

Keywords: Compound ring resonator with end reflector (CRRER) · High birefringence fiber (HBF) · Vernier effect · Free spectral range (FSR) · and Linewidth

1 Introduction

Erbium doped fiber lasers at 1550 nm are very attractive for fiber-based coherent lidar, fiber sensors, medical surgery and in communication applications. In general these fiber lasers are designed based on two popular configurations viz linear and ring cavity configuration.Out of these configurations the former one has a problem of spatial hole burning effect due to the counter-propagating waves in the gain medium, while in the later case the introduction of an optical isolator ensures unidirectional operation of the laser system [1–4]. In comparison to the linear configuration fiber laser unidirectional ring lasers have excellent lasing efficiency, and are free from back scattering and special hole burning problems. Consequently these lasers have better potential for achieve in single longitudinal mode oscillations. The main drawbacks reported in these unidirectional ring lasers using optical isolator have been the high cost and intrinsic loss of an optical isolator.

© ICST Institute for Computer Sciences, Social Informatics and Telecommunications Engineering 2022
Published by Springer Nature Switzerland AG 2022. All Rights Reserved
M. L. Berihun (Ed.): ICAST 2021, LNICST 411, pp. 173–183, 2022.
https://doi.org/10.1007/978-3-030-93709-6_12

In past, different configurations based on the combination of fiber couplers and Fiber rings utilizing vernier effect have been reported. Urquhart [2] proposed a vernier fiber ring resonator composed of two single-ring resonators in tandem. While compound double-ring resonators based on three couplers with improved characteristics have also been suggested [3, 4]. In order to achieve verniar operation, Y. H. Ja [5] used S-shape double-ring double-loop resonator based on degenerate two wave mixing. Their a photorefractive fiber has been utilized into common segment of two fiber loops. In order to achieve ultra-narrow linwidth spectrum, Wang et al. [6, 7] have demonstrated a Single-longitudinal-mode (SLM) fiber laser with an ultra-narrow linewidth system using different shapes and ring configurations. In order to increase free spectral range (FSR), Zhang and lit, [8] have studied all fiber compound ring (AFCR) resonator constructed from three single mode coupler by inserting a double-coupler fiber ring filter into the primary resonator ring. Further, Zhang et al. [9] have extended their theory of AFCR to the doped fiber ring laser where theoretical and experimentally also they have obtained the SLM operation with side mode reduction factor of 3 dB.

Also Sun et al. [10] proposed high birefringence fiber (HBF) ring resonator with an inline reflector for the generation of narrow band reflection peaks. These have taken an advantage of intrinsic vernier effect between the travelling orthogonally polarized light of HBF. In order to alleviate the losses of the passive components which degrade the properties of compound ring filters. The main drawback with this setup is dependence of output characteristic of cavity on polarization state of the input signal. Further, in order to eliminate this problem, feedback HBF loop mirror concept has been newly proposed and analysed by Sun et al. [10] for its application in single-frequency fiber lasers.

In this paper, we have exploited the concept of feedback HBF loop mirror suggested by Sun et al. [10] for the design of narrow line-width compound fiber ring EDF laser. The laser cavity is composed of compound ring structure with an end reflector. Which utilises a piece of EDF in the main cavity and HBF to provide feedback in the loop. This configuration will enable the single frequency operation with comparatively large FSR through the vernier effect. Jones matrix formulation has been used to obtained the varies physical parameter of fiber laser viz, loss difference, resonant condition and frequency spectrum property. The proper choice of coupling coefficient for couplers have been worked out by doing optimization of loss difference using Genetic Algorithm and hence obtained the increased value of loss difference 94 dB.

2   Fiber Laser Configuration and Theoretical Modeling

The configuration of fiber laser is a travelling wave fiber ring lasers which incorporates double coupler double ring resonator with a reflector as shown in Fig. 1. The two couplers have intensity coupling coefficients k_1 and k_2, respectively.The two ring cavities viz. primary and secondary are composed of a piece of EDF in length L3 and

SMF of length L1 with a common HBF of length L_2. The primary and secondary rings have the total length $L_p = L_2 + L_3$, and $L_s = L_1 + L_2$, respectively. The FBG is used as end reflector with a reflectivity of 99% and 3 dB bandwidth of 0.1 nm at 1550 nm. The difference between presently investigated resonator and Sun et al. [9] resonator lies in the fact that they utilized EDF instead of SMF in secondary ring and no end reflector in there resonator. Further in the present work the compound ring resonator has been analyzed for the SLM operation of doped laser. The pump light is injected into one end of the gain medium which is the EDF through a 980/1550 nm wave-length division multiplexer (WDM). A polarization controller (PC) is used to manipulate the polarization state of an input light beam and couple the resultant linearly polarized light into input port of PM coupler.

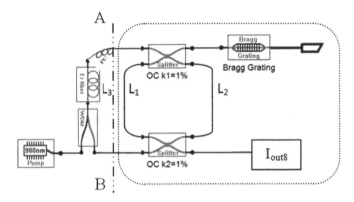

Fig. 1. Schematic diagram of narrow-linewidth compound ring EDF laser with $L_3 = 7.75$ m $L_1 = 0.25$ m (SMF) $L_2 = 0.25$ m (HBF)

Pump power at 980 nm is launched into the Erbium doped fiber through WDM coupler and the output of Er is given into the compound ring laser cavity. For mathematical simplification we will assume that below lasing threshold intensity at points A and B is same due to amplified spontaneous emission. Directionality of the resonator can be seen by analyzing the beams at point A and B. Amplifier spontaneous emission (ASE) beam coming from EDF at point B travels in the counter clockwise (ccw) direction through L_2 and emerges at point A while a part of the beam will travel L_1 and emerges as the output from OC2 where the reflector has no effect. However, the ASE input at point A travelling in clockwise (cw) direction will have an additional contribution due to ccw beam reflected backed by FBG. Therefore the non-reciprocal loss between the two directions is introduced, which will result in unidirectional oscillation in the ccw direction without the use of optical isolator.

2.1   Resonator Loss Difference

The loss difference for the resonator shown in dotted box in Fig. 1 is calculated by considering the input beam at point A and the direction of beam in the resonator to be ccw. The loss difference (LD) is defined as

$$LD = 10\log\left(\frac{RI_A}{RI_B}\right),\tag{1}$$

Where RI_A and RI_B are the returned intensities at points A and B defined as given below.

$$RI_A = I_{out1}^{cw} + I_{out1}^{cw}; \quad RI_B = I_{out5}^{cw}.\tag{2}$$

Loss difference in term of the coupling coefficients of OC1 and OC2 is derived as

$$LD = 10\log\left(\frac{R^2[x_1 - x_2(1 - \gamma_1)p_1p_2]^4}{(y_1y_2p_2)^2(1 - x_1x_2p_1p_2)^2} + 1\right),\tag{3}$$

Where the effective transmission coefficient and reflection coefficient of the ith coupler are $x_i = \sqrt{(1 - k_i)(1 - \gamma_i)}$ and $y_i = \sqrt{k_i(1 - \gamma_i)}$, respectively with i^{th} coupler intensity loss coefficient γ_i. p_i are defined as transmission factor for length L_i with $i = 1, 2$ and R is the reflectivity of FBG.

Form Fig. 2(a) and (b), it can be seen that the high loss difference can be obtained if K1 and K2 are chosen to be very small. If the two coupling coefficient is chosen to be very close to the optimum coupling coefficient $K_{opt} = 0.21$, it tell us that at optimum condition, the feedback intensity I_{out2}^{ccw} is going to be zero, and I_{out6}^{cw} becomes maximum which leads to minimum LD of zero. This can be seen from the intersecting point on x-axis in Fig. 2(a) and (b). when k_1 and k_2 are $\ll K_{opt}$ I_{out2}^{ccw} and I_{out6}^{cw} will become maximum and minimum, which will lead to large values of LD.

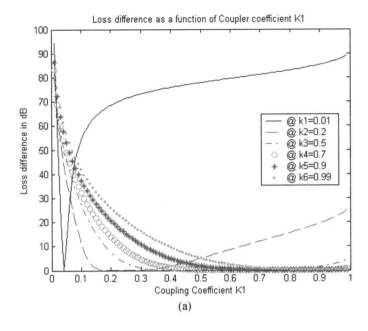

(a)

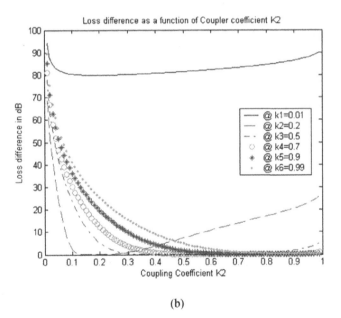

(b)

Fig. 2. Shows the loss difference: a). as a function of K1 for various values of K2 b). as a function of K2 for various values of K1 c) as a function of R for K2 = 0.1 and various values of K1. D). as a function of R for K1 = 0.1 and various values of K2. Other parameters are $p_1 = p_2 = p_3 = 0.995$, $\gamma_1 = \gamma_2 = 0.005$, and R = 0.99.

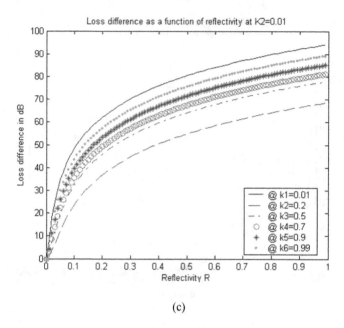

(c)

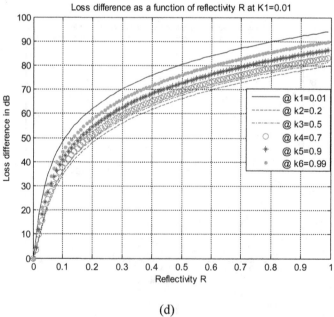

(d)

Fig. 2. (*continued*)

Also in Fig. 2(c) and (d), illustrates loss difference Vs reflectivity(R) at various values of K_1 for $K_2 = 0.01$ and K_2 for $K_1 = 0.01$, respectively. In both case, It clearly indicates that loss difference increase along with the reflectivity, and also it shows that, if reflectivity tends to zero, the loss difference reduced to zero. It tells as, FBG is the critical component in this configuration.

Moreover, we used the globalization optimization technique called genetic algorithm to determine the appropriate values of the corresponding coupling coefficient that can maximize the loss difference as it is indicated in Fig. 3 below. We have chosen the coupling coefficient $K_1 = K_2 = 1\%$ to maximize the loss difference to about 94 dB.

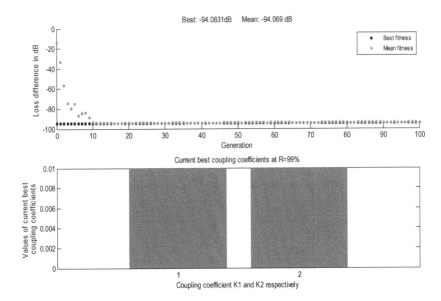

Fig. 3. Shows optimization result using Genetic algorithm

2.2 Fiber Laser Characteristics

Incorporating the double ring double resonator described in above section in the laser cavity, the intensity expression at the output port 8 of the laser has been derived using Jones matrix formulation.

$$I_{out1_{s+}^{f+}} = \frac{(x_1 - (1 - \gamma_1)x_2 p_1 p_2)^2 + 4x_1 x_2 g(1 - \gamma_1)p_1 p_2 \sin^2(\emptyset_{s_{so}^{fo}}/2)}{((1 - x_1 x_2 p_1 p_2)^2 + 4x_1 x_2 p_1 p_2 \sin^2(\emptyset_{s_{so}^{fo}}/2))} \qquad (4)$$

$$I_{out1} = I_{out1}^{f+} \sin^2(\theta) + I_{out1}^{s+} \cos^2(\theta) \qquad (5)$$

$$I_{out8_s}^f = \frac{1}{D_s^f}\left[\left\{(x_1x_2p_3 - y_1y_2p_1 - (1-\gamma_1)(1-\gamma_2)p_sp_3)^2\right.\right.$$
$$\left(4x_1x_2y_1y_2p_1p_3g\sin^2\left(\left(\emptyset_{p_{so}^{fo}} - \emptyset_{s_{so}^{fo}}\right)/2\right)\right)$$
$$+\left(4x_1x_2(1-\gamma_1)(1-\gamma_2)p_1p_2p_3^2g^2\left(\frac{\emptyset_{s_{so}^{fo}}}{2}\right)\right)$$
$$\left.\left.-(4(1-\gamma_1)(1-\gamma_2)y_1y_2p_1^2p_2p_3g\sin^2\left(\frac{\emptyset_{p_{so}^{fo}}}{2}\right))\right\}((R^2I_{out3}.\right] \tag{6}$$

Where,

$$D_s^f = (1 - x_1x_2p_1p_2 + y_1y_2p_2p_3g)^2 - 4y_1y_2p_2p_3g\sin^2\left(\frac{\emptyset_{p_{so}^{fo}}}{2}\right) + 4x_1x_2p_1p_2\sin^2\left(\frac{\emptyset_{s_{so}^{fo}}}{2}\right)$$
$$+ 4x_1x_2y_1y_2p_1p_2^2p_3g\sin^2\left(\frac{\emptyset_{p_{so}^{fo}}}{2} - \frac{\emptyset_{s_{so}^{fo}}}{2}\right) \tag{7}$$

Hence the laser intensity at the output port 8 is given as

$$I_{out8} = I_{out8}^f\sin^2(\theta) + I_{out8}^s\cos^2(\theta) \tag{8}$$

Where: $\emptyset$ is the beam phase on the primary and secondary ring.

$$\varphi_{pf0} = \frac{2\pi(n_fL_2 + n_0L_3)}{\lambda}, \varphi_{ps0} = \frac{2\pi(n_fL_2 + n_0L_3)}{\lambda}$$

$$\varphi_{sf0} = \frac{2\pi(n_fL_2 + n_0L_1)}{\lambda}, \quad \varphi_{sf0} = \frac{2\pi(n_fL_2 + n_0L_1)}{\lambda}$$

λ is the beam wavelength, $\theta =$ the rotation angle of HBF with the reference of SMF and the subscript numbers indicate the corresponding port in Fig. 1. The superscript letters f and s tell the corresponding intensity in the fast and slow axis of HBF. It follows from Eq. (8) the resultant FSR of I_{out8} is dominated by the secondary ring and it can be enhanced if θ is between 0 and 90^0 $(0 < \theta < 90^0)$. For example, considering a scenario when there is no rotation of the birefringence axes $\theta = 0^0$, the second term of the Eq. (8) is null. On the other hand when $\theta = 90^0$, the first term of the function is suppressed. From the above analysis, the transmission spectrum is a combination of the two spectrums which are governed by the function $sin^2(\theta)$ and $cos^2(\theta)$. As a result the enhancement factor relies on the ratio $\emptyset_{so}/\emptyset_{fo}$ which is assumed to be p/q (p and q are relatively prime numbers). The effective FSR is greatly enhanced by q times compared with the FSR along the slow axis.

The output intensities as functions of wave length are shown in Fig. 4. It demonstrates the mode suppression by use of the vernier effect between the traveling orthogonally polarized lights along the fast and slow axes of the HBF in L_2 as well as between the primary and secondary rings. The ratio of the two cavity length is 16:1 and the coupling coefficients are chosen to be K1 = K2 = 1% $\theta = 45^\circ$ from Fig. 4, it can be seen that the effective FSR of the narrow-linewidth compound ring EDF laser is

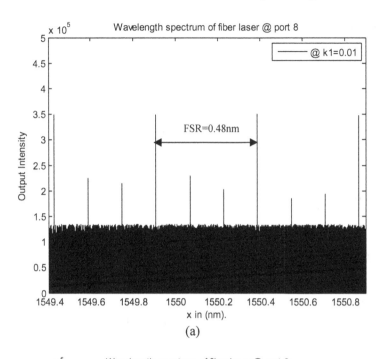

(a)

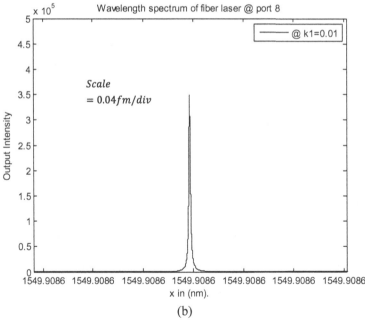

(b)

Fig. 4. Output intensity of fiber laser Vs wavelength at $p_1 = 0.995$, $p_2 = 0.995$, $p_3 = 0.995$, $R = 99\%$, and $\gamma_1 = 0.001$

determined by the FSR of the small ring. This can be written $L_p : l_s = m : n$ where m and n are two integers which do not have common factors. For each ring, the FSR is inversely proportional to its length. Therefore, the effective FSR of the compound ring cavity is:

$$FSR = nFSR_l = mFSR_L$$

The main peak occurs when only the primary ring resonates. From the configuration and simulation result, we have got FSR of 59.5 GHz with a full width half maximum (FWHM) of about 3 kHz at the expense of reduction factor (about 0.37) as shown in Fig. 4. The back reflection of the CRRER with HBF as a feedback is as small as ≤ 94 dB. It is also observed that when the ratio of the cavity lengths increases, the reduction factor will increase.

3 Conclusion

According to the directionality analysis, a high loss difference can be obtained by choosing the appropriate value of coupling cofficents k_1 and k_2, we used a Genetic Algorithm optimization technique to select the appropriate value of coupling coefficient and it doubles the loss difference to 94 dB.

Moreover, the effects of the coupling coefficients, losses and resonance numbers on the resonance are investigated. The results show the, reduction factor (≈ 4.32 dB), and the back-reflection is obtained to be < -94 dB. It is also observed that when the ratio of the cavity lengths increases, the reduction factor will increase.

Based on the CRRER, We have designed a narrow-linewidth compound ring fiber laser. The laser is basically structured on a compound-ring resonator, and uses the vernier principle to effectively increase its free spectral range. The single longitudinal mode(SLM) selection in this laser is achieved by compound ring resonator with end reflector which uses HBF as a feedback. As a result, securely attained with a narrow linewidth of less than 3 kHz with FSR of 59.5 GHz that can be used in sensing and communication applications.

References

1. Ou, P., Jia, Y., Cao, B.: Narrow line width single polarization frequency modulated Er-doped fiber ring laser. Chin. Opt. Lett. **6**(11), 845–847 (2008)
2. Urquhart, P.: Compound optical-fiber-based resonator. J. Opt. Soc. Am. A **5**, 805–812 (1988)
3. Barbarossa, G., Matteo, A.M., Armenise, M.N.: Theoretical analysis of triple coupler ring-based optical guide-wave resonator. J. Lightwave. Tech. **13**, 148–157 (1995)
4. Wang, Z., Shang, J., Li, S., Mu, K., Yu, S., Qiao, Y.: All-polarization maintaining single-longitudinal-mode fiber laser with ultra-high OSNR, Sub-kHz linewidth and extremely high stability. Optical Society of America (2020)
5. Ja, Y.H.: A vernier S-shaped fiber double-loop resonator with double couplers and degenerate two-wave mixing. J. Lightwave. Tech. **11**, 728–736 (1993)

6. Wang, Z.K., Shang, J.M., Tang, L.H., Mu, K.L., Yu, S., Qiao, Y.J.: Stable single-longitudinal-mode fiber laser with ultra-narrow linewidth based on convex-shaped fiber ring and sagnac loop. IEEE Access. **7**(1), 166398–166403 (2019)
7. Wang, Z.K., Shang, J.M., Mu, K.L., Yu, S., Qiao, Y.J.: Single-longitudinal-mode fiber laser with an ultra-narrow linewidth and extremely high stability obtained by utilizing a triple-ring passive subring resonator. Opt. Laser Technol. **130**, 106329 (2020)
8. Zhang, J., Lit, J.W.Y.: All-fiber compound ring resonator with a ring filter. J. Lightwave. Tech. **12**, 1256–1262 (1994)
9. Sun, G., Moon, D.S., Chung, Y.: High birefringence fiber ring resonator with an inline reflector For single-frequency fiber lasers". Opt. Commun. **280**(2007), 157–160 (2007)
10. Sun, G., Moon, D.S., Chung, Y.: Theoretical analysis of feedback high birefringence fiber loop mirror for application in single frequency fiber lasers. Opt. Commun. **283**, 1047–1049 (2009)

Design and Performance Analysis of 125 MW Floating Photovoltaic Power Plant in Ethiopia: Metema vs Lake Tana

Tewodros G. Workineh$^{(\boxtimes)}$, Biniyam Z. Taye, and Abraham H. Nebey

Bahir Dar Institute of Technology, Bahir Dar University, Bahir Dar, Ethiopia

Abstract. Floating solar PV power plants are currently emerging form of photovoltaic technologies that uses the surface of water bodies such as irrigation, canals, water reservoirs, lakes and failing ponds, ocean, water treatment plants, etc. Uses of man-made reservoirs for floating solar PV have significant advantages over land-based and other water body's installation. Ethiopian power authority planned to install 125 MWp grid connected battery-less land-based PV solar systems at Metema in Amhara region. In this paper, output performance of the solar PV plant at Metema and on Lake Tana is compared. Factors that affect the PV power plant efficiency such as wind speed and temperature are modelled and simulated in MATLAB/ SIMULINK. Panels and inverters are selected and the system components are configured to generate 125 MW. The system is modeled by MATLAB/SIMULINK to show the efficiency variations of solar PV. Due to high temperature and wind speed, solar PV efficiency drops. The efficiency of solar PV on water surface is improved by 2.88%, 3.6 MW from 125 MW plant, over the land surface. This indicates that temperature and wind speed are the major factors that affects the output performance of solar PV generation systems.

Keywords: Floating solar PV · PV power plant · Wind and temperature effects

1 Introduction

In the last few years, renewable energy capacity installed from sun has increasing and in 2017 the PV market practiced a further worldwide growth with an installed capacity over 400GW [1]. The promising alternative energy technology, solar photovoltaic system, is now becomes a very reasonable choice for harnessing the resource by utilizing obtainable water surface [2].

Though premium, loss of efficiency at high operating PV cell temperature and during tracking 50–60% increase in land occupancy are some of the factors that limits the growth of PV penetration around the world [2, 3]. Thus, the combination of solar PV and floating technology on water surface is best solution to overcome the above-mentioned problems [4].

Japan was the first to install floating PV system in 2007 in Achi, followed by France, Italy, South Korea, Spain and USA, all of which have tested small scale for research and development. Recently, China takes the lead with plant capacity of 73%

© ICST Institute for Computer Sciences, Social Informatics and Telecommunications Engineering 2022
Published by Springer Nature Switzerland AG 2022. All Rights Reserved
M. L. Berihun (Ed.): ICAST 2021, LNICST 411, pp. 184–195, 2022.
https://doi.org/10.1007/978-3-030-93709-6_13

of the world (around 1752 MW). The world solar generation plant capacity could reach up to 1.2 TW by the end of 2020, according to solar power Europe reports [1].

Floating solar PV power plants are currently emerging form of photovoltaic technologies that uses the surface of water bodies such as irrigation, canals or remediation, water reservoirs, lakes and tailing ponds, ocean, water treatment plants [2, 5]. Floating PV system has lower ambient temperature in virtue to the cooling effect of water and thus reduces cell temperature of the PV panel. Consequently, efficiency of floating solar PV panel is 11% higher than the land based solar panels [5, 6].

In addition to improving generation efficiency, the systems provide other environmental benefits such as reducing evaporation by up to 70% and improve water quality. It also reduces the growth of algae by shading the water from sun [7].

Uses of dam reservoir for floating solar PV have significant advantages over land based and other water body's installation. Water conservation, PV variability compensation, peak load demand support and facilitation of black start for hydropower are the main advantages of integrating floating PV on existing infrastructure of hydroelectric dam [8, 9].

A countrylike Ethiopia, where agriculture leads the economy and food insecurity is critical issues. Floating solar power plant technology on the surface water bodies is not a choice. Therefore, the aim of this paper is to show the floating solar PV at Lake Tana has better performance over land-based systems at Metema.

2 Methodology

Detail sizing and configuration of the various components of the floating PV power plant is carried out. ABB central inverter and HCP78X9-400W PV module specification are used to show the effect of temperature performance in energy production of the plant [10, 11]. MATLAB/SIMULINK is used to simulate the model the overall system. Finally, the floating solar panel performance is compared with land-based installation.

2.1 Study Area

Metema is a city in the Amhara region in Ethiopia. Metema is located at 12°58′0″ N and 36°12′0″ E. The temperature ranges between 36 to 45 °C. The area intensively used to farm peanut, cotton, incense and sesame [12]. They are the major export products of the country. To preserve this precious land and improve energy production due to high ambient temperature, the design is proposed on the surface of Lake Tana.

Lake Tana is the largest and one of the tourist destinations in Ethiopia, which is found in Amhara regional state nearby the capital city Bahir Dar, located at 11.5742°N latitude and 37.3614°E longitude [13]. The location map of Metema and Lake Tana is shown in (Fig. 1).

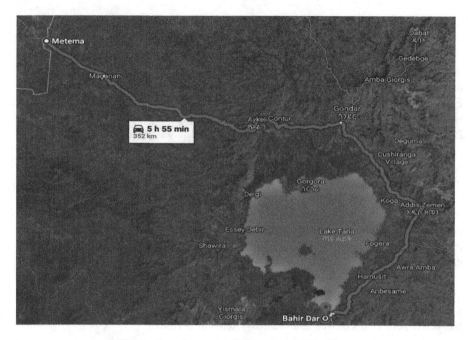

Fig. 1. Location map of Metema and Lake Tana

2.2   Study Area

The average solar radiation (Table 1) and maximum ambient air temperature (Table 2) for the last 20 years for the Bahir Dar city and Metema are taken from NASA surface meteorology and solar energy data base [14, 15]. Temperature and wind speed are corrected to fit surface temperature of the water.

Table 1. Monthly average daily insolation incident on horizontal surface (KWh/m²/day) of Bahir Dar/Metema

Lat & Lon	Jan	Feb	Mar	Apr	May	Jun
Bahir Dar						
Lat 11.5742°N						
Lon 37.3614°E	6.4	6.7	7.0	6.9	6.6	5.6
Metema						
Lat 12.9545°N						
Lon 36.1573°E	7.0	7.2	6.73	7.3	6.9	7.5

Table 2. Maximum daily temperature (°C) of Bahir Dar/Metema

Lat & Lon	Jan	Feb	Mar	Apr	May	Jun
Bahir Dar						
Lat 11.5742°N						
Lon 37.3614°E	29	31	32	32	32	29
Metema						
Lat 12.9545°N						
Lon 36.1573°E	35.7	39.5	40.3	40.3	39	36

2.3 Components of Floating Photovoltaic Power Plant

To improve efficiency of the plant and preserve the land for agriculture, the solar PV generation structural modification is required to install the plant over the water surface [3, 6]. This installation of PV plant over treasurable land is replaced by using floating system.

2.3.1 Solar Module and Associated Components

It is common to use standard crystalline PV module with aluminum frame. However, on the salty environment specially fabricated module and polymer made frame are applied to resist corrosion. Other associated elements in a system such as inverters, DC disconnect and protection equipment's are the same as it is applied in land-based installation [16–18].

Floating

A floating body with effective buoyancy to the safe weight ratio that allows installation of PV module can be used. It is usually made from steel, aluminum, HDPE or glass reinforced plastic. Low cost, good durability in wet and salty as well as humid environment, low weight and good strength per unit of weight make HDPE and glass reinforced plastic a preferred choice [18, 19].

Mooring

Floating PV technology requires the technical capability to secure structural stability and durability on the water. The mooring system keeps the panel structure fixed in the same position to adapt the change to water level using nylon wire rope slings to be tied to bollards on bank or bottom [3, 6, 20].

Underwater Cable and Connection System

Extremely robust resistance, high mechanical load and abrasion, high temperature resistance and excellent weather proof cables are used to transfer generated power from water bodies to the substation. The weatherproof IP67 junction boxes and high current capacity connectors are used for power plant cable connection if available under water [3, 16, 18, 21].

2.4   Mathematical Modeling of Temperature and Wind Effect

The efficiency of solar PV power plant is highly dependent on temperature and wind speed. For silicon modules, a typical reduction of efficiency with temperature is 0.4–0.5%/°C. Therefore, estimation of the temperature of the PV panel to assess the efficiency of the system due to temperature rise is important [22–24]. The efficiency of PV panel, η_{PV} is given by

$$\eta_{PV} = \eta_{STC}\left[1 + \beta\left(T_{panel} - 25\,°C\right)\right]\left[1 + \gamma \ln\left(\frac{G_T}{G_o}\right)\right] \tag{1}$$

Where:

η_{STC}– Module/panel efficiency at STC.
T_{panel}– Module temperature.
G_T– Irradiance received by a module.
G_o– Reference solar irradiance taken as 1000 W/m^2.
β– Temperature coefficient at maximum power point.
γ– Azimuth angle ($\gamma = 0$ for surface facing to south).

In this study, it is assumed that the PV module are fixed with tilting angle 11.5742° and 12.9545° facing south for Bahir Dar and Metema respectively and the efficiency is [17].

$$\eta_{PV} = \eta_{STC}\left[1 + \beta\left(T_{panel} - 25°C\right)\right] \tag{2}$$

But the operating cells temperature $Tpanel$, of the PV panel is determined by

$$T_{panel} = T_{amb} + \frac{\left(N_{OCT} - 20°\right)}{0.8\,\text{KW/m}^2} * G_o \tag{3}$$

In this study, it is assumed that the PV module are fixed with tilting angle 11.5742° and 12.9545° facing south for Bahir Dar and Metema respectively and the efficiency is [17].

Where N_OCT is nominal operating cell temperature defined by the manufacturer for the exploitation condition for each PV panel, it is usually set to 45 °C.

Floating PV module were situated in a boundary air layer and the lake surface, whose surface temperature >20 °C [17, 18]. In this paper the ambient temperature is assumed $a\ T_{amb} = T_{lakearea}$. High wind location, is not considered in this work, the precise temperature estimation formula for free standing mounting type is given by

$$T_{Panel} = T_{amb}\left(\frac{0.32}{8.91 + 2V_f}\right)G_T \tag{4}$$

Where V_f- free steam wind speed.
Wind speed value can be adjusted at the required height according to the measured height using power law formula [17].

$$\frac{V_f}{V_{ref}} = \left(\frac{Z}{Z_{ref}}\right)^n \tag{5}$$

$$n = \frac{0.37 - 0.0881 \ln(V_{ref})}{1 - 0.0881 \ln\left(\frac{Z_{ref}}{10}\right)} \tag{6}$$

Where:

Z_{ref}- Reference height measured from ground.

Z- Required height in meter.

V_{ref}- Known wind speed at the reference height.

The sea temperature T_w is given in relation to the air (land) temperature T_a, air-water regression model based on daily and weekly water temperature data resulted [25, 26].

$$T_w = 5 + 0.75 T_{amb} \tag{7}$$

Due to the thermal inertia of the water, response of water temperature is damped and delayed, which is depicted in coefficients in a given formula. As shown in the formula above, the water temperature will be warmer than the temperature if the air temperature is below 20 °C [26].

Annual average temperature (Table 2) is 28.75 °C

$$T_w = 5 + 0.75 * 28.75 = 26.56 \,^{\circ}C$$

The velocity of wind in the sea is always higher than that of the land. The wind on sea V_{ws} in terms of land wind speed V_{wl} [17] is given by

$$V_{ws} = 1.62 + 1.17 * V_{wl} \tag{8}$$

$$V_{ws} = 1.62 + 1.17 * 6.14 = 8.8 \,\text{m/s}$$

Energy production (E) at any time of hour using floating PV panel can be defined by the following equation [17, 19].

$$E = G_T * A * \eta \tag{9}$$

Where:

A- is surface area (m^2) of the solar array

$$\eta = \eta_{mod} * \eta_{Pv} * \eta_{inv} \tag{10}$$

Where:

η_{mod}- Module efficiency (15–18% recommended or can be taken from module specification).

η_{inv}- Inverter efficiency (>95% recommended for solar application or can be taken from inverter specification).

The power generated by the PV panels is given by [17, 19].

$$P_{PVout} = P_{R.PV} * \frac{G_T}{G_o} * \left[1 + \beta_T \left(T_{panel} - 25\,^{\circ}\text{C}\right)\right] * \eta_{inv} * \eta_{mod} \tag{11}$$

Where $P_{R.PV}$- PV rated power at required condition.

2.5   Panel and Inverter Specification

Mono crystalline silicon module HCP78X9-400W made in China with 400 Wp per panel capacity and ABB central inverter of PVS 980–58.5.0 VA (10 MW) is selected for this research [6, 27, 28] (Tables 3 and 4).

Table 3. Solar photovoltaic specification

Module type	HCP78X9-400W
Maximum power *Pmax*	400 W
Open-circuit voltage *Voc*	51.6 V
Maximum power voltage *Vmp*	42.0 V
Short-circuit current *Isc*	9.95 A
Maximum power current *Imp*	9.53 A
Module efficiency (%)	18.38%
Power tolerance	0 ∼+ 5 W
Temperature coefficient of *Isc*	0.05%/°C
Temperature coefficient of *Voc*	−0.31%/°C
Temperature coefficient of *Pmax*	−0.38%/°C
Standard test environment	Irradiance 1000 W/m^2, cell temperature 25 °C, Spectrum AM 1.5

Table 4. Inverter specification

Inverter type	PSV980-58-4348-5000 KVA
Max power input	10 MWp
Voltage range	978–1250 V
Max DC voltage	1500 V
Max DC current	5700 A
Nominal AC power output	5000 KVA
Nominal AC current	3700 A
Nominal AC voltage output	690 V
Efficiency	98.5%

2.6   Design of 125 MWp Floating Solar PV

Ethiopian power authority planned to install, 125 MWp grid connected battery-less land-based at Metema. 125 MW power was estimated by Ethiopian electric power to electrify Metema and surrounding community. This estimated power is used in the paper.

2.6.1   System Sizing

Required number of modules to generate 10 MW peak power

$$Number\ of\ PV\ modules = \frac{Pinverter}{Pmodule} = \frac{10\,\text{MW}}{400\,\text{W}} = 25,000\,modules \qquad (12)$$

Number of modules in series

$$N_{ms} = \frac{V_{inverter}}{V_{mp}} = \frac{1250}{42} = 29.76 \approx 30\,modules \qquad (13)$$

Number of modules in parallel

$$N_{mp} = \frac{N_m}{N_{ms}} = \frac{25,000}{30} = 833.33 \approx 834\,modules \qquad (14)$$

The total number of modules for 10 MW inverter = 834 * 30 = 25,020 modules. To generate 125 MW power, 312,750 modules are required. Thus, system components are arranged so as to generate 125 MW power.

2.6.2   String and Component Arrangement

The configuration shown in Fig. 2 indicates that 834 strings are clustered in to 13 inverters to be coupled with 1.25/15 KVA distribution transformer.

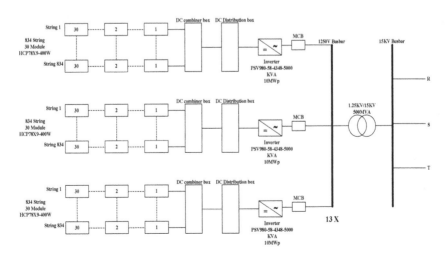

Fig. 2. String and system component arrangement

2.7 MATLAB Modeling Solar PV

Solar PV is modeled for Metema at an average temperature of 36.7 °C and Lake Tana at an average temperature of 26.56 °C. MATALAB/Simulink is used to model the system in both cases (Fig. 3).

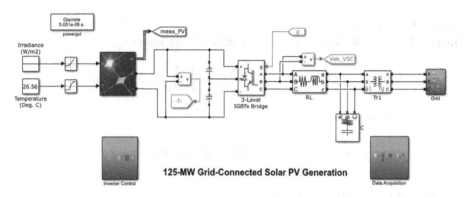

Fig. 3. MATLAB/Simulink model of 125 MW Solar PV system

3 Result and Discussion

To generate 125 MW power at Metema and Lake Tana, 312,750 modules of HCP78X9-400W and 13 number of 10 MW, ABB - PSV980-58-4348-5000 KVA are required. The generated power at Metema with 36.7 °C is 116.4 MW (Fig. 4) and at Lake Tana with 26.56 °C is 120 MW (Fig. 5). Therefore, generated power using a floating solar PV system is improved by 2.88%, which is 3.6 MW more compared with Metema (Table 5).

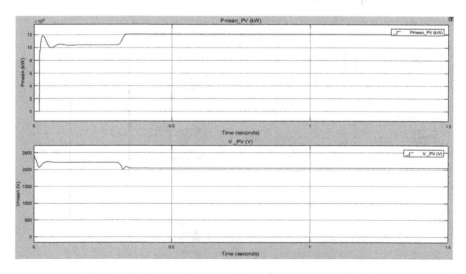

Fig. 4. Mean power and Voltage simulation result at 36.7 °C

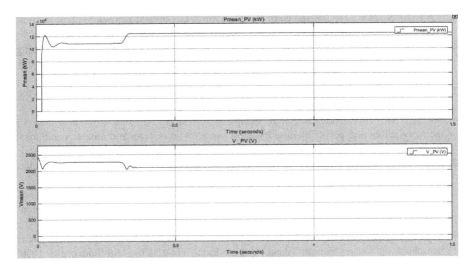

Fig. 5. Mean power and voltage simulation result at 26.56 °C

Table 5: Comparison of 125 MW solar photovoltaic generation at Metema and Lake Tana

Place	Ta (°C)	Pmean (MW)	Vmean (V)	Performance ratio (%)
Metema	36.7	116.4	2079	93.12
Lake Tana	26.56	120	2138	96

4 Conclusion

Ethiopian government proposed to install land-based solar power plants in selected areas. This leads to loss of fertile land and solar PV plants efficiency drops. Temperature and wind speed effects are the dominant factor for efficiency drops. Thus, installing solar photovoltaic systems at Lake Tana instead of Metema, improves the efficiency of power generation, reduces evaporation of water, more economical and saves the fertile land for agriculture. The performance ratio of power generation at Metema and Lake Tana to the proposed power generation is 93.12% and 96% respectively at different temperature.

References

1. Gaetan, M., Sinead, O., Manoel, R.: Global market outlook for solar power/2018–2022, p. 60. EPIA - Eur. Photovolt. Ind. Assoc. (2018). http://www.solarpowereurope.org/global-market-outlook-2018-2022/, Accessed Sep 2020. www.africa-eu-renewables.org
2. Sahu, A., Yadav, N., Sudhakar, K.: Floating photovoltaic power plant: a review. Renew. Sustain. Energy Rev. **66**, 815–824 (2016). https://doi.org/10.1016/j.rser.2016.08.051

3. Schlisske, S., et al.: Design and color flexibility for inkjet-printed perovskite photovoltaics. ACS Appl. Energy Mater. **2**(1), 764–769 (2019). https://doi.org/10.1021/acsaem.8b01829
4. Cazzaniga, R., Cicu, M., Rosa-Clot, M., Rosa-Clot, P., Tina, G.M., Ventura, C.: Floating photovoltaic plants: performance analysis and design solutions. Renew. Sustain. Energy Rev. **81**, 1730–1741 (2018). https://doi.org/10.1016/j.rser.2017.05.269
5. Yousuf, H., et al.: A review on floating photovoltaic technology (FPVT). Curr. Photovolt. Res. **8**(3), 67–78 (2020). https://doi.org/10.21218/CPR.2020.8.3.067
6. Mirzaei, M., Mohiabadi, M.Z.: A comparative analysis of long-term field test of monocrystalline and polycrystalline PV power generation in semi-arid climate conditions. Energy Sustain. Dev. **38**, 93–101 (2017). https://doi.org/10.1016/j.esd.2017.01.002
7. Aznar, A.Y., Lee, N., Booth, S.S.: International applications for floating solar photovoltaics. Golden, CO (United States) (2019). https://doi.org/10.2172/1526906
8. Mondal, M.H.A., Gebremeskel, A.G., Gebrehiwot, K., Ringler, C.: Ethiopian universal electrification development strategies, p. 4 (2018). http://ebrary.ifpri.org/cdm/ref/collection/p15738coll2/id/132767
9. Taye, B.Z., Nebey, A.H., Workineh, T.G.: Design of floating solar PV system for typical household on Debre Mariam Island. Cogent Eng. 7(1) (2020). https://doi.org/10.1080/23311916.2020.1829275
10. EECE 550: Topics in Power Electronics (2004). http://courses.ece.ubc.ca/550/, Accessed 18 Mar 2021
11. On Stability of Voltage Source Inverters in Weak Grids—Aalborg University's Research Portal. https://vbn.aau.dk/en/publications/on-stability-of-voltage-source-inverters-in-weak-grids, Accessed 18 Mar 2021
12. Kala-azar among labour migrants in Metema-Humera region of Ethiopia. | Semantic Scholar. https://www.semanticscholar.org/paper/Kala-azar-among-labour-migrants-in-Metema-Humera-ofMengesha-Abuhoy/82242b3cadfd04df18851d850f52592f1e9b931e, Accessed 18 Mar 2021
13. Geremew, A., Triest, L.: Hydrological connectivity and vegetative dispersal shape clonal and genetic structure of the emergent macrophyte Cyperus papyrus in a tropical highland lake (Lake Tana, Ethiopia). Hydrobiologia **843**(1), 13–30 (2017). https://doi.org/10.1007/s10750-017-3466-y
14. Mahmoudi, H., et al.: Assessment of wind energy to power solar brackish water greenhouse desalination units: a case study from Algeria. Renew. and Sustain. Energy Rev. **13**(8), 2149–2155 (2009). https://doi.org/10.1016/j.rser.2009.03.001
15. Frid, S.E., Rakhimov, E.Y., Boliev, B.B.: Actinometric data for flat receivers solar energy units performance estimation. Appl. Sol. Energy (English Transl. Geliotekhnika) **55**(1), 78–82 (2019). https://doi.org/10.3103/S0003701X19010079
16. Hermanu, B.A.C., Santoso, B., Suyitno, W., Wicaksono, F.X.R.: Design of 1 MWp floating solar photovoltaic (FSPV) power plant in Indonesia. In: AIP Conference Proceedings, vol. 2097, no. 1, p. 030013 (2019). https://doi.org/10.1063/1.5098188
17. Siecker, J., Kusakana, K., Numbi, B.P.: A review of solar photovoltaic systems cooling technologies. Renew. Sustain. Energy Rev. **79**, 192–203 (2017). https://doi.org/10.1016/j.rser.2017.05.053
18. Mittal, D., Saxena, B.K., Rao, K.V.S.: Comparison of floating photovoltaic plant with solar photovoltaic plant for energy generation at Jodhpur in India. In: Proceedings of 2017 IEEE International Conference on Technological Advancements in Power and Energy: Exploring Energy Solutions for an Intelligent Power Grid, TAP Energy 2017, June 2018, pp. 1–6 (2018). https://doi.org/10.1109/TAPENERGY.2017.8397348

19. Yadav, N., Gupta, M., Sudhakar, K.: Energy assessment of floating photovoltaic system. In: International Conference on Electrical Power and Energy Systems, ICEPES 2016, May 2017, pp. 264–269 (2017). https://doi.org/10.1109/ICEPES.2016.7915941
20. Liu, L., Wang, Q., Lin, H., Li, H., Sun, Q., Wennersten, R.: Power generation efficiency and prospects of floating photovoltaic systems. Energy Procedia **105**, 1136–1142 (2017). https://doi.org/10.1016/j.egypro.2017.03.483
21. Sharma, P., Muni, B., Sen, D.: Design Parameters OF 10 Kw Floating Solar Power PlanT Conference (2016)
22. Dubey, S., Sarvaiya, J.N., Seshadri, B.: Temperature dependent photovoltaic (PV) efficiency and its effect on PV production in the world - a review. Energy Procedia **33**, 311–321 (2013). https://doi.org/10.1016/j.egypro.2013.05.072
23. Green, M.A., Bremner, S.P.: Energy conversion approaches and materials for high-efficiency photovoltaics. Nat. Mater. **16**(1), 23–34 (2016). https://doi.org/10.1038/nmat4676
24. Hirst, L.C., Ekins-Daukes, N.J.: Fundamental losses in solar cells. Prog. Photovoltaics Res. Appl. **19**(3), 286–293 (2011). https://doi.org/10.1002/pip.1024
25. Abdoli, A., Farokhnejad, M.R., Nazari, H., Hassanzadeh Kiabi, B.: The role of temperature and daytime as indicators for the spawning migration of the Caspian lamprey Caspiomyzon wagneri Kessler 1870. J. Appl. Ichthyol. **33**(3), 553–557 (2017). https://doi.org/10.1111/jai.13078
26. Fawzy, D., Moussa, S., Badr, N.: WFEC: wind farms economic classifier using big data analytics. In: 2017 IEEE 8th International Conference on Intelligent Computing and Information Systems, ICICIS 2017, Jul. 2017, vol. 2018-January, pp. 154–159. https://doi.org/10.1109/INTELCIS.2017.8260046
27. Chondrogiannis, S., Barnes, M.: Specification of rotor side voltage source inverter of a doubly-fed induction generator for achieving ride-through capability. IET Renew. Power Gener. **2**(3), 139–150 (2008). https://doi.org/10.1049/iet-rpg:20070104
28. Kobougias, I., Tatakis, E., Prousalidis, J.: PV systems installed in marine vessels: technologies and specifications. Adv. Power Electron. **2013** (2013). https://doi.org/10.1155/2013/831560

Efficiency Analysis of a Solar Photovoltaic DC and Existing AC Distribution System for Bahirdar University Data Center

Tewodros G. Workineh[1($\boxtimes$)], Tefera T. Yetayew[2], and Tesfaye B. Sisay[3]

[1] Bahirdar Institute of Technology, Bahirdar University, Bahir Dar, Ethiopia
[2] Adama Science and Technology University, P.O. 1888, Adama, Ethiopia
[3] Debreberhan University, Debreberhan, Ethiopia

Abstract. Data centers are multipurpose internet based centers which needs to perform different tasks without any perturbation of electric power. It is a very fast growing structures with significant contribution to the world's energy consumption. For this paper, Bahirdar University data center is selected for reliability and efficiency evaluation of both AC and DC distribution system architecture. The study is based on the existing AC power distribution layout of the selected case area which gets supply from Ethiopian electric utility (EEU) with a nearby diesel generator as a backup power supply system in a case of power outage from the utility system as well as the proposed data center power distribution model with an off grid solar powered 380 V DC distribution system. Results show that an AC distribution system has an average efficiency of 72.96% while a proposed DC distribution system has an average efficiency of 82.63%. This demonstrated that a DC power distribution system is 9.67% efficient than AC power distribution architecture. The simulation analysis was done in MATLAB.

Keywords: Data center · DC distribution · Efficiency analysis

1 Introduction

Recently, DC distribution system has many advantages over an AC distribution system. An improved power quality, higher efficiency and reliability are some of the merits listed in DC distribution systems. It has also reduced installation costs as it requires fewer power conversion stages, less copper, no reactive power or skin effect and smaller floor space. Integration of renewable energy sources and energy storage systems are simple in DC distribution since it does not require any synchronization. Telecommunication systems and data centers are among the few surviving examples of DC distribution systems [1]. Data centers are very fast growing structures with significant contribution to the world's energy consumption. The main source of electricity for a data center is usually the grid connection which is provided by utility companies, although there are some exceptions like Apple's data centers which claim to use 100% renewable energy [2].

© ICST Institute for Computer Sciences, Social Informatics and Telecommunications Engineering 2022
Published by Springer Nature Switzerland AG 2022. All Rights Reserved
M. L. Berihun (Ed.): ICAST 2021, LNICST 411, pp. 196–214, 2022.
https://doi.org/10.1007/978-3-030-93709-6_14

Now a day, the renewable energy sources such as solar PV, wind, geothermal, biomass energy and other sources of energy leads to replace the dependency of electricity from utility system. Power convertors like rectifiers, inverters and choppers are also more applicable to change the voltage type and level from one state to another. These convertors are now more applicable for DC distribution systems [2].

A data center is a multipurpose internet based center which needs to perform different tasks without any perturbation of electric power that comprises critical and sensitive load comprises of IT equipment's such as servers, switches storage devices and UPS systems that are typically DC-based loads. Thus, this study leads to push on the design of DC distribution for data center power distribution architecture to improve the efficiency and reliability of the system For this paper, Bahir Dar University data center is selected for reliability and efficiency evaluation of AC and DC distribution system by properly designing an off grid solar power with a backup diesel generator to supply the data center loads to replace utility power supply.

Bahir Dar University gets electric power supply from Ethiopian electric power industry at a nearby substation through 15 kV distribution line. Bahir Dar University data center is one of the large loads of the university which is very sensitive to the power interruption in the utility side. In most cases the power is interrupted due to different faults at the feeder lines of the substation which feeds the university loads leads to fail the data center power supply. System failure is the problem of data center power reliability. High reliability requirement of a data center can be achieved by appropriate design of the data center electric power distribution architecture.

The availability of power is increased by using multiple main supplies, alternative energy sources such as solar and wind, and standby diesel generators [3].The many cascaded power conversion stages and the low efficiency of each converter are the causes of low data center efficiency. All power conversion stages in the power distribution system should be high-efficiency in order to achieve high overall efficiency. Hence, implementation of a DC distribution system instead of AC distribution system results in elimination of a number of conversion stages, thereby reducing the distribution losses resulting in efficient distribution system [3].

2 Data Center Topologies and Components

One of the major concerns of data centers is to ensure continuous energy supply to its load and to improve the energy efficiency [7]. As servers in data center runs applications for flow of information and data to and from different parts of the world, continuous supply of power to the server load and supporting infrastructure (cooling and lighting loads) is needed at all times. Nowadays, there are different topologies used in data center's power distribution system. An appropriate power supply option has been chosen based on the reliability and availability of the power distribution topologies and type and size of a data center.

Tier Classifications: Uptime Institute standardized the Tier classification system for data centers as a means to evaluate data center infrastructure in terms of their availability. The Uptime Institute has defined four Tier system topologies for describing the availability as shown in Fig. 1 [7]. These are Tier I, Tier II Tier III and Tier IV. Each tier has a specific function and its appropriate criteria for power, cooling, maintenance, and capability to withstand a fault. Tiers are progressive, meaning each Tier incorporates the requirements of all the lower Tiers.

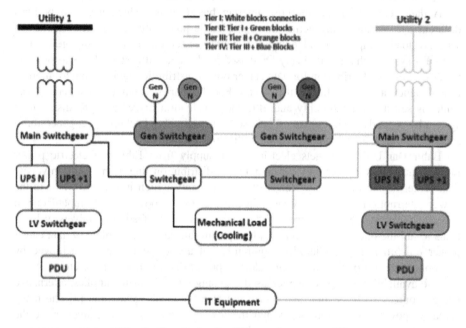

Fig. 1. Topologies for different tier systems [8]

The comparison of different Tier systems is shown in Table 1.

Table 1. Comparison of Tier systems [8]

	Tier I	Tier II	Tier III	Tier IV
Distribution paths	Only one	Only one	1 active and 1 Alternative	2 simultaneously active
Concurrently maintainable	No	No	Yes	Yes
Fault tolerance	No	No	No	Yes
Annual IT downtime	28.8 h	22 h	1.6 h	0.4 h
Site Availability	99.67%	99.75%	99.98%	99.99%

The data center in case of this study is a Tier II standard which has one active supply system with two sources, one from utility and the other is a diesel generator as a backup source. Throughout this study Tier standard listed in Table 1 has been used.

Components of a Typical Data Center: The components of any data center can be broadly categorized into energy source, power distribution path and data center load. These components are described in the next section.

3 Resource Assessment and System Parameter Metrics

The load profile and solar radiation data has been collected. To supply all data center loads using solar energy, all procedures and mathematical equations of solar design/sizing are considered. The electrical power distribution architecture of existing (AC) system and a proposed solar powered DC distribution would be explained. The preference of DC distribution over an AC distribution and the standard selection of DC voltage for distribution system have been described. Finally, the proposed distribution system could be compared with an existing AC power distribution system in terms of efficiency and reliability.

3.1 Data Center Load Profile

As explained above a data center consist both IT load and supporting infrastructures. IT load comprises of server load, switches, and routers and so on. It is a critical or sensitive load of a data center. Other loads such as computer room air-conditioners (CRACs), lighting, and switchgears are known as supporting infrastructure for IT load. Table 2 below shows the load profile data for selected study case area.

Table 2. Data center load profile

Load	Watts	H/day	Number	Watt – Hr
Air Conditioner	3200	24	2	7600
IT load	120	24	70	201600
Un interruptible Power Supply (UPS)	16000	0.0916	2	2931.2
Lighting	18	12	10	2160
Computer (Desktop)	120	8	4	3840
Security System	120	24	1	2880
—	—	—	—	—
Total daily watt and Watt-Hr/day	**45,910 W**			**220,931.2 Wh/day**

Based on Table 2, data center consists of 12 racks for the IT critical loads and each rack contains 10 servers with peak power usage of 120 W on the data nameplate. From the table above, estimated energy capacity at full load, is 220.931.2 Wh/day or 289.4112 KWh/day.

3.2 Solar Resource Assessment of Selected Site

Bahir Dar area gets enough sun for standalone as well as grid-connected photovoltaic systems to operate well. The site location from NASA is shown in Fig. 2. The data center is installed in one sectional room of a large building in the university compound and it is free from shading and also gets sun in all times of a day.

Table 3. Monthly averaged radiation (kWh/m²/day)

Months	Jan	Feb	Mar	Apr	May	Jun	Jul	Aug	Sep	Oct	Nov
KWh/m²/day	6.4	6.7	7.0	6.9	6.6	5.6	4.6	4.8	6.03	6.6	6.4

Fig. 2. Solar resource potential and site map of the case study area

The data center is located at the 11.5742°N latitude and 37.3614°E longitude and has the following Monthly Averaged Radiation (kWh/m²/day) is indicated in Fig. 2. From the above table, the maximum average radiation is 6.14 kWh/m²/day in January and minimum radiation is 4.6 kWh/m²/day at August.

3.3   System Parameter Metrics and Estimation Methods

The system efficiency and reliability analysis is based on the power distribution components. Their power distribution system (AC or DC) determines both efficiency and reliability of data center. This will further discussed by the next sections.

Data Center Efficiency: The efficiency of a system is expressed as the fraction of its input that is converted to the desired useful output. For data centers, the input is electricity and the useful output is power for the IT load.

$$\text{Data center efficiency} = \frac{\text{IT load power}}{\text{Total data center power}} \qquad (1)$$

Data Center Efficiency Metrics: The large portion of energy consumption by data centers is causing a significant impact on the electrical grid and the environment. Hence, there should be metrics to measure data center's effectiveness. Metrics are used to measure and improve the effectiveness of some value, function or parameter. Power Usage Effectiveness (PUE), Water Usage Effectiveness (WUE), Energy Reuse Effectiveness (ERE), Data Center Compute Efficiency (DCCE), and Clean Energy Index are most widely used metrics nowadays to measure data center effectiveness. PUE is the most common metric used in data centers [13].

Power Usage Effectiveness (PUE): When compared to electricity utilized by cooling, lighting, and other extra plant within the data center, PUE reflects how much of this power is actually used by the IT equipment [13]. The ideal value of PUE is 1 and a lower PUE value indicates a more efficient data center. PUE is calculated by:

$$\text{PUE} = \frac{P_{total}}{P_{ITload}} \qquad (2)$$

where, P_{total}, is the total power consumed by the data center and.
$P_{IT\,load,}$ is the power consumed by the IT load.

Data Center Infrastructure Efficiency (DCiE): Data Center Infrastructure Efficiency (DCiE), the inverse of PUE, is a metric used to determine the energy efficiency of a data center. The ideal value of DCiE is 1.[13] DCiE is also expressed as a percentage, is calculated by dividing IT equipment power by total facility power.

$$\text{DCiE} = \frac{1}{\text{PUE}} = \frac{P_{ITload}}{P_{total}} \qquad (3)$$

Data Center Compute Efficiency (DCcE): Server in data centers are designated to perform specific task known as primary services. For example, primary service of an email server is to provide email services when requested [13]. Depending upon the primary service provided by the server, the server compute efficiency can be calculated by:

$$\text{SCE} = \frac{\sum_{i=1}^{n} Pi}{m} \times 100 \qquad (4)$$

where Pi is the number of primary service provided by the server, *n* is total number of sample taken over time. Also, for given data center having *m* servers, DCcEis calculated by averaging the *ScE* values from all servers during the same time period calculated by:

$$DCcE = \frac{\sum_{j=1}^{n} SCEj}{m} \times 100 \tag{5}$$

4   Sizing and Models of Proposed DC-System Components

4.1   Sizing System Components

The first step is to estimate daily electrical demand. Thus, according to Table 2 the daily estimated energy capacity at full load is 220,931.2 Wh/day or 289.4112 KWh/day. For this design, August is the design month that is 4.6 KWh/m^2/day given in Table 3 for 25 years life span. A typical module is selected for design purpose and its specification also shown in Table 4. The performance of PV modules and arrays is generally rated according to the maximum DC power output and current. 300 Wp-*JSSP-24300, e*asily available Module in Ethiopian market, is selected as shown in Table 4 with important specifications.

Table 4. Specification of typical PV- module for design purpose (JSSP-24300) [24]

Specification	Value
Maximum power current (I_{mp})	8.3 A
Maximum power voltage (V_{mp})	36 V
Max. Power (P_{max})	300 W
Short circuit current (I_{sc})	8.9 A
Open circuit voltage (V_{oc})	44 V

The following constants are also taking into consideration for the general design of PV system [15].

- Battery efficiency (%) = (0.8 < × < 0.85) for round trip average efficiency of a new battery. Typical percentages of the losses in a PV system are temperature losses = 0.9 and wiring losses = 0.97
- Combined efficiency = 0.85 * 0.9 * 0.97 = 0.74, Inverter efficiency = 0.9 and Output efficiency, η_{out} = 0.85 * 0.9 = 0.765
- Depth of discharge, DOD = 0.65

For the most efficient and reliable power distribution in modern data centers with standalone PV system case, 380 V is selected as off grid supply of data center loads since 380 V has relatively better performance compared to 120 V, 48 V, 24 V and 12 V DC distribution systems. The procedures summarized in Table 5 are step by step methods for which to design/size PV array, Charge controller, Battery capacity and other necessities to supply the proposed system from standalone solar power system [15].

Table 5. Procedures for sizing the PV system

Step	Expression	Description
PV- array sizing [11]	$P_{pv} = \frac{E_{pv}}{G_{min}} \times 1000 \ w/m^2$	P_{pv} is the total power of PV array in watts E_{pv} is the total energy required from PV array and G_{min} is the minimum solar radiation of a month
PV array (w) = *fill factor* × *PV array* (w)		By considering fill factor (FF) as 0.77
Battery sizing [11]	$E_{bat} = \frac{E_t \times days\ of\ autonomy}{DOD \times \eta_{out}} \ Wh/day$	E_{bat} is battery energy storage capacity DOD is maximum permissible depth of discharge η_{out} is the output efficiency of the battery
Number of batteries required		$N = \frac{C_{bat}}{rating}$
Sizing of charge controller [11]	$I_{controller} = N_{parallel} \times I_{sc} \times 1.3$	I_{sc} - represents the size of solar charge controller $N_{parallel}$ is the number of parallel solar modules
Inverter sizing [11]	$P_{inv} = P_{acload} \times CF$	P_{inv} - the rating of inverter in watt CF - the correction factor for safety $P_{ac\ load}$ represents the total ac electrical load in watt

Accordingly, summary of sizing results are presented in Table 6.

Table 6. A summary for PV system component sizing

Component	Description of component	Result
Load	Total estimated load (kW)	45.9
	Total estimated energy (kWh)	220.93
PV Array	Capacity of PV array (kW)	52.8
Number of modules in series		16
Number of modules in parallels		11
Total number of modules		176
Battery Bank	Battery bank capacity (Ah)	1334.8
Number of batteries in series		16
Number of batteries in parallel		4
Total number of batteries required		72
Inverter	Capacity of the inverter (kW)	9

4.2 System Component Models

Existing (AC) Power Distribution System of a Data Center: Figure 3(a) shows the single line diagram of existing AC power distribution system for Bahirdar University Data Center which has one main source from the utility system (EEU) and a diesel generator as aback up source. One distribution transformer is used in this model. The distribution transformer steps down the 15 kV AC bus voltage to distribution level voltage, 400 V before connecting to the 400 V AC bus of the data center input.

The Proposed 380 V DC Power Distribution System Model: The proposed system contains a designed solar array as a main source of supply and one diesel generator as a backup source. The renewable energy source (in this case solar array) is used to replace the utility source in order to independently supply the data center loads to eliminate power interruptions from the utility system. The data center has a load of 45.9 KW power with DC power distribution architecture with a backup diesel generator and is designed to have 196 solar panels each having 300 W power ratings with 16 strings to be connected to the 380 V DC bus to achieve the required load capacity as shown in Fig. 3(b). It consists of three converters which lead to have relatively good efficiency as compared to AC distribution with five converters.

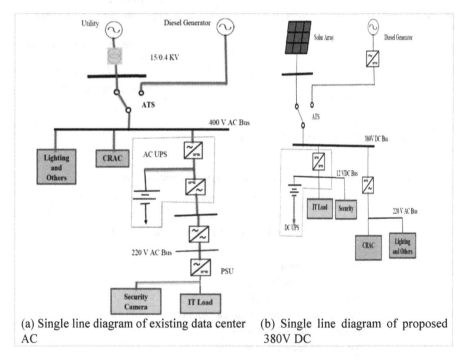

(a) Single line diagram of existing data center AC

(b) Single line diagram of proposed 380V DC

Fig. 3. Single line diagram representations for the existing AC and the proposed DC system

4.3   Main Components Loss and Efficiency Modeling

The data center's efficiency can be determined empirically by summing up the power consumption of all IT equipment and dividing by the total power input of the data center. This method is simple, but gives an overstated efficiency result of data centers. Another approach is to use manufacturer provided efficiency for the data center main components such as UPSs, inverters, rectifiers and PSUs. Manufacturers provide efficiency data for the data center components which underestimate the losses [17].

Components Loss Model:
The accuracy of data center efficiency estimation is determined by the validity of each data center component's efficiency models. As illustrated in Eq. 6, a component's losses can be evaluated as the total of three losses: no-load loss, proportional loss, and square-law loss [17].

$$Component's\ loss = No-load\ loss + Proportional\ loss + Square-law\ loss \quad (6)$$

Now, the component loss can be computed by using Eq. 7.

$$P_{loss} = K_0 + K_1 L_\% + K_2 L_\%^2 \quad (7)$$

where L % is the component load as a percentage of its rated active power, and K0, K1 and K2 are the no-load, proportional loss, and square-law term coefficients, respectively, that are determined through regression analysis of the loss data provided by the manufacturer at multiple load levels, which are 0% (no-load), 25%, 50%, and 75%. (full load). The component losses are computed by subtracting the output power from the input power using Eq. 8.

$$P_{loss} = P_{in} - P_{out} \quad (8)$$

The component loss can also be expressed as the percentage of its rated power and the results in Eq. 9.

$$P_1 = K_{p0} + K_{p1} L_\% + K_{p2} L_\%^2 \quad (9)$$

where,

$$P_1 = \frac{P_{loss}}{P_{rated}} \quad And \quad K_{pz} = \frac{K_z}{P_{rated}}; \quad z = 0,\ 1,\ 2$$

As the values of the per-unit component losses P_1 and the component's per unit load $L_\%$ are known, regression analysis is used to determine the values of the loss term coefficients: K_{p0}, K_{p1} and K_{p2}.

From Eq. 9, as the values of the per-unit component losses P_l and the component's per unit load $L_\%$ are known, regression analysis is used to determine the values of the loss term coefficients: K_{p0}, K_{p1} and K_{p2}. The following tables describe the mathematical model of loss and efficiency of main data center components which is provided by this

Load (p.u.)	0.25	0.50	0.75	1.0
Loss (p.u.)	0.0364	0.0631	0.0946	0.1312

(a) Measured AC UPS loss data (p.u.) at multiple load levels (p.u) [19]

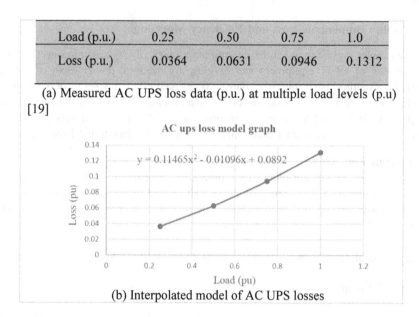

(b) Interpolated model of AC UPS losses

Fig. 4. Measured AC UPS and interpolated model

study. The UPS loss data is considered here for both AC and DC type UPS. Loss data of typical double conversion AC UPS was extracted from [18]. The loss data expressed in per unit value at different loadings are shown in Fig. 4(a). A regression analysis (or

Load (p.u.)	0.25	0.50	0.75	1.0
Loss (p.u.)	0.01767	0.02576	0.04114	0.06157

(a) Measured 380V DC UPS loss data (p.u.) at multiple load levels (p.u.)

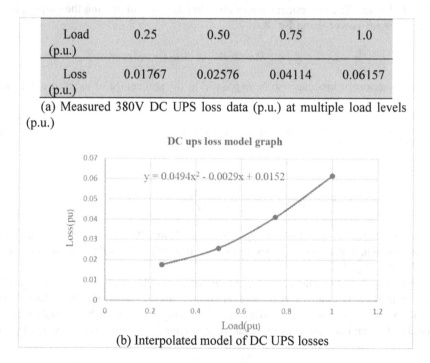

(b) Interpolated model of DC UPS losses

Fig. 5. Measured 380 V DC UPS and interpolated loss model

second order polynomial fit) was done for this loss data and plotted in Fig. 4(b). It can be seen from the figure that the values of K_{p0}, K_{p1} and K_{p2} for AC UPS loss model are respectively 0.0892, −0.01096 and 0.11465.

Similarly, loss data of a DC UPS was extracted from efficiency data in [18]. The loss data expressed as percentage of the rated load at different loadings are shown in Fig. 5(a). A regression analysis (or second order polynomial fit) was again done for this loss data and plotted in Fig. 6. From Fig. 5(b), it can be seen that the values of K_{p0}, K_{p1} and K_{p2} for DC UPS loss model are respectively 0.0152, 0.029 and 0.0494.

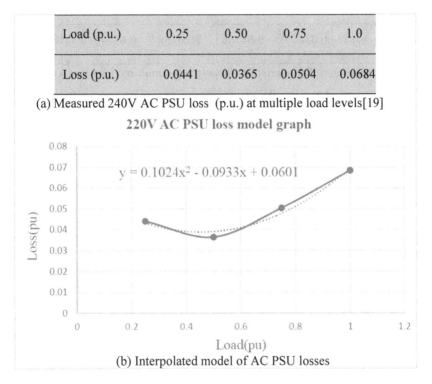

Load (p.u.)	0.25	0.50	0.75	1.0
Loss (p.u.)	0.0441	0.0365	0.0504	0.0684

(a) Measured 240V AC PSU loss (p.u.) at multiple load levels[19]

220V AC PSU loss model graph

$y = 0.1024x^2 - 0.0933x + 0.0601$

(b) Interpolated model of AC PSU losses

Fig. 6. Measured AC PSU and interpolated loss model

Power supply unit: The loss data and their second order polynomial fit of AC power supply unit in the model used in this paper is given in Fig. 6. For AC power supply unit, a measured 240 V loss data was extracted from [18] which is approximated with 220 V supply unit and its polynomial fit is constructed as shown in Fig. 6(a). The interpolated second order polynomial fit of this AC PSU loss is plotted in the following graph.

Load (p.u.)	0.25	0.50	0.75	1.0	1.20
Loss (p.u.)	0.03409	0.04765	0.06788	0.09649	0.12597

(a) Measured PV inverter loss data (p.u.) at multiple load levels (p.u.)

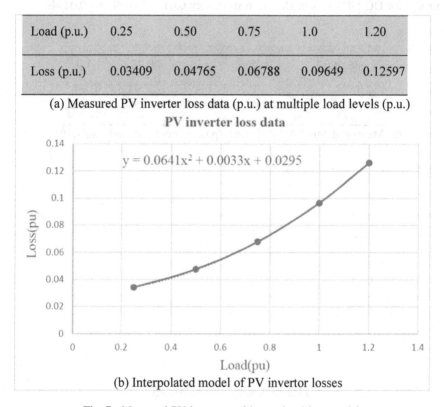

(b) Interpolated model of PV invertor losses

Fig. 7. Measured PV inverter and interpolated loss model

The loss data taken for the inverter is a loss data from a 240 V type inverter which is extracted in [19] approximated with 220 V inverter to determine the component loss coefficients. Based on this data, a regression analysis graph was done as shown in Fig. 7(b).

The loss data of distribution transformer was obtained from [20] and it is shown in Fig. 8(a). A regression analysis (or second order polynomial fit) was again done for this loss data and plotted in Fig. 8(b).

Load	0.10	0.20	0.30	0.40	0.50	0.60	0.70	0.80	0.90	0
Loss	0.002	0.003	0.003	0.004	0.005	0.007	0.008	0.010	0.013	0.015

(a) Measured distribution loss data (p.u.) at multiple load levels (p.u)

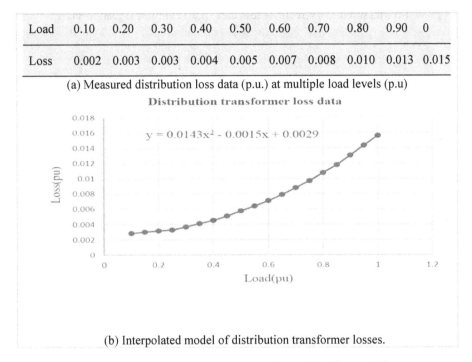

(b) Interpolated model of distribution transformer losses.

Fig. 8. Measured distribution loss and interpolated loss model

The loss data of 380 V DC rectifier is extracted from [21] and it is tabulated in Fig. 9(a).This loss data is based on a measured 400 V DC rectifier and has the following losses which is expressed in per unit value at different loading conditions. Similarly a regression analysis (or second order polynomial fit) was again done for this loss data and plotted in Fig. 9(b).

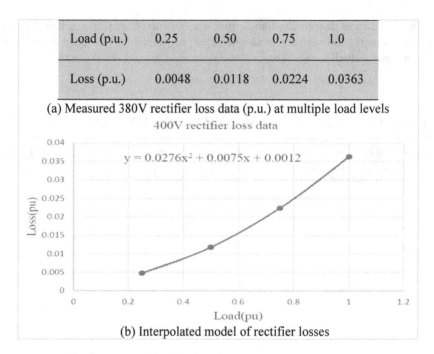

Load (p.u.)	0.25	0.50	0.75	1.0
Loss (p.u.)	0.0048	0.0118	0.0224	0.0363

(a) Measured 380V rectifier loss data (p.u.) at multiple load levels

400V rectifier loss data

$y = 0.0276x^2 + 0.0075x + 0.0012$

(b) Interpolated model of rectifier losses

Fig. 9. Measured rectifier loss data and interpolated loss model

ii) Component Loss Coefficients: Regression analysis (or second order polynomial fit) had been done for all the loss data recorded. The no-load, proportional and square-law term coefficients for the components are listed in Table 7.

Table 7. No-load, proportional and square-law item coefficients

Converter	Loss item coefficients		
	$Kp0$	$Kp1$	$Kp2$
AC UPS	0.0892	−0.01096	0.11465
DC UPS	0.0152	−0.0029	0.0494
AC PSU	0.0601	−0.0933	0.1024
PV Inverter	0.0295	0.0033	0.0641
Distribution transformer	0.0029	−0.0015	0.0143
380 V DC rectifier	0.0012	0.0075	0.0276

5   Results and Discussions

5.1   Efficiency Analysis of Existing Distribution System (Base Case Scenario)

The efficiency analysis results of existing AC distribution systems is done by following the different component loss model described in above sections. The efficiency analysis of the data center for different load conditions was carried out based on multiplying the efficiency of the individual components used by the data center distribution system. By considering the efficiency plot of different equipment's used by the existing system at different load conditions, the total efficiency of the AC system is summarized in Table 8.

Table 8. Efficiency data of different components

Components	Efficiency (%) at multiple load level				
	25%	*50%*	*75%*	*100%*	*Average*
AC UPS	73.10	81.90	84.00	84.10	80.775
DC UPS	93.44	95.04	94.84	94.19	94.38
AC PSU	85.27	92.76	94.02	93.53	91.39
DC rectifier	98.12	97.69	97.11	96.50	97.36
PV Inverter	87.93	88.96	91.68	91.17	89.94
Distribution Transformer	98.44	98.87	98.75	98.45	98.63

Figure 10 shows the result of efficiency plot for the data center power distribution system (existing AC distribution system and the proposed DC system). The result demonstrated that the minimum efficiency is 61.4% at 25% load and maximum efficiency is 77.97% at 75% load condition. The average efficiency becomes 72.96%.

5.2 Efficiency Analysis of DC Distribution System (Proposed Case Scenario)

As a result the total efficiency of proposed DC power distribution system is based on the individual component efficiency. The following table is constructed to get the data points for total efficiency of the proposed system.

Figure 10 shows the result of efficiency plot for the data center power distribution system (proposed DC distribution system). The result indicated that the minimum efficiency is 80.6% at 25% load and maximum efficiency is 84.44% at 75% load condition. The average efficiency becomes 82.63%. Figure 10 compares the efficiency of AC and DC power distribution designs for various loading scenarios. In data centers, 380 V DC power distribution system is more efficient than a normal AC power distribution system.

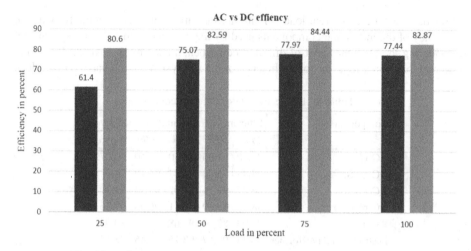

Fig. 10. Efficiency plot of AC and proposed DC distribution system.

Taking the average efficiency of both cases, a DC power distribution system is more efficient than AC power distribution architecture by 9.67%.

5.3 Energy Cost Analysis

The assessed Life Cycle Cost (LCC) of the arranged independent PV framework is portrayed in this segment. The lifetime cost of proprietorship and activity of an article, expressed in the present cash trade, is the LCC of that thing. Procurement, working, upkeep, and substitution costs are completely remembered for the expense of an independent PV framework.

The total present worth (PWs) of the costs of PV modules, storage batteries, battery charger, and inverter, the cost of installation, and the system's maintenance and operation cost (M&O) are all included in the LCC of the PV system. All of the products' lifetimes are estimated to be 25 years, except for the battery, which is estimated to be 5 years. Thus, an extra 2 groups of batteries (each of 2 batteries) to be purchased, after 5 years, 10 years, 15 years and 20 years, assuming inflation rate i of 3% and a discount or interest rate d of 10%.

Therefore, the LCC of the system can be calculated as the following equation.

$$LCC = C_{PV} + C_B + C_{B1PW} + C_{B2PW} + C_{B3PW} + C_{B4PW} + C_C + C_{Inv} + C_{Ins} + C_{MPW}.$$
(10)

And

$$C_{MPW} = \left(\frac{M}{yr}\right) x \left(\frac{1+i}{1+d}\right) x \left(\frac{1 - \left(\frac{1+i}{1+d}\right)^N}{1 - \left(\frac{1+i}{1+d}\right)}\right)$$
(11)

where,

C$_{PV}$ - PV array cost
CB - Initial cost of batteries
CB1PW - Group of battery to be purchased after N years
CC-Charge controller cost
CInv - Inverter cost
CInst - Installation cost
C$_{MPW}$ - maintenance cost

It is sometimes useful to calculate the LCC of a system on an annual basis. The annualized LCC (ALCC) of the PV system in terms of the present day dollars can be calculated using the following equation.

$$ALCC = LCC \times \left(\frac{1 - \left(\frac{1+i}{1+d}\right)}{1 - \left(\frac{1+i}{1+d}\right)^N} \right) \tag{12}$$

Hence,

Once the ALCC is known, the unit electrical cost (cost of 1 kWh) can be calculated, to be $0.238/kWh, from Eq. (13).

$$Unit\ Electrical\ Cost = \frac{ALCC}{365E_L} \tag{13}$$

It is to be noted that this price is very high compared to the current unit cost of electricity in Ethiopia for 15 kV customer is 0.8008 Birr/kWh or **$0.0235/kWh**. PV energy generation for data center is important due to its better efficiency and reliability to the power distribution system. This price is also free from interruption and fuel cost.

6 Conclusions

In this study the improvement method of data center's efficiency and reliability has been presented. A 380 V solar powered DC power distribution architecture has been proposed to obtain improved efficiency and better reliability in data center power distribution system. The design of solar power for overall data center loads has also been included. The efficiency analysis shows that solar powered DC distribution system is more efficient than the typical AC distribution system at different load levels. Results show that 380 V solar powered DC distribution has an average of 9.67% efficient than AC power distribution architecture of a selected data center for different loading level typically 25%, 50%, 75% and at full load (100%). This improvement is due to the reduction of number of convertors and high component efficiency of the proposed DC distribution system for a selected data center.

References

1. Prabhala, V., et al.: An overview of direct current distribution system architectures & benefits (2018)
2. HiroyaYajima, T.B., et al.: Energy-saving and efficient use of renewable energy by introducing a 380 vdc power-supply system in data centers. IEEE (2015)
3. Deng, C.S.N., Li, J.: Concentrating renewable energy in grid-tied datacenters. In: International Symposium on Sustainable Systems and Technology(ISSST). IEEE (2011)
4. Levente, S.B., et al.: Sustainable data centers powered by renewable energy. IEEE (2012)
5. Jones, K.M.: AC versus DC Power Distribution in the Data Center (2013)
6. Robert, A.F.P., et al.: Reliability of example data center designs selected by tier classification. IEEE (2010)
7. Rytoft, C.: Data centers and critical technologies. ABB Review (2013)
8. Santosh, A.G., et al.: Data center energy systems: current technology and future direction. IEEE (2015)
9. Ailee, G., Tschudi, W.: 380 Vdc brings reliability and efficiency to sustainable data centers. IEEE Power Energy Mag. **10**, 50–59 (2012)
10. Ebtesam, L.M.K., et al.: Information technology and stand-alone solar systems in tertiary institutions. ScienceDirect (2013)
11. Gont*, S.D.: Design of a standalone photovoltaic system for a typical household around Dessie City Ethiopia. Am. J. Electric. Electron. Eng. **7**, 1–7 (2019)
12. Ali Najah, S.M., et al.: Design & sizing of stand-alone solar power systems a house Iraq (2015)
13. Brotherton, P.H.: Datacenter Efficiency Measures," Heather Brotherton Purdue University: College of Technology, West Lafayette, USA (2015)
14. Shrestha, R.: Reliability analysis of 380 V DC distribution in data centers. IEEE (2016)
15. Patterson, D.A., et al.: Solar PV standardised training manual developed by, SNV for the Rural Solar Market Development (2012)
16. Parimita, K.R.S., et al.: PV system design for off-grid applications. ResearchGate (2015)
17. Shrestha, B.R., Tamrakar, U.: Efficiency and reliability analyses of AC distribution in data centers. IEEE (2018)
18. Rasmussen, N., Spitaels, J.: A quantitative com parison of high efficiency AC vs. DC power distribution for data centers. White Paper 127 (2013)
19. Driesse, P.J.A.: Beyond the curves: modeling the electrical efficiency of photovoltaic inverters. IEEE (2015)
20. Bush, J.W., et al.: Transformer efficiency assessment, Okinawa, Japan (2012)
21. Hamidi, S.A., Nasiri, A., Tiefu, Z.: Rectifier efficiency analysis for DC distributed data centers. In: 3rd International Conference on Renewable Energy Research and Applications (2014)
22. Boxwell, M.: Solar Electricity Handbook. Green stream Publishing, United Kingdom Ltd. (2017)
23. Richardson, L.: Solar panel costs. https://news.energysage.com/how-much-does-the-average-solar-panel-installation-cost-in-the-u-s/, Accessed 20 May 2020
24. Richardson, L.: Storage battery systems pricing. https://www.energysage.com/solar/solar-energy-storage/what-do-solar-batteries-cost/, Accessed 20 May 2020

Design of Genetic Algorithm Based Robust LQG Controller for Active Magnetic Bearing System

Enderias Alemayehu Workeye[1(✉)], Tamiru Getahun G/Meskel[1], and Yakob Kiros T/Himanot[2]

[1] Adama Science and Technology University, Adama, Ethiopia
[2] Ethiopian Institute of Technology-Mekelle, Mekelle University, Mekelle, Ethiopia

Abstract. The Active Magnetic Bearing system (AMB) is a mechatronic device which is used to suspend rotating parts of a machine so that they rotate without contact to the stationary part of the machine. AMBs are highly non-linear, non-minimum phase and inherently unstable. This paper has aimed to obtain a robust optimal state-feedback control system for the stabilization of the AMB System, with the help of Genetic algorithm (GA) as an optimization tool which will solve the tedious manual tuning of the weighting matrices in the design of linear quadratic regulator (LQR) and linear quadratic Gaussian (LQG).

The system's mathematical model has been developed and also the properties of the uncontrolled system have been analyzed. Since AMB is a MIMO system, the interaction of the inputs with the outputs has been analyzed using relative gain array analysis and frequency domain analysis of the system transfer functions. Then, the optimal state feedback controllers have been developed. Here, LQR and LQG controllers are developed.

Finally, Comparative analysis between the controllers and between the design methods was carried out. The proposed GA based design methodology has resulted good Performance. In addition, the GA based design has also resulted improvements in robustness of the control systems. As far as gain margin (GM) and phase margin (PM) are concerned GA has resulted increase of $8.0*10^{-4}$ db and $6.02*10^{-3}$° in GM and PM respectively for LQR. Whereas, in LQG GA has resulted an increase of $3.8*10^{-5}$ db and $2.54*10^{-4}$°.

Keywords: Active magnetic bearing · Genetic algorithm · Linear quadratic Gaussian · Kalman filter

1 Introduction

Bearings are machine elements of a mechanism. They constrain the relative motion of a certain mechanical structure only to the desired motion, and reduce friction between moving and stationary parts.

There are many types of bearings which differ based on their operation, the motions allowed, or the directions of the loads (forces) applied to the parts. Despite the diverse types, Ball bearings are the oldest and most common types [1]. Ball bearings use balls

M. L. Berihun (Ed.): ICAST 2021, LNICST 411, pp. 215–236, 2022.
https://doi.org/10.1007/978-3-030-93709-6_15

to maintain separation between the bearing races. Mostly they have two races to contain the balls and transfer the load forces through the balls.

Most electrical machines and wheels use ball bearings. In such applications, one race is stationary and the other is attached to the rotating machine part (e.g., a rotor or shaft). As one of the bearing races rotates it causes the balls to rotate as well, as a result the coefficient of friction will be reduced compared to two flat surfaces sliding against each other.

In Magnetic Bearings (MBs), the balls between the two races are replaced by a magnetic field. One of the two races will be suspended/levitated by a magnetic force. Such mechanisms provide all the functions of the ball bearings and since there is no physical contact, the friction will be almost zero. The magnetic field used to maintain the separation between the two races can be supplied either by permanent magnets or electromagnets.

Implementing magnetic bearings using permanent magnets requires intense design effort, the highest quality (almost ideal) of materials and gives no possibility to actively control the system in order to dump disturbances [3]. Due to this most magnetic bearings are powered by electromagnets.

Active magnetic bearings (AMBs) are mechatronic systems that support a rotating shaft with a magnetic field generated by electromagnets controlled in feedback. The rotor is levitated in an air gap. As shown in Fig. 1, using the feedback loop the performance is actively controlled. In the name of the AMBs the term active represents the continuous and active control action required in order to make the system functional and the use of electric power to energize the levitation.

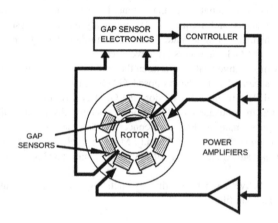

Fig. 1. The AMB control system [3].

2 Active Magnetic Bearings

AMBs are applied for enhancing the speed and efficiency of electrical machines. Therefore, they are used to suspend the rotor at a fixed air gap from the stator so that it rotates without any contact.

The AMB system considered in this paper has four electromagnetic actuators, as shown in Fig. 1, on both ends of the rotor. In reference to the horizontal axis the current in the upper half electromagnetic actuators produce a magnetic force which counteracts the force of gravity and enables the ferromagnetic rotor shaft to levitate. Whereas current in the lower half electromagnetic actuators produce a magnetic force which acts along with gravity to make sure the magnetic force by the upper actuators does not cause unnecessary upward displacement [2].

T. Schuhmann, et al. (2012), has proposed "Improving Operational Performance of Active Magnetic Bearings Using Kalman Filter and State Feedback Control," [6]. In this paper, the application of optimal state estimation using extended Kalman filter and optimal state feedback algorithms (LQG) for real-time active magnetic bearing control is considered. It is shown that this controller yields improved rotor positioning accuracy, better system dynamics, higher bearing stiffness, and reduced control energy effort compared to the conventionally used proportional-integral-derivative (PID) control approaches. In addition, a method for compensating unbalance caused by forces and vibrations of the magnetically levitated rotor is presented which is based on the estimation of unknown disturbance forces. In this paper a methodology on how to tackle the optimization problem along with noise compensation has been presented; however, the robustness of the controller designed has not been addressed and the design approach of the LQG was based on the trial and error tuning of the weighting matrices.

İ. Sina Kuseyri, in his paper titled "Robust control and unbalance compensation of rotor/active magnetic bearing systems", [7] has designed, analyzed and compared the performance of various stabilizing robust controllers for the model of a horizontal rotor with active magnetic bearings. Two H∞ controllers are designed for the nominal system using different structures. The uncertainties in the system dynamics due to changes in the model parameters are two-fold: gyroscopic forces due to different rotor speeds within the range of operation, and the changing spring stiffness of the electromagnetic bearings due to different conditions during the operation. To ensure robust stability of the closed-loop system for all possible values of parameters that can change during the operation, an H∞ controller based on the model incorporating uncertainty in the system is designed. The limits for the allowable parameter changes for robust stability are tested and established with μ-analysis. The paper is highly focused on the stability and robustness of the system; however, it has not proposed about optimization of the control effort of the controller designed.

A paper titled "Active Magnetic Bearing Online Levitation Recovery through μ-Synthesis Robust Control" [8] by Alexander H. Pesch, et al. (2017), has presented in the event of momentary loss of levitation in Active magnetic bearings due to an acute exogenous disturbance or external fault, reestablishing levitation may be prevented by unbalance forces, contact forces, and the rotor's dynamics. A novel robust control strategy is proposed for ensuring levitation recovery. The proposed strategy utilizes model-based μ-synthesis to find the requisite AMB control law with unique provisions to account for the contact forces and to prevent control effort saturation at the large deflections that occur during levitation failure. The proposed strategy is demonstrated experimentally with an AMB test rig and the proposed control strategy shows a marked improvement in re-levitation transients. However, the μ-synthesized controllers are high order [9]. For industrial implementation, further reduction of the weighted plant model or the synthesized controller may be required; therefore, practical implementation is not going to be feasible.

In this paper, Genetic Algorithm (GA) based Robust Linear Quadratic Gaussian (LQG) Controller that has good performance and robustness with minimum possible control effort for an Active Magnetic Bearing (AMB) system is designed, thus the AMB will levitate and maintain central position for the rotor despite the plant disturbance and measurement noises.

3 Problem Formulation

Active magnetic bearings have a significant advantage in increasing the efficiency of different machines. They practically avoid the loss due to frictional force, but the systems are highly nonlinear, non-minimum phase, and unstable system [2].

In the case of high speed rotating machines the rotor must be regulated in the desired position for smooth operation. Beside the nonlinearity and un-stability, the model uncertainty and neglecting of some higher frequency dynamics due to simplification for computation may make the system unrealistic when implemented in real system, therefore robustness is another problem.

It is possible to overcome the above mentioned properties of the AMB with the design of controller with a very high control effort in order to guarantee robustness. But still, the control effort should be as minimum as possible. Therefore, here optimization comes in to the picture. Furthermore, the controller designed should be realizable and lower order. Since, higher order control systems are quite difficult and costly to implement.

The control of AMB systems mostly has not tried to solve the Robustness and optimization problems fully at once. Therefore, this will not give the full picture on the performance and appropriateness the controller for the AMB system.

In addition, in the design of optimal state feedback controllers like LQR and LQG, the selection of the values of the weighting matrices Q and R is done by trial and error. This is done by setting them on some value and observing the performance of the closed loop step response. Such methodology is tedious and time consuming.

Therefore, observer based state feedback controllers (LQGs) are designed to stabilize the system with optimal control effort. In the design of the LQG the selection of the weighting matrices has been under taken by using the genetic algorithm (GA). In addition, the robustness of the control systems will be analyzed.

4 Mathematical Model of Amb

The active magnetic bearing system has (AMB) has three main system components.

The power amplifier, electro-magnetic actuator and the rotor as illustrated in Fig. 2 below.

The block diagram of AMB control system. The plant consists of power amplifier, AMB actuator and the rotor mass system. Vectors r, u, i, f and y represent the reference input, plant input (control current), coil current, magnetic force, and plant output (rotor displacement), respectively. In addition, the additive measurement noise is represented by v.

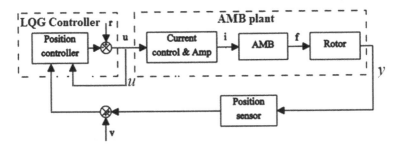

Fig. 2. The Block diagram of the AMB control system

4.1   Modeling of the AMB Actuator

The electromagnetic actuators in Active Magnetic Bearings accept current signal from the power amplifiers and then the flow of current via the coils generates a magnetic force. The AMBs considered in this paper are two sided bearings. In two sided bearings the upper bearings are used to overcome the weight of the rotor due to gravity and suspend it. The fixed current required by the upper bearing to overcome the weight of the rotor due to gravity is determined by the non-linear equation of electromagnetic force given below.

$$f = \frac{k * i^2}{2x^2} \tag{1}$$

After the linearization of (1) at the equilibrium points (the biasing current 'i_0' and the nominal air gap 'x_0') the linear force equation is given by the following relation.

$$f = K_s x_x + K_i i_x \tag{2}$$

Where K_s and K_i are given by:

$$K_s = \frac{k * i_0^2}{2 * x_0^3} \quad and \quad K_i = \frac{k * i_0}{2 * x_0^2}$$

4.2   Modeling the Power Amplifiers

The amplifier model accepts the voltage signal from the controller and outputs the current signal to the actuator coil. It does so by employing a closed loop control of its own. The current control is usually a pure proportional control. Under the assumption that the coil resistance R_C is small and the inductance L is constant, the following transfer function in (3) is obtained [5].

$$G_a(s) = \frac{Kp}{sL + (Kp + Rc)} = \frac{Kp}{sL + Kp} \tag{3}$$

Where, KP is the proportional gain of the amplifier. KP is highly dependent on the band-width of the amplifier denoted by ω_{bw}.

$$Ga(s) = \frac{(\omega_{bw})}{(s + \omega_{bw})} \qquad (4)$$

Where,

$$\omega_{bw} = \frac{Kp}{L} \qquad (5)$$

In order to determine the bandwidth of the power amplifier,

$$\omega_{bw} = \frac{Cos(\alpha) * P_{max}}{X_0 * F_{max}} \qquad (6)$$

Where, α is the angle between consecutive poles of the electromagnetic actuators and P_{max} and F_{max} are the maximum power by the amplifier and the maximum force required by the actuator respectively.

$$F_{max} = K_i * i_{max} + K_s * X_{max} \qquad (7)$$

$$i_{max} = 2 * i_0 \ and \ X_{max} = 2 * X_0 \qquad (8)$$

Using the state space representation, the model of the amplifier will be:

$$\frac{d}{dt}\begin{vmatrix} i_A \\ i_B \end{vmatrix} = \begin{vmatrix} -\omega_{bw} & 0 \\ 0 & -\omega_{bw} \end{vmatrix}\begin{vmatrix} i_A \\ i_B \end{vmatrix} + \begin{vmatrix} \omega_{bw} & 0 \\ 0 & \omega_{bw} \end{vmatrix}\begin{vmatrix} u_A \\ u_B \end{vmatrix} \qquad (9)$$

4.3 Modeling the Rigid Rotor

The rotor mass system is supported with two radial AMBs. As shown in Fig. 3 the axial support is not considered here. This is justified by the negligible coupling of the axial and radial dynamics.

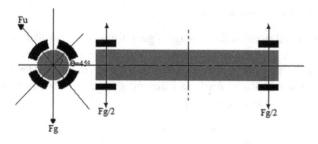

Fig. 3. Sectional view for the rotor mass-bearing system

Moreover, this analysis is restricted to rigid rotors at stand still. Such approach is taken to avoid the coupling that occurs between radial motions in the two perpendicular planes. As a result, it is possible to analyze the motion in one plane.

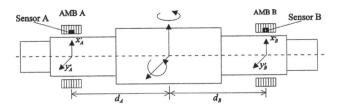

Fig. 4. Cross-sectional view of the AMB-rotor assembly [2].

The radial motion in one plane can be completely described by a rigid beam model, i.e. by the displacement X of the rotor and the rotation of the rotor about an axis through the center of gravity as shown in Fig. 4.

The forces and displacement that put effect on the rotor are resolved along the X and Y planes. Bearings A and B are separated from the center of gravity of the rotor by d_A and d_B respectively.

The mathematical model of the rotor mass system is done by integrating it with the electromagnetic actuator model. Therefore, the force balance equation of the actuator-rotor system is given as:

$$M * \ddot{X} = f \tag{10}$$

$$M * \ddot{X} = K_s x + K_i i$$
$$\ddot{X} = M^{-1} K_s x + M^{-1} K_i i \tag{11}$$

Where, M is the mass matrix of the rotor given as:

$$M = \begin{vmatrix} m_1 & m_3 \\ m_3 & m_2 \end{vmatrix} \tag{12}$$

And m_1, m_2 and m_3 are given by;

$$m_1 = \frac{M * d_B^2 + I_r}{(d_A + d_B)^2} \tag{13}$$

$$m_2 = \frac{M * d_A^2 + I_r}{(d_A + d_B)^2} \tag{14}$$

$$m_3 = \frac{M * d_A * d_B - I_r}{(d_A + d_B)^2} \tag{15}$$

Ir represents the radial moment of inertia of the rotor. In this paper, the center of gravity of the rotor is assumed to be at the center of the axial length of the rotor. As a result, 'd_A' and d_B' will have equal length.

The Non-linear model is based on the non-linear force equation given in (1).

$$\begin{vmatrix} \ddot{X}_A \\ \ddot{X}_B \end{vmatrix} = \begin{vmatrix} f(X_A, i_A) \\ f(X_B, i_B) \end{vmatrix} * M^{-1} \tag{16}$$

From Eq. (1) we can write $f(X_A, i_A)$ and $f(X_B, i_B)$ as follows:

$$f(X_A, i_A) = k\frac{i_A^2}{X_A^2} \tag{17}$$

$$f(X_B, i_B) = k\frac{i_B^2}{X_B^2} \tag{18}$$

Then Eq. (16) becomes (Table 1);

$$\ddot{X}_A = \left(\frac{m_2}{m_1 * m_2 - m_3^2}\right) * k\frac{i_A^2}{X_A^2} - \left(\frac{m_3}{m_1 * m_2 - m_3^2}\right) * k\frac{i_B^2}{X_B^2}$$

$$\ddot{X}_B = \left(\frac{-m_3}{m_1 * m_2 - m_3^2}\right) * k\frac{i_A^2}{X_A^2} + \left(\frac{m_1}{m_1 * m_2 - m_3^2}\right) * k\frac{i_B^2}{X_B^2}$$

Table 1. AMB parameter values

No	Parameter	Symbol	Value [Unit]
1	Mass of Rotor	M	$1.39*10^1$ [Kg]
2	Moment of inertia	I_x	$1.34*10^{-2}$ [Kg.m^2]
3	Rotor length	L	$2.6*10^{-1}$ [m]
4	Permeability of free space	μ_0	$4\pi*10^{-7}$ [H/m]
5	Number of coil	n_c	269 [turns]
6	Area of coil	A_c	$5.7375*10^{-4}$ [m^2]
7	Steady air gap	x_0	$3*10^{-3}$ [m]
8	Biasing current	i_0	3 [A]
9	Number of poles	p	8 [number]
10	Power Amplifier BW	ω_{bw}	300 [Hz]

Finally, the overall model of the AMB system is obtained by combining all state equations of the sub-systems. Therefore, using the state space representations obtained on (9) and (16) we obtain the overall system state space representation.

$$
\frac{d}{dt}
\begin{vmatrix} i_A \\ i_B \\ X_A \\ X_B \\ \dot{X}_A \\ \dot{X}_B \end{vmatrix}
=
\begin{vmatrix}
-300 & 0 & 0 & 0 & 0 & 0 \\
0 & -300 & 0 & 0 & 0 & 0 \\
0 & 0 & 0 & 0 & 1 & 0 \\
0 & 0 & 0 & 0 & 0 & 1 \\
10.7206 & -9.5648 & 10.7206 & -9.5648 & 0 & 0 \\
-9.5648 & 10.7206 & -9.5648 & 10.7206 & 0 & 0
\end{vmatrix}
\begin{vmatrix} i_A \\ i_B \\ X_A \\ X_B \\ \dot{X}_A \\ \dot{X}_B \end{vmatrix}
+
\begin{vmatrix}
300 & 0 \\
0 & 300 \\
0 & 0 \\
0 & 0 \\
0 & 0 \\
0 & 0
\end{vmatrix}
\begin{vmatrix} u_A \\ u_B \end{vmatrix}
$$

$$
Y =
\begin{vmatrix}
0 & 0 & 1 & 0 & 0 & 0 \\
0 & 0 & 0 & 1 & 0 & 0
\end{vmatrix}
\begin{vmatrix} i_A \\ i_B \\ X_A \\ X_B \\ \dot{X}_A \\ \dot{X}_B \end{vmatrix}
+
\begin{vmatrix}
0 & 0 \\
0 & 0
\end{vmatrix}
\begin{vmatrix} u_A \\ u_B \end{vmatrix}
$$

The Active magnetic bearing represented by the above state-space model has right hand side poles and zeroes which will make the system to be unstable and non-minimum phase.

5 Interaction and Coupling

One of the most challenging aspects of MIMO systems control is the interaction between different inputs and outputs. In the AMB control system the control action on bearing A not only affects the position of the rotor at bearing A but, it will also have effect on the position of the rotor at bearing B and the vice-versa.

A certain MIMO system is totally decoupled when the non-diagonal elements of the square transfer matrix functions are zero. In other words, if the transfer matrix is a diagonal matrix the system is said to be decoupled [14].

The RGA will show the measure of process interaction and gives indication of control loop pairings [14].

$$
\Lambda(G) = G(0) .* G^{-T}(0) \tag{19}
$$

For the AMB system with transfer matrix the RGA is calculated as:

$$
\Lambda(G) =
\begin{bmatrix} \lambda_{11} & \lambda_{12} \\ \lambda_{21} & \lambda_{22} \end{bmatrix}
=
\begin{bmatrix} \lambda_{11} & 1 - \lambda_{11} \\ 1 - \lambda_{11} & \lambda_{11} \end{bmatrix} \tag{20}
$$

Therefore, the relative gain array (RGA) will be:

$$
\Lambda(G) =
\begin{bmatrix} 1 & 0 \\ 0 & 1 \end{bmatrix} \tag{21}
$$

From the RGA result obtained above $\lambda_{11} = \lambda_{22} = 1$ indicates that coupled inter-action does not affect the pairing of U1 with Y1 and U2 with Y2. Therefore, it is a clear that we should select the two loops since we can sufficiently manipulate the outputs Y1 and Y2 using the input control signals U1 and U2 respectively.

6 Controller Design

The controllers designed for AMBs supply the electro-magnetic actuators the appro-priate control signal to maintain the rotor at the desired central position.

6.1 LQR Design

Linear quadratic regulators as the name indicates, they are linear state feedback con-trollers. The LQR is the extension of pole placement technique that tends to find the control input u(t) so as to place the poles of the system at a desired optimal position. This is done by minimizing a quadratic cost function J given below.

$$J = \frac{1}{2} \int_{to}^{tf} [x^T(t)Q(t)x(t) + u^T(t)R(t)u(t)]dt \tag{22}$$

And the control input u(t) is given as:

$$u(t) = r - K * x(t) \tag{23}$$

The cost function is the time integral of the sum of the transient energy and control energy. The LQR should minimize this cost function while obtaining the state feedback gains K that drives the system to the desired operating point.

$$K = R^{-1}B^T P \tag{24}$$

The optimal state feedback control gain matrix K of LQR can be found by solving the following arithmetic Riccati equation.

$$A^T P + PA + Q - PBR^{-1}B^T P = 0 \tag{25}$$

Where, P is the solution of the Arithmetic Riccati equation.

The selection of the weighting matrices Q and R for the LQR design is done by; first keeping the R matrix constant (R = diag([1, 1])) and checking for different Q values.

Q matrix values are going to be selected based on the performance of the LQR. Therefore, Q values are kept constant at 0.01 and LQR is designed for different R matrix values.

It can be observed that the rise time, settling time, steady state error and peak responses are improved as magnitude of the values of R matrix increases. Thus, it can be observed that the best result out of the four cases is obtained at $R_i = 10$.

This method is burdensome, time consuming and difficult to know whether it results in optimum performance or not. In order to address this problem, here it has been proposed genetic algorithm (GA) based optimization for selecting the weight matrices of LQR based on the time domain specifications of the system to be controlled.

Genetic algorithm (GA) is an intelligent optimization technique developed by John Holland. It is based on the principles of natural selection and genetic modification. The evolutionary theory attributes the process of the natural evolution of populations to Darwin's principle of natural selection, "survival of the fittest," and Mendel's genetics law of transfer of the hereditary factors from parents to descendants [10].

Compared with the traditional (enumeration, heuristic, etc.) genetic algorithm, optimization method has very good convergence. It has the advantages of less computing time, higher robustness in the calculating accuracy. So this paper uses constrained genetic algorithm, to search the optimal value of Q and R. The weighting matrices are generally used in the form of a diagonal matrix. For the Active magnetic bearing system, the parameters Q and R are optimized by using the following representation.

$$Q = diag(q_1, q_2, q_3, q_4, q_5, q_6) \quad and \quad R = diag(q_7, q_8)$$

The need for using constrained GA is that sometimes the work of basic genetic algorithm cannot solve the problem of large amount of calculation very well, the optimization result could produce results away from the actual or desired result.

The step in genetic algorithm optimization begins by creating a random initial population. The algorithm then creates a new generation or population using the individuals of the current population. To create new generation, the algorithm performs crossover and mutation in between the individuals of the current generation. Then the current generation is replaced by the children of the next generation. The children of the next generation are chosen on the basis of their best fitness value. The algorithm stops when one of the stopping criteria is met.

Genetic algorithm can be implemented in different ways. One can implement the algorithm by coding it in any desirable programming language. In the case of this paper, the MATLAB™ optimization toolbox has been used to implement the algorithm.

To implement the GA optimization, first the fitness function must be defined. The fitness function is the objective function that needs to be minimized. In this case the objective function contains the cost function J defined in (21) and also contains a function that represents the ISE (integral square of error) of the response of the system to a unit step input. Beside the fitness function the number of variables to be optimized should also be specified. The variables to be optimized are the diagonal elements of the Q and R matrices (Fig. 5).

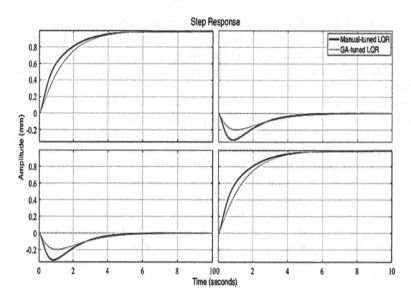

Fig. 5. Unit step response of GA-tuned LQR vs. Manually-tuned LQR

For the highly interacting input-output pairs, it can be observed that the performance of GA-tuned LQR is slightly degraded. The manually tuned LQR has a better response. The rise time and settling time of the GA-tuned LQR have shown slight increase compared to the manually-tuned LQR even though the result obtained satisfies the control objective.

Whereas, for the loosely interacting I/O pairs the GA-tuned LQR has managed to reduce the undershoot caused by input 1 on output 2 and input 2 on output 1 by 64.54%. This shows that the GA-tuned has reduced the unwanted effect of the inputs on the outputs in a significant manner.

Generally Linear Quadratic Regulators are designed for systems having a perfectly known model and also if all states of the system are available for measurement. In the case of Active magnetic bearings, the model of the system has its own level of uncertainty. This is due to the rejected model components during the linearization process. In addition, employing measurement techniques and devices to extract measurement of each and every state makes the control system quite expensive. Thus, this problem can be addressed by another controller design approach known as the Linear Quadratic Gaussian (LQG) Regulator.

6.2   LQG Design

Linear quadratic Gaussian regulators are optimal observer (Kalman Filter) based optimal state feedback controllers (LQR). In the design of LQG, based on the separation principle; the state estimator and state feedback controller are designed independently.

In LQG the Kalman filter estimates the states of the system by taking the control signal and the output of the system. The estimation of the states is undertaken in the presence of both process disturbance (d) and measurement noises (n). The stochastic noises i.e. the disturbance and measurement noises are modeled as white Gaussian noise.

For this controller design problem, the state-space model of the system has the following form (Fig. 6).

$$\frac{d}{dt}X = A*X + B*U + V_d*d \tag{26}$$

$$Y = C*X + D*U + V_n*n \tag{27}$$

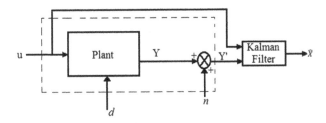

Fig. 6. State estimation using Kalman filter.

The kalman filter takes the control signal u and the plant output Y and gives out the estimate of the plant states. In Fig. 7 there are two parts, the augmented system with disturbance and noise, indicated by the dashed area and the Kalman filter.

Once the gains (L) of the Kalman filter are obtained, The KF will have the following state-space representation.

$$\frac{d}{dt}\hat{X} = (A - L*C)\hat{X} + [BL]U \tag{28}$$

$$Y' = eye(6)\hat{X} + 0*[BL]U \tag{29}$$

The inputs of the Kalman filter are the control signals u and the plant outputs **y**.

$$U = [uy]^T$$

In order to inject the disturbances in to each state the augmented plant model can be developed as follows:

$$\frac{d}{dt}X = AX + [Bf]U \tag{30}$$

$$Y = eye(6)X + DU \tag{31}$$

Where, $[Bf]$ is an augment inputs to include disturbance and noise along with the plant input.

$$[Bf] = [BV_d 0 * B]$$

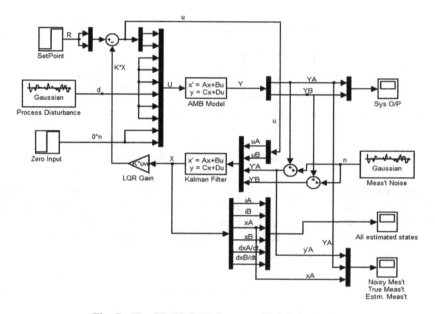

Fig. 7. The SIMULINK diagram of LQG for AMB

The performance of the Kalman filter designed has been evaluated in both noisy and less noisy conditions. The noisy condition the disturbance signal has a variance of 0.1. When the system is subjected to such process disturbances and measurement noises the Kalman filter was able to extract the output measurement out of the noise (Figs. 8 and 9).

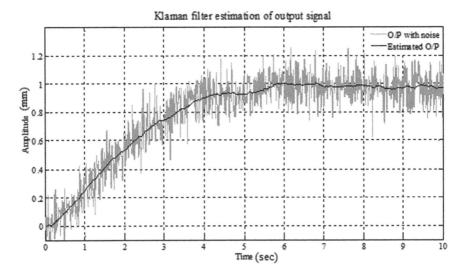

Fig. 8. Kalman filter estimation of the output signal out of the noisy measurement signal

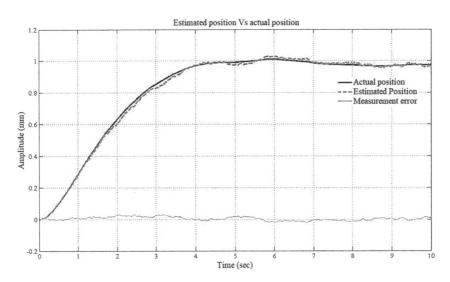

Fig. 9. Estimated state vs Actual state and estimation error in noisy condition

The performance of the LQG depends on how well the states are being estimated and on the performance of the LQR. The performance of the Kalman filter has already been established, and also in the LQR design the GA-based LQR was selected (Fig. 10).

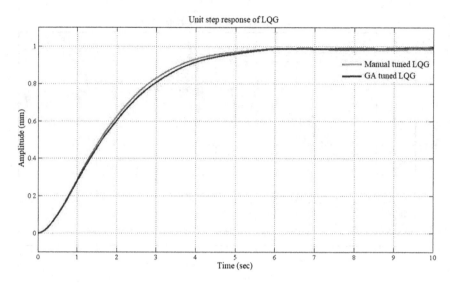

Fig. 10. Unit step response of GA-tuned LQG and manually tuned LQG

The GA-tuned LQG takes an advantage over not only by steady state performance but also the control effort required is also lower compared to manually tuned LQG (Table 2).

Table 2. Comparison of the performance of GA-tuned LQG and manually tuned LQG.

Specifications	GA-tuned LQG	Manual-tuned LQG
Settling time (t_s)	4.66 s	4.35 s
Rise time (t_r)	3.05 s	3.02 s
Steady state error (e_{ss})	0.006 mm	0.015 mm
Peak Response (Y_p)	0.994 mm	0.985 mm

7   Robustness Analysis

Robustness is the measure of how well the controller will perform if it is implemented in the actual AMB system. Prior to the analysis of robustness, the cases which may make the system to be not robust (model uncertainties) will be identified.

The model uncertainty in the AMB system can arise due to (Fig. 11):

1. Model parameter uncertainty
2. Neglected high frequency dynamics
3. Non-linearity
4. Changing operating conditions
5. Neglected dynamics
6. Setup variations

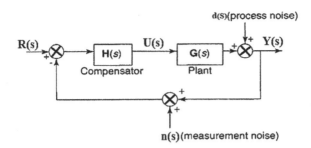

Fig. 11. A multivariable feedback control system with process and measurement noise

The sensitivity of the output of the system Y(s) with respect to the process disturbance d(s) and measurement noise n(s) depend on the sensitivity function given by $[I + G(s)H(s)]^{-1}$. While the sensitivity of the input control signal U(s) depends on the sensitivity function $[I + H(s)G(s)]^{-1}$.

In a certain closed loop system the larger the magnitude of the two sensitivity functions, the larger will be the sensitivity of the plant output and the input control signal to process disturbance d(s) and measurement noise n(s).

Return ratio matrix can be defined to analyze robustness. In order to simplify the measure of robustness, we can assign scalar measure of robustness than dealing with return difference matrix or return ration matrix. In order to accomplish this we can assign the scalar values (Singular Values) by defining matrix norm.

The most common way of identifying the singular values of a certain matrix is using singular value decomposition (SVD) algorithm. Singular values are very important to analyze property of multivariable feedback system. In the analysis of robustness the largest and smallest singular values of the return difference matrix as providing upper and lower bounds on the scalar return difference matrix.

7.1 Robustness at the Output

When we analyze robustness with respect to process disturbance d(s) and measurement noise n(s) independently, it has been summarized as follows:

- To maximize robustness with respect to process disturbance d(s) δmin[G(s)H(s)] should be maximized
- To maximize robustness with respect to measurement noise n(s) δmax[G(s)H(s)] should be minimized

The conditions stated in (a) and (b) conflict to each other. However, measurement noise usually has predominantly high frequency content. Therefore we can threat robustness for measurement noise and process disturbance in high frequency and low frequency respectively. Thus, it is compromised by minimizing **δmax** of [G(s)H(s)] at high frequency and by maximizing **δmin** of [G(s)H(s)] at low frequency.

Table 3. The singular values of [G(jw)H(jw)] for different nominal frequencies.

Design methods	$\omega = 0.01$ rad/s		$\omega = 10$ rad/s		$\omega = 100$ rad/s	
	δmin	δmax	δmin	δmax	δmin	δmax
Manual LQR	1.9723	1.9843	0.1456	0.7189	0.0019	0.0138
GA-LQR	1.9801	1.9911	0.2056	0.7348	0.0023	0.0175
Manual LQG	0.6965	1.8533	0.1161	0.2221	$3.05*10^{-8}$	$1.334*10^{-7}$
GA-LQG	0.6754	1.8416	0.1184	0.2323	$3.14*10^{-8}$	$1.778*10^{-7}$

From the results given in Table 3 the output robustness the control systems with respect to the process disturbance can be compared. In the results, the one with largest δ_{min} has a better robustness. Generally it can be observed that LQR has a better robustness compared to LQG. In fact this has been a well-established point by many scholars and in different journals [11].

The GA tuned LQR has the best robustness to process disturbance compared to the other three controllers. The manually tuned LQR has the next better robustness while manually tuned LQG and GA tuned LQG follow.

For output robustness with respect to measurement noise, the LQG controllers tend to have better measurement noise rejection. Thus, it must have the smallest δ_{max} at higher frequency range. As it can be observed from the table the LQG controllers have very small values of δ_{max} which shows that the LQG designed has better noise rejection capability compared to LQG. This is due to the ability of the Kalman filter being able to extract the states from a noisy measurement signal.

7.2   Robustness at the Input

The return difference matrix can be maximized which is maximizing the minimum singular value in the return difference matrix [12].

- The input robustness with respect to process noise or model uncertainty is improved if $\delta_{min}[H(s)G(s)]$ is maximized.
- The input robustness with respect to measurement noise is improved if $\delta_{min}[H(s)G(s)]$ is maximized (Table 4).

Table 4. The singular values of [H(jw)G(jw)] for different nominal frequencies.

Design methods	$\omega = 0.01$ rad/s		$\omega = 10$ rad/s		$\omega = 100$ rad/s	
	δ_{min}	δ_{max}	δ_{min}	δ_{max}	δ_{min}	δ_{max}
Manual LQR	1.9723	1.9843	0.1456	0.7189	0.0019	0.0138
GA-LQR	1.9801	1.9911	0.2056	0.7348	0.0023	0.0175
Manual LQG	0.6965	1.8533	0.1161	0.2221	$3.05*10^{-8}$	$1.334*10^{-7}$
GA-LQG	0.6754	1.8416	0.1184	0.2323	$3.14*10^{-8}$	$1.778*10^{-7}$

For input robustness unlike to the output robustness, the GA tuned LQR and LQG have better robustness over the manually tuned LQR and LQG respectively. The Genetic algorithm based tuning of the weighting matrices Q and R has managed to improve the measurement noise rejection capability as far as the input control signal is concerned.

7.3   Gain Margin and Phase Margin

The singular values of the return difference matrix at the output in the frequency domain, $\delta[I + G(jw)H(jw)]$, can be used to estimate the gain and phase margins of a multivariable system [12]. By plotting singular value plots against frequency, for all frequencies, ω, in the frequency range of interest.

The gain and phase margins are defined using singular values, by taking the smallest singular value, δ_{min}, of all the singular values of the return difference matrix at the output. Then a real constant, a is determined, such that $\delta_{min}[I + G(jw)H(jw)] > a$. Then the gain and phase margins are defined as follows [12]:

Figure 12 and Fig. 13 show the singular values of the return difference ratio of the AMB control systems. From the first figure it can be observed that the smallest singular value of manually tuned LQR reaches minimum of −40.6725 dB at frequency of 100 rad/s. The smallest singular value of the manually tuned LQG reaches minimum value −77.9141 dB at 100 rad/s.

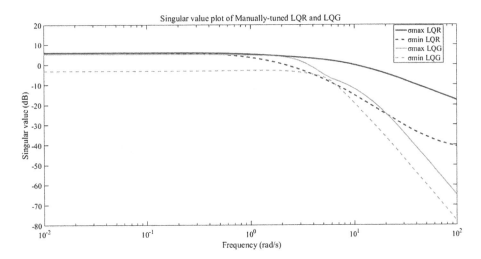

Fig. 12. Singular value plot of [I + G(s)H(s)] of manually tuned LQR and LQG

Similarly as shown in the Fig. 13 the smallest singular value of GA-tuned LQR reaches a minimum of −40.722 dB at 0.01 rad/s. The GA-tuned LQG's smallest singular values reach minimum of −77.7643 dB at 0.01 rad/s.

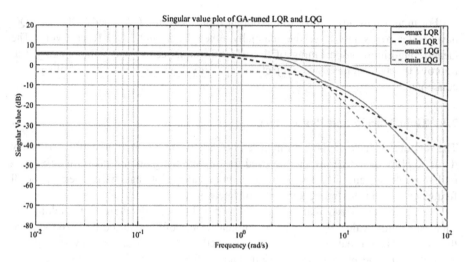

Fig. 13. Singular value plot of [I + G(s)H(s)] of GA-tuned LQR and LQG

Table 5. The minimum and maximum gain and phase margins of the four controllers

Design methods	δ_{min} (dB)	A	Gain margin (dB)	Phase margins (deg)
Manual LQR	−40.7220	0.009202	0.1606	1.05452
GA-LQR	−40.6725	0.009255	0.1614	1.06054
Manual LQG	−77.9141	$1.2714*10^{-4}$	0.002208	0.01457
GA-LQG	−77.7643	$1.2935*10^{-4}$	0.002246	0.014824

Observing the results from Table 5, the GM and PM of LQR obviously exceeds the GM and PM of LQG. On the other hand, concerning on the tuning methodologies, the GA tuning has relatively a better GM and PM in both LQR and LQG case compared to manual tuning. Observing the results from Table 5, the GM and PM of LQR obviously exceeds the GM and PM of LQG. On the other hand, concerning on the tuning methodologies, the GA tuning has relatively a better GM and PM in both LQR and LQG case compared to manual tuning.

This narrow range of gain margin and phase margin indicates that the control system for the Active magnetic bearings cannot tolerate an appreciable variation in the phase and gain of the return difference matrix [G(s)H(s)] before its eigen value cross into the right-half s-plane. Though, GA-tuning has slightly improved the gain margin and phase margin compared to manually tuned LQG.

8   Conclusion

Active Magnetic bearings are very important mechatronic element of a machine. In this paper with some assumptions, the model of the AMB system is developed and it is shown that, the system is 2-input and 2-output MIMO system. State feedback controllers are designed for the AMB system. Before the controllers are designed the appropriate control loop was selected by the RGA analysis. From the RGA analysis it has been found that to control y1, u1 should be manipulated and u2 is manipulated to control y2.

Linear quadratic regulators (LQR) are designed by tuning the weighting matrices manually and using genetic algorithm (GA). The GA tuned LQR designed has managed to reduce the magnitude of the undesired undershoot almost by half and the overall performance is also as good as the manually tuned LQR.

LQG has better performance than LQR. As far as the tuning mechanisms are concerned in GA-tuned LQG the rise time and settling time are as good as the manually tuned LQG. In addition, the steady state error in GA-tuned LQG has a better value.

The genetic algorithm tuning has managed to improve the robustness of the manually tuned LQR. Although in the case of the LQG design, the manually tuned LQG has better robustness. Although, it has been observed that, the weighting matrices (Q and R) of the LQR design have small effect in improving the robustness of the LQG.

References

1. 6 Most Popular Types of Mechanical Bearings - Craftech Industries. Craftech Industries (2017). http://www.craftechind.com/6-most-popular-types-of-mechanical-bearings/, Accessed 01 Oct 2017
2. Bleuler, H.: A survey of magnetic levitation and magnetic bearing types. JSME Int. J. Ser. III **35**(3), 335–342 (1992)
3. Thrust Bearings Information | Engineering360. Globalspec.com (2017). http://www.globalspec.com/learnmore/mechanical_components/bearings_bushings/thrust_bearings, Accessed 05 Feb2017
4. Schuhmann, T., Hofmann, W., Werner, R.: Improving operational performance of active magnetic bearings using kalman filter and state feedback control. IEEE Trans. Ind. Electron. **59**(2), 821–829 (2012)
5. Kuseyri, I.S.: Robust control and unbalance compensation of rotor/active magnetic bearing systems. J. Vib. Control **18**(6), 817–832 (2012)
6. Pesch, A.H., Sawicki, J.T.: Active magnetic bearing online levitation recovery through μ-synthesis robust control. In: Multidisciplinary Digital Publishing Institute(MDPI) Actuators, vol. 6, no. 2, pp. 1–14 (2017)
7. Pesch, A.H.; Hanawalt, S.P.; Sawicki, J.T.: A case study in control methods for active magnetic bearings. In: Proceedings of the ASME Dynamic Systems and Control Conference, San Antonio, TX, USA, pp. 22–24 (2014)
8. Schweitzer, G.: Active magnetic bearings - chances and limitations. In: International Centre for Magnetic Bearings, ETH Zurich, CH-8092 Zurich (2002)
9. Skogestad, S.: Multivariable Feedback Control Analysis and Design, 2nd edn. John Wiley & Sons, Hoboken (2001)

10. Michalewicz, Z., Janikow, C.: GENOCOP: a genetic algorithm for numerical optimization problems with linear constraints. Commun. ACM **39**(12), 175 (1996)
11. Doyle, J.: Guaranteed margins for LQG regulators. IEEE Trans. Autom. Control **23**(4), 756–757 (1978)
12. Tewari, A.: Modern Control Design with MATLAB, 1st edn. John Wiley & Sons, Hoboken (2002)
13. Hutterer, M., Hofer, M., Nenning, T., Schrödl, M.: LQG control of an active magnetic bearing with a special method to consider the gyroscopic effect. In: ISMB14, 14th International Symposium on Magnetic Bearings, Linz, Austria, 11–14 August 2014 (2014)
14. Schweitzer, G.: Applications and research topics for active magnetic bearings. In: Proceedings IUTAM-Symposium on Emerging Trends in Rotor Dynamics, Indian Institute of Technology, Delhi, India, 23–26 March 2009. Springer, Heidelberg (2011)

Pitch Angle Control for Optimal Power of Horizontal Axis Variable Speed Wind Turbines Using Fuzzy Tuned PID Controller

Tamiru Getahun G/Meskel[(✉)], Tefera Terefe Yetayew,
and Endrias Alemayehu Workeye

Adama Science and Technology University, Adama, Ethiopia

Abstract. Energy is the firewood for development of a country. An increased access to electricity boosts chances for industrial development and improves quality of health and education. Renewable energies have a large potential to maintain sustainable energy. Wind turbine is a system which is used to change kinetic energy that exists in airstream into Mechanical Energy. The system is complex, unstable and highly nonlinear involving some random wind speed. Because of this reason, the output power from the system is fluctuated and also the mechanical part of the turbine become structurally overloaded as well as damage itself physically at strong wind condition. Pitch control is the most popular and extensively used practical technique to Control the output Power especially, when the wind velocity is beyond the rated value. It is considered as the most competent and common power regulation method. This paper suggests optimal power control method through pitch angle control of Horizontal-axis variable speed wind turbine system to extract constant energy between rated and maximum wind speed using a Fuzzy tuned PID controller. The Performance of the proposed controller is evaluated by simulation results for 1.5 MW Wind Turbine using MATLAB ™/SIMULINK. After implementing and validating, the results obtained shows that the performance of the proposed controller was much better than the conventional PID and Fuzzy controllers.

Keywords: Horizontal-axis variable speed wind turbine · PMSG · Pitch angle and Fuzzy-PID controller

1 Introduction

Wind is one of the most gifted renewable energy sources for generating electricity due to its cost attractiveness compared with other types of energy resources [1]. It is Environment Friendly. According to Global Wind Energy data, Currently, around 743 GW of wind power capacity worldwide, this helping us to remove over 1.1 billion tonnes of CO_2 worldwide. And also, the installed capacity of wind power is growing at an average rate of 53% year over the year 2020 [3].

© ICST Institute for Computer Sciences, Social Informatics and Telecommunications Engineering 2022
Published by Springer Nature Switzerland AG 2022. All Rights Reserved
M. L. Berihun (Ed.): ICAST 2021, LNICST 411, pp. 237–255, 2022.
https://doi.org/10.1007/978-3-030-93709-6_16

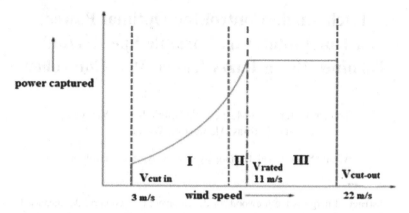

Fig. 1. Power Captured vs. wind speed characteristic

In recent years, Pitch adjusted VSWT have become the dominating type of yearly installed wind turbines. The process and control mechanisms of variable speed wind turbine differs along the wind speed range. Figure 1 shows a characteristic of Power captured to wind speed curve. In Region one, the system is in partial load and the objective is to maximize the captured Energy. The change between low and high wind speed Region is exposed by region two. The 3rd region is named full load region. In this region, the objective is to control the turbine at its rated power and to keep the turbine components within safety limits. Unceasing turning of turbine higher than the rated speed will yield high aerodynamic torque such that the mechanical structure of turbine may get hurtle or damaged. To overcome this problem and limit the aerodynamic power captured in region three, many pitch angle control approaches can be proposed. Practically, PID based pitch angle controllers are often used for power regulation.

In this paper work, a Fuzzy tuned PID method is suggested for optimal power condition through pitch control of wind power system under various wind speed conditions.

2   Mathematical Modeling

2.1   Aerodynamic Model

In this system, the wind turbine blades structurally designed in different shape and number. It extracts the kinetic Energy in the wind and converts in to Mechanical Energy.

In Fig. 2, the mass flow rate is constant for upstream, on the rotor and downstream of the blade. Mathematically expressed as follows:

$$A_0 V_0 = A_1 V_1 = A_2 V_2 \tag{1}$$

Then,

$$m = PA_0V_0 = PA_1V_1 \tag{2}$$

Where m is mass flow rate, p is pressure difference, A is area and V is velocity of air.

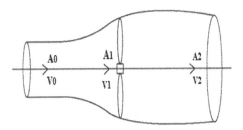

Fig. 2. Airstreams around a turbine [5, 20]

Assume, all the air particles are moving at the same direction and speed before bear upon the rotor blades of the wind turbine.

The kinetic energy stored in the wind can be stated as follows:

$$E = \frac{1}{2}mv^2 \tag{3}$$

But, the total mass of the particles expressed as follows:

$$m = \rho Avt = \rho \pi R^2 vt \tag{4}$$

Sub. (4) into (3) then, the kinetic energy become:

$$E = \frac{1}{2}\rho \pi R^2 v^3 t \tag{5}$$

2.2   Captured Power by Wind Turbines

The harvested Power in the moving air is proportional to the cube of the wind Velocity:

$$P_w = \frac{dE}{dt} = \frac{1}{2}mv2 = \frac{1}{2}\rho Av3 = \frac{1}{2}\rho \pi R^2 v^3 \tag{6}$$

According to Betz limit, a wind turbine can extract maximum 59.3% of power stored in wind energy [13]. This fraction is defined by the power coefficient of the turbine, (Cp). Consequently, the Mechanical power is mathematically expressed by

$$P_m = P_w c_p(\lambda, \beta) \tag{7}$$

Substitute (6) into (7), then we have

$$P_m = \frac{1}{2}\rho A v^3 c_p(\lambda, \beta) = \frac{1}{2}\rho\pi R^2 v^3 c_p(\lambda, \beta) \tag{8}$$

The rotor torque T_a, can be computed as:

$$T_a = \frac{P_m}{\omega_m} \tag{9}$$

Substitute (8) into (9), then we have

$$T_a = \frac{\frac{1}{2}\rho\pi R^2 v^3 c_p(\lambda, \beta)}{\omega_m} \tag{10}$$

Then,

$$\lambda = \frac{\omega_m R}{V} \tag{11}$$

Now, C_p can be defined as a function of λ, β:

$$C_p(\lambda, \beta) = c_1\left(c_2\frac{1}{\lambda_i} - c_3\beta - c_4\right)e^{\frac{-c_5}{\lambda_i}} + c_6\lambda \tag{12}$$

Where:

$$\frac{1}{\lambda_i} = \frac{1}{\lambda + 0.08\beta} - \frac{0.035}{1 + \beta^3}$$

the values of a wind turbine constants $(c_1 - c_6)$ depend on the design of the wind turbine. For this work, we take the following value $c_1 = 0.5176$, $c_2 = 116$, $c_3 = 0.4$, $c_4 = 5$, $c_5 = -21$, $c_6 = 0.0068$ [8]. This power coefficient governs the efficiency of the turbine to convert the kinetic energy contained in the wind to Mechanical Energy. Figure 3 shows the relationship between C_p, λ and β.

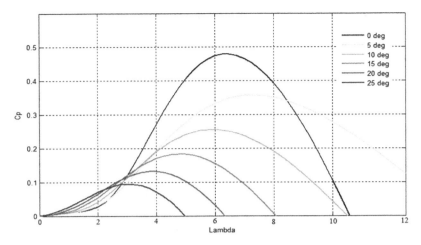

Fig. 3. Cp Vs TSR at different β angles

2.3   Drive Train

The fundamental dynamic equation is described by:

$$\frac{d(w_r)}{dt} = \frac{1}{J}(T_m - Bm * w_r - T_e) \tag{13}$$

$$\frac{d(\theta)}{dt} = w_r \tag{14}$$

Where J is Combined inertia of rotor & generator, Bm is combined viscous friction of rotor & generator, θ is angular position of rotor and T_m is mechanical torque (Table 1).

Table 1. Wind turbine data set

WTG Version	GW 1.5/77
Wind turbine nominal power (MW)	1.5
Number of wind turbines	34
Wind turbine inertia constant (H(s))	4.32
Rotor diameter (m)	77
Wind turbine rotor radius(m)	37.3
Tower height(m)	65
Cut-in wind speed	3 m/s
Rated wind speed	11m/s
Optimal speed ratio (λ_{opt})	6.14
Maximum Power coefficient ($C_{p,max}$)	0.45
Cut-out wind speed	22 m/s
Swept area	4649m²
Number of blades	3
Power control	Collective pitch control/rotor speed control

2.4   Permanent Magnet Synchronous Generator

The mathematical model of a PMSG was developed both in three phase and two reference frames (dq synchronously rotating reference frame) by using Park and clark transformation techniques. Some parameters of the generators like magnetic saturation, eddy current and hysteresis effect, damping effect are neglected [4, 6] (Fig. 4).

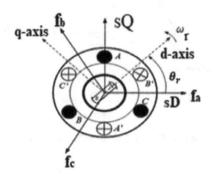

Fig. 4.   Cross-section view of the PMSM [6]

2.4.1   Modeling PMSM in the Dq-Axes Synchronously Rotating
Reference Frame

In the 3-phase systems like PMSMs, the phase quantities are time varying quantities. This makes our system complex. So, by applying Park's transformation, we can transform from 3-phase in to dq synchronously rotating reference frame.

$$\begin{bmatrix} X_{ds} \\ X_{qs} \\ X_{0s} \end{bmatrix} = \sqrt{\frac{2}{3}} \begin{bmatrix} \cos(\theta_r) & \cos\left(\theta_r - \frac{2\pi}{3}\right) & \cos\left(\theta_r + \frac{2\pi}{3}\right) \\ -\sin(\theta_r) & -\sin\left(\theta_r - \frac{2\pi}{3}\right) & -\sin\left(\theta_r + \frac{2\pi}{3}\right) \\ \frac{\sqrt{2}}{2} & \frac{\sqrt{2}}{2} & \frac{\sqrt{2}}{2} \end{bmatrix} \begin{bmatrix} X_{as} \\ X_{bs} \\ X_{cs} \end{bmatrix} \tag{15}$$

In Eq. (15), $X_{(abc)s}$ represent stator voltages, currents or flux linkages of the AC machines. Since, the system is under balanced conditions, $X_{0s} = 0$, the voltage equation of the PMSM in the dq-axis reference frame become like this [6]:

$$V_{ds} = R_s i_{ds} + L_d \frac{di_{ds}}{dt} - \omega_r i_{qs} L_q \tag{16}$$

$$V_{qs} = R_s i_{qs} + L_q \frac{di_{qs}}{dt} + \omega_r i_{ds} L_d + \omega_r \lambda_r \tag{17}$$

where V_{ds}, V_{qs}, i_{ds}, and i_{qs}, are the instantaneous stator voltages and current in the dq-axis reference frame respectively. Whereas, L_d and L_q are the d-axis and q-axis inductances respectively.

2.4.2 Power and Torque Analysis

The power in dq-axis is written as follows:

$$P_{dq} = \frac{3}{2}\left(i_{qs}V_{ds} + i_{ds}V_{qs}\right) \tag{18}$$

The torque produced by the PMSM (Table 2)

$$T_e = \frac{3}{2}P\left(i_{qs}\lambda_{ds} - i_{ds}\lambda_{qs}\right) \tag{19}$$

$T_e = \frac{3}{2}P\left(\lambda_r i_{qs} - \left(L_d - L_q\right)i_{ds}i_{qr}\right)$ Where, P is number of poles

Table 2. Generator data set

Generator Type	PMSG, 1.5 MW, 620 V, 12.7 Hz, multi - pole (non-salient pole)
Rated Mechanical Power	1.5MW
Rated Apparent Power	1.6 MVA
Generator inertia	35000(J(kg.m^2))
Rated Power Factor	0. 97
Speed Range	9-17.3 rpm
Rated rotor speed	17.3
Shaft stiffness (pu)	0.3
Number of Pole Pairs	44
Rated Rotor Flux Linkage	1.48
Stator Winding Resistance	0.006Ω
d axis Synchronous Inductance	0.395mH
q axis Synchronous Inductance	0.395mH
Rated current	680 A
Static friction	0.01
Viscous damping	1.5

2.5 Actuator

The Actuators model defines the dynamic behavior between a pitch demand (β_d) from the pitch controller and the pitch angle (β). This is written mathematically as follows:

$$\frac{d\beta}{dt} = \frac{\beta_d - \beta}{\tau_\beta} \tag{20}$$

By applying Laplace transforms, we get

$$\beta_d(s) = \tau_\beta s \beta(s) + \beta(s) = \beta(s)(\tau_\beta s + 1) \tag{21}$$

Then, the transfer function of the actuator is

$$\frac{\beta(s)}{\beta_d(s)} = \frac{1}{(\tau_\beta s + 1)} \tag{22}$$

$$\frac{\beta(s)}{\beta_d(s)} = \frac{1}{(0.01s + 1)} \tag{23}$$

Many authors used different values of time constant τ_β based on their logic. But, for this work we used small amount of time constant ($\tau_\beta = 0.01$) to increase the control effort.

3   Controller Design

3.1   Conventional Controller (PID)

Correcting the pitch angle of the blades as shown in Fig. 5, brings an operative means of regulations (limiting the operation of the turbine in strong wind velocity). In conventional system, PID controller with pitch servos are in use to set the blades into the ideal position. In normal operation, blade pitch adjustments with rotational speeds of approximately 5–10°/s are expected [23]. The conventional blade pitch angle control approaches are shown in Fig. 5.

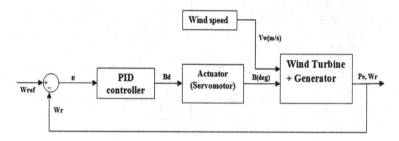

Fig. 5. Wind energy conversion system with PID controller

3.2   Fuzzy Logic Controller

Complex physical systems are very difficult to model by an accurate and precise mathematical equation. This is due to the complication of the system structure, uncertainty, nonlinearity, randomness, etc. Fuzzy logic control solves non-linear systems problem by requiring little prerequisite knowledge of inputs and crisp mathematical description of the system. In case of wind turbine, the wind velocity is a changing quantity this makes the system output unpredictable and nonlinear (Fig. 6, Table 3).

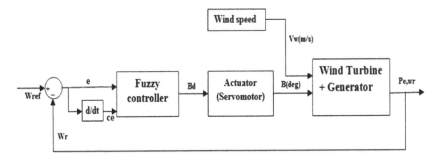

Fig. 6. Wind energy conversion system with Fuzzy controller

Table 3. Fuzzy logic controller rule base.

Bd		\multicolumn{6}{c}{Error}
		nvb	nb	nm	ns	ze	p
Change in error	nb	PVL	PL	PVB	PB	ZE	ZE
	ns	PVL	PVVB	PB	PS	ZE	ZE
	ze	PL	PVB	PB	PS	ZE	ZE
	ps	PVL	PVVB	PB	PS	ZE	ZE
	pb	PVL	PL	PVB	PB	ZE	ZE

3.3 Fuzzy Tuned PID Controller

Conventional PID controller is the simplest and robust controller but its function is limited based on the application area (plant). In this work, PID itself can't control the overall system because the system is highly nonlinear. Which means the gains of the PID controller are not regularly tuned for the nonlinear plant with random parameter variations. In addition to this, PID controller is offline controller. To solve this problem, we have used Fuzzy tuned PID controller which can able to tune automatically the gains (K_p, K_I, K_D) of the PID controller with the supervision of fuzzy controller online over wider range of operating conditions [18, 19] (Fig. 7).

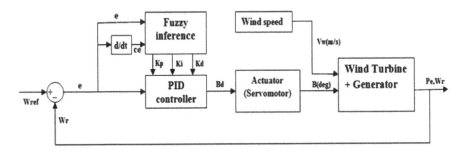

Fig. 7. Wind energy conversion system with Fuzzy Tuned PID controller

The rule base for each parameter have been carried out & shown in the tables below (Tables 4, 5 and 6).

Table 4. Rule base for Kp.

K_p		error							
		NL	NVVB	NVB	NB	NM	NS	ZE	PO
Change in error	NB	NEL	NVVL	NVVL	NVVL	NVVB	NVVB	ZE	ZE
	NS	NVVL	NVVL	NVVL	NVL	NVVB	NVB	ZE	ZE
	ZE	NVVL	NVL	NVL	NVL	NVB	NVB	ZE	ZE
	PS	NVL	NVL	NVL	NL	NVB	NB	ZE	ZE
	PB	NVL	NL	NL	NL	NB	NB	ZE	ZE

Table 5. Rule base for Ki.

K_i		error							
		NL	NVVB	NVB	NB	NM	NS	ZE	PO
Change in error	NB	NL	NL	NVB	NVB	NB	NB	ZE	ZE
	NS	NL	NVB	NVB	NB	NB	NM	ZE	ZE
	ZE	NVB	NVB	NB	NB	NM	NS	ZE	ZE
	PS	NVB	NB	NB	NM	NM	NS	ZE	ZE
	PB	NB	NB	NM	NS	NS	ZE	ZE	ZE

Table 6. Rule Base for Kd.

K_d		error							
		NL	NVVB	NVB	NB	NM	NS	ZE	PO
Change in error	NB	PM	PS	PS	ZE	NS	NS	ZE	ZE
	NS	PS	PS	ZE	NS	NS	NM	ZE	ZE
	ZE	PS	ZE	NS	NS	NM	NM	ZE	ZE
	PS	ZE	NS	NS	NM	NM	NB	ZE	ZE
	PB	NS	NS	NM	NM	NB	NB	ZE	ZE

4   Result and Discussion

4.1   Uncontrolled Wind Turbine

In Fig. 8, the dynamic performances of the system without controller have been study under variable wind speed and uniform wind direction to compare the validity of the proposed method.

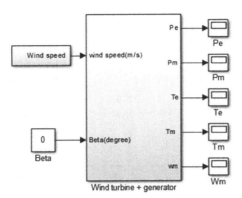

Fig. 8. Simulation diagram of uncontrolled system under different wind speed

The simulation result in Fig. 9 Shows as, the extracted power mainly depends on the magnitude of the velocity of the wind. Once the wind velocity is goes beyond rated wind speed, the torque and captured power go up above rated valued. This leads very big fatigue loads to the components of the turbine and this results a short fatigue life.

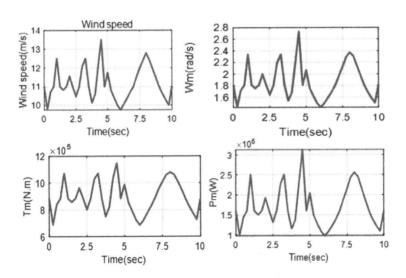

Fig. 9. Uncontrolled system response under variable wind speed

4.2   The Conventional PID Controller of Wind Turbine

In this simulation diagram, the gains of the PID controller are auto tuned based on the inflow wind speed velocity (Fig. 10).

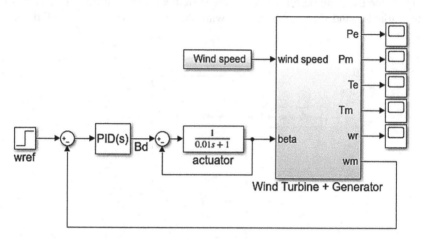

Fig. 10. Simulation diagram of overall system with PID controller

The results obtained from the simulation are depicted in Fig. 11 below. System with PID controller perform batter compared with uncontrolled system. However, still there is power and torque above rated values. This means there is power and torque ripples. This makes the system under pressure and give an impact on wind turbine system.

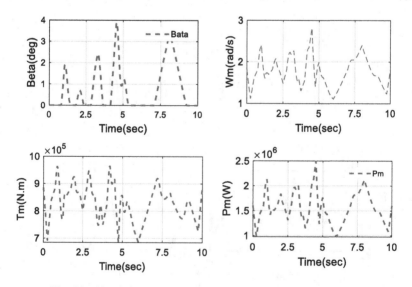

Fig. 11. Simulation results of overall system using PID controller

4.3   The Fuzzy Controller Design of Wind Power System

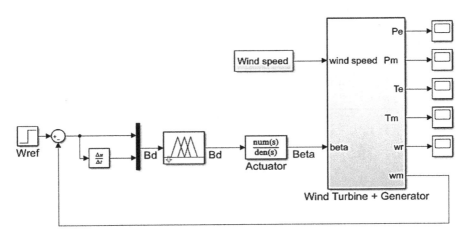

Fig. 12. Simulation diagram of overall system with fuzzy controller

The inputs/output membership function, the rule editor and the simulated results of overall system using Fuzzy controller are shown as follows (Figs. 12 and 13).

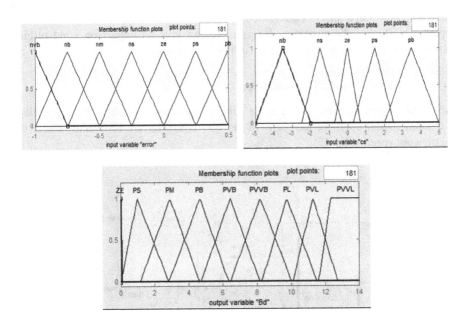

Fig. 13. Input/output fuzzy membership function

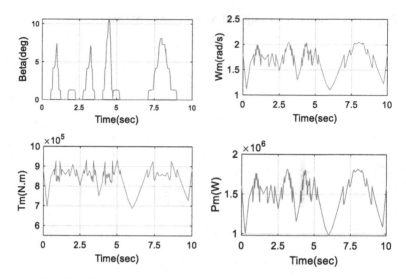

Fig. 14. Simulation results of overall system using Fuzzy controller.

From the above results, system with fuzzy controller perform batter compared with system with PID controller. The time taken to reach rated value of rotor speed, torque and output power are very small compared with PID controller. However, there is still a problem in power and torque values. Due to variable nature of the wind, there is torque ripples. This makes the system under pressure and give an impact on wind turbine system. This tells as, the system needs further improvement (Fig. 14).

4.4   The Fuzzy Tuned PID Controller

This research proposed fuzzy to tune the gains of the main controller (PID controller). In this simulation diagram, the gains of the PID controller are auto tuned under the inflow wind speed (Fig. 15).

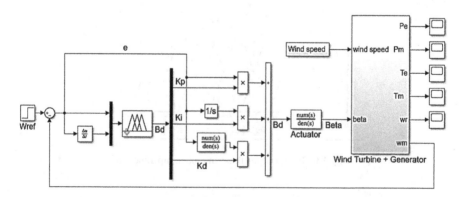

Fig. 15. Simulation diagram of overall system with fuzzy tuned PID controller

The inputs/output membership function, the rule editor and the simulated results of overall system using Fuzzy tuned PID controller are shown as follows (Fig. 16 and 17).

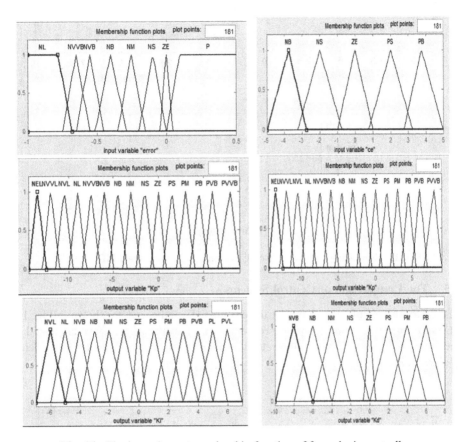

Fig. 16. The inputs/output membership function of fuzzy logic controller

The result obtained from the proposed controller are much better than PID and fuzzy controllers in terms of regulation or limiting. The time taken to reach rated value of rotor speed, torque and output power are very small compared with PID and fuzzy controller. With this controller, we can able to regulate the output power to the rated value up to cutoff wind speed value (22 m/s). The comparison between the proposed controller and the other two controllers are clearly stated in Sect. 4.5 below.

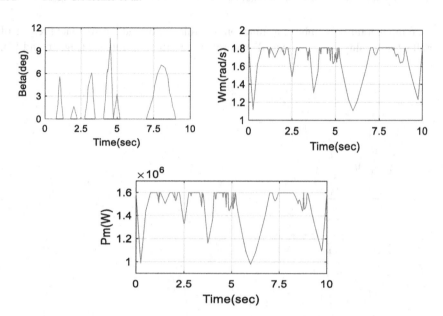

Fig. 17. Simulation results of overall system using fuzzy tuned PID controller

4.5 The Comparison of Control Systems

The performances of each controller under different wind speed are shown in Fig. 18. Standing from this result, the proposed controller has better performance compared to the other controllers. Table 5, illustrates the characteristics of each controller in detail (Tables 7, 8 and 9).

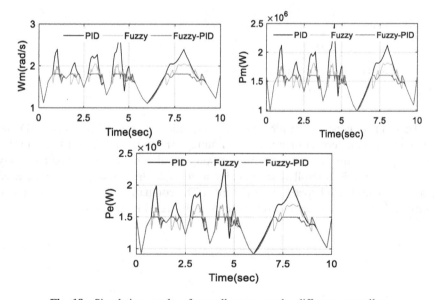

Fig. 18. Simulation results of overall system under different controllers

Table 7. Performance of PID, Fuzzy and Fuzzy-PID controller in case of below rated wind speed.

Power optimization (maximum power tracking)							
V_w (m/s)	Λ	C_p	$\beta^{\bar{o}}$	w_m(rad/s)	Electrical power (w)		
					PID	Fuzzy	Fuzzy-PID
3	1.675	0.45	0	0.1347	935.8	935.8	935.8
4	2.233	0.45	0	0.2394	4375	4375	4375
5	2.791	0.45	0	0.3741	$1.911 * 10^4$	$1.911 * 10^4$	$1.911 * 10^4$
6	3.349	0.45	0	0.5387	$6.415 * 10^4$	$6.415 * 10^4$	$6.415 * 10^4$
7	3.907	0.45	0	0.7333	$1.655 * 10^5$	$1.655 * 10^5$	$1.655 * 10^5$
8	4.465	0.45	0	0.9577	$3.487 * 10^5$	$3.487 * 10^5$	$3.487 * 10^5$
9	5.024	0.45	0	1.212	$6.312 * 10^5$	$6.312 * 10^5$	$6.312 * 10^5$
10	5.582	0.45	0	1.496	$1.018 * 10^5$	$1.018 * 10^5$	$1.018 * 10^5$
11	6.14	0.45	0	1.811	$1.5 * 10^6$	$1.5 * 10^6$	$1.5 * 10^6$

Table 8. Performance of PID and Fuzzy controller in case of above rated wind speed.

V_w (m/s)	Λ	C_p	PID			Fuzzy		
			β^o	w_m	Power (w)	β^o	w_m	Power (w)
11.48	5.884	0.293	1.52	1.72	$1.42 * 10^6$	1.67	1.743	$1.405 * 10^6$
11.75	5.748	0.257	1.14	2	$1.65 * 10^6$	1.88	1.532	$1.512 * 10^6$
12	5.629	0.235	1.46	2.017	$1.71 * 10^6$	3.6	1.822	$1.454 * 10^6$
12.42	5.438	0.217	3.03	2.14	$1.77 * 10^6$	6.35	1.755	$1.543 * 10^6$
12.52	5.404	0.214	1.54	2.4	$1.99 * 10^6$	6.96	1.936	$1.512 * 10^6$
12.8	5.277	0.205	1.98	2.4	$1.98 * 10^6$	8.37	1.825	$1.51 * 10^6$
13.5	5.003	0.186	3.64	2.827	$2.34 * 10^6$	10.5	1.696	$1.4 * 10^6$

Table 9. Performance of Fuzzy-PID controller in case of above rated wind speed.

V_w (m/s)	Λ	C_p	Fuzzy-PID		
			β^o	$w_m(rad/s)$	Power(w)
11.48	5.884	0.293	1.18	1.78	$1.47 * 10^6$
11.75	5.748	0.257	1.8	1.81	$1.495 * 10^6$
12	5.629	0.235	4.1	1.811	$1.5 * 10^6$
12.38	5.456	0.218	6.8	1.811	$1.5 * 10^6$
12.42	5.438	0.217	7	1.811	$1.5 * 10^6$
12.52	5.404	0.214	7.22	1.811	$1.5 * 10^6$
12.8	5.277	0.205	8.36	1.811	$1.5 * 10^6$
13.5	5.003	0.186	10.1	1.811	$1.5 * 10^6$

5 Conclusions

We start this work by modeling the system (pitch controlled HAVSWT) with some assumptions. It has been shown that the system is nonlinear & also the outputs are mainly depended on the aerodynamic torque and rotor speed of the shaft. To control this system under different wind condition, we proposed Fuzzy tuned PID controller. To compare the efficiency of the anticipated controller, we use conventional PID & Fuzzy controller. The simulation is done by using MATLAB/SIMULINK. Results obtained from simulation illustrates that fluctuations of output power and Mechanical Torque is very high in conventional controller (PID). In case of Fuzzy controller, the output reaches target value after 1.15 s. But, due to quick change of the value of change of error there are still some fluctuations in both outputs. However, when a fuzzy tuned PID is used, the power output reaches target value very quickly (before 1.15 s) and fluctuation gets reduced. Numerically, at 13.5 m/sec wind velocity by using conventional PID controller we get 2.827 rad/s angular velocity and $2.34 * 10^6$ output power, when the controller is replaced by fuzzy controller, we get 1.696 rad/s angular velocity and $1.4 * 10^6$ output power. Finally, when we use the proposed controller, we get 1.811 rad/s angular velocity and $1.5 * 10^6$ output power. Based on this result, the proposed controller has better performance than other two controllers.

References

1. Bisoyi, S.K., Jarial, R.K., Gupta, R.A.: Modeling and Analysis of Variable Speed Wind Turbine equipped with PMSG. Int. J. Current Eng. Technol., February 2014
2. "U.S. Energy Information Administration (EIA) - Ap", Eia.gov (2018). https://www.eia.gov/environment/emissions/carbon/. Accessed 01 Jan 2018
3. Saur Energy International: GWEC's 16th Edition Global Wind Report 2021: Key Highlights (2021). https://www.saurenergy.com/solar-energy-news/gwecs-16th-edition-global-wind-report-2021-key-highlights. Accessed 6 July 2021
4. Wu, B., Lang, Y., Zargari, N., Kouro, S.: Power Conversion and Control of Wind Energy Systems. Wiley, Hoboken (2011)
5. Hongbin, W., Ming, D.: Modeling and control of distribution system with wind turbine generators. In: Proceedings of the 3rd International Conference on Deregulation and Restructuring and Power Technologies (DRPT '08), pp. 2498–2503, April 2008
6. "Simulation of Power Control of a Wind Turbine Permanent Magnet Synchronous Generator System" Nantao, Huang. http://epublications.marquette.edu/theses_open/215. Accessed 23 Dec 2017
7. Duong, M.Q., Grimaccia, F., Leva, S., Mussetta, M., Ogliari, E.: Pitch angle control using hybrid controller for all operating regions of SCIG wind Turbine system. J. Renewable Energy **70**, 197–203 (2014)
8. Hwas, A., Katebi, R.: Wind Turbine control using PI pitch angle controller. IFAC Conf. Proc. Vols. **45**(3), 241–246 (2012)
9. Akhmatov: Modelling and ride-through capability of variable speed wind turbines with permanent magnet generators. Wind Energy, vol. 9, no. 4, pp. 313–326 (2006)

10. Yin, M., Li, G., Zhou, M., Zhao, C.: Modeling of the wind turbine with a permanent magnet synchronous generator for integration. In: Proceedings of the IEEE Power Engineering Society General Meeting (PES 2007), pp. 1–6, June 2007
11. Makvana, V.T., Ahir, R.K., Patel, D.K., Jadhav, J.A.: Study of PID controller based pitch actuator system for variable speed HAWT using MATLAB. Int. J. Innov. Res. Sci. Eng. Technol. **2**(5), 5 (2013)
12. Anderson, P.M., Anjan, B.: Stability simulation of wind Turbine systems. IEEE Trans. Power Oprators Syst. **PAS-102**(12), 3791–3795 (1983)
13. Muhando, E.B., Senjyua, T., Urasakia, N., Yonaa, A.K., Funabashi, T.: Gain Scheduling Control of Variable Speed WTG Under Widely Varying Turbulence Loading. Renew Energy, **32**(14), 2407 (2007)
14. Pao, L.Y., Johnson, K.E.: Control of Wind Turbines: Approaches, Challenges and Recent Development. IEEE Control Systems Magazine April (2011)
15. Zafer Civelek, et al, "a new fuzzy controller for adjusting of pitch angle of wind turbine", Journal of Science and Technology, Volume 6, Issue 3, July, 2016
16. Lakshmi, K., Srinivas, P.: Fuzzy adaptive PID control of pitch system in variable speed wind turbines. In: International Conference on Issues and Challenges in Intelligent Computing Techniques (ICICT), April 2014
17. Beltran, B., Ahmed-Ali, T., El Hachemi Benbouzid, M.: Sliding mode power control of variable-speed wind energy conversion systems. IEEE Trans. Energy Conversion **23**(2), 551–558 (2008)
18. Chen, G., Pham, T.: Introduction to Fuzzy Sets, Fuzzy Logic and Fuzzy Control Systems. CRC, Boca Raton (2001)
19. Sinthipsomboon, K., Hunsacharoonroj, I., Khedari, J., Po-ngaen, W., Pratumsuw, P.: A hybrid of fuzzy and fuzzy self-tuning PID controller for servo electro-hydraulic system. Fuzzy Controllers- Recent Advances in Theory and Applications (2012)
20. Baldo, F.: Modeling of load interfacs for a Draiv Train of a wind Turbine. Master's Thesis, Department of Applied Mechanics Division of mechanics, Chalmers University of Tchenology, Guthenburg, Sweden (2012)
21. Mamdani, et al.: An experiment in linguistic synthesis with a fuzzy logic controller. Int. J. Man Mach. Stud. **7**(1), 113 (1975)
22. Saad, A.S.B.: Three phase inverter for induction motor control using fuzzy-pi controller with Arduino. universiti tun hussein onn Malaysia july 2014
23. Heier, S.: Grid Integration of Wind Energy Conversion Systems, 2nd edn. Wiley, Chichester (2006)

A Concise Evaluation of Auto-tuned PID and Fuzzy Logic Controllers for Speed Control of a DC-Motor

Tefera T. Yetayew[1($\boxtimes$)], Tamiru G. G/Meskel[1],
and Dawit M. G/michael[2]

[1] Adama Science and Technology University, P.O 1888 Adama, Ethiopia
[2] Dire Dawa University, P.O 1888 Dire Dawa, Ethiopia

Abstract. This paper presents the dynamic performance evaluation of the auto tuned conventional PID controller and fuzzy logic based speed control of a permanent magnet dc (PMDC) motor. Analytically designed PID controllers and fuzzy logic based controllers need final tuning until the response of the plant to be controlled meets the performance specifications set during design stage. Usually, fuzzy logic based controllers need more tuning activities than analytically designed conventional PID based controllers. The alarming advancement in automation tools provided a number offers to simplify the manual activities to be solved automatically within a short period of time. In this regard, MATLAB software provided automatic tuning features for conventional PID controllers by which the trial and error tuning period can be shorten. In this research, a conventional PID controller for a PMDC motor speed control application is tuned using one of auto tuning feature of MATLAB, i.e., SISOtool. And also, fuzzy logic based controllers is also designed using the fuzzy control system design approach. The performance of both controllers is evaluated for the conditions of no load and loaded conditions of the PMDC motor. The results reveal that application of fuzzy logic based controller has better response than PID based system response.

Keywords: Fuzzy Logic controller · PID controller · SISOtool · Dynamic performance

1 Introduction

Dc motors are widely in use in different industries that require high starting torque such as electric transportations, electric vehicles, and electric trains. And also applicable in areas that may require adjustable speed drives such as in printers, paper industry and floppy drives [1–5]. Among different Dc motor permanent magnet Dc motors are widely in use for different industrial applications that may require adjustable speed drives using power electronics converters. To provide adjustable speed drives, control of the current loop in addition to the outer speed control loop may be required. Usually, the control algorithm may use conventional PID controllers [1, 2]. However, conventional PID controllers may not give whenever parameter changes such as load changes mainly due to nonlinearity of the system to be controlled. To overcome such

© ICST Institute for Computer Sciences, Social Informatics and Telecommunications Engineering 2022
Published by Springer Nature Switzerland AG 2022. All Rights Reserved
M. L. Berihun (Ed.): ICAST 2021, LNICST 411, pp. 256–268, 2022.
https://doi.org/10.1007/978-3-030-93709-6_17

problems a number of controllers that are appropriate for non-linearity cases are devised. Among the number of controllers, fuzzy logic based controllers are appropriate for systems with no models since the main idea behind fuzzy logic based controllers is to model expert's knowledge for a particular application [4–7]. Usually, conventional PID controllers are designed analytically and followed by tuning tasks. However, advancement in automation application tools such as MATLAB provided offers of automatic tuning tasks for linear and nonlinear controllers [5, 8].

In this paper performance evaluation of auto tuned conventional PID controller and fuzzy logic based controllers for speed control application of a PMDC motor is proposed. The overall system architecture and descriptions are presented in the second section. Dynamic models of the power processing unit, the motor, the mechanical load and MATLAB/Simulink model of the open-loop system are presented in third section. Section four described the controller design procedures bot of the PI and fuzzy logic based systems. The MATLAB/Simulink model of the closed-loop system for implementation, simulation results and discussions are presented in section five of the paper. Summary of the findings in this paper is presented in section six.

2 System Description

The system given in Fig. 1 comprises of the controller, power processing unit (PPU), the dc motor and mechanical load. The controller consists of error amplifier and controller (PI or fuzzy logic based). The output speed is sensed and feedback to be compared with the reference speed. The difference between the feedback and reference input (error) signal is amplified and fed to controller by which output of the controller (PWM signal) will be input to the power processing unit [1, 2].

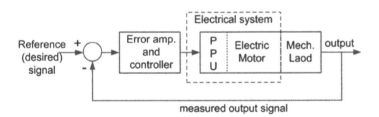

Fig. 1. Basic structure of the proposed system [1]

The speed controller responds to the inputs, disturbances and other changes that may arise due uncertainty. Due to mechanical load in general, the system is non-linear [1, 2]. To design the controller, the most common procedures can be summarised as:

- Linearization of the non-linear system (small-signal modelling).
- Controller design, further tuning, large signal simulation and evaluation.

3 Mathematical Model of the System

Developing mathematical model of the system helps to perform the required dynamic performance evaluation of the controller for the system to be controlled. In this research, Dc motor is considered as a system to be controlled. The Dc motor comprises of electrical and mechanical characteristics and to model these physical laws using energy balance principle are applied [2, 3].

The schematic diagram in Fig. 2 shows the basic electrical components of the Dc motor considered. The variables: V_a is voltage source across the coil of the armature, L_a represents equivalent inductance of armature coil, R_a is the series armature resistance and V_C represents induced voltage that opposes the voltage source generated by the rotation of the electrical coil through magnetic field due to the permanent magnet and this voltage usually known as back-emf or electromotive force [2–5].

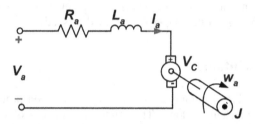

Fig. 2. Electrical diagram of a dc motor [3]

Applying Kirchhoff's voltage law around the electrical loop of schematic diagram in Fig. 2, we can get the Eq. (1).

$$V_a - V_{Ra} - V_{La} - V_c = 0 \tag{1}$$

Applying ohm's law, we can develop the relations for voltage across armature resistance, R_a (V_{Ra}), voltage across the armature inductance, L_a (V_{La}) considering the relation that voltage across inductor is proportional to time rate of change in current and back-emf (V_C) can be represented by expressions in Eq. (2) respectively.

$$\begin{cases} V_{Ra} = i_a R_a \\ V_{La} = L_a \dfrac{d}{dt} i_a \\ V_C = k_v \omega_a \end{cases} \tag{2}$$

where i_a is the armature current, L_a is the inductance of the armature coil, k_v is the velocity constant (determined by the flux density of the permanent magnets, the reluctance of the iron core of the armature, and the number of turns of the armature winding) and ω_a is the rotational velocity of the armature. Substituting, expressions in

Eq. (2) to electrical Eq. (1) derived by applying Kirchhoff's voltage law, we can get the differential Eq. (3) representation of electrical characteristics of the motor.

$$V_a - i_a R_a - L_a \frac{d}{dt} i_a - k_v \omega_a = 0 \tag{3}$$

Mechanical characteristic can be developed from energy balance that the sum of torques of the motor is zero. Thus, Eq. (4) torque equations of the motor.

$$T_e - T_{\omega'} - T_\omega - T_L = 0 \tag{4}$$

where T_e is the electromagnetic torque, $T_{\omega'}$ is the torque due to rotational acceleration of the rotor, T_ω is the torque produced from the velocity of the rotor, and T_L is the torque of the mechanical load. Considering the proportional relation between the electromagnetic torque and armature current we can develop expression for electromagnetic torque (T_e), the relation of torque due to rotational acceleration ($T_{\omega'}$) with inertia of the motor, and the relation between torque and velocity can be given by expressions in Eq. (5) respectively.

$$\begin{cases} T_e = k_t i_a \\ T_{\omega'} = J \dfrac{d}{dt} \omega_a \\ T_\omega = B \omega_a \end{cases} \tag{5}$$

where k_t is the torque constant, where J is inertia of the motor equivalent to mechanical load and where B is the damping coefficient associated with mechanical rotation of the machine. Substituting the torque Eqs. (5) to torque Eq. (4) for balance of energy we can get the differential Eq. (6) representation of the mechanical system.

$$k_t i_a - J \frac{d}{dt} \omega_a - B \omega_a - T_L = 0 \tag{6}$$

Expressions in Eq. (6) are differential equations given in Eq. (7) for armature current and angular velocity to describe the dc-motor system respectively.

$$\begin{cases} \dfrac{d}{dt} i_a = -\dfrac{R_a}{L_a} i_a - \dfrac{k_v}{L_a} \omega_a + \dfrac{V_a}{L_a} \\ \dfrac{d}{dt} \omega_a = \dfrac{k_t}{J} i_a - \dfrac{B}{J} \omega_a - \dfrac{T_L}{J} \end{cases} \tag{7}$$

Arranging the differential expressions in Eq. (7) in state space form can be represented using Eq. (8).

$$\frac{d}{dt} \begin{bmatrix} i_a \\ \omega_a \end{bmatrix} = \begin{bmatrix} -\frac{R_a}{L_a} & -\frac{k_v}{L_a} \\ \frac{k_t}{J} & -\frac{B}{J} \end{bmatrix} \begin{bmatrix} i_a \\ \omega_a \end{bmatrix} + \begin{bmatrix} -\frac{1}{L_a} & 0 \\ 0 & -\frac{1}{J} \end{bmatrix} \begin{bmatrix} V_a \\ T_L \end{bmatrix} \tag{8}$$

$$\begin{bmatrix} y_1 \\ y_2 \end{bmatrix} = \begin{bmatrix} 1 & 0 \\ 0 & 1 \end{bmatrix} \begin{bmatrix} i_a \\ \omega_a \end{bmatrix} + \begin{bmatrix} 0 & 0 \\ 0 & 0 \end{bmatrix} \begin{bmatrix} V_a \\ T_L \end{bmatrix}$$

Symbolically can be represented using Eq. (9) where, $\bar{x}$ and $\bar{u}$ represent input vector and $\bar{y}$ is the output vector.

$$\frac{d}{dt}\bar{x} = A\bar{x} + B\bar{u}$$
$$\bar{y} = C\bar{x} + D\bar{u}$$

(9)

Block diagram can be developed using differential expressions above. Taking Laplace transform of these differential expressions we can get expressions in Eq. (10).

$$\begin{cases} sI_a(s) - i_a(0) = -\dfrac{R_a}{L_a}I_a(s) - \dfrac{k_v}{L_a}\omega_a(s) + \dfrac{1}{L_a}V_a(s) \\[3mm] s\omega_a(s) - \omega_a(0) = \dfrac{k_t}{J}I_a(s) - \dfrac{B}{J}\omega_a(s) - \dfrac{1}{J}T_L(s) \end{cases}$$

(10)

Consider small perturbations around steady-state condition, initial conditions will be approximated to zero and small changes around the reference state for other variables expressions in Eq. (10) can be represented using Eq. (11).

$$\begin{cases} I_a(s) = \dfrac{-k_v\omega_a(s) + V_a(s)}{L_aS + R_a} \\[3mm] \omega_a(s) = \dfrac{-k_tI_a(s) - T_L(s)}{Js + B} \end{cases}$$

(11)

The block diagram of the motor can be easily developed using transfer functions given in Eq. (11). Figure 3 shows the block diagram representation of the motor considered. Thus, based on dynamic characteristics of electrical and mechanical

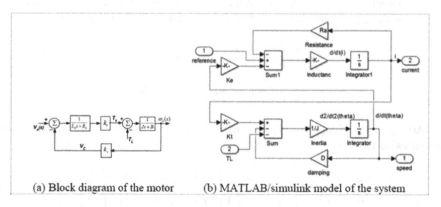

(a) Block diagram of the motor   (b) MATLAB/simulink model of the system

Fig. 3. Block diagram representation and MATLAB/Simulink model of the open-loop system

characteristic of the dc-motor, simulation model for the proposed system is developed in MATLAB/Simulink. Figure 3(b) shows the Simulink model of the dc-motor.

4 Design of Speed Controllers

The objective of controller is to achieve system performance of:

- Fast response – (large bandwidth)
- Minimum overshoot, good gain margin ($>60^0$)
- Zero steady state error – very large DC gain

The power processing unit, the dc-motor and mechanical load considered have parameter values given in Table 1.

Table 1. System parameter values.

System parameter	Value
R_a	2Ω
L_a	5.2 mH
B	1×10^{-4} kg.m^2/sec
J	152×10^{-6} kg.m^2
K_E	0.1 V/(rad/s)
k_T	0.1 Nm/A
V_d	60 V
V_{tri}	5 V
f_S	33 kHz

Based on the design objectives (specifications) and given parameter values of the system controllers of PI and fuzzy logic based are designed and presented in the following sections.

4.1 PI Controller Design

Summary of related works in motion control systems generalizes that PI controller is enough for systems involving Dc motor for motion control application. The controller acts on the error signal and compensates the system response until the required response is achieved [1, 4–7].

In this research, the PI controller is designed using control system designer tool box (SISO) of MATLAB/Simulink [8]. Based on the basic procedures and requirements the controller is designed. Requirements include the model of plant in MATLAB work space and design specifications. Accordingly, the PI controller is designed using automated tuning option of control and estimation tools manager. The closed loop performance of the system, controller parameters, performance and robustness are given in Fig. 4. Following the procedures of automated PID tuning technique, the closed loop response given in Fig. 4(a) is tuned until the performance parameters are within the limits of design specifications.

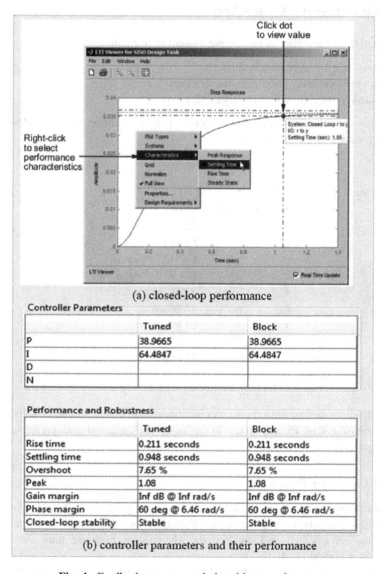

(a) closed-loop performance

Controller Parameters

	Tuned	Block
P	38.9665	38.9665
I	64.4847	64.4847
D		
N		

Performance and Robustness

	Tuned	Block
Rise time	0.211 seconds	0.211 seconds
Settling time	0.948 seconds	0.948 seconds
Overshoot	7.65 %	7.65 %
Peak	1.08	1.08
Gain margin	Inf dB @ Inf rad/s	Inf dB @ Inf rad/s
Phase margin	60 deg @ 6.46 rad/s	60 deg @ 6.46 rad/s
Closed-loop stability	Stable	Stable

(b) controller parameters and their performance

Fig. 4. Feedback structure and closed loop performance

4.2 Fuzzy Logic Controller Design

System non-linearity and systems with no accurate mathematical model can be better handled using artificial intelligent algorithms like fuzzy logic and neural network.

Fuzzy logic models operator's taught and the process of control system can be interpreted and widely used. Fuzzy logic for control application comprises of procedures of fuzzification, rule execution, inference and defuzzification [9–15] where all these procedures can be described in Fig. 5.

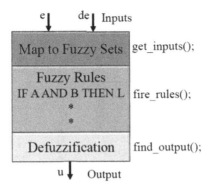

Fig. 5. Schematic diagram of basic tasks in fuzzy logic controller

Centre of gravity technique is widely applied defuzzification technique [9, 10]. Mathematically, the approach can be represented by Eq. (12).

$$y_{out} = \frac{\sum_{i=1}^{n} y_i(x_i) * x_i}{\sum_{i=1}^{n} y_i(x_i)} \tag{12}$$

The general rules for Dc motor speed control is that if motor speed is less than desired speed then speed up the motor and if motor speed is more than reference speed then slows it speed. If we consider a general unit step response of under damped case given in Fig. 6(a), we can have nine possible conditions as given in table form in Fig. 6 (c) from which based on the magnitude and polarity of error and change in error, it is possible to determine the fuzzy output. The error versus change in error plot given in Fig. 6(b) can give the active regions (range) of the universe of discourse for the fuzzy membership functions.

Following similar procedure, we can fill the possible fuzzy controller output for the error and change in error combinations. This concept can be used to set the rule table for the fuzzy logic controller. In this paper, triangular membership functions for the inputs and the output having each seven linguistic variables of negative large (nl), negative medium (nm), negative small (ns), zero (ze), positive small (ps), positive medium (pm) and positive large (pl) are designed. Accordingly, the corresponding membership functions and the rule table are given in Fig. 7.

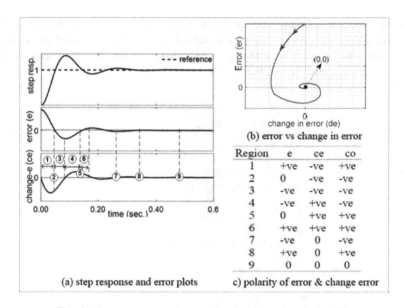

Fig. 6. Step-response and error signal plots and analysis table

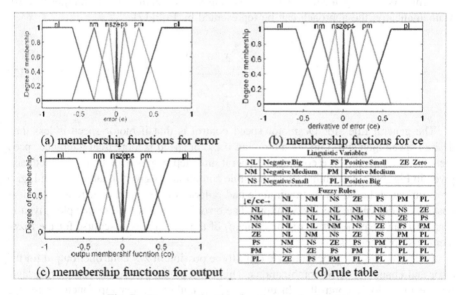

Fig. 7. Fuzzy membership functions and rule table

5   Results and Discussions

Performance evaluation of the proposed controllers is done using MATLAB/Simulink simulation for the test conditions of no load and loaded conditions. The complete MATLAB/Simulink model of the closed-loop system using PI and fuzzy logic controllers is given in Fig. 8.

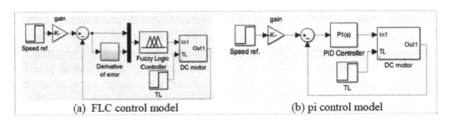

(a) FLC control model   (b) pi control model

Fig. 8. MATLAB/Simulink Models for speed control of a DC motor

5.1   Responses at No-Load Condition

Step-input of reference speed 800 and 1500 rad/sec are applied for both cases: PI and fuzzy logic based control systems. Figure 9 shows the step-response plots at no-load conditions.

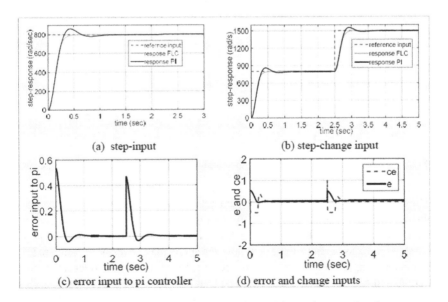

Fig. 9. Step responses at no-load and error/change in error signals

The broken line shows the reference (step-input) plot and the black curve shows the response using PI controller and the red curve with no-overshoot shows the response using fuzzy logic controller. From the responses, fuzzy logic controller based system has zero steady state error; zero percentage overshoot compared with PI based system. Figures 9(c) and (d) show the error plots for the corresponding controllers.

5.2 Response at Loaded Condition

At loaded condition, a reference speed of 800 and 1500 rad/sec and torque of load of 5 Nm is applied at time t = 4 s of the simulation time. The response plot with overshoot and black colour is the response using PI controller and the response with no overshoot and red colour is using fuzzy logic controller. Accordingly, the response plot for a loaded case, step reference input of 800 rad/sec and step-change in reference input from 800 rad/sec to 1500 rad/sec is given in Fig. 10.

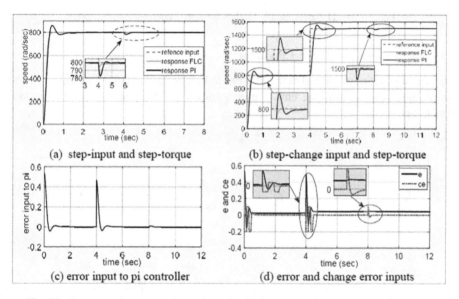

Fig. 10. Response for a step-change input/applied torque and the corresponding error

The results reveal that performance parameter values of using both controllers are within the specified limits. But using fuzzy logic has short settling time ($\approx$0.61 s) where as using PI has settling time of $\approx$1.4 s. For both conditions of loaded and no-load, fuzzy logic based controller has almost zero percentage overshoot compared 7.3% of overshoot using PI controller. This is because, fuzzy based controller has slow rise time compared to PI controller that may result in increasing peak over reference speed value. From performance parameters value for step reference speed input of 800rad/sec, the system takes short time to settle compared to using PI controller. And also the system using FLC has almost zero overshoot where as using PI has some overshoot even though it is within the limit specified. The result verifies that using FLC for the specified system has better dynamic performance and zero steady-state error compared to PI based system under the no-load and loaded conditions of the system.

6 Conclusions

Dynamic performance evaluation of the conventional PID controller and the intelligent fuzzy logic controllers based speed control of a permanent magnet DC motor using MATLAB/Simulink tool has been done. To evaluate their performance, measuring parameter values of rise-time, settling time, percentage overshoot and peak speed have been evaluated for the corresponding controllers. Controller having system performances of reduced percentage overshoot, short settling time and zero steady state-error are the required performances. From the performance evaluations done, the results shows that using fuzzy logic controller has small rise time which cause to reduce the peak speed and percentage overshoot and small settling time compared to using PI controller.

In summary, using fuzzy logic controllers as speed controller of dc motor has superior dynamic performance than using PID controllers.

References

1. Mohan, N., Undeland, T.M., Robbins, W.P.: Power Electronics: Converter, Applications and Design. Wiley and Sons
2. Lakshmi, G.R.P., Puttalakshmi, G.R., Paramasivam, S.: Speed control of brushless Dc motor using fuzzy controller. Indian Journal Appl. Res. (3)(11), 1–5 (2013)
3. Zhang, R., Song, L., Yang, J., Hoffman, T.: DC motor speed control system simulation based on fuzzy self-tuning PID. Fuzzy Info. Eng. **2**, AISC 62, 967–975 (2009)
4. Dökmetaş, B., Akçam, N., Faris, M.: Speed control of DC motor using fuzzy logic application. In: 4th International Symposium on Innovative Technologies in Engineering and Science 3–5, pp. 734–740, November 2016
5. Bitara, Z., Al Jabia, S., Khamisb, I.: Modeling and simulation of series DC motors in electric car. Energy Procedia **50**, 460–470 (2014)
6. Jilani, A., Murawwat, S., Jilani, S.O.: Controlling speed of DC motor with fuzzy controller in comparison with ANFIS controller. Intell. Control Autom. **6**, 64–74 (2015)
7. Guillemin, P.: Fuzzy logic applied to motor control. IEEE Trans. Ind. Appl. **32**(1), 51–56 (1996)
8. MATLAB Documentation "SISO Design Tool" (2017)
9. Orlowska-Kowalska, T., Szabat, K.: Optimization of fuzzy-logic speed controller for DC drive system with elastic joints. IEEE Trans. Ind. Appl. **40**(4), 1138–1144 (2004)
10. Gupta, R.A., Kumar, R., Bansal, A.K.: Artificial intelligence applications in Permanent Magnet Brushless DC motor drives. Artif. Intell. Rev. **33**, 175–186 (2010)
11. Jamali, N., Amlashi, S.: Design and implementation of fuzzy position control system for tracking applications and performance comparison with conventional PID. IAES Int. J. Artif. Intell. (IJ-AI) **1**(1), 31–44 (2012)
12. Sun, X., Koh, K., Yu, B., Matsui, M.: Fuzzy-logic-based *V/f* control of an induction motor for a DC grid power-leveling system using flywheel energy storage equipment. IEEE Trans. Industr. Electron. **56**(8), 3161–3168 (2009)

13. Ramya, A., Balaji, M., Kamaraj, V.: Adaptive MF tuned fuzzy logic speed controller for BLDC motor drive using ANN and PSO technique. J. Eng. **2019**(17), 3947–3950 (2019)
14. Kahveci, H., Okumus, H.I., Ekici, M.: Improved brushless DC motor speed controller with digital signal processor. Electron. Lett. **50**(12), 864–866 (2014)
15. Nag, T., Santra, S.B., Chatterjee, A., Chatterjee, D.: Fuzzy logic-based loss minimisation scheme for brushless DC motor drive system. IET Power Electron. **9**(8), 6 29, 1581–1589 (2016)

Genetic Algorithm Tuned Super Twisted Sliding Mode Controller (STSMC) for Self-balancing Control of a Two-Wheel Electric Scooter

Tefera T. Yetayew[1](✉) and Daniel G. Tesfaye[2]

[1] Adama Science and Technology University, P.O. 1888, Adama, Ethiopia
[2] Wolayta Sodo University, Sodo, Ethiopia

Abstract. Two wheel self-balancing electric scooter is based on inverted pendulum system and this system is a nonlinear and unstable. An inertial measurement unit (IMU) which is combination of accelerometer and gyroscope measurement is used in order to estimate and obtain the tilt angle of the scooter. Super twisted sliding mode controller (STSMC) is applied to correct the error between the desired set point and the actual tilt angle and adjust the brushless direct current (BLDC) motor speed accordingly to balance the scooter, when scooter is tilted forward, motor is move forward to catch up in order to balance the scooter and proportional integral derivative (PID) controller is used to control direction of scooter that means to turn left or right. The STSMC parameters and PID parameters are tuned using genetic algorithm (GA) and controllers performance evaluation is done using MATLAB/Simulink. The pitch and yaw angle with changes in magnitude of 0.1 rad and zero reference angle, almost the steady state error are 7.965×10^{-08} and 5.677×10^{-07} respectively for both controllers tuned by GA. GA tuned controllers are compared with analytically tuned controlled for initial pitch angle of 0.3 rad. The magnitude of steady-state errors at time 2 s are 7.71×10^{-07} and 0.004648 respectively, which is an indication of parameters tuned using global optimization algorithms, in this case GA are more optimal than analytically tuned parameters.

Keywords: Scooter · Genetic algorithm · STSMC and PID controller

1 Introduction

In today's society transportation is undoubtedly a fast-growing industry. Due to the rapid growth in the demand for personal transporter vehicles, self-balancing personal transporter scooters were introduced by the Segway Company. For the intention of increasing the efficiency of human's transportation and to reduce the cost, the self-balancing personal transporter which is also a great representation of the personal mobility device concept is now widely used in many industries and institutions such as police departments, tourism industry, factories and so on. The benefits which are offered by this personal transporter vehicle such as higher accessibility and zero fuel consumption can be considered as the ultimate solutions for the upcoming global issues

© ICST Institute for Computer Sciences, Social Informatics and Telecommunications Engineering 2022
Published by Springer Nature Switzerland AG 2022. All Rights Reserved
M. L. Berihun (Ed.): ICAST 2021, LNICST 411, pp. 269–287, 2022.
https://doi.org/10.1007/978-3-030-93709-6_18

caused by the growth of traffic and the environmental pollution happening all around the world. Even though the self-balancing transporter represents a better version of the personal transporter type vehicles that are being used nowadays, it simply failed in reaching the hands of the majority of society due to the expensive price range and the safety issues pointed out by the existing users of these self-balancing transporter models [1, 2].

The self-balancing personal transporter models (mainly Segway models) are comprised of multiple gyroscope and accelerometer sensors (few as additional) to obtain the angular rate and acceleration readings along different axes. The drawback which comes along using multiple sensors is the additional cost and the extra computational power required by the control unit. The two-wheeled self-balancing robot is a nonlinear MIMO under actuated system; thus, it is very challenging to keep balance when it climbs or descends on a slope and, especially, in the presence of no measurable disturbances. Two-wheeled scooters are one of the modern research topics in the robotic fields due to the natural unstable dynamic systems around the world [2–5]. Two-wheeled self-balancing robot based on inverted pendulum theory and dynamic balancing systems.

The contents of the research organizes the basics lay-out, components and principles in section two of the research and the dynamic models of the self-balance scooter in section three. The controllers design, tuning both analytically and GA based is presented in section four of the research. The results with the corresponding discussions and concluding remarks of findings are presented in sections five and six of the research.

2   Two-Wheel Self-balancing Scooter Basics

The research in recent years reveals the idea of self-balancing scooters. The two wheel self-balancing scooter is represented schematically in Fig. 1. Once system balance is achieved the system can move forward and back ward directions [6, 7].

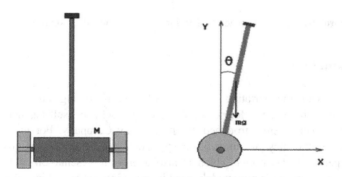

Fig. 1. Side and front views of the ideal two wheeled inverted pendulum system [6]

The pendulum that may cause system instability, the main body of the scooter that carries the drive system and the wheels for forward and backward movement are the main components of the two wheel self-balancing scooter considered in this research [6–8].

In principle, the controller for the self-balancing two wheel scooter, reads the tilt and compensates for the error so that the required upright position of the system will be kept. And also should respond to external forces as disturbance to the normal motion of the scooter by which the required position of the scooter can be maintained [7, 8] (Fig. 2).

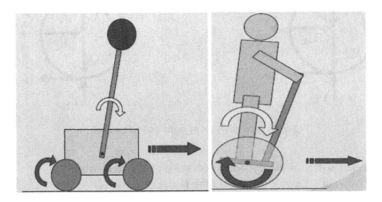

Fig. 2. Working principle of scooter [8]

3   Mathematical Model of the System

3.1   Mathematical Model of Scooter

To design the controller and perform the required analysis, the electrical actuator and the mechanical system of the scooter needs to be represented mathematically. Table 1 gives the required parameters of the scooter.

Table 1. Parameter and descriptions of scooter [8–10].

Parameters	Description	Unit
T_L and T_R	Input torque of the left and right wheel	N.m
H_{TR} and H_{TL}	Friction between the ground and the right and left wheels	N
H_R and H_L	Reaction forces impact on the right and left wheels	N
J_{TL} and J_{TR}	Inertial moment of the rotating masses with respect to the z axis	N.m
θ_{WR} and θ_{WL}	Pitch angle of the right and left wheels	rad
J_B	Inertial moment of the chassis with respect to the z axis	N m

The mathematical model of scooter is separated into 3 parts.

1. Wheel
2. Body
3. Dc motor (actuator)

In order to determine mathematical model of the electric scooter newton method is applied (Fig. 3).

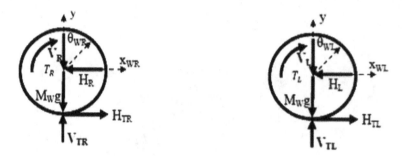

Fig. 3. Force analysis of right and left-wheel [8]

For the left wheel of the eScooter (the same as the right wheel):
Using Newton's Law of motion on the horizontal axis X

$$\sum F_x = ma$$

$$M_W \ddot{x}_{WL} = H_{TL} - H_L \tag{1}$$

Using Newton's Law of motion on the vertical axis Y

$$\sum F_Y = ma$$

$$M_W \ddot{y}_{WL} = V_{TL} - V_L - M_W g \tag{2}$$

And the sum of the Moments around the wheel's center gives:

$$\sum M_O = I\alpha$$

$$J_{WL} \ddot{\theta}_{WL} = T_L - H_{TL}R \tag{3}$$

By transforming any linear motion component to an angular motion component by using

$$x_{WL} = \theta_{WL}R \tag{4}$$

Moment of inertia of left wheel

$$J_{WL} = \frac{1}{2}M_{WL}R^2 \tag{5}$$

And for the rotation

$$\delta = \frac{x_{WL} - x_{WL}}{D} \tag{6}$$

From (1) sum the left and right wheel equation

$$+\begin{cases} M_W\ddot{x}_{WL} = H_{TL} - H_L & \text{for the left wheel} \\ M_W x_{WR} = H_{TR} - H_R & \text{for the right wheel} \end{cases}$$
$$\text{than}$$
$$M_W(\ddot{x}_{WL} + \ddot{x}_{WR}) = (H_{TL} + H_{TR}) - (H_L + H_R) \tag{7}$$

From (3)

$$\begin{cases} J_{WL}\ddot{\theta}_{WL} = T_L - H_{TL}R & \text{for the left wheel} \\ J_{WR}\ddot{\theta}_{WR} = T_R - H_{TR}R & \text{for the right wheel} \end{cases} \tag{8}$$

Solve (8) as follow (Fig. 4)

$$H_{TL} = \frac{T_L - J_{WL}\theta}{R}$$
$$H_{TR} = \frac{T_R - J_{WR}\theta}{R} \tag{9}$$

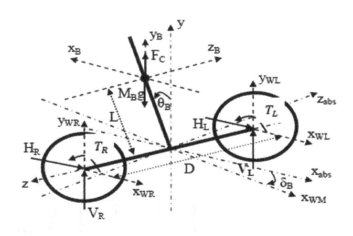

Fig. 4. Coordinate system of body of scooter [8].

For the body of the Scooter:
Using Newton's Law of motion on the horizontal axis X

$$\sum F_x = ma$$

$$M_B \ddot{x}_B = H_L + H_R \tag{10}$$

Using Newton's Law of motion on the vertical axis Y

$$\sum F_y = ma$$

$$M_B \ddot{y}_B = V_L + V_R - M_B g + \frac{T_L + T_R}{L} \sin(\theta_B) \tag{11}$$

The sum of moments around the center of mass of the body

$$\sum M_O = I\alpha$$

$$J_B \ddot{\theta}_B = (V_L + V_R)L \sin(\theta_B) - (H_L + H_R)L \cos(\theta_B) - (T_L + T_R) \tag{12}$$

$$x_B = L \sin(\theta_B) + \frac{x_{WL} + x_{WR}}{2} \tag{13}$$

$$y_B = -L(1 - \cos(\theta_B)) \tag{14}$$

Moment of inertia of chassis

$$J_B = \frac{1}{3} M_B L^2 \tag{15}$$

$$\theta = \theta_B = \theta_W = \theta_{WL} = \theta_{WR} \tag{16}$$

$$x_{WM} = \frac{x_{WL} + x_{WR}}{2} \tag{17}$$

For the chassis rotation:

$$J_\delta \ddot{\delta} = \frac{D}{2}(H_L - H_R) \tag{18}$$

After Solve (8) for $V_L + V_R$ and (7), (13) into (9) than

$$J_B \ddot{\theta} = \left(M_B \ddot{y}_B + M_B g - \frac{T_L + T_R}{L} \sin(\theta) \right) L \sin(\theta) - M_B \ddot{x}_B L \cos(\theta) - (T_L + T_R)$$

$$J_B \ddot{\theta} = M_B L(\ddot{y}_B \sin(\theta) - \ddot{x} \cos(\theta)) + M_B g L \sin(\theta) - (T_L + T_R)(1 + \sin^2(\theta)) \tag{19}$$

Substitute (14) into (10) than differentiate both side

$$x_B = L\sin(\theta) + x_{WM}$$

$$\dot{x}_B = L\dot{\theta}\cos(\theta) + \dot{x}_{WM}$$

And again differentiate both side

$$\ddot{x}_B = L\ddot{\theta}\cos(\theta) - L\dot{\theta}^2\sin(\theta) + \ddot{x}_{WM} \tag{20}$$

And the same way as x_B differentiate y_B than

$$\ddot{y}_B = -L\ddot{\theta}\sin(\theta) - L\dot{\theta}^2\cos(\theta) \tag{21}$$

Multiply (17) by $\cos(\theta)$ and multiply (18) by $\sin(\theta)$ and subtract both equation than we get

$$\ddot{y}_B\sin(\theta) - \ddot{x}_B\cos(\theta) = -L\ddot{\theta} - \ddot{x}_{WM}\cos(\theta) \tag{22}$$

Substitute (19) and (12) into (16)

$$\frac{4}{3}M_B L^2\ddot{\theta} + M_B L\cos(\theta)\ddot{x}_{WM} = M_B g L\sin(\theta) - (T_L + T_R)\left(1 + \sin^2(\theta)\right) \tag{23}$$

From (10)

$$H_L + H_R = M_B\ddot{x}_B \tag{24}$$

Substitute (9) and (24) into (7)

$$M_W(\ddot{x}_{WL} + \ddot{x}_{WR}) = \left(\frac{T_L + T_R - (J_{WL}\theta + J_{WR}\theta)}{R}\right) - M_B\ddot{x}_B$$

Where $\begin{aligned} J_W &= J_{WL} + J_{WR} \\ M_W &= M_{WL} + M_{WR} \end{aligned}$ than

$$2M_W\ddot{x}_{WM} = -M_B\ddot{x}_B + \frac{(T_L + T_R)}{R} - \frac{2J_W\ddot{\theta}}{R} \tag{25}$$

From (5)

$$\begin{cases} J_{WL} = \frac{1}{2}M_{WL}R^2 & \text{for left wheel} \\ J_{WR} = \frac{1}{2}M_{WR}R^2 & \text{for right wheel} \end{cases}$$

Sum the two equation

$$J_{WL} + J_{WR} = R^2(M_{WL} + M_{WR})$$
$$J_W = R^2 M_W \tag{26}$$

Substitute (20) and (26) into (25) than we get

$$(M_B L \cos(\theta) + R M_W)\ddot{\theta} + (2M_W + M_B)\ddot{x}_{WM} = M_B L \dot{\theta}^2 \sin(\theta) + \frac{(T_L + T_R)}{R} \tag{27}$$

Solve (23) for $\ddot{x}_{WM}$ and substitute into (27) than

$$\left((2M_W + M_B) - \frac{0.75(M_B L \cos(\theta) + M_W R)\cos(\theta)}{L}\right)\ddot{\theta} = \frac{0.75g(2M_W + M_B)\sin(\theta)}{L}$$
$$-0.75M_B \sin(\theta)\cos(\theta)\dot{\theta}^2 - \left(\frac{0.75(2M_W + M_B)(1 + \sin^2(\theta))}{M_B L^2} + \frac{0.75\cos(\theta)}{RL}\right)(T_L + T_R) \tag{28}$$

Solve (23) for $\ddot{\theta}$ and substitute into (27) than

$$\left(-0.75\frac{\cos(\theta)(M_B L \cos(\theta) + M_W R)}{L} + (2M_W + M_B)\right)\ddot{x}_{WM} = -0.75(M_B L \cos(\theta) + M_W R)$$
$$\frac{g \sin(\theta)}{L} + M_B L \sin(\theta)\dot{\theta}^2 - \left(0.75\frac{(M_B L \cos(\theta) + M_W R)(1 + \sin^2(\theta))}{M_B L^2} + \frac{1}{R}\right)(T_L + T_R) \tag{29}$$

Solve H_{TL} from (1)

$$H_{TL} = M_W \ddot{x}_{WL} + H_L \tag{30}$$

Differentiate (4)

$$\ddot{\theta}_{WL} = \frac{\ddot{x}_{WL}}{R} \tag{31}$$

Substitute (30) into (3) than

$$\begin{cases} H_L = \frac{T_L}{R} - \ddot{x}_{WL}\left(M_W + \frac{J_W}{R^2}\right) & \text{for the left wheel} \\ H_R = \frac{T_R}{R} - \ddot{x}_{WR}\left(M_W + \frac{J_W}{R^2}\right) & \text{for the right wheel} \end{cases} \tag{32}$$

Subtract two equation of (32) and then substitute into (18) than

$$\left(J_\delta + \frac{1}{2}D^2\left(M_W + \frac{J_W}{R^2}\right)\right)\ddot{\delta} = \frac{1}{2}D\frac{T_L - T_R}{R} \tag{33}$$

We have

$$J_W = \frac{1}{3}M_B R^2 = J_\delta = \frac{1}{3}M_B \left(\frac{D}{2}\right)^2 = \frac{1}{12}M_B D^2 \tag{34}$$

Substitute (34) into (33) than we get

$$\ddot{\delta} = \frac{6}{(M_B + 9M_W)DR}(T_L - T_R) \tag{35}$$

The basic system of equations are (28), (29) and (35).

Let $x_1 = \theta$, $x_2 = \dot{\theta}$, $x_3 = x$, $x_4 = \dot{x}$, $x_5 = \delta$ and $x_6 = \dot{\delta}$. State equations of the e-scooter is rewritten as

$$\begin{cases} \dot{x}_1 = x_2 \\ \dot{x}_2 = f_1(x_1) + f_2(x_1, x_2) + g_1(x_1)(T_L + T_R) \\ \dot{x}_3 = x_4 \\ \dot{x}_4 = f_3(x_1) + f_4(x_1, x_2) + g_2(x_1)(T_L + T_R) \\ \dot{x}_5 = x_6 \\ \dot{x}_6 = g_3(T_L - T_R) \end{cases} \tag{36}$$

$$f_1(x_1) = \frac{\left(\frac{-0.75g(\sin x_1)}{L}\right)}{\left(\frac{0.75(M_W R + M_B L(\cos x_1))(\cos x_1)}{(2M_W + M_B)L} - 1\right)}$$

$$f_2(x_1, x_2) = \frac{\left(\frac{0.75 M_B L(\sin x_1)(\cos x_1)}{(2M_W + M_B)L}(x_2)^2\right)}{\left(\frac{0.75(M_W R + M_B L(\cos x_1))(\cos x_1)}{(2M_W + M_B)L} - 1\right)}$$

$$g_1(x_1) = \frac{\left(\frac{0.75(1 + (\sin x_1)^2)}{M_B L^2} + \frac{0.75(\cos x_1)}{(2M_W + M_B)RL}\right)}{\left(\frac{0.75(M_W R + M_B L(\cos x_1))(\cos x_1)}{(2M_W + M_B)L} - 1\right)}$$

$$f_3(x_1) = \frac{\left(\frac{-0.75g(M_W R + M_B L(\cos x_1))(\sin x_1)}{L}\right)}{\left(2M_W + M_B - \frac{0.75(M_W R + M_B L(\cos x_1))(\cos x_1)}{L}\right)}$$

$$f_4(x_1, x_2) = \frac{M_B L(\sin x_1)(x_2)^2}{\left(2M_W + M_B - \frac{0.75(M_W R + M_B L(\cos x_1))(\cos x_1)}{L}\right)}$$

$$g_2(x_1) = \frac{\left(\frac{0.75(M_W R + M_B L(\cos x_1))(1 + (\sin x1)^2)}{M_B L^2} + \frac{1}{R}\right)}{\left(2M_W + M_B - \frac{0.75(M_W R + M_B L(\cos x_1))(\cos x_1)}{L}\right)}$$

$$g_3 = \frac{6}{(M_B + 9M_W)DR} \quad \text{where} \quad \begin{cases} U1 = T_L + T_R \\ U2 = T_L - T_R \end{cases}$$

3.2   Dc Motor Modeling

Dc motor is the most common type of actuator in electric drives mainly because of high starting torque and wide range of speed control. The couples system with the Dc motor may change the rotational motion to translational motion [11, 12]. In this research, Dc motor is considered as the main actuator for the specified application. The schematic diagram of the electric and mechanical components of a Dc motor is given in Fig. 5.

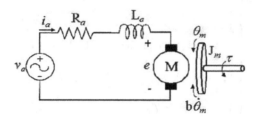

Fig. 5. Schematic diagram of a DC-motor [12]

Applying Kirchhoff's law we can get the electrical equation,

$$v_a = R_a i_a + L_a \frac{d}{dt} i_a + e \tag{37}$$

To drive the mathematical representation of the mechanical part of the motor, the direct proportion relation of the torque with armature current is considered. For the specified application in this research, constant magnetic field is considered and the torque can be affected by the armature current as shown in Eq. (38).

$$T_e = k_t I_a \tag{38}$$

The relation between back emf and angular velocity of the shaft can be represented using Eq. (39).

$$e = k_b \omega \tag{39}$$

Usually, the back emf constant and torque constant are assumed to have same value [11]. Using physical laws, Newton's second law, the expression for the torque can be given by Eq. (40).

$$T_e = J\frac{d\omega}{dt} + B\omega \tag{40}$$

Substitute (39) into (37) and solve I_a of (38) and substitute again into (37) then

$$V_a = \frac{R_a}{K}T_e + \frac{L_a}{K}\frac{dT_e}{dt} + K\omega \tag{41}$$

Now, taking the Laplace transform of (40) and (41)

$$V_a(s) = \frac{R_a}{K}T_e(s) + \frac{L_a}{K}sT_e(s) + K\omega(s) \tag{42}$$

$$T_e(s) = (Js + B)\omega(s) \tag{43}$$

Solve for $\omega(s)$ of (43) and substitute into (42) and solve transfer function of input $V_a(s)$ and output $T_e(s)$ than

$$V_a(s) = \left(\frac{R_a}{K} + \frac{L_a}{K}s + \frac{K}{Js + B}\right)T_e(s)$$

Then

$$T_e(s) = \frac{K(Js + B)}{R_a(Js + B) + L_as(Js + B) + K^2}V_a(s) \tag{44}$$

From motor dynamics, the torque driving the right and left wheel can be expressed as [12].

$$U_1 = \frac{K(Js + B)}{R_a(Js + B) + L_as(Js + B) + K^2}(V_L + V_R)$$

$$U_2 = \frac{K(Js + B)}{R_a(Js + B) + L_as(Js + B) + K^2}(V_L - V_R) \tag{45}$$

System Decoupling: The state-space representation indicates that two wheel scooter is a high coupled nonlinear system. The decoupling the whole system into two separate sub-systems. Similar to the work in [17, 18] the following decoupling transformation is used to convert V_θ and V_δ to the voltages of the left and right wheels V_L and V_R. Where as

$$\begin{cases} V_\theta = V_L + V_R \\ V_\delta = V_L - V_R \end{cases} \tag{46}$$

So

$$\begin{cases} V_L = \dfrac{1}{2}(V_\theta + V_\delta) \\ V_R = \dfrac{1}{2}(V_\theta - V_\delta) \end{cases} \tag{47}$$

where,

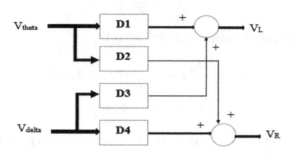

Fig. 6. Decoupling unit

$$D1 = D2 = D3 = 0.5 \text{ and}$$
$$D4 = -0.5$$

The parameter values of the scooter and the dc-motor specifications for the proposed system drive are given Tables 2 and 3 respectively.

Table 2. Parameter of scooter with specified value [1, 8].

symbol	Value (unit)	Description
θ	Degree	Pitch angle (user defined)
δ	Degree	Yaw angle (user defined)
M_W	6kg	Mass of the wheel
M_B	Up to 90kg	Mass of the body
R	0.2m	Radius of the wheel
L	1m	Distance between z-axis and e gravity center
D	0.6m	Distance between contact patches of the wheel
g	9.8m/s^2	Acceleration due to Gravity

Table 3. DC motor value

Parameters	Description	Value (unit)
Ra	Armature Resistance	$2.5\,\Omega$
La	Armature Inductance	0.0005H
Va	Armature Voltage	V
e	DC motor Back Emf	V
Kb	DC motor back emf constant	0.58V s/rad
Kt	DC motor torque constant	0.58 N m/A
ω	DC motor rated speed	rad/s
J	Moment inertia of the motor	$0.02\ \text{kg.m}^2/\text{s}^2$
B	Damping ratio of the mechanical system	0.04 Nms

4 Controller Design

4.1 Design Super Twisted Sliding Mode Controller (STSMC) for Balancing Scooter

Firstly, we design the sliding mode function as,

$$S = c\dot{e} + e \qquad (48)$$

where S is sliding surface, e is error and c must satisfy the Hurwitz condition.
Define tracking error for the pitch angle as

$$\begin{cases} e = x_1 - x_{1ref} \\ \dot{e} = \dot{x}_1 - \dot{x}_{1ref} \\ \ddot{e} = \ddot{x}_1 - \ddot{x}_{1ref} = \dot{x}_2 - \ddot{x}_{1ref} \end{cases} \qquad (49)$$

where $x_{1ref} = \theta_{ref}$, the reference value of pitch angle.
Therefore, we have

$$\dot{S} = c\dot{e} + \ddot{e} = c(\dot{x}_1 - \dot{x}_{1ref}) + (\dot{x}_2 - \ddot{x}_{1ref})$$

But

$$\dot{x}_2 = f_1(x_1) + f_2(x_1, x_2) + g_1(x_1)U1$$

$$\dot{S} = c(\dot{x}_1 - \dot{x}_{1ref}) + f_1(x_1) + f_2(x_1, x_2) + g_1(x_1)U1 - \ddot{x}_{1ref} \qquad (50)$$

$$\dot{S}S = S(c(\dot{x}_1 - \dot{x}_{1ref}) + (f_1(x_1) + f_2(x_1, x_2) + g_1(x_1)U1 - \ddot{x}_{1ref})) \qquad (51)$$

In order to make the balancing scooter remains on the surface the Lyapunov stability requirement must be fulfilled i.e. to satisfy the condition $\dot{S}S < 0$, then 1st design conventional sliding mode control as.

$$U1 = \frac{c\left(\dot{x}_{1ref} - \dot{x}_1\right) - f_1(x_1) - f_2(x_1, x_2) + \ddot{x}_{1ref} - \eta \mathrm{sgn}(s)}{g_1(x_1)} \tag{52}$$

$$\mathrm{sgn}(s) = \begin{cases} 1, & s > 0 \\ 0, & s = 0 \\ -1, & s < 0 \end{cases}$$

where c and η are constant

From (41) designed controller has two parts.

$$U1 = u_c + u_{eq}$$

So

$$u_c = \eta \mathrm{sgn}(s) \text{ and} \tag{53}$$

$$u_{eq} = \frac{c\left(\dot{x}_{1ref} - \dot{x}_1\right) - f_1(x_1) - f_2(x_1, x_2) + \ddot{x}_{1ref}}{g_1(x_1)} \tag{54}$$

The Super-twisting sliding mode controller [13–16] is given by:

$$\begin{cases} u_c = -C_1 |s|^{\frac{1}{2}} \mathrm{sgn}(s) + v \\ \dot{v} = -C_2 \mathrm{sgn}(s) \end{cases} \tag{55}$$

where c_1 and c_2 are constant

From (48) and (55) we have

$$u = -C_1 |s|^{\frac{1}{2}} \mathrm{sgn}(s) - C_2 \int_0^t \mathrm{sgn}(s) d\tau \tag{56}$$

Therefore from (54) and (56) the proposed super twisted sliding mode controller is given by

$$U1 = u_c + u_{eq}$$

$$U1 = \frac{c\left(\dot{x}_{1ref} - \dot{x}_1\right) - f_1(x_1) - f_2(x_1, x_2) + \ddot{x}_{1ref}}{g_1(x_1)} - C_1 |s|^{\frac{1}{2}} \mathrm{sgn}(s)$$

$$- C_2 \int_0^t \mathrm{sgn}(s) d\tau \tag{57}$$

The parameter of STSMC C1, C2 and c are tuned using genetic algorithm (GA). And STSMC are used to control balancing of scooter.

4.2   Design PID Controller for Turn Left and Right Direction

Proportional, integral and derivative controller is also designed to compare the performance of the proposed modern optimization algorithms based tuned controller. The mathematical representation of the PID controller comprising of all actions on the error is given by Eq. (58), defining "u" as the controller output and Kp, Ki and Kd as the corresponding constants [12].

$$U = Kpe(t) + Ki \int e(t)dt + Kd\frac{d}{dt}e(t) \tag{58}$$

4.3   Controller Parameters Tuning Sung GA

The most crucial step in applying GA is to choose the objective functions that are used to evaluate fitness of each chromosome. Some of this objective function are

$$IAE = \int_0^\tau |e(t)|dt$$

$$ISE = \int_0^\tau e(t)^2 \tag{59}$$

$$ITAE = \int_0^\tau t|e(t)|dt$$

The STSMC and PID controller is used to minimize the error signals, or we can define more carefully, in the term of error criteria: to minimize the value of performance indices mentioned as below for our system.

$$ITAE = \int_0^t t(|e_1(t) + |e_2(t)||)dt \tag{60}$$

where $e_1(t) = \theta_{ref} - \theta(t)$ and $e_2(t) = \delta_{ref} - \delta(t)$

Pseudo code for GA to tune parameter of controller:

1. Generate an initial, random population of individuals for a fixed size
2. Evaluate their fitness.
3. Select the fittest members of the population.
4. Reproduce using a probabilistic method
5. Implement crossover operation on the reproduced chromosomes (choosing probabilistically both the crossover site and the.mates.).
6. Execute mutation operation with low probability.
7. Repeat step 2 until a predefined convergence criterion is met.

The genetic algorithm parameters, the convergence characteristic of the fitness function and tuned parameters are given in Fig. 6. In Fig. 6(b) analytically tuned parameters are also included. From the response the convergence curve, the algorithm converged with best value of 0.0158945, mean value of 0.0162138 and seventh generation (Fig. 7).

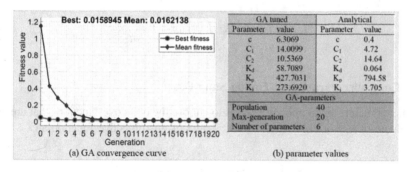

(a) GA convergence curve   (b) parameter values

Fig. 7. Convergence curve and parameter values

5   Results and Discussions

The simulation is performed based on parameter of scooter described in tables above. STSMC is used for balancing of scooter and PID controller is used for direction control (turn left and turn right). Performance evaluation of the corresponding controllers is done using MATLAB/Simulink.

5.1   GA Tuned Controllers with Initial Pitch and Yaw Angles

Figure 8(a) shows the response of the scooter with small initial pitch angle ($\theta = 0.1$ rad), and the corresponding error plot with reference angle of zero rad. And the response plot for zero reference angle and with initial pitch angle of $\theta = 0.3$ rad is presented in Fig. 8(b).

For both cases of initial pitch angles $\theta = 0.1$ and $\theta = 0.3$, the steady state errors are 7.965×10^{-08} and 9.372×10^{-08} respectively. Which is nearly zero and indicates that for the given reference angle of zero radian, the pitch angle of scooter converge to zero for both initial pitch angle values. It is also indication that the scooter can keep the balance.

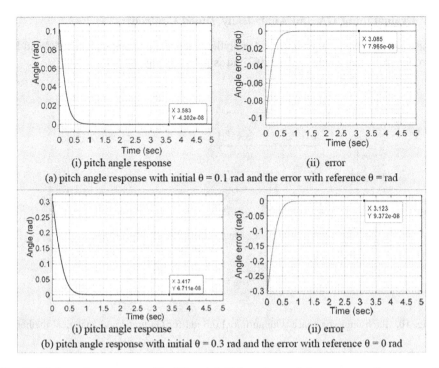

Fig. 8. Pitch angle response with different initial angles and the corresponding error with reference angles

Figure 9 shows the response plot and the corresponding error values of the initial yaw angle, $\delta = 0.1$ rad again for zero reference angel. The direction (turn left and right) of scooter successfully converge to zero.

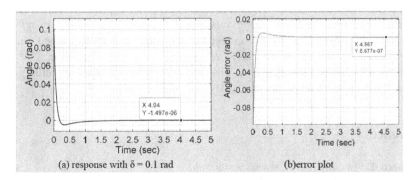

Fig. 9. Yaw angle response with an initial 0.1 rad and the corresponding error from reference angle

5.2   Evaluation of GA and Analytically Tuned Controllers

Comparison of genetic algorithm and analytical method of tuning for STSMC and PID controller for initial pitch angle of 0.3 rad is given in Fig. 10.

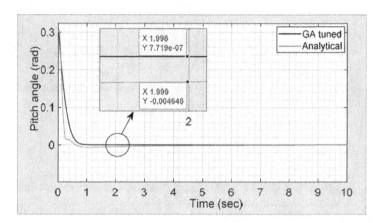

Fig. 10. Pitch angle response with an initial 0.3 rad for Ga tuned and analytical method

The performance evaluation of GA tuned and analytically tuned controllers for the proposed application show that GA tuned parameters gives almost zero steady state error (7.719×10–07) compared to analytically tuned controllers (-4.648×10–03).

6   Conclusions

Mathematical models of self-balancing scooter, controllers of supper twisted sliding mode add PID design using genetic algorithm and analytical tuning methods has been done. Performance evaluation of controllers tuned in both approaches has been evaluated for initial pitch and yaw angle values of 0.1 and 0.3 rad with zero reference angles has been done. The simulation results show that for both GA tuned and analytically tuned controllers have nearly zero steady state error. However, GA tuned parameters give better convergence to zero and fast dynamic response (settling time) compared with system response with analytically tuned controllers.

References

1. Kamen, D.: Segway (2001). www.segway.com
2. Jmel, I., Dimassi, H., Hadj-Said, S., M'Sahli, F.: Adaptive observer-based Sliding mode control for a two-wheeled self-balancing Robot under terrain inclination and disturbances. Math. Prob. Eng. **2021**, 1–15 (2021)
3. Goher, K.M., Tokhi, M.O., Siddique, N.H.: Dynamic modeling and control of a two wheeled robotic vehicle with a virtual payload. Arpn J. Eng. Appl. Sci. **6**(3), 7–41 (2011)

4. Kim, S., Kwon, S.: Robust transition control of under actuated two-wheeled self-balancing vehicle with semi-online dynamic trajectory planning. Mechatronics **68**, 102366 (2020)
5. Tsai, C.-C., Huang, H.-C., Lin, S.-C.: Adaptive neural network control of a self-balancing two-wheeled scooter. IEEE Trans. Ind. Electr. **57**(4), 1420–1428 (2010)
6. Khaled, M., Mohammed, A., Ibraheem, M.S.: Balancing a two wheeled robot do (July 2009). https://doi.org/10.13140/rg.2.2.25634.63683
7. Rigatos, G., Busawon, K., Pomares, J., Abbaszadeh, M.: Nonlinear optimal control for the wheeled inverted pendulum system. Robotica **38**(1), 29–47 (2019)
8. Son, N.N., Anh, H.P.H.: Adaptive backstepping self-balancing control of a two-wheel electric scooter. Int. J. Adv. Robot. Syst. **11**(10), 165 (2014)
9. Asali, M.O., Hadary, F., Sanjaya, B.W.: Modeling, simulation, and optimal control for two-wheeled self-balancing robot. Int. J. Electr. Comput. Eng. (IJECE) **7**(4), 2008–2017 (2017)
10. Lin, S., Tsai, C.: Development of a self-balancing human transportation vehicle for the teaching of feedback control. IEEE Trans. Educ. **52**(1), 157–168 (2009)
11. Kankhunthod, K., Kongratana, V., Numsomran, A., Tipsuwanporn, V.: Self-balancing robot control using fractional-order PID Controller, 13–15 March 2019, pp 77–82 (2019)
12. Srisertpol, J.: PI controller plus adaptive fuzzy logic compensator for torque controlled system of DC motor, November 2013 (2013)
13. Ouchen, S., Benbouzid, M., Blaabjerg, F., Betka, A., Steinhart, H.: Direct power control of shunt active power filter using space vector modulation based on super twisting sliding mode control. IEEE J. Emerg. Sel. Top. Power Electron. **9**(3), 3243–3253 (2021). https://doi.org/10.1109/JESTPE.2020.3007900
14. Humaidi, A.J., Hasan, A.F.: Particle swarm optimization–based adaptive super-twisting sliding mode control design for 2-degree-of-freedom helicopter. Measur. Control **52**(9–10), 1403–1419 (2019)
15. Zhao, Y., Huang, P., Zhang, F.: Dynamic modeling and super-twisting sliding mode control for tethered space robot. Acta Astronaut. **143**, 310–321 (2018)
16. Zheng, Z., Teng, M.: Modeling and decoupling control for two-wheeled self-balancing robot. In: 2016 28th Chinese Control and Decision Conference (CCDC) (2016)
17. Chen, L., et al.: Robust hierarchical sliding mode control of a two-wheeled self-balancing vehicle using perturbation estimation. Mech. Syst. Sig. Process. **139**, 106584 (2020)
18. Ali, M.I., Hossen, M.M.: A two-wheeled self-balancing robot with dynamics model. In: 2017 4th International Conference on Advances in Electrical Engineering (ICAEE), Dhaka, 2017, pp. 271–275 (2017)

Artificial Neural Network Based Rotor Flux Estimation and Fuzzy-Logic Sensorless Speed Control of an Induction Motor

Tefera T. Yetayew[(⊠)] and Rahel S. Sinta

Adama Science and Technology University, P.O. 1888, Adama, Ethiopia

Abstract. This paper aims to design rotor flux estimation based on artificial neural network (ANN) and fuzzy-logic based sensor less speed control of control for an induction motor drive. Induction motors are widely used for industrial applications with better reliability compared with DC-motor drives. However, control techniques for wide range speed control are complex. To achieve wide speed control range, field oriented control techniques are recommended. From the areas of application point of view, field sensors may not operate properly may be due to frequent failure that needs sensor less control technique. Thus, the research in this paper focuses on application of artificial neural network for flux estimation and fuzzy logic sensor less speed control of induction motor drive system. Performance evaluation of the control and flux estimation is done using MATLAB tool. The training of ANN for the flux estimation converged with epochs of 1000 and mean squared error of 0.00061617. The simulation results for the reference step input of 100 rad/s, the system with PI controller showed 5.851% percentage overshoot and 0.2 s settling time. Whereas the fuzzy based system resulted in 0.505% percentage overshoot and 0.085 s settling time. In summary, the controller performance reveals better dynamic response can be achieved using fuzzy logic based system than the system based on the conventional proportional integral (PI) controller.

Keywords: ANN · Fuzzy logic · Induction motor drive · Sensor less indirect field-oriented control

1 Introduction

Three-phase induction motor has been a reliable electromechanical energy conversion device for over 100 years. Induction motors, particularly the squirrel cage induction motors (SCIM) have been widely used in industrial applications because of their several inherent advantages such as their simple construction, robustness, reliability, low cost, and less maintenance needs [1]. The induction motor control methods are broadly classified into two categories i.e., scalar control and vector control. Scalar control: one of the primary ways of controlling induction motor was the Volts/Hertz speed control during which the motor was excited with constant voltage to frequency ratio to take care of a constant air gap flux and hence provide maximum torque sensitivity. This method is comparatively simple but doesn't yield satisfactory results for a high- performance application. This is often the fact that within the scalar control,

M. L. Berihun (Ed.): ICAST 2021, LNICST 411, pp. 288–303, 2022.
https://doi.org/10.1007/978-3-030-93709-6_19

an inherent coupling exists between the torque and air gap flux, which results in a sluggish response of the induction motor. Vector control (field-oriented control), overcome the limitation of the scalar control method [2, 3].

High performance vector control induction motor drives require speed or position information for its operation. However, these Sensors mounted on the machine shaft are not desirable for a variety of reasons. First of all, the cost is substantial. Secondly, their mounting requires a machine with two shaft ends available - one for the sensor and therefore the other one for the load coupling. Thirdly, electrical signals from the shaft sensor need to be taken to the controller and therefore the sensor needs an influence supply these require additional cabling. Finally, the presence of a shaft sensor reduces the mechanical robustness of the machine and its reliability [4–6]. Due to these reasons, speed sensor less systems, in which rotor speed measurements are not available, are preferred and find applications in many areas for speed regulation, load torque variation, and speed tracking purposes.

This paper addresses flux estimation technique using artificial neural network and speed control using fuzzy logic. And the contents are organized as dynamic models and control techniques in Sect. 2, flux estimation and controller design parts are presented in Sects. 3 and 4 respectively. The simulation results with the corresponding discussions and conclusions of findings in the research are presented in Sects. 5 and 6 respectively.

2 Dynamic Model of Induction Machine and Control Techniques

Assumptions made to produce mathematical model of the induction motor are summarized as follows:

- Copper loss is neglected.
- Spatial distribution of fluxes and amper turns wave are considered sinusoidal.
- Neglect all losses.
- Permeability of the rotor and stator are assumed infinite.

2.1 Dynamic Model of Induction Machine

Synchronous frame [7–10];

Equation (1) and (2) shows, the stator dq0 equations of voltage,

$$v_{ds}^e = R_s i_{ds}^e - \omega_e \varphi_{ds}^e + \frac{d\varphi_{ds}^e}{dt} \tag{1}$$

$$v_{qs}^e = R_s i_{qs}^e - \omega_e \varphi_{qs}^e + \frac{d\varphi_{qs}^e}{dt} \tag{2}$$

where v_{ds}^e, v_{qs}^e is stator voltages along d, q-axis respectively

Equation (3) and (4) shows, the rotor dq0 equations of voltage,

$$v_{dr}^e = R_r i_{dr}^e - (\omega_e - \omega_r)\varphi_{dr}^e + \frac{d\varphi_{dr}^e}{dt} \tag{3}$$

$$v_{qr}^e = R_r i_{qr}^e + (\omega_e - \omega_r)\varphi_{qr}^e + \frac{d\varphi_{qr}^e}{dt} \tag{4}$$

where v_{dr}^e, v_{qr}^e is rotor voltages along d, q-axis respectively.

Matrix form representation for the stator and rotor flux linkage is given by Eq. (5).

$$\begin{bmatrix} \varphi_{ds}^e \\ \varphi_{qs}^e \\ \varphi_{dr}^e \\ \varphi_{qr}^e \end{bmatrix} = \begin{bmatrix} L_s & 0 & L_m & 0 \\ 0 & L_s & 0 & L_m \\ L_m & 0 & L_r & 0 \\ 0 & L_m & 0 & L_r \end{bmatrix} \begin{bmatrix} i_{ds}^e \\ i_{qs}^e \\ i_{dr}^e \\ i_{qr}^e \end{bmatrix} \tag{5}$$

The torque developed in the q-axis current can be represented by Eq. (6),

$$T_e = \frac{3}{2}\frac{P}{2}\frac{L_m}{L_r}(\varphi_{rd}i_{sq} - \varphi_{rq}i_{sd}) \tag{6}$$

The mechanical system torque is given by Eq. (7),

$$T_e = J\frac{dw_r}{dt} + fw_r + T_L \tag{7}$$

where, w_r is rotor speed in RPM and J-is moment of inertia and f-friction coefficient.

2.2   Clark and Park Transformations

Clarke-park transformation transforms three-phase to two axis of α and β stationary and rotary by which complexity of analysis can be reduced [11].

A. Clarke transformation.
Equations (8)–(10) show the corresponding voltage expressions for an induction motor under unbalanced condition,

$$V_a = \sqrt{2}V_{rms}\sin(\omega t) \tag{8}$$

$$V_b = \sqrt{2}V_{rms}\sin(\omega t - \frac{2\pi}{3}) \tag{9}$$

$$V_c = \sqrt{2}V_{rms}\sin(\omega t + \frac{2\pi}{3}) \tag{10}$$

The result of clark transformation of V_{abc} to $V_{\alpha,\beta}$ is presented in Eq. (11),

$$\begin{bmatrix} V_\alpha \\ V_\beta \end{bmatrix} = \frac{2}{3} \begin{bmatrix} 1 & -\frac{1}{2} & -\frac{1}{2} \\ 0 & \frac{\sqrt{3}}{2} & -\frac{\sqrt{3}}{2} \end{bmatrix} \begin{bmatrix} V_a \\ V_b \\ V_c \end{bmatrix} \tag{11}$$

Equation (12) shows inverse Clark transformation results,

$$\begin{bmatrix} V_a \\ V_b \\ V_c \end{bmatrix} = \begin{bmatrix} 1 & 0 \\ -\frac{1}{2} & -\frac{\sqrt{3}}{2} \\ -\frac{1}{2} & -\frac{\sqrt{3}}{2} \end{bmatrix} \begin{bmatrix} V_\alpha \\ V_\beta \end{bmatrix} \tag{12}$$

B. Park transformation.

In the dq reference frame, Eq. (13) shows the system voltages,

$$\begin{bmatrix} V_d \\ V_q \end{bmatrix} = \begin{bmatrix} \cos(\theta) & \sin(\theta) \\ -\sin(\theta) & \cos(\theta) \end{bmatrix} \begin{bmatrix} V_\alpha \\ V_\beta \end{bmatrix} \tag{13}$$

Result of inverse park transformations results in,

$$\begin{bmatrix} V_\alpha \\ V_\beta \end{bmatrix} = \begin{bmatrix} \cos(\theta) & -\sin(\theta) \\ \sin(\theta) & \cos(\theta) \end{bmatrix} \begin{bmatrix} V_d \\ V_q \end{bmatrix} \tag{14}$$

2.3 Scalar Control of Induction Motor

Achieving wide speed control range like Dc motors for induction motor can be achieved by applying field oriented control techniques that may need relatively complex implementation of the controller but can provide the required control performance compared to scalar control approaches [3].

2.4 Field Oriented Control of Induction Motor

The field orientated control consists of controlling the stator currents represented by a vector. This control is based on projections that transform a three-phase time and speed-dependent system into a two co-ordinate (d and q co-ordinates) time-invariant system. These projections lead to a structure similar to that of a DC machine control. Field orientated controlled machines need two constants as input references: the torque component and the flux component [12]. There are two approaches to obtain the flux vector, one direct measurement, and the other is indirect. According to the field-oriented control can be classified as direct field orientation control (DFOC) and indirect field orientation control (IFOC).

A) Direct Field Oriented Control

The direct field-oriented control approach is based on by direct measurement of the air gap flux using appropriate sensor that is the hall effect sensor [14–17]. Schematic diagram in Fig. 1 shows the basic principle of how direct field oriented control technique operates.

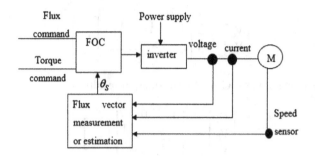

Fig. 1. Direct FOC method [17]

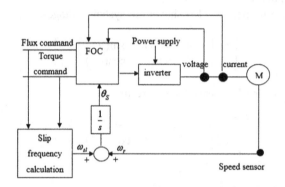

Fig. 2. Indirect FOC [17]

B) Indirect Field Oriented Control

Indirect field oriented approach computes the rotor flux by computing the slip speed [14, 17]. Figure 2 shows the schematic arrangement of the IFOC control approach.

The angular position, Θe, of the rotor flux vector is expressed as

$$\theta_e = \int \omega_e = \int (\omega_r + \omega_{sl}) \tag{15}$$

where, ω_r is the rotor speed, which is easy to measure using a shaft position sensor, and ω_{sl} is the slip frequency speed.

The procedures for indirect control approach can be summarized as follows [18]:

1. Stator current measurement and the required transformations.
2. Compute rotor angle using Eq. (15).
3. Error computation between the reference and rotor speed.
4. Quadrature current computation using Eq. (16),

$$I_{qs}^* = \left(\frac{2}{3}\right)\left(\frac{2}{P}\right)\left(\frac{L_r}{L_m}\right)\left(\frac{T_e^*}{\varphi_r}\right) \tag{16}$$

5. Compute the direct current component using Eq. (17),

$$I_{ds}^* = \frac{\lambda_r^*}{L_m} \tag{17}$$

where, λ_r^* is reference nominal flux linkage.

6. I_{ds}^* and I_{qs}^* are references for the current controller. The output of the current controller is the voltage. V_{ds}^* and V_{qs}^* voltage references are converted to $V_{\alpha s}^*$ and $V_{\beta s}^*$ using inverse park transformation and feed to SVPWM inverter to produce the inverter gating signals.

3 Flux and Speed Estimation for Sensor-Less IFOC of Induction Motor

3.1 Flux Estimation of the Three-Phase Induction Motor

Equations (18) and (19) show how to compute stator flux linkage [19].

$$\varphi_{ds}^{s,v} = \int \left(u_{ds}^s - i_{ds}^s R_s - u_{comp,ds} \right) dt \tag{18}$$

$$\varphi_{qs}^{s,v} = \int \left(u_{qs}^s - i_{qs}^s R_s - u_{comp,qs} \right) dt \tag{19}$$

Equations (20) and (21) are the expressions for rotor flux linkages,

$$\varphi_{dr}^{s,i} = \varphi_{dr}^{e,i} \cos(\theta_{\varphi r}) - \varphi_{qr}^{e,i} \sin(\theta_{\varphi r}) = \varphi_{dr}^{e,i} \cos(\theta_{\varphi r}) \tag{20}$$

$$\varphi_{qr}^{s,i} = \varphi_{qr}^{e,i} \cos(\theta_{\varphi r}) + \varphi_{dr}^{e,i} \sin(\theta_{\varphi r}) = \varphi_{dr}^{e,i} \sin(\theta_{\varphi r}) \tag{21}$$

where, $\theta_{\varphi r}$ is the rotor flux angle (rad).

Expressions (22) and (23) are for the compensated voltages,

$$u_{comp,ds} = K_p \left(\varphi_{ds}^{s,v} - \varphi_{ds}^{s,i} \right) + \frac{K_p}{T_i} \int \left(\varphi_{ds}^{s,v} - \varphi_{ds}^{s,i} \right) dt \tag{22}$$

$$u_{comp,qs} = K_p \left(\varphi_{qs}^{s,v} - \varphi_{qs}^{s,i} \right) + \frac{K_p}{T_i} \int \left(\varphi_{qs}^{s,v} - \varphi_{qs}^{s,i} \right) dt \tag{23}$$

Equations (24) and (25) are for rotor flux calculations,

$$\varphi_{dr}^{s,v} = -\left(\frac{L_s L_r - L_m^2}{L_m} \right) i_{ds}^s + \frac{L_r}{L_m} \varphi_{ds}^{s,v} \tag{24}$$

$$\varphi_{qr}^{s,v} = -\left(\frac{L_s L_r - L_m^2}{L_m}\right) i_{qs}^s + \frac{L_r}{L_m} \varphi_{qs}^{s,v} \tag{25}$$

Equation (26) is for rotor flux angle calculation on the voltage model,

$$\theta_{\varphi r} = \tan^{-1}\left(\frac{\varphi_{dr}^{s,v}}{\varphi_{qr}^{s,v}}\right) \tag{26}$$

The research in this paper applied artificial neural network for rotor flux estimation purpose by replacing the voltage and current models by which the voltage model will be less sensitive to variations of stator resistance and omit pure integrations. Application of ANN needs training data and in this research the training data set is generated using the current and voltage model equations.

3.2 Speed Estimation of the Three-Phase Induction Motor

Equation (27) shows the calculation for the synchronous speed,

$$W_e = \frac{d\theta_{\varphi r}}{dt} = \frac{1}{\left(\varphi_r^s\right)^2}\left(\varphi_{dr}^s \frac{d\varphi_{dr}^s}{dt} - \varphi_{qr}^s \frac{d\varphi_{qr}^s}{dt}\right) \tag{27}$$

The equation for rotor speed computation is given in Eq. (28),

$$\therefore w_r = w_e - \frac{L_m}{T_r}\left(\frac{\varphi_{dr}^s i_{qs}^s - \varphi_{qr}^s i_{ds}^s}{\left(\varphi_r^s\right)^2}\right) \tag{28}$$

where, $\frac{L_m}{T_r}\left(\frac{\varphi_{dr}^s i_{qs}^s - \varphi_{qr}^s i_{ds}^s}{\left(\varphi_r^s\right)^2}\right)$ is the slip.

3.3 Artificial Neural Network for Flux Estimation

Artificial neural network is a crude approximation of human network of neurons. In the artificial representation, training of neurons followed by the long term memory weight adjustment is required [20]. In this research, ANN is adapted for rotor flux estimation purpose using the required training data set and supervised learning. Figure 3 shows, the flow chart of application of ANN for the intended application in this paper.

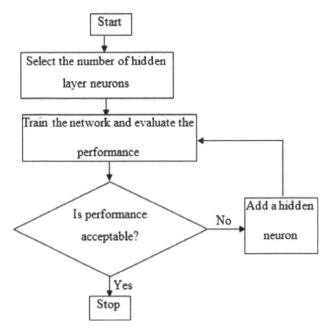

Fig. 3. Flow chart of the neural network training

The network structure in this paper with sigmoidal function as an activation function is given in Fig. 4.

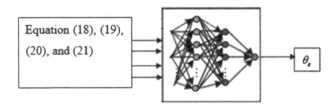

Fig. 4. Neural network structure

In this system the input layer, which is not neural, has 3 nodes; input layers, hidden layer, and output layer. The procedure to create and train a network using the toolbox is as follows:

- Training data sets of input and output are loaded in work space of MATLAB.
- Back propagation network comprise of four layers is created.
- Trainlim and Tansig were chosen as training and transfer function, respectively.
- Introduce training data set.
- Training parameters of convergence goal and epoach set.
- Training the system with data set and requirements set and evaluate the output.

Table 1 shows the required specifications for the induction motor considered in this paper.

Table 1. Induction motor parameters

Parameter	Symbol	Unit	Value
Types of rotor	$\bar{p}$	–	Squirrel cage
Number of pole pairs	$\bar{p}$	–	2
Frequency	F	Hz	50
Stator resistance	R_s	Ω	0.966
Stator inductance	L_s	H	0.00439
Rotor resistance	R_r	Ω	1.45
Rotor inductance	L_r	H	0.00439
Mutual inductance	L_m	H	0.002373
Moment of inertia	J	kgm^2	0.009
Rated voltage	V_r	v	400
Rated speed	ω_r	RPM	1460
Rated power	P_r	KW	2.2
Friction factor	F	N.m.s	0.00061
PWM frequency	Fs	KHz	20

The training results given in Fig. 5 shows 1000 epoach with the convergence value of 0.00061617.

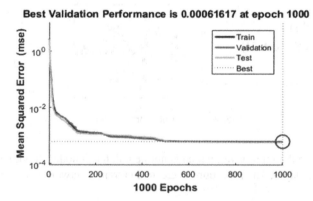

Fig. 5. Validation of the mean squared error

4   Design of PI and Fuzzy Logic Speed Controller

In this research, the controller is based on fuzzy logic algorithm with ANN for flux estimation application. To evaluate the performance of fuzzy based controller, PI based controller is designed and evaluated along with.

4.1   Designing a Proportional-Integral (PI) Controller

Conventional controllers of PID type are widely in use for different applications being simple in implementation and design the required constants of the controller. There various approaches of determining the required parameter values of a conventional PID controller. These can be analytical, manual tuning and application of auto-tuning approach using appropriate computation tool [21]. Block diagram representation of a typical PID controller is presented in Fig. 6.

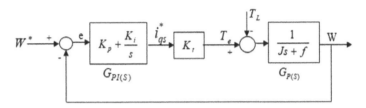

Fig. 6.   Model of Speed PI Controller block diagram

where W^* is the reference rotor angular speed, W is the rotor angular speed, $e = W^* - W$ is the tracking speed error, K_P is the proportional gain of speed, K_i is the integral gain, f is the total damping coefficient, T_L is load torque, K_t denotes torque constant, T_e denotes the electromagnetic torque. From Fig. 8.

$$T_e = K_t i_{qs}^* \tag{29}$$

$$i_{qs}^* = \frac{2}{3} * \frac{2}{p} * \frac{L_r}{L_m} * \frac{T_e}{\varphi_r} \tag{30}$$

$$\phi_r = L_m i_{ds} \tag{31}$$

From Eqs. (29)–(31) K_t is given by:

$$K_t = \left(\frac{3pL_m^2}{4L_r}\right) i_{ds}^* \tag{32}$$

The parameters K_P and K_i of the continuous controller are obtained by the following steps;

Step 1: Open loop transfer function.
Step 2: Controller parameters for the closed loop system.

Equation (33) shows the open-loop transfer function of the system at no load condition.

$$Go(s) = G_{PI}(s) \times G_P(s) = K_t \left(\frac{sK_P + K_i}{Js^s + sf} \right) \tag{33}$$

Equation (34) shows the closed loop system transfer function,

$$G_C(s) = \frac{Go(s)}{1 + H(s)Go(s)} = \frac{\frac{K_t}{J}(sK_p + K_i)}{s^2 + \left(\frac{f + K_t K_p}{J} \right)s + \frac{K_t K_i}{J}} \tag{34}$$

By comparing with a second order closed loop transfer function and setting $\xi = 1$, values of the PI controller are computed and presented in Table 2.

Table 2. Proportional (K_P) and Integral (K_i) gain for PI controller

PI controller	Kp	Ki
Speed control loop	2	563
Inner $d_e - q_e$ current loops	0.135	265.09

4.2   Designing Fuzzy Logic Speed Controller

Artificial intelligence based algorithms such as ANN and fuzzy logic have better capability in handling non-linearity compared with classical algorithms. However, implementation complexity and more computation requirement are major draw backs of intelligent algorithms. Fuzzy based controller is to model the operator knowledge for control application having basic procedures of fuzzification, rule base, inference and defuzzification activities as shown in Fig. 7 [22, 23].

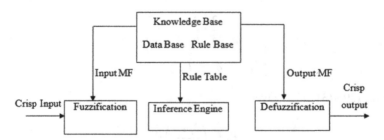

Fig. 7. Basic structure of the fuzzy logic controller

In this research, the fuzzy based controller comprises of two inputs of error and change is error and one output. Triangular member ship function of seven variables for both inputs and output and mamdani based inference is considered. Plot of membership functions and the rule table are summarized in Fig. 8.

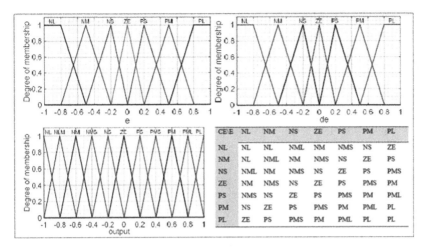

The rule table portion of Fig. 8:

CE\E	NL	NM	NS	ZE	PS	PM	PL
NL	NL	NL	NML	NM	NMS	NS	ZE
NM	NL	NML	NM	NMS	NS	ZE	PS
NS	NML	NM	NMS	NS	ZE	PS	PMS
ZE	NM	NMS	NS	ZE	PS	PMS	PM
PS	NMS	NS	ZE	PS	PMS	PM	PML
PM	NS	ZE	PS	PMS	PM	PML	PL
PL	ZE	PS	PMS	PM	PML	PL	PL

Fig. 8. Membership functions of input error (e), change in error (de), output and rule table.

5   Results and Discussions

Schematic diagram of the system for implementation in MATLAB/Simulink is given in Fig. 9.

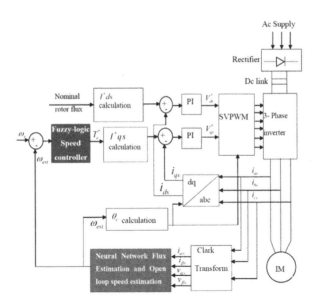

Fig. 9. Schematic diagram of the proposed system

The simulation results of the proposed sensorless speed control of indirect field-oriented control of induction motor drive are discussed in terms of:

- Space vector pulse width modulation.
- Setpoint tracking capability.
- Step response at no load.
- Step response when loaded.

The equivalent space-vector modulations of waveforms spaced 1200 is given in Fig. 10.

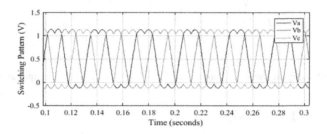

Fig. 10. Voltage for three phases (PWM Duty cycles)

Figures 11, 12 and 13 shows the estimated parameters of the motor.

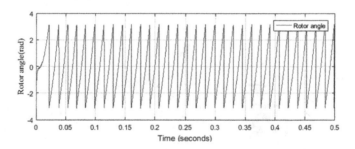

Fig. 11. Estimated rotor flux angle vs time

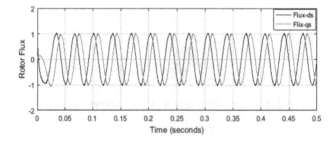

Fig. 12. Estimated rotor flux in dq-axis reference frame vs time

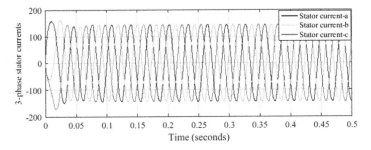

Fig. 13. Three-phase stator current vs time at 100 rad/s.

The angle of rotor flux to the stationary frame d-axis is estimated with the proposed flux linkages in the rotating reference frame are found by using voltage and current flux estimation and then the rotor flux angle improved by using an artificial neural network. The estimated rotor flux with a reference speed of 100 rad/s is shown as in Fig. 12. Both the dq-axis fluxes are 90-degree out of phase.

Three phase stator currents generated using voltage source inverter are given in Fig. 13. The three phase currents are equal and 120° phase displaced generated using the voltage source inverter controlled using space vector modulation technique.

At the same time the controllers' performance for the reference set point of 100 rad/s at no-load condition is presented in Fig. 14.

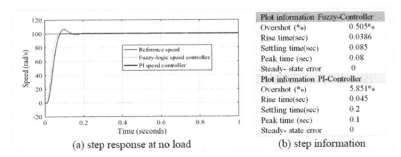

(a) step response at no load   (b) step information

Fig. 14. PI and fuzzy logic speed controller Vs time for 100 rad/s at no-load condition

From the control system theory, the system is said to have better dynamic performance if it has a lower rise time, lower percent overshoot, lower settling time, and lower peak time. The PI speed controller has poor performance than the fuzzy logic speed controller. It has a 5.851% overshoot and settling time of 0.2 s. The fuzzy logic controller has a better result in the case of overshoot (0.505%) and settling time (0.085 s) than the PI controller. The system response at load of 5Nm with reference set point of 100 rad/s is given in Fig. 15. The dynamic measurement criterion are also presented in the right side of the simulation result, Fig. 15(b).

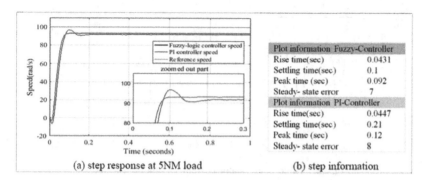

(a) step response at 5NM load   (b) step information

Fig. 15. PI and fuzzy logic speed controller vs time for 100 rad at (5 NM) load condition

The settling time, rise time, and peak time values are increased when compared to the system simulated under no-load condition. This shows that when the load is increased the system performance will be decreased. There is no variation in the case of overshoot but there is a steady-state error in the result with the system simulated under no-load condition.

6 Conclusion

In this research, flux estimation is done using artificial neural network and the sensor less speed control of the induction motor based on indirect field-oriented control is done with fuzzy logic. The performance of speed control of the indirect vector control of an induction motor using conventional PI and Fuzzy control has been compared. Accordingly, the PI speed controller has a settling time 0.2 s, 5.851% overshoot, 0.045 s rise time, 0.1 s peak time, and 0% steady-state error for 100 rad/s at no-load condition. On the other hand, the fuzzy logic speed controller has a settling time of 0.085 s, 0.505% overshoot, 0.0386 s rise time, and 0% steady-state error for 100 rad/s at no-load condition. Thus, values show that the fuzzy-logic based speed control of indirect vector control of induction motor gives a better speed response than that of the conventional PI controller at no-load condition. The performance of PI and fuzzy-logic controller evaluated under the application of sudden load (5 Nm) change and constant set point condition for both performed control systems. The settling time, rise time, and peak time values are increased when compared to the system simulated under no-load condition. This shows that when the load is increased the system performance will be decreased. There is no variation in the case of overshoot but there is a steady-state error.

References

1. Rashid, M.H.: Power Electronics Devices Circuits and Applications, 4th edn. (2014)
2. Fitzgerald, A.E.: Electrical Machine, 6th edn. (5 March 2006)

3. Mohan, N.: Advanced Electric Drives, 2nd edn. Wiley, Hoboken, New Jersey (2014)
4. Filippich, M.: Digital Control of Three Phase Introduction Motor, Thesis University of Queensland (October 2002)
5. Li, M.: A Differential-Algebric Approach to Speed and Parameter Estimator of Induction, Thesis University of Tennessee (2005)
6. Chapman, S.J.: Electric Machinery Fundamentals, 5th edn. (2004)
7. Blaschke, F.: The principle of field orientation as applied to the new trans-vector closed loop control systems for rotating machines. Siemens Rev. **39**(5), 217–220 (2001)
8. Chourasia, A., Srivastava, V., Choudhary, A., Praliya, S.: Comparison study of vector control of induction motor using rotor flux estimation by two different methods. Int. J. Electr. Electr. Eng. **7**(3), 201–206 (2014)
9. Mishra, A., Choudhary, P.: Speed control of an induction motor by using indirect vector control method. Int. J. Emerg. Technol. Adv. Eng. **2**(12), 144–150 (2012)
10. Campbell, S., Toliyat, H.A.: DSP-Based Electromechanical Motion Control. CRC Press (2004)
11. Krouse, P.C., Wasynczuk, O., Sudhoff, S.D.: Analysis of Electric Machinery and Drive Systems. Wiley, United States of America (2002)
12. Kazmierkowski, M.P., Krishnan, R., Blaabjerg, F.: Control in Power Electronics Selected Problems. Acadamic Press (2002)
13. Popescu, M.: Induction motor modeling for vector control purposes. Laboratory of Electromechanics, Department of Electrical and Communications Engineering, Helsinki University of Technology (2000)
14. Bose, B.K.: Modern Power Electronics and AC Drives, 4th edn. Pearson Education (2004)
15. Umanand, L., Bhat, S.: Online estimation of stator resistance of an induction motor for speed control applications. IEE Proc. Electr. Power Appl. **142**, 97–103 (2001)
16. Zhang, P., Lu, B., Habetler, T.G.: A remote and sensorless stator winding resistance estimation method for thermal protection of soft-starter-connected induction machines. IEEE Trans. Ind. Electr. **55**(10), 3611–3618 (2008)
17. Gopal, B.T.V.: Comparison between direct and indirect field oriented control of induction motor. Int. J. Eng. Trends Technol. **43**, 364–369 (2017)
18. Kassa, G.: Design and comparative analysis of genetic algorithm tuned fractional and integer order PI controllers with adaptive neuro fuzzy controller for speed control of indirect vector controlled induction motor. Addis Ababa Institute of Technology (January 2019)
19. Hambissa, T.: Analysis and DSP implementation of sensor-less direct FOC of three-phase induction motor using open-loop speed estimator. Addis Ababa Institute of Technology (17 May 2017)
20. Sonawane, P.P., Joshi, S.D.: Sensorless speed control of induction motor by artificial neural network. Int. J. Ind. Electr. Electr. Eng. **5**(2), 2347–6982 (2017)
21. Mhaisgawali, M.L.: Speed control of induction motor using PI and PID controller. IOSR J. Eng. **03**(05), 25–30 (2013)
22. Mishra, A., Zaheeruddin: Design of speed controller for squirrel-cage induction motor using fuzzy logic based techniques. Int. J. Comput. Appl. **58**(22), 10–18 (2012)
23. Hamood, M.A., Faris, W.F., Badran, M.A.: Fuzzy logic based speed control system for three phase induction motor. EFTIMIE MURGU (2013). ISSN 1453-7397

Performance Analysis of Microstrip Antenna with Semi-eliptical Slotted Patch and Defected Ground Structure at 28 GHz for 5G Communication Systems

Ayane Lebeta Goshu, Mulugeta Tegegn Gemeda,
and Kinde Anlay Fante[✉]

Faculty of Electrical and Computer Engineering, Jimma Institute of Technology,
Jimma University, PO Box 378, Jimma, Ethiopia
{ayane.goshu, mulugeta.geneda, kinde.anlay}@ju.edu.et

Abstract. The fifth-generation (5G) wireless communication networks are required to support ultra-high speed broadband communications. The utilization of millimeter wave (mm-wave) bands is needed to meet these requirements. However, communication in the mm-wave band has different propagation properties such as relatively high path losses and atmospheric absorption; the signals are easily blocked by the obstacle and low diffraction around the objects. It is crucial to design compact size antennas with high gain and bandwidth to mitigate these effects. In this paper, a semi-elliptical slotted microstrip patch antenna with defected ground structure configuration operating in the millimeter waveband is proposed. The antenna is designed using Rogers RT5880 substrate material with a thickness of 0.34490 mm and a dielectric constant of 2.2 to operate at 28 GHz. The semi-elliptical slotted radiating patch is mainly used to improve bandwidth and radiation efficiency. The defected-ground structure is used to enhance both the bandwidth and gain of the antenna. The defect structure (slot) positions and sizes are optimized to obtain considerably high bandwidth and gain. The inset-fed input matching network becomes easy due to introducing semi-elliptical slots in the radiating patch and defected ground structure. The overall structure of the antenna has a size of $(5.8 \times 6.4 \times 0.3449)$ mm. The proposed microstrip patch antenna (MPA) with a defect structure is simulated using CST-MW studio and found that its return loss, bandwidth, and gain are −37.784 dB, 1.132 GHz, 7.128 dBi; whereas a typical rectangular MPA without defect structure achieves −34.189 dB, 0.978 GHz, 6.67 dBi, respectively. The simulation results show that simultaneously introducing defected structures in the patch and ground plane of the proposed MPA significantly influences its performance. As compared to existing works, the proposed antenna shows significantly improved performance. It shows a suitable characteristic, in terms of size, bandwidth, and gain, for the needs of IoT applications offered by 5G technology.

Keywords: Bandwidth · Gain · Etched structure · Fifth-generation (5G) · Microstrip patch antenna

© ICST Institute for Computer Sciences, Social Informatics and Telecommunications Engineering 2022
Published by Springer Nature Switzerland AG 2022. All Rights Reserved
M. L. Berihun (Ed.): ICAST 2021, LNICST 411, pp. 304–317, 2022.
https://doi.org/10.1007/978-3-030-93709-6_20

1 Introduction

In the current 5G and future 6G systems, a large number of mobile devices are expected to be connected to the current cellular networks, which increase data traffic and system connections, resulting in the need for massive resources in the upcoming years [1, 2]. One of the promising technologies for meeting these system requirements is the use of millimeter-wave frequency band, and the fifth-generation of wireless technology is rolling out and has already been launched in some parts of developed countries [3]. In 5G communication systems, the mm-wave frequency band, which can provide unauthorized bandwidth of up to 1 GHz and low latency, is considered a key factor in resolving exponential data traffic increment. Thus, by using the mm-wave frequency band, the 5G system supports three major usage scenarios. These are enhanced high-speed movable and fixed broadband, low latency communications, and machine to machine (M2M) communications [4].

The first usage scenario is the key characteristic of this platform, particularly in the early stage of its deployment. Thus, the productivity and efficiency of device connectivity in society will be improved by the 5G infrastructure's superiority over existing cellular networks. The second one offers a minimal delay, in which several end-users within the range of the same base station can use up to 1Gbps internet connection for low latency applications such as drone control and unrestricted call rates. In the last usage scenario, a large number of links from low-power machines can be assisted by 5G technology. In this technology, the supported data rate will reach a up to one hundred times the bandwidth of the 4G networks. Thus, for instantaneous connectivity, 5G frameworks and advancements migrate to advanced mobile networks, allow large machine-type interactions, and encourage network applications that demand ultra-high reliability and minimal latency [5, 6].

To achieve the 5G wireless communication systems' anticipated performances, three frequency bands are considered: low, medium, and high-frequency bands. However, the selection of a band relies on its characteristics, precisely the capacity of spectrum resources and radio signal propagation. Accordingly, under 3GPP release 15, two new frequency bands have been defined for 5G communication systems. These are frequency band one (450 MHz–6 GHz, in which the upper limit can be extended up to 7.125 GHz) and frequency band two (24.25 GHz–52.6 GHz). Recently, the initial deployment of 5G communication systems has been launched in China, South Korea, and Japan using the first frequency band as the working frequency. However, in order to meet the demands of different applications, primarily for fixed/mobile 5G applications that need significant bandwidth to support higher speeds (greater than 1.0 Gbps) with lower latency, the FCC approved the reallocation of wide bandwidths of more than one GHz at 28, 37, and 39 GHz [5, 7].

Thus, for the next phase deployment of indoor broadband access point applications, introducing fixed point-to-point and point-to-multipoint high-speed backhaul connectivity at home, and mid-sized cell outdoor applications, the 28 GHz frequency band has got high research interest from the scientific research community. This frequency band contains large bandwidth and provides the opportunity of assigning bulky spectrum resources. The size of the antenna at this frequency band is very compact; therefore, the antenna designer can integrate a large number of array elements to construct massive antenna arrays, which can be easily integrated into tiny IoT devices.

Moreover, the 28 GHz band could be made available by reallocating the local multipoint block distribution service, which is suitable for various applications. Mobile applications, which are currently a core aspect of 5G deployment endorsed by national carriers and other organizations, may use the 28 GHz band [8, 9]. More specifically, the complete deployment of a 5G scheme needs antenna infrastructure planning and the introduction of new technological resolutions, which can be more reliable to build inside the public service buildings such as train stations, stadiums, and shopping malls. Antennas for 5G wireless technology at a higher frequency are expected to be wideband to achieve high-speed connectivity [10].

In applications where a strong connection with low latency is needed, an antenna with a high gain is required to mitigate the radio wave impediment, such as human beings, which are likely barriers to the mm-wave system, causing more significant transmission loss due to high operating frequency [11]. In general, wireless technology advancements require less weight, low cost, easy for mass manufacturing, compatible with planar and non-planar surfaces, and mechanically stable while mounted on rigid surfaces [12]. Microstrip patch antennas are one of the proposed solutions and are considered a good option in this regard. They are ideal for spacecraft, satellites, aircraft, vehicles, and lightweight, portable communication types of equipment. The MPA, therefore, continues to play a vital role in the fastest-growing field of wireless communication [13, 14].

However, compared to traditional microwave antennas, MPA has some drawbacks. The substrate thickness affects the antenna bandwidth and radiation efficiency by increasing surface waves and spurious feed radiation of the feeding lines. Consequently, undesired cross-polarized radiation is caused by feed radiation effects. The MPA also experiences losses such as dielectric, conductor, and radiation losses resulting in bandwidth and gain reduction. These pose a design challenge for the MPA designers to meet the broadband and high gain requirement of 5G mm-wave communication systems [15–18].

With an aim to overcome the limitations of MPA and enhance its performance for 5G systems, several research studies have been carried out in [3, 9, 11, 19–29]. These studies have employed various approaches, including a U-slotted patch [3], adding extra structure on radiating patch [11], modifying the feeding techniques [19, 20], the defected ground structure and Y-shaped patch [21], X-shape slotted [22], introducing multiple slots [23, 24], etched patch [25], various substrate material types [26], a substrate integrated waveguide patch [27]. The antenna designs in [9, 11, 20, 26, 28, 31] show high gain and directivity from reported simulation results. High radiation efficiency is achieved in [26], and a wide bandwidth antenna is reported in [9, 32]. However, the magnitude of VSWR of antennas reported in these studies is large.

Likewise, works in [11, 20, 28, 29] achieved narrow bandwidth. Therefore, to improve the bandwidth, various MPA designs appeared in [21–25] and achieved wide bandwidth. Nevertheless, low gain and large magnitude of return loss and VSWR are achieved in [21, 22] because of their inefficient impedance matching. The radiation efficiency of the antennas in [9, 21, 24, 29] is low. Antenna with significantly improved radiation efficiency was proposed in [11, 22, 25, 26]. Lastly, a good performance in gain, directivity, and VSWR is achieved [3, 21, 24].

To sum up, the performance of existing single-element MPA reported in recent scientific literature reveals that the bandwidth is narrow, gain and directivity of the radiation pattern are low to be used in the 5G wireless communication systems. The existing patch antenna studies show no single antenna with good performance in all key performance metrics. Therefore, the scientific research community has continued its effort to boost the performance of MPA in terms of all performance metrics.

This study's main focus is to enhance the bandwidth and gain of single element rectangular MPA for 5G communication systems. Defect structure is introduced in both the patch and the ground plane, and also, the antenna key physical dimensions are tuned to enhance these performance parameters. The remaining sections of this paper are presented as follows. Section 2 discusses the design specification and the proposed microstrip patch antenna. In Sect. 3, the simulation result analysis and discussions are revealed. Lastly, Sect. 4 presents the conclusion and remarks of the study.

2 Materials and Methods

The basic procedure of patch antenna design starts with \selecting the resonant frequency and substrate material type with its thickness and dielectric constant. Next, by substituting the selected four initial design parameters in the governing equation given in [17, 31], all the remaining preliminary physical dimensions of the antenna such as width and length of the patch, ground plane, microstrip feeder line, and feed point of the antenna are determined. Design parameters and fundamental governing equation used to calculate MPA dimension are given in Table 1 [5, 17, 31].

Table 1. Design parameters and fundamental governing equations.

Designed parameters	Symbols	Governing equations
Substrate thickness	SH	$SH = \frac{0.3C}{2\pi F_o \sqrt{\varepsilon r}}$
Patch width	PW	$PW = \frac{C}{2F_o\sqrt{\frac{\varepsilon r+1}{2}}}$
Patch length	PL	$PL = PL_{eff} - 2\Delta PL$
Length microstrip transmission line	LMTL	$LMTL = \frac{\lambda 0}{4\sqrt{\varepsilon r}}$
Width of microstrip transmission line	WMTL	$WMF = \frac{5.98SH}{\exp\left(ZMHF_{\sqrt{\varepsilon_r+1.41}}\right)}t$ $\frac{87}{0.8}$
Inset length	IL	$IL = \left(\frac{PL}{\pi}\right)Cos^{-1}\left(\sqrt{\frac{Z_O}{Z_L}}\right)$
Ground plane width	GPW	$GPW = PW + 6SH$
Ground plane length	GPL	$GPL = PL + 6SH$

Where C denotes the speed of light (3×10^8 m/s), Fo is the operating frequency (28 GHz).

Accordingly, in this study, Rogers RT5880 substrate material with a thickness of 0.3449 mm and a dielectric constant of 2.2 is selected. A 28 GHz is chosen as a resonant frequency. Therefore, using these initial design parameters, all physical dimensions of substrate thickness, length, and width of the radiating patch, feeder-line, inset and ground plane, and feed point location can be calculated using the equations given in Table 1. After obtaining the preliminary dimensions of the patch antenna, the dimensions are tuned to optimize its performance using the CST Microwave Studio simulator. Table 2 shows the initially calculated and optimized dimensions of the rectangular microstrip patch antenna.

To enhance the performance of the rectangular MPA in terms of directivity, bandwidth, and gain, different shapes of defect structures can be incorporated in the radiating patch or/and the ground plane. After optimizing the rectangular MPA, a semi-elliptical slot is introduced to both the radiating element and group plane of rectangular MPA. This half-ellipse part on both the radiating element portion and the ground plane has been etched out to boost some of the performance characteristics, indicated in Fig. 1.

Table 2. Initial calculated and tuned dimension of typical and modified MPA.

Design parameters	Typical MPA		Semi-elliptical Slotted MPA	
	Calculated values (mm)	Optimized values (mm)	Calculated values (mm)	Optimized values (mm)
PW	4.23519	4.7	4.23519	4.73
PL	3.40451	3.3398	3.40451	3.66
LMTL	1.80589	1.861	1.80589	1.67
WMTL	0.82137	0.821	0.82137	0.8
IL	0.89268	0.89268	0.89268	1
IW	0.02475	0.3	0.02475	0.2
GPW	6.30459	6.4	6.30459	7
GPL	5.47391	5.8	5.47391	7

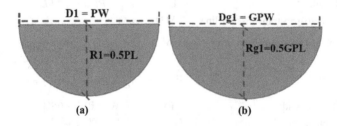

(a)   (b)

Fig. 1. The defected structure on the patch (a) and ground plane (b).

The defect structure dimension is half-ellipse with the diameter of the major axis is equal to the patch width for the radiating element (D1 = PW) and ground plane width for the ground plane part (Dg1 = GPW). Similarly, the diameter of the minor axis equal to the patch length for the radiating element (R1 = 0.5PL) and ground plane length for the ground plane part (Rg1 = 0.5 GPL) as shown in Fig. 1. The complete physical structures of the proposed rectangular and modified semi-elliptical slotted MPA are shown in Fig. 2. After setting the dimensions of the slot, CST Microwave Studio simulator is used to determine the optimal dimensions of the slots. The optimal performance of the antenna is obtained when the diameter of the major axis of the slot is 3.15 mm for radiating element and 4.67 mm for the ground plane structure; and when the diameter of minor axis of the slot is 1.22 mm for the radiating element and 2.33 mm for the ground plane structure. Inset-fed structure is used to improve the reflection coefficient of the antenna.

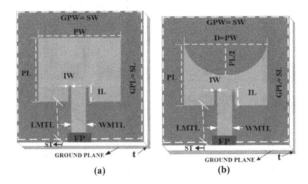

Fig. 2. (a) Typical rectangular MPA and (b) Semi-elliptical slotted MPA.

3   Simulation Result Analysis and Discussions

In this section, simulation-based performance analysis of MPA with a different configuration for 5G communication systems is discussed. The performance of MPA structures shown in Fig. 3 is compared. Frequency-domain solver of the CST Microwave Studio simulator has been used to analyze the performance of these antenna structures in terms of S-parameter plot (return loss), bandwidth, radiation efficiency, VSWR, gain, and directivity of the radiation pattern. As described in Sect. 2, the design of the proposed antenna started with rectangular MPA with an inset-feed structure, as shown in Fig. 2 (a). A semi-elliptical slot is introduced in the ground plane in Fig. 3 (a). Then, a semi-elliptical structure is introduced in the radiating patch of the antenna, as shown in Fig. 3 (c). In a similar pattern, we have introduced semi-elliptical slots of different sizes, as shown in Fig. 3 (d–f).

The impact of introducing different structures in MPA is studied, and comparative analysis is performed. Figure 3 (a–c) shows the effect of introducing defect structures on the performance of the microstrip patch antenna. The simulated reflection coefficients of the three structures are shown in Fig. 4. Among the three structures, the structure without defect (Fig. 3a) has achieved the lowest reflection coefficient, bandwidth, directivity, gain, and radiation efficiency. Introducing a semi-elliptical slot on the ground structure (Fig. 3b) improves the bandwidth, gain and directivity of the antenna. The semi-elliptical slot on the radiating patch of the antenna (Fig. 3c) improves the bandwidth and radiation efficiency, as indicated in Table 3.

Further study was conducted to analyze the effect of the size of the slot on the performance of the MPA. The size of the semi-elliptical slot is varied as shown in Fig. 3 (d–f) and its effect is analyzed as depicted in Fig. 5. The performance of the optimized antenna structure (Fig. 3 (e)) achieves the best performance among all the other structure as depicted in Fig. 5. Making the slot size above or below the optimal dimension of the antenna, deteriorates the performance of the antenna.

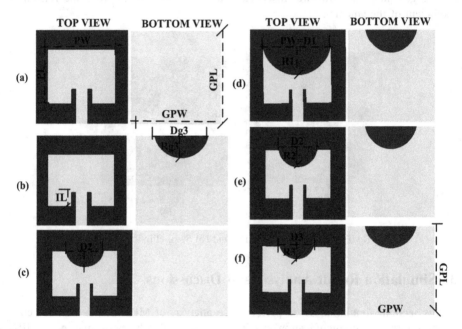

Fig. 3. Physical structure of examined MPA: (a) Typical MPA, (b) Typical MPA with DGS, (c) Defected patch with Typical Ground Plane, and (d, e, f) varying patch defect dimension size with DGS with D1 = PW, R1 = 0.5PL, D2 = 2 * PW/3, R2 = PL/3, D3 = PW/2, R3 = PL/4, and Rg3 = 2 * GPL/3, Dg3 = GPW/3.

The simulated results reveal that the analyzed regular and semi-elliptical slotted MPA's return loss is less than -10dB between 27.522 GHz and 28.5 GHz, as shown in Fig. 6a and between 27.419 GHz and 28.551 GHz as shown in Fig. 6b, respectively. At the operating frequency (28 GHz), the return losses are −34.189dB and −37.784dB, respectively. Therefore, as can be seen from these results, the optimized semi-elliptical slotted MPA achieved minimum return loss compared to the other structures.

In addition, from Table 4, it is evident that the return loss of the proposed antenna is lower than the simulation results achieved in [3, 5, 9, 11, 18, 20, 22, 24, 26, 28–30]. However, it is large as compared to the results of antenna designs reported in [19, 23, 25, 31, 32]. Furthermore, the −10dB bandwidth of the proposed antenna is 1.132 GHz

(4.043%) as shown in Table 3. The obtained bandwidth of modified antenna is wide as compared to the previous similar works reported in [9, 11, 18–20, 26, 29–32] as listed in Table 4. Conversely, achieved bandwidth is narrow compared to designs demonstrated in [3, 5, 22–25].

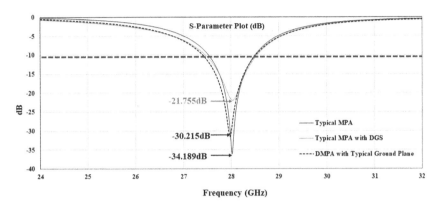

Fig. 4. The simulation results of the reflection coefficients (S_{11}) of the structures shown in Fig. 3 (a–c).

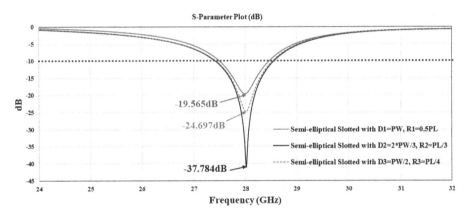

Fig. 5. Simulation results of the reflection coefficients of the antenna structures shown in Fig. 3 (d–f).

Generally, the minimum return loss and wide bandwidth have been attained since poor impedance matching at the feeder point, and patch edge has been minimized using the inset-feed impedance matching technique and tuning the design parameters. Besides, by creating the defect on both the patch antenna and ground plane and the fringing patch width, which is used to change the current distribution of both structures, the high input impedance at the resonant frequency is minimized. Accordingly, considerable input power is transferred to the transmission line, and small input power is returned as a return loss. Thereby, the antenna's radiation efficiency is increased, which leads to enhanced bandwidth.

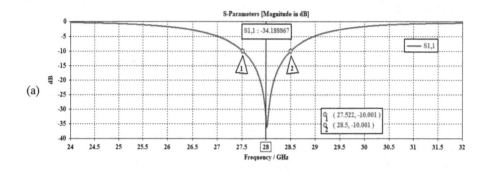

(a)

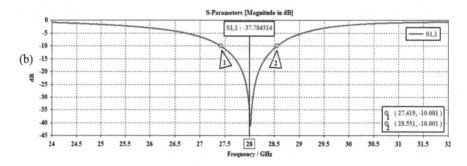

(b)

Fig. 6. Return loss plot of typical (a) and modified (b) single MPA.

Table 3. Comparison of the performance of different MPA structures.

Antenna structures (Fig. 3)	Performance metrics					
	S_{11} (dB)	BW (GHz)	G (dBi)	D (dBi)	VSWR	ηtot(%)
(a)	−34.189	0.978	6.667	6.689	1.039	98.22
(b)	−21.755	1.092	7.038	7.121	1.178	98.37
(c)	−30.215	1.117	6.931	6.942	1.064	99.66
(d)	−19.565	0.959	7.112	7.174	1.235	97.49
(e)	−37.784	1.132	7.128	7.183	1.026	98.74
(f)	−24.697	1.085	7.094	7.132	1.124	98.79

The VSWR plot of the proposed modified single rectangular MPA is shown in Fig. 7. As observed from the plot, at the resonant frequency, the VSWR of the modified single rectangular MPA is 1.026. In a rigorous way of description, as the feeder-line is moved to the patch's center, the impedance mismatch between the patch's transmission line and the edge will be reduced [17]. In this study, the patch and ground plane's introduced defect highly influences input impedance at the resonant frequency (Fig. 7).

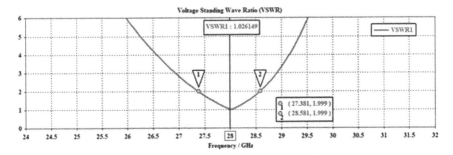

Fig. 7. VSWR plot of the optimized MPA with semi-elliptical slotted patch and DGS.

Also, the patch width, the inset length, and the inset gap have been carefully tuned, and then the impedance mismatch between the feeder line of the microstrip and the patch edge becomes a matched point, i.e., the input power is passed to the patch with lower standing waves of voltage. Consequently, maximum power is transferred to the radiating patch. Compared to the design reported in [9, 18, 20, 22, 26, 28–30], the optimized MPA has achieved a minimum magnitude of VSWR.

Figure 8 shows the 3D radiation pattern of the proposed optimized MPA. As displayed in Fig. 8, the MPA gain is 7.128 dBi, and the achieved directivity of the antenna is 7.183 dBi. As shown in Table 4, the gain of the proposed antenna out-performs the reported designs of [5, 9, 18, 22, 23, 25, 29, 30]. But, it is low as compared with simulation results given in [3, 19, 20, 26, 31, 32].

The improved radiation pattern directivity is achieved as compared to designs demonstrated in [22, 28]. Nevertheless, it is lower than the directivity of antenna designs in [11, 30]. Besides, the radiation efficiency and total radiation efficiency of the proposed antenna structure are –0.05442 dB (98.75%) and –0.05513 dB (98.74%), respectively, which is higher than antennas cited in [9, 11, 25, 26, 29–32].

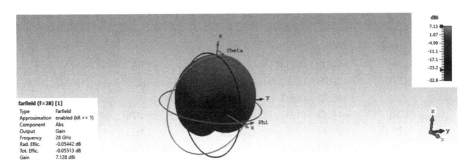

Fig. 8. 3D radiation pattern of the proposed typical (a) and modified (b) single MPA.

Generally, in this study, the proposed single element rectangular MPA has attained better and improved results in terms of directivity, radiation efficiency, and gain.

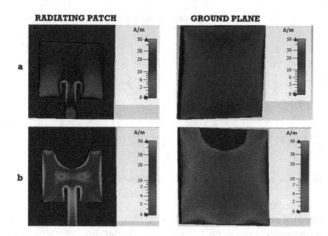

Fig. 9. Current distributions of typical (a) and semi-elliptical slotted (b) rectangular MPA.

As shown in Fig. 9, simultaneously introducing defect structure on patch and ground plane significantly alters the current distributions of both structures and then increases the radiatixon efficiency of the antenna. Besides, good impedance matching has been made in the middle of the edge of the patch and the microstrip transmission line. The dimensions of key design parameters have been tuned, which minimize the magnitude of the return loss, VSWR, and raise the radiation efficiency and bandwidth.

Table 4. Comparison of Reported Works and the Proposed Modified Single MPA.

Ref.	S_{11} (dB)	BW (GHz)	G (dBi)	D (dBi)	VSWR	η_{rad} (%)
[3]	−32	5.82	9.49	-	-	-
[5]	−22.51	5.57	3.6	-	-	-
[9]	−13.48	0.847	6.63	-	1.5376	70.18
[11]	−12	0.5	-	8.33	1.01	85.33
[18]	−14.15	0.8	6.0611	7.767	1.48784	-
[19]	−59.37	0.43	8.5	-	-	-
[20]	−34.05	0.582	8.00	-	1.75	-
[22]	−20.03	2.1	5.2	6.16	1.22	-
[23]	−48.25	4.07	5.61	-	-	-
[24]	−28.47	1.9	7.63	7.632	1.078	-
[25]	−39.37	2.46	6.37	-	1.022	86.73
[26]	−17.83	0.44	12.013	-	1.2994	92.655
[28]	−22.2	-	-	6.85	1.34	-
[29]	−27.7	0.463	6.72	-	1.22	75.87
[30]	−20.24	0.572	7.18	7.404	1.2156	94.95
[31]	−38.86	1.046	7.587	-	1.023	98.214
[32]	−54.492	1.062	7.55	-	1.011	98
This work	**−37.784**	**1.132**	**7.128**	**7.183**	**1.026**	**98.75**

Where S_{11} denotes return loss, BW denotes bandwidth, D denotes directivity, G is gain, VSWR denotes voltage standing wave ratio, and η_{rad} denotes radiation efficiency.

4 Conclusions

In this paper, bandwidth and gain enhancement of the single element rectangular MPA for 5G communication systems have been performed successfully. Simulation results of this study reveal that the bandwidth, return loss, gain, and radiation efficiency of the proposed modified single element MPA are 1.132 GHz (4.043%), −37.784 dB, 7.128 dBi, and (98.75%), correspondingly. As compared to designs reported in [11, 18–20, 26, 29, 30], and [31], in this study the bandwidth is increased by 632MHz, 332 MHz, 702 MHz, 550 MHz, 285 MHz, 669 MHz, 560 MHz, 86 MHz, respectively. Likewise, the gain has been boosted by 3.528 dBi, 0.98 dBi, 1.066 dBi, 1.928 dBi, 1.518 dBi, 0.758 dBi, as compared with the antenna design presented in [5, 9, 18, 22, 23], and [25], respectively.

Furthermore, the magnitude of the return loss is minimized by −15.584 dB, −24.304 dB, −25.78 dB, −23.63 dB, −17.754 dB, −19.95 dB, −15.584 dB, −17.544 dB, as compare to work presented in [5, 9, 11, 18, 22, 26, 28, 30], respectively. Lastly, as seen as simulation result reported in [9, 11, 25, 26, 29] the radiation efficiency has been increased by 28.5%, 13.42%, 12.02%, 6.095%, 22.9%, respectively. Therefore, in general, it can be concluded that by introducing etched structure on radiating element and ground plane structures and tuning the key design parameters simultaneously, the rectangular MPA's performance is greatly improved compared to other related works in terms of the bandwidth, gain, and radiation efficiency. The designed MPA provides highly competitive performance with a very compact size suitable for the emerging 5G communication systems.

References

1. Xiaoxiong, G.: A multilayer organic package with 64 dual-polarized antennas for 28 GHz 5G communication. In: Proceedings of the IEEE International Microwave Symposium, pp. 1899-1901. IEEE (2018)
2. Mungur, D., Duraikannan, S.: Microstrip patch antenna at 28 GHz for 5G applications. J. Sci. Technol. Eng. Manage. Adv. Res. Innov. 1(1), 20–22 (2018)
3. Hussain, W.: Multiband microstrip patch antenna for 5G wireless communication. Int. J. Eng. Works 01(01), 15–21 (2020). https://doi.org/10.34259/ijew.20.7011521
4. Sohail, A., Hamid, K., Khan, U., Muhammad, I., Nasir, S., Jamal, A.: Design and analysis of a novel patch antenna array for 5G and millimeter-wave applications. In: 2019 2nd International Conference on Computing, Mathematics and Engineering Technologies, IEEE, pp. 30–31, Sukkur, Pakistan (2019)
5. Przesmycki, R., Bugaj, M., Nowosielski, L.: Broadband microstrip antenna for 5G wireless systems operating at 28 GHz. Electronics 10(1), 1 (2020). https://doi.org/10.3390/electronics10010001
6. Liu, Y., et al.: Non-Orthogonal Multiple Access for 5G and Beyond. In: Proceedings of the IEEE October 2017, pp. 1-33(2017)

7. Hakanoglu, B., Sen, O., Turkmen, M.: A square microstrip patch antenna with enhanced return loss through defected ground plane for 5G wireless networks. In: 2nd URSI AT-RASC, Gran Canaria, 28 May-1 June 2018

8. Zhang, J., Ge, X., Li, Q., Guizani, M., Zhang, Y.: 5G millimeter-wave antenna array: design and challenges. In: IEEE Wireless Communication, pp. 106-112 (2017)

9. Omar, D., Dominic, B., Onyango, K., Franklin, M.: A 28GHz rectangular microstrip patch antenna for 5G applications. Int. Res. Publ. House. J. Eng. Res. Technol. 12(6), 854–857 (2019)

10. Ershadi, E., Keshtkar, A., Abdelrahman, A., Xin, H.: Wideband high gain antenna sub-array for 5G applications. Progr. Electromagn. Res. C 78, 33–46 (2017)

11. Abdelsalam, M., Abdalla, M., Essam, H.: Design and analysis of millimeter-wave microstrip patch antenna for 5G applications. In: International Conference on Technical Sciences (ICTS2019), pp. 137-142, Tripoli, Libya (2019)

12. Sridevi, S., Mahendran, K.: Design of millimeter-wave microstrip patch antenna for MIMO communication. Int. Res. J. Eng. Technol. 4(10), 1513–1518 (2017)

13. Shanthi, S., Jayasankar, T., Christydass, P., Venkatesh, P.: Wearable textile antenna for GPS application. Int. J. Sci. Technol. Res. 8(11), 3788–3791 (2019)

14. Jones, S., Gunavathi, N.: Codirectional CSRR inspired printed antenna for locomotive short-range radar. In: ICICI (2017)

15. Johari, S., Jalil, M., Ibrahim, S., Mohammad, M., Hassan, N.: 28GHz Microstrip Patch Antennas for Future 5G. Malaysian. J. Eng. Sci. Res. 2(4), 01–06 (2018). https://doi.org/10.26666/rmp.jesr.2018.4.1

16. Vamsi, N., Sravanthi, G., Narmada, K., Kavya, K., Swamy, G., Durgarao, M.: A microstrip patch antenna design at 28 GHz for 5G mobile phone applications. Int. J. Electron. Elect. Comput. Syst. 7(3), 1–10 (2018)

17. Balanis, C.: Antenna Theory Analysis and Design, 3rd edn. John Wiley and Sons Inc, Hoboken, New Jersey (2005)

18. Kavitha, M., Kumar, T., Gayathri, A., Koushick, V.: 28 GHz printed antenna for 5G communication with improved gain using array. Int. J. Sci. Technol. Res. 9(03), 5127–5133 (2020)

19. Jeyakumar, P., Chitraand, P., Christina, G.: Design and simulation of directive high gain microstrip array antenna for 5G cellular communication. Asian J. Appl. Sci. Technol. 2(2), 301–313 (2018)

20. Chaitanya, N., Poornima, M., Prahelika, P., Monika, R., Rozy, T.: Inset feed compact millimeter-wave microstrip patch antenna at 28 GHz for future 5G applications. Int. Res. J. Eng. Technol. 06(03), 3137–3141 (2019)

21. Wahaj, A., Abir, Z., Abdennaceur, B.: Patch antenna with improved performance using DGS for 28GHz applications. IEEE Access, International Conference on Wireless Technologies, Embedded and Intelligent Systems, Fez, Morocco, 3-4 April 2019

22. Gupta, V., Vijay, S., Gupta, P.: A Novel Design of Compact 28GHz Printed Wideband Antenna for 5G Applications. Int. J. Innov. Technol. Explor. Eng. 9(3), 3936–3700 (2020)

23. Ghazaoui, Y., El Alami, A., El Ghzaoui, M., Das, S., Barad, D., Mohapatra, S.: Millimeter wave antenna with enhanced bandwidth for 5G wireless application. J. Instrum. 15(01), T01003–T01003 (2020). https://doi.org/10.1088/1748-0221/15/01/T01003

24. Karthikeyan, V., Vignesh, S., Ayyavar Reddy, K., Bhargavi Reddy, G., Aparna Sekhar, R. S.: A millimeter wave based circular slot loaded microstrip patch antenna for 5G communication. IOP Conf. Ser. Mater. Sci. Eng. 590(1), 012059 (2019). https://doi.org/10.1088/1757-899X/590/1/012059

25. kaeib, A.F., Shebani, N.M., Zarek, A.R.: Design and analysis of a slotted microstrip antenna for 5G communication networks at 28GHz. In: 19th International Conference on Sciences and Techniques of Automatic Control and Computer Engineering, March 24-26, 2019

26. Subramaniam, S., Selvaperumal, S., Jayapal, V.: High gain compact multi-band microstrip patch antenna for 5G network. Int. J. Adv. Sci. Technol. **29**(1), 1390–1410 (2020)

27. Mohamed, B., Hegazy, E.A.: Design and analysis of 28GHz rectangular microstrip antenna. WSEAS Trans. Commun. **17**, 2224–2864 (2018)

28. Sarade, S.S., Ruikar, S.D., Bhaldar, H.K.: Design of microstrip patch antenna for 5G application. In: Pawar, P.M., Ronge, B.P., Balasubramaniam, R., Vibhute, A.S., Apte, S.S. (eds.) Techno-Societal 2018, pp. 253–261. Springer, Cham (2020). https://doi.org/10.1007/978-3-030-16848-3_24

29. Darsono, M., Wijaya, A.R.: Design and simulation of a rectangular patch microstrip antenna for the frequency of 28 GHz in 5G technology. J. Phys. Conf. Ser. **1469**(1), 012107 (2020). https://doi.org/10.1088/1742-6596/1469/1/012107

30. Mulugeta, T.: Comparative performance assessment of different rectangular microstrip patch antenna array configurations at 28GHz for 5G wireless applications. Master's thesis, Jimma University, Jimma Institute of Technology, Jimma, Ethiopia (2020)

31. Gemeda, M.T., Fante, K.A., Goshu, H.L., Goshu, A.L.: Design and Analysis of a 28GHz microstrip patch antenna for 5G communication systems. Int. Res. J. Eng. Technol. **8**(02), 881–886 (2021)

32. Fante, K.A., Gemeda, M.T.: Broadband microstrip patch antenna at 28GHz for 5G wireless applications. Int. J. Elect. Comput. Eng. **11**(3), 2238–2244 (2021)

Data-Driven Based Optimal Placement and Performance Evaluation of FD-MIMO for Enhanced 4G Mobile Networks Under Realistic Environment

Seifu Girma Zeleke[(✉)], Beneyam B. Haile,
and Ephrem Teshale Bekele

Addis Ababa Institute of Technology, Addis Ababa University,
Addis Ababa, Ethiopia
{seifu.girma, beneyamb.haile,
ephrem.bekele}@aait.edu.et

Abstract. To accommodate the increasing mobile user data rate demand, various capacity enhancing technologies have been developed and incorporated in enhanced fourth generation (4G) and fifth generation technology standards. For mobile operators, to achieve user satisfaction and then a successful business, planning and using the advanced antenna techniques in a cost effective manner is important. To that end, the planning work needs to accurately consider spatiotemporal distribution of user demand, propagation characteristics of the planning area and existing network capability and configuration. Although benefits of advanced antenna techniques are researched well, approaches to exploit their benefits in a cost-effective way considering realistic network environment is rarely reported. In this article, we present a practical multi-objective based FD MIMO antenna placement for enhanced 4G mobile network. We use Matlab to implement the proposed method and performance comparisons are performed considering 1800 MHz and C-band. Performance results show that the proposed method that can be applied for gradual deployment can be achieved considering the trade-off between users satisfaction and cost while maximizing aggregate throughput. It is observed that, implementing 3D vertical sectors in all sites with different operating band provides up to 319.93% aggregate system capacity gain compared to the existing macro only horizontal sectorized antenna configuration.

Keywords: 4G · 5G · Vertical beams · Multi-objective · FD MIMO · Antenna planning

1 Introduction

Global mobile data traffic has been increasing and is predicted to increase significantly in the coming years due to rise in penetration of various traffic-intensive applications [1, 2]. For instance, International Telecommunication Union predicts mobile traffic will grow up at an annual rate of around 55% in 2020–2030 and global mobile traffic per month is projected to reach to 607 EB in 2025 and 5016 EB in 2030, see Fig. 1 [2].

M. L. Berihun (Ed.): ICAST 2021, LNICST 411, pp. 318–330, 2022.
https://doi.org/10.1007/978-3-030-93709-6_21

The monthly average consumed traffic per user is also estimated to be 39.4 GB and 257 GB in 2025 and 2030, respectively [2]. Similar to the global trend, mobile traffic is also significantly increasing in emerging market like Ethiopia (especially in cities) mainly due to the increasing penetration of social media services [3, 4].

To successfully accommodate this increasing traffic and guarantee mobile users satisfaction, mobile network operators need to improve their network capacity in a cost effective manner. For that, various capacity enhancing mobile technologies have been developed and incorporated in enhanced fourth generation (4G) and fifth generation (5G) technology standards. Technologies that desnsify base stations, expand operating bandwidth up to 400 MHz and apply advanced antenna techniques with up to tens of antennas are among the most important ones [5–9].

Benefits and challenges of different use cases of 3D beamforming capability of advanced antenna system are investigated and presented in literature, e.g. [10, 13]. Densifying cells not only in the vertical domain but also in the horizontal domain considering spatial distribution of demand is one of the most practical use cases of 3D beamforming to considerably improve network performance, [12]. Traditionally, such approach is called vertical sectorization where macro cells are divided into two or more vertical beams (sectors) with different down tilt and beam width but same frequency resource [14, 15]. Unlike small cell densification, macro cell densification using vertical sectorization does not require additional sites and associated network elements which simplify deployment and reduce network cost.

Authors in [14–20] investigate the capacity impact of macro cell densification using active antenna system (AAS) under synthetic environments. In [21–25], performance of tilt, beam width and transmit power optimization methods for the vertical beams is analyzed. Field trial experiments have also undertaken to understand and characterize actual performance cell densification [26, 27]. These performance investigation, optimization and field trial works show that significant network capacity improvement can be achieved by macro cell densification. However, cell splitting can also limit cell coverage and the data rate of cell edge users due to additional co-channel interference unless different carrier configuration is applied among neighboring cells [21]. Although capacity benefits of macro cell densification using advanced antenna technique are researched well, planning approaches to exploit their benefits in a cost-effective manner considering realistic network environment and C-band is rarely reported. For small cell densification, planning framework and analysis considering realistic network environment including Addis Ababa and different network performance and cost objectives are presented in [29–34].

Inspired by aforementioned small cell planning framework, in this work we present a data-driven antenna planning approach for cost-effective gradual deployment of multiple vertical cells on top of existing macro cells. The planning approach is demonstrated using a practical case study for selected urban area in Addis Ababa. We implement the approach for the case study using Matlab and performance analysis is performed considering 3D buildings and existing network data for the selected area. Network data is collected from network management system (NMS) of Addis Ababa. We make the analysis considering currently used 1800 MHz band and C-band which is the most popular band for 5G deployment. Performance results show that gradual deployment of vertical beams with different antenna configuration is cost-effective. For example, for all macro cells (54 cells) 1800/1800 MHz configuration, a relative gain of about 33.1%, 39.6% and 86.3 at 10%-ile, 50%-ile and 90%-ile are obtained, whereas for 28 macro cells 1800/3600 MHz configuration, a relative gain of about 58.6%, 98.2% and 151.7% at 10%-ile, 50%-ile and 90%-ile are obtained. While being cost-effective, up to 319.93% aggregate network capacity improvement can be achieved compared to existing LTE network.

The rest of the paper is organized as follows. Section 2 discusses and illustrates a multi-objective problem formulations and optimization algorithm for macro cell densification. Section 3 describes the planning study area, spatial user demand distribution and applied simulation assumptions. Section 4 presents performance results and discussion. Finally, Sect. 5 provides concluding remarks and potential future works.

2   System Model and Deployment Scenarios

2.1   Multi-objective Problem Formulation

In this article, to study the data driven antenna planning approach, a downlink LTE network is considered. A 3x1cellular network having K number of macro sites will have 3K numbers of total macro LTE cells. Let, the notation C refer to a macro LTE cell and a cell with conventional cell index i is denoted by c_m^i, where, m indicates, if a cell is replaced with two vertical sectors (inner and outer beams) and i = 1, 2..., 3K. For the conventional cell layout, the value of m will be zero, but if a cell is replaced, m takes a non-zero value of m = 1 and m = 2 to specify the outer and the inner beams respectively [35]. When, cell splitting is applied on M number of macro LTE cells, total numbers of macro cells and vertically divided sectors becomes 3K + M. If M = 0, there are only macro LTE cells and if M = K, all cells are replaced with inner and outer beams.

For macro LTE cell having a coverage area of (A) and L number of user nodes, SINR performance of a user located at u is given by [35],

$$\text{SINR} = \frac{p(U,\ c_0^z)}{\sum_{i \neq z} p(U,\ c_o^i) + N} \tag{1}$$

Where, $p(u, c_0^z)$ is the received power of a user from serving cell (c_0^z) at a location of u. When a macro LTE cell is replaced with vertical sectors, SINR performance of a user located at u is given by

$$\text{SINR} = \begin{cases} \dfrac{p(U, c_1^z)}{\sum_{i \neq z} \left(\sum_{m=1}^{2} p(U, c_m^i) \right) + N} & \text{when user is associated with outer beam} \\ \dfrac{p(U, c_2^z)}{\sum_{i \neq z} \left(\sum_{m=1}^{2} p(U, c_m^i) \right) + N} & \text{when user is associated with inner beam} \end{cases} \tag{2}$$

Where, $p(u, c_1^z)$ and $p(u, c_2^z)$ are received signal powers of the users from outer and inner sectors respectively and, throughput (TP) performance of the user located at u from macro LTE cell using Shannon formula is given by [36].

$$TP = BW_{eff} N_{PRB} B_{PRB} log_2 \left(1 + \frac{SINR}{SINR_{eff}}\right) \tag{3}$$

When cell is replaced with inner and outer beams, a user located at u connects to either inner or outer beam depending on the the received signal strength and consequently will have a different $SINR$ performance. As a result, the TP performance after cell spliting is given by [35],

$$TP' = BW_{eff} N_{PRB} B_{PRB} log_2 \left(1 + \frac{SINR'}{SINR_{eff}}\right) \tag{4}$$

Where, BW_{eff} is bandwidth efficiency, N_{PRB} is number of Phsical Resource Block (PRBs), B_{PRB} is the bandwidth per PRB, and $SINR_{eff}$ is $SINR$ efficiency.

$$\Gamma = \frac{TP' - TP}{TP} \tag{5}$$

When M numbers of macro LTE cells replaced by inner and outer beams, L_1 number of users are served by $3K\text{-}M$ macro LTE cells and L_2 numbers of users are served by $2M$ numbers of replaced beams. Hence aggregate throughput (TP'_{agg}) of the network is given by

$$TP'_{agg} = \sum_{n=1}^{L1} TP(u_n) + \sum_{n=1}^{L2} TP'(u_n) \tag{6}$$

Where, $\sum_{n=1}^{L_1} TP(u_n)$ is an aggregate user throughput served by macro cells and $\sum_{n=1}^{L_2} TP'(u_n)$ is an aggregate user throughput served by replaced beams. For every M number of macro cells selections, there will be P number of options given by

$$P = \frac{3k!}{3k - M! \; * M!} \tag{7}$$

Equation 7 leads to the following question: from those P options how optimal sets are identified fulfilling cell edge and average user throughput constraints given by

$$TP'_{ce} = T([0.05 \, N_{ut}]) \text{ and } TP'_{au} = T([0.5 \, N_{ut}]) \tag{8}$$

Where, T is a vector containing user throughputs sorted in ascending order. This is a kind of multi-objective problem having multiple objectives: Minimizing number of splitting cells (f_1) and maximizing aggregate throughput (f_2) which can be formulated as:

$$Min_x \; f(x) = [f_1(x), \; -f_2(x)] \tag{9}$$

Where, x shows whether a macro LTE cell is replaced or not. To solve a problem in (9), evolutionary algorithms are effective meta-heuristics as the mathematical structure of the objective functions does not feature convexity or continuity [29]. According to [37] non dominated sorting genetic algorithm II (NSII GA) has less complexity, fast convergence, good scalability and empirically very near optimal compared with other compared algorithms. As a result the popular multi-objective evolutionary algorithm called NSII GA is selected.

2.2   Application of NSII GA on Antenna Planning

Non dominated sorting genetic algorithm II (NSII GA) accepts initial populations, fitness function and stopping condition as an input and gives an individual's that can give best fitness values as an output. To come up with the final results the algorithm performs a number of iteration. While the algorithm performs iterations, it uses reproduction option to bring new generations. Those reproduction options are elite count, cross over and mutation. For our case, the initial populations are denoted by X and given by

$$
X = \begin{bmatrix} x_{1,1} & x_{2,1} & \cdots x_{i,1} & \cdots & x_{3k,1} \\ \vdots & \vdots & \vdots & \ddots & \vdots \\ x_{1,1} & x_{2,2} & \cdots x_{i,z} & \cdots & x_{3k,z} \\ & & \vdots & & \\ & & \vdots & & \\ & & \vdots & & \\ & & \vdots & & \\ & & \vdots & & \\ x_{1,z} & x_{2,z} & x_{i,z} & \cdots & x_{3k,z} \end{bmatrix} \tag{10}
$$

Where, $z = 1,2,\ldots\ldots Z.$, number of population and $x_{i,z}$ are macro LTE cell status whether cell splitting is applied or not at each cell having a cell index i and denoted by c^i.

$x_{i,z} = 1$, If a macro LTE cell is replaced by inner and outer beams.
$x_{i,z} = 0$, If a cell is not replaced.

Thus, X consists of Z number of randomly selected populations with different combination of 0 and 1 which indicates status of $3k$ macro LTE cells. The fitness function is given by Eq. (6).

2.3   FD-MIMO Antenna Model

In general the antenna pattern is determined by element pattern and array factor. Let antenna elements are uniformly spaced in the horizontal direction with a spacing of d_H and in the vertical direction with spacing of d_v as shown in Fig. 1 [12].

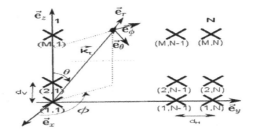

Fig. 1. 2D antenna array system [12].

By defining $u_y = \sin\theta \sin\phi$ and $u_z = \cos\theta$, the beam pattern can be expressed as [10–12].

$$G(u_y, u_z) = \cdots \sum_{m=1}^{M} \sum_{n=1}^{N} A_E(\theta, \phi) w_{m,n}^* e^{\frac{j2\pi}{\lambda}(md_H u_y + nd_V u_z)} \tag{11}$$

$A_E(\theta, \phi) + AF(\theta, \phi)$ (dB).

Where, ϕ and θ are the azimuth and elevation angles respectively. $A_E(\phi, \theta)$ is the 3D element pattern that can be obtained from resulted azimuth and elevation pattern. According to [11, 12], the azimuth and elevation radiation pattern for a single element are formulated as:

$$A(\phi) = -\min\left[12, \frac{\phi}{\phi_{3dB}}, A_m\right], \qquad A_m = 25 \text{ dB} \tag{12}$$

$$A(\theta) = -\min\left[12, \frac{\phi}{\phi_{3dB}}, SLA_v\right], \qquad SLA_v = 20 \text{ dB} \tag{13}$$

Then 3D element pattern can be formulated as follows:

$$A_E(\phi, \theta) = -\min\left\{-[A(\phi) + A(\theta)], A_m\right\} \tag{14}$$

3 Simulation Environments

To study the performance impact of gradual densification of macro cells with vertical sectors with C-band, a realistic network environment in Addis Ababa, Ethiopia with dense hotspots is selected. The studied area is about 5.47 Km^2 and consists of 18 macro sites with real-location of the existing Addis Ababa LTE network. The location of macro sites are shown in Fig. 2 below.

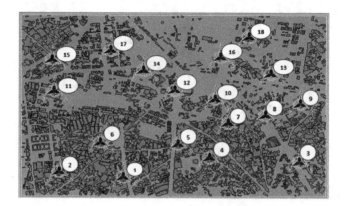

Fig. 2. Performance studied area

3.1 User Distribution

User's locations or demand nodes are one of the important parameters that can have an impact on performance of mobile network. Thus, in cellular network performance analysis, a careful selection of user distributions model is important to be more realistic. In this work, we use a reference [38] to locate demand nodes which uses telecom operator's data as an input parameter.

According to the procedures set in the reference, numbers of demand nodes are found as follows. First the studied area is divided into 8 rows and 11 columns based on pixel wise collected data from Ethio-telecom. The area of each pixels are considered as the same and denoted by a. Then, for each pixel, the corresponding traffic density ($g_{(m, n)}$) per Km^2 is obtained. Finally, number of demand nodes is obtained by [35].

$$N(m, n) = \cdots \frac{a \times g(m, n)}{r} \tag{15}$$

Where, r is the individual data rate requirements in Kbps which is assumed equal for all individual pixels (less than the minimum traffic density). The subscripts n and m represents longitude and latitude of the studied area respectively. Once the number of demand node obtained according to Eq. (13), users are distributed randomly in their respective pixel.

3.2 Studied Scenarios and Simulation Parameters

Performance of the proposed mulit-objective based planning method is studied using simulation parameters and technology usage option of different inner and outer band configurations stated under Tables 1 and 2 below.

Table 1. Simulation parameters

Parameters	Values/Assumptions
Transmit power	46 dBm
UE-height	1.5 m
UE-number	1337
Noise frigure	9 dB
Band width efficiency	0.5
SINR efficiency	0.85
Fast fading	8 dB
Shadow fading	Rayleigh fading
Cell association	RSRP
Scheduling	Round robin
Resolution	5 m

Table 2. Studied scenarios.

Scenarios	Inner and outer band configuration	Band width (Inner/outer beams)
Case 1	1800/1800 MHz	20/20 MHz
Case 2	3600/3600 MHz	20/20 MHz
Case 3	1800/3600 MHz	20/(20/60) MHz

4   Results and Discussions

This section presents performance impact of gradual densification of macro LTE cells with 3D vertical sectors, for antenna configurations listed in Table 2. For comparisons purpose, aggregate capacity of all macro only (MO) and replaced 3D vertical sectors are used. To come up with the results, the following Matlab based system level simulations are performed. First path loss of each user is obtained using Proman. Next, users are associated with their serving cell based on received signal power level. Then, resource blocks are scheduled using frequency domain round robin. Finally, SINR and throughput performance are calculated using Eqs. (1), (2), (3) and (4). This process is repeated a number of times and the statics are collected. Throughput performance is used as a fitness value to find the Pareto frontier while optimization is performed.

Figure 3 and 4 are plotted to compare UE SINR of the existing MO configuration and studied scenarios indicated in Table 4. Simulation result shows that, configuring VS with different operating bands significantly improve UE SINR at all percentile. For example, UE SINR values of MO, 1800/1800 MHz and 1800/3600 MHz, at 10%-ile are: -3.44 dB, -5.04 dB and -2.76 dB, at 50%-ile: 1.46dB, 0.51dB and 3.24 dB and at 90%-ile: 10.12 dB, 8.96 dB and 11.99 dB respectively (see Figs. 5 and 6).

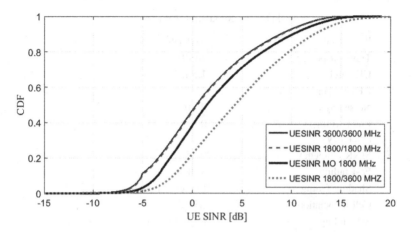

Fig. 3. CDF of UE-SINR for different inner and outer band configurations

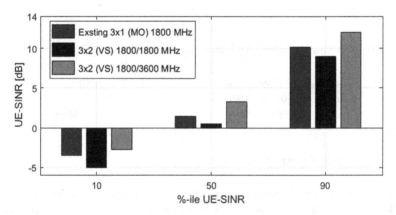

Fig. 4. UE-SINR at 10%-ile, 50%-ile and 90%-ile

The aggregate capacities of the studied scenarios are compared with the existing 3x1 LTE mobile network as shown in Table 3. Result shows that, aggregate capacity of MO, 1800/1800 MHz 1800/3600(20/20) MHz, and 1800/3600(20/100) MHz are 1.6224 Gbps, 2.4058 Gbps, 3.9595 Gbps and 6.813 respectively. Based on these values, the corresponding relative aggregate capacity gains of the studied configurations are 48.3, 144.1 and 319.93 respectively (see Table 3).

Table 3. Aggregate capacity and gain

Configurations	Aggrigate capacity(Gbps)	Gain w.r.t macro configuration (%)
Macro only	1.6224	Reference
1800/1800 MHz	2.4058	48.3
1800/3600 (20/20 MHz)	3.9595	144.1
1800/3600 (20/60 MHz)	6.1830	319.93

Pareto frontiers of 1800/1800 MHz and 1800/3600 MHz with their corresponding aggregate capacity are shown in Fig. 5. Aggregate capacity of MO network, all VS 1800/1800 MHz and all VS 1800/3600 MHz are used as an asymptotic value. This figure also shows how aggregate capacity of pareto frontier behaves while the number of vertical beams is increasing. In general, as numbers of vertical beams increased, aggregate capacity also increased. However as the number progress, the studied scenarios tend to close their respective asymptotic value differently (see Fig. 5).

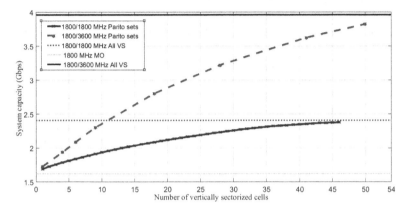

Fig. 5. Aggregate capacity and Pareto points of studied scenarios

UE throughput gain of commonly 28 pareto location of 1800 MHz/1800 MHz and 1800/3600 MHz are compared at different percentiles as depicted in Fig. 6. Both cases provide significant user throughput gain compared to the existing MO configuration. For example, for the case of 1800/1800 MHz, a relative gain of about 33.1%, 39.6% and 86.3 at 10%-ile, 50%-ile and 90%-ile respectively, whereas for the case of 1800/3600 a gain of 58.6%, 98.2% and 151.7% at 10%-ile, 50%-ile and 90%-ile are obtained compared with the existing macro only configuration.

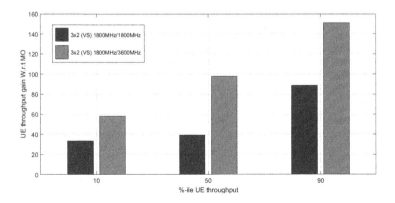

Fig. 6. CDF of UE-SINR for different inner and outer band configurations

5 Conclusion

In this paper, a data driven antenna planning approach for a stepwise deployment of vertical sectors under realistic network environment for selected area of Addis Ababa LTE mobile network have been analyzed. The analysis is accompanied with literatures survey, mutiobjective problem formulation and demand node location using the real data from Ethio-telecom network management system. Simulations are performed to find Pareto frontier that can maximize system capacity and analyze the performance impact of applying vertical sectors on the top of the existing macro LTE network. The result provides different parito frontier that can maximize system capacity. While number of pareto sets increase, system capacity also increase. It is also observed that, 3D vertical sectors with different operating bands significantly improve system performance. For example, for the case of 1800/1800 MHz, a relative gain of about 33.1%, 39.6% and 86.3 at 10%-ile, 50%-ile and 90%-ile respectively whereas, for the case of 1800/3600 a gain of 58.6%, 98.2% and 151.7% at 10%-ile, 50%-ile and 90%-ile are obtained. This is because, co-channel interference between inner and outer beams does not occur in the case of different band configuration, unlike the same operating band configuration. Performance impact of static 3D beams in high rise building and dynamic user centric 3D beams in 5G mobile network from planning and optimization perspective are an important future work.

References

1. Cisco white paper: Cisco Visual Networking Index: Forecast and Methodology. 2016–2021. Cisco public, June 2017
2. ITU: IMT Traffic estimates for the years 2020 to 2030. Report M.2370, July 2015
3. Adam, L.: Underst anding what is happening in ICT in Ethiopia. A supply and demand side analysis of the ICT sector. Evidence for ICT Policy, Action Policy Paper, April 2012
4. Beneyam, B.H., Dinkisa, A.B., Bekele, M.Z.: On the relevance of capacity enhancing 5G technologies for Ethiopia. In: 10th Ethiopian ICT Annual Conference, Addis Ababa, Ethiopia, June 2017
5. Whitepaper: 5G vision and requirements. IMT-2020 (5G) Promotion Group, Feburary 2015
6. Qualcomm and Nokia: Making 5G a reality: addressing the strong mobile broadband demand in 2019 & beyond. White paper of Qualcomm Technologies, Inc. and Nokia Oyj, September 2017
7. 5G Americas: 5G Services and Use Cases. 5G Americas white paper, Technical report, November 2017
8. Nokia: 5G deployment below 6GHz. White paper of Nokia, August 2018
9. Zaidi, A., Athley, F., Medbo, J., Gustavsson, U., Durisi, G., Chen, X.: 5G Physical Layer: Principles, Models and Technology Components, 1st edn. Academic Press Inc, USA (2018)
10. Koppenborg, J., Halbauer, H., Saur, S., Hoek, C.: 3D beamforming trials with an active antenna. In: International ITG Workshop on Smart Antennas (WSA), Dresde, pp.110–114. IEEE, April 2012
11. Kelif, J.,Coupechoux, M., Mansanarez, M.: A 3D beamforming analytical model for 5G wireless networks. In: 14th International Symposium on Modeling and Optimization in Mobile, Ad Hoc, and Wireless Networks (WiOpt), Arizona, pp.1–8. IEEE, June 2016

12. Nadeem, Q., Kammoun, A., Alouini, M.: Elevation beamforming with full dimension MIMO architectures in 5G systems: a tutorial. IEEE Commun. Surv. Tutorials. **21**, 3238–3271 (2019)
13. Lee, C., Lee, M., Huang, C., Lee, T.: Sectorization with beam pattern design using 3D beamforming techniques. In: Asia-Pacific Signal and Information Processing Association Annual Summit and Conference, Kaohsiung, pp.1–5.IEEE, January 2014
14. Fangchao, Z., et al.: A system level evaluation of vertical sectorization for active antenna system. In: 2015 IEEE/CIC International Conference on Communications, China, pp.126–131. IEEE, November 2015
15. Yilmaz, O., Hamalainen, S., Hamalainen, J.: System level analysis of vertical sectorization for 3GPP LTE. In: 6th International Symposium on Wireless Communication Systems, Tuscany, pp.453–457. IEEE, September 2009
16. Youqi, F., Jian, W., Zhuyan, Z., Liyun, D., Hongwen, Y.: Analysis of vertical sectorization for HSPA on a system level: capacity and coverage. In: IEEE Vehicular Technology Conference (VTC Fall), Quebec, pp. 1–5. IEEE, September 2012
17. Caretti, M., Crozzoli, M., Del, G., Orlando, A.: Cell splitting based on active antennas: performance assessment for LTE system. In: WAMICON 2012 IEEE Wireless & Microwave Technology Conference, Florida, pp. 1–5. IEEE, April 2012
18. Ahn, M., Lee, I.: Vetrical sectorization techniques for active antenna systems. In: 2014 International Conference on Information and Communication Technology Convergence, Busan, pp. 765–767. IEEE, December 2014
19. Zeleke, S.G., Haile, B.B.: Performance analysis of vertical sectorization for LTE realistic deployment scenario. In: Mekuria, F., Nigussie, E., Tegegne, T. (eds.) ICT4DA 2019. CCIS, vol. 1026, pp. 154–163. Springer, Cham (2019). https://doi.org/10.1007/978-3-030-26630-1_13
20. Wei, Z., Wang, Y., Lin, W.: Optimization of downtilts adjustment combining joint transmission and 3D beamforming in 3D MIMO. In: IEEE/CIC ICCC 2014 Symposium on Wireless Communications Systems, Shanghai ,p. 728–732. IEEE, January 2015
21. Deng, J., Lv, G., Li, G., Zhang, G.: Vertical sectorization using beam steering in cellular communication systems. In: IEEE/CIC International Conference on Communications in China - Workshops (CIC/ICCC), Shangha, pp.21–25, May 2015
22. Guo, W., Fan, J., Li, G.Y., Yin, Q., Zhu, X., Yusun, F.: MIMO transmission with vertical sectorization for LTE-a downlink. IEEE Wirel. Commun. Lett. **5**(4), 372–375 (2016). https://doi.org/10.1109/LWC.2016.2560841
23. Nai, S.E., Lei, Z., Wong, S.H., Chew, Y.H.: Optimizing radio network parameters for vertical sectorization via taguchi's method. IEEE Trans. Veh. Technol. **65**(2), 860–869 (2016). https://doi.org/10.1109/TVT.2015.2401030
24. Joydeep, A., Salam, A.: Optimizing vertical sectorization for high-rises, international conference on computing. In: Networking and Communications (ICNC), Garden Grove, pp.1–5, IEEE, February 2015
25. Jinping, N., Geoffrey,Y., Li, F., Wei, W., Weike, N., Xun, L.: Downtilts optimization and power allocation for vertical sectorization in AAS-based LTE-a downlink systems. In: IEEE 86th Vehicular Technology Conference (VTC-Fall), Toronto, pp.1–5. IEEE, September 2017
26. Fengyi,Y., Jianmin, Z., Weiliang, X., Xuetian, Z.: Field trial results for vertical sectorization in LTE network using active antenna system. In: IEEE International Conference on Communications (ICC), Sydney, pp. 2508–2512. IEEE, June 2014
27. Xie, W., Cui, Q., Yang, F., Bi, Q., Yuan, Y.: Experimental investigation on a vertical sectorization system with active antenna. IEEE Commun. Mag. **54**(9), 89–97 (2016). https://doi.org/10.1109/MCOM.2016.7565254

28. Usman, M., Ruttik, K., Jäntti, R.: Performance analysis of vertical and higher order sectorization in urban environment at 28 GHz. In: 26th International Conference on Telecommunications(ICT), pp.8–10. IEEE, April (2019)

29. González, D.G., Mutafungwa, E., Haile, B., Hämäläinen, J., Poveda, H.: A planning and optimization framework for ultra dense cellular deployments. Mobile Inf. Syst. **2017**, 1–17 (2017). https://doi.org/10.1155/2017/9242058

30. Biruk, E.T., Beneyam, B.H., Mutafungwa, E., Hämäläinen, J.: Comparison of multiobjective optimal and collocated 4G and 5G small cells using street lampposts as candidate locations. In: 2019 IEEE AFRICON, Accra, Ghana, pp. 1–5, September (2019)

31. Ashagrie, G.F, Beneyam, B.H., Dereje, H., Mutafungwa, E., Hämäläinen, J.: Capacity demand based multiobjective optimal small cell placement under realistic deployment scenario. In: 2019 IEEE AFRICON, Accra, Ghana, pp. 1–5,September (2019)

32. Fulle, T.A., Haile, B.B.: Performance evaluation of 6-sector site and small cell for addis ababa UMTS network. In: Mekuria, F., Nigussie, E., Tegegne, T. (eds.) ICT4DA 2019. CCIS, vol. 1026, pp. 176–187. Springer, Cham (2019). https://doi.org/10.1007/978-3-030-26630-1_15

33. Beneyam, B.H, Mutafungwa, E., Hämäläinen, J.: A data-driven multiobjective optimization framework for hyperdense 5G network planning. In: IEEE Access, IEEE, September (2020)

34. Zeleke, S.G., Haile, B.B., Bekele, E.T.: Performance analysis of vertical sectorization in Sub-6-GHz frequency bands for 4g mobile network under realistic deployment scenario. In: Delele, M.A., Bitew, M.A., Beyene, A.A., Fanta, S.W., Ali, A.N. (eds.) ICAST 2020. LNICSSITE, vol. 384, pp. 231–243. Springer, Cham (2021). https://doi.org/10.1007/978-3-030-80621-7_17

35. Dereje, W.K., Wegmann, B., Viering, I., Klein, A.: Mathematical model for vertical sectorization (VS) in AAS based LTE deployment. In: 11th International Symposium Wireless Communication Systems, Barcelona, pp. 100–105. IEEE, October (2014)

36. Preben, M., et al.: LTE system capacity compared to Shannon bounds. In: IEEE VTC Spring, Dublin, pp. 1234–1238. IEEE, April (2007)

37. Fei, Z., Li, B., Yang, S., Xing, C., Chen, H., Hanzo, L.: A survey of multi-objective optimization in wireless sensor networks: metrics, algorithms and open problems. IEEE Commun. Surv. Tutorials. (2016)

38. Dongheon, L., Sheng, S., Xiaofeng, Z., Zhisheng, N.: Spatial modeling of the traffic density in cellular networks. IEEE Wirel. Commun. **21**, 80–88 (2014)

Optimization of Dualband Microstrip mm-Wave Antenna with Improved Directivity for Mobile Application Using Genetic Algorithm

Arebu Dejen[1(✉)], Jeevani Jayasinghe[2], Murad Ridwan[1], and Jaume Anguera[3,4]

[1] School of Electrical and Computer Engineering, Addis Ababa University, Addis Ababa, Ethiopia
murad.ridwan@aait.edu.et
[2] Department of Electronics, Wayamba University of Sri Lanka, Kuliyapitiya, Sri Lanka
jeevani@wyb.ac.lk
[3] Technology and Intellectual Property Rights Dep't, Fractus Antennas, Barcelona, Spain
jaume.anguera@salle.url.edu
[4] Telecommunication Engineering, Unversitat Ramon LLull, Barcelona, Spain

Abstract. The demand of high data rate requirement and spectrum scarcity in the current wireless communication drives the next generation communication technology to mm-wave frequencies. Researches in directivity improvement and multi-functionality of antenna are the determinant factor to provide high data rate and quality of services. This research discourses directivity optimization of a single microstrip rectangular patch antenna with dualband service for mm-wave mobile communication using binary-coded genetic algorithm. Optimization has been done by dividing the patch geometry into 100 small circular cells and assigning them as conducting and none conducting. The proposed antenna was iteratively simulated using a combination of HFSS and MATLAB, and obtained $S11 < -10$ dB bandwidth (BW) of 2.9% at 28.0 GHz with peak directivity 8.6dB and BW of 1% at 31.1 GHz with peak directivity 10.9dB.

Keywords: Dualband antenna · Genetic algorithm optimization · Mm-wave antenna · Microstrip antenna

1 Introduction

In the global telecommunications industry the fastest growing and the most dynamic sector is wireless communication. Though the global system of mobile communication has passed many modifications till the existing 4G, the demand for a high data rate, connecting everywhere with everything is still not satisfied due to spectrum scarcity at microwave frequency. The next-generation wireless communication (5G) will answer such high-end demands using the plenty of spectrum existing in mm-wave [1].

M. L. Berihun (Ed.): ICAST 2021, LNICST 411, pp. 331–340, 2022.
https://doi.org/10.1007/978-3-030-93709-6_22

Figure 1 shows that the predicted mm-wave frequencies available for 5G mobile communication in the range of 20–50 GHz [2]. In spite of having a huge spectrum, this band is vulnerable for various challenges including high propagation loss, blockage, and atmospheric loss. Research studies on antenna directivity improvement are among the key factors for overcoming some of the propagation challenges, increase the spectrum efficiency and provide higher data rates for mobile broadband services [3].

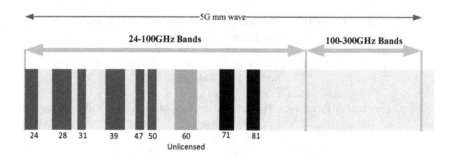

Fig. 1. Predicted spectrum for 5G mobile communication

Investigation of multiband antenna with low profile also another research area due to the increasing demand for multifunctional devices. Accordingly, microstrip patch antenna technology is an attractive solution since it is advantageous over low volume, low cost, simple planar configuration, low weight, ease of fabrication [4]. However, the conventional microstrip patch antenna inherently has a narrow bandwidth, low efficiency, low gain and less directivity [5]. Therefore, it is always a challenging task to develop high directive and multiband microstrip patch antennas. A number of techniques to improve a directivity of patch antenna were reported in the literature. Among them, fractal shaped geometry were presented in [6–8] and frequency selective surface (FSS) were reported in [9, 10]. Besides the above, directivity improvement was also done using TModd-0 modes reported in [11] and genetic algorithm optimization as presented in [12–14].

This paper proposes a dual-band patch antenna optimization using binary coded genetic algorithm for mm-wave frequency with improved directivity. The proposed antenna was analyzed and modeled on high frequency structure simulator (HFSS) software in combination with MATLAB to build a genetic algorithm optimizer code and Visual Basic Script (VBS) files. VBS files called into HFSS for simulation and export analyzed antenna parameter to MATLAB which will be input for genetic algorithm optimization as shown in Fig. 2 for each iteration. The optimizer checks the fitness values continuously for every population until the end of the iterations or the termination criteria is reached. As far as the authors' knowledge there is no related work on optimization of patch antenna for mm-wave dual-band frequency with improved directivity using genetic algorithm. This paper is organized as a brief introduction of genetic algorithm in Sect. 2, and antenna configuration, optimization and genetic algorithm setup are presented in Sect. 3. Section 4 will explain the detail analysis of simulation result and lastly, conclusion will be drawn.

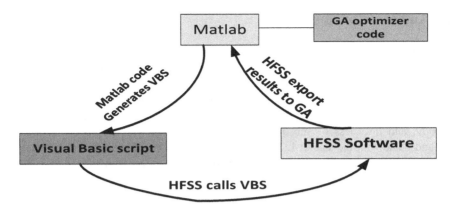

Fig. 2. Optimization procedure for single iteration

2   Genetic Algorithm

A genetic algorithm reflects the process of natural selection where the fittest individuals are selected for reproduction of offsprings for the next generation. It is a powerful, robust, stochastic-based optimization method, which was used to handle the common characteristics of electromagnetic optimization problems for the last two decades. Each individual in genetic algorithm is represented by a chromosomes or a string of bits (gens) [15]. The first generation is created by a random mechanism and the following generations are reproduced from more fit and selected individuals who have a greater chance to produce better offsprings based on the cost (fitness). Crossover and mutation are used to improve the cost [16]. The best individual may be passed unchanged to the next generation. This iterative process creates successive generations until a stop criterion is reached [17]. A flowchart of genetic algorithm optimizer is presented in Fig. 3.

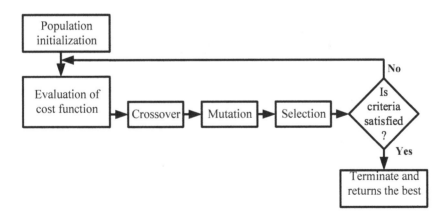

Fig. 3. Flowchart of genetic algorithm

3 Antenna Configuration

The optimized dimension of the radiating patch is L_{xp} = 3.36 mm ($\sim$0.32λ_0) and W_{yp} = 5.26 mm ($\sim$0.50λ_0) where the patch is made of thin copper having thickness of 0.00032 λ_0 < < λ_0 (λ_0 is free space wavelength at 28 GHz) located on the top side of a thin non-conducting substrate with the size of $\lambda_0 \times \lambda_0$. In the proposed design, the Roger RT/duriod 5880 (tm) substrate with a dielectric constant of 2.2, a tangent loss 0.0009, and thickness of substrate is 0.3 mm (0.028λ_0) was employed on a finite ground plane with the size of $L_{xg} \times W_{yg}$. The dimensions of microstrip patch antenna shown in Fig. 4, which is proposed for genetic algorithm, are summarized in Table 1.

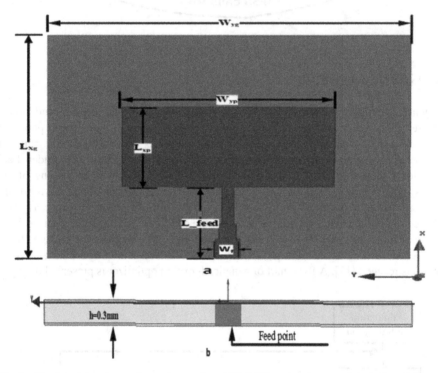

Fig. 4. Single patch antenna element operating at 28.0 GHz printed on a substrate (h = 0.3 mm, ε_r = 2.2, tan δ = 0.0009) (a) top view and (b) side view.

Table 1. Proposed antenna dimension summary

Parameter	L_{xp}	W_{yp}	h	L_{xg}	W_{yg}	$L_{\_feed}$	W_f
Dimensions(mm)	3.36	5.26	0.30	10.7	10.7	3.52	0.74

3.1   Genetic Algorithm Procedure

In order to optimize the patch geometry, an array (10×10) of random and non-uniform small circular cells are positioned on the patch surface as shown in Fig. 5. The probability of diameter of the cell to be 0.35 mm is 0.8 and 0.27 mm is 0.2. This helps to creates varieties of circular geometries on the patch surface. These cells are subtracted from the rectangular patch if and only if they are non-conducting. The conducting and non-conducting cell is defined by a binary coding algorithm. If the cell is conducting '1' is assigned to the corresponding gene whereas if it is non-conducting gene '0' represents the cell [18]. In this research, the fitness function (F) is defined to maximize the directivity D (f) and negative of reflection coefficient $S_{11}(f)$ in the two bands (27.5 GHz–29.5 GHz and 31 GHz–31.5 GHz) of frequencies.

$$F = \sum_{f} [D(f) - S_{11}(f)] \tag{1}$$

$$S_{11}(f) = \begin{cases} S_{11}, & \text{if } S_{11} > -10dB \\ -10dB, & \text{if } S_{11} \leq -10dB \end{cases} \tag{2}$$

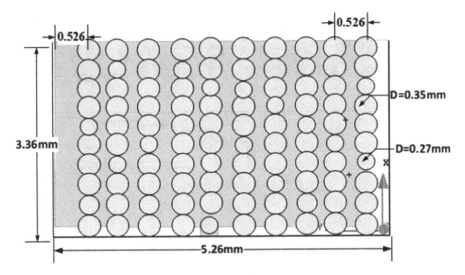

Fig. 5. Placement of 100 circular cells on rectangular patch surface

3.2   Optimization Setup

The population size clustered as a generation is set to 20 individuals and each individual is represented by 100 genes. A single point crossover with a 70% probability and a 0.02 mutate rate have been used to create a diversity of the population in each generation. The tournament selection mechanism has been applied to select individual parents that fit to reproduce offspring for the next new generation. The simulation is carried out until 150 generations. The simulation convergences after 130 iteration as shown in Fig. 6-b and the best-fit individual is shown in Fig. 6-a.

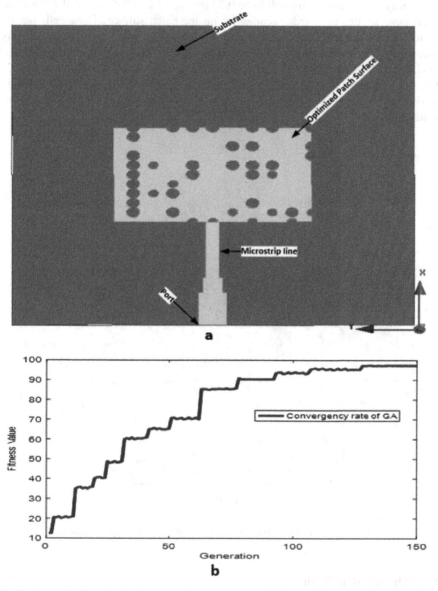

Fig. 6. a) genetically optimized proposed patch geometry, b) fitness value vs number generation.

4   Simulation Result and Analysis

The proposed genetically engineered patch antenna shown in Fig. 6-a was simulated using HFSS software. The result proves that directivity of the antenna was improved and it resonates at two frequencies. As Fig. 7 illustrates the reflection coefficient of the reference antenna resonates at 28.0 GHz only with $S_{11} = -17.9$ dB whereas genetically optimized antenna resonates at two frequencies of 28.0 GHz and 31.1 GHz with BW = 2.9% and BW = 1% respectively. At both range of frequencies 27.6 –28.4 GHz and 31.0–31.3 GHz VSWR is less than 2. Furthermore, in Fig. 8 directivity improvement in both operating bands was verified. A broadside direction directivity of 8.6 dB at 28.0 GHz, is demonstrated (Fig. 8-a) and a directivity of 10.9dB was verified at 31.1 GHz along broadside direction (Fig. 8-b). The performance of both reference and the genetically optimized antenna is summarized in Table 2.

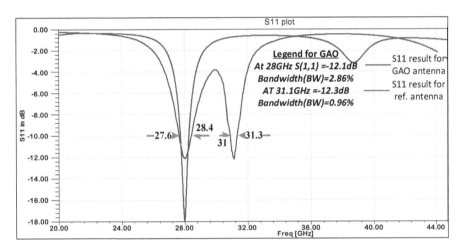

Fig. 7. Simulated S_{11} of the GAO dual-band patch antenna resonates at 28.0 GHz and 31.1 GHz

Table 2. Overall performance of genetically optimized proposed antenna

	Overall Size of antenna (mm^3)	Resonant frequency	BW(%, S11 <– 10 dB)	Directivity
Reference patch antenna	10.7 × 10.7 × 0.3	28.0 GHz	2.1%	6.8 dB
Genetically optimized patch antenna	10.7 × 10.7 × 0.3	28.0 GHz	2.9%	8.6 dB
		31.1 GHz	1%	10.9 dB

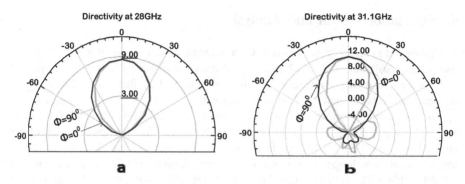

Fig. 8. Directivity of genetically optimized patch antenna a) at 28.0 GHz b) at 31.1 GHz

The surface current distribution of the reference antenna at 28 GHz is presented in Fig. 9-a. The surface current distributions of genetically optimized antenna at 28GHz and 31.1 GHz are shown in Fig. 9-b and Fig. 9-c respectively.

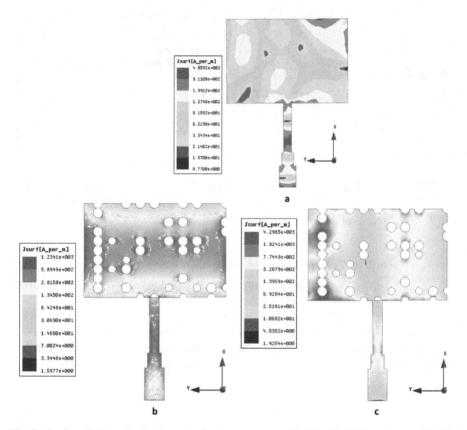

Fig. 9. Surface Current distribution: **a)** reference antenna at 28 GHz, **b)** GAO antenna at 28 GHz and **c)** GAO antenna at 31.1 GHz

4.1 Conclusion

Directive antennas are vital to solve some propagation challenges of mm-wave signals. At the same time multiband antennas for 5G mobile devices also becoming a good glance of research due to the increasing demand of multi-functional mobile service. This paper presents dual-band directivity improvement using genetic algorithm optimization. The proposed genetically optimized antenna was simulated in HFSS and compared to a reference antenna. The result explores that the optimized antenna is operated in two resonant bands where $S_{11} < -10$ dB at 28.0 GHz with BW = 2.9% and 31.1 GHz with BW = 1%. The directivity of a proposed antenna is improved to 8.6 dB and 10.9 dB at 28.0 GHz and 31.1 GHz respectively when compared to 6.8 dB of the reference antenna making the proposed antennas advantageous for mm-wave mobile communication.

References

1. Wei, L., Hu, R.Q., Qian, Y., Geng, W.: Key elements to enable millimeter wave communications for 5g wireless systems. IEEE Wirel. Commun. **21**(6), 136–143 (2014). https://doi.org/10.1109/MWC.2014.7000981
2. Mashade, M.B.E., Hegazy, E.A.: Design and analysis of 28 GHz rectangular microstrip patch array antenna. WSEAS. Trans. Commun. **17**, 1–15 (2018)
3. Dejen, A., Anguera, J., Ridwan, M., Jayasinghe, J.: Genetically engineered dual-band microstrip antenna with improved directivity for 5g mm-wave mobile applications: In:1st Women in Engineering Symposium, Sri lanka (2020)
4. Rappaport, T.S., Xing, Y., MacCartney, G.R., Molisch, A.F., Mellios, E., Zhang, J.: Overview of millimeter wave communications for fifth-generation (5G) wireless networks—with a focus on propagation models. IEEE Trans. Antennas Propag. **65**(12), 6213–6230 (2017). https://doi.org/10.1109/TAP.2017.2734243
5. Hu, C.-N., Chang, D.-C., Hu, C.-H., Hsaio, T.-W., Lin, D.-P.: Millimeter-wave microstrip antenna array design and an adaptive algorithm for future 5g wireless communication systems. Int. J. Antennas Propag. **2016**, 1–10 (2016). https://doi.org/10.1155/2016/7202143
6. C.Borja, G. Font, S. Blanch and J. Romeu: High directivity fractal boundary microstrip patch antenna. Electronics Letters 36(9), (2000)
7. Anguera, J., Montesinos, G., Puete, C., Borja, C.: andJordi Soler: an undersampled high-directivity microstrip patch array with a reduced number of radiating elements inspired on the Sierpinski fractal. Microw. Opt. Technol. Lett. **37**(2), 100–103 (2003)
8. Anguera, J., Puente, C., Borja, C., Montero, R.: Bowtie Microstrip patch antenna based on the Sierpinski Fractal. Microw. Opt. Technol. Lett. **31**(3), 239–241 (2001)
9. Errifi, H., Baghdad, A., Badri, A., Sahel, A.: Directivity enhancement of aperture coupled microstrip patch antenna using two layers dielectric superstrate. In: 14th IEEE Proceedings of 2014 Mediterranean Microwave Symposium (MMS2014), Marrakech, Morocco, (2014)
10. Kurra, L., Abegaonkar, M.P., Basu, A., Koul, S.K.: FSS properties of a Uni-planar EBG and its application in directivity enhancement of a microstrip antenna. IEEE Antennas Wirel. Propag. Lett. (2016)
11. Anguera, J., Andujar, A., Jayasinghe, J.: High-directivity microstrip patch antennas based on TModd-0 Modes. IEEE Antennas Wirel. Propag. Lett. **19**(1), 39–43 (2020). https://doi.org/10.1109/LAWP.2019.2952260

12. Jayasinghe, J.M.J.W.: Disala Uduwawala, Jaume Anguera: Increasing the directivity of a microstrip patch array by genetic optimization. J. Natl. Sci. Found. **43**(1), 83–89 (2015)
13. Jayasinghe, J.W., Anguera, J., Uduwawala, D.N.: A High-directivity microstrip patch antenna design by using genetic algorithm optimization. Progr. Electromagn. Res. C **37**, 131–144 (2013)
14. John, M., Ammann, M.J.: Design of a wide-band printed antenna using a genetic algorithm on an array of overlapping sub-patches. In: IEEE International Workshop on Antenna Technology Small Antennas and Novel Metamaterials, New York (2006)
15. Haupt, R.L.: An introduction to genetic algorithms for electromagnetics. IEEE Antennas Propag. Mag. **37**(2), 7–15 (1995). https://doi.org/10.1109/74.382334
16. Saraereh, O.A., Al, A.A., Saraira, Q.H., Alsafasfeh, A.A.: Bio-inspired algorithms applied on microstrip patch antennas: a review. Int. J. Commun. Antennas Propag. (IRECAP) **6**(6), 336 (2016). https://doi.org/10.15866/irecap.v6i6.9737
17. Johnson, J.M., Rahmat-Samii, Y.: Genetic algorithms in engineering electromagnetics. IEEE Antenna Propag. Mag. **39**(4), 1–10 (1997)
18. Jayasinghe, J.M.J.W., Anguera, J., Uduwawala, D.N.: A simple design of multi band microstrip patch antennas robust to fabrication tolerances for GSM, UMTS, LTE, and Bluetooth applications by using genetic algorithm optimization. Progr. Electromagn. Res. M. **27**, 255–269 (2012)

ICT, Software and Hardware Engineering

N-Neuron Simulation Using Multiprocessor Cluster

Derara Senay Shanka[✉]

College of Engineering and Technology, Electrical and Computer Engineering Department, Bule Hora University, Bule Hora, Ethiopia

Abstract. A growing number of research effort has been made to make the Simulation of the astonishing biophysical activities of the massively interconnected organic neurons on various computational platforms such as Field programmable Gate Arrays (FPGAs) and General Purpose Graphics Processing Unit (GP-GPU). Nonetheless, to make efficient and realistic simulation of this biophysical activities, a considerable amount of processing power and memory space is incurred. Although computational platforms come with an advanced solutions such as high performance cluster, and super computers, they come with high establishment cost. Hence, biologically realistic and computationally efficient simulation on consumer level cluster of microprocessor nodes would be helpful, as they give a room for a better performance of compute intensive applications in a relatively cheaper cost as compared to dedicated High performance computing facilities. Accordingly, in this work, large scale simulation of spiking neural network (SNN) on a cluster of 8 physical cores enabled with hyper threading (16 logical cores) is presented. The neural network is composed of the biologically plausible and computationally efficient Izhikevich single neuron model. To improve the performance of the simulation and effectively exploit the computational capacity of the cluster, we have used two parallel programming techniques: distributed parallel programming using Message Passing Interface (MPI) library and distributed shard (hybrid) parallel programming using MPI in tandem with Open Multi-Processing (OpenMP) library. Moreover, to harness the combined memory and computation power of the cluster the neurons were distributed across the nodes using static load balancing mechanism. Hence, we were able to simulate up to 160,000 neurons and 3.2M synapses connection per neuron. Performance evaluation for different configuration of the SNN with a purely MPI and Hybrid Parallelization method was presented. Our performance result show that for 160K neurons with 200 synapses connections, using purely MPI parallelization with 16 MPI processes the sequential simulation has improved by 43.12% and using the hybrid parallel programming the sequential simulation has improved by 69.58%. Hence, comparing the performance results the hybrid parallelization approach demonstrated to be a good programming solution for simulation of SNNs on a cluster of consumer level multiprocessors.

Keywords: Spiking neural network · MPI · OpenMP · Hybrid parallelization

M. L. Berihun (Ed.): ICAST 2021, LNICST 411, pp. 343–367, 2022.
https://doi.org/10.1007/978-3-030-93709-6_23

1 Introduction

The mammalian cerebral cortex, the largest portion of the organic brain, contains a massive interconnection of information processing element called neuron. It is now understood that these neurons incorporate computational and memory units as well. Moreover, a single neuron is connected to as many as 1000–10,000 to other neurons, creating massively parallel, and extensively interconnected network of biological neurons.

It has long been since an effort was being reported to model the computational power of this biological phenomena. From the earliest McCulloch Pitts neuron based network of artificial neurons to the latest biologically realistic spiking neural networks (SNN). Be that as it may, the need to have biologically accurate simulation is computationally demanding. This fact have further led researchers to crave in finding a way to realize an efficient large-scale simulation of biologically plausible neural networks both on software and hardware platforms.

Advancements in the computational efficiency of the present day multiprocessor computers and the increasing understanding of computational principles of the organic brain in the past decades have led to an ever growing efforts in simulating the physiological activities of biological neuronal networks using various computational platforms. For instance, R. Ananthanarayanan and et al. [1] simulated 55 million neurons with a 442 billion synapses on a BlueGene/L computer which has more than 32,000 cores with a reasonable time.

Inspired by the astounding physiological activity of network of biological neural networks there is a proliferated effort to mimic this activity using a variety of mathematical models on a range of computational platforms both on software development approaches and specialized hardware architectures like Field Programmable Gate Array (FPGA) and General Purpose Graphics processing Unit (GP-GPU).

In line of this effort, there exists a tradeoff between realizing biologically realistic simulations and computational cost, where such simulations require a considerable amount of processing power and memory space. Conventional processors do not have enough parallelism and memory bandwidth for real-time simulation of SNNs with large number of neuron population. Modern parallel architectures (such as clusters, supercomputers, or high-performance processors) promise powerful alternatives for speeding spiking neural network simulation, but incur high price cost to establish them. Therefore, simulation on consumer level cluster of microprocessors would be helpful and relatively less expensive than high performance facilities.

This research work seeks to speed up the simulation using message passing interface (MPI) library and hybrid MPI + Open Multi-processing (OpenMP) library and measure and compare the performance of the simulation on different neural network configuration. Moreover, Performance Measurement and comparison of the simulation on varying number of MPI processes and OpenMP threads.

In the ensuing section, we present a brief discussion of literatures related with other works done by manifold researchers on large-scale simulation of SNN on various computational platforms in general and on multiprocessor cluster in particular followed by the theoretical background of how biological neural networks function from computational neuroscience perspective. Three prominent mathematical model of spiking neurons are discussed in brief. The methodology section discusses regarding parallel programming fundamentals on shared memory and distributed shared memory computers. Moreover the experimental setup of the simulation is also presented.

2 Literature Review

Simulation of how biological neural networks function in organic brain has been an interest of study for decades. The effort to efficiently make large scale simulation of spiking neural networks has a long history that spans from hardware implementations to the more popular distributed compute cluster implementations. A growing body of literatures exist regarding the various approaches followed by different research groups. These approaches, particularly parallel simulations, are broadly categorized as hardware and software based implementations. In this section, we present notable works demonstrated using these platforms.

2.1 Literatures on Simulation of SNN Using Hardware Platforms

Parallel simulation of SNNs on different hardware architectures and platforms have saw three major approaches. For instance in [2], digital signal processing (DSP) accelerator based simulation was reported. On the other hand in [3], using one category of very large scale-integration(VLSI) technology, application-specific integrated circuit (ASIC), 512k neurons with up to 104 synaptic connections was demonstrated. Furthermore, field programmable arrays (FPGAs) have been a major class of hardware-based approach that are used to significantly accelerate SNN algorithms. For example two notable works [4] & [5] can be mentioned.

2.2 Literatures on Simulation of SNN Using Software Implementations

Several SNN software simulators have been developed using different programming languages which can be categorized based on the computational platform in which they are implemented. These could be on a single dedicated computer or a network of distributed computers. In addition, graphics card enabled computers and supercomputing facilities are used for large scale simulations. The paragraph that right follows goes through prominent researches made on the mentioned platforms. Starting from the earliest HH-neuron based SNN simulation environments like GENESIS [6] and NEURON [7], several sequential SNN software packages written in C++ and Python programming languages have been developed, and are currently in a widespread use.

The advent and ubiquity of multi-core computers have drawn the attention of a growing number of computational neuroscientists aiming to harness the increased processing power of these machines. Accordingly, a plethora of software based neural network simulators that are made on a parallel computers have been presented in various times. For instance, PGENESIS [6]: the parallel version of GENESIS and a parallel version of NEURON [8] have been reported. Simulation efforts that came later one have targeted multiprocessor computers. One quintessential example of such parallel software technologies for large-scale SNN simulation works on multiprocessor computers is Neural Simulation Tool (NEST) [9].

Another category of work that fall under software-based neural network simulation package are the one that were made on a cluster of distributed multi-processor computers. Accordingly, the research work presented in [10], proposed coarse grained nature of parallelism in which a groups of neurons are mapped on to different processors and made to be solved independently and hence in parallel. This approach was tested and have resulted a 10x speed up using a cluster of 16 processors and the authors pointed out that further speed up can be achieved.

In 2007, Plesser and his colleagues [11], were able to map NEST simulation software on a cluster of multiprocessor computers. A hybrid programming which combines multi-threading and distributed parallel computing techniques using MPI and Pthread APIs respectively was introduced to the simulation. An event driven benchmark simulation of a network composed of 12,500 leaky-integrate and fire neuron model on a cluster of four Sun × 4100 computer nodes with a capability of dual core AMD Opteron processors. In this work, the neural network was partitioned and distributed over the "virtual processes", which are a combination of MPI process and Pthread threads in each processes. They have used maximum of 20 processes and 4 threads in each process. Eventually the performance of the simulation was evaluated and a super linear scaling up to 16 "virtual processes" was observed regardless of the order of combination of MPI processes and Pthread threads in the hybrid penalization and up to 8 "virtual processes" in the purely MPI implementation. Moreover, they've reported that the hybrid parallel programming has outperformed the purely MPI based distributed simulation.

Another biophysically realistic parallel simulation effort that uses two parallel programming APIs was reported in a paper [12] by Jingzhen Hu in 2012. In this work more than 100,000 Hodgkin-Huxley neurons were simulated using distributed memory parallel programming using MPI API and distributed shared memory parallel programming using MPI together with OpenMp API on a multiprocessor cluster of 52 nodes each with 32 processors. Due to the parallel strategy employed, it was reported that the execution time of the simulation has shown an improvement of 10% using a hybrid approach than the purely MPI implementation. Moreover, it was reported that the hybrid approach was 31× faster than the serial implementation when used on 32 processors.

Another distributed simulation of SNN that exhibit time locked spiking behavior was demonstrated in 2014 [13]. This simulation was made on cluster made of up to 128 processors running at 2.5 GHz. The neural network was arranged as a bi-dimensional column of Izhikevich neurons and this neurons were distributed to the processors in the cluster using a collective communication MPI primitive. In this paper, the simulation performance of the network varied from 6.6 Giga synapses down to 200k synapses was demonstrated to be scalable and fast for the maximum number of synapses used. Performance evaluation by varying the number of MPI processes for a fixed network size and fixing the number of MPI processes for a varying number of neurons and synapses was made. A speed-up of 41.5 was reported for a simulation of 204M synapses on a cluster of 128 cores. The authors have attributed the deviation from the theoretically expected speed up of 128 to the communication cost between the processors in the cluster.

Ever since NVIDIA introduced the first graphics processing unit (GPUs) in to the main stream computing arena at the end of the 20thcentury, it has got the attention of a sizeable number of researchers from the computing community for the implementation of computationally demanding applications. The reason for this is its flexibility for parallel implementations. So much so that, several GPU-based simulation of SNN were reported at various times. In the paragraphs that follow, we present popular and notable studies under this category.

A. K. Fidjeland and M. P. Shanahan [14], demonstrated biologically realistic large-scale simulation of a network of Izhikevich spiking neurons on GPU. In this study, they were able to made real-time simulation of around 55,000 neurons with 1000 synapses per neuron. Similarly in [15], 4,096 Izhikevich neurons were simulated on an NVIDIA GTX260 GPU that resulted a real-time performance with a 9 times speedup compared to a CPU-based simulation.In 2009 T. B. Vekterli [16], has showed parallelization of SNNs both on CPU and GPU. The method involves parallelization of SNN model using OpenMp implementation of up to 100,000 neurons on CPU and 70,000 neurons for GPU Computer Unified Device Architecture (CUDA) implementation each with synaptic connection of 100, 200 and 300 every time the network simulation was made to run. In this work, the OpenMp implementation have exhibited a speed ups of nearly 2x with four threads over the single threaded results. On the other hand, the CUDA implementation have proved to be the fastest alternative in the simulation process.

Another domain of simulation is employed on super computers in big research facilities like IBM research center using software-based techniques. For instance, IBM C2 simulator [1] demonstrated a rat-scale cortical simulation with a 55 Million neurons and 442Billion synapses using a Blue-Gene supercomputer having more than 32K processors. Such computational devices are due to their cost to make unfortunately the cost and development time make these approaches impractical for general purpose, large-scale simulations.

Although the idea of performing large scale neuron simulation is not and different techniques and successes have been reported, the prior works that exist on the simulation of spiking neural network on multiprocessor CPU cluster use the integrate and fire neuron model to simulate the neural dynamics. Using IF neuron model as a base for the simulation of large scale SNN is computationally efficient than the HH model but lacks biological realism. Another important and distinguishing issue with our work is that, previous works on distributed parallel computation use either Pure Message passing Interface/interaction or MPI with POSIX thread (Pthreads). In this work, we follow a hybrid parallel programming model that brings both a multithreading with OpenMP library and distributed MPI on polychronous Izikevich spiking neuron. Furthermore, the simulation effort targets a cluster consumer level multiprocessor clusters than costly high performance compute nodes.

3   Biological Background

Neurons which are the elementary building block of the cognitive system have different shapes and form, but they share common anatomical appearance and physiological activities. This specialized nerve cells constitute mainly the central nervous system (CNS) of animals, particularly the primary information processing "machine", the brain. Their number ranges from handful in invertebrates to 100 billons in human brain.

A biological neuron has four main parts (see Fig. 1) viz. dendrite, an axon, synapse and soma. Dendrite is a "tree" like structure in which a neuron receives an electro-chemical signal from other neurons where connection is established.

Soma is the cell body of a neuron where protein and other important substances are produced. It is also a place where electrochemical progress occurs. Moreover, electrical pulses are generated and incoming electrical signals are processed by the soma. An axon is a cable like extension where electrochemical pulse signal called action potential is sent through. In addition, it has a protective fatty white substance called myelin sheath which serves as an electrical insulation. Synapse is a narrow gap between one neuron's axon terminal and another neuron's dendrite. Individual neuron is "connected" to 1000–10,000 other neurons through synapse. It is also a place where the neuron passes its signal to other neurons by a means of special chemical substance called neurotransmitters.

The information processing and communication between these interconnected neurons is done by a means of electrochemical pulse signal called "spikes".

3.1   Spiking Neural Networks

In order to aid our understanding of the complexities and information processing capability of biological neural networks, different efforts have been made so far for so long to represent it at various levels of abstraction. Among them, the conventional Artificial Neural Networks (ANNs) are the popular and most widely used one for a variety of applications including real world problems. Since it was first introduced back in 1943 by McCulloch-Pitts [17], ANNs have evolved in to three generations along the past seven decades, distinguishing their computational unit from one generation to the other. For instance, the first generation of ANNs were based on applying a non-linear function (threshold or perceptron) to a weighted sum of inputs.

Experimental results from neurobiology: information processing in biological neural system depends on the timing of action potential (spike) of a neuron, have led to an emergence of Spiking Neural Networks (SNNs) that fall under the third generation of ANNs which take into account the spiking nature of real neurons and are able to encode spatial-temporal information into both spike timing and spiking rates. This makes SNNs more biologically plausible in mimicking the physiological activity of biological neural networks than previous generations [18]. Moreover, the information processing ability in general and cognitive capability specifically in organic brain is achieved through the weighted and complex interconnection of SNNs.

3.1.1 Single Neuron Model

In Computational models can be a paramount tool for comprehending the complex properties and activities that happen in organic brain. Several models exist that characterize neural dynamics of an individual biological neuron in multiple levels of abstraction. Here we present only the three most popular and widely used classes of computational single neuron modeling of neural dynamics starting from the oldest Hodgkin Huxley model to the recent Izhikevich model.

Detail discussion of this models and review of various mathematical models is beyond the scope of this research work. For further read, see [19].

3.1.1.1 Hodgkin-Huxley Neuron Model

Hodgkin-Huxley (HH) model [20], is a pioneering model in describing ionic processes and voltage dependent conductance during the generation and propagation of action potential, which was studied by Hodgkin and Huxley on a giant squid axon in 1952. It explains how a neuron responds by producing various spiking patterns to current stimuli. The model uses four differential equations and tens of parameters that describe the corresponding physiological measurements. The parameters introduced are biologically meaningful and measurable. Thus, it is considered to be the most biologically plausible model. However, the number of ordinary differential equations (ODE) used in the model incur high computational cost for simulation purpose using different computational platforms. For this reason, only a few number of neurons can be simulated using HH model [19].

3.1.1.2 Integrate-And-Fire Neuron Model

Despite the fact that HH model is biologically plausible, it incurs a considerable computational cost. Moreover, it is difficult to implement it on hardware devices. Therefore, more simplified models are needed. In Integrate- and-fire (IF) model [21] the four dimensional HH model is reduced to a two-dimensional model. As its very name suggests, this model proposes two steps that abstract the neural dynamics. The first stage is the integration stage, where by inputs are summed up. The next stage that rightly follows is the firing phase, in which the neuron fires if the summed value exceeds a predetermined threshold and reset the membrane potential. After the firing state the neuron enters into a refractory condition.

Because LIF models are simple to implement and easy to analyze they are the most widely used Spiking neuron models for a wide range of applications, however, IF model fails short to exhibit all neural dynamics and literatures so conclude that this model is not good enough for computer simulation if we are concerned of biologically realistic simulation [22].

3.1.1.3 Izhikevich Neuron Model

In a paper presented in 2003 [23], Izhikevich proposed a new model which is almost as accurate as the highly detailed Hodgkin-Huxley neuron model and also which has an efficient computational cost.

The Izhikevich (here after called "IZ") neuron model is based on the knowledge of bifurcation mechanisms [3], which enables to reduce HH neuron model in to a two-dimensional system of first order ordinary differential equations (FODEs).

Accordingly, IZ neurons are represented by the following expressions:

$$v' = 0.04v^2 + 5v + 140 - u + I \qquad (1)$$

$$u' = a(bv - u) \qquad (2)$$

With the auxiliary after-spike resetting.

$$\text{If } v \geq 30\,\text{mV}, \text{then} \{u^v \leftarrow^{\leftarrow} u^c + d \qquad (3)$$

Where v is the membrane potential, u is the recovery variable where the membrane potential is adjusted to. The dimensionless parameters a and b represent the sensitivity of the recovery variable and the time scale of the recovery variable respectively.

Represents the after-spike reset value of the membrane potential v. The common value of c = −65"m" V. The parameter d describes the value in which the recovery variable u is update after a particular spike has occurred.

The firing state of the neuron is determined if the membrane potential exceeds over a certain threshold, in this case + 30 mV. After reaching this apex, the membrane voltage and the recovery variable are reset according to Eq. (3).

By varying the values of a and d various spiking patterns that correspond to a particular type of neuron can be produced. For instance, for excitatory Regular spiking (RS) neurons, which are a typical neuron that reside in the cerebral cortex, we use the values a = 0.02 and d = 8. In addition, for inhibitory Fast Spiking (FS) cortical neurons we use the a = 0.1 and d = 2.

Two important factors must be taken in to consideration when choosing single neuron model for SNN implementation. That is the model has to biologically realistic by yield a reach set of firing patterns as exhibited in biological neurons and it has to be computationally simple and efficient when being implemented on various computational platforms [19]. Therefore, the models are scrutinized in light of the above two metrics when choosing a particular model for large scale simulation. In light of the above to criteria, HH model is biologically plausible yet computationally prohibitive. IF and its variant models are computationally simple and efficient but, fall short of being biologically plausible [4]. In the contrary, IZ single neuron model is both biologically realistic and computationally efficient. Therefore, we have so chosen it for this research work.

3.2 Learning in Spiking Neural Network

Any neural network gains functionality through learning or training function. Learning in conventional ANN is performed through back propagation or gradient descent in which errors are propagated backwards in the network. However, the learning and memory capabilities of the organic brain are substrate essentially on the plasticity of synapses (weight/conductance modification) between pre-synaptic and post-synaptic neurons. The first study regarding synaptic weight modification depending on the relative spiking of pre-synaptic and post- synaptic neurons was introduced by Hebb in 1949 [24]. In this paper, Hebb formulated a synapses weight adjustment which states: a synapse weight should be strengthened if a pre-synaptic neuron repeatedly takes part in firing before a postsynaptic neuron fires. This scenario is apparently dubbed as long-term potentiation (LTP). Nonetheless, Hebb didn't addressed about synaptic weakening. Since then, a detailed explanation of the mechanism in which synaptic weight modification occur has been developed. One commonly used unsupervised Hebbian learning approach which uses spike timing information to set the synaptic weights for SNNs is called spike time dependent plasticity (STDP) [25]. STDP can be viewed as a more quantitative form of Hebbian learning. It emphasizes the importance of causality in synaptic strengthening or weakening; the relative spike timing of pre-synaptic and post-synaptic neurons leads to changing synaptic weight of the neurons [26]. Whenever STDP is invoked the synapses weight is either depreciates or potentiates. This phenomenon is hailed as long-term potentiation (LTP) and long-term depression (LTD), of synaptic weight value, respectively.

Another main characteristic of synaptic connection is the axonal conduction delay. After a pre-synaptic neuron has fired and before this spike signal reaches to the point of post synaptic neuron, a certain amount of time elapses. H.A. Swadlow [27] have reported regarding this study; the value of an axonal conduction delay in mammalian cortex depends on the neuron type and their location and this value ranges between 0.1 ms to 44 ms. Hence, when modeling dynamics of spiking neurons, a conduction delay has to be considered. For this reason, unlike conventional ANNs that discard axon conduction delay, when modeling biological SNNs it is essential to consider the time required for an action potential to travel from its initiation of presynaptic neuron to the axon terminals of the post-synaptic neuron. This feature makes possible the generation of stable, and time locked spatio-temporal neural firing patterns [28].

Regarding inhibitory neuron to allow the inhibitory connections to provide sufficient inhibition to their postsynaptic neurons, all their M synapses have a fixed conduction delay of 1 ms. As in the work in [23], for our network simulation the axonal conduction delay is as low as 1ms and as large as 20 ms.

One of the issues that determine the overall behavior of neural network simulation is the network structure. In this work, we have adopted the neural network structure used in [28]. Unlike the conventional feed forward neural network, this neural network structure involves neurons which are randomly connected, with axonal conduction delay and having polychromous property, which is briefly discussed in the ensuing section.

4   Parallel Programming Fundamentals

Parallel programming is a programming paradigm in which large and compute intensive problem is divided in to multiple smaller simultaneously executed tasks. This model can be implemented through one of the following ways; shared memory parallelism, distributed shared memory parallelism, and hybrid: shared-distributed memory parallelism. Different software technologies have been introduced to aid the implementation of these methods. The following section discusses briefly about these methods.

4.1   Shared Memory Parallelization

The architecture of recent decades consumer-level multicore computers have more than one processor inside each individual core. This feature makes them suitable for speeding up computations by concurrently executing independent tasks on these processors. There are different hardware and software approaches that are known to realize parallelization in a multiprocessor computer. One is multithreading parallel programming model: generation of multiple threads and assigning tasks to this threads for simultaneous execution.

A typical process; an instance of program execution in many of operating systems (OS) available have a single master thread in which instructions are executed sequentially. This thread has its own program counter to keep track of which instruction to execute next, system registers which hold its current working variables, and a stack which contains the execution history. To execute a computational task single threaded processes tasks a lot of resource than multiple threaded process. This is because, the creation of multiple threads provide a suitable foundation for parallel execution of applications on shared memory multiprocessors. Threads are "light weight" processes. Threads created in the same process share the same address space.

4.1.1   Open Multi-processing (OpenMP)

OpenMP is the de facto industry standard API for parallel programming paradigm which targets shared memory multiprocessors [29]. It provides a set of compiler directives, run-time library functions and environment variables that enables the Transformation of a sequential source code written in FORTRAN, C, or C++ programming language in to a parallel application. This feature makes it easy to implement compared to other parallel programming APIs like Pthread for multithreaded parallel programming. It is essentially based on fork-and-joint parallelism model, where threads in a particular process are categorized as master and slave. In this model, program execution commences as a single process or thread which is hailed as master thread and continues the execution sequentially. When "Parallel" parallelization directive is encountered in the sequential source code, a block of slave threads are forked/created under this master thread and continue the program execution in a parallelized manner until the end of the parallel region. When this team of threads finish execution of job, they join back together again and only a single thread continues.

4.2   Distributed Parallel Programming Model

In distributed memory parallel programming paradigm, a program runs as a separate, independent process with a private memory can be considered as separate serial programs. Parallelization for distributed memory computer systems is done by distribution of computational task and data on the processors through message passing programming model. This processes communicate via message passing programming model: a coordinated communication between processes inside a network of computer nodes.

In the message passing model, resource on a networked computers have their own local memory and they communicate and coordinate to execute a set of tasks through exchange of data by sending and receiving messages between the nodes. Among the various message passing software approaches that run on a distributed compute nodes, Message passing Interface (MPI) is the popular and widely used one. In message passing model processes in compute nodes share data and coordinate/synchronize their operation.

4.2.1 Message Passing Interface

Message passing Interface (MPI) [30] is a message-passing library interface specification used to handle data communication between distributed shared memory computers. Currently, it is the *defacto* industry standard API for distributed parallel programming. Essentially, it comes with different library functions which allow coordinated message passing between distributed nodes. This includes a protocol and semantic specifications for how its features behave in any implementation. Depending on the type of the operating system a process contains a program counter and address spaces. In addition, a single process can have multiple threads sharing a common address spaces. MPI parallel programming model enables a communication between separate and distribute processes. In an MPI application processes that are allowed to communicate with each other do the communication through a default MPI communicator function. Processes that are bound in a communicator will have a unique identifier called rank, numbered from 0 to n–1. By default in an MPI program, initially all the processes belong to the MPI_COMM_WORLD communicator.

MPI API offers two communication schemes namely, point to point communication and collective communication. Point-to-point communication scheme involves exclusive sending and receiving of messages between two processes. Conversely, in collective communication scheme all processes do part-take in passing message from one processes to all processes in a more efficient manner. For instance data can be scattered to all other processes using a single communication routine, MPI_scatter with reduces the communication overhead had it been used in a point-to-point communication. Among open source MPI implementations, LAM-MPI [31] and MPICH [32] are the most widespread use ones, where the former is for Unix-based systems and the later for Windows systems. Hence, for our simulation, we have used MPICH that is based on MPI 3.1 standard.

4.3 Hybrid Parallel Programming Model

It is intuitive to assume employing both shared and distributed parallel programming models to work in tandem for a performance improvement of a computer program at hand. Such a programming approach is hailed as a hybrid/mixed mode parallel programming model. It is the use of two distinct parallel programming models in a complimentary way for a cluster of multiprocessor computer nodes. Unlike pure multithreading parallelization approach inside a shared memory programming node, message passing between nodes will also occur in this model.

Through this hybrid programming model, multiple threads are forked inside each process in each multiprocessor node while MPI API controls the communication between this processes.

This scenario is shown as below in Fig. 5, how a two-dimensional array is decomposed in two four processes and three threads in individual process.

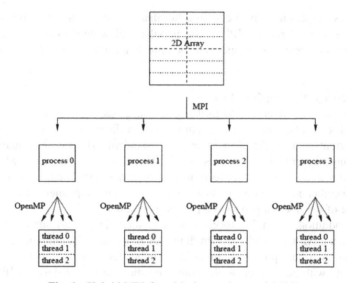

Fig. 1. Hybrid MPI OpenMp integration model [33]

5 Methodology

Different techniques have been proposed and implemented as for the parallel simulation is concerned. For instance, a paper by A. Jahnke and et al. [28] States that parallel simulation of SNN can be realized through three approaches namely, neuron parallelism (n-parallel), synapses parallelism (s-parallel), pattern parallelism (p-parallel). In n-parallel approach each neuron are mapped to a processing element and associated computations are processed in parallel while their corresponding computations with synapses state update are executed serially. In s-parallel approach the synapses state update of each neuron is executed using parallel processing element. As individual neuron will have more than one synapses connections, this approach gives an additional opportunity for parallelization. The third approach, p-parallel approach uses the above two approaches in tandem i.e. when the neuron state update is required the process is executed in a parallel fashion so will be the case for synapses state updates. In this work we have used the n-parallel approach for the pure MPI parallelization and p-parallel approach for the hybrid MPI +OpenMp parallelization.

Moreover, another perspective about simulation techniques of SNN can have a different categories. According to [34], two class of methods do exist in SNN simulation viz. time-step driven, and event-driven.

In time-step driven simulation the state variable of individual neuron in the SNN is updated at every discrete time step. On the contrary, in an event - driven simulation the state of SNN is updated only at the instant of spike occurrence at a particular neuron. The later gives a speed up advantage as update to the neural network only occurs when event/spike is emitted or arrives. Moreover, it suits the IZ single neuron model used in this research work. The mixed mode simulation approach amalgamates the above two methods. The important feature of this method is that, it renders an opportunity to use the advantages of both time-step driven simulation and event driven simulation. Therefore, in our simulation we have adopted this approach for the reason mentioned just above.

The real-time simulation value for both network construction and simulation phase of the purely serial execution and parallel execution for simulating 10s of model time was recorded. To keep the stochastic nature of neuron connection, the simulation were run five times with different random number seed and the average of five run was taken at the end for each number of varying synapses and neuron value.

An effort to get the average sequential execution time for a large problem size faces a hindrance due to both high memory requirement and time restrictions. For instance, for synapses value of 100 it was possible to measure average execution time of only 120,000 neurons on a single process. Moreover, it was also impossible to get an average sequential execution time for neuron size of more than 80,000 with 200 synapse connection. Consequently, to get the speed up gain for exceeding network sizes, we need to extrapolate based on the value we got for lesser problem sizes. Execution time for sequential simulation that exceeds running capability of a single processor can be found by extrapolating the result gained from less work load [35]. The extrapolation was done using a second order polynomial extrapolation as it takes in to consideration the entire data points of the simulations average runtime before the compute intensive network size.

5.1 MPI Based Parallel Simulation

The SNN simulation passes through two main steps: network construction and actual simulation steps. This section outlines the steps followed to make a solely MPI based parallel implementation. The original MATLAB/C++ algorithm used in [28] passes through two main stages namely; network construction and network simulation. The following paragraph discusses the steps used to map this two stages on to a cluster of multiprocessors using MPI API. Before making the actual network simulation, a network of spiking neuron is constructed under network construction section using the steps mentioned below.

Step 1:- Array of N neuron holding the index of ith individual neuron were distributed equally with static load balancing in mind among the MPI processes using the MPI_scatter routine. In this step the number of neuron population was based on the 4:1 ratio of excitatory and inhibitory neuron type of the total neuron population (i.e. 80% are excitatory neuron and 20% are inhibitory neuron in each node) Ne = N*0.8 and Ni = N*0.2.

Step 2:- For each N neuron, M number of synapses which resides in the i index holding the index of the post-synapses neuron j projecting from neuron i is distributed among the MPI processes in the cluster in which neuron j will exist [36]. In this way the data structure that contains a neuron and synapses that it is post-synaptic do exist in on the same processes rank.

Step 3:- Initialization of neural dynamics parameters a and d. For Ne: a = 0.02 and d = 8, For Ni: a = 0.1 and d = 2. This determines the behavior of each neurons.

Step 4:- A call to the MPI_all_to_all collective communication routine will create awareness about a connection from the incoming axon of neuron N will be created. Impliedly, this will establish the connection between neurons that reside in different process. In addition, excitatory neurons (Ne) connect to other model processes in compute nodes share data and coordinate/synchronize their operation. Excitatory (Ne) and inhibitory neurons (Ni) but, inhibitory neurons only connect to excitatory neurons.

Step 5:- Initial synaptic weight (s) of 6.0 mV is assigned for every excitatory connections and –5.0 mV for every inhibitory connections. The synaptic weight derivative; the value the synapse weight to be modified (*sd*) is also set to zero at this stage.

Step 6:- For each neuron in same MPI process an axonal conduction delay (D) in a range from 1ms-20ms was assigned with a uniform distribution of M/D axon conduction delay table. For inhibitory neuron an axonal conduction delay of 1ms was assigned.

Step 7:- For each neuron in the same MPI process an initial value of the activity variables like the membrane potential v = 65 mV and recovery variable u = 0.02*v was assigned according to the IZ neuron model. This will make neurons to wait in the reset state until a triggering signal reaches and makes it to spike. In addition, the STDP functions LTP and LTD were made to be zero at this stage.

The network simulation Stage can be broken down in to a category of steps:
For each simulation second:

Step 1:- Reset Input step:
For every neuron N the value of input to the neurons is reset to zero.

Step 2:- Spike generation step:
For a randomly picked neuron thalamic input current with a value of 20 mV is supplied.

Step 3:- Spike detection step:
The membrane potential, v, of individual neuron is checked whether it has reached at its apex vt, which is set to cause a spike at greater than or equal to the value of vt. If any neuron have fired during this time step (i.e. $v \geq vt$), then:
The membrane potential value is re-set to parameter c, membrane recovery is incremented by parameter d,
The time step associated with this neuron is updated and the neuron index is added to the list of fired neurons.
STDP variables of the neuron; LTP and LTD are reset to their maximum values of 0.1 and 0.12 respectively, according to the STDP rule.
Synapse derivative sd connections with the neuron are potentiated according to STDP LTP according to the time signature the last spike has occurred relative to the current firing.

Step 4:- Spike Exchange between processes:
All neurons that have fired in the D previous time steps are processed.
Each MPI process containing the fired neuron broadcasts spike input to other MPI processes holding the post synaptic neurons.

The total current introduced by the sent input spike to the target neuron are calculated and stored to be used for the neuron state update stage.

Step 5:- Neuron state update step:

For each individual neuron in the subset of each MPI process.

Membrane potential v is updated according to IZ model numerically using a forward Euler method based on input from previous simulation stage.

Step 6:- Synapses state update step:

For every Ne, their synapses s and their derivative Sd is updated as:

$$s \leftarrow s + 0.001 + Sd \text{ and } Sd = 0.9 * Sd \qquad (4)$$

The constants 0.01 represents activity independent increase of synaptic weight and 0.9 a simulation parameter as suggested in [35].

If $s \geq 10$ mV, then $s \leftarrow 10$ mV

If $s < 10$ mV, then $s \leftarrow 0$ mV

5.1.1 Spike Exchange between Processes

Each MPI processes communicate by sending and receiving spike messages. In order to make a spike exchange between MPI processes, address event representation (AER) scheme which was first rolled out for communication in neuromorphic chips [36] was adopted. In this mechanism a spike message from neuron N will be represented by the neuron id of spike origin and the time signature of the spike that has occurred. Hence, Information about all the neuron that have fired in the same simulation time step is gathered by MPI processes using MPI_All_to_all communication routine and distributed to all the neuron that they have established a connection.the parallel region. When this team of threads finish execution of job, they join back together again and only a single thread continues.

The single neuron model's FODE is not suitable for use in a computer program. Therefore, the ODE was approximated using a numerical method that fits to a computer program. Among the available numerical integration methods for ODE, forward Euler's method was used because it demands less number of iterations unlike its counterpart backward Euler's Method. Moreover, in our simulation, in order to update the membrane potential value we have used four iterations and 0.1 time step for the sake of minimizing the numerical error incurred due to the method we followed.

5.1.2 Hybrid MPI+OpenMP Parallelization Simulation

In the purely MPI based simulation there are portion of the SNN simulation were we can take advantage of multithreaded parallel programming. In the network construction/initialization phase(initialization of neuron dynamic parameters, synapses and synapses weight derivatives) and in the simulation phase it contains for loops including neuron and synapses state updates which can be executed in a parallel fashion on more than one thread. Consequently, an additional loop level parallelization is introduced inside the pure MPI based implementation. As it was mentioned above in Sect. 4.3.1, MPI API supports a multithreaded parallel programming.

In order to use OpenMp API to parallelize the source code, the integrated development environment (IDE) used for source code compilation and editing has to be enabled to support it. The IDE used in this work, visual studio 2013, supports OpenMp 2.0 hence was enabled for multithreaded execution.

In this approach a omp_set_num_threads routine will be called to specify the number of threads to be used in each processes. In this regard, among the available 4 logical processors in side each the cluster, a thread number of 2, and 4 are forked in each simulation experiment with in each MPI process of combination for 8 and 4 MPI processes respectively.

To ensure work load balance between threads in each process dynamic work scheduling was incorporated using dynamic clause (#pragma omp parallel for schedule (dynamic, 1). This scheduling mechanism is a good way to reduce work load imbalance between OpenMP threads created in MPI processes.

To get the execution time of both the network construction, and the actual simulation phases on the master node, an MPI routine, MPI_wtime was used.

5.2 Experimental Setup

To achieve efficient parallelization and scale up in simulation time of SNN with a considerable amount of neurons and synapses connections, we have used a cluster of nodes with multiprocessors where the nodes are connected in separate private network.

The simulation was conducted on a 4-node cluster, each of which are configured with Intel core i3 3.30 GHz processors enabled with hyper threading and having 2 GB RAM. MPICH API was installed on each nodes in the cluster and the processes were managed using MPICH process manager.

8-Port 10/100Mb fast Ethernet switch which enables a communication between the connected nodes in the network was used. This communication between the computer nodes was made using Transmission Control protocol (TCP)/Internet Protocol (IP) protocol version 4. The server management software we used was Microsoft windows server 2012 standard edition. In order to have a network of computers to function suitably for our experiment, the following services were installed and configured with an appropriate setting on it; Active Directory Domain Service (ADDS) for role management of nodes, DNS (Domain Name System) for resolving host names and to group host computers into domains, Network File System (NFS) for sharing files between nodes in the cluster network and DHCP (Domain Host Configuration protocol) to dynamically assign IP addresses to the nodes that exist in the cluster network. The head node serve as a domain controller for the cluster and slave nodes are made to join the domain. The issue of a proper mechanism of process mapping among the multiprocessor nodes and the communication between the nodes in performance is important. In this research work maximum of one process is created per logical processors in each node in the cluster and a thread number of 2 and 4 created in each process employed in the cluster. The main reason in doing so is that this mechanism enables a better communication control among the individual process in the nodes.

6 Result and Discussion

Pursuant to the methodologies followed in the previous section, this section presents the performance results of the simulation of N-spiking neural network using two parallelization methods on a multiprocessor cluster. Moreover, we elucidate the observations made based on these results.

One of the goals of using parallel programming and multiprocessor cluster in an application is performance improvement. The two important quantities that allow to make performance evaluation are speedup and efficiency.

A speed up gain from using n number of processing elements can be gained as:

$$\text{Efficiency} = (\text{Speed up } (n))/(\text{No. of processors}) \qquad (5)$$

In this regards, the results of both purely MPI and hybridized MPI + OpenMp implementation is presented accordingly below.

6.1 MPI Implementation

The following paragraphs entail the results from solely MPI implementation of the simulation of different SNN configuration on a multiprocessor cluster. In order to observe the performance of the cluster implementation we have calculated the speed up based on the average execution time of the simulation both for the serial and parallel implementation on different network sizes by varying number of MPI processes.

The following figure depicts the speed up gain from MPI processes of 2, 4, 8 and 16 when used in a network of increasing number of neurons of 20k, 40k, 80k and 160k with 100 synapses connections per each neuron.

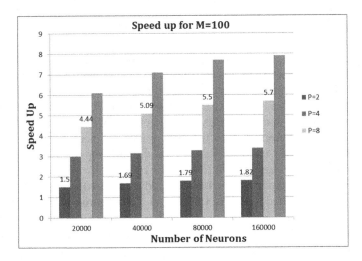

Fig. 2. Speed up of scaling number of neurons and increasing MPI processes

$$Speedup(n) = Ts/Tp \tag{6}$$

Where, Ts is the sequential execution time and Tp is the execution time for n number of processing elements

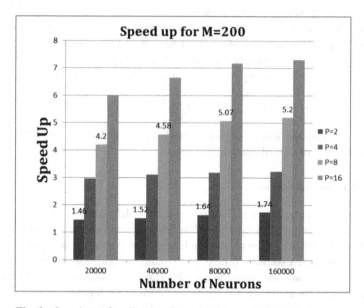

Fig. 3. Speed up of scaling number of neuron and MPI 200 Synapses

The efficiency of a parallel implementation can be calculated as follow:

Figure 2 shows the speed up gain for MPI processes of 2, 4, 8 and 16 when used in a network of increasing number of neurons of 20k, 40k, 80k and160k with 200 synapses connections per each neuron.

A parallel program is considered as scalable if the speed up increases with increasing number of parallel processing elements. Accordingly, for an ideal speed up of a parallel application using four processes will be four but, most applications exhibit sub linear speedup. In this regard, we could observe from Figs. 7 and 8 that the speed up of both network configuration scales as the number of MPI process increases. But a better scalability was observed in an increased number of neuron and when a lesser number of MPI processes are used. For instance, the speed up for 2 MPI processes on 20k neuron with 100 synapses was 1.5 while for 160k neuron with 100 synapses was 1.82, which is closer to the ideal speed up. Similarly, the speed up for 2 MPI processes on 20k neuron with 200 synapses is 1.46 and on 160k neuron with 200 synapses is 1.74.

As illustrated in both figures we could observe that increasing the number of synapses from 100 to 200 while keeping the neuron population fixed in the network makes the overall speed up to decrease. For example the speed up for N = 80,000 has decreased from 5.5 to 5.07 when 8 MPI processes are used. The prime reason for this would be the bandwidth and memory requirement due to increased connection per neuron so that more spike messages has to traverse from one MPI processes to another.

Figure 3 illustrates reduction in average execution time using different number MPI process implementation on varying number of neurons with 100 synapses connections per neuron. To use this approach. This saturation issue in scalability could be addressed by introducing threads in each processes Fig. 4 shows a strong scaling evaluation the effect of increasing synapses connection per neuron. In this regard, the speed up for network size that contains 160k neurons with 100 and 200 synapses connection for scaling MPI processes is presented.

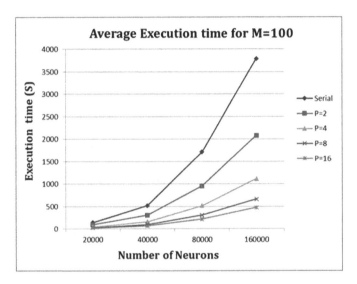

Fig. 4. Average execution time in seconds for increasing number of number of neurons simulated under different MPI processes

We can observe from the above figure that a significant decrease in execution time of the simulation for 2 and 4 MPI process. Even though the average execution time beyond 8MPI process does not decreased as per the theoretically expected level, the time saved for running the simulation still does worth to use this approach. This saturation issue in scalability could be addressed by introducing threads in each processes.

Figure 4 shows a strong scaling evaluation the effect of increasing synapses connection per neuron. In this regard, the speed up for network size that contains 160k neurons with 100 and 200 synapses connection for scaling MPI processes is presented.

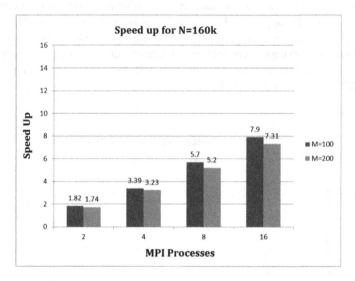

Fig. 5. Speed up for N = 160K neuron with M = 100 and M = 200.

Accordingly, a speed up gain from the MPI implementation for 160,000 neurons with 100 and 200 synapses values. The speed up scales very good for a less number of process. But, as the synapses per neuron increases from 100 to 200 and the number MPI processes increases the speed up scalability decreases more noticeably.

6.2   Hybrid MPI+OpenMP Implementation

Below we present performance evaluation for the hybrid MPI +OpenMP implementation for a network size of 160K, neurons with 100 and 200 synapses values per each neuron. In this experiment the number of OpenMP threads per process is limited by the number of cores in each nodes. Figure 11 shows the speed up of the simulation for various combination of MPI processes and OpenMp threads (Fig. 6).

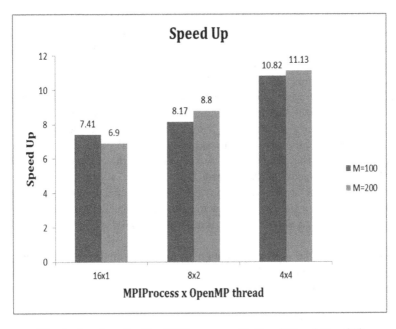

Fig. 6. Speed up for N = 160K neuron with M = 100 and M = 200

Figure 7 depicts the efficiency of a hybrid parallel programming for a network size of 160K neuron with 100 and 200 synapses connections in each neuron using a hybrid parallelization strategy for varying number of MPI processes and OpenMp threads in each process.

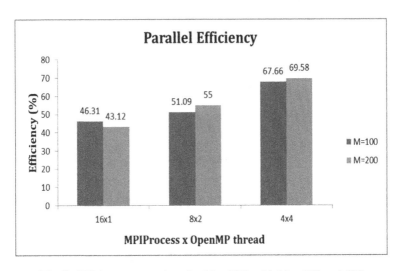

Fig. 7. Efficiency comparison for N = 160k with M = 100 and 200

From the figure we can observe that the hybrid parallel programming approach has improved the efficiency of the purely MPI implementation for 160k neuron with 100 synapses by 4.69% when 2 OpenMP threads were used in 8 MPI process and by 21.35 % when 4 OpenMP threads were used in 4 MPI processes.

Similarly, the efficiency of purely MPI implementation for 160k with 200 synapses was raised by 11.88% when 2 OpenMP threads are used in 8 MPI processes and by 26.46% when 4 OpenMP threads were used inside the 4 MPI processes. As it can be noticed from the results the speed up for all the performance measurement of the parallel implementations is below the theoretically expected value which is also dubbed as sup linear scaling. The usual suspect for such issues is the communication overhead of the MPI processes and OpenMp threads.

Better performance was observed in the hybrid parallel programming approach when 4 MPI process was used in tandem with 4 number of threads. Moreover, a significant drop in average execution time was observed in increased number of threads.

Figure 13 shows the average execution time of the simulation on sequential and hybridized parallel execution. As the result shows the execution time decreases significantly when threads along with MPI processes used on the sequential execution.

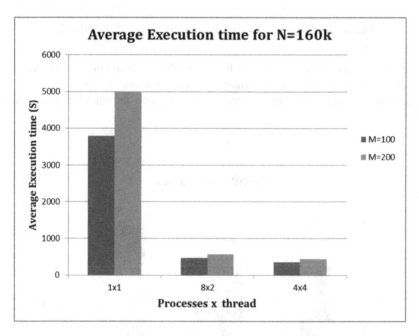

Fig. 8. Average execution time of serial and hybrid implementation

7 Conclusion and Recommendations

In this research work, we have demonstrated biologically realistic large scale simulation of spiking N-neurons on a multiprocessor cluster using distributed memory and distributed shared memory parallel programming through two APIs viz. MPI and OpenMP. The original simulation effort done on a single processor was mapped on a consumer level cluster of multiprocessors with the relatively cheaper price cost for making such compute intensive simulations using supercomputing facilities or specialized hardware platforms.

The performance of our simulation was analyzed for different configurations of the SNN, first for MPI based implementation then followed by a Hybrid MPI +OpenMp based implementation is presented in terms of speed up or efficiency for varying arrangement of MPI processes and OpenMp threads.

From the experimental results the purely MPI based implementation scales good and demonstrated performance gains until 8 MPI processes. Beyond 8 MPI processes the scalability suffers mainly from communication overhead and by the virtue of the fact that the actual processors used are logical processors. But still it does worth to go for the solely MPI based simulation than the sequential simulation as it has allowed more number of neuron and synapse connections.

The scalability issue in the purely MPI based simulation with increasing MPI processes is addressed using Hybridized parallel programming approach. Furthermore, our performance evaluation shows that the hybrid programming out performs the purely distributed programming for the simulation of SNNs. For 160K neuron with 100 synapses and 200 synapses the best performance was gained at 4 thread with 4 MPI processes. Hence, it is an ideal candidate for a multiprocessor cluster based SNN simulation.

The achievements reported in this paper can be further enhanced by developing an easy to use tool set can be developed on the top of the implementation. Moreover, further analysis on memory consumption of both parallel programming approaches can be conducted. Additionally, future research might consider employing different load balancing mechanisms particularly when using purely MPI implementation.

References

1. Ananthanarayanan, R., Modha, D.S: Anatomy of a cortical simulator. In: Proceedings of the 2007 ACM/IEEE Conference on Supercomputing, p. 3 (2007)
2. Wolff, C., Hartmann, G., Rückert, U.: ParSPIKE-a parallel DSPaccelerator for dynamic simulation of large spiking neural networks. In: MicroNeuro 1999 Proceedings of the Seventh International Conference on Microelectronics for Neural, Fuzzy and Bio-Inspired Systems, pp. 324–331 (1999)
3. Jahnke, A., Roth, U., Klar, H.: A SIMD/dataflow architecture for a neurocomputer for spike-processing neural networks (NESPINN). In: Proceedings of Fifth International Conference on Microelectronics for Neural Networks, pp. 232–237 (1996)

4. Cheung, K., Schultz, S.R., Leong, P.H.: A parallel spiking neural network simulator. In: Proceedings of International Conference on Field-Programmable Technology (FPT), pp. 247–254 (2009)
5. Thomas, D.B., Luk, W.: FPGA accelerated simulation of biologically plausible spiking neural networks. In: 17th IEEE Symposium on Field Programmable Custom Computing Machines, 2009 FCCM 2009, pp. 45–52 (2009)
6. Bower, J.M., Beeman, D.: The Book of GENESIS: Exploring Realistic Neural Models with the GEneral NEural SImulation System, 2nd edn. Springer Science & Business Media, New York (2003)
7. Hines, M.L., Carnevale, N.T.: The NEURON simulation environment. Neural Comput. 9(6), 1179–1209 (1997)
8. Migliore, M., Cannia, C., Lytton, W., Markram, H., Hines, M.L.: Parallel network simulations with NEURON. J. Comput. Neurosci. 21(2), 119–129 (2006)
9. Diesmann, M., Gewaltig, M.-O.: NEST: an environment for neural systems simulations. Forsch. Wisschenschaftliches Rechn. Beitr. Zum Heinz-Billing-Preis 58, 43–70 (2001)
10. Thomas, E.A.: A parallel algorithm for simulation of large neural networks. J. Neurosci. Methods 98(2), 123–134 (2000)
11. Plesser, H.E., Eppler, J.M., Morrison, A., Diesmann, M., Gewaltig, M.-O.: Efficient parallel simulation of large-scale neuronal networks on clusters of multiprocessor computers. In: Kermarrec, A.-M., Bougé, L., Priol, T. (eds.) Euro-Par 2007. LNCS, vol. 4641, pp. 672–681. Springer, Heidelberg (2007). https://doi.org/10.1007/978-3-540-74466-5_71
12. Hu, J.: BIOPHYSICALLY ACCURATE BRAIN MODELING AND SIMULATION USING. A&M University, Texas (2012)
13. Paolucci, P.S., et al.: Distributed simulation of polychronous and plastic spiking neural networks: strong and weak scaling of a representative miniapplication benchmark executed on a small-scale commodity cluster (2013). arXiv Prepr. arXiv13108478
14. Fidjeland, A.K., Shanahan, M.P.: Accelerated simulation of spiking neural networks using GPUs. In: The International Joint Conference on Neural Networks (IJCNN), pp. 1–8 (2010)
15. Yudanov, D, Shaaban, M, Melton, R, Reznik, L.: GPU-based simulation of spiking neural networks with real-time performance & high accuracy. In: IJCNN, pp. 1–8 (2010)
16. Vekterli, T.B.: Parallelization of artificial spiking neural networks on the CPU and GPU. Master's Research, Norwegian University of Science and Technology, Department of Computer and Information Science, Trondheim (2009)
17. McCulloch, W.S., Pitts, W.: A logical calculus of the ideas immanent in nervous activity. Bull. Math. Biol. 52(1–2), 99–115 (1990)
18. Paugam-Moisy, H.: Spiking neuron networks: a survey. Rapp. Tech. RR-11 IDIAP Martigny Switz (2006)
19. Izhikevich, E.M.: Which model to use for cortical spiking neurons? IEEE Trans. Neural Netw. 15(5), 1063–1070 (2004)
20. Hodgkin, A.L., Huxley, A.F.: A quantitative description of membrane current and its application to conduction and excitation in nerve. J. Physiol. 117(4), 500–544 (1952)
21. Burkitt, A.N.: A review of the integrate-and-fire neuron model: I. Homogeneous synaptic input. Biol. Cybern. 95(1), 1–19 (2006). https://doi.org/10.1007/s00422-006-0068-6
22. Feng, J.: Is the integrate-and-fire model good enough?—a review. Neural Netw. 14(6), 955–975 (2001)
23. Izhikevich, E.M., et al.: Simple model of spiking neurons. IEEE Trans. Neural Netw. 14(6), 1569–1572 (2003)
24. Hebb, D.O.: The Organization of Behavior: A Neuropsychological Theory. Wiley, Hoboken (1949)

25. Song, S., Miller, K.D., Abbott, L.F.: Competitive Hebbian learning through spike-timing-dependent synaptic plasticity. Nat. Neurosci. **3**(9), 919–926 (2000)
26. Bi, G., Poo, M.: Synaptic modifications in cultured hippocampal neurons: dependence on spike timing, synaptic strength, and postsynaptic cell type. J. Neurosci. **18**(24), 10464–10472 (1998)
27. Swadlow, H.A.: Physiological properties of individual cerebral axons studied in vivo for as long as one year. J. Neurophysiol. **54**(5), 1346–1362 (1985)
28. Izhikevich, E.M.: Polychronization: computation with spikes. Neural Comput. **18**(2), 245–282 (2006)
29. Dagum, L., Enon, R.: OpenMP: an industry standard API for sharedmemory programming. Comput. Sci. Eng. IEEE **5**(1), 46–55 (1998)
30. Message Passing Interface (MPI) Forum Home Page. http://www.mpi-forum.org/. Accessed 19 May 2016
31. Burns, G., Daoud, R., Vaigl, J.: LAM: An open cluster environment for MPI. Proc. Supercomput. Symp. **94**, 379–386 (1994)
32. Gropp, W., Lusk, E., Doss, N., Skjellum, A.: A high-performance, portable implementation of the MPI message passing interface standard. Parallel Comput. **22**(6), 789–828 (1996)
33. Smith, L.A.: Mixed mode MPI/OpenMP programming. UK High-End Computing Technological Report, pp. 1–25 (2000)
34. Brette, R., et al.: Simulation of networks of spiking neurons: a review of tools and strategies. J. Comput. Neurosci. **23**(3), 349–398 (2007)
35. de Velde, E.F.V.: Concurrent Scientific Computing. Springer Science & Business Media, Berlin (2013)
36. Merolla, P.A., Arthur, J.V., Shi, B.E., Boahen, K.A.: "Expandable networks for neuromorphic chips. IEEE Trans.Circuits Syst. Regul. Pap. **54**(2), 301–311 (2007)

A SVM Based Model for COVID Detection Using CXR Image

Sudhir Kumar Mohapatra[1], Beakal Gizachew Assefa[2(✉)], and Getamesay Belayneh[3]

[1] Faculty of Emerging Technology, Sri Sri University, Cuttack 754006, Odisha, India
sudhir.mohapatra@srisriuniversity.edu.in
[2] School of Information Technology and Engineering, AAiT, Addis Ababa, Ethiopia
beakal.gizachew@aait.edu.et
[3] School of Health, Dire Dawa University, Dire Dawa, Ethiopia

Abstract. Covid-19 is among the few global pandemic that has caused a massive adverse economic, social, and psychological effect. Nearly hundred million people are affected and out them a minimum of 2 million people lost their lives. The 2nd and 3rd wave of the spread of the virus has been recorded in the western world. Despite the countless efforts and very few successes in preparation of vaccine, the number of people who have access is very much limited even in the developed countries. The RT-PCR and antigen test are impractical in developing and underdeveloped countries because of high cost and less accuracy, respectively. Chest XRay (CXR) has been used for detection of Covid-10, however, it needs a domain expert. In this paper, we propose an Artificial Intelligent assisted automatic radiology system based on CXR images using Support Vector Machines (SVM). Experimental results conducted on real world CXR image data set shows that, our proposed system have achieved an accuracy and sensitivity of 99.4% and 86% respectively..

Keywords: CXR · Image procession · Segmentation · COVID · Support vector machine

1 Introduction

The covid-19 situation is not settled to date. In the world by 19-01-2021, 93,805,612 people were infected by the virus and 2,026,093 precious lives were lost. The figure clearly shows the alarming situation. Many European countries face the 2nd and 3rd phases of the wave. The world is still struggling to contain the virus. Though two to three vaccines are approved in the world, vaccination is restricted to a limited number of countries. The World Health Organization's advisory for the containment of the virus recommendations is testing and isolation. From different available testing methods, Reverse Transcription Polymerase Chain Reaction (RT-PCR) is considered as the golden standard [1]. Due to the challenge of building RT-PCR infrastructure and its high testing cost, developing and underdeveloped countries largely resort to an alternative low-cost testing method like testing the antigens. However, this is impractical

M. L. Berihun (Ed.): ICAST 2021, LNICST 411, pp. 368–381, 2022.
https://doi.org/10.1007/978-3-030-93709-6_24

because of the very low accuracy exhibited. The Sofia antigen test had a sensitivity of less than 37% as compared to RT-PCR tests when used for screening of asymptomatic persons [2].

The cause of COVID because of the virus SARS-CoV-2. It is a respiratory disease which affect the lungs the most. Traditionally for existing respiratory disease like tuberculosis we use Chest X-Ray (CXR) as a diagnosis method. The diagnostic center with X-Ray are adequately available in private and public health care facilities. For the identification of the disease, manual examination of CXR by a radiologist is required. The limited availability of test-kits and domain experts in the hospitals and rapid increase in the number of infected patients necessitates an automatic screening system, which can act as a second opinion for expert physicians to quickly identify the infected patients, who require immediate isolation and further clinical confirmation. It can act as an alternative screening modality for the detection of nCOVID-19 or to validate the related diagnosis, where the CXR images are interpreted by expert radiologists to look for infectious lesions associated with nCOVID-19. In this work, we proposed an AI assisted COVID-19 lung X-ray image-based detection method using SVM. The contribution of this work is as follow.

- Proposed a computer added diagnosis model for COVID-19 detection
- SVM classifier is used to avoid high computational resources and huge training and testing data set.
- Conducted experiments on a real-world data set. Experimental results show that, the proposed system exhibited an accuracy of 99.4% and sensitivity of 86%.

The remainder of the paper is organized as follows; Sect. 2 shows the related work. Sections 3 and 4 presents the proposed system and the experimental results on a real world CXR image data sets. Conclusion and future work directions are put on Sect. 5.

2   Related Works

All the world still fighting to contain and control COVID-19 pandemic. Every branch of science are contributing to it day by day. The world health organization already declare that we have to habituate to live with this virus. In this direction many research a has been done for proper diagnosis of the disease. Researcher proposed computer added diagnosis system using machine learning. The radio imaging and epidemiology findings using ML are reported by many researcher [3–6]. Going further Deep Learning models are also used for analysis of the characteristic of theses radiology images [7, 8]. with a good diceindex of 0.67, Xue et al. (2018) assign class level in CXR image for detection of a localize tuberculosis-infected regions in CXR images [9]. They use Deep Learning for this. Purkayastha, Buddi, Nuthakki, Yadav, and Gichoya (2020) successfully assigns one level out of fourteen to the uploaded CXR images [10]. Pesce et al. (2019), also able to level the images using two proposed model [11].

DL is applied by many researchers for early detection of COVID-19 [12–16]. But the main challenge face by their models are annotated images (CXR). Availability of less annotated CXR images and requirement of large data by DL increase the difficulty of the researcher. To overcome this problem different overfitting avoidance method are applied by researcher. Method like random photometric transformations like blurring, sharpening, contrast adjustment, are implemented in their model [13, 14, 17]. The CXR images are further used to perform in-depth volumetric analysis of subtle disease responses (similar to viral pneumonia or other inflammatory lung diseases) [13, 14, 18].

After study for the available literature we find the following gaps.

- Lack of availability of enough dataset (Annotated CXR Image)
- Deep learning is data hungry which requires huge amount of data.
- Deep learning requires high computational resource which may not be easily available in developing and under developed country.

In this study, we proposed a SVM based COVID diagnosis system. The major benefit of the proposed system is low computational resource requirement and also can be trained correctly with less available annotated images.

3   Proposed Model

The application of image processing in medical diagnosis is require different processing than normal image processing. Here the CXR images are overlapped with many different organs, which make the processing difficult. The proposed model for COVID detection using CXR image will pass through many image processing steps. These steps are discuss in the following (see Fig. 1).

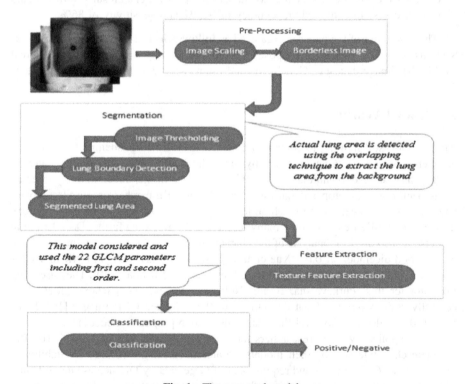

Fig. 1. The proposed model

The details of each image processing steps are discussed in the following subsections.

3.1 Preprocessing

The images in the dataset are of different resolution. For processing all the images should be made uniform by applying normalization. In the preprocessing step consist of basic and intensive task of image processing, where the model scales the image from variable resolution to uniform resolution. In this phase nonzero pixels connect to border are also removed. The model normalizes the image with 1024×1024 resolution because the classification is based on statistical or textural feature. The next step is to identify the lung area. To achieve it the image, need to be sharpen. The model use dilation and erosion technique of open CV. This sharpen the lung object particularly left and right side of the lungs.

3.2 Segmentation

The distortion in the CXR image para-medical professional, quality of medical equipment, poor contrast, different lung size, different shape of lung due to age of the patient are challenge for CXR image segmentation. This distorted images are display in the following (see Fig. 2).

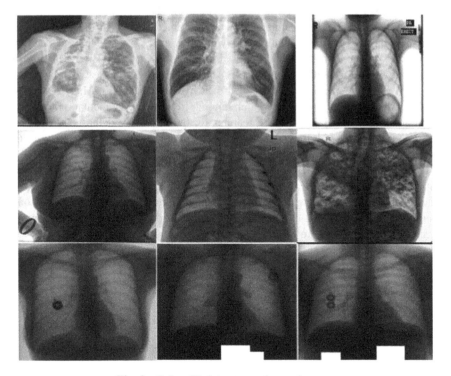

Fig. 2. Cohen JP dataset sample raw images.

The CXR image contains lung in the foreground and also some background information. The background information of the lungs need to be removed. The background information has a property i.e. these are lighter than its neighboring. To identify, remove it there are existing technique. This article applies popular clear border algorithm [19]. This algorithm is effective in cleaning of the structure. It compares the surrounding of the structure with the border of the images. The proposed model use scikit-image library of python to remove background information. Next for thresholding, Otsu thresholding [20, 21] for global and local thresholding are applied. Thresholding make it easier to extract the lungs are from the CXR image. In CXR, it is challenging to separate the lung fields using pure pixel-based approaches. Overlapping technique is used in our model for separation of lung area from the background objects (Like other organs coms in the CXR images).

3.3   Feature Extraction

Normal and abnormal images have different graylevel. In case of CXR images, the distinction of these two (Normal and Abnormal) is lie in the depth of actual color. This is because some part of the lungs are affected by SARS-CoV-2. Statistical Methods are used in our model for analysis of the appearance of a segmented region. For this the proposed model use a combination of first-order and second-order textural features extraction parameters. The effect of basic statistical methods clues to high representations of textures in an image and the gray-level histogram labels the texture of an image. The first five parameters from first order and another five from the grey level co-occurrence matrix (GLCM) features extraction parameters used in our model. These techniques shows the pixel relationship with graylevel. Grey level co-occurrence matrix was proposed was primary proposed by Haralick al. [22]. The researcher first proposed four second-order parameters such as contrast, energy, correlation and entropy. Another 22 parameters are added to it by Soh et al. [23]. Many researchers used GLCM successfully in their research ranging from image segmentation to textural feature analysis [24–26]. The texture features using GLCM are determined by seeing the rate of pixel pairs with the values which agrees the grey level in spatial connection of an image and extracting the factors from the matrix [27].

This model used other seventeen second order parameters of GLCM and they are cluster shade, difference-entropy, contrast, correlation, cluster prominence, difference-variance, dissimilarity, energy, entropy, information measure of correlation, homogeneity, maximum probability, sum average, sum entropy, sum of squares: variance and sum variance. These are used and suggested by researchers [28].

3.4 Classification

In this model, classification of lungs in terms of infected and non-infected is to achieve. The Support vector machine (SVM) classifier is better in binary classification among available classifier [29, 30]. The classification of normal and abnormal images is done by the help of hyper plane generate by SVM with a linear classifier. The scikit-learn library in python is used to apply SVM using Radial Basis Function Kernel. The performance evaluation of the model is done by separating the dataset into train and test set. The K-fold technique of cross validation is used.

4 Experiments and Results

Google Colaboratory GPU environment used for the experiment purpose. The model is implemented in Python3 with scikit-learnlibrary. The next subsection discuss about the details of individual sub-process.

4.1 Dataset Preparation

The public datasets of CXR imagesare considered for experiment [32]. The CXR images collected from Github repository of Cohen JP[1] is used for training and validation of our model. It is continuously updated by different researcher from different geographical area. This open dataset is having normal, infected and pneumonia affected images (see Fig. 3).

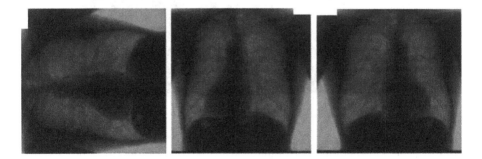

Fig. 3. Slicing image for the dataset

---

[1] https://github.com/muhammedtalo/COVID-19.

4.2 Preprocessing

The model requires standardized uniform images. To achieve it, CXR images from the data set are resize to 1024×1024 using OpenCV. The images then go through a process of removal of lighter information. This is done by first assuming lighter information as background information and looking into its connection to the border (see Fig. 4).

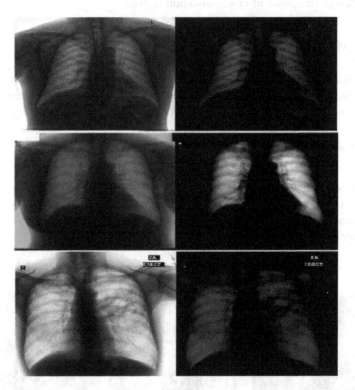

Fig. 4. The dataset images after sampling

Next using Otsu threshold algorithm and threshold value of 0.01, 0.001 the borderless image are change to binary image [20, 33]. Then, filtering method is used to the two lungs with a input value of 2. The filtering further applies hole fill method find out hole. The presence of hole in lungs indicate the presence of infection of COVID or distortion of image. All the above discussion are presented with input output images (see Fig. 5).

4.3 Detection of Lung Region

After identifying the lungs object, next issue may be unclear boundary. To achieve this python and OpenCV is used. The input and output of the process are presented in

A) Original Image	B) Border less Image	C) Binaries	D) Thresholding With 0.01	E) Thresholding With 0.001	F) Global Otsu's threshold

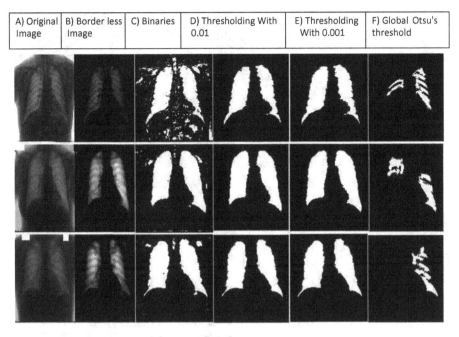

Fig. 5. Image after different filtering method

Fig. 6. The first column A contains original image, column B contains detected object and the last column(c) contains (see Fig. 6).

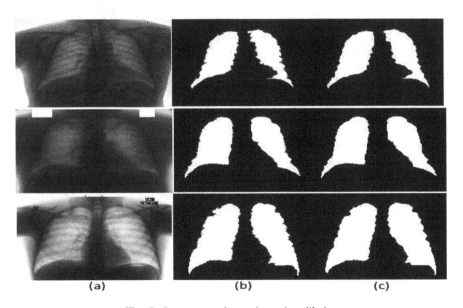

Fig. 6. Lungs area sharpening using dilation

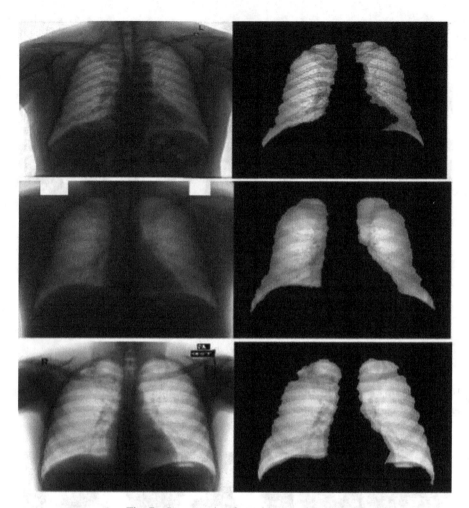

Fig. 7. Segmentation from the open data set.

4.4   Segmentation

In segmentation the lung object is extracted from the CXR images. It is a process where except the lung object all other organs are treated as background object. As the lung area in the binary image is in white in color, the model extracts the white region only. In the process the same white intensity area with actual intensity is considered. The other area intensity makes 0 or black. Figure 7 present the whole segmentation steps (see Fig. 7).

4.5   Feature Extraction

Python3 and Scikit-image is used to apply the feature extraction step. Allthe first order and second order parameter are stored in a excel file for SVM processing. Figure 8 present a sample extracted feature (see Fig. 8).

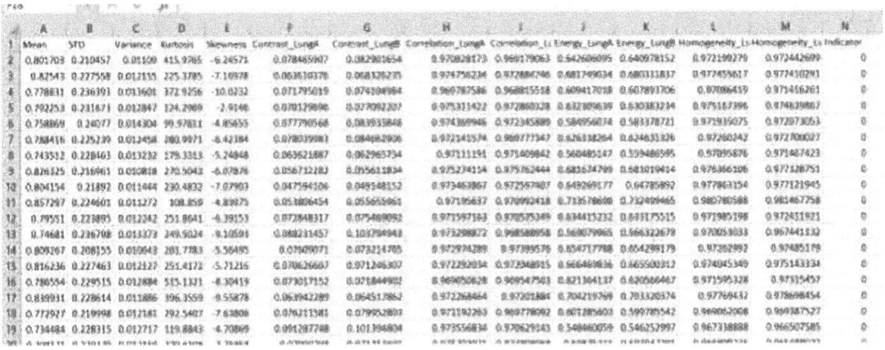

Fig. 8.   Sample of extracted feature in an Excel format.

4.6   The Performance Evaluation

The datasets are separated as train and test sets. The cross-validation [31], particularly the kfolds technique was used is used in our model. This model use 10-fold method.

4.7   Result

After feature extraction the confusion matrix of the pubic dataset with train and test dataset is shown in Table 1. From the table out of total 662 instance 522 images are correctly detected, 6 are incorrectly detected. These are also crosscheck by human expertise. The following Table 1.

Table 1.   Confusion matrix.

Dataset		Positive	Negative	Total
Cohen JP	Normal	324	2	662
	Abnormal	4	332	

The confusion matrix shows a performance of around 99.4 accuracy and 86% sensitivity. The performance matrix in the following Table 2.

Table 2. Performance analysis of the model

Dataset	Area under curve (AUC)	Specificity (%)	Accuracy (%)	Sensitivity (%)
Cohen JP	0.99	81	99.4	86

The overall performance of the proposed model is shown in the (see Fig. 9) by a AUC curve.

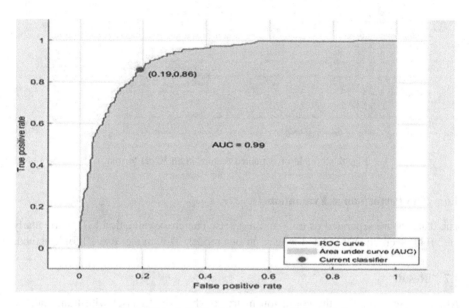

Fig. 9. ROC and AOC of the model on Cohen JP dataset

4.8   Comparison with Other Existing Models

The result achieve by the proposed model are compared with 5 deep learning model (Hemdan et al. [34], Narin et al. [35], Wang and Wong [36], Ozturk et al. [39], Nayak et al. [16]), two deep learning model combine with SVM (Sethy and Behera [37], Toğaçar et al. [38]). The comparison is presented in the Table 3. This article proposed model is classify the data set into 326 COVID 19 and 336 normal images. The proposed model use more image than all the compared technique except that of Wang et al.. But Wang et al. drawback is the technique leads to a class imbalance problem. The researcher also go for multi classification. Using binary classification and SVM our model our model performance is more than 99%. The following Table 3.

Table 3. Comparison with other models.

Authors	Hemdan et al. [37]		Wang and Wong [39]		Sethy and Behera [40]		Narin et al. [38]		Ozturk et al. [42]		Toğaçar et al. [41]		Nayak et al.[16]		Proposed Model	
Used Method	COVIDX-Net		COVID-Net		ResNet-50 and SVM		ResNet-50		Dark Covid Net		SqueezeN et and MobileNe tV2	SMO and SVM	ResNet-34		SVM	
Number of class	COVID-19	Nor mal	COVI D-19	Nor mal	COVI D-19	Nor mal	COVI D-19	Nor mal	COVI D-19	Nor mal	COVID-19	Nor mal	COVI D-19	Nor mal	COVI D-19	Nor mal
Sample Used	50	C: 25 and N: 25	13800	C: 183	C: 25 and N: 25	50	100	C: 50 and N: 50	625	C: 125 and N: 500	458	C: 295, N: 65 and P: 98	406	C: 203 and N: 203	662	C: 552 and N: 110
Accuracy (%)	90		92.6		95.38		98		98.08		98.25		98.33		99.4	

5 Conclusion

The respiratory disease COVID-19 is still a global threat. This article proposed a novel SVM classifier for screening of COVID-19 patient. The study use CXR images from public dataset. The result shows accuracy of 99.4%, which is more than other Deep learning models. The model can be used in computer aided diagnosis, thereby reducing the workload of frontline health worker. It will be helpful in early identification and isolation of COVID19 patient, when all the world struggling to get vaccinated. Besides, the model requires low computational resources.

References

1. Jameel, T., Baig, M., Gazzaz, Z.J.: Persistence of reverse transcription-polymerase chain reaction (RT-PCR) positivity in COVID-19 recovered patients: a call for revised hospital discharge criteria. Cureus 12(7), 9048 (2020). https://doi.org/10.7759/cureus.9048

2. Pray, I.W.: Performance of an antigen-based test for asymptomatic and symptomatic SARSCoV-2 testing at two university campuses—Wisconsin, September–October 2020. MMWR Morbid. Mortal. Wkly. Rep. **69** (2021)
3. Chen, N., et al.: Epidemiological and clinical characteristics of 99 cases of 2019 novel coronavirus pneumonia in Wuhan, China: a descriptive study. Lancet **395**(10223), 507–513 (2020). https://doi.org/10.1016/S0140-6736(20)30211-7
4. Huang, C., et al.: Clinical features of patients infected with 2019 novel coronavirus in Wuhan, China. Lancet **395**(10223), 497–506 (2020). https://doi.org/10.1016/S0140-6736(20)30183-5
5. Kooraki, S., Hosseiny, M., Myers, L., Gholamrezanezhad, A.: Coronavirus (COVID-19) outbreak: what the department of radiology should know. J. Am. Coll. Radiol. **17**(4), 447–451 (2020). https://doi.org/10.1016/j.jacr.2020.02.008
6. Yoon, S.H., et al.: Chest radiographic and CT findings of the 2019 Novel Coronavirus Disease (COVID19): analysis of nine patients treated in Korea. Korean J. Radiol. **21**(4), 494 (2020). https://doi.org/10.3348/kjr.2020.0132
7. Chouhan, V., et al.: A novel transfer learning based approach for pneumonia detection in chest X-ray images. Appl. Sci. **10**(2), 559 (2020). https://doi.org/10.3390/app10020559
8. Jaiswal, A.K., Tiwari, P., Kumar, S., Gupta, D., Khanna, A., Rodrigues, J.J.P.C..: Identifying pneumonia in chest X-rays: a deep learning approach. Measurement **145**, 511–518 (2019). https://doi.org/10.1016/j.measurement.2019.05.076
9. Xue, Z., et al.: Localizing tuberculosis in chest radiographs with deep learning. In: Zhang, J., Chen, P.-H. (Eds.), Medical Imaging 2018: Imaging Informatics for Healthcare, Research, and Applications, vol. 3, p. 28 (2018). https://doi.org/10.1117/12.2293022
10. Purkayastha, S., Buddi, S.B., Nuthakki, S., Yadav, B., Gichoya, J.W.: Evaluating the implementation of deep learning in LibreHealth radiology on chest X-rays. Adv. Intell. Syst. Comput. **943**, 648–657 (2020). https://doi.org/10.1007/978-3-030-17795-9_47
11. Pesce, E., Joseph Withey, S., Ypsilantis, P.P., Bakewell, R., Goh, V., Montana, G.: Learning to detect chest radiographs containing pulmonary lesions using visual attention networks. Med. Image Anal. **53**, 26–38 (2019). https://doi.org/10.1016/j.media.2018.12.007
12. Abbas, A., Abdelsamea, M.M., Gaber, M.M.: Classification of COVID-19 in chest X-ray images using DeTraC deep convolutional neural network (2020). Retrieved: http://arxiv.org/abs/2003.13815
13. Wang, S., et al.: A deep learning algorithm using CT images to screen for corona virus disease (COVID-19). MedRxiv (2020). https://doi.org/10.1101/2020.02.14.20023028
14. Xu, X., et al.: Deep learning system to screen coronavirus disease 2019 pneumonia. Arxiv (2020). Retrieved: https://arxiv.org/abs/2002.09334
15. Mishra, A.K., Das, S.K., Roy, P., Bandyopadhyay, S.: Identifying COVID19 from chest CT images: a deep convolutional neural networks based approach. J. Healthc. Eng. **2020**, 1–7 (2020). https://doi.org/10.1155/2020/8843664
16. Nayak, S.R., Nayak, D.R., Sinha, U., Arora, V., Pachori, R.B.: Application of deep learning techniques for detection of COVID-19 cases using chest X-ray images: a comprehensive study. Biomed. Signal Process. Control **64**, 102–365 (2020)
17. Chowdhury, M.E.H., et al.: Can AI help in screening Viral and COVID-19 pneumonia? (2020). Retrieved|: http://arxiv.org/abs/2003.13145
18. Maghdid, H.S., Asaad, A.T., Ghafoor, K.Z., Sadiq, A.S., Khan, M.K.: Diagnosing COVID-19 pneumonia from X-Ray and CT images using deep learning and transfer learning algorithms. Arxiv.Org. (2020). Retrieved: https://arxiv.org/abs/2004.00038
19. Soille, P.: Morphological Image Analysis: Principles and Applications. Springer Science & Business Media (2013)

20. Otsu, N.: A threshold selection method from gray-level histograms. IEEE Trans. Syst. Man Cybern. **9**(1), 62–66 (1979). https://doi.org/10.1109/TSMC.1979.4310076
21. Bradley, D., Roth, G.: Adaptive thresholding using the integral image. J. Graph. Tools **12**(2), 13–21 (2007). https://doi.org/10.1080/2151237X.2007.10129236
22. Haralick, R.M., Shanmugam, K., Dinstein, I.: Textural features for image classification. IEEE Trans. Syst. Man Cybern. **SMC-3**(6), 610–621 (1973). https://doi.org/10.1109/TSMC.1973.4309314
23. Soh, L.-K., Tsatsoulis, C.: Texture analysis of SAR sea ice imagery using gray level co-occurrence matrices. IEEE Trans. Geosci. Remote Sens. **37**(2), 780–795 (1999). https://doi.org/10.1109/36.752194
24. Tuceryan, M., Jain, A.K.: The Handbook of Pattern Recognition and Computer Vision, Chapter 2.1, Texture Analysis. World Scientific Co., pp. 207–248 (1998)
25. Hiremath, P.S., Pujari, J.: Content based image retrieval based on color, texture and shape features using image and its complement. Int. J. Comput. Sci. Secur. **1**, 25–35 (2007)
26. Palanivel, M., Duraisamy, M.: Adaptive color texture image segmentation using α-cut implemented interval type-2 fuzzy C-means. Res. J. Appl. Sci. **7**, 258–265 (2012)
27. Tsaneva, M.: Texture features for segmentation of satellite images. Cybern. Inf. Technol. **8**, 73–85 (2008)
28. Karargyris, A., et al.: Combination of texture and shape features to detect pulmonary abnormalities in digital chest X-rays. Int. J. Comput. Assist. Radiol. Surg. **11**(1), 99–106 (2016). https://doi.org/10.1007/s11548-015-1242-x
29. Kotsiantis, S.B., Zaharakis, I.D., Pintelas, P.E.: Machine learning: a review of classification and combining techniques. Artif. Intell. Rev. **26**, 159–190 (2006)
30. Hearst, M.A., Dumais, S.T., Osuna, E., Platt, J., Scholkopf, B.: Support vector machines. IEEE Intell. Syst. Appl. **13**, 18–28 (1998)
31. Golub, G.H., Heath, M., Wahba, G.: Generalized cross-validation as a method for choosing a good ridge parameter. Technometrics **21**, 215–223 (1979)
32. Jaeger, S., Candemir, S., Antani, S., Wang, Y.-X.J., Lu, P.-X., Thoma, G.: Two public chest X-ray datasets for computer-aided screening of pulmonary diseases. Quant. Imaging Med. Surg. **4**, 475–477 (2014)
33. Cheremkhin, P.A., Kurbatova, E.A.: Comparative appraisal of global and local thresholding methods for binarisation of off-axis digital holograms. Opt. Lasers Eng. **115**, 119–130 (2019)
34. Hemdan, E.E.-D., Shouman, M.A., Karar, M.E.: COVIDX-Net: a framework of deep learning classifiers to diagnose covid-19 in X-ray images, arXiv preprint arXiv:2003.11055 (2020)
35. Narin, A., Kaya, C., Pamuk, Z.: Automatic detection of coronavirus disease (COVID19) using X-ray images and deep convolutional neural networks, arXiv preprint arXiv:2003.10849 (2020)
36. Wang, L., Wong, A.: COVID-Net: a tailored deep convolutional neural network design for detection of COVID-19 cases from chest X-ray images, arXiv preprint arXiv:2003.09871 (2020)
37. Sethy, P.K., Behera, S.K.: Detection of coronavirus disease (COVID-19) based on deep features (2020). https://doi.org/10.20944/preprints202003.0300.v1
38. Toğaçar, M., Ergen, B., Cömert, Z.: COVID-19 detection using deep learning models to exploit social mimic optimization and structured chest X-ray images using fuzzy color and stacking approaches. Comput. Biol. Med. **121**, 103805 (2020)
39. Ozturk, T., Talo, M., Yildirim, E.A., Baloglu, U.B., Ozal Yildirim, U., Acharya, R.: Automated detection of COVID-19 cases using deep neural networks with X-ray images. Comput. Biol. Med. **121**, 103792 (2020). https://doi.org/10.1016/j.compbiomed.2020.103792

Simultaneous Indoor Localization Based on Wi-Fi RSS Fingerprints

Nooria Rafie[✉] and Bang Wang

Department of Information and Communication Engineering,
Huazhong University of Science and Technology, Wuhan 430074, Hubei, China
{rafie_n,wangbang}@hust.edu.cn

Abstract. Indoor localization has been extensively investigated over the last few decades, especially in the industrial area of wireless sensor networks. For indoor positioning, many techniques have been proposed over the Wi-Fi signal's deployment. Wi-Fi Received Signal Strength (RSS) fingerprinting approach especially the deterministic algorithms have received much attention. However, as the deterministic algorithms use RSS of the test point (TP) by ignoring the other TPs, two or more TPs will take the same location while physically far apart, and the reverse can also be true. Thus, to improve positioning accuracy, this study proposes Wi-Fi RSS fingerprint based simultaneous indoor localization (SIL). The proposed approach was tested on the data collected from Huazhong University of Science and Technology teaching buildings. Experimental results show error reduction upto 9.8%, and 13.2% in MDE (Mean Distance Error) and standard deviation, respectively.

Keywords: Indoor localization · Simultaneous localization · Wi-Fi Fingerprinting · RSS · Multidimensional scaling

1 Introduction

Location recognition has become a necessity for today's Internet of Things (IoT) applications. Location estimation and prediction are investigated in two separate indoor and outdoor categories. Comparatively, there has been considerable development in positioning through satellite deployment and use for global positioning systems (GPS). This GPS improvement is unlikely to provide accurate indoor positioning due to weak signal propagation in a complex indoor environment. The short-range signal, such as Bluetooth, Wi-Fi, and RFID, are used to estimate the locations in an indoor environment [10]. From the signals above, Wi-Fi RSS has received significant attention for its massive penetration of wireless local area networks (WLAN) and has become a victorious procession of signal accumulation and aggregation with the indoor environment without the requirement for additional infrastructure.

© ICST Institute for Computer Sciences, Social Informatics and Telecommunications Engineering 2022
Published by Springer Nature Switzerland AG 2022. All Rights Reserved
M. L. Berihun (Ed.): ICAST 2021, LNICST 411, pp. 382–400, 2022.
https://doi.org/10.1007/978-3-030-93709-6_25

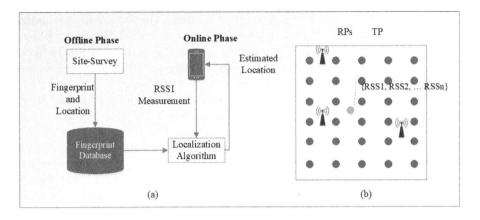

Fig. 1. (a) Fingerprinting workflow (b) TP allocation.

Many research and investigation endeavors have been concerned with the construction of indoor positioning systems (IPS) based on the RSS from the access points (AP) in wireless local area networks [14]. Furthermore, in the past decade, the fingerprint technique has been extensively investigated for most RSS-based indoor positioning schemes. The fingerprinting is implemented in two separate phases: offline phase (site-survey), which is done through the site-survey, or recently, the most used crowdsourcing approach. In this phase, the RSS vectors are collected from all detected Wi-Fi signals from different APs at many RPs in known locations as the fingerprint or signature. Therefore, each fingerprint represents each RP in an indoor environment. All collected RSS vectors that make up the site-survey fingerprints will be stored in the database or radio map for consultation in the online phase. In the online phase (signature-match): the server measures the RSS vector of TP with a location from the pre-built database or radio map. It uses a specific similarity metric in the signal space to compare the TP with the fingerprints, such as the Euclidean distance [2]. Figure 1 illustrates the fingerprint approach workflow.

Furthermore, two types of algorithms, deterministic and probabilistic, are used for fingerprinting localization[16]. The traditional deterministic indoor localization algorithms use a similarity metric to compare the online signal measurement with a fingerprint in the fingerprint database. For instance, it measures the TP location to the nearest RP's fingerprint location in the signal space. Euclidean distance, Manhattan distance, cosine similarity, and Tanimato similarity have been implemented to compare and analyze signal space. Deterministic algorithms are simple for implementation, can be easily applied based on K nearest neighbors (kNN), and often low in terms of computational complexity. Other advanced, accurate, and low computational cost deterministic algorithms are support vector machines and linear discriminant. Probabilistic algorithms use statistical inference between the measurement of the TP signal and the stored fingerprints in the online phase [24]. These algorithms find the location of the

TP with the highest probability of the training data. Moreover, each estimated location can be indicated by a confidence interval in probabilistic algorithms. Probabilistic algorithms with high precision are the Bayesian network, the maximization of expectations, the Kullback-Leibler divergence, the Gaussian process, and the conditional random field [3].

Most of the current research on Wi-Fi fingerprint-based indoor localization is based on an independent location estimation, and each TP's location is located independently. Indoor localization occurs regardless of the location of the relative RPs, or the location of other TPs. Subsequently, the TP localization is usually considered independently in the approach mentioned above. This measurement noise or uncertainty may lead to a spatially dispersed set of neighboring points, which significantly reduces the localization accuracy [9]. As a result, this inaccurate location estimation can lead to an error-prone indoor localization. It can delegate one location to two physically distanced TPs or assign different locations to two physically close TPs. For all of these reasons, it should acquire and use the information of RPs or neighboring relative TPs as a solution. The result of the location estimation can be improved and become reliable by using this approach. Additionally, this will also drive the localization process to high precision concerning the precision of the indoor localization based on Wi-Fi RSS fingerprints.

The remainder of this paper is organized as follows. Section 2 describes related work on Indoor Localization based on Wi-Fi RSS Fingerprints. The detailed structure of SIL architecture is discussed in Sect. 3. In Sect. 4, there is an explanation of performance evaluation and results. Finally, we draw conclusion in Sect. 5.

2   Related Work

Technically, the utilized indoor localization methods are divided into range-based and range-free [22]. The range-based method is the most used between these methods. The range-based technique is appropriate for applications that need high accuracy. The current prevalent types of range-based localization techniques are Received Strength Signal (RSS), Angle of Arrival (AOA), Time of Arrival (TOA), and Time Difference of Arrival (TDOA). Compared to these methods, the TOA is more accurate than the other methods. Unlike other time-synchronized methods, the TOA and TDOA are less strict time synchronization, which makes it easy to implement [4,13,23].

As discussed in the [8], the collaborative indoor localization is classified into two categories: Distance-based and proximity-based schemes.

Distance-based Scheme: Advanced sensors of smartphones or IoT devices are used for indoor localization in this scheme, and these sensors include Bluetooth, Wi-Fi direct, ultrasound. Although this scheme has been impressive in using the distance for localization, it often lacks an accurate distance measurement compared to the proximity-based scheme. The [9] has proposed a Wi-Dist, a generic framework applicable to a wide range of sensors such as peer-assisted and

INS, and the wireless fingerprint Wi-Fi, CSI, RFID. Wi-Dist indoor localization approach fuses on the noisy fingerprint of wireless technology with uncertain mutual distances achieved from their bounds. It collaboratively considers the distance limits and noisy fingerprints to reduce the indoor localization error. The system requires the mean and variance of fingerprint's RSS and optimize its location using Semi-Definite Programming (SDP). Figure 2 depicts peer-assisted localization.

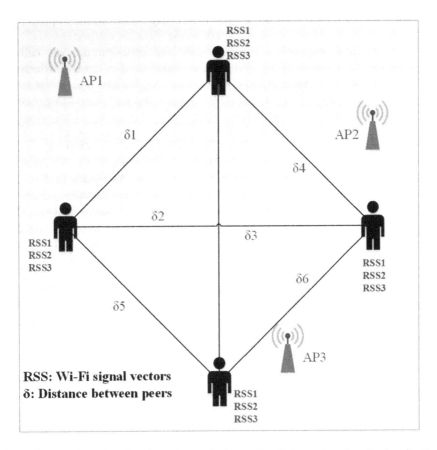

Fig. 2. Peer-assisted localization scheme that uses the distance to refine the localization error.

In [19], the privacy-preserving multi-model has been proposed based on the Wi-Fi RSS, Cellular RSS, light, and sound. This work has also developed its system based on an infrastructure-free model of indoor localization. The system uses the existing Wi-Fi RSS of the access point with the data from the smartphone's light and sound sensors to increase indoor localization's granularity. The system helps the areas with low Wi-Fi signal coverage to distinguish themselves in a region or room level. Besides, this system has used weighted fusion for further improvement of the localization accuracy. Moreover, to degrade the energy consumption for footprint, it has automatically used a Wi-Fi scan to generate it when the device Wi-Fi is on. Another collaborative Bluetooth-based approach is proposed in [17], which aggregates multiple Bluetooth devices' location information. The system takes advantage of the enhanced kNN algorithm to localize devices based on Bluetooth distance measurements. The work in [23] details another system that has proposed Multi-Anchor Nodes Collaborative Localization (MANCL). MANCL system has divided the localization procedure into four-part: ordinary node localization, iterative localization, improved 3D Euclidean distance estimation, and 3D DV-Hope distance estimation.

Paper [18] has proposed a system based on infrastructure-free collaborative indoor localization. This system has determined a case in which the infrastructure-based indoor localization is not applicable. The system has designed a novel algorithm called Collaborative Indoor Positioning Scheme (CLIPS), which uses the RSS map as a reference. It uses the dead reckoning to disqualify the invalid candidates. Compared to peer-assisted, this system's unique advantage is that this algorithm does not require any additional infrastructure for localization. Peer-assisted (PA) localization method in [18], and [15] use sound for distance measurement between devices. As shown in Fig. 2, it transmits an audio signal to its close peers. First, the server initializes the peer's location with the Wi-Fi fingerprint, then measures the distance between them through the acoustic ranging, and finally calculates the new location. The high localization precision in the PA indoor localization depends on the high precision of distance measurement. Hence, the graph's shape is rigid, and if there are distance measurement errors, the location estimation will be significantly influenced. Moreover, pairwise measurements are needed to build a complete graph. Accordingly, the synchronization in the PA approach becomes complicated and can be exposed to measurement error. Range-based collaborative localization is considered as non-linear minimum optimization. Thus, many methods are introduced to solve this problem, such as maximum likelihood in [21] and multidimensional scaling in [7].

Proximity-based Scheme: The user temporary stops to measure the internode distance between each other based on this scheme [11]. The proximity scheme can be used for dynamic measurement as [5]. It proposes a collaborative localization system to enhance position estimation by taking advantage of more accurate information from neighboring nodes within the same cluster. The system uses ZigBee radio to detect its neighboring nodes in the cluster. Accordingly, the system computes and attaches a confidence score to the system's calculated position (e.g., Ekahau). The mentioned confidence measures the probability of estimated location. Finally, a collaborative error correction adjusts the TP's estimated location using the estimated locations of neighboring nodes. Figure 3 depicts the design of the ZigBee Collaborative localization system.

Furthermore, in range-free paper [24] introduces a Probabilistic Neural Network-based localization approach that eliminates the RSS distance relationship noise and inconsistency. The approach features two processes: Global

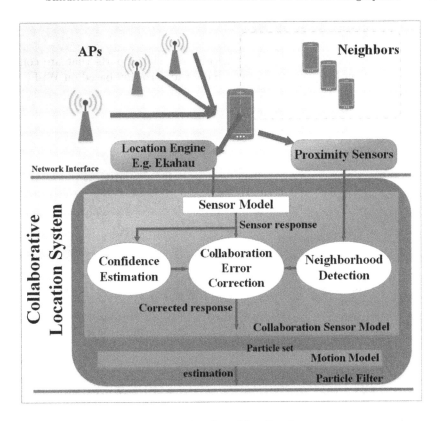

Fig. 3. ZigBee based localization.

Optimization and Regional Compensation. In this method, the APs are exchanging information about the TP to localize it collaboratively.

To summarize, the collaborative localization emerging in the above works has shown a significant improvement in localization precision even though several issues need to be considered in actual deployment. Computational complexity is one of those issues that must be considered in collaborative localization. Due to the pairwise communication and synchronization, the computational complexity is high for collaborative localization [9]. User mobility also makes the node collaboration challenging, as the relative positions of peer users change frequently. During the social interaction, smartphone's sensor collaboration may also unleash the information of the device owners [6]. Therefore, to address the privacy issues, smartphone collaborative localization in future work requires a specific security protocol for the information sharing [19].

3   MDS-based Model: SIL

This part examines the proposed model and its related parts that are coming up with a solution for the simultaneous indoor localization based on Wi-Fi RSS fingerprints.

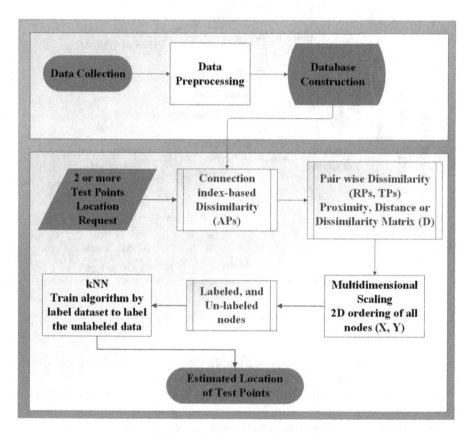

Fig. 4. System architecture.

3.1   SIL Architecture

The general architecture of the indoor fingerprinting localization based on Wi-Fi RSS involves two phases. The first phase is the offline phase, consisting of two sub-phases: data collection and database construction. The second phase is the online phase, which localizes the TP's RSS based on matching the database data. Therefore, this proposed simultaneous indoor localization model also consists of the same two general phases. The offline phase of the model implements the data collection and data pre-processing. The RSS data for this simulation has been retrieved from the smartphone's Wi-Fi sensors. Smartphones and IoT devices are commonly used in indoor localization to adapt to different applications, and indoor environment data collection is one of its applications. Following this, the users' smartphones are used to measure the required data as a signature at each point in the indoor area and build the indoor localization radio map or fingerprinting database. The RSS of the Wi-Fi signal as a signature to build the radio map from those IoT devices is available through the previously developed android or iOS application using application programming interfaces (APIs). These applications will scan the Wi-Fi signal available in the indoor environment from the APs, and this information consists of the Wi-Fi signal BSSID, SSID, and RSS [19]. The RSS is utilized as the signature for each measured point from the data retrieved through the smartphone. RSS vector with their related location is being used to construct the radio map. Since the measured data consists of extensive records of the RSS vector and its location, it must be pre-processed to construct a precise radio map for the online phase use. During the pre-processing process, the noisy data have been evacuated from the dataset. Moreover, each point's signature in the database becomes shrunk in the number of RSS received from the APs. In the online phase, the TPs would be localized with the aid of the proposed model.

In the online phase, an adaptive MDS-based model like [7], and [12] has been proposed, which builds the process of matching for the fingerprints. The new point or the collaboration of two points is localized based on the adapted dissimilarities among the points and the database RPs. The proposed adaptive MDS-based model is localizing points based on the previous mappings of the sampled data in terms of the adaptive dissimilarities (D), and by the Euclidean distance between the interpolated points.

In addition to the original MDS algorithm in which other points influence the mapping of a point, it uses kNN to label the unlabeled point with the position of its neighboring RPs that have been interpolated by the MDS dissimilarity function. Figure 4 details the flowchart of the proposed model for simultaneous indoor positioning based on Wi-Fi RSS the fingerprints.

3.2 Preprocessing of Data

The simulation data should be analyzed and processed in order to build the fingerprint database. The dataset collected by the site-survey is pre-processed to deduct the sensitivity of data's initial values for the simulation to validate the feasibility and effectiveness of the proposed model [20]. In data collection, testbed 1 was collected ten times for the offline phase and twenty times for the online phase at each point, and the zero was delegated to the non-received RSS. Moreover, the data for testbed 2 was collected ten times for offline and online phases at each point, respectively. Since the RSS varies due to indoor environmental reflections, here for the fingerprint database construction, the number of RSS measurements from each AP at each point is averaged using Eq. 1. Moreover, the zero value is also replaced with the value of -100 (dBm), which indicates the extremely poor signal. Identically, Fig. 5 illustrates the RSS instability during different time stamps (Table 1).

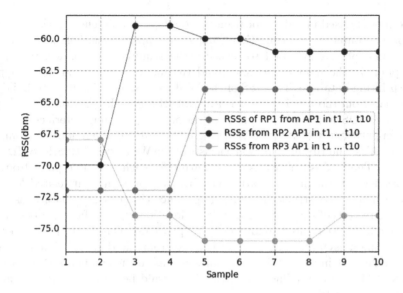

Fig. 5. Behavior and variance of the RSS measurements.

$$RSS_l = \frac{1}{t} \sum_{n=1}^{t} RSS_n \qquad (1)$$

3.3 SIL Algorithm

For the MDS-based localization, the dataset consists of $N1$ RPs, and $N2$ TPs from the L APs. The RPs are with their known location coordinates as a label, and the TPs are with unknown location coordinates. Therefore, here the dataset is consisting of $N = N1 + N2$ points from $L = L1 \cap L2$ APs.

In this implementation, the MDS-based model goal is to estimate the TP location based on the RP fingerprints and pairwise RSS distance measurement from all localization points. In contrast, non-MDS based localization estimates TP's location based on the distance measurement between the TPs and RPs.

The simultaneous indoor localization problem can be formulated in the MDS problem. It has been assumed that the Eq. 2 is the RSS vector of N points in L dimensional space:

$$X = \begin{bmatrix} rss_1 \; rss_2 \ldots rss_L \end{bmatrix}^T \qquad (2)$$

Each point continuously estimates its inter-point distances with the Euclidean-distance using Eq. 3, and exchanges this information with other points on the fingerprint map. Therefore, all points involved in collaboration share their pair-distances, and it will be stored in a matrix (D) called the dissimilarity matrix which is shown in Eq. 4.

Table 1. List of notations.

Notations	Descriptions
N	Number of points
L	Number of access points
$L1$	Access points, numbers of access points in RP fingerprint
$L2$	Access points, number of access points in TP fingerprint
$N1$	Reference Points, number of RPs
$N2$	Test Points, number of TPs
X	$N \times M$ Configuration matrix
D	Dissimilarity Matrix
rss_N	Measured RSS vector of N points
$S_{rss(X)}$	MDS configuration matrix
θ_i	Location of i node
$d_{ij(X)}$	Euclidean distance between two RSS vector of points
rss_l	Measured RSS of l AP
$\theta_i^{n2}, \widehat{\theta}_i^{n2}$	Real and estimated locations of i TP

$$d\left(rss_i, rss_j\right) = \sqrt{\sum_{i=1}^{n}\left(rss_{il} - rss_{jl}\right)^2} \tag{3}$$

where $i, j = 1, 2, ..., n$ and $i \neq j$

$$D = \begin{bmatrix} 0 & \ldots & d_{ij} & \ldots & d_{1n} \\ \vdots & \ddots & \vdots & \ddots & \vdots \\ d_{i1} & \ldots & 0 & \ldots & d_{in} \\ \vdots & \ddots & \vdots & \ddots & \vdots \\ d_{n1} & \ldots & d_{nj} & \ldots & 0 \end{bmatrix} \tag{4}$$

Moreover, the $\theta_i = \begin{bmatrix} \theta_{i1} & \theta_{i2} \end{bmatrix}^T$ is the location coordinates of ith point. As it mentioned before, here the dataset is consisting of N points, which are the summation of N_1 points as a RP and N_2 as a test point. So then, here the signatures are $rss_i, 1 \leq i \leq N1$ with the known location as its label, and $rss_i, N1 + 1 \leq i \leq N$ with the unknown location. The MDS solution of the configuration matrix X can be obtained by minimization of the following STRESS function:

$$S_{rss(X)} = \sum_{i=1}^{N-1} \sum_{j=i+1}^{N}\left(d_{ij(X)} - \delta_{ij}\right)^2 \tag{5}$$

Where $d_{ij(x)} = \|rss_i - rss_j\|$ is the distance between rss_i, and rss_j, and δ_{ij} is the distance measurement between i, and j. Finally, the simple kNN algorithm needs to be applied to the MDS solution of dissimilarity function of $S_{rss(x)}$ to estimate each test point's location coordinates from known coordinates of the reference points. Algorithm 1 details the MDS solution for simultaneous indoor localization based on the fingerprints.

Algorithm 1. MDS-based fingerprint localization.

Input: LocationSet N1, Fingerprint (), double (temp, sim = POSITIVE-INFINITY)
Output: DissimilaritySet (), Coordinate c
1: **procedure D** DISSIMILARITY CONSTRUCTION
2:     $N \leftarrow$ length(X)
3:     $d < 1$
4:     **for** $i \leftarrow 1, N - 1$ **do**
5:         **for** $j \leftarrow i + 1, N$ **do**
6:             $V_d \leftarrow X_i - Y_j$
7:             $d \leftarrow d + 1$
8:         **end for**
9:     **end for**
10: **end procedure**
11: **procedure c** DISSIMILARITY BASED LOCALIZATION
12:     **for** $i \leftarrow 1, N_1$ **do**
13:         **for** $1 \leftarrow 1, 2$ **do**
14:             $temp+ = square(V_{N2}(r) - V_{N1}(r))$
15:         **end for**
16:         $temp = sqrt(temp)$
17:         **if** $temp < sim$ **then**
18:             $sim = temp$
19:             $N2 = N1$
20:         **end if**
21:     **end for**
22:     $c = N1.getCoordinates()$
23: **end procedure**

---

4   Experiments and Results

In this section, the necessary RSS data collection, evaluation parameters, and positioning results are discussed for the proposed SIL method of indoor localization. The performance evaluation of the proposed SIL is compared to the traditional RSS-based indoor localization scheme. Moreover, two scenarios have been considered for the proposed method's performance evaluation, one is based on testbed 1, and another is testbed 2.

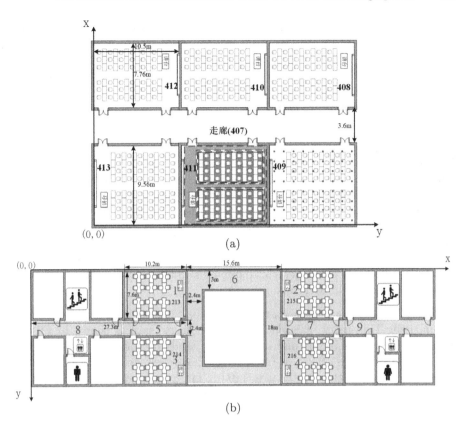

Fig. 6. Experimented environment layouts (a) Building D, fourth floor and (b) Building N, second floor.

4.1 Experimental Setup

The data collection and processing, and simulation measurements have been conducted to validate the proposed SIL system based on the fingerprinting method. Here, the proposed system's experimental setup divides into two parts: the data collection and processing and its simulation. The data collection step has been previously done through the site-survey method for indoor localization by our school's lab. The retrieved data is then processed to prepare the desired data for experimentation and performance measurement. The system simulation step and then evaluation of the obtained results are carried out to reach the desired outcome. This research's experimental setups are built on two testbeds, the fourth floor of Building D (east teaching building) and the second floor of Building N (south first teaching building) of Huazhong University of Science and Technology. Therefore, the data has the required diversity to evaluate the proposed model and measures its performance.

The required data from sampling includes a list of Wi-Fi APs along with SSID, BSSID (MAC address), RSS, and the sample's location coordinates. Later, the two crucial datasets (RSS vector and its location) are used as a fingerprint or signature to validate the system. The RSS vector heard from a list of APs have the values started from 0 (dBm) as an excellent signal to the −100 (dBm) as an extremely weak signal. Many factors affect the RSS signal as the distance between APs and sample points, but the fingerprint-based localization degrades these side effects. The Wi-Fi network has different RSS measurements in different frequency channels, but here, for this experiment, the RSS measurement is taken at a data frequency of 1 (Hz) for both testbeds.

Testbed 1: As Fig. 6a shows, the area includes six classrooms and one corridor, and the total area is 717 (m²). The width of concrete walls between the areas is 0.3 (m). The smartphone has been held flat right on the agent's chest, and all samples are collected in the same orientation. The offline phase's sampling process is conducted between 0.6 (m), and for the online phase in between 1 (m). Huawei Hol T00 is used to collect sampling data in testbed 1 for this research. Moreover, the device has collected two types of data, site-survey data for the offline phase to build the fingerprint database and test data for the online phase to evaluate the system performance.

Testbed 2: The second testbed area is the second floor of the south 1st building of Huazhong University of Science and Technology, as it is shown in Fig. 6b. It includes four classrooms and one corridor, and the total area is 592 (m²). The classroom size is 10.2   7.6 (m²). The other labels are shown in the same figure. The origin of the coordinates is (0,0). The x and y axes are shown in the picture. Oppo R9sk (Op9) is used to collect sampling data in testbed 2 for model evaluation in this paper. Moreover, the distance between two adjacent sampling points is 0.6 (m) and 1 (m) for offline and online sampling, respectively.

4.2   Evaluation Metrics

In order to evaluate the SIL method localization accuracy, the Mean Distance Error (MDE) and Standard Division (STD) are used as evaluation metrics in this paper. If the (N), are considered as number of TPs, real location of TP and estimated location of TP, the MDE and STD have been calculated as follows:

$$MDE = \frac{1}{n2} \sum_{n2=1}^{N2} \|\theta_n^{n2} - \widehat{\theta}_n^{n2}\|^2 \tag{6}$$

$$\sigma = \sqrt{\frac{\sum_{n2=1}^{N} \left(\widehat{\theta}_n^{n2} - MDE\right)^2}{N2}} \tag{7}$$

4.3   Performance Evaluation

In this section, to evaluate the proposed method's performance, the cumulative distribution functions (CDF) of the proposed method and the kNN method have been plotted. Testbed 1 consists of 288 RPs and 110 TPs from 30 APs, and testbed 2 contains 221 RPs and 50 TPs from 27 APs as a fingerprint in the fingerprint database. Moreover, for all algorithms in the simulation of testbed 1, the kNN metric has been considered in two cases k = 2 and k = 8. In contrast, in the simulation of testbed 2, the k value is equal to 1, and for both testbeds, the metric of kNN for labeling the new fingerprint with the position is Euclidean distance.

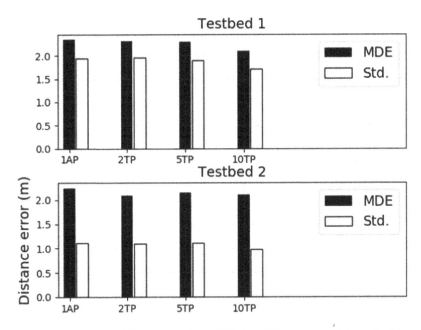

Fig. 7. MDE and Std. of different number of TP in MDS-based model, testbed 1 and 2.

Figure 7 demonstrates the localization error upon the collaboration of the different number of TPs in the MDS-based model. It shows the more TPs share the information for interpolation; the higher accuracy would gain the algorithm. The first line of CDF shows one TP per time localization, the second line 2 TPs per time, the third line 5 TPs per time, and 4th line 10 TPs per time. Form all clusters in a time localization, the 10 TPs per time localization shows the highest accuracy in MDE and standard deviation. Likewise, the MDEs and standard deviations related to the different number of TP information sharing in the MDS-based model are listed in Table 2. As the number of TPs for simultaneous localization increases, the error would decrease in the fingerprinting localization.

Table 2. Positioning error of TP collaboration in MDS-kNN, testbed 1 and 2.

	Testbed 1				Testbed 2			
	1TP	2TP	5TP	10TP	1TP	2TP	5TP	10TP
MDE (m)	2.34	2.31	2.29	2.10	2.24	2.09	2.14	2.09
STD (m)	1.95	1.95	1.89	1.71	1.10	1.09	1.11	0.97

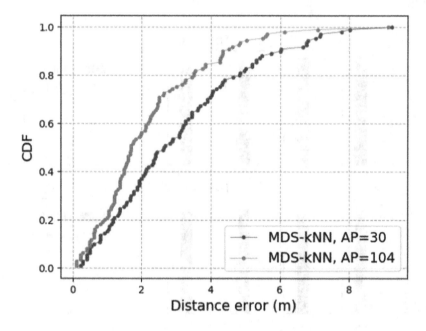

Fig. 8. The effect of AP removal on localization accuracy, testbed 1.

Figure 8 indicates the effect of number APs deployment on fingerprint positioning accuracy based on the k-nearest neighbor algorithm. As shown in Fig. 8, the smaller the number of AP, the better the accuracy for indoor positioning. The 104 APs CDF contains the APs, which has no signal transmission (0 dBm) or stopped sending the signal. Moreover, for building the database for simulation of models, it had been assigned to –100 dBm as the weakest RSS signal. In contrast, in the 30 AP approach, all those APs that had no signal, or stopped working in more than half of the database's RP, have been removed from the database. Therefore, the effect of noise and inconsistency over the fingerprint vectors of TP and RP has been degraded from the fingerprint database. For all of those reasons, the accuracy of fingerprinting has increased.

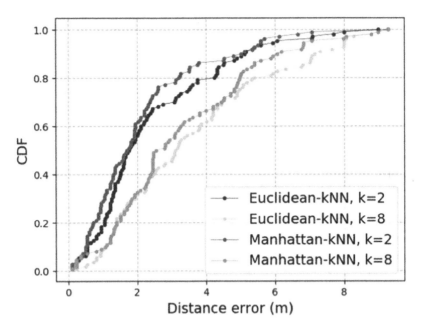

Fig. 9. The comparison of the Euclidean and Manhattan distance metrics in kNN, Testbed 1.

Figure 9 compares the used metric of kNN algorithm. The RSS signal similarity between the TP and selected votes of neighboring is calculated using Euclidean distance and cumulative Manhattan distance. The result shows that the Manhattan distance gains more accuracy than the Euclidean distance. Moreover, this result indicates that the cumulative Manhattan distance metric can provide the best similarity between the TP and RPs in the deterministic kNN algorithm. Besides, according to the paper [1], the cumulative Manhattan distance provides the best discrimination in high-dimensional data space than the Euclidean distance.

The CDF for the MDS-based and traditional kNN are shown comparatively in Fig. 10. The CDF indicates huge precision differences between both of the used methods of this paper. The CDF curve for the MDS-based model displays less inaccuracy than the kNN curve. The accuracy increase in both testbed 1 and testbed 2 demonstrates improved accuracy in mean distance error of 9.8% and 19.6%, respectively. The improvement of accuracy according to the standard deviation of 13.2% and 20.9% increase in testbed 1 and 2, accordingly. Both testbed's experimentation indicates that the proposed MDS-based model takes advantage of information-sharing and collaboration between TPs and RPs to increase the fingerprinting approach reliability and consistency in indoor localization. Finally, Table 3 records the mean distance error and standard deviation of the mentioned methods on testbed 1 and 2, respectively.

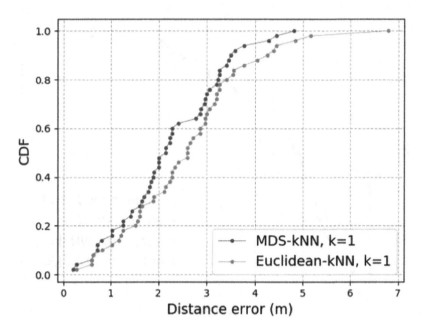

Fig. 10. The comparison of CDFs of the MDS-based and kNN models, testbed 2.

Table 3. MDE and Std. of experimented models, testbed 1 and testbed 2.

Method	Testbed 1 k = 2		Testbed 2 k = 2	
	MDE (m)	**STD (m)**	**MDE (m)**	**STD (m)**
MDS-kNN	2.21	1.64	2.09	1.02
kNN	2.45	1.89	2.60	1.29

5   Conclusion

In the fingerprinting approach, TP's localization has been done independently without consideration of other TPs and RPs. Thus, the collaboration concept helps the fingerprinting method leverage information-sharing among points to increase the localization precision. Therefore, in this paper, the effort has put into finding an approach to include the collaboration concept in fingerprinting and increase the localization precision.

This paper analyzes previous works and researches of indoor localization based on the Wi-Fi RSS fingerprints to find the solution for the mentioned fingerprinting problem. The literature review results come out with pre-summarized collaboration usage: Distance-scheme and Proximity-scheme. This paper's proposed method has been built on the proximity scheme of collaborative localization that is utilized the RSS distance in the MDS-based algorithm to build collaboration among RSS's fingerprints. This method integrates the TPs and the RPs information to localize the test points. This method's experimentation has been conducted on data collected from Huazhong University of Science and Technology teaching buildings as testbed 1 and testbed 2. The result demonstrates improvement in the MDS-based method compared to the deterministic kNN algorithm. The error results show up to 9.8%, and 13.2% error reduction in MDE, and standard deviation, respectively, for testbed 1. Moreover, the error results of testbed 2 show up to 19.6% and 20.9% error degradation in MDE, and standard deviation, respectively, for testbed 2. Several experiments have been conducted in both testbeds with different numbers of RPs, TPs, APs, and algorithmic metrics.

References

1. Aggarwal, C.C., Hinneburg, A., Keim, D.A.: On the surprising behavior of distance metrics in high dimensional space. In: Van den Bussche, J., Vianu, V. (eds.) ICDT 2001. LNCS, vol. 1973, pp. 420–434. Springer, Heidelberg (2001). https://doi.org/10.1007/3-540-44503-X_27
2. Beder, C., Klepal, M.: Fingerprinting based localisation revisited: a rigorous approach for comparing RSSI measurements coping with missed access points and differing antenna attenuations. In: 2012 International Conference on Indoor Positioning and Indoor Navigation (IPIN), pp. 1–7. IEEE (2012)
3. Belmonte-Hernández, A., Hernández-Peñaloza, G., Alvarez, F., Conti, G.: Adaptive fingerprinting in multi-sensor fusion for accurate indoor tracking. IEEE Sens. J. 17(15), 4983–4998 (2017)
4. Buehrer, R.M., Wymeersch, H., Vaghefi, R.M.: Collaborative sensor network localization: algorithms and practical issues. Proc. IEEE 106(6), 1089–1114 (2018)
5. Chan, L., Chiang, J., Chen, Y., Ke, C., Hsu, J., Chu, H.: collaborative localization: enhancing WiFi-based position estimation with neighborhood links in clusters. In: Fishkin, K.P., Schiele, B., Nixon, P., Quigley, A. (eds.) Pervasive 2006. LNCS, vol. 3968, pp. 50–66. Springer, Heidelberg (2006). https://doi.org/10.1007/11748625_4
6. Gu, F., Niu, J., Duan, L.: Waipo: a fusion-based collaborative indoor localization system on smartphones. IEEE/ACM Trans. Networking 25(4), 2267–2280 (2017)
7. Hamaoui, M.: Non-iterative MDS method for collaborative network localization with sparse range and pointing measurements. IEEE Trans. Signal Proc. 67(3), 568–578 (2018)
8. He, S., Chan, S.-H.G.: Wi-fi fingerprint-based indoor positioning: recent advances and comparisons. IEEE Commun. Surv. Tutorials 18(1), 466–490 (2015)
9. He, S., Chan, S.-H. G., Yu, L., Liu, N.: Fusing noisy fingerprints with distance bounds for indoor localization. In: 2015 IEEE Conference on Computer Communications (INFOCOM), pp. 2506–2514. IEEE (2015)
10. Jung, S.-H., Han, D.: Automated construction and maintenance of Wi-Fi radio maps for crowdsourcing-based indoor positioning systems. IEEE Access 6, 1764–1777 (2017)
11. Kampis, G., Kantelhardt, J.W., Kloch, K., Lukowicz, P.: Analytical and simulation models for collaborative localization. J. Comput. Sci. 6, 1–10 (2015)
12. Koneru, A., Li, X., Varanasi, M.: Comparative study of RSS-based collaborative localization methods in sensor networks. In: 2006 IEEE Region 5 Conference, pp. 243–248. IEEE (2006)

13. Kotwal, S., Verma, S., Sharma, A., et al.: Region based collaborative angle of arrival localization for wireless sensor networks with maximum range information. In: 2010 International Conference on Computational Intelligence and Communication Networks, pp. 301–307. IEEE (2010)

14. Li, Z., Zhao, X., Liang, H.: Automatic construction of radio maps by crowdsourcing PDR traces for indoor positioning. In: 2018 IEEE International Conference on Communications (ICC), pp. 1–6. IEEE (2018)

15. Liu, H., et al.: Push the limit of wifi based localization for smartphones. In: Proceedings of the 18th Annual International Conference on Mobile Computing and Networking, pp. 305–316 (2012)

16. Liu, X., Cen, J., Zhan, Y., Tang, C.: An adaptive fingerprint database updating method for room localization. IEEE Access **7**, 42626–42638 (2019)

17. Mair, N., Mahmoud, Q.H.: A collaborative bluetooth-based approach to localization of mobile devices. In: 8th International Conference on Collaborative Computing: Networking, Applications and Worksharing (CollaborateCom), pp. 363–371. IEEE (2012)

18. Noh, Y., Yamaguchi, H., Lee, U.: Infrastructure-free collaborative indoor positioning scheme for time-critical team operations. IEEE Trans. Syst. Man Cybern. Syst. **48**(3), 418–432 (2016)

19. Sadhu, V., Pompili, D., Zonouz, S., Sritapan, V.: Collabloc: privacy-preserving multi-modal localization via collaborative information fusion. In: 2017 26th International Conference on Computer Communication and Networks (ICCCN), pp. 1–9. IEEE (2017)

20. Wang, W., Bai, P., Zhou, Y., Liang, X., Wang, Y.: Optimal configuration analysis of AOA localization and optimal heading angles generation method for UAV swarms. IEEE Access **7**, 70117–70129 (2019)

21. Wu, Z., Zhou, Y., Wang, X., Zhu, J., Xue, L.: Location accuracy on collaborative positioning in wireless sensor networks. In: 2014 9th IEEE Conference on Industrial Electronics and Applications, pp. 738–742. IEEE (2014)

22. Xu, L., Yao, L., He, J., Wang, P., Long, K., Wang, Q.: Collaborative geolocation based on imprecise initial coordinates for internet of things. IEEE Access **6**, 48850–48858 (2018)

23. Zhang, C., Han, G., Jiang, J., Shu, L., Liu, G., Rodrigues, J.J.: A collaborative localization algorithm for underwater acoustic sensor networks. In: 2014 International Conference on Computing, Management and Telecommunications (ComManTel), pp. 211–216. IEEE (2014)

24. Zhao, P., Jiang, C., Chen, H., Ren, Y.: Probabilistic neural network for RSS-based collaborative localization. In: 2012 IEEE 75th Vehicular Technology Conference (VTC Spring), pp. 1–5. IEEE (2012)

Posture Prediction for Healthy Sitting Using a Smart Chair

Tariku Adane Gelaw[1,2(✉)] [iD] and Misgina Tsighe Hagos[3,4] [iD]

[1] Department of Information Engineering and Computer Science, University of Trento, Trento, Italy
taru2004@protonmail.com
[2] Fondazione Bruno Kessler, Povo, Italy
[3] Science Foundation Ireland Centre for Research Training in Machine Learning at University College Dublin, Dublin, Ireland
misgina.hagos@ucdconnect.ie
[4] School of Computer Science, University College Dublin, Dublin, Ireland

Abstract. Poor sitting habits have been identified as a risk factor to musculoskeletal disorders and lower back pain especially on the elderly, disabled people, and office workers. In the current computerized world, even while involved in leisure or work activity, people tend to spend most of their days sitting at computer desks. This can result in spinal pain and related problems. Therefore, a means to remind people about their sitting habits and provide recommendations to counterbalance, such as physical exercise, is important. Posture recognition for seated postures have not received enough attention as most works focus on standing postures. Wearable sensors, pressure or force sensors, videos and images were used for posture recognition in the literature. The aim of this study is to build Machine Learning models for classifying sitting posture of a person by analyzing data collected from a chair platted with two 32 by 32 pressure sensors at its seat and backrest. Models were built using five algorithms: Random Forest (RF), Gaussian Naïve Bayes, Logistic Regression, Support Vector Machine and Deep Neural Network (DNN). All the models are evaluated using KFold cross validation technique. This paper presents experiments conducted using the two separate datasets, controlled and realistic, and discusses results achieved at classifying six sitting postures. Average classification accuracies of 98% and 97% were achieved on the controlled and realistic datasets, respectively.

Keywords: Sitting posture · Smart chair · Pressure sensor · Deep neural networks · Prediction

1 Introduction

Many people spend a large portion of their daily time, sitting in an office chair, lounge chair, car seat or on wheelchairs. Due to this reason, seat comfort has gained particular attention for nursing homes, military, workplace, and assistive technology applications. Sore muscles, heavy legs, uneven pressure, stiffness, restlessness, fatigue, and pain was considered as symptoms which are caused due to seating discomfort in the office environment [1–3].

© ICST Institute for Computer Sciences, Social Informatics and Telecommunications Engineering 2022
Published by Springer Nature Switzerland AG 2022. All Rights Reserved
M. L. Berihun (Ed.): ICAST 2021, LNICST 411, pp. 401–411, 2022.
https://doi.org/10.1007/978-3-030-93709-6_26

Everyone needs to be more active but at the same time they also wanted to spend less time sitting down. A person in the developed world who primarily works using a computer could reasonably sit for up to 15 h a day [4]. Other studies also showed that some older adults (aged 65 and over) spend 10 h or more each day sitting or lying down, making them the most sedentary population group. All of this sitting comes with significant health costs, both from inactivity and from poor posture.

Long periods of sitting have been linked to obesity, cardiovascular disease and premature mortality. Although there is also evidence that these adverse effects can be mitigated by short standing breaks [5, 6]. Poor sitting posture has been identified as a risk factor for musculoskeletal disorders [7], and particularly for lower back pain. Musculoskeletal disorders can cause chronic pain in the limbs, neck and back. In general, this shows us that postural imbalance has a great impact on the health of individuals by causing different diseases. Specially, senior citizens (older adults) and people with disabilities are impacted with this. So, finding a solution to improve postural imbalance of an individual is the key for achieving a healthy and active life. As a result, the aim of this study is also to focus on finding ways to prevent or treat the postural distortions that has a greater impact on the individuals' health and daily activities.

This paper is structured into five sections. Section 2 presents related works found in the literature and the research gap that we worked on in this paper. Our proposed methodology is discussed in Sect. 3. Experiment results are presented in Sect. 4. Finally, conclusion of our work and recommendations for future work are presented in Sect. 5.

2 Related Work

A study by [8] used 19 pressure sensors to identify sitting postures. This study used an approximation algorithm for a near-optimal sensor placement. The researchers used a dataset which contains pressure data for ten postures, collected from 52 participants. In this study the researchers achieved an accuracy of 82%. Another research by Kazuhiro et al. [9] used a pressure sensor seat on a chair for identifying sitting postures. In their experiments, [9] classified nine postures, including leaning forward/backward/right/left and legs crossed. In this study, they obtained a classification accuracy of 98.9% when the sitting person was known and 93.9% when the person was not known. A study by [10] also designed a personalized smart chair system to recognize sitting behaviors. The system can receive surface pressure data from the designed sensor and provide feedback for guiding the user towards proper sitting postures. They used a liquid state machine and a Logistic Regression (LR) classifier to construct a spiking neural network for classifying 15 sitting postures. The experimental results consisting of 15 sitting postures from 19 participants show that a prediction precision of 88.52%. Yong et al. developed a system for classifying sitting postures for children using CNN, Naïve Bayes, Decision Tree (DT), Multinomial Logistic Regression (MLR), Neural Network (NN), and Support Vector Machine (SVM) machine learning algorithms [11]. Ten children participated in this research and achieved an accuracy of 95.3% using CNN. Another researcher [12] proposed a system that uses a specialized Arduino-based chair to predict and analyze the sitting posture of the user and provides appropriate videos to help them correct their posture by analyzing the user statistics on their overall posture data. They used deep CNNs and LBCNet (Lower-Balanced Check Network).

A research conducted by Griffiths et al. [13], in a laboratory study with 18 participants, evaluated a range of common sitting positions to determine when heart rate and respiratory rate detection was possible and evaluate the accuracy of the detected rate. Griffiths et al. employ conductive fabric on the chair's armrests to sense heart rate and pressure sensors on the back of the chair for sensing respiratory rate. Arnrich et al. used detected chair information for understanding stress level of individuals during office work [14]. A collective of 33 subjects were involved while a set of physiological signals was collected. In [14], Self-Organized Map (SOM) and XY-fused Kohonen Network were used and a classification accuracy of 73.75% achieved for discriminating stress from cognitive load. Another research by [15] used sitting postures to identify emotion expressions. The sitting postures have the semantic factors: "arousal", "pleasantness", and "dominance", so emotion expressions of the sitting postures are like those of the facial expressions [15].

Our proposed approach differs from the existing literature in two main aspects: (1) most of the above works focused their study on office workers but our study, in addition to office workers, targets older people who spend much of their time at home; (2) we employ different algorithms for modeling our posture classifier using several pressure sensors both at the seat and backrest of the chair (32 × 32). Furthermore, in addition to the traditional techniques, we also implemented Deep Neural Network (DNN) algorithm for building predictive models. In the current computerized world, even while involved in leisure or work activity, people tend to spend most of their daily life sitting at computer desks. Therefore, a means to remind people about their sitting habits and provide recommendations that can counterbalance, such as physical exercise, is important. In this work, we propose to identify six sitting postures, which are back, empty, left, right, front and still. An identified sitting posture could potentially be used by an end-user or researcher towards putting solutions to bad sitting posture habits.

3 Proposed Method

3.1 Data Collection

In this study, pressure sensors were used for collecting the pressure distribution data from a sensor plated chair. The pressure mat was built by members of the Micro Electro-Mechanical-Systems (MEMS) unit of Fondazione Bruno Kessler (FBK) research institute. The dataset was collected at the Intelligent Interfaces and Interaction (I3) research unit of FBK. These mats have a 32 by 32 pressure sensors, which are placed at the seat (bottom) and backrest of the chair. These 64 sensors cover the seat and backrest body of the chair and are able to detect every pressure which is placed on it. In this study, we have tried to investigate whether it is possible to predict sitting postures using the collected information from the pressure sensors. In order to collect both the controlled and realistic datasets, we involved a total of 50 participants, 11 and

39 individuals for each respectively. In the controlled dataset collection, participants were told what positions to hold in a controlled lab setting. Similarly, the realistic dataset were collected in a controlled lab environment by employing a wizard Oz method where participants perform activities to change a television channel by simply moving/changing their body position (moving right corresponds to channel+, moving left for channel-, moving forward for channel page up and moving backward for channel page down). The channels of the television were changed when the button (corresponding to the body movement) was clicked.

3.2 Dataset Description

A total of 1980 and 4875 data examples were collected, from two set of participants, for the controlled and realistic datasets, respectively. The controlled dataset was collected from 11 individuals who were told to hold a certain posture for 15 s. For every sitting posture, including empty and still positions, data were recorded for the 32 sensor values in every half a second. So, we have 30 snapshots of sensor values. For the realistic dataset collection, we only used five sitting postures excluding the empty posture class. From a total of 39 participants, 25 examples were recorded for each of the five postures resulting in a total of 125 data examples in each participant's file. The dataset was collected within an interval of 0.75 seconds as at time t01, t02, t03, t04 and t05. The assumption in this data collection was that at t01, which is the 1st recurrent element, a participant might not have moved yet or might just be starting to move. At time t05 participant might already be moving back to "center". We found t03, the 3rd recurrent element, and element t234, which is a combination of 2nd, 3rd, and 4th recurrent elements, to be less noisy than the other timestamps, good representatives of the final posture and hence easier to predict and useful for learning.

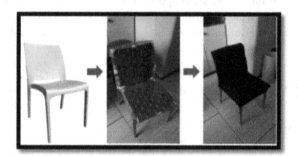

Fig. 1. Sensor mounted smart chair.

We used the still sitting posture to normalize both datasets by subtracting it from the other sitting postures. The empty sitting posture data was collected from the empty chair (while there was no one sitting on it). Although the data collected from empty chair were supposed to be empty, there were some sensor reading values. These data were collected from a sensorized chair which was built by members of the Micro Electromechanical-Systems (MEMS) unit of FBK research institute. The chair has a 32 by 32 pressure sensors, which are placed at the seat (bottom) and backrest of the chair as indicated in Fig. 1. These 64 sensors cover the whole body of the chair and able to detect every pressure which is placed on it.

3.3 Data Preprocessing

Since the goal of this study is to investigate whether it is possible to predict sitting postures using data collected from sensor slipped chair (from both the seat and back of the chair), unnecessary columns and invalid sensor readings and outliers are removed from the datasets. The 8 × 8 matrix where the data collected from each of the 32 sensors is mapped on (see Table 1), does not contain missing values.

Inside each individual file, there are 125 examples collected for each of the five sitting postures. The raw data has a total of 80 features. Since, our goal in this study is to investigate whether it is possible to predict or classify person's sitting posture, we only consider the 64 back and seat sensor features and the class label posture feature. As a result, we removed a total of 15 features from the dataset. After we extracted all of the initial features, we then continued to read the sensor values from each individual for each posture and put them into a nested list which we then mapped to an 8 × 8 matrix for ease of manipulation. Then we merged all individual files into a single Comma-Separated Values file.

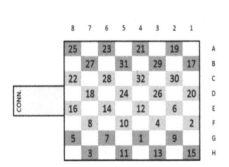
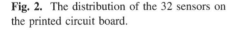

Fig. 2. The distribution of the 32 sensors on the printed circuit board.

Fig. 3. A person seated on a sensor plated smart chair (mirror view.)

In the raw collected sensor data, we saw that some of the sensor readings were outliers that deviate from most of the values of a particular sensor in each person's file. In order to handle this, we first calculate the average still value of each sensor column by summing the sensor values in that column for a single person file (which contains 125 data records) and we set a certain threshold. Then we replace the sensor's values which are above the threshold, with the average still value. We did this for the entire 64 seat and back sensors. In addition to this, to avoid discrepancies of sensor readings due to weight variation and fluctuating seating habits of individuals, we normalize each column sensor's for each person with the average still value of the column sensor's that we calculated before. Using these average values, we then subtract it from each of the other posture values of the individual. Normalizing using these still posture values helps to avoid some defects that come due to weight variation between individuals, fluctuating sitting habits and others. The numbers in Table 1 are the positions of the sensors on the printed circuit board of the Texas instrument board. As can be seen in Fig. 2 and Fig. 3, we can visualize the back sensors projection as the face of the sitting person coming out of the mirror.

3.4   Feature Generation

In addition to the 64 sensor features, we generate other features that will better describe our dataset and contribute to improve classification accuracy. Since the pressure distribution of sensors on the chair has a great impact, we generate four other features by calculating the center of mass of the 32 sensors of the seat and 32 sensors of the back. We calculated the center of mass for both the seat and back sensors separately. We also extracted features for each of the seat and back sensors dividing the given 32 sensors into four quadrants and edges. Each category in both the quadrant and the edge contains 8 sensor readings. Concerning the quadrant features, each of them are extracted by taking half of the rows and half of the columns from the 8×8 matrix as indicated in Table 2.

Table 1. Projection of the seat and back sensors on an 8x8 matrix.

	Left leg/right shoulder				Right leg/left shoulder			
	Col 1	Col 2	Col 3	Col 4	Col 5	Col 6	Col 7	Col 8
Row 1	16		31		9		14	
Row 2		24		23		1		12
Row 3	18		29		11		10	
Row 4		26		21		3		8
Row 5	20		27		15		6	
Row 6		28		17		5		4
Row 7	22		25		13		2	
Row 8		30		19		7		0
Bottom								

We used the Random Forest (RF) Classifier algorithm to evaluate the importance of each of the features in both the controlled and realistic datasets.

3.5   Model Development and Testing

The study is conducted using both the controlled and realistic datasets separately. In both cases, we have conducted various experiments using different combinations such as using normalized and non-normalized dataset, using full sensor features, using selected features, and using selected features with a portion of class labels (two, four, five and all of the classes) with all the five machine learning algorithms used in the study. Specifically, the different experiment settings conducted on the controlled dataset are the following: non-normalized and normalized dataset and 3 other features, non-normalized and normalized sensor and top 10 features, normalized dataset for the whole 55 feature sets, top selected features for non-normalized and normalized datasets, selected features with selected class labels for non-normalized and normalized dataset, and using a DNN on top selected features with the full class labels normalized dataset, five class label normalized dataset with top selected features, and four class label normalized dataset with top selected features.

Table 2. Features from the 32 sensors of seat/back divided into four quadrants.

	Col 1	Col 2	Col 3	Col 4	Col 5	Col 6	Col 7	Col 8
Row 1	16		31		9		14	
Row 2		24		23		1		12
Row 3	18		29		11		10	
Row 4		26		21		3		8
Row 5	20		27		15		6	
Row 6		28		17		5		4
Row 7	22		25		13		2	
Row 8		30		19		7		0

Like the experiments on the controlled dataset, the following experiment settings were used on the realistic dataset: non-normalized and normalized dataset, experimentation using seat, back or both seat and back sensors dataset, using senior, young or both age groups, using full, 234th and 3rd recurrent elements, experimentation using various length class labels of the posture feature, and using third recurrent element with varying number of classes. All of these experiments are conducted considering number of participants, age group, class label, recurrent element, printed circuit board (seat or backrest), extracted features, and normalized or non-normalized dataset. Unlike the controlled dataset collection (which uses only the 32 sensors of the seat), we use both the 32 by 32 sensors for the realistic dataset collection. In the realistic dataset, five different postures (two before the click and 3 after the click) were collected within five different time frames for each particular posture. Click is a wizard of Oz technique that we employ to perform the position change. As a result, we conduct experiments by using different levels of recurrent elements of the data.

We used five different algorithms and several classifier models are built using RF, Gaussian Naïve Bayes (GNB), Logistic Regression, SVM and DNN. All the models are evaluated using the KFold cross validation technique. Scikit-learn and TensorFlow libraries were used. Accuracy of the five classifiers, which were trained with top selected feature sets on the normalized controlled dataset, is reported in Table 3. We train our models with a total of 1800 data examples where 1620 are used for training and the rest 180 are used for testing. As can be seen in Table 3, DNN scores superior performance measure compared to all the other methods, be it on the full class labels or a portion of them. The front, left and right postures are relatively easy to predict in all of the classifiers compared to classifying the back posture. Table 4 shows the result of the RF algorithm using the realistic dataset 3rd recurrent element with the left and right class labels.

Table 3. Summary classification accuracy results using the normalized controlled dataset.

Selected feature sets (normalized dataset)	Classifiers				
	RF	GNB	SVM	LR	DNN
Full class label	82%	88%	75%	81%	93%
Five class label	86%	95%	82%	88%	95%
Four class label	85%	88%	83%	89%	98%

Table 4. Classification report of the RF algorithm using the 3rd recurrent element with left and right class labels normalized realistic dataset.

	Precision	Recall	F1-score	Support
Left	0.98	0.95	0.97	195
Right	0.95	0.98	0.97	195
Avg/total	0.97	0.97	0.97	390

4   Results

We have conducted a total of eight experiments in the study using the controlled dataset while we performed a total of six experiments in the study with the realistic dataset using the five classifiers. From all the experiments, the one we did using the DNN algorithm with normalized dataset and four class labels scored the highest result with 98% prediction accuracy. Among the five classifiers, DNN, GNB and RF scored the highest performance in most of our experiments. Although most of the models trained on the controlled dataset were able to classify most of the sitting postures, it was also difficult to easily predict the back posture. The main reason for this might be the usage of only the seat sensors in the data collection, which resulted in the incomplete representation of back postures.

The study using the realistic dataset the highest score was recorded by the RF algorithm with an accuracy score of 97% from a model developed using the third recurrent element and only the left and right class labels as indicated in Table 5. Classifying sitting postures using the full timeframe dataset with all the five class labels was very difficult. As we have seen in our experimentations, the models performance improved when we used varying length of class labels and different portions of the timeframe dataset. The reason for not correctly classifying the full postures might be due to the nature of the dataset as well as the participant's motionless character. Figure 4 shows the plot of the postures using the 3rd recurrent element with left and right class labels normalized dataset.

Table 5. Summary accuracy of the models using the 3rd recurrent element with full/4/3/2 class labels (realistic dataset.)

Recurrent element		Classifiers				
		RF	GNB	LR	SVM	DNN
3rd	Full	77%	66%	67%	69%	56%
	4	77%	66%	70%	71%	64%
	3	87%	78%	82%	84%	79%
	2	97%	95%	93%	94%	96%

As it can be observed from the results of the two studies, the one with the controlled dataset seems to perform better than the one with the realistic dataset in classifying sitting postures. Specially, the DNN performed much better in most of the experiments involving the controlled dataset. In addition to this, it was difficult to predict back sitting posture in the case of controlled dataset, but it was relatively easier using the realistic dataset. The reason for this is due to the addition of the 32 back sensors dataset. Variations in the number of class labels does not seem to have that much impact in the case of classifying the controlled dataset while it is important in the realistic dataset.

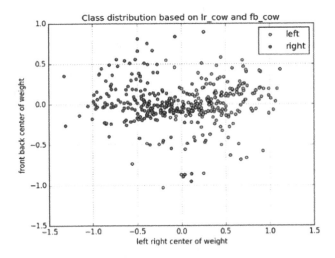

Fig. 4. Plot of the postures using only the third recurrent element with left and right class labels normalized realistic dataset.

These differences exist due to the different nature of the two datasets. There is a visible difference in each sensor readings in each of the different data examples in the controlled dataset. This might be associated with a participant performing movements to a certain degree. In the case of the realistic dataset, sensor readings in the different data examples seem closer, meaning participants were in relatively steady sitting conditions compared to the controlled dataset. In addition to the above reasons, we associate performance differences with the variations in dataset size. In the controlled dataset, we have used a total of 1800 data examples while we have a total of 4875 records in the realistic dataset for training and testing the models.

5   Conclusion and Recommendations

The main goal of this study was to build a predictive model which can classify the sitting posture of a person and enable individuals to monitor their sitting habits for healthy living. For this purpose, we have collected two datasets from 32 and 64 sensor coated chairs and carried out two separate studies. In addition to the sensor data, we have also generated new features in both studies depending on the center of weight of the seat and back sensors, partitioning the seat and back of the chair into four quadrants and edges.

We have conducted experiments using the sensor and the generated features to build predictive models for both studies. As a result, the model that we built using controlled dataset was able to classify six sitting postures (back, empty, left, right, front and still) with an accuracy score of 93% using a DNN. The highest accuracy score of 98% was achieved in classifying four of the basic sitting postures (back, left, right and front) using DNN. In the second study, our predictive model was able to classify five sitting postures (back, front, left, right and still) with a classification accuracy of 77% using the 3rd recurrent element. The model built on the 3rd recurrent element with only two class labels was able to classify the left and right sitting postures with the highest accuracy score of 97% using RF classifier.

In general, we have achieved good results for both studies in classifying sitting postures, particularly using the controlled dataset. However, performance variation exist between the two studies probably due to differences in dataset size, number of class labels used, data collection method and participants' sitting habit.

In this study, we used a dataset collected within a controlled lab environment, employed limited numbers of participants, and identified six sitting postures. For future work, our method can be extended by collecting real world dataset, employing increased number of participants, and sitting postures. Different sitting activities can also be considered towards developing a full system that can work with variety of chair types and environments.

Acknowledgements. This publication has emanated from research supported in part by a grant from Science Foundation Ireland under Grant number 18/CRT/6183. For the purpose of Open Access, the author has applied a CC BY public copyright license to any Author Accepted Manuscript version arising from this submission.

References

1. Zemp, R., et al.: Application of Machine Learning Approaches for Classifying Sitting Posture Based on Force and Acceleration Sensors. Hindawi Publishing Corporation BioMed Research International, Zurich, Switzerland (2016)
2. Halender, M.G., Zhang, L.: Field studies of comfort and discomfort in sitting. Ergonomics **40**(9), 895–915 (1997)
3. Yong, M.K., Son, Y., Kim, W., Jin, B., Yun, M.H.: Classification of Children's Sitting Postures Using Machine Learning Algorithms. Applied Sciences, MDPI, Basel, Switzerland (2018)
4. Hamilton, M.T., Healy, G.N., Dunstan, D.W., Zderic, T.W., Owen, N.: Too little exercise and too much sitting- inactivity physiology and the need for new recommendations on sedentary behavior. Curr. Cardiovasc. Risk Rep. **2**(4), 292–298 (2008)
5. Owen, N., Healy, G.N., Matthews, C.E., Dunstan, D.W.: Too much sitting: the population health science of sedentary behavior. Exerc. Sport Sci. Rev. **38**(3), 105–113 (2010). https://doi.org/10.1097/JES.0b013e3181e373a2
6. Matuska, S., Paralic, M., Hudec, R.: A Smart System for Sitting Posture Detection Based on Force Sensors and Mobile Application. Hindawi Mobile Information Systems (2020)
7. Wahlström, J.: Ergonomics, musculoskeletal disorders and computer work. Occup. Med. **55** (3), 168–176 (2005)
8. Bilge, M., Krause, A., Forlizzi, J., Guestrin, C., Hodgins, J.: Robust, low-cost, non-intrusive sensing and recognition of seated postures. In: Proceedings of the 20th Annual ACM Symposium on User Interface Software and Technology, pp. 149–158. Carnegie Mellon University, 5000 Forbes Avenue Pittsburgh, PA 15213 USA (2007)
9. Kamiya, K., Kudo, M., Nonaka, H., Toyama, J.: Sitting posture analysis by pressure sensors. IEEE (2008)
10. Wang, J., Hafidh, B., Dong, H., El Saddik, A.: Sitting Posture Recognition Using a Spiking Neural Network. IEEE Sensors Journal. University of Rochester (2020)
11. Huang, Y.R., Ouyang, X.F.: Sitting posture detection and recognition using force sensor. In: 5th International Conference on Biomedical Engineering and Informatics. IEEE (2012)
12. Cho, H., Choi, H.J., Lee, C.E., Sir, C.W.: Sitting posture prediction and correction system using Arduino-based chair and deep learning model. In: 12th Conference on Service-Oriented Computing and Applications (SOCA). IEEE (2019)
13. Griffiths, E., Scott Saponas, T., Bernheim Brush, A.J.: Health Chair-Implicitly Sensing Heart and Respiratory Rate. UBICOMP'14, Seattle, USA (2014)
14. Arnrich, B., Setz, C., La Marca, R., Troster, G., Ehlert, U.: What does your chair know about your stress level? IEEE Trans. Inf. Technol. Biomed. **14** (2009)
15. Shibata, T., Kijima, Y.: Emotion recognition modeling of sitting postures by using pressure sensors and accelerometers. In: 21st International Conference on Pattern Recognition (ICPR), Tsukuba, Japan (2012)

Agricultural Domain-Specific Jargon Words Identification in Amharic Text

Melaku Lake[(⊠)] and Tesfa Tegegne

ICT4D Research Center, Bahir Dar Institute of Technology,
Bahir Dar University, Bahir Dar, Ethiopia

Abstract. Domain-specific jargon words are lists of words used in formal communication of a particular domain with domain experts and non-domain experts; however, it is difficult to understand by non-experts and society. Experts of an organization use jargon words in scientific and science communication to keep the protocol of the communication within a domain. The domain-specific Amharic jargon words negatively impact people out of the domain experts to understand the main theme of the disseminated content in science communication. We followed a design science research approach to conduct our study. We prepared a knowledge base with a list of domain-specific Amharic Jargon Words and the meaning of the word. Machine learning classifier algorithms are employed for model development with Support Vector Machine, Artificial Neural Network, and Naïve Bayes with TFIDF feature selection that returns a classification accuracy of 96.2%, 95.2%, and 94.7% respectively. The knowledge-based system best performs when a smaller number of test sentences are entered into the system. For the input of 20, 40, 60, and 80 test sentences, an accuracy of 88.2%, 86.7%, 85.4%, and 83.1% is observed. So that with the hybrid of machine learning and knowledge-based, identification of domain-specific Amharic jargon words is performed. Therefore, we observed promised result with the hybrid of machine learning and knowledge base for the identification of jargon words in jargony text.

Keywords: Natural language processing · Domain-specific jargon words · Science communication · Knowledge base · Machine learning

1 Introduction

The research in the area of NLP addresses problems in line with language modeling, morphological processing, syntactic processing, and semantic processing [1]. These days, NLP strives to obtain effective communication and accurate knowledge like human beings with increased use of human language in computational language processing to obtain human-like language processing [2]. We use scientific and science communication for communicating science [3]. Scientific communication is written by experts for experts and simple to understand for receivers. In science communication, experts of a domain in an organization communicate to the people outside the domain, and non-experts using domain-specific words to keep the protocol of communication. We attempted science communication to provide prominent information to non-domain

Published by Springer Nature Switzerland AG 2022. All Rights Reserved
M. L. Berihun (Ed.): ICAST 2021, LNICST 411, pp. 412–423, 2022.
https://doi.org/10.1007/978-3-030-93709-6_27

experts. In science communication, jargon words are used intentionally or unintentionally. Usage of jargon words in formal communication makes the communication cumbersome as the meaning of the jargon words are unknown for the communicants and jargon words hamper the interaction [4].

Jargon words are defined by the Oxford English dictionary as "words or expressions that are used by a particular profession or group of people, and are difficult for others to understand". Jargon words are defined as a list of domain terminologies used by experts of an organization that is necessary for the communication of a particular field; however, it needs meaning for users of text out of the field [5]. Experts use the words to explore their ideas besides organizational related tasks and also the readers of the text have a common understanding of the words used in a text. Scientists that use domain terminologies in workshops, meetings are stressed to reach a non-expert reader with the target theme [4].

1.1 Motivation

Communication with a particular language requires the combination of words for communicants. The selection of words is the responsibility of writers for prominent communication between communicants. We attempted Amharic domain-specific jargon words to alienate the communication barrier between agricultural domain experts and non-expert readers. We considered agricultural domains that are highly vulnerable to the occurrence of Amharic jargon words. The agricultural domain in Ethiopia has huge customers because the domain is the dominant source of income for an estimated 85% of the people. Clear and precise communication between agricultural experts and the people in Ethiopia is fundamental to maximize yield and achieve food security [7].

1.2 Amharic Agricultural Jargon Words Justification

We surveyed non-experts such as farmers, non-domain experts, and agricultural domain experts to know the level of knowing and using agricultural jargon words in communication. We use judgmental sampling and random sampling techniques for selecting samples from a large size population to fill the prepared questionnaire. We prepared a questionnaire for selected respondents and we collected and analyzed the responses.

We randomly selected 40 Amharic agricultural domain-specific jargon words around 9% of the total from the knowledge source. We prepared different close-ended questionnaire formats for the agrarian society (farmers), non-experts, and domain experts. We selected 3 samples from each group of respondents. The following figure depicts the analysis of collected data from the respondents. The rate depicted in the following figure is based on the agreement of all respondents. For example, 92.5% of the randomly selected jargon words are known by all of the regional bureau expert respondents; all regional bureau expert respondents use 70% of the randomly surveyed words for communication. So that we observed equal treatment for usual and rare usage of words on the respondents (Fig. 1).

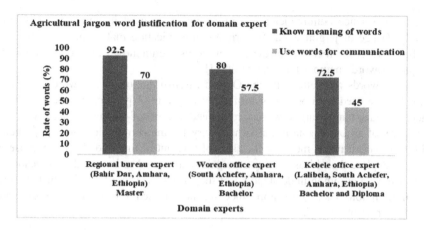

Fig. 1. Agricultural jargon word justification for domain-experts

Though knowing the meaning of jargon words is a challenge for agrarian society, the words are available in a text that confuses readers to understand the target theme. Based on the survey, we found the use of DSAJW in agricultural discourse is a weighty problem for domain experts, non-domain experts, and society.

Experts that use domain-specific jargon words on the letter, advertisement, reports, and social media are stressed to reach a non-expert reader [4]. The existence of jargon words in a text return wastage of time and money for the reader, increase the traffic of searching words. The proposed system considered literate farmers in which the ability of reading and writing is possible. The running industry-leading business of the government attempt to literate Ethiopian farmers such as the launching adult's education curriculum in Ethiopian general education.

Experts of the agricultural domain handle simple communication with non-experts and society. Readers of news, advertisement, business reports, working manuals, periodicals, magazines, social media are full of information besides the theme of the content. The developed DSAJWI system motivates experts to use domain terminology in organizational discourse to handle simple communication with customers. For the Amharic language, the usage of domain terminology used for the development and usage of Amharic language in a domain.

The following are the main contributions of our study.

- We assured the problem is weighty for experts and non-experts with the survey.
- We developed a system for the agricultural society for both experts and non-experts.
- We integrated the machine learning and knowledge-based component.

The rest of this paper is organized as follows. Section 2, presents reviews of related work made on domain-specific jargon words, Sect. 3, presents the proposed system, and a description of the function of phases in the proposed system. Section 4, discusses the experimentation and dataset preparation. Section 5 discusses on evaluation. Section 6 discusses on discussion of performance results. Finally, Sect. 7 presents the conclusion and recommendation of future works.

2   Related Work

The use of domain-specific jargon words in a text increases the frustration of the people during reading documents, emails; It returns a wastage of time and money to understand the accurate meaning of words. Removing jargon words is impossible because the words are formal languages of organizations; jargon with new concepts is invented in various domains at different times. Besides, experts are expected to minimize the use of more jargon in organizational discourse to increase the content to be understandable by the targeted user [8].

Physicians and patients require effective communication to come up with the best outcomes of the treatment and consultancy process. Translation of clinical jargon-to-layperson understandable language is essential to improve the communication between physician and patient in the process of treatment, and consultation. This clinical jargon translation is also used for physicians with the active involvement of patients to increase their decision-making ability concerning the patient's health conditions. The authors use unsupervised learning for unseen datasets using representation learning, bilingual dictionary induction, and statistical machine translation. The authors use unsupervised bilingual dictionary induction (BDI) to learn a mapping dictionary for the alignment of embedding spaces and return a precision of 82.7% at the subword level [9].

Web-based treatment and patient consultation today have increased [10]. In a web-based application, physicians use many medical jargon words for treatment and consultation; this results in the patient's frustration and confusion. The use of medical words in the digital world using different platforms on the internet is increasing. Because of the confusion and frustration of patients, the authors generate new Consumer Healthcare Vocabulary (CHV) using predefined lexical source or ontology for the medical jargon in the online consultation process to increase the understanding of patients. The authors use word embedding with GloVe Iterative Feedback (GloVeIF) and basic GloVe. The GloVeIF outperforms by 8.7% F-measure from the basic GloVE [6].

Dark Jargon words are benign-looking words that have hidden meaning to the user and require clean words. The authors use the word distribution model with Kullback-Leibler Divergence (KL), and cross-context lexical analysis (CCLA) methodology to detect the presence of jargon words in a text and mapped to the word meanings. Binary mapping of dark words to clean words is investigated using dark corpus and clean corpus. The word distribution of KL methodology outperforms around 90% of MRR from CCLA for all words and simulated dark words, however, the CCLA performs better for all words of 97.4% and performs worse for simulated dark words. So that KL outperforms the CCLA for the target dark jargon words detection and identification to provide meaning [11].

Medical words are challenging to understand by ordinary people (by non-medical people). Biological concepts require induction of meaning to be understandable to non-experts using predefined ontologies by domain expert annotators. The authors use dictionary-based Variable-step Window Identification Algorithm (VWIA) for biomedical concepts. Datasets are collected by crawling the URL of the necessary website. After the necessary preprocessing techniques are performed the developed system returns biomedical concepts based on the constructed dictionary with an F-measure of 95%. However, this work is intended for biomedical concept classification for further analysis, there is no meaning of concepts [12].

To the best of our knowledge, there are no prior works in domain-specific Amharic jargon word identification (DSAJWI) using texts in a particular domain. So that we are motivated to do our work on domain-specific Amharic jargon word identification.

3 Proposed System

The three main components in the proposed domain-specific Amharic jargon words identification (DSAJWI) system are preprocessing component, model development component, and knowledge base component. The following Fig. 2 describes the main phases and necessary steps in the DSAJWI system.

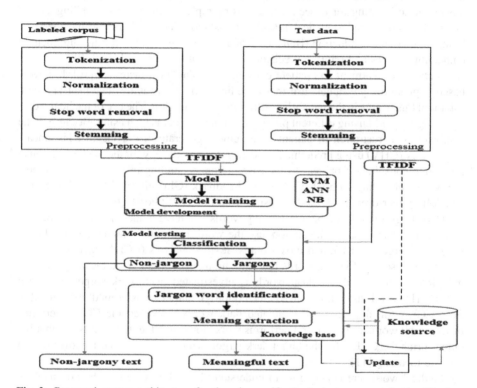

Fig. 2. Proposed system architecture for domain-specific Amharic jargon words identification system

3.1 Preprocessing

Preprocessing components make the input sentence suitable for further analysis with different preprocessing techniques that include tokenization, normalization, stop word removal, and stemming [13]. Tokenization is the first step in the preprocessing technique that can be performed right next to the input sentence to segment an input sentence into a list of tokens [13]. The target DSAJW can be generated from the list of tokens. Normalization is the process of making words having similar pronunciations to have similar representation [13]. Variant forms of Amharic characters have different meanings in a language. So that further work is required to represent variant forms of Amharic characters as per their meaning. The Amharic language use various forms of morphologically generated stop words and stop words are removed to work with content-bearing words that include DSAJW [14].

Amharic is a morphologically complex language and removing affixes of words and generating morphemes from inflectional Amharic words inline to bound morphemes is a challenging task in Amharic morphological analysis. We collected a list of prefixes and suffixes from Amharic language experts, and we removed these affixes to get the stem of the Amharic word.

TFIDF: We used a powerful feature engineering technique Term Frequency Inverse Document Frequency (TFIDF) to identify the important and precisely rare words in the text data [15]. For our work, we used the techniques to convert the strings of a text into numbers so that the developed SVM, ANN, and NB machine learning models consume the input data in numerical formats. The TFIDF feature selection technique is used for scoring words in machine learning models for Amharic language processing.

3.2 Knowledge Base

Amharic Jargon Machine Readable Dictionary (AJMRD) is a knowledge-based lexical resource used to store Amharic agricultural jargon words and the words meaning collected from various agricultural sources to employ for computational linguistics. The meaning of Amharic agricultural jargon words is sourced from agricultural domain experts. Agricultural erudite reviewed the constructed knowledge source on the behalf of the meaning of words obtained from domain experts. The AJMRD helps users to extract the meaning of an exact jargon word with binary lexical mapping, and an over-stemmed jargon word with the help of a close match to the stored words. Because there is no prior AJMRD developed for any of the reasons, we developed interactive AJMRD.

The meaning of collected jargon words in the text are stored in the knowledge source. However, jargon word is invented for different reasons besides the organization's business. The newly invented jargon words by agricultural domain experts and the jargon words that are not included in our knowledge source require meaning for users of text. So that the knowledge source becomes updated as new words occur in the input text and domain experts are required to provide meaning.

The Amharic jargon identification phase is the first phase in the knowledge base component of DSAJWI. The input of the jargon identification phase is a list of tokens passed from the classification phase of the machine learning component. So that the existence of each list of tokens in the input sentence is checked from the knowledge source to extract the meaning of words. Amharic jargon identification phase is used to identify a particular jargon word from the input text hence, AJMRD is the main lexical knowledge source for our identification.

The meaning extraction phase of DSAJWI extracts the meaning of the identified jargon word from the knowledge source. Meaning extraction is performed from the knowledge source when a word is identified as a jargon word. So that for the occurrence of DSAJW in a text of domain, the meaning of the word is extracted. Therefore, Amharic text containing DSAJW with prominent meaningful text is returned to the user.

Over-stemming: though stemming is a challenge for the meaning extraction from the knowledge source, we handle the problem with entering the over-stemmed word.

4   Experiment

4.1   Experiment Setup

We use python version 3.82 programming language for our implementation because Python is the former programming language in the current computing environment and it supports many open-source libraries. We use anaconda distribution and Jupyter notebook editor to work with our experiment. We imported various python libraries that are compatible with our experiment. Domain-specific Amharic jargon word identification has been done with a hybrid approach using the labeled trained corpus and the knowledge source. So that we used machine learning techniques to develop a model with labeled trained corpus and also, we used a knowledge base for meaning extraction.

4.2   Dataset Preparation

Table 1. Dataset prepared for machine learning and knowledge base

Dataset	Machine learning			Knowledge base	
	Training	Testing	Total	Testing	AJMRD
Sentences	832	208	1040	80	–
Jargon word	–	–	–	59	358

The experiments are done with SVM, ANN, and NB machine learning classifiers with the TFIDF feature selection technique. The performance of the ML classifiers is compared with precision, recall, f1-score, and accuracy for the two-way classification (Table 1).

We collected sentences manually from agricultural reports, training manuals, working guidelines, advertisements of product and service delivery processes that contain Amharic agricultural jargon words. Labeled trained corpus was prepared from sentences with and without Amharic agricultural jargon words. We collected 1.04k dataset that comprises jargon and non-jargon words. In this study, the 80/20 split ratio is used for training and testing sets/phases.

We collected 358 domain-specific Amharic agricultural jargon words from different agricultural sources with the help of agricultural domain expert curators to prepare the AJMRD. We randomly prepared a total of 80 test sentences of different lengths for different experiments to test the knowledge base performance.

5 Evaluation

Performance evaluation is required for our developed system to know the effectiveness and efficiency of the system. The performance of the proposed system is evaluated with machine learning to classify the input text as jargony or non-jargony and also, evaluated with the knowledge-based system. The evaluation of the knowledge-based component is based on the capability of the system to extract the meaning of identified jargon words from the predefined explanatory lexical knowledge source. We used precision, recall, f1- score, and accuracy to evaluate the machine learning and knowledge base component of our proposed system [16]. We used precision, recall, f1-score, and accuracy that calculated the correctness and completeness of the test set to evaluate the performance.

5.1 Machine Learning Evaluation

The evaluation of our proposed system on the machine learning component is committed with the comparison of models developed from the machine learning algorithms. We developed machine learning models to select the most likely model for the classification of the input text. So that we selected SVM, ANN, and NB machine learning algorithms to compare the classification result and select the outperformed model. The performance result of three supervised ML models is compared for the same labeled input corpus for the agricultural domain. The same algorithm for feature vector representation with TFIDF vectorizer was employed. The algorithms are compared with precision, recall, f1-score, and accuracy (Table 2).

Table 2. Precision, recall, f1- score result of SVM, ANN, and NB

Performance metrics	Support Vector Machine (SVM)	Artificial Neural Network (ANN)	Naïve Bayes (NB)
Precision	96	95	94
Recall	96	95	94
F1-score	96	95	95
Accuracy	96.2	95.2	94.7

We observed that SVM outperforms the other model. Because of the performance result of the models, SVM is selected to predict the input test data for the knowledge base.

5.2   Knowledge Base Evaluation

The performance evaluation on the knowledge-based component measures the capability of the knowledge-based system to extract the meaning of jargon words for the input text with the AJMRD.

We randomly used a total of 80 test sentences of different lengths for different experiments to test the performance of the knowledge base system with 20, 40, 60, and 80 test sentences. The different lengths of sentences are used to evaluate the performance on the behalf of the number of input test sentences. We performed different experiments to measure the knowledge base performance. For the occurrence of 17 Amharic agricultural jargon words in 20 test sentences, a knowledge base extracts the meaning of jargon words with a performance of 88.2% accuracy. We prepared 40 sentences containing 30 agricultural jargon words, and the meaning of words are extracted with the performance 86.7%. The following figure depicts the number of input test sentences and the performance (Fig. 3).

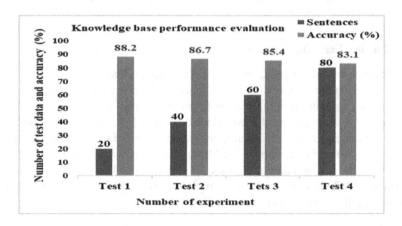

Fig. 3. Performance result of the knowledge base for test 1, test 2, test 3, and test 4

The result of the knowledge base shows as the number of domain-specific Amharic jargon words in the input test sentences and the number of test sentences increases, we observed a decrease rate of performance. Over-stemming on some of the jargon words is committed because of the nature of the word and binary lexical mapping between the over-stemmed jargon word in the input text and the jargon word in the knowledge source is impossible.

6 Discussion

Experimental results described that the hybrid system for DSAJWI is affected by the labeled trained corpus to classify a text as jargony or non-jargony text. The machine learning component of our proposed system minimizes the workload of the knowledge-based system by discarding non-jargon text without entering the knowledge-based system. The developed machine learning model identified the input text as jargony solely entered to the knowledge-based system for further analysis and extraction of meaning. We observed machine learning models predict the input text with 96.2%, 95.2%, and 94.7% accuracy using SVM, ANN, and NB respectively. For the prepared labeled trained data, SVM model outperformed the other developed models because SVM works well for binary classification [17]. We selected SVM for the model testing phase of our proposed system to classify unseen test data as jargony and non-jargony. The knowledge-based component of our proposed system best performs when fewer input sentences are entered into the system. We observed accuracy of 88.2%, 86.7%, 85.4%, and 83.1% for the input of 20, 40, 60, and 80 test sentences respectively.

Therefore, the proposed hybrid system works well for the identification of jargon and non-jargon text. The machine learning model decreases the workload of the knowledge base by discarding non-jargon text from entering the knowledge base system. Texts classified as jargony text are entered into the knowledge-based system. So that for every occurrence of a jargon word in a jargony text, the meaning of the word is extracted from the knowledge source.

7 Conclusion and Future Work

The study focused on the identification of jargon words in a text and provide meaning of words for agriculture domains. We performed operations using both the machine learning and knowledge-based approach. Evaluation of the developed machine learning models are performed and we selected the outperformed model. We have developed models with SVM, ANN, and NB. First, we evaluated the machine learning model and we achieved an accuracy of 96.2%, 95.2%, and 94.7% using SVM, ANN, and NB respectively. We selected the outperformed SVM model.

We observed the best performance of the knowledge-based system for the input of the small number of test sentences. For the input of 20, 40, 60, and 80 test sentences, an accuracy of 88.2%, 86.7%, 85.4%, and 83.1% is observed. So that for a few sentences entered into the knowledge-based system, the best performance of the system is observed. Therefore, we observed the best performance of our proposed system with the knowledge base to extract the meaning of jargon words from the predefined explanatory lexical knowledge source for jargon text with less amount input test data. Therefore, we have achieved a promised result for domain-specific Amharic jargon word identification. In our current study, we only consider Amharic jargon word identification in the agricultural domain with a hybrid of machine learning and knowledge-based. For future work, we are intended to consider other domains in which Amharic is the working language of a domain by increasing features for our proposed system. Additionally, we will compare our result with other techniques inline to provide the meaning of jargon words in a text of domain. The limitation of the proposed system is that the knowledge base is created manually to retrieve meaning. This problem can be alleviated by using other techniques. We recommend for the future, automatic generation of the meaning of domain-specific jargon words in various domains and select best hyperparameter value combination to benefit customers.

Acknowledgment. The routine tasks of this paper are surely granted by the great contribution of agricultural domain experts, erudite, and agrarian society in Ethiopia.

References

1. Sparck Jones, K.: Natural language processing: a historical review. In: Zampolli, A., Calzolari, N., Palmer, M. (eds.) Current Issues in Computational Linguistics: In Honour of Don Walker, pp. 3–16. Springer Netherlands, Dordrecht (1994). https://doi.org/10.1007/978-0-585-35958-8_1

2. Kevitt, P.M., Partridge, D., Wilks, Y.: Approaches to natural language discourse processing. Artif. Intell. Rev. **6**(4), 333–364 (1992). https://doi.org/10.1007/BF00123689

3. Burns, T.W., O'Connor, D.J., Stocklmayer, S.M.: Science communication: a contemporary definition. Public Underst. Sci. **12**(2), 183–202 (2003). https://doi.org/10.1177/09636625030122004

4. Rakedzon, T., Segev, E., Chapnik, N., Yosef, R., Baram-Tsabari, A.: Automatic jargon identifier for scientists engaging with the public and science communication educators. PLoS One **12**(8), 1–13 (2017). https://doi.org/10.1371/journal.pone.0181742

5. Helmreich, S., Llevadias Jané, J., Farwell, D.: Identifying jargon in texts. Identif. Jarg. Texts **35**(35), 425–432 (2005)

6. Ibrahim, M., Gauch, S., Salman, O., Alqahatani, M.: Enriching consumer health vocabulary using enhanced glove word embedding. In: CEUR Workshop Proc., vol. 2619 (2020)

7. Demeke, M., Ferede, T.: Agricultural Development in Ethiopia : Are There Alternatives to Food Aid? (2014)

8. Willoughby, S.D., Johnson, K., Sterman, L.: Quantifying scientific jargon. Public Understand. Sci. **29**(6), 634–643 (2020). https://doi.org/10.1177/0963662520937436

9. Weng, W.H., Chung, Y.A., Szolovits, P.: Unsupervised clinical language translation. In: Proc. ACM SIGKDD Int. Conf. Knowl. Discov. Data Min., pp. 3121–3131 (2019). https://doi.org/10.1145/3292500.3330710

10. Cyr, A.: Social media: don't discount the benefits! Oncol. Times **34**(8), 1–3 (2012). https://doi.org/10.1097/01.COT.0000414683.49317.3b

11. Seyler, D., Liu, W., Wang, X., Zhai, C.: Towards Dark Jargon Interpretation in Underground Forums, pp. 1–8 (2020). Available at: http://arxiv.org/abs/2011.03011

12. Gong, L., Yang, R., Liu, Q., Dong, Z., Chen, H., Yang, G.: A dictionary-based approach for identifying biomedical concepts. Int. J. Pattern Recognit. Artif. Intell. **31**(9), 1–12 (2017). https://doi.org/10.1142/S021800141757004X

13. Hermawan, R.: Natural language processing with python, vol. 1, no. 1 (2011)

14. El-Khair, I.A.: Effects of Stop Words Elimination for Arabic Information Retrieval: A Comparative Study (2006, 2017). Available at: http://arxiv.org/abs/1702.01925

15. Jing, L.P., Huang, H.K., Shi, H.B.: Improved feature selection approach TFIDF in text mining. In: Proc. 2002 Int. Conf. Mach. Learn. Cybern., vol. 2, pp. 944–946 (2002). https://doi.org/10.1109/icmlc.2002.1174522

16. Dalianis, H.: Evaluation metrics and evaluation. In: Dalianis, H. (ed.) Clinical Text Mining, pp. 45–53. Springer International Publishing, Cham (2018). https://doi.org/10.1007/978-3-319-78503-5_6

17. Holts, A., Riquelme, C., Alfaro, R.: Automated text binary classification using machine learning approach. In: Proc. Int. Conf. Chil. Comput. Sci. Soc. SCCC, pp. 212–217 (2010). https://doi.org/10.1109/SCCC.2010.30

Design Event Extraction Model from Amharic Texts Using Deep Learning Approach

Amogne Andualem[1,2(✉)] and Tesfa Tegegne[1,2]

[1] Faculty of Computing, Bahir Dar Institute of Technology, Bahir Dar
University, Bahir Dar, Ethiopia
[2] ICT4D Research Center, Bahir Dar Institute of Technology, Bahir Dar
University, Bahir Dar, Ethiopia

Abstract. Every day, a massive amount of information is reported in the form of video, audio, or text through various media such as television, radio, social media, and web blogs. As the number of unstructured documents on those media has grown, finding relevant information has become more difficult. As a result, extracting relevant events from large amounts of unstructured text data is essential. We proposed an event extraction model, which aims to detect, classify and extract various types of events along with their arguments from Amharic text documents. In this paper, the researchers first come up with Amharic language-specific issues and then proposed Bidirectional Long Short Memory (BiLSTM) with a Word2vec model to detect and classify Amharic events from unstructured documents. To achieve this research 9,050 Amharic documents were used for event detection and extraction purpose. In addition to event detection and classification, the model also extracts event arguments that contain additional information about events such as Time and Place. The experimental results showed that the Bidirectional long short-term memory approach with Word2vec word embedding shows a promising result in terms of Amharic event detection and event classification, with 94% and 89% accuracy, respectively.

Keywords: Natural language processing · Information extraction · Event extraction · Bidirectional long short-term memory · word2vec

1 Introduction

Natural language Processing (NLP) applications aids in the extraction of relevant information from large, unstructured text documents. Event extraction is one of the NLP applications that makes detecting and extracting events and their arguments, as well as classifying and tracking similar events from different texts. Events have many definitions among those the actual or contemplated fact of anything happening or occurrence at a specific time and place [1]. The ideal goal of Event extraction systems in the presence of huge volume digital text in the news, social media, and blogs are to produce the best possible extraction of text events with their arguments with minimal human intervention.

It can be done automatically using Natural Language Processing(NLP) and other machine learning algorithms to extract events with their arguments from text, including

M. L. Berihun (Ed.): ICAST 2021, LNICST 411, pp. 424–434, 2022.
https://doi.org/10.1007/978-3-030-93709-6_28

details on what happened, when it happened, and where it happened [2]. The most important sub tasks of event extraction in the NLP domain include extracting event arguments and identifying their roles, as well as classifying and tracking similar events from different texts. Another important aspect of event extraction is event arguments, which discuss what happened, when it happened, where it happened, and who took part during the occurrence of the event [3]. Event argument extraction is the process of locating incidents that occurred at a specific time and location, extracting a set of properties from those incidents, and converting unstructured texts into a structured representation of those incidents [4]. Currently, this task is performed manually by media analysts, digital news editors, collecting, interpreting, and presenting news from multiple news sources.

This manual task is tedious and time-consuming for journalists and news staff. Amharic event extraction researchers recently used a machine learning algorithm for binary classification and some rule-based techniques for identifying and extracting events in Amharic text documents [5, 6].

2   Related Studies

Due to the wide availability of resources in various European languages, event extraction research has gained popularity in the last decades. Because of the differences in the language's morphological structure, we cannot use the existing techniques and tools developed for other languages without modification for our work.

Until today, several event extractions studies have been developed using machine learning algorithms and deep learning with some limitations. Furthermore, to the best of our knowledge, no deep learning-based event extraction model for Amharic text events has been proposed previously. Besides this, Hordofa in [5] proposed a model for extracting events from Amharic News articles that uses traditional machine learning techniques as a binary classifier and an ontology technique for event detection. However, there are some limitations on this research. (1) some sub-tasks of Event Extraction, such as Argument Role classification and event classification, are not included; (2) handcrafted feature engineering is used as a feature extractor, resulting in incorrect event detection prediction probability. Similar approaches have also been adopted in [6], in this work was related to Amharic event extraction from unstructured Amharic texts using machine learning and a rule-based called hybrid approach. However, in this research, the researchers did not incorporate basic sub-tasks of event element extraction, event classification, and Argument Role classification.

Other than those studies, there has been no other work in Amharic event extraction until today. However, many works on event extraction have been proposed in other resourceful languages such as English, France, and others [7–10]. The majority of research has been focused on detecting, extracting, and matching event slots on predefined templates in domain-specific event extractions [11]. There are several traditional machine learning text classification models that have been employed for text events extraction tasks such as the K-Nearest Neighbor classification algorithm, Support Vector Machine algorithm, Bayesian classification algorithm, Decision Tree, and others have been used.

Before years, many researchers developed many event extraction systems using an unsupervised machine-learning algorithm for Event Detection, Event classification, Argument identification, and argument role classification tasks [15–17]. However, existing machine learning approaches, on the other hand, have a variety of drawbacks for text classification applications. The major flaw in the traditional machine learning approach is it extracts text features using handcrafted rules, which rely heavily on the designer's prior knowledge and make big data use nearly impossible.

Deep learning has a strong nonlinear mapping capability on different NLP application development and is capable of extracting abstract hierarchical features from complex text data [18]. It improves the accuracy of the event detector by checking whether every token in a given input sentence is an event trigger of some pre-defined event type or not using convolutional neural networks (CNN) and recurrent neural networks (RNN) [19].

Recently, many researchers have applied recurrent neural networks to automatically extract different text features such as distribution of words, capture word syntax, and semantics of words from natural language written texts, and improving the performance of event detector and event classifier models [20, 21].

3   Proposed Event Extraction Model

The proposed Amharic Event Extraction Model consists of many subtasks: Dataset Preparation, Preprocessing, Event detection, Event Classification, and Event argument Extraction. The following figure depicts the overall proposed Amharic event extraction model.

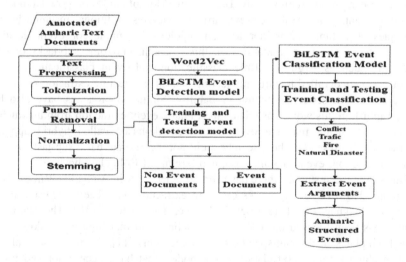

Fig. 1. Proposed Amharic event extraction model

3.1 Dataset Preparation

Data set for Natural Language Processing (NLP) tasks is crucial, specially to train and test the model using traditional machine learning and deep learning approaches. To determine the system's accuracy, event extraction requires a large corpus for training, validation, and testing. For event classification, we focus on disaster and accident data namely fire accident (የእሳት አደጋ), conflict (ግጭት), car accident (የመኪና አደጋ), Natural Disaster (የተፈጥሮ አደጋዎች). All collected Amharic documents were annotated by Amharic language experts using annotation guidelines prepared by the researchers.

3.2 Preprocessing

Data preprocessing is a crucial and fundamental step in the event extraction model development process. Because the Amharic texts collected have a variety of formats and characteristics. To produce structured Amharic texts documents, it is necessary to analyze the collected raw texts using various techniques. Under the preprocessing module the following sub tasks have been performed tokenization, punctuation removal, stop word removal, character normalization, and stemming.

Tokenization. It is the process of identifying all words in a document by using space as the primary separator factor. Furthermore, in the Amharic language writing system, not only space but also Amharic punctuation marks are used to separate words or phrases. To tokenize or convert an Amharic document into a sequence of words, the proposed algorithm used space and other special characters as delimiters.

Remove Punctuations. Amharic language writing system uses different punctuation marks for different purposes. For example, አራት ንጥብ ።(full stop) used for end of the sentence, የጥያቄ ምልክት(?) (question mark) used for interrogative sentences, ነጥላ ሰረዝ ፤(semicolon) used for separate the list object, etc. When the model is being trained, those punctuations in the sentence cause ambiguity. As a result, the developed punctuation removal algorithm removes punctuation from the Amharic text document.

Remove Stop Words. Stop words are extremely common words across document collections that have no discriminatory power from the collection. Amharic stop words have little semantic content in the document, high-frequency words, or highly occurred in the document collection. To avoid those words from the document we prepared 226 Amharic stop word lists. Following that, we proposed an algorithm for removing those words from the training and testing documents.

Character Normalization. There are characters in the Amharic language that have similar roles and redundant in similar words. Such as ኅ, ሀ, ሐand ስ, ሠand አ, ዐand ጸ, ፀare superficial difference along with their sequences. Those character representations may have different meanings in NLP tasks including event extraction. As a result, such inflections must be normalized to a single common character. To avoid this type of inflection, we replaced a set of characters with the same meaning as the most common characters by using the previously proposed normalization algorithm.

Stemming. It is the process of reducing morphological variants to a single root word in natural language processing. It is language-dependent, which means that different stemming techniques are required for each language due to morphological differences. Amharic words can take on a variety of morphologies by adding a prefix, suffix, or infix. As a result, the researchers proposed a rule-based stemmer algorithm by collecting different root words from various domains to address the aforementioned issue by finding their root from the collection and stem the prefix and suffix of a word.

3.3   Word Embedding

As shown in Fig. 1, after completing the text preprocessing module, each word must be numerically valued using appropriate embedding techniques. Words are essential units of letter formed language and sequence of characters like ' በላ' (he ate), ' መጣ' (he came), etc. To understand by machine learning algorithms, each word in a document must be represented as a real-valued vector.

As a result, word embeddings have been successfully used in a variety of natural language processing and it is a vector that not only represents syntactic but also semantic similarities between words in a document [22]. In our study after performed preprocessing steps, we change the word into vector form using Word2vec- Continuous Bag of a Word (CBOW) to use vectors as input for deep learning models called BiLSTM and classify Amharic text events effectively.

We have used 420,910 documents to proposed word2vec word embedding model with 200 Embedding dimensions and other important setups. Amharic Event Detection model

Event detection is a subcomponent of the event extraction model that identifies events in a text document. We proposed a Bidirectional Long Short-Term Memory (BiLSTM) recurrent neural network algorithm to extract context information from an Amharic text sequence. It is a special type of neural network that is proved to be extremely effective in capturing long and short-term dependencies in sequential data in a forward and backward direction.

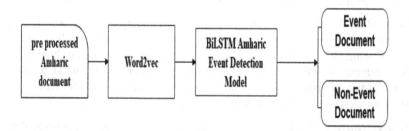

Fig. 2. Event detection model using Bi-LSTM techniques

As shown in Fig. 2, Bi-LSTM binary event classification component, the goal is to determine whether a given input Amharic text document contains an event or not called event detection.

3.4 Amharic Event Classification Model

The event and non-event documents are identified by the event detection model from the previously mentioned BiLSTM based event detection model. The outputs of the Bi-LSTM layer are merged and combined into a single matrix and passed to the fully connected layer. In Bi-LSTM independent event classification model takes events for the BiLSTM event detection model and classify events in the four predefined event type such as traffic (ትራፊክ), fire (እሳት), conflict (ግጭት), and natural disaster (የተፈጥሮ አደጋዎች).

3.5 Event and Event Argument Extraction

As we mentioned above Event extraction has many components including event detection, event classification, and event Argument identification. Event Arguments are an important component of event extraction, discussing what happened, and when the event happened. The event arguments, on the other hand, are another component of the event that provides additional information about the event. For our study, we created a predefined list of all possible values of a named entity, referred to as a gazetteer. Using Named Entity Recognition, the model uses some specific rules to identify and extract arguments from the input Amharic text.

3.6 Event Extraction Experiment and Results

The word embedding, event detection, and event classification models are all sub-components of the proposed EE model, and they were all evaluated using appropriate evaluation metrics. For the Word2vec word embedding model, both the Continuous Bag of Words and the Skip-gram models were evaluated, and the CBOW model performed better, so it was used from each embedding layer of the event detection and classification model. For the event detection and event classification model we used precision, Recall, F1-score, and Accuracy as evaluation metrics and compare the three popular deep learning text classifier algorithms such as convolutional neural network (CNN), Long short-term memory (LSTM), and Bidirectional long short-term memory (BiLSTM).

3.7 Event Detection Model Experimental Results

We used 9,050 Amharic data sets for Event detection training and testing phase. The total data set were preprocessed and split into training, validation, and test sets. The training set is composed of 7,318 (80%) sentences, the validation set consists of 813 (10%) sentences, and the test set contains 919 (10%). By using zero post padded techniques, each sentence has a sequence length of 50 tokens. In the embedding layer used designed CBOW word embedding with 200 dimensions. The detailed experiment result from the BiLSTM with Word2vec Event detection and Classification model is discussed in the following table (Tables 1 and 2) respectively.

Table 1. BiLSTM event detection model evaluation result

Document size		Class	Evaluation metrics with Result		
			Precision	Recall	F-score
Training data	7,318	Event	0.93	0.97	0.95
Validation data	813	None event	0.97	0.90	0.93
Testing data	919	Testing accuracy			**94%**

To achieve the best model performance, we have changed the hyperparameter values that have a significant impact on our models, such as dropout value (0.4), optimizer (Adam), and learning rate values (0.001), Batch Size (128), number of epoch (20) and those values of each hyperparameter achieve the optimal performance value of the proposed Amharic Event detection model. Finally, as shown in the graph below, we trained the model to achieve optimal training and validation accuracy. One of the challenges we faced when training the model is avoiding overfitting between training and validation accuracy.

To solve such a problem, we used the dropout regularization technique that prevents neural networks from overfitting problems by modifying the cost function of the dropout value.

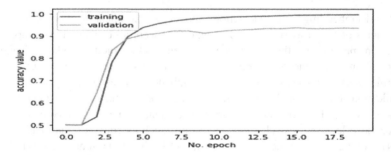

Fig. 3. Training and validation Accuracy graph

The above figure (Fig. 3) depicts that, the training and validation accuracy increase from one epoch to the next epoch. This shows that the model learns more Amharic event features from one epoch to the others. The following graph also shows that how to minimize the loss value from one epoch to the next epoch.

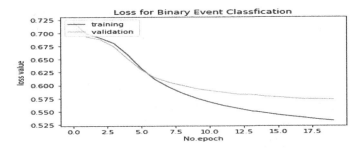

Fig. 4. Training and validation Loss from event detection BiLSTM model

The above figure (Fig. 4), shows the loss value of both validation and training is decreasing from one epoch to the next epoch. This graph shows that the event detection model learns more features from each epoch during the training phase and detect the input sentence without overfitting and underfitting problem.

3.8 Event Classification Model Experimental Results

The output of the BiLSTM event detection model is fed into another BiLSTM model, which identifies event types like traffic accidents, fire accidents, conflicts, and natural disaster accidents. On the training set, we begin training the BiLSTM classification model with four event classes label datasets. The dataset distribution for Amharic event classification experiment is shown in the diagram below (Fig. 5).

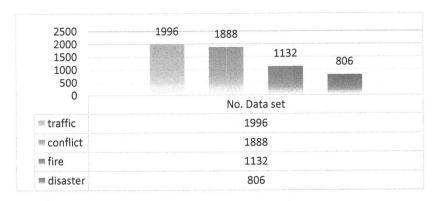

Fig. 5. Dataset distribution for event classification

This event classification experiment used a total dataset of 5815 event data as input to the BiLSTM event classification model. From the total data set, 4,159 used for training, 462 for validation, and 1194 were used for testing purposes. The distribution of the dataset over four classes as traffic (ትራፊክ), fire (እሳት), conflict (ግጭት), Natural Disasters (የተፈጥሮ አደጋዎች). The data was split 80% for training, 10% for validation, and 10% for testing the splitting ratio.

Finally, we combined BiLSTM deep learning Amharic event classification with CBOW word embedding and found that the predicted model performed well, as shown in the table below.

Table 2. BiLSTM event classification experimental result

Class	Label	Precision	Recall	F-score
Traffic accident	0	0.94	0.88	0.92
Conflict	1	0.89	0.90	0.92
Fire	2	0.92	0.91	0.91
Natural disaster	3	0.79	0.84	0.78
Testing accuracy	89%			

The following figure (Fig. 6) shows that, the training and validation accuracy improves from one epoch to the next epochs.

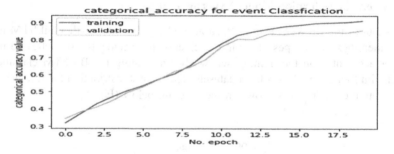

Fig. 6. Training and validation accuracy for BiLSTM event classification model

The last sub-component of event extraction, as mentioned in the previous section, is event argument extraction. In this paper, we develop a rule for extracting event arguments such as location and time. The rule can take an Amharic sentence or document as input, analyze each token, and then extract event arguments from the input document automatically.

After the three extensive experiments of the proposed model for Amharic event extraction, we observe that the BiLSTM with Word2vec outperforms the best result when comparing the other selected deep learning techniques LSTM and CNN.

4 Conclusion

The problem of event extraction for Amharic texts has been addressed in this paper. We proposed a BiLSTM deep learning approach for Amharic event detection and classification that can capture text contextual information. For the BiLSTM embedding layer, we used a proper text preprocessing technique and proposed the word2vec word embedding model. The event detector model also detects events, and the classification model categorizes them into pre-defined categories like traffic accidents, conflict, fire, and natural disasters. To evaluate the performance of the proposed Amharic event extraction model, experiments are conducted on both event detection and classification of Amharic text data sets. The experiments show that BiLSTM combined with Word2vec is effective for both event detection and classification. In this study, the BiLSTM-word2vec model was compared to some current state-of-the-art deep learning methods.

The proposed model can detect events in the Amharic testing data set 82%, 83%, 92%, 94.2%, LSTM, CNN, BiLSTM and Word2vec BiLSTM respectively. Another proposed event classification model can classify events in the Amharic testing dataset 81%, 78%, 87.6%, and 89.4% for, CNN, LSTM, BiLSTM, and Word2vec-BiLSTM respectively. This may have an impact on the event extraction model. We also plan to propose an event extraction model that includes an Amharic grammar checker as well as a subcomponent called Name Entities Recognition (NER).

References

1. Polakof, A.C.: Why are events, facts, and states of affairs different? Disputatio **9**(44), 99–122 (2017). https://doi.org/10.2478/disp-2017-0029
2. Zhou, D., Chen, L., He, Y.: A simple Bayesian modelling approach to event extraction from Twitter. 52nd Annu. Meet. Assoc. Comput. Linguist. ACL 2014 - Proc. Conf., vol. 2, pp. 700–705 (2014). https://doi.org/10.3115/v1/p14-2114
3. Sahoo, S.K., Saha, S., Ekbal, A., Bhattacharyya, P.: A platform for event extraction in hindi. Proc. 12th Conf. Lang. Resour. Eval. (LREC 2020), no. May, pp. 11–16 (2020)
4. Petroni, F., et al.: An extensible event extraction system with cross-media event resolution. Proc. ACM SIGKDD Int. Conf. Knowl. Discov. Data Min., pp. 626–635, (2018). https://doi.org/10.1145/3219819.3219827
5. Hordofa, B.A.: Event extraction and representation model from news articles. **16** (3, 1–8 (2020)
6. Tadesse, E., Aga, R.T., Qaqqabaa, K.: Event extraction from unstructured amharic text. no. May, pp. 2103–2109 (2020)
7. Nguyen, V.Q., Anh, T.N., Yang, H.J.: Real-time event detection using recurrent neural network in social sensors. Int. J. Distrib. Sens. Networks **15**, 6 (2019). https://doi.org/10.1177/1550147719856492
8. Björne, J., Salakoski, T.: Biomedical event extraction using convolutional neural networks and dependency parsing. 98–108 (2019). https://doi.org/10.18653/v1/w18-2311
9. Huang, L., et al.: Liberal event extraction and event schema induction. 54th Annu. Meet. Assoc. Comput. Linguist. ACL 2016 - Long Pap., vol. 1, pp. 258–268 (2016). https://doi.org/10.18653/v1/p16-1025
10. Zhang, Y., Liu, Z., Zhou, W.: Event recognition based on deep learning in Chinese texts. PLoS ONE **11**(8), 1–18 (2016). https://doi.org/10.1371/journal.pone.0160147
11. Wang, W., Ning, Y., Rangwala, H., Ramakrishnan, N.: A multiple instance learning framework for identifying key sentences and detecting events. Int. Conf. Inf. Knowl. Manag. Proc., vol. 24–28-Octo, pp. 509–518 (2016). https://doi.org/10.1145/2983323.2983821

12. Ji, H., Grishman, R.: Refining event extraction through cross-document inference. ACL-08 HLT – 46th Annu. Meet. Assoc. Comput. Linguist. Hum. Lang. Technol. Proc. Conf., no. June, pp. 254–262 (2008)
13. Sahnoun, S., Elloumi, S., Yahia, S.B.: Event Detection Based on Open Information Extraction and Ontology. In: Nguyen, N.T., Chbeir, R., Exposito, E., Aniorté, P., Trawiński, B. (eds.) ICCCI 2019. LNCS (LNAI), vol. 11683, pp. 244–255. Springer, Cham (2019). https://doi.org/10.1007/978-3-030-28377-3_20
14. Ribeiro, S., Ferret, O., Tannier, X.:. Unsupervised event clustering and aggregation from newswire and web articles. pp. 62–67 (2018). https://doi.org/10.18653/v1/w17-4211
15. Zhou, D., Chen, L., He, Y.: An unsupervised framework of exploring events on Twitter: filtering, extraction and categorization. Proc. Natl. Conf. Artif. Intell. **3**, 2468–2474 (2015)
16. Valenzuela-Escárcega, M.A., Hahn-Powell, G., Hicks, T., Surdeanu, M.: A domain-independent rule-based framework for event extraction. ACL-IJCNLP 2015 – 53rd Annu. Meet. Assoc. Comput. Linguist. 7th Int. Jt. Conf. Nat. Lang. Process. Proc. Syst. Demonstr. pp. 127–132 (2015). https://doi.org/10.3115/v1/p15-4022
17. Miwa, M., Thompson, P., Korkontzelos, I., Ananiadou, S.: Comparable study of event extraction in newswire and biomedical domains. COLING 2014 – 25th Int. Conf. Comput. Linguist. Proc. COLING 2014 Tech. Pap. pp. 2270–2279 (2014)
18. Minaee, S., Kalchbrenner, N., Cambria, E., Nikzad, N., Chenaghlu, M., Gao, J.: Deep learning based text classification: a comprehensive review. arXiv, 1(1), pp. 1–43 (2020)
19. Nguyen T.H., Grishman, R. Modeling skip-grams for event detection with convolutional neural networks. EMNLP 2016 – Conf. Empir. Methods Nat. Lang. Process. Proc. no. January, pp. 886–891 (2016). https://doi.org/10.18653/v1/d16-1085
20. Nguyen, T.H., Fu, L., Cho, K., Grishman, R.: A two-stage approach for extending event detection to new types via neural networks. pp. 158–165 (2016) https://doi.org/10.18653/v1/w16-1618
21. Nguyen, T.H., Cho, K., Grishman, R.: Joint event extraction via recurrent neural networks. 2016 Conf. North Am. Chapter Assoc. Comput. Linguist. Hum. Lang. Technol. NAACL HLT 2016 – Proc. Conf. pp. 300–309 (2016). https://doi.org/10.18653/v1/n16-1034
22. Ma, J., Wang, S.: Resource–Enhanced Neural Model for Event Argument Extraction (2018)

Identification of Nonfunctional Requirement Conflicts: Machine Learning Approach

Getasew Abeba[1]([✉]) and Esubalew Alemneh[2]

[1] Faculty of Computing,
Bahir Dar Institute of Technology, Bahir Dar University, Bahir Dar, Ethiopia
Getasew.abeba@wldu.edu.et
[2] ICT4D Research Center,
Bahir Dar Institute of Technology, Bahir Dar University, Bahir Dar, Ethiopia
esubalew.alemneh@bdu.edu.et

Abstract. The most common causes of software failure in system development are requirements issues. One of these issues is requirement conflicts, which results in expensive costs and a long development time. This is because contradicting requirements make it difficult to design, test, and maintain a software system, which almost always results in software failure. Using manual and semi-automated methods, many researchers attempted to overcome the challenge of detecting conflicting requirements. We've suggested a machine learning-based model for detecting conflicts between non-functional requirements in a Software Requirement Specification (SRS) document. To build the model for identifying non-functional requirement conflicts; text preprocessing, vectorization, and classification are included. The text from the document is preprocessed into a series of words using natural language processing (NLP). Then, using vectorization techniques to give words weight, a series of words are stored in numeric representation and utilized as input for classification algorithms. The prepared dataset is used to test traditional machine learning and deep learning classification techniques. Bi-LSTM with pre-trained SO word2vec embedding performs 84.74% accurately, according to a comparative experimental investigation. Future research directions in the problem domain include identifying the relationship between quality attributes and resolving nonfunctional requirements conflict through experiments.

Keywords: Nonfunctional requirements · Requirement conflict · Machine learning · Conflict catalog · Natural language processing (NLP) · Pre-trained so word2vec embedding

1 Introduction

Non-functional requirements (NFRs) must be considered in software projects to deliver a system that meets the needs of its users [1]. NFRs are the specifications that define the level of quality that a software system must meet [2]. System restrictions, company business rules, quality attributes, and any other requirements that do not specify the system's operation are all included in NFRs [2]. Even if functional requirements are well-documented, many software systems have failed due to a poor set of quality

M. L. Berihun (Ed.): ICAST 2021, LNICST 411, pp. 435–445, 2022.
https://doi.org/10.1007/978-3-030-93709-6_29

attribute criteria [3]. Requirement conflicts are one of the most common causes of software project failure [4]. Non-functional requirements represent a software system's efficiency and effectiveness in completing a task [5].

The relationship between requirements that can result in a negative or unwanted outcome of the system is known as requirement conflict [6]. The three core actions of NFR conflict management are conflict identification, conflict analysis, and conflict resolution [7]. Identifying or detecting a possible conflict is the goal of conflict identification. The goal of conflict analysis is to assess and examine the risk of a conflict. The goal of conflict resolution is to avoid a possible conflict [7]. Different reasons cause conflicts between stakeholders' requirements. Those are:

- The large size of requirements can lead to conflicts in NFR.
- The occurrence of one NFR affects the other NFR
- Complex system domains can lead to a misunderstanding of requirements.
- The system has different stakeholders with diverse interests that usually interact with each other and cause conflicts [8].

The model's performance is affected by the different types of conflict. As a result, the focus of this study is on detecting tradeoffs between quality attributes. A tradeoff is a decision that entails sacrificing one component of a system design in exchange for improvements in other areas [1].

Shah [11] has just published research on building a knowledge-based Quality Attributes Relationship Matrix to Identify Conflicts in Non-functional Requirements. This study uses NLP to identify quality attributes features in a document and rule-based techniques to classify the conflict status of the retrieved quality attributes sub-features. To classify the conflicted relationship, the rules in this study used catalogs or quality attribute relationship matrix (QARM) from the literature. Similarity measures combining string similarity and ontology-based semantic similarity are used to describe the weight for the quality attribute feature. To classify conflict relationships, the rule used a similarity measure value. The conflicting relationship that depends on the similarity measure of terms in a sentence is the problem of this study. The rule used to classify conflict situations is static. As a result, static rules are predetermined and cannot learn new requirement correlations from data.

2   Related Works

Different literature [5, 7] clearly describes the presence of conflict in NFRs and its impact on system growth. Although many academics are attempting to identify conflicts, create a catalog of conflict relationships, and resolve conflict, it remains a hot study subject due to the unavoidable occurrence of conflict in non-functional requirements.

The literature in this domain mainly differs in terms of conflict management strategy, application domain, and scope. The literature may utilize a manual, automated, or general framework, depending on the technique. Manual procedures involve stakeholders and software engineers manually negotiating, discussing, and analyzing requirements to identify any conflicts [3]. The alternative option is to use software tools to automatically identify NFR conflicts. Some researchers look for functional requirement conflict, while others look for non-functional requirement conflict, depending on the type of requirement. Some researchers are attempting to apply for both functional and non-functional positions. As a result, we attempted to describe literature only under the scope of conflict identification for non-functional requirements in this study.

Mairiza et al. [2], has Proposed To manage the conflicts between security and usability requirements, the researcher suggested an ontological framework called Security-usability requirement conflicts management (sureCM). Lists of conflicts, the nature of the conflict based on the influence of the conflicts on different components in software development, and a conflict resolution approach are the system's outputs. SureCM is a framework for identifying and characterizing conflicts between security and usability criteria, as well as determining the best strategy for resolving those conflicts. This research identifies a catalog for conflict between the subcategory of usability and security requirements. The gaps in this research are that it is not scalable, manual-based and it is not evaluated.

Liu et al. [10], proposed a conflict detector in non-functional requirement evolution (CDNFRE) system that uses ontologies as a theoretical foundation for automatically detecting conflicts. Metadata of requirements, conflict detection rules, and conflict detection processes are described for the CDNFRE tool. The integration of ontology and rule in this research is used to identify conflict in non-functional requirements using the CDNFRE tool. The gaps in this research are scalability of the identification which means limited to pre-defined ontology and rules. And also, this research mainly solves conflict that happens as a result of semantic inconsistency of requirements, but it is difficult to identify tradeoffs which means interference of requirements when applying both at the same time.

Aldekhail and Ziani [9], proposed an approach that works at two levels; a rule-based system to detect the conflicts in functional requirements, and the application of a genetic algorithm to resolve conflicts and optimize the set of functional requirements to produce minimum conflicts. The gaps in this research are rule-based approaches are deterministic, cannot learn from the data, used for only functional requirements, and not evaluated with different requirements.

3 Methodology

We employed experimental approaches in our study, which are widely used in computing science. To evaluate innovative solutions to challenges, this methodology incorporates two phases. The first phase is the exploratory phase, during which the researcher collects data to assist determine what questions should be answered about the system being evaluated. These questions were then answered in the second step, which was the evaluation phase. A well-designed experiment begins with a list of questions to be answered by the experiment [12]. To assess the research, we used an experimental method.

3.1 Dataset Preparation

The NFR dataset used in this study relates to quality attributes in the SRS document that conflict with one another. Quality attribute tradeoffs are the problem that this research automates using NLP and machine learning classification techniques, even if the nature of the NFR conflict is different. The NFR dataset used in this study relates to quality attributes in the SRS document that conflict with one another. To prepare the dataset different tasks are done.

- Identifies the research's main and sub-quality attributes.
- The catalog of main quality attribute relationships is identified.
- Identify sub-quality attribute relations from various works of literature if the relationship of attributes is relative conflict.
- For each sub-quality attribute, build NFRs.
- Prepare a dataset of a pair of NFRs, then use the catalog to determine whether they conflict or not.
- Individual NFR conflicts from various studies are being identified to improve the dataset quality.

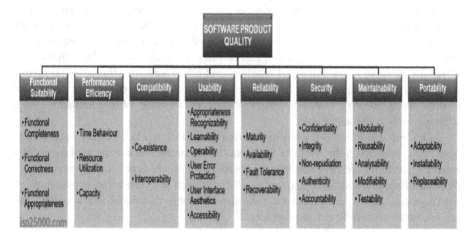

Fig. 1. ISO 25010 quality attribute model [13]

Quality Attributes: For requirement engineering, there are a variety of quality attribute models that identify and define quality attributes. The latest ISO/IEC 25010 model is utilized to identify the major and sub-quality criteria in this study. As a result, all main and sub-quality attribute conflicts are taken into account in this study. Figure 1 shows the ISO/IEC 25010 model.

Conflict Catalog: The Conflict Catalog is the primary source for determining whether NFRs conflict or not. It is based on the most up-to-date conflict relationships between quality and sub-quality attributes. The relationship is described by absolute conflict, relative conflict, and never conflict in the most recent catalog of NFRs [2]. As a result, the absolute conflict relationship indicates that the two NFRs are always in conflict, requiring prioritizing and a conflict resolution technique. Conflicting requirements are defined as any pair of NFRs that are incompatible. Quality attributes that are in relative conflict, but not always, are called relative conflict quality attributes. It's difficult to tell if this kind of conflict relationship is conflicting or not. As a result, conflict interactions are labeled based on the relationship between sub-quality attributes. Never conflict quality attributes are supposed to be conflict-free at all times.

Prepare NFRs for Each of the Sub-quality Attributes: The NFR statements for the dataset are prepared for each sub-quality attribute. Because the relationships of NFRs are between sub-qualities attributes. After preparing NFR statements for each sub-quality attribute, the relation is labeled based on the catalog of relationships. In this research NFR statements for main quality attributes select from an official tera-promise dataset. Some sub-quality attribute statements select from the tera-promise dataset based on the definition of sub-quality attributes.

Identifying Statement-Level NFR Conflicts from Literature: Most of the dataset is finally labeled based on catalogs. But to improve the quality of the dataset we gather available examples of conflicts from different literature.

3.2   The Proposed Model

The model for NFR conflict Identification has the following architecture (Fig. 2).

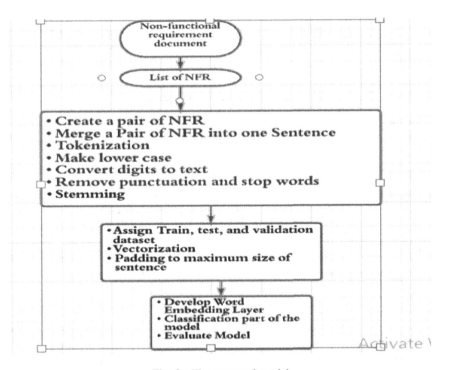

Fig. 2. The proposed model

3.3   Dataset Preprocessing

The textual dataset used in our model is not directly analyzed by the classification techniques [14]. So, the data must be preprocessed to remove noise, and easily accessed by the classification techniques. So, convert the text to lowercase, remove punctuation, tokenization, convert a numeric value to text, remove stop words and steaming the word, and split train, test, and validation data.

Tokenization: Tokenizing separate text into units such as sentences or words [14]. It gives structure to previously unstructured text. The feature selection algorithm vectorizes the word based on different weighting techniques. To do this the sentence must be tokenized into words. We used Punkt tokenizer to remove punctuation and tokenize sentences to words.

Converting Texts to Lowercase: Converting texts to lowercase is important because cases affect the data representation [14].

Remove Stopwords: Stopwords are common words that will likely appear in any text [14]. They don't tell us much about our data so we remove them.

Converting Numerical Value to Text: Since numeric values are significant for our model, we change them to text.

Stemming: To reduce similar words that have the same meaning in the model, we use the steaming approach to reduce the corpus of words but often the actual words get neglected.

3.4   Vectorization and Feature Weighting Techniques

Vectorizing is the process of encoding text to integer i.e., numeric form to create feature vectors [14]. So that machine learning algorithms can understand our data. The machine or deep learning algorithms can only accept inputs in the form of numeric values. So, in this research, we use two ways of encoding.

Vectorizing Data Using TF-IDF: It computes the "relative frequency" that a word appears in a document compared to its frequency across all documents [14]. It is more useful than "term frequency" for identifying "important" words in each document (high frequency in that document, low frequency in other documents). But it cannot understand the semantic of the word at the time of encoding. We implement this encoding with traditional machine learning classification algorithms (SVM, KNN, NB).

Word Embeddings: This method represents words as dense word vectors (also called word embeddings) [14]. The word embeddings collect more information into fewer dimensions. Note that the word embedding does not understand the text as a human would, but rather maps the statistical structure of the language used in the corpus. They aim to map semantic meaning into a geometric space. This geometric space is then called the embedding space [14]. This would map semantically similar words close to the embedding space like numbers. We use Kara's built-in word embedding and the pre-trained word2vec model we used to be SO word2vec from Word Embeddings for the Software Engineering Domain [15]. The SO word2vec is developed for software engineering research word embedding techniques. A pre-trained word embedding model is selected, then the model needs to be loaded into the system from the external model file. We use Genism's Keyed Vectors implementation to load a model into a common lookup table format.

3.5 Classification Model

The classification portion of the model began once the dataset had been prepared, preprocessed, and vectorized. The numerical encoding weight of each word in a sentence pad with the longest sentence in the dataset is used as the model's input. We used text to sequence, count vectorizer plus tfidf weighting, and a pre-trained word2vec model (SO word2vec) as input to traditional machine learning classification algorithms (NB (nave Bayes), SVM (support vector machine), KNN (K-nearest neighbor)), and deep learning classification models (CNN (convolutional neural network), LSTM (long short-term memory), BI-LSTM (bi-directional long short-term memory)).

In this research, shallow machine learning models like K-Nearest Neighbors, Naive Bayes, and Support Vector Machines Classifier using python and scikit-learn are implemented with TF-IDF vectorizer. Naive Bayes simplifies the calculation of probabilities by assuming that the probability of each attribute belonging to a given class value is independent of all other attributes. This is a strong assumption but results in a fast and effective method. KNN Algorithm is based on feature similarity: choosing the right value of k is a process called parameter tuning, and is important for better accuracy. The k-nearest neighbor's algorithm uses a very simple approach to perform classification. When tested with a new instance, it looks through the training data and finds the k training instance that is closest to the new instance. It then assigns the most common class label (among those k-training instances) to the test instance.

CNN, LSTM, and Bi-LSTM deep learning classification models are constructed using Keras embedding and pre-trained word2vec embedding.

4 Experiment and Evaluation

The reason behind comparing all recent classification and embedding algorithms is that the best-performing algorithm depends on the behavior of the dataset [16].

4.1 Experimental Setup

Various tools are required to create the model, as explained in the methodology section. TensorFlow, NLTK, Scikit-Learn, and Genism are the key packages installed in the Anaconda environment, which also includes Jupiter notebook editors.

4.2 Dataset Setup

A total of 200 NFR statements were evaluated in this experiment. The sentence is a collection of the ISO/IEC 25010 model's sub-quality attributes. There are a total of 11,753 statement pairs when all 200 requirements are combined. The pair of statements is labeled using sub-quality attribute catalogs from several sources. To improve the dataset's quality, 50 pairs of contradictory requirements were collected from the literature. The data is manually split to train and test data. The validation data is split from data using a train_test_split () method. There is no optimal split percentage for train, test, and validation data, but we use the recommended percentage of 70% for train, 20% for a test, and 10% for validation [14].

4.3 Discussion and Result

The experiments that are done in this research to solve the research objective are.

- SVM, KNN, and NB classifier with TF-IDF vectorizer
- CNN, LSTM, and Bi-LSTM classifier with Keras embedding
- CNN, LSTM, and Bi-LSTM classifier with SO word2vec embedding

NFR conflict identification using machine learning with TF-IDF vectorization comparison results:

Table 1. Machine learning experiment output

Classification techniques	Precision	Recall	F1 score
SVM with TFIDF	71%	72%	72%
NB with TFIDF	68%	68%	68%
KNN with TFIDF	68%	68%	68%

When comparing the classification performance of machine learning algorithms, SVM came out on top in binary classification tasks [17, 18]. The experimental outcome in our dataset likewise reveals that SVM has the best F1 score of 72%.

Conflict identification model using deep learning techniques comparison results:

Table 2. Deep learning classification result

Classification techniques	Testing accuracy
CNN with Keras Embedding	81%
CNN with SO word2vec Embedding	79.82%
LSTM with Keras Embedding	83.33%
LSTM with SO word2vec Embedding	84%
Bi-LSTM with Keras Embedding	82.23%
Bi-LSTM with SO word2vec Embedding	84.74%

Bi-LSTM classifier with SO word2vec embedding Model Accuracy Graph.

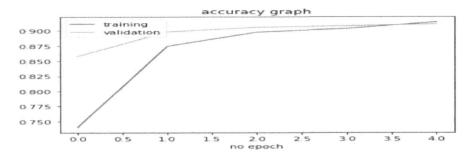

Fig. 3. Bi-LSTM with SO W2V accuracy graph

Bi-LSTM classifier with SO word2vec embedding Model Loss Graph.

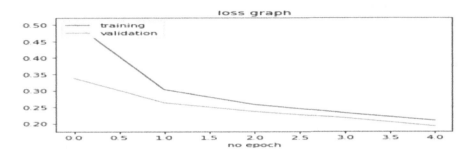

Fig. 4. Bi-LSTM with SO W2V loss graph

With large datasets, deep learning algorithms outperform shallow machine learning techniques in terms of accuracy [19]. According to the quantitative experimental comparison, deep learning techniques outperform shallow machine learning approaches. With an accuracy of 84.74%, Bi-LSTM with SO word2vec outperforms all other tests.

Because bi-LSTM is a sequence processing model that consists of two LSTMs, one of which takes the input in a forward direction and the other in a backward direction, it outperforms. Furthermore, Bi-LSTMs efficiently increase the amount of data supplied to the network, hence improving the content of the algorithm [18].

Because SO word2vec has 15 GB of rich textual data and can transform words to vectors, it performs best. This allows the researchers to learn about software engineering terminology from big vocabularies [15].

5   Conclusions

Conflicts in nonfunctional requirements have a significant impact on the successful development of systems. Numerous researchers attempted to solve the problem, but there is still no method for automatically detecting conflicts in SRS documents. In recent research, NFR conflict identification can identify only attributes from a document and uses a knowledge base to identify conflicts. This automatic method of identifying conflicts only identifies a pair of requirements based on a predetermined rule. Techniques based on rules are predetermined. As a result, the techniques are not scalable or adaptable to new NFR conflict identification needs. In this study, we solved the previous research's NFR conflict identification problem by using NLP for preprocessing tasks and a machine learning classification algorithm to predict the relationship. We designed a proposed model architecture that incorporates preprocessing, vectorization, and classification tasks. Following comparative experimental results, Bi-LSTM with pre-trained SO word2vec outperforms with an accuracy of 84.74%.

6   Contributions

The main contributions of this study are:

- The labeled dataset of a pair of NFRs conflict relationship
- We develop NFR conflict identification model using machine learning-based feature selection and classification algorithms.
- Models and datasets are used as input for next-level research areas (conflict resolution, testing, etc.).
- How to build a model for conflict identification is also used as knowledge for the research community.

7   Recommendations

We recommend, preparing a large vocabulary dataset and performing an experimental analysis of different algorithms improves the model's performance. It is also preferable to include other conflict characteristics, such as semantic inconsistency. Working on experimental analysis for sub-quality attributes and identifying catalogs for the relationships is also a good research area due to the limited number of catalogs. It is also possible to research by broadening this research into conflict analysis and resolution.

References

1. Zhang, X., Wang, X.: Tradeoff analysis for conflicting software non-functional requirements. IEEE Access **7**, 156463–156475 (2019). https://doi.org/10.1109/ACCESS.2019.2949218
2. Mairiza, D., Zowghi, D., Nurmuliani, N.: Non-Functional Requirements, pp. 20–29 (2010)
3. Boehm, H.I.B.: Identifying requirement conflicts (1996)

4. Butt, W.H., Amjad, S., Azam, F.: Requirement Conflicts Resolution : Using Requirement Filtering and Analysis, pp. 383–397 (2011)
5. Xu, L., Ziv, H., Alspaugh, T.A., Richardson, D.J.: An architectural pattern for non-functional dependability requirements. J. Syst. Softw. **79**(10), 1370–1378 (2006). https://doi.org/10.1016/j.jss.2006.02.061
6. Kim, M., Park, S.: Managing requirements conflicts in software product lines : a goal and scenario-based approach. **61**, 417–432 (2007). https://doi.org/10.1016/j.datak.2006.06.009
7. Mairiza, D., Zowghi, D., Nurmuliani, N.: Managing Conflicts among Non-Functional Requirements, pp. 11–19 (2007)
8. Alkubaisy, D.: A Framework Managing Conflicts between Security and Privacy Requirements. (February 2018) https://doi.org/10.1109/RCIS.2017.7956571
9. Aldekhail, M., Ziani, D.: Intelligent method for software requirement conflicts identification and removal : proposed framework and analysis. **17**(12), 91–98 (2017)
10. Liu, C.: Computer standards & interfaces CDNFRE: con fl ict detector in non-functional requirement evolution based on ontologies. Comput. Stand. Interfaces **47**, 62–76 (2016). https://doi.org/10.1016/j.csi.2016.03.002
11. Shah, U.: Constructing a Knowledge-Based Quality Attributes Relationship Matrix to Identify Conflicts in Non- Functional Requirements (2018)
12. Williams, N.: Non-Representational Theory Why Do Experiments ? Experimental Design : Overview (2020)
13. Estdale, J., Georgiadou, E.: Applying the ISO/IEC 25010 quality models to software product. In: Communications in Computer and Information Science. vol. 896, pp. 492–503. (2018) https://doi.org/10.1007/978-3-319-97925-0_42.
14. Sarkar, D.: Text Analytics with Python (2019)
15. Efstathiou, V., Chatzilenas, C., Spinellis, D.: Word Embeddings for the Software Engineering Domain, pp. 38–41 (2018)
16. Sakr, S., et al.: Comparison of machine learning techniques to predict all-cause mortality using fitness data: the henry ford exercise testing (FIT) project. BMC Med. Inform. Decis. Mak. **17**(1), 1–15 (2017). https://doi.org/10.1186/s12911-017-0566-6
17. Huang, S., Nianguang, C.A.I., Penzuti Pacheco, P., Narandes, S., Wang, Y., Wayne, X.U.: Applications of support vector machine (SVM) learning in cancer genomics. Cancer Genomics and Proteomics. **15**(1), 41–51 (2018). https://doi.org/10.21873/cgp.20063
18. Mandal, A, Nigam, M.K.: Comparison between SVM & other classifiers for SER. **1**(10), 46–54 (2018)
19. Menger, V.: Applied Sciences Comparing Deep Learning and Classical Machine Learning Approaches for Predicting Inpatient Violence Incidents from Clinical Text (2018). https://doi.org/10.3390/app8060981

A Survey of Stroke Image Analysis Techniques

Henok Yared Agizew[1] and Asrat Mulatu Beyene[1,2(✉)]

[1] AI & Robotics CoE, Addis Ababa Science and Technology University,
Addis Ababa, Ethiopia
asrat.mulatu@aastu.edu.et
[2] Department of Electrical and Computer Engineering, Addis Ababa Science
and Technology University, Addis Ababa, Ethiopia

Abstract. Stroke is one of the instantaneously shocking and spiking cerebrovascular diseases having substantial residual effects. Image analysis techniques have the ability to diagnosing and providing proper treatment for stroke patients. To lighten the problem, various techniques of image analysis have been proposed. Thus, this survey intended to analyze these proposed image analysis approaches intending to thoroughly examine the state-of-the-art image analysis techniques. To prepare this survey, the systematic literature review method was employed. Based on the reviewed literature, several clinical and biological image datasets are found to be used in the process of stroke diagnosis. However, there are very few publicly accessible datasets are available currently. In this survey, each image analysis technique used for stroke image analysis processes is briefly discussed. Finally, open research challenges are identified that could be addressed in the future.

Keywords: Image analysis · Systematic literature review · Stroke image analysis

1 Introduction

Stroke is one of instantaneously shocking and spiking cerebrovascular diseases having substantial residual effects. Globally, 15 million people suffer from stroke each year [1]. Among these, five million die and another five million are left permanently disabled placing a burden on family and community. Stroke is also one of the publicly and widely known reason for death and disability around the globe [2]. The stroke burden in Africa, including Ethiopia, is likely to increase because of demographic changes and the inadequate control of major risk factors for stroke including hypertension, cardiac disease, obesity, diabetes, and smoking [3]. Basically, the two commonly known types of strokes are Ischemic and Haemorrhagic strokes. When an artery is congested in our brain it causes ischemic stroke. Whereas, a broken blood vessel causes a Haemorrhagic stroke. Recently, the concept of artificial intelligence is being incorporated into many fields, including health and medicine to provide potent tools that aid professional decision making processes. Artificial intelligence techniques such as Machine Learning had become popular tools for inferring medical images to recognize various forms of imaging information rendering medical diagnosis. Thus, we are motivated to provide this comprehensive review of image analysis techniques for stroke diagnosis in terms

M. L. Berihun (Ed.): ICAST 2021, LNICST 411, pp. 446–467, 2022.
https://doi.org/10.1007/978-3-030-93709-6_30

of current efforts and future directions. As a result, the following research questions are identified.

RQ1: How image analysis techniques and modalities are used for stroke imaging?
RQ2: What existing image analysis techniques are applied for stroke imaging?
RQ3: What datasets are available in stroke image analysis?

The main aim of this survey is to identify the state-of-the-art in image analysis techniques as applied in stroke diagnosis and the dataset being used thereof. Specifically,

– To identify and compare the applicability of image analysis techniques and imaging modalities on stroke disease management (diagnosis).
– To analyze and assess the state-of-the-art in image analysis techniques as applied to stroke imaging.
– To find out and show open research challenges for further study.

2 Methodology

This survey work adopted the structured literature review approach to examine the application of image analysis techniques and modalities in stroke diagnosis and management. For finding the entire population of scientific papers that are relevant to the identified research questions, proper searching strategies was employed on six different electronic databases such as Google Scholar, Archivx, IEEE Xplore, Springer, PubMed and Web of Science. The research string patterns used were: ("STROKE DIAGNOSIS") AND ("IMAGING TECHNOLOGIES") AND ("STROKE IMAGE ANALYSIS TECHNIQUES") AND ("IMAGING MODALITIES OR STROKE IMAGING MODALITIES") AND ("APPLICATION OF IMAGE ANALYSIS TECHNIQUES IN STROKE DIAGNOSIS"). Totally the search retrieved 81 papers, among which unduplicated and relevant papers in terms of the research questions are 76. The inclusion and exclusion criteria are summarized in Table 1.

Table.1 Inclusion and exclusion criteria

Inclusion criteria	Exclusion criteria
Type of studies Journals, Conf. Proc., and Book Chapters that are published on peer-review basis	– Short papers, experience reports, summaries of workshops, & papers in the form of abstracts, tutorials, or talks
Documents in the area of stroke image analysis techniques	– Documents in the area of image analysis that do not deal with the techniques
Documents in the area of imaging modalities applied to stroke	– Documents in the area of image analysis that mention analysis techniques as an example but do not discuss in detail
The scientific material that has been published since 2004	– Documents that do not match the search string
	– Studies with low relevance to the RQs
	– Studies that do not fulfill the inclusion criteria

Table.2 Study selection

Database	Round One	Round Two	Used	Excluded
IEEE Explore	11		8 (72.73%)	3 (27.27%)
Springer	16	3	9 (47.36%)	7 (52.63%)
Google scholar	8		2 (25%)	6 (75%)
Archivx	12		3 (25%)	9 (75%)
Web of science	7		1 (10%)	6 (90%)
PubMed	22	2	7 (29.17%)	17 (29.83%)
Total	76	5	30 (37.04%)	51 (62.96%)

As shown in Table 2, two different rounds have been used to identify the relevant works. Firstly, 76 non-redundant works were identify for further evaluation. After a critical evaluation of these papers, extra five papers are obtained from the citations. Finally, however, only 30 papers are considered for review in this work. Table 3 shows those selected studies arranged in order.

Table.3 List of article identifiers

Id.	Ref.	Id.	Ref.	Id.	Ref.	Id.	Ref.	Id.	Ref.
P1	[1]	P7	[8]	P13	[16]	P19	[22]	P25	[32]
P2	[2]	P8	[9]	P14	[17]	P20	[24]	P26	[33]
P3	[3]	P9	[10]	P15	[18]	P21	[26]	P27	[34]
P4	[5]	P10	[11]	P16	[19]	P22	[29]	P28	[35]
P5	[7]	P11	[13]	P17	[20]	P23	[30]	P29	[36]
P6	[8]	P12	[14]	P18	[21]	P24	[31]	P30	[37]

The rest of this report is organized as follows. The section that follows, section three, discussed stroke imaging modalities and section four highlighted stroke image analysis techniques and related works. Finally, open challenges and gaps that have not yet been fully addressed in existing works are summarized.

3 Stroke Diagnosis

In stroke diagnosis process there are three main phases, viz., clinical diagnosis, laboratory diagnosis, and imaging [30, 67]. The clinical diagnosis phase is the first step used to check weather a patient has a stroke or not through an assessment of symptoms. Symptoms of a stroke can be different for different people. The most common symptoms of stroke includes speaking trouble, paralysis, seeing problem of one or both eyes, headache and walking problems. In laboratory diagnosis phase, blood testing is conducted. Complete blood count and clotting time tests are performed in this phase. These tests are used to know the level of platelets and how quickly the blood clots, respectively. The third phase is imaging. It is used to identify which type of stroke is occurred in the patient (Fig. 1).

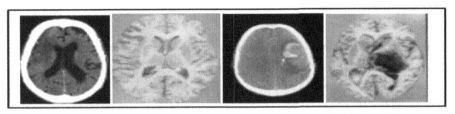

a) Ischemic stroke   b) Haemorrhagic stroke

Fig. 1. Stroke images [4]

3.1   Stroke Imaging Modality

Basically, screening a patient with stroke disease is to decide whether the patient is feeling an ischemic or Haemorrhagic stroke in order to give the right treatment. The two known stroke imaging modalities are discussed as follows [6].

3.1.1   Computed Tomography (CT)

It is a way of scanning internal body with multiple scenes through essential x-ray tools integrated with computers. Using CT scan, experts can identify a stroke from a blood clot or bleeding within the brain. CT scan tests show abnormalities in the brain, and can aid to determine if these parts are caused by inadequate blood flow (ischemic stroke), a burst blood vessel (haemorrhage), or a different kind of problem [7]. In contrast to other techniques, CT and Magnetic Resonance Imaging (MRI) scans can display the internals of the head showing the details of soft tissues, bones, brains and blood vessels. It is a primary method of determining whether a stroke is ischemic or haemorrhagic. It is also used to show other attributes of brain defects such as spots and sizes influenced through extra factors like cancers, and clots, among others.

3.1.2   Magnetic Resonance Imaging (MRI)

MRI uses a potent magnetic field, radio frequency pulses and a computer to yield detailed images of organs, soft tissues, bone and almost all other internal body structures. It is among the most known and high level tools used to give the required image viewing including three dimensional (3D) views. Mostly, this tool is used for medical purposes. It works without using any rays unlike computed tomography replacing the rays by magnets that provide strengths as high as 20,000 times. It could be managed using appropriate tools or machines with internal instructions that help them capture images, displaying appropriate body parts or tissues showing their internal workings as needed [12].

3.1.3   Advancements in Stroke Imaging Modalities and Associated Performance Evaluation Metrics

Image analysis processes require imaging modalities and techniques to analyze stroke images by capturing the targeted body parts using MRI or CT scan devices. Advancements are observed with both modalities.

Table.4 Summary of stroke imaging modalities with sensitivity and time onset of symptoms

Sensitivity	Time	Stroke type	Modalities	Citation
100%	>3 h	Hemorrhagic	CT (CTA, CTP)	[40, 44, 47]
86%–90%	>6 h	Hemorrhagic		
93%	<48 h	Hemorrhagic		
17%–58%	>48 h	Hemorrhagic		
64%–85%	>3 h	Ischemic		[40, 47]
47%–80%	>6 h	Ischemic		
23%–81%	<48 h	Ischemic		
53%–74%	>48 h	Ischemic		
–	>3 h	Hemorrhagic	MRI (MRA, MRP, DWI)	[44, 45]
86%–90%	>6 h	Hemorrhagic		
46%	<48 h	Hemorrhagic		
38%–97%	>48 h	Hemorrhagic		
–	>3 h	Ischemic		[45, 47]
65%	>6 h	Ischemic		
84%–88%	<48 h	Ischemic		
94%-98%	>48 h	Ischemic		

Key: CTA = Computed Tomography Angiography, CTP = Computed Tomography Perfussion, MRA = Magnetic Resonance Angiography, MRP = Magnetic Resonance Perfussion, DWI = Deffusion Weithed Imaging

Recently, studies were conducted on MRI modalities showing its various advancements to stroke imaging as discussed in [17, 18, 20, 23]. CT has also shown advancements as addressed in previous studies [19, 21, 22]. There are several performance evaluation metrics of imaging modalities. Among these metrics, some of them are discussed in Table 4. In the Table, the most known stroke imaging modalities such as CT and MRI are examined based on their range of sensitivity with the time onset of stroke symptoms for both Haemorrhagic and Ischemic stroke types.

4   Image Analysis

The process of image analysis has grown dramatically as its applicability increased on several fields of science and technology. The main points with image analysis is improving the visual quality of an image to extract useful information or features based on different image properties such as color, gloss, morphology of the objects, and texture [13]. Figure 2 depicts the main steps of image analysis.

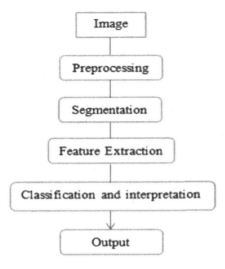

Fig. 2. Image analysis steps [13]

4.1   Image Analysis Techniques

Since image analysis is used as a tool for recognizing, differentiating, and quantifying various types of images it involves, on each step of analysis, various computing techniques.

4.1.1   Pre-processing

In image analysis pre-processing is the term for operations on images at the lowest level of abstraction. These operations do not increase image information content but they decrease it if entropy is an information measure. The aim of pre-processing is an improvement of the image data that suppresses undesired distortions or enhances some image features relevant for further processing and analysis task. There are 4 different types of Image Pre-Processing techniques such as;

- *Pixel brightness transformations (PBT)* [13, 68]: which is used to modify pixel brightness and the transformation depends on the properties of a pixel itself. In PBT, output pixel's value depends only on the corresponding input pixel value.
- *Gamma correction* [13, 68]: it is a non-linear adjustment to individual pixel values. While in image normalization we carried out linear operations on individual pixels, such as scalar multiplication and addition/subtraction, gamma correction carries out a non-linear operation on the source image pixels, and can cause saturation of the image being altered.
- *Image Filtering and Segmentation* [13, 68]: The goal of using filters is to modify or enhance image properties and/or to extract valuable information from the pictures such as edges, corners, and blobs. A filter is defined by a kernel, which is a small array applied to each pixel and its neighbors within an image
- *The Fourier Transform* [13, 68]: it is an important image processing tool which is used to decompose an image into its sine and cosine components. The output of the

transformation represents the image in the Fourier or frequency domain, while the input image is the spatial domain equivalent. In the Fourier domain image, each point represents a particular frequency contained in the spatial domain image [68].

4.1.2 Segmentation

The crucial step in image analysis processes is segmentation. It is a method used to divide an image into its constituent parts or segments having similar features [14]. The reason behind using segmentation technique is to identify the object of interest that depends on the specified application constraints. Since the main goal of image segmentation is to separate images in to its constituent parts, identifying and using the appropriate image segmentation technique is very important. There are two different image segmentation types such as local segmentation and global segmentation. Local segmentation deals with image's local properties which are characterized by the interactions of neighboring pixels and the image edge. It is also deals with particular region of image only. While, the mean values of different pixel classes and the continuous boundary of the region are the focus of global segmentation. Global segmentation also concentrated by partitioning overall image poses highest amount of pixels. The most popular image segmentation techniques are discussed below.

- *Thresholding Method:* it is one of the common image segmentation methods preferred based on our prior knowledge of image features to identify the lighter front object from the background images. It has three varieties as global, variable and multiple thresholding. In global thresholding the threshold values are constant or not changed. In variable thresholding the threshold values can vary over the image. While in multiple thresholding values are used to compute the correct result in multiple thresholding [14, 15]. In global thresholding, the threshold values are constant or not changed.

$$q(x,y) = \left\{ \begin{array}{l} 1, \ if \ p(x,y) > T \\ 0, \ if \ p(x,y) \leq T \end{array} \right\} \tag{1}$$

Adapted from [15]

In variable thresholding, the threshold values can vary over the image. While, values are used to compute the correct result in multiple thresholding [14, 15].

$$q(x,y) = \left\{ \begin{array}{l} m, \ if \ p(x,y) > T1 \\ n \ if \ p(x,y) \leq T1 \\ o \ if \ p(x,y) \leq T0 \end{array} \right\} \tag{2}$$

Adapted from [15]

- *Edge Based Method:* it is an edge detection technique used based on the quick fluctuation of intensity of the image. This happens because it is difficult to have useful details of edges using a single value of intensity. The first step in edge based segmentation techniques is detecting all edges and then connecting them together for the sake of making boundaries of that object. This properly scatters the required image portions [15, 16].

- *Region Based Method:* as its name implies, this technique is the key image segmentation used for segmenting the image depending on pixel similarity properties. It can be classified into region growing and split & merge methods. Region growing methods are used for segmenting the image into several regions based on the growth of seeds. That means, firstly, it groups image pixels that are selected from the original image. Second, after selecting the similarity criteria feature sets it grows regions by appending together those seeds or pixels that have similar predefined properties. It finally, stops the region growing process when there is no more inclusion criteria to be achieved [16, 17].

- *Clustering Based Method:* It is a process of organizing groups of image pixels based on their attributes. Usually, a group of similar pixels fit a region being different from others creating a cluster [16].

4.1.3 Feature Extraction

A feature of an image is the basic identification property. Having a big sized image needs more time to analyze. Accordingly, in order to have an easy and quick analysis process it is mandatory to have the required quantitative details of the object. Through identifying the portion required for analysis, it is possible to minimize the computational requirements of detecting objects. This further enhances its efficiency.

Features can be categorized as low level and high level features. Since a low-level feature is extracted directly from the source image, it is quite different from the high-level one. On the other hand, the extraction of high-level features is based on those low-level features [19, 20].

Handcrafted features have been used for more than a decade in a number of computer vision applications, including object detection and image classification. Over time, the number of features has increased to better adapt to the various tasks being tackled by researchers. Different types of the handcrafted features are used in machine learning approaches. Some of the most common types are; Local Binary Pattern (LBP) [35], Local Ternary Pattern (LTP) [36] and Local Phase Quantization (LPQ) [37]. Many state-of-the-art descriptors are based on LBP [38]. These approaches extract features that are general-purpose and are, therefore, most suitable for building a generic computer vision systems.

According to [35], LBP has rapidly become a popular descriptor mainly because of its low computational complexity and ability to code fine details. The canonical LBP operator [35] is computed at each pixel location by considering the values of a small circular neighborhood (with radius R pixels) around the value of a central pixel. One variant that has inspired many others is the Local Ternary Patterns (LTP), proposed by Tan and Triggs [36], which utilizes a 3-valued encoding scheme that includes a threshold around zero for the evaluation of the local gray-scale difference.

The LPQ operator, first proposed by Ojansivu and Heikkila [37], is based on the blur invariance property of the Fourier phase spectrum and uses the local phase information extracted from the 2-D short-term Fourier transform (STFT) computed over a rectangular neighborhood at each pixel position of the image.

4.1.4 Classification

Classification is one of the methods that comes after image feature extraction and segmentation. It helps us classify an image based on problem types. Image classification technique are applied for prediction and detection purposes in stroke diagnosis and management processes [1, 24–27].

4.2 Image Analysis Techniques for Stroke Diagnosis

Among the emerging image analysis techniques is machine learning approaches. In this section the most known machine learning techniques that are used for stroke diagnosis are briefly revised. Thus, the trends of image analysis is discussed based on their learning ability.

– *Manual image analysis:* there are several methods of image analysis applied in stroke diagnosis using traditional Machine Learning techniques. Basically, these machine learning processes are start with preprocessing. The next feature extraction step is followed using hand crafted methods and the final classification step is continued to classify normal and abnormal stroke slices. Accordinglly, some extracted features like intensity, texture and wavelet transform are inserted to the specific model as input. Those algorithms are limited in processing the natural images in their raw form, because they require expert knowledge and lots of time for tuning the features [48, 66].
– *Semi-automatic image analysis:* Since the advancement of image acquisition equipment are rapidly changing, the system's ability to come up with those tools is also enhanced. Thus, machine lerning techniques that are capable to learn features have emerged [48]. In semi-automatic analysis, the system can learn features and perform its own activities, but it needs expert support to learn and accomplish the needed tasks [48, 66].
– *Automatic image analysis:* It is an emerging trend of machine learning approaches that are capable of reducing or eliminating experts support completely. In this method, the machine has the ability to learn each feature automatically. Some machine learning approaches can apply automatic learning techniques. Currently, among the most known automatic image analysis techniques is deep learning [26, 48]. It has minimized the challenges faced in conventional machine learning approaches in the analysis of complex images like those found in medical domains which are subjective, and error prone.

Deep learning algorithms such as Convolutional Neural Network (CNN), Recurrent neural Network (RNN), Long-Short-Term Memory (LSTM), Extreme Learning Model (ELM), Generative Adversarial Networks (GANs) and the likes are fed with raw data, have automatic features learning ability that is done considerably faster [26]. These algorithms can learn multiple levels of abstractions, representations and information automatically from large set of images that exhibit the desired behavior of data [26, 48]. The most popular techniques that are being used for stroke image analysis are discussed as follows.

4.2.1 Convolutional Neural Networks (CNNs)

It is a type of neural network that effectively performs image classifiction and recognition. It is also used to automatically detect important features without any human intervention. There are three different layers in a CNN; convolutional, pooling and fully connected layers. In order to build a fully functional CNN architecture those different layers should be stacked. CNNs are one of the best learning algorithms for understanding image content and have shown exemplary performance in image segmentation, classification, detection, and retrieval tasks [62]. In CNN, there are many different types of architectures identified based on their own purposes. Some of the most popular CNN architectures are;

- *LeNet-5* [34, 62]: it is the first architecture of CNN produced to overcome the drawbacks of image recognition. The main motivations of this model includes shared weight ideas and back propagation optimization with neural networks. It plays a great role by introducing CNN with its full layers.
- *AlexNet* [34, 62]: the emergence of this architecture reduces the problems with large margin and scale recognition with tasks of detecting an object. It was the initial point for computer vision concepts because it deals with large complex datasets. It is different from LeNet-5 by its ability to provide ReLU (Rectified Linear Unit) and DropOut in CNN.
- *GoogleNet* [34, 62]: it is also called Inception. It was developed by the team of Google Brain. It contributes by reducing the number of parameters needed to implement CNNs.
- *VGGNet* [34, 62]: it is a well known neural network identified in ImageNet Large Scale Visual Recognition Challenge (ILSVRC) in 2014. It is primarily used in image localization and image classification purposes.
- *ResNet* [34, 62]: supports the idea that very deep classical CNNs are harder to optimize mostly due to the vanishing gradient problem. To solve this challenge, the new residual block was introduced in this model.
- *Xception* [34, 62]: it is a.k.a. Extreme Inception model. It achieved better results than ResNet on big Google dataset called JFT, through verifying the concept of correlation with cross channels that could be decoupled from corelations of spatial data.
- *NasNet* [34, 62]: this model explores the hypothesis that is possible to create an efficient learning architecture directly from dataset of interest.

4.2.2 Recurrent Neural Networks (RNNs)

RNN is empowered with recurrent connections which enable the network to memorize the patterns form last inputs. The fact that the Region of Interest (ROI) in medical images which is usually distributed over multiple adjacent slices, as in CT or MRI, results in having correlations in successive slices. Accordingly, RNNs are able to extract inter-slice contexts from the input slices as a form of sequential data. The most popular types of RNNs are:

- *Long Short-Term Memory (LSTM):* is an architecture of recurrent neural network used in deep learning approaches. The main diffirentiating feature of LSTM from standard feed forward neural networks is the occurence of feedback connections. It has the ability to process both single image and entire sequences of data. The reason behind the creation of LSTM is to overcome the problem of gradient vanishing that occur while training traditional RNNs. It is also used to add new useful information and erase the previously saved memory [63].
- *Gated Recurrent Unit (GRU):* it is similar with LSTM by its erase (forgete) gate. But, it has very limited number of parameters. The reason for that is it lacks an output gate. It also perform well in less frequent and small datasets. But it could not perform good in unbounded counting unlike LSTM. This makes it fail to learn some languages that could be simple for LSTM [60].

4.3   Related Works

Various studies are employed on medical imaging throughout the world previously. But, the intention, application area, approaches used and scope of those studies varies accordingly. Among the employed several works on this area, most of them are concentrated on both Machine Learning and Deep Learning based image analysis techniques used for stroke diagnosis as seen and discussed here below separately.

4.3.1   Machine Learning Based Stroke Image Analysis

The machine learning approaches have been applied in several types of medical image analysis including stroke disease diagnosis. The main intention of this section is to review the relevant related works of machine learning techniques applied on stroke diagnosis and treatments. In stroke image analysis process different stages are there as we have seen previously. As a result there is various machine learning studies have been employed on stroke imaging. Those studies were concentrated mostly on the detection and prediction tasks by using image analysis pathways such as; segmentation, feature extraction and classification. Here below, the related works on machine learning approaches for stroke detection and stroke prediction are reviewed and discussed as follows.

In [18], the study aims to provide appropriate approach used for assisting the physician during stroke diagnosis. As a main problem, the rising medical mistakes specifically for stroke diagnosis were mentioned in this study. To overcomming this problem the study proposed the accurate way used for stoke diagnosis. Accordingly, the segmentation method was used for imaging brain stroke by using MRI devices for capturing the required images. For the sake of writing and implimenting the program the MATLAB tool with its own language was also used to achieve the good result through having clear images with more details for the brain. Finally in this study, fifteen (15) images of brain stroke with thresholding and morphological segmentation methods were used. There is no any evaluation metrices are used and mentioned on this study.

In [19], the automatic detection mechanism of stroke disease was proposed through using CT images. According to the study, selecting appropriate features from large datasets were challenging. As a result the proposed approach, collecting 92 extracted features and overcame the problem existed with selection complexity. Thus, the proposed particle swarm optimization (PSO) method was used for the 98 brain CT images. Finally SVM (Support Vector Machine) was employed for testing purposes. The study performed a good result of 92% accuracy by comparing with previous studies.

In [20], since the accurate classification of the stroke section with problems is needed for aids quick diagnosis processes, this study came with stockwell transform based method used for detecting ischemic stroke. The proposed study concentrated to diagnosis or detection of ischemic stroke in the brain. In this study, the SEA (Skull Elimination Algorithm), CLSA (Central Line Sketching Algorithm), FCM (Fuzzy C-Means), and DOST (Discrete Orthonormal Stockwell Transform) were used for extracting the tissue part only in the brain, splitting the MR image qually, extracting the lession part, and extracting the features like mean, median and standard deviation respectivelly. In this study 20 MR images samples with 2D view of axes were used for expriment, and implimented by using MATLAB tool. The evaluation results of the proposed approach was not mentioned in this study.

In [23], the study for detecting stroke diseases by using segmentation and classification methods were proposed. The study aims to automatically segmenting and classifying stroke diseases through using DWI imaging modality. The 3D image was constructed to view the captured imagein three different axes. Fuzy C-means method was used for segmenting the image and the spatial features were also extracted from the region of interest. The rule based method was used to classify the extracted features. In this study both acute and chronic lesion are analyzed to achieve accuracy results 90% and 70% respectively. The study performed the overall sensitivity and specifity results of 84.38% and 83.33% for the classification respectively. The image samples of 30 acute and 20 chronic slices were used with MATLAB analysis tool here.

In [28], the ways of detecting ischemic stroke using DWI images was proposed for stroke diagnosis. This proposed way is working automatically through using computer aided system. The stroke detection process consists both segmentation and classification methods. The expectation maximization approaches were used for segmentation issue. The classification activities concentrated to classify into partial and total anterior circulation syndrome and lacunar syndrome stroke using random forest classifier method. Once the part of affected image region was segmented, the remaining process is followed by using FODPSO (Fractional-Order Darwinian Particle Swarm Optimization) technique. In this study, 192 MRI scan for evaluation was used. The study achieved 94.3%, 92% and 94% of accuracy, sensitivity and dice similarity index results respectively. Finally, the challenging activity of determining the 3D volumetric value of lesions was recommended as a future works of line.

In [49], the problem of cerebral edema to the deterioration of neurology and death after stroke was mentioned. Also, the lack of effective ways of preventing and predicting the occurrence of the disease accurately were presented. The study deals with an automation of imaging the brain in order to attain proper volumetric data saved for big stroke patient's repository. CT was used as a modality in this study. A random forest segmentation approach with 400 CT images for testing purpose was used. A machine learning algorithm with the capability of segmenting and computing cerebrospinal fluid (CSF) volume from sequential CT scans of stroke patients could be created to support the proposed approach.

In [50], the main aim of this study was, to provide an efficient hybridization model able for the purpose of classifying MR brain image as normal and abnormal. Accordingly, for the sake of extracting features the digital wavelet transform was used. For decreasing the feature space the principal PCA was used. Finally for the parameter optimization kernel support vector machine and radial basis function kernel was used. The performed results were; 98.79% sensitivity, 96.29% specificity, 98.65% accuracy.

Some relevant works have been conducted on forecasting or predicting stroke disease risks and the mortality rates by using classification algorithms with the machine learning ways such as; DT (Decision Tree), NN (Neural Network) and NB (Naive Bayes) with various useful attributes. In [52], the study aims to identify weither or not the ischemic stroke location and infraction volume helps the prediction processes related to functional outcome was proposed. Here, a multi class SVM technique with 68 MR images of ischemic stroke was used. The proposed study score good result comparatively than conventional methods.

In [53], the study concentrated on improving the prediction efficiency of stroke risk classification by using machine learning algorithms was proposed. The proposed study used two steps to doing the required activities. The datasets used for training and testing purposes were first developed using both under and over sampling techniques. Then some other methods were created to classify stroke levels of risk. Such methods are; DT, NN, NB, LR (Logistic Regression), RF (Random Forest), BN (Bayesian Network) and both voting and boosting models. The study attain 99.94%, 97.33% and 98.44% boosting model recall with DT, RF based precision and recall respectively.

As shown here, most of the studies employed on diagnosis and prognosis purposes only through using image analysis processes. Which means [18–20, 23, 28, 38, 49, 50] deals with stroke diagnosis and some studies [52, 53] were intended to the issue of prognosis. This indicates that, there is no works aimed to provide stroke treatment and used for prevalence issues in this regard. The accuracy result of those previous studies shows that, all works employed by using 3D images [23, 49] were performed poor results than those used 2D images [19, 28, 50].

This indicates, analyzing stroke images with 3D views were challenging activities for conventional machine learning techniques. In addition, only little work was conducted with stroke image registration and retrieval techniques. Registration of stroke images is a common image analysis task in which a coordinate transform is calculated from one image to another. This ignored process is very useful for clinical issues of experimental design. Several types of modalities have the ability to imaging; this might deserve its own role for facilitating the process of health care. Currently, the size of accumulated images are growing dramatically, this extracted images could be collected globally in any information system developed for the purpose of health care services. But there is no adequate works available regarding this in stroke imaging.

Table.5 Summary of existing machine learning image analysis techniques applied for stroke imaging

Ref.	For	Process	Mod	Type	Technique	Size	DM	Acc.
[17]	Dia	SG	MRI	B-Stroke	TR	–	2D	–
[19]	Dia	FE	CT	Ischemic	PSO + SVM	98	2D	92%
[20]	Dia	SG + FE + CL	MRI	Ischemic	SEA,CLSA,FCM + DOST	20	2D	–
[23]	Dia	SG + CL	DWI	B-Stroke	FCM	50	3D	90%
[28]	Dia	SG	MRI	Ischemic	EM-FODPSO	192	2D	94.3%
[38]	Dia	RG	CT	Ischemic	TR	37	2D	–
[49]	Dia	SG	CT	Ischemic	RF	400	3D	–
[50]	Dia	FE + CL	MRI	B-Stroke	DWT + K-SVM + R-SVM	–	2D	98.65%
[52]	Pro	CL	MRI	Ischemic	Multi-class SVM	68	–	85%
[53]	Pro	PR	–	Stroke	RF	–	–	99.94%

Key: Acc = Accuracy, B-Stroke = Brain Stroke, CL = Classification, Dia = Diagnosis, DM = Dimension, DWT = Digital Wavelet Transform, EM = Expectation Maximization, FE = Feature Extraction, K = Kernel, Mod = Modality, PR = Prediction, Pro = Progonosis, PSO = Particle-swarm optimization, R = Radial, RG = Registration, SG = Segmentation, TR = Thresholding

4.3.2 Deep Learning Based Stroke Image Analysis

Since this study is concerning with image analysis techniques, the most relevant deep learning based studies for stroke imaging are reviewed and discussed here below. In [54], the proposed study aims to detect ischemic stroke disease by using image analysis technique. Here, the main problems of manual segmentation processes were mentioned and novel automatic method was proposed for overcoming problems. Automatic segmentation process with FCNN (Fully Convolutional Neural Network) was used to segment CTP images with 2D view. Since it could be provide contextual information publicly, the model with PSPNet (Pyramid-Scene-Parsing Network) was used in this study. For learning different and challenging shapes the concept of focal function was also used. The proposed study achieved the DSC (Dice Similarity Coefficient) result of 0.54%.

In [55], this study proposed the detection of ischemic stroke through segmenting lesion from images. The CNN approaches with DenseUnet model was used for successful segmentation purposes in this study. The multi-modal MR modalities with 2D image views also applied for imaging the required brain part. The overall dataset size used in the study was totally 94 samples, which means 83 training and 11 validation samples. The proposed study achieved 0.635% with a DSC result finally.

In [56], another study aims to detecting ischemic stroke disease by using the segmentation processes with PCNet model. This new model was proposed to overcome the challenges with multi-modality, occurrences and the small size of the image to segmenting lesion automatically. The study used CNN approaches and 304 multi-modal MR images with 3D views were collected. The proposed study was performs 0.902% of DSC result.

In [57], the proposed study aims detecting ischemic stroke by using CNN approaches. The imaging modality used with the proposed study was CTA and the image captured has three dimensional views. Totally 60 image samples were collected, which are 30 training samples and 30 testing images. The highest result of DSC was 0.61 for the proposed approaches.

In [34], the concept of an IoT (Internet of Things) is presented this study. As a method, the CNN approach with Machine Learning classifiers was used to identifying a brain into a normal, ischemic stroke or hemorrhagic stroke. Totally 800 image samples were used here using CT imaging modality. The idea behind transfer learning was also applied here through integrated with other machine learning techniques. The intention of this study is detecting the stroke online without any challenge. As stated in the paper, the system performed 100% accuracy. But the proposed work is limited to 2D images. It is also challenging to deal with big 3D datasets.

In [50], there is also another study conducted for the purpose of detecting acute ischemic stroke automatically using CTA images. For this purpose a model that was very sensitive to change is proposed for the balance between hemispheres of the brain. An experiment is conducted to show the capability of the proposed model regarding the structure of the brain. The proposed study achieves good AUC (Area Under Curve) result of 0.914%. Generally for this study, deep symmetry sensitive network and convolutional neural network model was utilized with 217 image samples.

According to [58], the concept of detecting ischemic stroke using semi-supervised learning strategy was proposed. In this study an automatic segmentation process was applied. The CNN approach with DPC-Net (Double Path Classification Network) model was proposed to do the given task. Herewith the study, 460 image samples with 3D views could be collected using MR imaging modality. The DSC performance of the proposed study was 0.642%.

In [25], the study proposed the automatic lesion outcome prediction for stroke disease based on deep learning approaches. The study used other clinical information in addition to MR images. The study aims to create a CNN-UNet model with awareness of collateral and principal dynamics of blood flows. Here, only 75 image samples were collected using MR imaging modality. These images are limited to 2D views. The proposed study was achieved below the expert performances of the 0.58% DSC result.

In [59], here is also another study conducted to forecast the functional outcome of thrombectom. The approach used for directly exploiting data with multi-modal ways. The comparative assessments were used in between unimodal and multimodal images for the sake of having good functional outcome prediction results. Finally the proposed study attained with 0.75% of AUC results. Most of the reviewed studies were used the concept of data augmentation to obtain large image sizes as we have seen in the table below. Accordingly in [51], the current advances in data-augmentation techniques applied to MRI of brain were discussed. The pros and cons of data-augmentation technique are also described. Accordingly, the main challenges or limitation of data augmentation are mentioned. Since the data augmentation methods are able to overcoming the overfitting challenges, it is also very time consuming, generative adversarial networks applicable only in training-time, and it can easily concentrate multiple similar samples.

To conclude, several studies have been explored the image analysis approaches for the purpose of solving stroke problems. Related and relevant studies applied on stroke disease are reviewed and well discussed in this section. As the previous works achieved good results on their application area, they have different own limitations also. Generally, the absence of large stroke dataset; best analysis technique used for stroke imaging with small size dataset, and the absence of proper studies conducted for providing treatments for stroke patients are the main limitations of existed deep learning based image analysis techniques for stroke imaging. For solving the problem of dataset size, the augmentation method have been applied in [54, 60, 61, 64, 65]. But, it could not shows proper changes in the performance result.

4.4 Summary of Stroke Image Analysis Techniques

Basically, in this section some interesting notions of existed stroke image analysis techniques, the approaches used for stroke imaging and their application areas were discussed. Thus, machine learning and deep learning approaches with image analysis processes such as segmentation, feature extraction, classification, detection and prediction were widely used in stroke image analysis researches. In both Tables 5 and 6, the existing machine learning and deep learning based image analysis techniques applied in which stroke types, using which imaging modalities, approaches, dataset size, image dimension and the performed results were also shown in order to answer the research question 2. Based on the objectives of this survey, these existed analysis techniques are analyzed and examined, their limitations are also identified in this section.

Table.6 Summary of deep learning based image analysis for stroke imaging

App	Model	Technique	Type	Mod	DM	Size	Aug	DSC	Ref.
CNN	UNet	Prediction	Both	MR	2D	75	–	–	[25]
CNN	PSPNet	Segmentation	Ischemic	CTP	2D	–	Yes	0.54	[54]
CNN	Dense-UNet	Segmentation	Ischemic	MM-MR	2D	94	No	0.635	[55]
CNN	Res-FCN	Segmentation	Ischemic	MM-MR	2D	212	Yes	0.645	[65]
CNN	CNN + ML	Detection	Ischemic	CT	2D	800	No	–	[34]
CNN	PCNet	Segmentation	Ischemic	MM-MR	3D	304	No	0.902	[56]
CNN	3DCNN	Detection	Ischemic	CTA	3D	60	–	0.61	[57]
CNN	DeepSymNet	Detection	Ischemic	CTA	–	217	–	–	[50]
CNN	cGNA	Segmentation	Ischemic	MR, CT	–	–	Yes	–	[60]
CNN	DeepMedic	Segmentation	Ischemic	MRP	–	75	Yes	0.34	[61]
CNN	DPC-Net	Segmentation	Ischemic	MR	3D	460	No	0.642	[63]
CNN	AB-DNN	Segmentation	Ischemic	CTP	2D	–	No	–	[58]
CNN	ResNet-50	Segmentation	Ischemic	CT	3D	400	Yes	–	[63]
CNN	ClinicDNN	Prediction	Ischemic	CT	3D	400	–	–	[59]
CNN	MPFN	Segmentation	Ischemic	MR	3D	–	Yes	0.622	[62]

Key: AB = Attention-Based,   App = Approach   Aug = Augmentation, cGNA = Conditional Generative Adversarial Network, CilinicDNN = Clinical-Deep Neural Network, DeepMedic = Deep Medical, DeepSymNet = Deep Symetry Network, DM = Dimension, MM = Multimodal, MPF = Multi Plane Fusion, ResFCN = Residual-Fully-Convolutional-Network

4.5   Stroke Data Availability

In machine learning processes when large datasets are available, good results can be obtained. Since the severity of stroke diseases, there should be significant amounts of data available for MRI and CT globally [32]. Accordingly in stroke imaging semi- or fully-automated algorithms that uses machine learning techniques require training and testing on large datasets could be applicable for analyses purposes. Unfortunately a small number of imaging datasets have been made public in stroke imaging. Those that are available often were reached from a few institutions and do not reveal the variety of imaging devices and clinical scenarios that will be met in global settings. As a result, several studies employed small data sets available locally and publicly accessible datasets of stroke imaging. In Table 7 lists the available stroke image dataset that are mentioned in terms of size, format and image modality used.

Table.7 Summary of available stroke datasets

Dataset	Size	Format	Modality	Ref.
ATLAS	304	XML	MRI	[42]
FCP-INDI	229	–	MRI	[42]
I-KNOW	102	VOI	MRI	[41, 43]
ISLES	26	NIfTI	multi-modal MRI	[43, 55]
SFB	23	NIfTI	MRI	[41, 46]

Key: ATLAS = Anatomical Tracings of Lesions After Stroke, FCP-INDI = Functional Connectomes Project International Data Sharing Initiative, I-KNOW = Interconnected Knowledge database, ISLES = Ischemic Stroke Lesion Segmentation, SFB = Sonderforschungsbereich

5   Open Research Challenges

5.1   Challenges in Imaging Modalities

During the process of image analysis for stroke diagnosis, the problem of divergent occurrence of the required organ could be considered as a great challenge. That means, size of the tissue, shape and it's occurrence location of the organ that planned to capture may not similar for all patients [39].

The vague borderline through inadequate contrast among aiming tissues and the nearby tissues is considered as a recognized essential imaging challenge.

5.2   Challenges in Analysis Techniques

In recent approach, artificial intelligence model effectively applied in medical signal and image analysis in object identification and classification directly from images by eliminating the step to extract the features, thus speed-up the process of classification [32, 34]. The importance of automated segmentation technique is stated in many studies and also technically applied for different purposes. The segmentation of image that centered on deep learning techniques has got enormous consideration and it acmes the necessity of having an inclusive review of it recently.

Segmenting aimed tissue from complex volumetric images require a model used to extract features with deep and extreme information. However, the challenges with those 3D models are train deep networks to accomplish the desired goal accordingly.

5.3   Challenges in Dataset Availability

5.3.1   Constructing a Big Stroke Imaging Dataset

Since there is only few publicly available stroke datasets are existed, there is a gap on analyzing large and ever changing data easily for providing accurate and quick results. So, more effective data collection, identification, and management of stroke images methods will be needed for research that could be easily findable, accessible, interoperable and reusable. Imaging is the crucial step in brain stroke diagnosis [32]. Furthermore, even there is a lot of magnetic resonance imaging or computed tomography sequences consists many slices with a particular brain image, a massive amount of imaging data could be stored rapidly through medical practice. However, there is no properly stowed stroke image in various health care sectors. Once the patients are diagnosed, their history was removed rather than storing. This conveys the absence of large size stroke datasets. Thus, accommodated efforts will be needed across the health care sectors globally.

5.3.2   Developing a New Algorithm

Based on its necessities, constructing a big dataset for stroke imaging is mandatory. It also needs cooperative efforts worldwide to overcome challenges with standardization of imaging protocols, and development of a user-friendly repository, leading and controlling the developed repository.

For having large stroke dataset several studies were also proposed data augmentation methods. This data augmentation method is capable to generate artificial data from the original data. Conversely, image augmentation outputs are depends only on estimation, and decisions made based on these results must be treated accordingly. As depicted in the Table 6, the augmentation method have been applied in [54, 60, 61, 64, 65] but, there is no changes shown with their performance results. Hence, new algorithm which can be applicable for small size stroke image dataset will be needed.

5.3.3   Developing the Full-Fledged System Used for Stroke Diagnosis and Treatment

All previous studies were focused on stroke diagnosis and forecasting issues. Accordingly, the absence of proper works conducted for stroke treatment was one of the most perceived gaps. In previous studies, only images data was used for investigation. But, it is difficult to mine every diagnosis and treatment knowledge from image data only. Some data about stroke treatments, clinical and blood investigation could be collected from domain experts and related medical literatures.

Through combining the image data, blood laboratory results, clinical and treatments information it could be possible to develop a full-fledged system used for stroke diagnosis and treatment accurately. Such systems will be very important and performs best results in the developing countries like Ethiopia, where there is a lack of professional domain experts and poor medical infrastructures.

6 Conclusions

In this survey study we have identified and analyzed the various techniques of image analysis approaches. As a result, the state-of-the-art in image analysis techniques has been summarized and analyzed. Moreover, several clinical and biological image datasets are found being used in stroke diagnosis. And yet, much of these data sets are publicly accessible begging for open access datasets and repositories. Finally, the most common open research challenges in the area are identified and briefly discussed.

References

1. Songhee, C., Jungyoon, K., Jihye, L.: The use of deep learning to predict stroke patient mortality. Int. J. Environ. Res. Public Health **16**(11), 1876 (2019). https://doi.org/10.3390/ijerph16111876
2. Namale, G., Kinengyere, A., Ddumba, E., Seeley, J., Newton, R.: Risk factors for haemorrhagic & ischemic stroke in Sub-Saharan Africa. J. Trop. Med. **18**, 1–11 (2018). https://doi.org/10.1155/2018/4650851
3. Gebremariam, S.A., Yang, H.S.: Types, risk profiles, and outcomes of stroke patients in tertiary teaching hospital in northern Ethiopia. eNeurologicalSci **3**(1), 41–47 (2016)
4. Ralph, L.S., Kasner, E.S.: An updated definition of stroke for the 21st century: a statement for healthcare professionals from American Stroke Association. Stroke **44**, 2064–2089 (2013). https://doi.org/10.1161/STR.0b013e318296aeca
5. Kitchenham, B.: Procedures for Performing Systematic Reviews. Emp. Soft. Eng. Nat. ICT, Australia, NICTA Technical Report 0400011T.1 (2004)
6. Stephan, P., Jochen, B., Fiebach, D.: Acute stroke MRI: current status & future perspective. Neuroradiology **52**, 189–201 (2010)
7. Chalela, A.J., et al.: MRI and CT in emergency assessment of patients with suspected-acute stroke: a prospective comparison. HHS Public Access **369**(9558), 293–298 (2007). https://doi.org/10.1016/S0140-6736(07)60151-2
8. Napel, S.: Principles and techniques of 3D spiral CT angiography, pp. 167–82. Raven, New York (2005)
9. Dora, K., Nikoleta, I.: Modern imaging modalities in the assessment of acute stroke. Folia Med. **56**(2), 81–87 (2014)
10. Mokli, Y., Pfaff, J., dos Santos, D., Herweh, C., Nagel, S.: Computer-aided imaging analysis in acute ischemic stroke – background and clinical applications. Neurol. Res. Pract. **1**(1) (2019). https://doi.org/10.1186/s42466-019-0028-y
11. Cenek, M., Hu, M., York, G., Dahl, S.: Survey of image processing techniques for brain pathology diagnosis: challenges & opportunities. Front. Robot. AI **5** (2018). https://doi.org/10.3389/frobt.2018.00120
12. Soni, N., Dhanota, D., Kumar, S., Jaiswal, A., Srivastava, A.: Perfusion MR imaging of enhancing brain tumors: comparison of arterial spin labeling technique with dynamic susceptibility contrast technique. Neurol. India **65**(5), 1046 (2017). https://doi.org/10.4103/neuroindia.ni_871_16

13. Prats-Montalban, J., de Juan, A., Ferrer, A.: Multivariate image analysis: a review with applications. Chemometr. Intell. Lab. **107**, 1–23 (2011)
14. Anjna, E., Rajandeep, K.: Review of image segmentation technique. Int. J. Adv. Res. Comput. Sci. **8**, 36–39 (2017)
15. Dilpreet, K., Yadwinder, K.: Various image segmentation techniques: a review. Int. J. Comput. Sci. Mobile Comput. **3**(5), 809–814 (2014)
16. Vairaprakash, G., Subbu, K.: Review on image segmentation techniques. Int. J. Sci. Mod. Eng. **1**(8), 1–8 (2014)
17. Whited, B., Rossignac, J., Slabaugh, G., Fang, T., Unal, G.: Pearling: stroke segmentation with crusted pearl strings. Pattern Recognit. Image Anal. **19**(2), 277–283 (2009). https://doi.org/10.1134/s1054661809020102
18. Abdulrahman, A.: Segmentation of brain stroke image. Int. J. Adv. Res. Comput. Commun. Eng. **4**, 375–378 (2015)
19. Homiera, K.: Feature selection from brain stroke CT images based on particle swarm optimization. Int. J. Adv. Stud. Comput. Sci. Eng. **5**(1), 8–13 (2016)
20. Jayaram, P.V., Menaka, R.: An experimental study of Stockwell transform-based feature extraction method for ischemic stroke detection. Int. J. Biomed. Eng. Technol. **21**(1), 40–48 (2016)
21. Marbun, J.T., Seniman, U., Andayani, J.T.: Classification of stroke disease using convolutional neural network. J. Phys. Conf. Ser. **978**, 012092 (2018). https://doi.org/10.1088/1742-6596/978/1/012092
22. Mayank, C., Saurabh, S., Kishore, L.: A method for automatic-detection and classification of stroke from brain CT-images. In: 31st Annual International Conference of the IEEEEMBS Minneapolis, Minnesota, USA, September 2–6 (2009)
23. Saad, N.M., Abdullah, A.R., Muda, A.F., Musa, H.: Segmentation and classification analysis techniques for stroke based on diffusion weighted images. Int. J. Comput. Sci. **3**(14), 1–8 (2018)
24. Lindenberg, R., Zhu, L., Rüber, T., Schlaug, G.: Predicting functional motor potential in chronic stroke patients using diffusion tensor imaging. Hum. Brain Mapp. **33**(5), 1040–1051 (2011). https://doi.org/10.1002/hbm.21266
25. Heiss, W., Kidwell, C.: Imaging for prediction of functional outcome and assessment of recovery in ischemic stroke. Stroke **45**(4), 1195–1201 (2014). https://doi.org/10.1161/strokeaha.113.003611
26. Pinto, A., Mckinley, R., Alves, V., Wiest, R., Silva, C., Reyes, M.: Stroke lesion-outcome prediction based on MRI combined with clinical information. Front. Neurol. **9** (2018). https://doi.org/10.3389/fneur.2018.01060
27. Rekik, I., Allassonniere, S., Carpenter, T., Wardlaw, J.: Medical image analysis methods in MR/CT imaged acute-subacute ischemic stroke lesion: segmentation, prediction and insights into dynamic evolution simulation models a critical appraisal. Neuro Image Clin. **1**(1), 164–178 (2012). https://doi.org/10.1016/j.nicl.2012.10.003
28. Subudhi, A., Dash, M., Sabut, S.: Automated segmentation and classification of brain stroke using expectation-maximization and random forest classifier. Biocybern. Biomed. Eng. **40**(1), 277–289 (2020). https://doi.org/10.1016/j.bbe.2019.04.004
29. Lemogoum, D., Degaute, J., Bovet, P.: Stroke – prevention, treatment, and rehabilitation in Sub-Saharan Africa. Am. J. Prev. Med. **29**(5), 95–101 (2005). https://doi.org/10.1016/j.amepre.2005.07.025
30. Government of Western Australia. Diagnostic Imaging Pathways – Stroke (2nd ed.). http://www.imagingpathways.health.wa.gov.au (2017)

31. Audebert, H.J., Fiebach, J.B.: Brain imaging in acute ischemic stroke—MRI or CT? Curr. Neurol. Neurosci. Rep. **15**(3), 1–6 (2015). https://doi.org/10.1007/s11910-015-0526-4
32. Lee, E., Kim, Y., Kim, N., Kang, D.: Deep into the brain: artificial intelligence in stroke imaging. J. Stroke **19**(3), 277–285 (2017). https://doi.org/10.5853/jos.2017.02054
33. Brazzelli, M.: Magnetic resonance imaging versus computed tomography for detection of acute vascular-lesions in patients presenting with stroke symptoms (Review). Cochrane Database Syst. Rev. **4**(4) (2009). Available: https://pubmed.ncbi.nlm.nih.gov/19821415/
34. Carlos, M.: Deep learning IoT system for online stroke detection in skull-computed tomography images. J. Comput. Netw. **152**(19), 25–39 (2019). https://doi.org/10.1016/j.comnet.2019.01.019
35. Celine, R.: Automated delineation of stroke lesions using brain CT images. Neuro Image Clin. **4**(14), 540–548 (2014). https://doi.org/10.1016/j.nicl.2014.03.009
36. Robert, L., Lin, L., Gottfried, S.: Predicting functional motor potential in chronic stroke patients using diffusion tensor imaging. Hum. Brain Mapp. **33**(1), 1040–1051 (2011). https://doi.org/10.1002/hbm.21266
37. Soni, N., Dhanota, D.P., Kumar, S., Jaiswal, A.K., Srivastava, A.K.: Perfusion MR-imaging of enhancing brain tumors: comparison of arterial spin labeling technique with dynamic susceptibility contrast technique. Neurol. India **65**, 1046–1052 (2017). https://doi.org/10.4103/neuroindia.ni_871_16
38. Harston, W.J., Minks, D., Sheerin, F., Payne, S.J., Chappell, M., Kennedy, J.: Optimizing image registration and infarct definition in stroke research. Ann. Clin. Transl. Neurol. **4**(3), 166–174 (2017)
39. Doyle, S., Forbes, F., Jaillard, A., Heck, O., Detante, O., Dojat, M.: Sub-acute and chronic ischemic stroke lesion MRI segmentation. In: Crimi, A., Bakas, S., Kuijf, H., Menze, B., Reyes, M. (eds.) BrainLes 2017. LNCS, vol. 10670, pp. 111–122. Springer, Cham (2018). https://doi.org/10.1007/978-3-319-75238-9_10
40. Sporns, P., et al.: Computed tomography perfusion improves diagnostic accuracy in acute posterior circulation stroke. Cerebrovasc. Dis. **41**(5–6), 242–247 (2016). https://doi.org/10.1159/000443618
41. Bastian, C., et al.: Influence of stroke infarct location on functional outcome measured by the modified Rankin scale. Stroke **45**, 1695–1702 (2014). https://doi.org/10.1161/STROKEAHA.114.005152
42. Liew, S., et al.: A large, open source dataset of stroke anatomical brain images and manual lesion segmentations. Sci. Data **5**, 180011 (2018). https://doi.org/10.1038/sdata.2018.11
43. Maier, O., Menze, B.H., Heinrich, P., Handles, H., Reyes, M.: ISLES 2015: a public evaluation benchmark for ischemic stroke lesion-segmentation from multispectral MRI. Med. Image Anal. **35**, 250–269 (2017). https://doi.org/10.1016/j.media.2016.07.009
44. Kidwell, C.S., Chalela, J.A., Saver, J.L.: Comparison of MRI and CT to detecting the acute intracerebral haemorrhage. JAMA **292**(15), 1823–1830 (2004)
45. Wardlaw, J.M., Keir, S.L., Seymour, J.: What is the best imaging strategy for acute stroke? Health Technol. Assess. **8**, 1–180 (2004)
46. Latchaw, R.E., Yonas, H., Hunter, G.J.: Guidelines and recommendations for perfusion-imaging in cerebral-ischemia: a scientific statement for healthcare professionals by the writing group on perfusion-imaging, from the Council on Cardiovascular Radiology of the American Heart Association. Stroke **34**, 1084–1104 (2005)
47. Adams, H.P., Adams, R.J., Brott, T.: The early management guidelines for patients with ischemic stroke. Stroke **34**, 1056–1083 (2005)
48. Madhu, L.: Prediction of stroke using deep learning model. Am. J. Neuroradiol. **3**(8), 1–9 (2017). https://doi.org/10.1007/978-3-319-70139-478

49. Steffanie, H., Benno, G., Corinne, B., Gemma, L., Marcoand, D., Arthur, L.: Automated morphologic analysis of microglia after stroke. Front. Cell. Neurol. **12**(106), 1–11 (2018). https://doi.org/10.3389/fncel.2018.00106

50. Arko, B.: Determining ischemic stroke from CTA imaging using symmetry sensitive convolutional networks. Researchgate, pp. 1–6 (2019). https://doi.org/10.1109/ISBI.2019.8759475

51. Jakub, N., Michal, M., Michal, K.: Data augmentation for brain-tumor segmentation: a review. Front. Comput. Neurosci. **13**(83), 1–18 (2019)

52. Forkert, N.D., Verleger, T., Cheng, B., Thomalla, G., Hilgetag, C.C., Fiehler, J.: Multiclass support vector machine-based lesion mapping predicts functional outcome in ischemic stroke patients. PLoS One **10**(6), e0129569 (2015). https://doi.org/10.1371/journal.pone.0129569

53. Li, X., Bian, D., Jinghui, Y., Li, M., Zhao, D.: Using machine learning models to improve stroke risk level classification methods of China national stroke screening. BMC Med. Inform. Decis. Mak. **19**(261), 1–7 (2019)

54. Abulnaga, S., Rubin, J.: Ischemic Stroke Lesion Segmentation in CT Perfusion Scans Using Pyramid Pooling and Focal Loss. arXiv:1811.01085v1 [cs.CV] (2018)

55. Dolz, J., Ben, I., Desrosiers, C.: Dense Multi Path U-Net for Ischemic Stroke Lesion Segmentation in Multiple Image Modalities. arXiv:1810.07003v1 [cs.CV] (2018)

56. Sharique, M., Pundarikaksha, B., Sridar, P., Rama, K., Ramarathnam, K.: Parallel CapsuleNet for Ischemic Stroke Segmentation (2019). https://doi.org/10.1101/661132

57. Öman, O., Mäkelä, T., Salli, E., Savolainen, S., Kangasniemi, M.: 3D convolutional neural networks applied to CT angiography in the detection of acute ischemic stroke. Eur. Radiol. Exp. **3**(1), 1–11 (2019). https://doi.org/10.1186/s41747-019-0085-6

58. Wang, G., Song, T., Dong, Q., Cui, M., Huang, N., Zhang, S.: Automatic Ischemic Stroke Lesion Segmentation from Computed Tomography Perfusion Images by Image Synthesis and Attention Based Deep Neural Networks. arXiv:2007.03294v1 [eess.IV] (2020)

59. Samak, A., Clatworthy, P., Mirmehdi, M.: Prediction of Thrombectomy Functional Outcomes using Multimodal Data. arXiv:2005.13061v2 [eess.IV] (2020)

60. Rubin, J., Abulnaga, S.: CT-To-MR Conditional Generative Adversarial Networks for Ischemic Stroke Lesion Segmentation. arXiv:1904.13281v1 [eess.IV] (2019)

61. Malla, P., Hernandez, C., Rachmadi, M., Komura, T.: Evaluation of enhanced learning techniques for segmenting ischemic stroke lesions in brain MRP images using a convolutional neural network scheme. Frontiers (2019). https://doi.org/10.1101/544858

62. Zhang, L., et al.: Ischemic-stroke-lesion segmentation using multi-plane information fusion. IEEE Access **8**, 45715–45725 (2020). https://doi.org/10.1109/ACCESS.2020.2977415

63. Zhao, B., et al.: Automatic Acute Ischemic Stroke Lesion Segmentation Using Semi-Supervised Learning

64. Suberi, M., Zakaria, W., Tomari, R., Nazari, A., Mohd, H., Fuad, N.: Deep transfer learning application for automated ischemic classification in posterior fossa CT images. Int. J. Adv. Comput. Sci. Appl. **10**(8), 459–465 (2019)

65. Liu, Z., Cao, C., Ding, S., Han, T., Wu, H., Liu, S.: Towards Clinical Diagnosis: Automated Stroke Lesion Segmentation on Multimodal MR Image Using Convolutional Neural Network. arXiv:1803.05848v1 [cs.CV] (2018)

66. Henok, Y.A.: Adaptive learning expert system for diagnosis and management of viral hepatitis. Int. J. Artif. Intell. Appl. **10**(2), 33–46 (2019). https://doi.org/10.5121/ijaia.2019.10204

67. Stroke Diagnosis. https://www.nhs.uk/conditions/stroke/diagnosis/. Retrieved 19 May 2020

68. Great Learning Team: Introduction to Image Pre-processing: What is Image Pre-processing? https://www.mygreatlearning.com/blog/author/greatlearning/ (2020)

Amharic Fake News Detection on Social Media Using Feature Fusion

Menbere Hailu Worku[1](✉) and Michael Melese Woldeyohannis[2]

[1] University of Gondar, Gondar, Ethiopia
menbere.hailu@uog.edu.et
[2] Addis Ababa University, Addis Ababa, Ethiopia
michael.melese@aau.edu.et

Abstract. These days, many people use social media as a source of information and medium of communication due to its easy to access, fast to disseminate and low-cost platform. However, it also enables the wide propagation of fake news which causes economic, political, and social crises to the society. As a result, many researchers have been working towards detecting fake news. Most of the researches concerned on linguistic analysis of news content to identify its credibility, however fake news is also written intentionally to mislead users by mimicking true news. Beside this, Amharic is one of the under-resourced language that suffer from the benefits of fake news detection. To overcome the problem of fake news using content feature and under-resourced language, this study uses a feature fusion of linguistic and social context feature of the publisher information to detect Amharic fake news. For this, a total of 4,590 instance has been collected from different Facebook pages in different domain. Each article have been annotated by professional journalists and linguist for the purposes of doing experiments. The experimental result of feature fusion-based experiment shows at least 94.13% and at most 98.7% with a high relative error reduction over the content-based approaches. The result obtained from the experiment shows that, it is promising to detect fake news using fusion feature. We are now working towards incorporating intentionally edited pictures to the news content as part of the fake news detection.

Keywords: Amharic · Amharic fake news · Content-social feature

1 Introduction

As a result of advancing technology, ease of access and a low-cost platform, many people choose social media as a source of information and medium of communication [1]. Due to this fact, the traditional news media such as TV and magazine are evolving to a digital form such as online news platforms, blogs, social media feeds, and other digital media formats to reach the consumer in different ways [2]. Among these digital medias, social media has the potential to reach large number of audiences over the traditional news media [1]. Moreover, Social media is a powerful tool, for both business and individual to share and disseminate information in a short period than ever before when approached with appropriate content. From the very nature of social media, the information that the consumers get over the social media are not always

M. L. Berihun (Ed.): ICAST 2021, LNICST 411, pp. 468–479, 2022.
https://doi.org/10.1007/978-3-030-93709-6_31

correct and may not reach promptly. However, spreading false information on social media is for influencing others opinion while earning a money which highly affect the economy [2].

Nowadays, the issue of social media and fake news has become critical and the major issue among concerned stakeholders in country like Ethiopia [3]. Social media networks and immediate messaging applications allow misleading content to reach several people [4]. Due to the appealing nature, fake news spreads rapidly and influence people's perceptions about various subject. This causes genocides and protests that leads to economic, social, and political crises. To further detect the spread of the fake news, a number of researches attempts have been made using content-based [5–7] and social feature-based [8, 9] detection techniques despite their own drawbacks. Content-based fake news detection uses the content to detect real or not while the social features of the news.

The main problem of content-based fake news detection is that, fake news are written intentionally to mislead consumer, which makes it nontrivial to detect based on news content [10]. These difficulties are probably the reason behind the limitation of the content-based methods for fake news detection on social media. In addition to this, under-resourced Ethiopian languages like Amharic highly suffer from the lack of fake news detection. The main reason behind is the morphological complexity of the Amharic language and unavailability of linguistic resources such as stop words, Amharic stemmer and standard dictionary.

Similarly, fake news detection model using social features of news such as "like", "dislike" and "share" better determines in the presence of the social feature and tends to fail when the data did not have a social response [8, 9]. Thus, there is a need to fill the gap to overcome these problems by combining the content and social feature to detect fake news from the real on social media using state-of-the-art tools for techno-logically unsupported, morphological rich and complex Amharic language.

2 Related Work

Fake news detection is the process of discriminate fake news from genuine one news that contains false information from a certain one [11]. According to Shu and Liu [11] fake news detection methods generally focus on using news contents-based, social contexts-based and hybrid-based. News content-based approaches extract features from linguistic and visual information. Social context-based approaches incorporate features from user profiles, author analysis, and social networks [12]. Hybrid based approach is a combination of technique, method and feature from content-based method and social context-based method, using auxiliary information from different perspective [13].

An automated fake news detection system primarily introduced under the name "FakeNew-Tracker" for understanding and detecting of fake news based on the confirmed fake news and real news from fact-checking websites such as PolitiFact [14]. Then using the advanced search API of Twitter, they gathered the fake/real news related tweets that spread over the Twitter, through social engagement such as tweet replies, retweets, and favorites. To detect fake news, Auto-encoders and the doc2vec features are used for the content of the article and RNN for social context. The experiment result shows a 71.7% accuracy. However, due to the language difference, morphological richness and complexity of the language, tweets, retweets used cannot be applied for Amharic language.

Another attempt has been made to classify the social media posts with better accuracy based on the users who "like" or "dislike" them and achieved significant accuracies even with a very small training dataset [15]. However, social interactions features cannot be used when a post has no likes, and probably perform worse when a post collects only a few social reactions. To overcome this problem, a content-based features were introduced only when the social-based methods perform poorly [16]. The model based entirely on only one type of feature at a time tested on real-world data and obtained an accuracy of 81.7%.

In the other case, content based fake news detection have been attempt and it concentrates only on political news articles and news articles from both false and truthful categories in the year 2016 [17]. The length of each article is more than 200 characters. The author utilizes the techniques of n-gram analysis and machine learning with two distinct linguistic based features extraction techniques. Term Frequency-Inverted Document Frequency (TF-IDF) and N-gram are studied and compared using six different machine classification techniques. Compared to other, TF-IDF and uni-gram as a feature extraction technique, and Linear Support Vector Machine (LSVM) as a classifier, with an accuracy of 92%, experimental evaluation produces the best performance. The study shows a good result but the feature extraction technique did not contain the semantics of the news content and also this study were not applicable in Amharic news.

Consequently, a content-based fake news detection used after preprocessing and feature extraction using twenty-three machine learning algorithms to build a model [7]. The performance evaluation has been performed on three readymade datasets called BuzzFeed dataset contains 1,627 news articles and achieved an accuracy score of 65% by zeroR algorithm, Random political news data contains 75 articles and achieved an accuracy score of 69.3% by sequential minimal optimization algorithm, and ISOT fake news data collection contains 44,898 article and achieved an accuracy score of 96.8% by decision tree algorithm.

In addition to this, a novel machine learning model based on the NLP technique for detection of fake news by using both content-based features and social features of news which consist of a headline and body [18]. To examine the social features of the news articles, their authenticity can be established by using Facebook Page ID, Source, and Face-book App ID. In data processing, a bag of words for feature extraction from headline and body and classification were performed using a probabilistic classifier and tested on the FakeNewsNet dataset and achieved an average accuracy of 90.62%. The performance of the experiment shows a good result but when we see the feature extraction, it works only by counting the occurrence of the word in the documents without the semantic and order of words in the news content. The above research study works either on the content or social context, however this study uses both content and social features to detect Amharic fake news article.

3 Amharic Language

Amharic is one of the Semitic languages spoken in many parts of Ethiopia and it is an official working language for the Federal Democratic Republic of Ethiopia [19]. It is also a working language of several regional states including Amhara, South Nation, and Nationalities. The language is also used for the interregional communication. According to [20], more than 25 million with up to 22 million native speakers speaks Amharic as their first language in Ethiopia and it has over 4 million second-language speakers within the country and a further 3 million around the world. The majority of Amharic speakers found in Ethiopia even though there are also speakers in a number of other countries, particularly Italy, Canada, the USA and Sweden. The language Amharic is also used in commerce, government, media, and national education. Amharic is written using a writing system called Fidel (ፊደል), adapted from the one used by the Ge'ez language [19].

3.1 Amharic Writing System

The language Amharic which is phonetic contains 34 base characters each of the characters ordered in the form of seven orders [16]. The seven orders represent syllable combinations consisting of a consonant following a vowel. In Amharic language seven vowels are used, each of them has seven distinct forms that reflect the seven vowel sounds. They are ኽ/a/, ኹ/u/, ኺ/i/, ኻ/a/ኽ/e/, ኽ/ə/, ኽ/o/. This vowel is fused to the consonant form in the form of diacritic markings. The diacritic markings are strokes attached to the base characters to change their order. In the Amharic writing system, there is no capital-lower case distinction. The 34 basic characters and their orders give 238 distinct symbols. In addition to the 238 symbols, Amharic script contains five-so called labiovelars which have five orders and 18 additional labialized consonants. These letters do not use more frequently. Table 1 presents the distribution of Amharic characters in the modern writing systems.

Table 1. Amharic writing system

	Character order						
	1	2	3	4	5	6	7
U	U(ha)	U-(hu)	ሂ(hi)	ሃ(hā)	ሄ(hé)	U(he/h)	ህ(ho)
ለ	ለ(la)	ሉ(lu)	ሊ(li)	ላ(lā)	ሌ(lé)	ል(le/h)	ሎ(lo)
ሐ	ሐ(ha)	ሑ(hu)	ሒ(hi)	ሓ(hā)	ሔ(hé)	ሕ(he/h)	ሖ(ho)
መ	መ(ma)	ሙ(mu)	ሚ(mi)	ማ(mā)	ሜ(mé)	ም(me/h)	ሞ(mo)

Amharic writing scheme has some issues that are difficult to process Amharic text. One of these challenges is the redundancy of characters used in Amharic, more than one character to represent the same sound. The various forms have their meaning in Ge'ez, but there is no clear rule that shows their purpose in Amharic [19]. The problem of the same sound with various characters is not only observed with core characters but also exhibited in the same order of characters. Those are, ሀ and ሃ; ሐ and ሕ; ኀ and ኃ; አ and ኻ; ሰ and ሠ. A word formed by using this character has the same meaning. For example, the word 'sun' could be written in a different way like ጸሀይ/S'ähay/, ፀሀይ/ Ts'ähay/ጸሃይ/Tse-hi/, ፀሃይ, ጸሐይ, ፀሐይ/Ts'ähay/, ፀሐይ, ፀኀይ.

In addition to the 238 symbols, Amharic script contains five-so called labiovelars which have five orders and 18 additional labialized consonants. These letters do not use more frequently. Those characters are ሏ፣ ሟ ፣ሷ ፣ጇ ፣ኟ.

3.2   Amharic Morphology

Amharic is one of the most morphological rich and complex languages that [19]. It shows a root-pattern morphological phenomenon. With a basic lexical meaning [19]. Amharic words are categorized under five categories based on the use of morphology and position of the word in a sentence. Amharic word categories are noun, verb, adjective, adverb, and preposition. Nouns are words used to name or identify any class of things, people, places or ideas or a particular of these. Verbs are the most important part of speech because which shows the action or state, a word that tells the listener or reader what is happening in the sentence and have more to do with mental processes and perceptions. The adjective is a word that comes before a noun and adds some kind of qualification to the noun. An adverb is a word that qualifies the verb by adding extra ideas from time, place, and situations point of view. A preposition is a word that can be placed before a noun and perform adverbial operations related to place, time, cause, etc.

4   Data Collection and Preparation

In the experimental research, it was possible to collect data from social media and identify dependent and independent variable then perform experimental analysis with different experimental setting and machine learning techniques [21] to detect the news article as real or fake using both content and social feature as independent variable. This work collected the data from Facebook then prepared and annotated by experts for the purpose of the experiment. During experimental analysis, features has been extracted from content and social context of collected data, then total of 8 experiments have been performed using machine learning techniques to train and classify the dataset as real or fake news. The evaluation techniques take place after the classification task to check the performance of the proposed model.

Gereme et al. [22] states that they collect and prepare publicly available datasets for the fake news detection in local language especially for Amharic content news, however the data is not accessible. So, we collect data from the Facebook platform and make available for expert (journalist) for labeling (annotation).

The Facebook pages are selected from different categories including news media, broadcasting pages, bloggers and journalist's pages, political parties, politicians and government office pages. The pages are selected based on the frequency of news post content and contain accepted news for real and fake news through observation of the domain experts specifically the journalist. The data is collected in specific periodic manner which enables collect data with in a specific range as per suggestion of different researchers [14]. Accordingly, the data for this study have been collected from those selected pages which contain Amharic news contents starting from April 10, 2020 up to August 25, 2020 which covers four months of data. The data collection is made by using Data-miner web scraper tool which have effective way to collect the news content and social context of the perspective news from social media platform. During the data collection process, 4,590 data with six attributes; news content, posted date, published page, created date, verification of the published Facebook pages, number of follower and like of published pages are collected from the selected pages.

After the data collection, the annotation process takes place to label the given article as real or fake, it is not easy to find well-organized true and fake Amharic news, especially getting the fake article was tedious, and however there are new pages created for promoting fake news based on the situation of the country. However, to get the clarity of the news, we checked those manually using senior journalists and linguist. There are six senior journalist who are news editor and organizer at Gondar FM and one linguist from the linguistic department of government institution. Each annotator takes 765 post that are randomly selected from the collected data's. Since, the annotation process is manual, tedious and needs detail analysis and clarity, the annotation process takes two months and annotated based on the guidelines those are, the annotator labeled as fake/false when one or more of the following conditions is met;

- The statement is fully contradict to the truth,
- The statement seems true but interpreted in the wrong context,
- The posted date event and the nature of the news is mismatch which means the news is true and it happened before and presented it as it hap-pens now,
- Check the date of event and the news.

Accordingly, from the total of 4,590 instances, 2,211 news has been labeled as Fake and 2,379 news has been labeled as Real. Figure 1 represented the distribution of fake and real news image.

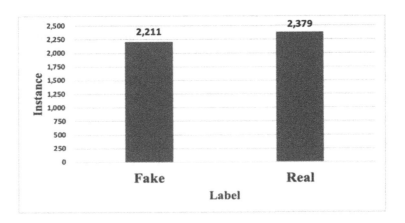

Fig. 1. Class label of distribution of the collected data

The challenge faced during the annotation was some post have written in both Amharic and Tigrinya language, in order to understand the meaning of full article it requires to translate those terms so it is the challenges for the annotator.

4.1 Data Preprocessing

In this work, two different kinds of preprocessing have been performed. One is for the content of the Amharic text and the other for the social features. Primarily, NLP based pre-processing used for the content of the article includes removing irrelevant characters. These characters include special symbol, emoji, Amharic and Arabic numbers and punctuation. In addition to this, Amharic character normalization were done to removes the Amharic character that made the same sound but different orthography. Consequently, content tokenization have been done after removing irrelevant and redundant characters. This is followed by the removal of Amharic stop words from the tokenized word and stemming using a rule-based Hornmorpho [23]. Finally, the output of content pre-processed data is used as an input for feature ex-traction process. The second one is handling categorical data that has been per-formed to convert categorical data of social-context information to numeric.

4.2 Features Extraction

In order to analyze the news content and verify the given news article, it is important to use feature extraction technique to extract features from the news content. In this study we used NLP-based feature extraction technique like TFIDF, N-gram weighted by TFIDF (i.e. unigram, bigram and trigram) and word2vec for the content. Beside content feature, for the social context features like number of like, follower, created date and credibility status of Facebook page that the news articles have been posted.

4.3 System Design

This system design for Amharic Fake News detection contain three different phase; pre-processing, feature extraction and classification. Those major phases are presented on the following figure.

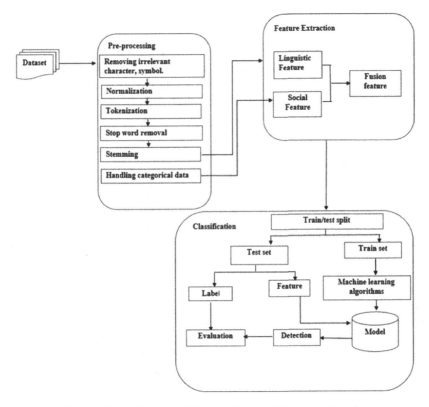

Fig. 2. The architecture of feature fusion of fake news detection

The above Fig. 2 shows the architecture of fake news which differ from other fake news detection by applying feature fusion to determine the reliability of the news article based on linguistic and social feature. Primarily, the dataset is collected from Facebook having news content and social information of news and it is annotated by expert (journalist).The news content in the dataset which have been preprocessed using Amharic data pre-processing technique including the removal of irrelevant character, normalization, tokenization, stop words removal beside stemming and social context information also preprocessed with handling categorical data technique. After all the preprocessing, feature extraction takes place to extract features from preprocessed news content using N-gram weighted by TFIDF and word2vec. The output of feature extraction of content-based and preprocessed social context information are combined and it makes an important feature vector of the dataset for training the model. After fusion of content and social feature, classification model has been built by training set and three machine learning algorithms, Logistic Regression (LR), Support Vector Machine (SVM), and Random Forest (RF). Finally, the performance of the model on the test set has been evaluated using accuracy, recall, F-measure, and precision.

5 Experiment and Discussion

In order to perform experiments, different python libraries for machine learning including the latest one Flair, Natural language processing toolkit (NLTK), Scientific computing (SciPy), and multidimensional processing (NumPy) has been used at different stages of the machine learning. Along with Python, the Jupyter notebook is used as a tool for an integrated development environment (IDE). Because of these advantages, the researcher uses python for preprocessing as well as for building models. Natural language processing uses for preprocessing the data like for tokenization, stemming, and normalizing the news content and analyzing some other social-context feature of data. In addition to this, LR, RF, and SVM, the machine learning algorithm has been used to create an Amharic fake news detection model.

To minimize the opportunity of creating over-fitting the dataset is first divided into two different datasets randomly, 80% of the data for training and the remaining 20% for evaluating the model. Once the dataset splitted, to investigate fake news detection for Amharic language, two independent experiment were conducted using three different machine learning algorithms. The first experiment is conducted using only content features s with three machine learning algorithms LR, SVM, and RF. Similarly, the second experiment also contain four experiments which is a hybrid feature of content and social-context features with three machine learning algorithms. Beside this, both experiments are conducted using n-gram weighted by TFIDF and word2vec. Table 2 presents the experimental result with respect to the linguistic feature, algorithm and content feature extracted against weighted n-gram and word2vec.

Table 2. Experiment result of fake news detection

Feature	ML algorithm	N-gram			w2vec
		Unigram	Bigram	Trigram	
Linguistic/content feature	LR	93.35	89.76	76.57	92.48
	SVM	89.76	81.69	74.94	92.48
	RF	91.5	86.71	79.52	94.33
Fusion feature	LR	96.84	96.84	96.84	93.79
	SVM	96.4	96.4	96.4	96.4
	RF	99.56	99.34	99.34	99.67

The above Table 2 presents the experiment result in terms of accuracy. The experiment result shows that the content/linguistic feature on the unigram and bi-gram with logistic regression achieves the highest accuracy 93.33% and 89.76% respectively. The reason behind the higher performance for LR is the ability to transform the class label using the probability measures of the unigram and bigram vectors. In addition to this, unigram and bigrams are relatively context independent. However, RF is much better than SVM but lower than LR.

Unlike the unigram and bigram, trigram and word2vec achieved the highest performance in the Random Forest. Because it is a capable to selecting the highest classification result among the selected decision tree results. In addition to that the word2vec features achieved the highest accuracy, because it uses the semantic information of the news content on the vectors than N-grams features. In other case, all fused feature achieves highest accuracy on RF.

The above Fig. 3 presents the comparison of the experimental result in terms of accuracy.

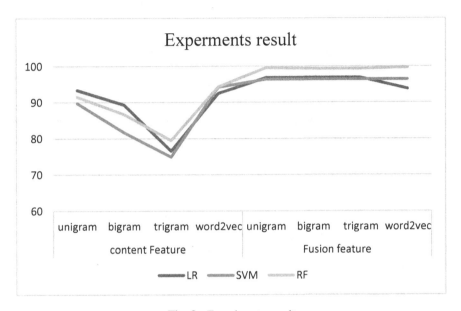

Fig. 3. Experiments result

The accuracy result has shown us which feature extraction technique, approach and model perform well than others. The result that has been observed while experimenting shows which technique should be used to build the prototype which received new data contain content news and social context. From the stated experiments, the content-based approach of the word2vec feature extraction technique with support vector machine achieves the highest accuracy 94.22% among other content-based feature extraction techniques like N-gram levels with TFIDF.

Because word2vec retains the semantic meaning of different words in a document. The context information is not lost and another great benefit of the word2vec approach is that the size of the embedding vector is very small. Each dimension in the embedding vector contains information about one aspect of the word. There is no need of huge sparse vectors, unlike the bag of words and TF-IDF approaches in addition to that trigram achieved the lowest accuracy among linguistic based analyses, because the occurrence of three consecutive words became. Whereas when we use a hybrid approach which means integrating the content-based feature with social con-text feature the accuracy is higher than content-based features. When we incorporate social context features to the content-based feature it performs higher than of con-tent-based feature.

The proposed model achieves its highest accuracy when using a fusion of word2vec and social context feature with Random Forest classifier because feature fusion get both content and social context feature other than of one of them. Among other machine learning algorithms Random Forest achieves the highest accuracy which is 99.67% because it enables to select the best classification result from random trees generated.

6 Conclusion and Future Work

This study proposed a solution for detecting fake news on social media especially Facebook by using a hybrid approach of fake news detection mechanism and ma-chine learning classification techniques for Amharic online news. 4,590 data are collected from 30 Facebook pages by using the "data_miner" tool that was posted with-in three months. When using the word2vec hybrid with social context and Random Forest classifier, the proposed model achieves 99.67% of the highest accuracy score. The first four experiment conducted on news content features (i.e. Uni-gram, Bigram, and Tri-gram word2vec). The rest of four experiments have done on incorporating of social context feature to content based feature. In addition to this, eight different experiments have been performed on three machine learning algorithms. The major contribution of this study is design a model for Amharic fake news detection using fused feature of both content and social context feature. In this research we only consider news text content and social information, it would be better for future re-searchers to incorporate also the image analysis as most of fake news distributer use unrelated and intentional edited pictures.

Acknowledgment. We would like to thank college of Informatics, University of Gondar for supporting the research work and Impact Amplifier Online Safety Project for sponsoring con-ference participation.

References

1. Perrin, A.: Social Media Usage: 2005–2015. Pew Research Center, Washington (2015)
2. Howell, L.: Digital wildfres in a hyperconnected world. WEF Report **3**, 15–94 (2013)
3. Abeselom, D.K.: The impacts of fake news on peace and development in the world: In the case of Ethiopia. Internal J. Curr. Res. **10**, 71356–71365 (2018)
4. Vosoughi, S., Roy, D., Aral, S.: The spread of true and false news online. Science **359**(6380), 1146–1151 (2018)
5. Ahmed, H., Traore, I., Saad, S.: Detection of online fake news using n-gram analysis and machine learning techniques. In: Traore, I., Woungang, I., Awad, A. (eds.) Intelligent, Secure, and Dependable Systems in Distributed and Cloud Environments, pp. 127–138. Springer International Publishing, Cham (2017). https://doi.org/10.1007/978-3-319-69155-8_9
6. Riedel, B., Augenstein, I., Spithourakis, G.P., Riedel, S.: A simple but tough-to-beat baseline for the Fake News Challenge stance detection task. arXiv preprint arXiv:1707.03264 (2017)
7. Ozbay, F., Alatas, B.: Fake news detection within online social media using supervised artificial intelligence algorithms. Physica A Stat. Mech. Appl. **540**, 123174 (2020)

8. Tacchini, E., Ballarin, G., Vedova, M.L.D., Moret, S., Alfaro, L.D.: Some like it hoax: automated fake news detection in social networks. In: Proceedings of the Second Workshop on Data Science for Social Good (SoGood), Skopje, Macedonia, 2017. CEUR Workshop Proceedings, vol. 1960 (2017)

9. Tlahun, A., Beshah, D.: Fake news detection model using machine learning approach: the caseof Amharic news on social media. unpublished masters thesis ,University of Gondar, Department of Information systems (2020)

10. Shu, K., Wang, S., Liu, H.: Exploiting Tri-Relationship for Fake News Detection (2017). arXiv:1712.07709 [cs]

11. Shu, K., Sliva, A., Wang, S., Tang, J., Liu, A.H.: Fake news detection on social media: a data mining perspective. In: KDD Exploration Newsletter (2017)

12. Zhou, X., Zafarani, R., Shu, K., Liu, A.H.: Fake news: fundamental theories, detection strategies and challenges. In: WSDM (2019)

13. Mahid, Z.I., Manickam, S., Karuppayah, S.: Fake news on social media: brief review on detection techniques. In: 2018 Fourth International Conference on Advances in Computing, Communication & Automation (ICACC). IEEE, Subang Jaya (2018)

14. Shu, K., Mahudeswaran, D., Liu, H.: FakeNewsTracker: a tool for fake news collection, detection, and visualization. Comput. Math. Organ. Theory **25**(1), 60–71 (2018). https://doi.org/10.1007/s10588-018-09280-3

15. Tacchini, E., Ballarin, G., Vedova, M., Della, S.M., Alfato, L.D.: Some like it hoax: automated fake news detection in social networks (2017). arXiv preprint arXiv:1704.07506

16. Vedova, D., Tacchini, E., Moret, S., Ballarin, G., DiPierro, M., de Alfaro, L.: Automatic online fake news detection combining content and social signals. In: 22nd Conference of Open Innovations Association (FRUCT), pp. 272–279 (2018)

17. Ahmed, H., Traore, I., Saad, S.: Detection of online fake news using n-gram analysis and machine learning techniques. In: Traore, I., Woungang, I., Awad, A. (eds.) ISDDC 2017. LNCS, vol. 10618, pp. 127–138. Springer, Cham (2017). https://doi.org/10.1007/978-3-319-69155-8_9

18. Shubham, B., Vijay, B., Jain, P., Chawla, M.: Natural language processing based hybrid model fordetecting fake news using content-based features and social features. Inf. Eng. Electron. Bus. **4**, 1–10 (2019)

19. Getahun, B.A., Fekade.: Event modeling from amharic news article. Unpublished Master's Thesis, Department of Computer Science, Addis Ababa University (2018)

20. ethiopiaonlinevisa   (2020).   https://www.ethiopiaonlinevisa.com/amharic-the-ethiopian-language/

21. Morrison, G.R., Ross, S.M.: Experimental Research Methods. Researchgate (2003)

22. Gereme, F., Zhu, W., Ayall, T., Alemu, D.: Combating fake news in "low-resource" languages: amharicfake news detection accompanied by resource crafting. Information **12**, 20 (2021)

23. Michael, G.: Hornmorpho 2.5 User's Guide. Indiana University, School of Informatics and Computing (2012)

24. Shu, K., Sliva, A., Wang, S., Tang, J., Liu, H.: Fake news detection on social media: a data mining perspective. In: KDD Exploration Newsletter (2017)

25. Potthast, M., Kiese, J., Reinart, K., Bevendorff, J., Stein, B.: A Stylometric Inquiry into Hyper partisan and Fake News (2017). arXiv preprint arXiv:1702.05638

Early Ginger Disease Detection Using Deep Learning Approach

Mesay Gemeda Yigezu[1]($\boxtimes$), Michael Melese Woldeyohannis[2],
and Atnafu Lambebo Tonja[3]

[1] Wachemo University, Hossana, Ethiopia
mesaygemeda@wcu.edu.et
[2] Addis Ababa University, Addis Ababa, Ethiopia
michael.melese@aau.edu.et
[3] Wolaita Sodo University, Wolaita Sodo, Ethiopia
atnafu.lambebo@wsu.edu.et

Abstract. Ethiopia is one of the countries in Africa which have a huge potential for the development of different varieties of crops used for traditional medicine and daily use in society. Ginger is one among the others which are affected by disease caused by bacteria, fungi, and virus being bacterial wilt is the most determinant constraint to ginger production. Detection of the disease needs special attention from experts which is not possible for mass production. However, the state-of-the-art technology can deploy to overcome the problem by means of image processing in a mass cultivates ginger crop. To this end, a deep learning approach for early ginger disease detection from the leaf is proposed through different phases after collecting 7,014 ginger images with the help of domain experts from different farms. The collected data passed through different image preprocessing to design and develop a deep learning model that can detect and classify with a different scenario. The experimental result demonstrates that the proposed technique is effective for ginger disease detection especially bacterial wilt. The proposed model can successfully detect the given image with a test accuracy of 95.2%. The result shows that the deep learning approach offers a fast, affordable, and easily deployable strategy for ginger disease detection that makes the model a useful early disease detection tool and this analysis is also extended to develop a mobile app to help a lot of ginger farmers in developing countries.

Keywords: CNN · Deep learning · Image detection · Image classification · Ginger disease

1 Introduction

Agriculture is one of the leading sector in Ethiopian economy accounting for about 68% of employment and 34% of GDP [1]. In addition to this, more than 3/4 of the Ethiopian population highly relies on the agriculture as a means of securing the necessities of life. In line with this, for the country like Ethiopia, the demand for economic growth of the agriculture sector is increasing at the alarming rate

© ICST Institute for Computer Sciences, Social Informatics and Telecommunications Engineering 2022
Published by Springer Nature Switzerland AG 2022. All Rights Reserved
M. L. Berihun (Ed.): ICAST 2021, LNICST 411, pp. 480–488, 2022.
https://doi.org/10.1007/978-3-030-93709-6_32

over the past decades. As a result, the rate of production in the agriculture sector has doubled in the last two decades [2]. This resulted in the expansion of land, labour and extension worker beside the modern inputs for the agriculture sector [3]. Accordingly, the production of cereals in last decode becomes three times more than that of the year 1995/16 while the yield produced increased by 86% for an increment of the 70% area cultivated [4]. Despite the increment of area, yield and modern inputs, the level of productivity remained low due to the unavailability and use of fertilizer and improved seeds [5]. Agriculture is one of the area that leads the economy of the country, but still it is done by using traditional techniques which leads to different structural problems including the quality and quantity [6]. The productivity of crops are highly affected by the disease that influence the quality of product.

Ethiopian farmers produce different crop and cereal products for the export market. Among these product, Ginger crop is one of that earns a sizeable amount of foreign exchange for the country. Traditional disease detection primarily depends on the skills and the visual inspection of the agricultural extension worker [7]. However, for the country like Ethiopia, with low logistical and human infrastructure capacity, detecting and classifying disease at the earliest stages are difficult and expensive to scale up specially when it comes to mass production. Similarly, smallholders farmers rely on the previous knowledge they have which make less effective in overcoming the challenges of farming. Therefore, early detection of pests and disease in the field is one of the crucial step for the early interventions resulting reduced impacts of food supply chain.

Ginger production in Ethiopia is handicapped by shortage of high yielding, absence of innovate technologies and weak role of private sectors in spices production [8]. In addition, the production of ginger is being affected by various disease. The decision-making capability of human inspector also depends on different condition. This include; the stability of the weather, work load, physical condition of the extension worker, such as fatigue and eyesight, and the biases. As a result, it is difficult to predict the type of disease by using observation which may leads also to biased prediction towards the disease type. This in turn leads farmers and extension worker to lose of money because of the wrong medicine which is difficult to control at its early stage.

Hence, it is not feasible and manageable to detect the ginger disease by digging out the root. Rather, it better to use the leaf of the plant because when plants become diseased. A diseased ginger displays a range of visual symptoms either in colored spots or streaks on different part of the plants [1,9]. The visual symptom of the disease continuously change in color, shape and size depending the progress of the disease.

In country like Ethiopia, farmers do not have proper facilities how and when they have to contact experts due to the high cost and time consuming to get the consultant. In such conditions, it is difficult to provide fruitfully ginger products specially when diseases are detected at the earliest stage. Different sectors benefits from the advancement of the state-of-the-art Artificial Intelligence (AI) technology which favours the high productivity and efficiency [10]. AI based solutions are supporting to overcome the challenges of traditional methods of detecting diseases and respond smartly to improve the efficiency while reducing the environmental hostile impacts. Deep learning is one of the technique for detecting and classifying the various crop diseases through image processing [11]. Previous research work has validated that, the AI-based detection and classification of crop diseases were effective to maximize production of goods [12,13]. Thus, there is a need to use a computerized early detection of disease in a short period by looking at the plant symptoms in easier and cheaper way to strengthen the agricultural fields and the economy of the country by increasing the productivity and quality of ginger crops.

2   Related Work

One of the research attempt is to detect cassava disease and used deep convolutional neural network approach through a transfer learning to train and detect the disease type [13]. As a result, an overall accuracy of 93% were achieved but experts extracted images manually from the dataset supported on the visibility of the most severe symptoms of every category.

In addition to this, under a controlled environment, a disease detection attempted on a public data set consisting of 54,306 using CNN through automatic feature extraction [14]. The first experiment conducted without any pretrained and has an accuracy of 99.35% on the test set. Beside these, using a transfer learning based approach using a ResNet50 and InceptionV2 pretrained models resulted a better performance than that of the MobileNetV1 [7].

Beside the use of deep learning, a classical machine learning has been applied in a cotton leaf disease classification using K-means clustering for segmentation and Support Vector Machine (SVM) for classification [15]. This has been achieved through the image converting from RGB to HSI, contrast enhancement and extracting a better features to identify disease through the process. Furthermore, groundnut disease identification and classification based on a back propagation [16]. However, the work were only applicable for limited diseases without the use of shape feature for the enhancement of image application.

In the research attempt [17], the researcher shows that, the application of image processing and Artificial Neural Network (ANN) to addresses the problem of cotton plant disease detection. The efficiency of the cotton plant disease detection were feasible with numerous techniques as well as ANN is employed as a classifier for testing using MATLAB to detect the kind of diseases on cotton leaf. The potency of the planned work were around 84% accuracy. Similarly, another the development of disease detection for maize disease [18]. The researcher collected massive amount of data for one plant disease from different platforms beside the data augmentation to assist the system for real-time observation. However, all the image dataset were collected from the single source using drones equipped with CNN model. This limit the generalizability of the data, as symptoms of equivalent disease in alternative regions could present in different ways.

In this review it has been observed that so many methods were proposed and implemented to identify, detect plant diseases using digital image processing. Most of the researchers used their datasets from internet that is publicly available databases such as in Plant Village. Using publicly available dataset is recommended but the images in most of the previously conducted researches are captured under controlled environments like in the laboratory setups; there are a lot of laborious pre-processing stages such as handcrafted feature extraction, color histogram, texture features, and shape features; most importantly the methods used by previously conducted research works are not state of the art, i.e. most of the studies in the literature of crop disease identification follows traditional image processing techniques.

As mentioned by different researcher [13,15,18], the studies shows that computer vision is widely used particularly for tasks like disease detection and identification has shown fascinating result specially in the field of agriculture. Moreover deep learning algorithms like CNN and ANN are most commonly used. Generally, a plant that has symptom seen on leaf as well as bacterial wilt however, currently there is a desire to come up with a model that is more correct and efficient. In general, more precise and efficient model development is necessary for a plant with symptoms on the leaf, such as leaf wilt and bacterial wilt.

3   Methodology

Deep learning techniques have obtained very high performance in different areas including image recognition, image segmentation, speech recognition, natural language processing and emotion recognition given sufficient data for learning [19]. We evaluate the pertinence of CNN from deep learning approach that is leading state-of-the-art in computer vision task. Before classification and prediction, traditional techniques to training classifiers need explicit extraction of the features to be examined from the image. CNN learns the feature hierarchy from pixels to classifier and train layers, which are made up of several consecutive layers, each of which changes one volume of activation to another using distinct functions. We have often utilized CNN layers such as the convolution layer, which is accomplished by sliding the feature detector on the provided image from left to right across dimension and computing between the filter and also the input image with dot product at every location to obtain a feature map.

Finally, we stake all the feature maps together and it is the final output of the convolution layer. The size of the output (the feature map) is controlled by the depth, stride, and padding parameters. These parameters should be decided before the convolution operation is performed [20]. Following the convolution layer, we used a pooling layer to reduce the size of the parameters and extract the main characteristics of a specific spatial location. The computational complexity of the model and to control the problem of over fitting in the CNN, we added it between some successive convolution layers [21]. In last, we flattened the matrix into a vector and sent it into a fully connected layer of a neural network, which contains neurons that are directly connected to neurons in the two adjacent layers but not to any layers within them.

In addition, We have used activation function on the hidden layer that is ReLU to apply non linearity and by using Sigmoid in last layer of fully connected we performed classification based on training data. Accordingly, the CNN architecture in this work has a of 11 layers, 5 convolutions, 3 pooling layers and 3 dense layers. Figure 1 presents a CNN based feature extraction and classification. The CNN algorithmic program extracts key features that are then used to classify images. The feature in this case has a different color mode than the given image. Then, to add non-linearity to the network, each feature map value is passed through a trigger function. Following non-linearity, the feature map is reintroduced into the pooling layer to minimize feature map resolution and network computational complexity. The extraction of useful features from a given image, which includes several similar steps such as cascaded convolutional layers, adding non-linearities, and layer pooling.

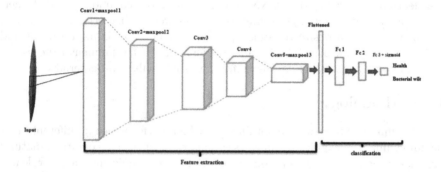

Fig. 1. CNN feature extraction and classification

The classification of the proposed model is performed in fully connected layers. As shown in the Fig. 1, we have a total of three fully connected layers, including the output layer. The main function of these layers is to classify the input image based on the features extracted by the convolutional layer and the detection layer. Before entering to the fully connected layer, the output layer is connected and flattened into a single vector value. The first fully connected layer accepts the output of the convolutional layer and the pooling layer. Each value of the vector represents the probability that a certain feature belongs to a class.

4   Data Preparation

Compared to the classical machine learning, deep learning requires large amount data to train the model [22]. For this, a data collected with the help of domain experts including; farmers, extension and agriculture researcher experts for the purpose of training the model. Accordingly, a total of 7,014 images the ginger dataset has been collected from Southern region of Ethiopia particularly from Boloso Bombe and Hadaro Tunto. From these, 7,014 dataset 2,734 images are labelled healthy while the remaining 4,280 images are labelled as infected. The image data has a 150 * 150 pixel size and Fig. 2 shows a leaf images collected for healthy and infected ginger.

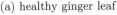

(a) healthy ginger leaf   (b) infected ginger leaf

Fig. 2. Healthy ginger leaf and infected ginger leaf

After collecting the data set, the leaf image passes through a number of images pre-processing task including; noise reduction, data labeling, data augmentation and data splitting takes place which is used to be the major and important task when we want to work with image processing. Before training a data to develop model, we pesrformed noise reduction from background of each images which may not predict accurately and all images sized uniform then labeled with appropriate label (healthy and bacterial wilt).

After labeling, Data augmentation were applied on the original image data to obtain other images and overcome the problem of small data as well as to get a better training and classifier model. For the detection of ginger diseases, a feature parameter namely color feature, is used. This feature is considered to be because the visual color distinction is used in the traditional system to identify whether the crop is infected with the disease through human vision. Therefore, the proposed model provides an output (pre-defined class) based on the color features of the input image learned during training.

5   Experimental Setup and Setting

In order to select a suitable tool to implement the CNN algorithm for ginger image classification, the entire experiment was tuned. Samsung galaxy S10 (16 Megapixel camera and 1440 * 3040 pixel display size and resolution) has been used to capture an images from the field. For building a classification model convolutional neural network were used. Along with this, a Python programming language with TensorFlow and Keras libraries on Google Colab environment which offered 12.72 GB RAM and 68.40 GB with GPU which is the most important hardware in deep learning for computer vision research. The proposed model has totally 974,561 parameters. Thus, the reason we had recommended the above experimental setting in order to handle the detection of ginger disease in more efficient manner and within short period of time using high computing.

5.1   Hyper-Parameter Setting

Before the start of the training process, experiments have been conducted with different hyperparameter settings. There is no standard rule for selecting the best hyperparameters for a given problem [23]. Therefore, many experiments have been done to select hyperparameters and improve the performance of the model. The hyperparameters selected for the model are described below.

Dataset Ratio:-Evaluate the results obtained from experiments using different ratio of training and testing, and get better results from experiments that use 80% for training and 20% for tests.

Learning Rate:-The result of the experiment is that by using different learning rates, when we apply a higher learning rate, its accuracy is lower than that of a smaller learning rate. Therefore, in the proposed model, a learning rate of 0.001 is considered the best.

Activation Function:-We examined different activation function which are Tanh, Softmax and Sigmoid and finally Sigmoid activation function in the output layer is better than others because this is more suitable for binary classification problems.

Batch Size:-It is too hard to give all the data to the computer in a single epoch therefore we want to divide the input into several smaller batches which is preferred in model training to reduce the computational time of the machine.We've used maximum number batch-size and got a good performance thus we should always strive with maximum batch size our GPU can handle; therefore, it depends on the memory of GPU. In this experiment can run until batch size 128.

Epochs:-In the experiment, the model was trained using different epochs from 10 to 50. During the training process, we see that when we use too small or too large epochs, there will be a big gap between the training error and the validation error of the model. After many experiments, the model reached its optimum at epoch twenty five.

Optimization Algorithms:-The proposed model is trained by using the Adaptive Moment Estimation (Adam) optimizer which updates the weight of the model and tunes parameters.

Loss Function:-The experiment was done by using Binary Cross Entropy (BCE) loss, Mean Squared Error (MSE), and categorical cross entropy (CCE) loss. we have chosen BCE loss as a loss function. It performed well for models that output possibilities.

6   Experimental Result

During the experiment, different classification scenarios were carried out to test the classification performance. The results obtained from the proposed model experiment are shown in the following table, using the classification accuracy metrics in the form of percentages of training data, validation data, and test data, respectively. Accordingly, the experimental result shows a training accuracy of 96.19% with 13.59% loss and validation accuracy 96.16% with 13.44% loss while the testing accuracy 95.22% with 11.67% loss. In this work we analyzed that the key feature to detect ginger disease is color because which appears on the leaf and can differentiate a healthy ginger from infected. Among deep learning approach, CNN is best approach to apply in ginger disease detection and after several experiments, all of the parameters were evaluated to find a good classifier result from developed model and achieved 95.22% accuracy of classifying ginger in the correct category during test data evaluation.

7   Conclusion and Future Work

A limited research attempt has been done on automatic detection of Ginger crop diseases using the symptoms are seen on the leaves. Therefore, this paper aimed to develop a model to detect ginger disease at early stage which are very useful to farmers, extension workers, pathologists and also agriculture scientists not only that, it increases both quality and quantity of ginger crops in agriculture production.

During the experiment, we used images collected directly from the farm with the help of agricultural experts. Thus, the experiment has two main phases. In the training phase, the data is repeatedly presented to the classifier, while the weights are updated to get the required response. In the testing phase, apply the trained algorithm to data that the classifier has not tested before to evaluate the performance of the trained algorithm and we have developed a model with a deep learning technique using CNN by improving the performance under different parameters.

Additionally, the size of data, using different pre-trained model, capturing in different angle of the leaf may increase the performance of the predictive model and considering other types of disease may be better model to identify disease and by extending this research, we hope to have a valuable impact on sustainable development and strengthen the ginger value chain.

References

1. Worldbank. World Development Indicators Data Catalog (2018). https://data.worldbank.org/country/ethiopia, Accessed 10 June 2021
2. Food and Agriculture Organization of the United Nations FAO. FAOSTAT database (2018). http://www.faostat.org, Accessed 19 June 2021

3. Cheru, F., Cramer, C., Oqubay, A.: The Oxford Handbook of the Ethiopian Economy. Oxford University Press, Oxford (2019). https://www.ebooks.com/en-us/book/209586650/the-oxford-handbook-of-the-ethiopian-economy/fantu-cheru/
4. CSA. Agricultural sample survey 2017/18 (2010 EC), Volume III: Report on farm management practices (Private peasant holdings, Meher season) (2018)
5. Dercon, S., Gollin, D.: Agriculture's Changing Role in Ethiopia's Economic Transformation. Oxford University Press, Oxford (2019)
6. Mengistu, A.D., Alemayehu, D.M., Mengistu, S.G.: Ethiopian coffee plant diseases recognition based on imaging and machine learning techniques. Int. J. Database Theory Appl. 9(4), 79–88 (2016)
7. Selvaraj, M.G., et al.: AI-powered banana diseases and pest detection. Plant Methods 15(1), 1–11 (2019)
8. M. Seiter et al.: We are IntechOpen, the world ' s leading publisher of Open Access books Built by scientists, for scientists TOP 1. Intech i, 13 (2019)
9. Camargo, A., Smith, J.S.: An image-processing based algorithm to automatically identify plant disease visual symptoms. Biosyst. Eng. 102(1), 9–21 (2009)
10. Gupta, J.: The Role of Artificial intelligence in Agriculture Sector. https://customerthink.com/the-role-of-artificial-intelligence-in-agriculture-sector/
11. Kamilaris, A., Prenafeta-Boldú, F.X.: Deep learning in agriculture: a survey. Comput. Electron. Agric. 147, 70–90 (2018)
12. Siricharoen, P., Scotney, B., Morrow, P., Parr, G.: A Lightweight Mobile System for Crop Disease Diagnosis (2016)
13. Ramcharan, A., Baranowski, K., McCloskey, P., Ahmed, B., Legg, J., Hughes, D.P.: Deep learning for image-based cassava disease detection. Front. Plant Sci. 8, 1852 (2019)
14. Mohanty, S.P., Hughes, D.P., Salathé, M.: Using deep learning for image-based plant disease detection. Front. Plant Sci. 7, 1419 (2016)
15. Oo, Y.M., Htun, N.C.: Plant leaf disease detection and classification using image processing. Int. J. Res. Eng. 5(9), 516–523 (2018)
16. Ramakrishnan, M.: Groundnut leaf disease detection and classification by using back propagation algorithm. In: IEEE ICCSP, pp. 1–19 (2015)
17. Mude, S., Naik, D., Patil, A.: Leaf disease detection using image processing for pesticide spraying. Int. J. Adv. Eng. Res. Dev. 4(4), 1129–1132 (2017)
18. Wiesner-Hanks, T., et al.: Image set for deep learning: field images of maize annotated with disease symptoms. BMC Res. Notes 11(1), 10–12 (2018)
19. Zhang, A., Lipton, Z.C., Li, M., Smola, A.J.: Dive into Deep Learning (2020)
20. Li, F.F., Krishna, R.: CS231n: Convolutional Neural Networks for Visual Recognition. https://cs231n.github.io/convolutional-networks
21. Prabhu.: Understanding of Convolutional Neural Network (CNN) - Deep Learning. https://medium.com/@RaghavPrabhu/understanding-of-convolutional-neural-network-cnn-deep-learning-99760835f148
22. Yu, D., Wang, H., Chen, P., Wei, Z.: Mixed pooling for convolutional neural networks mixed pooling for convolutional neural. Key Lab. Embed. Syst. Serv. Comput. Minist. Educ. (2014)
23. Josh, P., Adam, G.: Deep Learning A Practitioner's Approach. O'Reilly Media, Sebastopol (2017)

Towards Predicting the Risk of Cardiovascular Disease Using Machine Learning Approach

Hanna Teshager Mekonnen[1]([✉]) and Michael Melese Woldeyohannis[2]

[1] University of Gondar, Gondar, Ethiopia
[2] Addis Ababa University, Addis Ababa, Ethiopia
michael.melese@aau.edu.et

Abstract. Cardiovascular disease (CVDs) is one of the leading causes of mortality in the world taking around 18 million lives every year. As a result of the silent progression of CVDs, the rate of mortality is increasing at a higher rate than communicable, maternal, and neonatal diseases in a country like Ethiopia. The early stage detection and treatment, in turn, reduces the rate of mortality as well as the health care cost. For this, a total data set consisting of 10,029 unlabeled instances were analyzed from the Ethiopian Public Health Institution (EPHI). The data were collected by NCD STEPS survey. The population's demographic and behavioral characteristics and also each participant's physical and medical measurement data included in this dataset. Thus the given dataset doesn't have a target variable. Therefore, in order to identify the hidden patterns from unsupervised learning, we use the k-means clustering algorithm and specify the number of clusters to k = 3 and cluster the patient condition into high risk, medium risk, and low risk. The data is further experimented with five different machine learning (ML) algorithm to build a predictive model for the risk of CVDs. The result obtained from the experiment using an artificial neural network (ANN) shows a promising result which is 99.4% accuracy. This result shows it's possible to build an effective and efficient model for predicting the risk of having cardiovascular disease.

Keywords: Cardiovascular disease · Risk prediction · Machine learning techniques

1 Introduction

According to World Health Organization (WHO), health refers to a state of complete emotional and physical well-being. It's one of the most important aspects of thing in our day-to-day activities [1]. A health technology is the application of organized knowledge's in the form of devices, medicines, vaccines, procedures and systems developed to solve a health problem and improve quality of lives [2]. Thus, in the healthcare sector a lot of data are being generated every day. However, as data analytics come into existence, the hospitals and non-governmental organizations (NGOs) are making use of this data to generate useful information from the available resource [3]. Diseases might classify as communicable and non-communicable diseases. Non-communicable diseases (NCD's) are the leading cause of death globally, and one of the major health challenges of the 21st century [4]. According to WHO report each year, 15 million people die from NCD between the ages of 30 and 69 years; over 85% of these "premature" deaths occur in low- and middle-income countries [5]. In Ethiopia, NCDs cause 42% of deaths, of which 27% are premature deaths before 70 years of age. With no action, Ethiopia will be the first among the most populous nations in Africa to experience dramatic burden of premature deaths and disability from NCDs by 2040 [6].

Cardiovascular diseases (CVDs) are a group of disorders of the heart and blood vessels. CVD are the number one cause of death globally [1]. However, most cardiovascular diseases can be prevented by addressing behavioral risk factors such as tobacco use, unhealthy diet, physical inactivity and harmful use of alcohol [7]. The major modifiable risk factors are responsible for about 80% of coronary heart disease and cerebrovascular disease in emerging public health (PH) problems [8]. For instance, the major comorbidity of diabetes is CVD, which is estimated to affect about one-third (32.2%) of all people with diabetes. Besides cardiovascular complications also contribute substantially to the costs for managing diabetes [9]. CVDs are responsible for the majority of morbidity and mortality among NCDs in Ethiopia. Despite the rise of NCDs, the country's full attention was in combating the communicable diseases such as HIV, tuberculosis, and malaria [10]. According to a systemic review, CVD (24%), cancer (10 percent), diabetes (5%), and chronic obstructive pulmonary disease (3%) were found to be important causes of death in different parts of Ethiopia and managing multiple risk factors that are associated with CVD is difficult but could prevent numerous deaths [11]. The practice of medicine is changing with the development of new AI methods of machine learning [12]. Early identification of persons with higher risk of CVD is useful for timely strategies on preventing cardiac incidents that lead to death or disabilities.

Thus, there is a need to design and develop a machine learning model that detect and classify the CVD risk at earliest stage. Therefore, the main aim of this study is, to investigate the possibility to design and develop efficient predictive model that classifies the risk of CVD using machine learning techniques.

2   Related Works

Risk prediction on cardiovascular disease has been conducted over the past two decades with validated predictive models. Numerous multivariable risk scores have been developed to estimate a patient's risk of CVD based on certain key known risk factors using traditional approach [13]. For machine learning based researches, researcher [14] compared the Cox PH model that uses all variables, neural networks, AdaBoost, gradient boosting, and Auto-Prognosis; all achieved a significantly higher AUC-ROC compared to all other standard ML models which is 95%. These study conducted in the absence of cholesterol and other blood-based biomarkers which is used as a predictor. In addition, a prospective cohort study made using 378,256 patients on a routine clinical data in UK [15]. The study compares the established risk prediction using machine-learning technique and found a better prediction of the absolute number of cardiovascular disease cases correctly with neural network algorithm.

Besides this, heart disease diagnosis by utilizing Echocardiography (ECG) report attributes using hybrid data mining technology [16] conducted on a total of 6,987 patient's records using J48 decision tree which provides an accuracy of 96.72% in the absence of socio-demographic attributes on their dataset. Furthermore, institutional based cross sectional study conducted on a total of 416 study participants which are greater than or equal to 18 years from February to March 2017 [17]. These study reveals that Hypertension, dyslipidemia, and physical inactivity were common CVD risk factors in individuals with Type 1 and 2 diabetes malaises (DM). However, the study only refers to associations without inferring the causality.

In recognition of CVD risk prediction, different mechanisms were applied by many researchers for preventing and early detect the risk of having CVD through different algorithms. From the experimental result of these papers, the machine learning approaches resulted in good performance rather than the traditional or statistical approaches. Therefore, in this study, a wide ranging experiment is done to fill some gaps identified while reviewing the related works such as; integrating socio-demographic records, clinical measurement, associations and causal information variables of the patients to detect the risk of CVD's.

3   Methods

In this study, we employed experimental research to design and develop a model that detect and classify the risk of CVD after a set of step by step procedure from data collection to model development. The following section discuss the detail of data preparation, pre-processing, data engineering and feature engineering in attempt to develop the model.

3.1   Dataset

The dataset collected takes the 9 regional and 2 administrative cites in Ethiopia. The source is NCDs STEPS Survey made by Ethiopian public health institution (EPHI). The collected dataset is consisting of 437 attributes and 10,029 instances saved in Statistical Package for the Social Sciences (SPSS) software of unlabeled class. Each attribute is a potential risk factor containing demographic, behavioral and medical risk factors. The demographic attribute comprises of age, sex, educational background including address information. Similarly, behavioral attributes such as current smoking status, alcohol drinking status, and nutritional intakes of the patients. Beside the demographic and behavioral attributes, the survey data has clinical measurement histories like diabetes, high blood pressure, fast-bloodglucose, total cholesterol results etc.

3.2 Pre-processing

In machine learning, data preprocessing could be a significant step that makes a difference to enhance and advance the extraction of significant insights from the data [18]. It alludes to the procedure of cleaning and organizing the raw data to make it fitting for building a model. The dataset collected is pre-processed using different techniques such as identifying missing value, encoding categorical data, feature scaling, removing inconsistent and duplicated data. Among the given attributes, a number of duplicated attributes such as town, woreda and region has been removed from the total dataset. Consequently, to make the data appropriate for the machine learning process, we use alternate ways to remove missing data by re-placing with the most frequented data value for categorical variables and attributes with missing value above 60% has been removed. Similarly, for the missing value of continuous data, mean imputation method is used. Then we perform data transformation, normalization and scale categorical variables in to machine readable format. In the feature engineering phase, data transformation activities such as smoothing, feature construction, normalization and aggregation of the data were done to handle categorical variables using label encoder.

3.3 Feature Selection

Feature selection used to select the most relevant attributes and enable learning algorithms to operate faster and more effectively by reducing overfitting problem [19]. Once the redundant attributes are excluded during data cleaning tasks, again the remaining attributes were given to domain experts (internal medicine doctors) to identify relevant attributes which are highly recommended risk factors used for identifying if the patient is having cardiovascular disease risk warning signs. While we reduce the original dataset besides the domain expert's recommendation we consider the Framingham risk factor predictor features and American heart association (AHA/ACC) risk calculator. In addition to these 20 features were selected as important features by ExtraTreesClassifier feature selection algorithm. Figure 1 presents the selected 20 most important attributes.

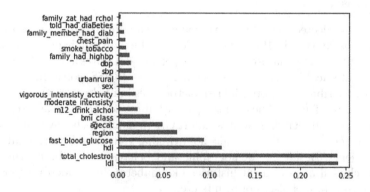

Fig. 1. Top 20 most important variables

However, for building best performing model five more relevant attributes (triglyceride, raised blood pressure, raised blood pressure medicated, raised glucose and raised glucose medicated) are added to the existing features. This relevant attributes are highly recommended risk factors for CVD risk prediction. Accordingly, out of the original dataset presented, we used 25 features and 10,029 instances.

3.4   Data Exploration

Exploratory data analysis is concerned with understanding the nature of data that we have to work with, try to find correlations between each variables, the distribution of the data [20]. To achieve this, mainly we use descriptive statistics, visual techniques, and modeling. These insights help in selecting the right ML algorithm based on our data. In this study for the data exploration and comparison with different variables we apply variety of techniques and we use Matplotlib and Seaborn library. Figure 2(a), 2(b) and 2(c) presents the detail distribution of patient age, gender and residence against the frequency in Fig. 2.

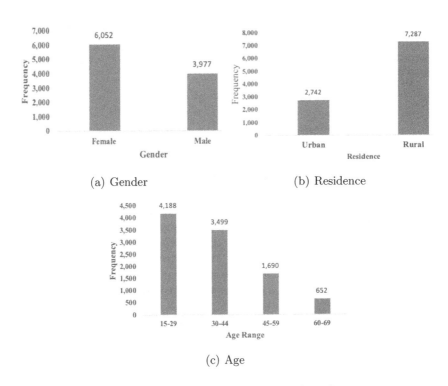

(a) Gender   (b) Residence

(c) Age

Fig. 2. Distribution of age, gender and residence

As depicted in Figure 2 out of 10,029 patients, 6,052 (60.35%) were female and 3,977 (39.65%) were male's. The majority of the patients were from rural areas of the country which accounts 7,287. In addition to this, from the total patients most of them are at the youngest age category which is from 15–29.

4   System Architecture

The system architecture includes various procedures such as labeling the unlabeled data, pre-processing, feature engineering and building a risk prediction model. Figure 3 presents the architecture of CVD risk prediction using different ML classification algorithms.

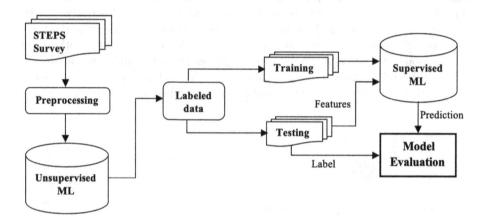

Fig. 3. Architecture of the system

As shown in Fig. 3 the flow of the architecture goes first by processing the unlabeled survey data and apply data preprocessing tasks using different ML data cleaning, transformation, and feature selection techniques and prepare the data for model building stage. After pre-processing, since our dataset doesn't have given target variable in order to find the hidden patterns, from unsupervised learning techniques k-means clustering algorithm were used. Afterwards, the labeled dataset is split for model building using five ML classification algorithms and then the performance of the model is evaluated with a standard evaluation metric's using accuracy.

5   Experiment

The experimental step includes both supervised and unsupervised learning techniques through the process ML model is selected, trained, and validated. From unsupervised learning we use K-Means clustering algorithm to partition and cluster our data based on attributes or features in to a K number of clusters [21]. Which is in our case three as high risk, medium (moderate) risk and low risk. The three class labels are selected based on previous CVD risk estimator studies and we also evaluate the clustering algorithm using silhouette score which is used to evaluate how well samples are clustered with other samples that are similar to each other. Giving this we get 0.45 silhouette score therefore, k=3 is the optimal numbers of the cluster. Figure 4 presents the dataset after applying k-means clustering.

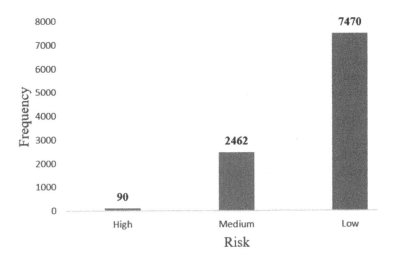

Fig. 4. Class distribution of target variable

After applying K-means clustering we get the clustered variables which is our target variable called risk which is classified as high, medium and low. Furthermore, the result of a cluster values has been evaluated with the help of domain experts, giving that from the high risk class which has 90 patients only 10 patients were misclassified as having high risk of CVD. Correspondingly for medium risk class which accounts 2469 patients the clustering model misclassified 3 of them as high risk class patients and 2 of them as low risk class patients. And as for the low risk form 7470 patients 23 patients were misclassified as medium risk class and 2 as high risk class. According to this the overall accuracy is 99.5%. As depicted in Fig. 4 the risk class levels are imbalance therefore, for improving the accuracy of the model and get accurate prediction result the Synthetic Minority Over-sampling Technique (SMOTE) [22] were used since these sampling method alleviates overfitting problems and we will not loss any information during sample creation. After making the data suitable for building a model we have done fifteen experiments using five supervised learning algorithms. Since all these five algorithms are well known classification algorithms we compare their performance by giving data obtained from k-means clustering algorithm. In model training we split our dataset using three methods, with single holdout random subsampling method the dataset split into two for training set which is used for model building 8,023 (80%), and the rest 2,006 (20%) is used to test or validate the models after training is complete. Correspondingly, in 70/30 for training 7,020 and 3,009 for testing additionally we also used Kfold splitting method. From supervised machine learning classification techniques five algorithms namely Decision Tree (DT), Naïve Bayes (NB), Support Vector Machine (SVM) and k-nearest neighbor's (KNN) and Artificial Neural Network (ANN) were used. Since our experimental method is multi class classification here for SVM algorithm we set the decision function shape argument to one vs one(ovo). Additionally, as for ANN we use Keras Classifier, the first procedure were to reshape the output attribute of each class by converting the vector of integers to a one hot encoding. Then we pass the parameters by specifying the number of layers and nodes for the classifier as hidden layer sizes = (150,100,50), also the number of epoches were set to 300, and the activation function for the hidden layers were set to Rectified Linear Unit (ReLu) since it induces a sense of non-linearity in the network. Another parameter Adam gradient descent weight optimization were given as a solver. Besides, the random state were also set to the default value which is 42. finally we fit our model to train the algorithm on our training data then make a prediction on our test data. Table 1 presents the results obtained from the experiments.

Table 1. Classification results

Algorithm	Split			Evaluation		
	80/20	70/30	k-fold	f-score	Precision	Recall
Decision Tree	88.3	86.4	85.5	92.0	88.0	89.0
Naive Bayes	83.0	84.0	68.8	90.0	83.0	86.0
SVM	98.0	97.5	98.2	98.0	98.0	98.0
KNN	98.8	97.8	98.4	98.0	98.0	98.0
ANN	99.4	99.2	99.0	99.0	99.0	99.0

Table 1 presented the classification results of each algorithms performance in terms of accuracy, precision, recall and f-measure. Giving that ANN achieves highest accuracy than the other algorithms and correctly predicts 1994 instances and missed 12 instances. When we see the performance of other four algorithms, DT algorithm correctly predicts 1772 instances and missed 234 instances. The SVM algorithm also correctly predict 1967 instances and missed 39 instances and the KNN algorithm correctly predicts 1966 instances and missed 40 instances. As for NB model it has less performance accuracy than the other algorithms, this algorithm correctly predicts 1659 instances and missed 345 instances.

6   Discussion of the Results

As discussed in the experimental setup we use five algorithms for the prediction model. Giving that the result shows DT, NB, SVM (One Vs One), KNN and

ANN classifier algorithms had performance accuracy of 88.3%, 83.0%, 98.0%, 98.8% and 99.4%. In order to evaluate the performance of all the models, specificity, sensitivity and average classification accuracy of each model was compared. From our experiments the obtained results show a good performance and this shows that it's possible to predict cardiovascular disease risk effectively and get good accuracy using ML algorithms. Figure 5 presents the experimental result of the five machine learning algorithm using three splitting techniques.

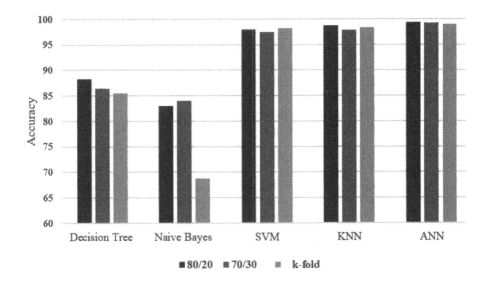

Fig. 5. Comparison of classifier algorithms

Based on the above comparison from the five algorithms used in this paper artificial neural network algorithm is the best performing model and Naïve Bayes got the least performance accuracy. Since neural networks able to deal with complex relations between variables, highly tolerance to noisy data, as well as their ability to classify patterns on which they have not been trained, makes the accuracy of the classifier better than other classifiers. In case of Naïve Bayes algorithm it has less performance level, we perform most of feature engineering techniques to handle categorical variables in our dataset yet, the NB algorithm seem to have difficulties on handling those variables since this algorithm assigns a zero probability and unable to make a prediction on those kind of variable data types. Therefore, this shows that this is the reason why we have less performance accuracy since most of our data include associations and causal information of patients. Additionally, as presented in Fig. 5 from the three splitting techniques the 80/20 splitting method get the highest score.

7   Conclusion and Recommendations

In this study, a wide ranging experimentation is done to fill some gaps identified while reviewing the related works and create better predictive model by integrating different socio-demographic, behavioral and clinical measurement variables. Besides, we also comprise different well known classification techniques to develop best performed classification model for predicting the risk of cardiovascular disease. As the result shown from all five algorithms used in this study ANN algorithm gets the highest accuracy score followed by KNN and SVM (One Vs One). Therefore, based on this results ANN is chosen as the best model at predicting the risk of cardiovascular disease. For future researchers in addition to this variable used in this study if echocardiography report variables have been added to this investigation we can extract more significant and useful information in the classification of each patient's risk. Similarly, additional deep learning algorithms with much larger data size needs to be taken to optimize the prediction of cardiovascular disease risk classification.

References

1. Organization Prevention of Cardiovascular Disease Guidelines for assessment cardiovascular risk (2020). https://www.who.int/about/who-we-are/constitution
2. Organization health-technology-assessment (2020). https://www.who.int/health-technology-assessment/about/healthtechnology/en
3. Dinesh, K., Arumugaraj, K., Santhosh, K., Mareeswari, V.: Prediction of cardiovascular disease using machine learning algorithms. In: 2018 International Conference on Current Trends Towards Converging Technologies (ICCTCT), pp. 1–7 (2018)
4. Organization, W., et al.: Noncommunicable diseases country profiles 2018. World Health Organization (2018)
5. Organization noncommunicable-diseases (2020). https://www.who.int/news-room/fact-sheets/detail/noncommunicable-diseases
6. Shiferaw, F., et al.: Non-communicable Diseases in Ethiopia: disease burden, gaps in health care delivery and strategic directions. Ethiopian J. Health Dev. **32** (2018)
7. Organization health topics (2020). https://www.who.int/health-topics/cardiovascular-diseasestab=tab
8. Baye, M.: Prevalence of overweight, obesity among urban civil servants in Southern Ethiopia. Ethiopian Med. J. **57** (2019)
9. Einarson, T., Acs, A., Ludwig, C., Panton, U.: Economic burden of cardiovascular disease in type 2 diabetes: a systematic review. Value Health **21**, 881–890 (2018)
10. Tefera, Y., Abegaz, T., Abebe, T., Mekuria, A.: The changing trend of cardiovascular disease and its clinical characteristics in Ethiopia: hospital-based observational study. Vasc. Health Risk Manag. **13**, 143 (2017)
11. Sung, J., et al.: Development and verification of prediction models for preventing cardiovascular diseases. PLoS One. **14**, e0222809 (2019)
12. Ahuja, A.: The impact of artificial intelligence in medicine on the future role of the physician. PeerJ **7**, e7702 (2019)
13. Tsao, C., Vasan, R.: The Framingham Heart Study: Past. Present and Future. Oxford University Press, Oxford (2015)

14. Alaa, A., Bolton, T., Di Angelantonio, E., Rudd, J., Schaar, M.: Cardiovascular disease risk prediction using automated machine learning: a prospective study of 423,604 UK Biobank participants. PloS One **14**, e0213653 (2019)
15. Weng, S., Reps, J., Kai, J., Garibaldi, J., Qureshi, N.: Can machine-learning improve cardiovascular risk prediction using routine clinical data? PLoS One **12**, e0174944 (2017)
16. Abrha, T.: School of Graduate Studies Faculty of Informatics. Addis Abeba University (2012)
17. Abdosh, T., Weldegebreal, F., Teklemariam, Z., Mitiku, H.: Cardiovascular diseases risk factors among adult diabetic patients in eastern Ethiopia. JRSM Cardiovasc. Dis. **8**, 2048004019874989 (2019)
18. Goyal, K.: Undefined. https://www.upgrad.com/blog/data-preprocessing-in-machine-learning/
19. Shrivastava, H., Sridharan, S.: Conception of data preprocessing and partitioning procedure for machine learning algorithm. Int. J. Recent Adv. Eng. Technol. (IJRAET) **1**, 2347–2812 (2013)
20. Education, I.: Undefined (2020). https://www.ibm.com/cloud/learn/exploratory-data-analysis
21. Greene, D., Cunningham, P., Mayer, R.: Unsupervised learning and clustering. In: Machine Learning Techniques For Multimedia, pp. 51–90 (2008)
22. Rendon, E., Alejo, R., Castorena, C., Isidro-Ortega, F., Granda-Gutierrez, E.: Data sampling methods to deal with the big data multi-class imbalance problem. Appl. Sci. **10**, 1276 (2020)

Rainfall Prediction and Cropping Pattern Recommendation Using Artificial Neural Network

Yohannes Biadgligne Ejigu[1](✉) and Haile Melkamu Nigatu[2]

[1] Bahir Dar University, Bahir Dar, Ethiopia
[2] Bahir Dar Institute of Technology, Bahir Dar, Ethiopia

Abstract. Ethiopia's economy is primarily agricultural, with agriculture employing more than 85% of the country's population. In a country like Ethiopia, where agriculture is the main source of income, reliable rainfall data is critical for water resource management, disaster avoidance, and agricultural productivity. In a circumstance where the amount of rainfall varies from time to time, cropping pattern recommendation is also highly important. In this paper we perform report, and discuss results of rainfall prediction and cropping pattern recommendation specifically for Amhara region using different combination of metrological parameters. Our Radial Basis Function Neural Network (RBFNN) prediction demonstrates better performance than the techniques used by Ethiopian National Metrological service agency (ENMSA) and other statistical techniques. For the recommendation system we used Model based collaborative filtering technique; that is K-means algorithm. We used Mean Squared Error (MSE), Mean Absolute Error (MAE), Root Mean Squared Error (RMSE) and Sum of Squared Errors (SSE) evaluation metrics to evaluate our prediction results. Generally, we can say that this is the first work which combines rainfall prediction and cropping pattern recommendation.

Keywords: Rainfall prediction · Artificial neural networks · Recommendation systems · RBFNN · K-means

1 Introduction

Ethiopia's economy is chiefly agricultural, with more than 85% of the country's population employed in this sector. Many people believe that agriculture is the backbone of the Ethiopian economy, and that its success influences all other sectors and, as a result, the entire national economy. Agriculture contributes a lot to the Ethiopian economy in terms of export, employment, and sustenance, according to the Ministry of Finance and Economic Development (MoFED). Despite the production challenges, agriculture contributes 50% of GDP, 85% of employment (the rural population of Ethiopia), 90% of earning from export, and 70% of raw material requirements for the large and medium industries which are agro processing [1,2].

© ICST Institute for Computer Sciences, Social Informatics and Telecommunications Engineering 2022
Published by Springer Nature Switzerland AG 2022. All Rights Reserved
M. L. Berihun (Ed.): ICAST 2021, LNICST 411, pp. 500–516, 2022.
https://doi.org/10.1007/978-3-030-93709-6_34

Crop production contributes for 60% of the agricultural sector's outputs in the country, while livestock accounts for 27% and other areas account for 13% of total agricultural value added. The sector is dominated by small-scale farmers who practice rain-fed mixed farming by employing traditional technology, adopting a low input and low output production system. The land tilled by the Ethiopian small-scale farmer accounts for 95% of the total area under agricultural use and these farmers are responsible more than 90% of the total agricultural output.

Given that the majority of Ethiopian farmers employ rain-fed mixed farming, rainfall data is critical for crop production, water management, and all other outdoor activities. The incident of extended dry period or heavy rain at the critical stages of the crop growth and development may lead to noteworthy reduction in the crop yield and hence affect the economy of the country. Actually, recently these problems are exacerbated by the impact of climate change in Ethiopia. This can be witnessed by the unpredictability of the rainy season and rain amount. This leads to a drought or flood that can impact large number of people in Ethiopia. Thus, an accurate and timely rainfall prediction and cropping pattern recommendation mechanisms could have a significant impact in the country's socioeconomic functioning in particular, food production.

This research paper aims to alleviate rainfall prediction and cropping pattern recommendation problems by modeling rainfall predictor using RBFNN and recommendation system by using model based clustering (K-means) algorithm.

2 Literature Review

2.1 ANN for Prediction

The use of ANN is a common data modeling approach that has been widely used to capture and depict complex input/output interactions in a variety of industries and research organizations. ANN for rainfall prediction have been used for a long time and have been proven to be more accurate than linear prediction models [3]. The pioneering work of applying ANN for rainfall prediction was done by French et al. [4], who used neural networks to predict two-dimensional rainfall one hour in advance. In 1999, Koizumi [5] using an ANN model that uses data from radar, satellite, and weather stations, as well as numerical products generated by the Japan Meteorological Agency (JMA) Asian spectral model, and used one-year data to train the model. The ANN abilities were found to be superior than the persistence forecast (after 3 h), linear regression forecasts, and numerical model precipitation prediction.

In 2000, Luk, Ball, and Sharma [6] to compare three different ANN models for rainfall prediction (Elman's partial recurrent neural network, multi-layer feedback neural network, and time-delay neural network) and concluded that this three networks can provide comparable performance results. E. Toth et al. [7] compared different forecasting models that use time series data for flood forecasting and found that artificial neural networks provide better results than other models. Chang, Liang and Chen [8] in 2001 tried to develop a rainfall model using data collected from the Lanyoung River and found that the radial basis function neural network is very effective in forecasting floods three hours ahead. In 2007, Ozgur Kisi et al. [9] examined two widely used ANN methods, namely feedback back propagation and radial basis for prediction tasks. According to their research work, Radial basis ANN provides the superior prediction performance, which resulted in significantly lower error (MSE and RMSE) compared with the feed-forward back-propagation ANN model.

In general, previous studies have clearly shown that artificial neural networks are a good method and have great potential in predicting precipitation. Artificial neural networks can model without specifying hydro-logical processes, capture complex nonlinear input and output relationships, and solve them without using differential equations [4,6,10]. Also, even if the input data contains errors or is incomplete, ANN can learn and generalize from examples to produce meaningful solutions [6]. Existing artificial neural network models for rainfall prediction are primarily event-based; the input for these models is filtered/generated data, which only includes the rainy season (i.e. rain events, rainy days, or monthly rain data). So far, various researchers have used RBFNN to make accurate rainfall predictions and have obtained valuable results.

2.2   Recommendation Systems

In recent years, recommendation algorithms have become highly popular. It assists customers in locating information and making decisions when they lack the necessary knowledge to evaluate a certain item [11]. Recommendation systems are commonly utilized in e-commerce as a tool to assist users in searching through knowledge data that are relevant to their interests and preferences [12]. However, it is difficult to find literature related with recommendation systems regarding cropping pattern recommendation. So, we can say that this is first work on this area. As depicted in Fig. 1. there are different types of recommendation system techniques.

2.3   Crop Water Needs

The crop water need (ET crop) is the depth (or amount) of water required to compensate for evapotranspiration losses. In other words, it is the amount of water needed by the various crops to grow optimally. Crop water needs always refer to a crop grown under ideal conditions, such as a uniform crop that is actively growing, completely shading the ground, disease-free, and in good soil (including fertility and water). The crop thus reaches its full production potential under the given environment. [13].

Crop water requirements are mostly determined by the climate, crop type, and crop growth stage. The following are the key climatic elements that influence crop water requirements:

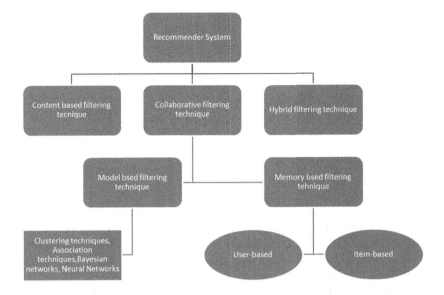

Fig. 1. Recommendation system techniques.

– Sunshine
– Temperature
– Humidity
– Wind speed

Table 1. Relationship between climatic factor and crop water need.

Climatic factor	Crop water needs	
	High	Low
Temperature	Hot	Cool
Humidity	Low (dry)	High (humid)
Wind speed	Windy	Little wind
Sun shine	Sunny (no clouds)	Cloudy (no sun)

As we can observe from Table 1, the highest crop water needs are thus found in areas which are hot, dry, windy and sunny. The lowest values are found when it is cool, humid and cloudy with little or no wind. Wheat, Maize, Sorghum and Barley are the major cereals which are produced by Ethiopian farmers. Table 2 will tabulate the water needs (mm/total growing period) and sensitivity to drought of these cereals for their total growing period.

Even though water needs of crops are influenced by sunshine, temperature, humidity and wind speed due to lack of information on those attributes, in this research we will consider only water consumption of the crop and their sensitivity to drought.

Table 2. Water needs and sensitivity to drought of different cereals.

Crop (cereal)	Water need (mm/total growing period)	Sensitivity to drought
Wheat	450–650	Low-Medium
Maize	500–800	Medium-High
Sorghum	450–650	Low
Barley	450–650	Low-Medium

3   Experimental Setup

3.1   Data

Currently large amounts of climate data of various types are becoming available for future research. There are different sources of climate data, ranging from single-site observations scattered across each country to climate model output. Each class of data has particular characteristics before it can be used or compared. A brief introduction to each type of data source was done [14].

The data source for this study is the Ethiopia national meteorology agency (NMA) data collected from weather stations found in West, North-East and South-East Amhara region. There are about one hundred fifty stations found in West, North-East and South-East Amhara Region (Gojjam, Gondor and Awi Zone, Semien Shewa). The stations record minimum temperature, maximum temperature, mean rainfall, sunshine and humidity.

The data obtained from weather stations are called Insitu data. Most of the stations are installed recently (Since 1999) and they do not have long period of time records. Some of the stations in capital cities and in some particular places are installed before 1980. However, they have high missing data and incomplete records. The study is limited to stations having complete record of monthly observations from 1980–2012. This gave a total of 15 recording stations. Among the 15 stations, 11 of them are selected for this study as representative weather conditions of Ethiopia.

The selected stations are taken from areas where there are dry and wet places that have different geographical variables to represent the weather conditions of Ethiopia. The selected stations and their geographical variables (Latitude (LAT), Longitude (LONG) and Elevation (ALT)) are shown in Table 3. For this study, we took monthly minimum temperature, maximum temperature, precipitation from the selected 11 places from 1980–2012.

3.2   Data Preprocessing

Data pre-processing is an important step in the data mining and machine learning process. The phrase "garbage in, garbage out" is particularly applicable to both of fields. Data-gathering methods are often loosely controlled, resulting in out-of-range values, impossible data combinations, missing values, etc. Analyzing data that has not been carefully screened for such problems can produce misleading results. Thus, the representation and quality of data is first and foremost before running an analysis [15].

Table 3. Geographical information of different metrological stations in Amhara region.

Station name	Altitude	Latitude	Longitude
AbaySheleko	1823.0	10°6' 46.8"	38°9' 25.2"
Aykel	2254.0	12°32' 24"	37°3' 32.4"
Bahir Dar	1800.000	11°35' 60"	37°21' 36"
Debre Birhan	2840.0	9°41'	39°32'
Debre Markos	2446.0	10°19' 33.6"	38°9' 25.2"
Debre Tabor	2612.0	11°52' 1.2"	37°59'42"
Debre Work	2508.0	10°39' 3.6"	38°9' 43.2"
Dessie	b/n2470 - 2550	11°8'	39°38'
Gondor	2128.0	12°36' 57.6"	37°27'32.4"
Kidamaja	1928.0	10°59' 56.4"	36°40' 44.4"
Metema	790.0	12°46' 30"	36°24' 50.4"

In general, the process of data preparation for a machine learning algorithm includes three steps:

- **Select data**: Consider what data is available, what data is missing and what data can be removed.
- **Preprocess Data**: Organize the selected data by formatting, cleaning and sampling from it.
- **Transform Data**: Transform preprocessed data ready for machine learning by engineering features using scaling, attribute decomposition and attribute aggregation.

There are different methods suggested in literature for treating missing values. Some of those methods include:

- **Ignore missed value**: This method usually done when class label is missed (assuming the task in classification).
- **Fill in the missed value manually**: This method is tedious, time consuming and infeasible.
- **Use a global constant to fill in the missing value**: This can be done if a new class is unknown.
- **Use the attributes' mean to fill in the missing value**: Replacing the missed values with the attributes' mean or mode (for numeric or nominal attributes, respectively).

In weather dataset, missing values are mostly due to equipment malfunction or users' error at the time of entry. Therefore, the appropriate method to fill the missing value in weather data is using the attributes' mean because all attributes in the weather dataset are numeric attributes and missing values of time series data has strong relation to its previous and next value in the series. In this research work we have used the attributes mean to fill the missing value.

Data transformation should be done to improve the speed, accuracy, efficiency, and performance of the model [16]. The performance of a neural network is often improved through data transformations. According to literature there are three existing data transformation methods.

- Linear transformation
- Statistical standardization and
- Mathematical function

Among the data transformation methods, the most commonly used one is scaling which is a type of linear transformation. Scaling is done to have a specific range, such as the range between –1 and 1 or 0 and 1, for the entire data set of a given station [17]. For this study we have used scaling technique to transform all the weather data sets (minimum temperature, maximum temperature, precipitation) to [xmin, xmax] scale.

$$Y = \frac{(Y_{max} - Y_{min}) * (X - X_{min})}{(X_{max} - X_{min}) + Y_{min}} \tag{1}$$

where Y is the scaled value, Mapminmax function processes matrices by normalizing the minimum and maximum values of each row to [xmin, xmax]. So, it processes data by mapping their values to minimum and maximum values (Fig. 2).

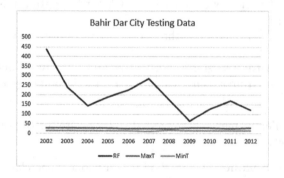

Fig. 2. Bahir Dar city testing data for June.

3.3   Setup the Dataset

Dividing the available sample dataset for training, and testing is common for prediction and classification in machine learning techniques. In [17] the selected data sets were randomly divided into two groups: 70% for training, 30% for testing after it had been first normalized into a certain range. In this study we have divided the data sets into training, and test set (70%, 30%) respectively. That means 22 years (1980–2001) of monthly data for training the neural network and 10 years (2002–2012) of monthly data for testing the prediction performance of our model (Fig. 3).

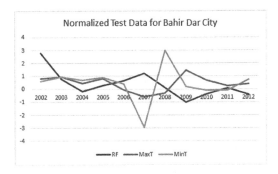

Fig. 3. Bahir Dar city normalized testing data for June.

3.4 Model Design

In this research work we developed two models:

- **Model-1 (Prediction model)**: this model is prepared to predict the upcoming year rainfall amount of a given month by using the previous year's similar month data as an input.
- **Model-2 (Recommendation model)**: by accepting the predicted values from the previous model it will recommend what crop to plant.

The First model uses ANN architecture (RBFNN structure), while the second model uses K-means clustering (Fig. 4).

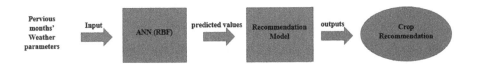

Fig. 4. General design of our proposed model.

Radial Basis Function Neural Network. Radial basis functions have been used as an important tool to solve problems which involve time series prediction and pattern recognition since late 1980s. An RBF network is basically an artificial neural network which uses radial basis function as activation function. Radial basis functions consist of three different layers: input layer, hidden layer and output layer. The hidden units in the network implement a radial basis function. While the output layer of the network is linear, the input layer of the network is non-linear.

In the time series modeling, the inputs are the data samples at certain time lapses and the output represents a signal value while in the pattern recognition, the input values represent the features of a point and output layer corresponds to the class label. The output is calculated by a linear combination. The weighted sum of the radial basis functions plus the bias according to the formula (Fig. 5).

$$Y(x_i) = \sum_{j=1}^{n} w_j \phi(||x_i - c_i|| + w_o) \tag{2}$$

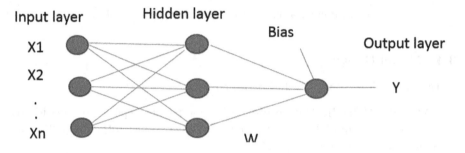

Fig. 5. RBFNN architecture.

Here the net input to the radbas transfer function is the vector distance between its weight vector w and the input vector x, multiplied by the bias b. The transfer function for a radial basis neuron is:

$$radbas(n) = exp(-n^2) \tag{3}$$

We design our RBFNN model with three inputs, twenty-two hidden and one output neurons.

We adjusted the RBFNN different parameters and select the best parameter values which gives better prediction results (P = 3; T = 1; GOAL = 0; SPREAD = 10; MN = 200; DF = 1;). Where P is input, T is the output, GOAL is Mean squared error goal, SPREAD - Spread of radial basis functions, MN - Maximum number of neurons, and DF - Number of neurons to add between displays.

K-means Clustering. Our recommendation system uses k-means clustering to recommend which crop to grow by accepting the predicted rainfall value of our RBF NN and the actual water needs of the selected crops. We used Orange3-3.6.0-Python34-win32 data mining tool for our K-means algorithm and Jaccard distance.

4 Experimental Results

Even though we conducted experiments for the four selected metrological stations namely Debre Birhan, Debre Markos, Gondar and Bahir Dar; for this research article we selected two cities only (Bahir Dar and Gondar). The results have been presented by using different evaluation metrics, graphs and tables.

4.1 Prediction Results

For the sake of saving some pages here we present the detailed prediction results for June month for both Cities (Bahir Dar and Gondar). Additionally MAE, SSE, MSE, and RMS results are presented for the three months (see Table 4).

Table 4. Prediction results using MAE, SSE, MSE, RMS for three months.

Months	Evaluation metrics			
	MAE	SSE	MSE	RMS
June	0.0098616201214	0.0048198015284	0.00043816377531	0.020932361914
July	0.3228689001455	10.61002822024	0.3228689001455	0.9821140565243
August	0.061528029425	0.38155200268	0.034686545698	0.18624324336

Prediction Results for Gondar City. In this section the detailed rainfall prediction results of Gondar city is presented. The results are depicted by Table 5 and Fig. 6.

Table 5. Prediction results for June month (Gondar).

Year	Actual values	Predicted values	Testing error (tE)
2002	197.40	197.397156684	0.00284331555940
2003	244.20	244.206224269	−0.00622426991512
2004	181.40	181.399202493	0.000797506273926
2005	137.50	137.566290411	−0.0662904111192
2006	98.70	98.7004967665	−0.000496766596697
2007	162.20	162.197409571	0.00259042812345
2008	228.50	228.498481883	0.00151811654302
2009	195.20	195.216542884	−0.0165428843431
2010	105.40	105.401297790	−0.00129779064215
2011	172.00	171.990342887	0.00965711205657
2012	160.90	160.900219220	−0.000219220163415

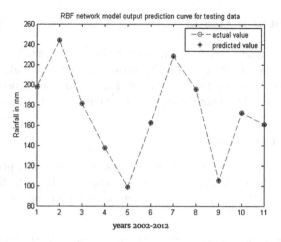

Fig. 6. Predicted results Vs actual value of June month from 2002–2012 (Gondar).

Prediction Results for Bahir Dar City. In this section the detailed rainfall prediction results of Bahir Dar city is presented. The results are depicted by Table 6 and Fig. 7.

Table 6. Prediction results for June month (Bahir Dar).

Year	Actual values	Predicted values	Testing error (tE)
2002	437.20	436.318262242423	0.881737757577184
2003	239.20	239.196520963533	0.00347903646749614
2004	144.30	144.288045159961	0.0119548400385838
2005	188.80	188.784253107786	0.0157468922142243
2006	225.50	225.502744965917	−0.00274496591691786
2007	285.60	286.475089324658	−0.875089324657836
2008	175.60	174.934988202164	0.665011797836257
2009	66.30	66.4235767290092	−0.123576729009173
2010	127.30	127.302742524422	−0.00274252442244460
2011	169.00	168.996294253586	0.00370574641419807
2012	122.00	121.990770264314	0.00922973568592056

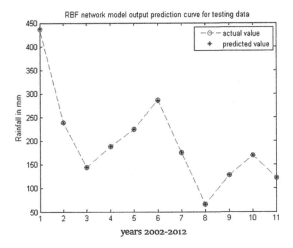

Fig. 7. Predicted results Vs actual value of June month from 2002–2012 (Bahir Dar).

4.2   Crop Recommendation Results

In this section we will present Crop recommendation results for Kiremt (Summer) Season. Because this is the main season that crops are grown in Ethiopia. Kiremt season consists of three months June, July and August. Table 7 shows the four seasons of Ethiopia and the months they constitute.

Table 7. Seasons and months of Ethiopia.

Season	Months
Kiremt or Meher (summer)	June, July, August
Belg (Autumn)	December, January, February
Bega (Winter)	December January, February
Tsedey(Spring)	March, April, May

Before we feed the output of our predictor model to the K-means recommendation system we have done three tasks.

- Sum-up the rainfall amount of each month in Kiremt season so as to get the aggregate amount of Rainfall of the season. Table 8 shows the aggregate results of Kiremt season from 2002–2012 for Gondar.
- Compute the average actual water needs of four crop types (Maize, Wheat, Sorghum and Barley). The actual water needs of crops and their sensitivity to drought is shown in Table 2.
- Scale the average actual water needs of crops based on their sensitivity to drought and the maximum and minimum amount of predicted rain fall values.

Means we use their sensitivity to drought as a scaling factor and predicted minimum rainfall and maximum rainfall as Domain. Table 9 shows the results of the above three tasks.

Table 8. Aggregate Rain Fall amount of Kiremt season from 2002–2012 (Gondar).

Year	Months	Predicted values	Season's total
2002	June	197.397156684	757.593482
	July	312.587723749	
	August	247.608601540	
2003	June	244.206224269	843.6054331
	July	318.701244177	
	August	280.697964651	
2004	June	181.399202493	871.9308527
	July	378.237761989	
	August	312.293888222	
2005	June	137.566290411	711.9952592
	July	300.8461206104	
	August	273.582848227	
2006	June	98.7004967665	695.497506
	July	291.497530851	
	August	305.299478341	
2007	June	162.19740957	857.9784652
	July	340.701462835	
	August	355.079592796	
2008	June	228.498481883	895.5232072
	July	365.533522626	
	August	301.491202686	
2009	June	195.216542884	788.6067698
	July	292.994018351	
	August	300.396208539	
2010	June	105.401297790	697.0017577
	July	266.607393999	
	August	324.993065879	
2011	June	171.990342887	670.8525965
	July	230.864035820	
	August	267.998217825	
2012	June	160.900219220	735.8973744
	July	296.397829111	
	August	278.599326048	

After we get the results of Scaled Rainfall amount for each crop we organize our data for clustering algorithm in the manner depicted on Table 10 and feed this data to the K-means Algorithm.

The last three rows of the table shows the scaled water needs of crops, while the remaining part of the table is the aggregated predicted value of Kiremt season for the respective years. Finally, we fed this data to Kmeans algorithm and found results shown in Fig. 8.

Table 9. Scaled rainfall amount for crops.

Crop type	Actual water need	Average water need	Sensitivity to drought	Scaling factor	Scaled RF amount
Wheat	450–650	550	Low-Medium	1.4	770
Maize	500–800	650	Medium-High	1.5	975
Sorghum	450–650	550	Low	1.3	715
Barley	450–650	550	Low-Medium	1.4	770

Table 10. Scaled water needs of crops and predicted values of Rainfall (Gondar).

Year/Crop Type	Amount of RF
2002	757.593482
2003	843.6054331
2004	871.9308527
2005	711.9952592
2006	695.497506
2007	857.9784652
2008	895.5232072
2009	788.6067698
2010	697.0017577
2011	670.8525965
2012	735.8973744
Wheat/Barley	770
Maize	975
Sorghum	715

As we can observe from Fig. 8 our recommendation system clusters the given data into three distinct groups C1 (sorghum), C2 (Wheat/Barley), C3 (Maize).

Analysis of the Results. In this section we will present the analysis based on the output of our recommendation system. According to our recommendation system farmers live in Gondar and nearby Gondar shall sow (see Table 11)

- Sorghum in 2005, 2006, 2010 and 2011.
- Wheat or Barley in 2002, 2009 and 2012.
- Maize in 2003, 2004, 2007 and 2008.

	Cluster	Year/Crop Type	RainFall/Centroids
1	C2	2002	757.5934820
2	C3	2003	843.6054331
3	C3	2004	871.9308527
4	C1	2005	711.9952592
5	C1	2006	695.4975060
6	C3	2007	857.9784652
7	C3	2008	895.5232072
8	C2	2009	788.6067698
9	C1	2010	697.0017577
10	C1	2011	670.8525965
11	C2	2012	735.8973744
12	C2	Wheat/Barly	770.0000000
13	C3	Maize	975.0000000
14	C1	Sorgum	715.0000000

Fig. 8. Recommendation results (Gondar).

Table 11. Analysis of recommendation results.

Clusters	Predicted rainfall	Year
C1 (sorghum)	715.0000000	
	711.9952592	2005
	695.497506	2006
	697.0017577	2010
	670.8525965	2011
C2 (Wheat/Barley)	770.0000000	
	757.593482	2002
	788.6067698	2009
	735.8973744	2012
C3 (Maize)	975.0000000	
	843.6054331	2003
	871.9308527	2004
	857.9784652	2007
	895.5232072	2008

5   Conclusion

Global climate fluctuations and their impacts on economic development have been a worldwide concern during the past several decades. The problem is more acute in developing countries in Africa, Asia, and Latin America, where alternating severe, droughts and floods have been persistent causes of severe economic hardships. To help mitigate the impacts of extreme weather and climate fluctuations requires routine timely and accurate monitoring and prediction. Especially countries like Ethiopia suffers from drought to many years, so rainfall prediction and cropping pattern recommendation systems can be used to alleviate this problem. The objective of this research was to develop such system and evaluate its performance.

In this research paper we presented our research results by using different graphs and tables. The results were presented for Bahir Dar and Gondar cities only for the sake of saving pages. But we also have conducted experiments for others cities and Woredas in Amhara region. The obtained results show that if we deploy such systems in the real life it will be helpful to increase the productivity of farmers and mitigate drought problems that are frequently occurring in our country.

As indicated in experimental results section, the prediction results were very good; means there is only a fractional point difference from the actual values. So, from this we can conclude that RBFNN is very good in predicting time series values. Generally, we can say that this is the first work which combines rain fall prediction and cropping patter recommendation.

References

1. Medic. Survey of the Ethiopian Economy: Review of Post Reform Developments 1992/3-1997/8. Addis Ababa. Ministry of Economic Development and Cooperation (Medic) (1999)
2. Gebre-Selassie, A., Bekele, T.: A review of Ethiopian agriculture: roles, policy and small-scale farming systems. Global Growing Casebook (2016)
3. Lee, S., Cho, S., Wong, P.M.: Rainfall prediction using artificial neural networks'. J. Geographic Inf. Decis. Anal. **2**(2), 233–242 (1998)
4. French, M.N., Krajewski, W.F., Cuykendall, R.R.: Rainfall forecasting in space and time using neural network. J. Hydrol. **137**, 1–31 (1992)
5. Koizumi, K.: An objective method to modify numerical model forecasts with newly given weather data using an artificial neural network. Weather Forecast. **14**, 109–118 (1999)
6. Luk, K.C., Ball, J.E., Sharma, A.: A study of optimal model lag and spatial inputs to artificial neural network for rainfall fore-casting. J. Hydrol. **227**, 56–65 (2000)
7. Toth, E., Brath, A., Montanari, A.: Comparison of short term rainfall prediction models for real-time flood forecasting'. J. Hydrol. **239**(1–4), 132–147 (2000)
8. Chang, F., Liang, J., Chen, Y.: Flood forecasting using radial basis function neural networks. IEEE Trans. Syst. Man Cybern. C **31**(4), 530–535 (2001)
9. Kisi, O., Cigizoglu, H.K.: Comparison of different ANN techniques in river flow prediction. Civil Eng. Environ. Syst. **24**(3), 211–231 (2007). https://doi.org/10.1080/1028660060088856
10. Hsu, K., Gupta, H.V., Sorooshian, S.: Artificial neural network modeling of the rainfall-runoff process. Water Resour. Res. **31**(10), 2517–2530 (1995)
11. Das, D., Sahoo, L., Datta, S.: A survey on recommendation system. Int. J. Comput. Appl. **160**(7), 6–10 (2017)

12. Schafer, J.B., Konstan, J., Riedl, J.: Recommender system in ecommerce. In: Proceedings of the 1st ACM Conference on Electronic Commerce, pp. 158–166 (1999)
13. FAO (2016). www.fao.org/docrep/s2022e/s2022e02.htm, Accessed 15 Mar 2021
14. Monteleoni, C., et al.: Climate Informatics, chapter 4 (2013). http://www.ldeo.columbia.edu/jsmerdon/papers/2013
15. Pyle, D.: Data Preparation for Data Mining. Morgan Kaufmann Publishers, California (1999)
16. Batista, G.E., Monard, M.C.: An analysis of four missing data treatment methods for supervised learning. Appl. Artif. Intell 17(5–6), 519–533 (2003)
17. Nkoana, R.: Artificial neural network modelling of flood prediction and early warning, Master dissertation, University of the Free State, Bloemfontein, South Africa (2011)

The Need for a Novel Approach to Design Derivation Lexicon for Semitic Languages

Enchalew Y. Ayalew[1(✉)], Laure Vieu[2], and Million M. Beyene[3]

[1] Software Engineering Department, Addis Ababa Science and Technology University, Addis Ababa, Ethiopia
enchalew.yifru@aastu.edu.et
[2] National Center for Scientific Research (CNRS), Institut de Recherche en Informatique de Toulouse, Toulouse, France
Laure.vieu@irit.fr
[3] School of Information Science, Addis Ababa University, Addis Ababa, Ethiopia
million.meshesha@aau.edu.et

Abstract. Morphology knowledge is relevant in language learning, information retrieval and natural language processing. Derivation lexicons are comprehensive and organized collections of the morphological variants of a language's vocabulary. These lexicons can be developed through either analysis-based synthesis of large text corpora or synthesis of surface forms from roots, stems, lemmas and morphological rules. Much of the research in developing derivation lexicon for Indo-European languages, which are concatenative, focus on analysis-based synthesis, as they do have well-developed preprocessing tools and organized text corpora. However, the methods for these languages are not appropriate for non-concatenative languages such as Semitic languages. Moreover, most of the Semitic languages, except Arabic and Hebrew, do not have well-developed text corpora and language processing tools. Hence, a novel approach that can cater for the root-pattern and rich morphology of these languages is necessary. This paper is therefore both a comprehensive survey of the literature and an analysis, motivating morphological synthesis approach coupled with a novel architecture with illustration. It is part of a larger project tailored for designing an innovative, generic, approach to derivation lexicon development for Semitic languages.

Keywords: Semitic computational morphology · Lexicon design · Derivation lexicon

1 Introduction

Lexical ontologies—dictionaries, thesauri or WordNets—have been used to improve various computational applications, such as information retrieval (IR) and natural language processing (NLP) [22]. Yet, these resources remain short of addressing certain NLP and IR tasks. This motivated researchers to develop *derivation lexicons*—organized clusters of part-of-speech (POS) variants; the "categorical variation of a word with a certain part-of-speech is a derivationally-related word with possibly a different part-of-speech" [18, p.1]. In an online version of CatVar 2.0—a derivation lexicon for

© ICST Institute for Computer Sciences, Social Informatics and Telecommunications Engineering 2022
Published by Springer Nature Switzerland AG 2022. All Rights Reserved
M. L. Berihun (Ed.): ICAST 2021, LNICST 411, pp. 517–531, 2022.
https://doi.org/10.1007/978-3-030-93709-6_35

English—the POS variants of 'break' are categorized into 39 clusters[1], indicating the word, the POS and the source lexicon in tabular form. For example, two clusters of "break" include break$_N$, break$_V$, broken$_{Adj}$, breaker$_N$, breakage$_N$, breakers$_N$, breaking$_N$, and breaking$_{Adj}$ as one cluster; and the second which encompasses breakable$_N$, breakable$_{Adj}$, breakability$_N$, breakableness$_N$. Habash and Dorr noted that a link-ability[2] principle was used to create these clusters [18] (see details on link-ability in Sect. 4.2).

As we shall see below, due to the successful use of morphology information in improving NLP and IR tasks, many language-specific derivation lexicons have been developed and are under development; and hence in this paper we propose a novel approach suited to design derivation lexicon for Semitic languages.

The rest of the paper is organized as follows. In Sect. 2, we briefly introduce Semitic languages and elaborate on their shared features. Section 3 looks at the major applications of derivation lexicons. Section 4 describes common approaches to non-concatenative morphological computations, including Semitic languages and existing approaches to derivation lexicon development. Section 5 presents our proposed approach and finally, in Sect. 6 future work directions are highlighted.

2 Overview of Semitic Languages

Semitic languages belong to the Afro-Asiatic language phylum. They are mainly spoken by over 336 million[3] people living in the Middle East, North and East Africa. They used to be spoken, as back in time as the 2500BC, by populations who lived in areas spanning from Ethiopia, Sudan and Saudi Arabia in the South to today's Syria in the North and what is known today as Iran and Iraq in the East [41].

According to Shimron [41], these languages are grouped into East and West Semitic. While the East Semitic languages spoken today are Amorite and Eblaite, the West Semitic group has more diverse languages and hence is sub-classified as Central and Southern Semitic. Surviving languages in the Central Semitic sub-group are Arabic and North Western Languages such as Hebrew and Aramaic. The languages that constitute the Southern Semitic sub-group are South Arabian (spoken in Yemen and Oman) and Western South Semitic which are spoken in Ethiopia. The Ethio-Semitic cluster constitutes the Northern (such as Tigre, Tigrinya and Geeze-an old liturgical language) and Southern (Amharic, Harari, Gurage, Chaha and Gura) languages. Bender and Fulass [6] also included Argoba to the list.

The most widely-spoken Semitic languages today are Arabic, Amharic, Tigrigna, Hebrew, Syriac and Maltese – an Arabic dialects influenced by Italian language [47], Modern Aramaic, Mandaic and different dialect of Modern South Arabian languages [41]. Arabic and Amharic are – respectively – the first and second widely spoken Semitic languages [47]. Hebrew is the fourth widely spoken language, next to Tigrigna, and is relatively well researched like Arabic.

---

[1] https://clipdemos.umiacs.umd.edu/catvar/, last accessed 2021/12/03.

[2] Link-ability [18] is the percentage of word-to-word links resulting from a specific source.

[3] Arabic (300 m), Amharic (22 m), Tigrigna (7 m), Hebrew (5 m) + over 2 m others https://en.wikipedia.org/wiki/Semitic_languages, accessed on 21/07/04.

2.1   Common Features

Languages that have closely-related features enable not only in speeding up language learning but also in sharing and adapting computational solutions easily. This is true of Semitic languages as they are related in their phonology, morphology, lexicon and syntax [41]. Narrowing our focus on morphology and lexicon tells us that these languages have complex morphologies and rich verbal lexicon. In addition, words of the same root have related semantics. These common features are illustrated taking Arabic, Amharic and Hebrew as examples.

Complex Morphology. Word formation in Semitic languages is so complex that it intensively involves both inflection and derivation. While derivation is mainly non-concatenative, inflection is dominated with suffixation and prefixation in addition to the reduplication of certain characters in the stem [5]. Inflection is meant to create variants of a lemma in the same syntactic category (showing person, number, tense, gender, etc.). On the other hand, derivation helps to create new lemmas with different syntactic categories (nouns, verbs, adjectives or adverbs) from verbal roots, patterns and linguistic rules. While roots are generally consonant characters, the pattern is a sequence of consonant-vowel (like CVC, CVCC, CVCVCV …) forms where actual consonant and vowel characters will be inter-digitized using rules to form stems or lemmas. When stems/lemmas are inflected, they form surface forms that is to say words.

For example, in Amharic from the tri-literal root '*m-k-r*': standing for 'advise', we can generate plenty of POS variants. To mention some, CVCC: "mIkr$_N$"[4]-advice; CVCVCV: "mekari$_{Adj}$"-advisor, one who advises; CVCVCV: "mekari$_N$"-adviser; CVCCVCV: "mekkere$_V$"-advised; CV-CVCCVCV: "te-mekkere$_{Adj}$"- advised or CV-CVC[C]VCV: "te-mek[k]ari$_N$"-advisee, V-CCVCVC-V: "a-mmakari$_{Adj}$"-advisory, V-CCVCVC-V: "a-mmakari$_N$"-advisory, etc.

Person, gender, number, etc. markers can be added to the above forms to show inflection: "mekari-occ: => mekariwocc$_N$"-advisors"; "a-mmakari-u-a: ammakariwa$_{Adj}$"-the advisor (feminine); "mekkere-cc: => mekkerecc$_V$"-advised (1st person, feminine).

Lexicon Rich in Verbs. The complexity of word formation in Semitic languages leads to a vocabulary rich in verbs. For instance, about 75% to 80% of Amharic dictionary entries consist of verbs or their de-verbal nouns/adjectives and hence an "exhaustive verb list is a substitute for a complete dictionary… the verb is the language" [45, p. 73]. There is even larger proportion of verbs in the Arabic vocabulary: "verbal roots and their derivative nouns and participles make up 80% to 85% of all Arabic words"[5]. It is also noted that "Hebrew is primarily a verbal language" and "every Hebrew verb (and every noun) is based on a three-consonant root … which encodes the basic semantic meaning or purpose of a given verb or noun"[6].

---

[4] Romanization is based on: The System for Ethiopic Representation in ASCII by Yitna Fird-yiwok and Daniel Yacob(1997). Amharic forms and English glosses are from Amsalu [1].

[5] https://www.memrise.com/course/110178/1500-arabic-verbs-by-frequency/, last accessed on 2021/03/01.

[6] https://www.hebrew4christians.com/Grammar/Unit_Ten/Introduction/introduction.html, last accessed 2021/03/04.

All verbs and most nouns have roots [41]; a verbal root serves to produce not only verbs but also nouns. In addition, adjectives are also produced from verbal roots [5], in a manner similar to nouns [14]. However, prepositions, conjunctions, simple nouns and adjectives, also known as "primitives" [10], are not derivable from verbs. For example, in Amharic, the noun '*bEt*: *house*' and the adjective '*bIIh*: *smart*' are not derivable from verbs [5]. In general, a Semitic lexicon built on verbal roots covers most of a language's vocabulary entries.

Semantic Relatedness. Words derived from a given root are, broadly speaking, related in meaning [10, 41]. For instance, the Arabic words *kataba*, *kaataba*, *maktabun*, *maktabatun*, *kitaabun*, *maktuubun*, and *kuttaabun* are derived from the same root *k-t-b*, representing not only similar morphological and phonological relation but also, at various degrees, similar semantic contents such as the semantic meaning of *writing* [10]. The equivalent English meanings respectively are *write, correspond, office, library, book, destiny*, and *Koran school*, which are not morphologically related. Except *destiny*, the rest of the terms are strongly related in meaning. Destiny is unrelated in meaning from the rest because it might be the result of "semantic drift" –deviation mainly due to "usage over time" [12]. The Hebrew root '*k-t-b*' produces surface forms which are related in meaning like '*ktb*'/*katav/*: write, '*hktib*'/*hiktiv/*: dictate,'*hktbh*'/ *haktava/*: dictation, *mktbh*: writing desk [18]. Similarly, the Hebrew words *zimər* ('sing'), *zamar* ('singer') and *ziməra* ('singing) are derived from the root *z-m-r* [36].

In Amharic *sella* ('sharp, have keen edge'), *sale* ('sharpen'), *selessele* ('wear thin, weak'), *sellele* ('become paralyzed, withered') with 'slender'as common meaning are derived from same root '*s-l*' [9][7]. The Arabic root '*k-t-b*' does have the equivalent Amharic root *S-h-f* [6, p. 122]. It is derived from the Geez *Sehafe*[8], which in Amharic translates to *Safe*, referring to "he wrote". Derivations from this root include *meShaf* ('Book'), *meSaSaf* ('correspond'), *meSaf*('write'), *Shuf/Sfet/* (anything written or inscription), *Sehafi* (writer), *meSafia*('instrument for writing'), *aSaSaf* ('manner/style of writing'), *maSaf* ('dictate').

Although words of the same root do have one shared lexical meaning [10] and the root stands out as the core lexical content of words [36], the root represents one aspect of lexical meaning shared by the derived stems [9]; the rest of a word's meaning for these languages come from templates [10].

3   Application of Derivation Lexicons

Language learning and computation (IR and NLP) equally benefit from using morphology information. The first sub-section illustrates benefits for language learning; the second and third sub-sections address the merits of morphology in computation.

---

[7] '*s-l*' is not in root corpus of Bender & Fulass [6]; instead there is '*sll*': gloss 'be paralyzed' in Kane [23, pp. 2249].

[8] Kane [23, pp. 2249].

3.1   Language Learning

Derivation morphology knowledge speeds up the ability of children to learn new vocabulary [8] and empower the analysis and understanding of language learning from infancy to adulthood [28]. It enhances second language learning [13], helps in reading and spelling accuracy [2], gives a key to the access and construction of sentence syntactic structure as well as organizes internal lexicons [43].

Language learners detect and understand morphological variants easily by analyzing words into their morphemes (morphological sub-structures), particularly detecting the root in the derived forms and then give definitions on the basis of the root [8].

3.2   Information Retrieval (IR)

Effective IR systems allow the retrieval of documents in a collection that match queries. However, some IR systems are unable to fully address users' information need either due to polysemy—a situation where there are multiple possible meanings for a word/phrase (e.g., bank-'financial organization' vs. bank-'river side')—or synonyms—multiple words having the same meaning (e.g., student vs pupil). While polysemy may confuse the IR system to retrieve irrelevant documents, synonymy may not allow the retrieval of all relevant documents in a collection. Lexical ontologies are used in IR to address these issues.

Morphological variants are also relevant both at indexing and querying time to address part of these problems. During document indexing morphological variants are conflated to a single indexing term, thereby allowing the retrieval of all possible documents with the variants. During querying time, users can reformulate their search by considering system suggested morphological variant alternatives.

In general, morphology information enhances IR through query expansion and conflation-based document indexing [33]; CatVar proves to be relevant for IR research [20].

3.3   Natural Language Processing (NLP)

In NLP, morphology knowledge is useful in machine translation, spell check, lexicon compilation, POS tagging and sentence construction [25]. CatVar improves natural language generation and machine translation [18], textual and lexical entailment [7], helps to enhance and induce semantic role resources for predicates of nouns [31] and paraphrase identification [32]. It has also the potential to constructing lexicons and enhancing WordNets [18]. The German DEriveBase is used in improving similarity prediction and synonym choice [35].

4   Approaches to Derivation Lexicon Development

Morphological computations are tailored either to form a word from the parts, i.e., synthesis or to break up a word into its components, i.e. analysis. Most NLP and IR research focus on analysis, by taking words of a text and breaking them up into their components and whenever necessary reproducing words from these components, thereby merging analysis and synthesis together [14]. When the goal is to develop a lexicon, however, analysis is conducted on finite text corpora and thus unable to produce comprehensive vocabulary entries. This is particularly true for most Semitic languages which do not have large-sized, organized corpora. Moreover, analysis involves using tools for a number of pre-processing phases such as sentence detection, tokenization, POS tagging and stemming or lemmatization.

On the other hand, synthesis takes on a collection of finite 'primitive' linguistic components—i.e., roots, stems or lemmas, along with linguistic rules—and then builds words resulting in a comprehensive coverage of a language's vocabulary. This is more so for Semitic languages, where word formation is based on the inter-digitations of consonantal roots with vowels, based on patterns, as explained in Sect. 2.

Both synthesis and analysis-based synthesis have the downside of producing out-of-vocabulary words. A machine learning technique—decision trees implemented in Weka[9]—has been used to reduce invalid word entries [37]. We plan to test a similar method. Alternatively, we also planned to experiment on a less data intensive valid word prediction method. This method should depend only on small learning seed data —instead of large corpora—from which the required "full valid" vocabulary of a language is built. This is the direction adopted in the study to which the work reported here belongs.

In the remaining subsections, we first briefly look into non-concatenative finite state morphology (FSM). The various forms of this technique have been widely used for Semitic Language morphology processing. This is followed by the specific approaches used in developing derivation lexicons for Indo-European languages; they focus mainly on analysis-based generation. Lastly, we look at the approaches used in generating various lexical resources for Semitic languages.

4.1   Non-concatenative Finite-State Morphology

The concept of finite-state morphology was proposed in the early 1980s. It was conceived to overcome the computational difficulties of morphologically complex languages in general. The idea was first tested on the Finish language [27] following a "Two-Level Morphology" approach. The model is based on a lexicon, a set of two-level rules processed in parallel and a small set of finite state automata (FSA) [41]; it handles both analysis and generation. However, this approach was not sufficient for Semitic languages which require more than two levels of representation.

Hence, Kay [24] proposed multi-level implementation based on the theory of auto-segmental [30] approach to Semitic morphology processing. It outlined a quadruple-tape finite state machine to describe the independent morphemes of Arabic, making it more palatable for other Semitic languages as well. However, the rules to control tape manipulation were arbitrary. Therefore, Kiraz [26] came up with "attractive rule" control of the four-level tapes by applying it to Arabic and Syriac languages.

---

[9] https://www.cs.waikato.ac.nz/ml/weka/, last accessed 2021/03/01.

Later on, Habash, Rambow and Kiraz [16] extended Kiraz's [26] idea by adding a fifth tape, with the goal of developing the Arabic morphological analyzer and generator named MAGEAD. The five levels have different purposes [16]: level 1 represents patterns and affixation morphemes, level 2 stands for roots, level 3 stands for vocalism, levels 4 and 5, respectively, stand for phonology and orthography. However, it is learnt that the complexity of transitions between levels exponentially increases with the number of tapes [21]. Therefore, Hulden [20] tried to simulate the representation of multiple levels with a single-tape, claimed to be realizable on available standard finite-automaton toolkits. On the other hand, the single FSA simulation has resulted in search speed limitations during surface forms generation and search-based analysis [21]. This tells us that simulating multiple tapes into a single tape simply makes the problem cyclic.

To tackle the inherent efficiency-problem of FSA for multi-tape representation, a Finite-State Registered Automata (FSRA) was proposed [11]. It involves supple-menting existing FSA with finite memory/registers so as to save space. The registers are made small in number and help to avoid the need to repeat paths in order to memorize a finite set of symbols. FSRA is efficient, reducing the quadratic time $O(r*p)$ for traversing arcs in an ordinary FSA to linear time $O(r + p)$, where r and p are the number of roots and patterns, respectively. To test the benefits claimed, this technique would be used to implement the first two phases (i.e., synthesis of derived and inflected forms) in our approach.

4.2   Derivation Lexicon for Indo-European Languages

Indo-European languages have concatenative word-formation morphology. These languages rely on analysis-based synthesis as the dominant approach to derivation lexicon development. This may be attributed to the availability of sufficient corpora, effective preprocessing tools and the relative "simplicity" of reducing words to basic forms—stems or lemmas. In the following paragraphs, we describe the most influential derivation lexicon development research for this group of languages.

A suffixation-based probabilistic unsupervised machine learning technique was used to strip off suffixes from words of an inflectional lexicon aiming to produce French's derivational families [15]. The main intuition to clustering words to relational families is to add words into a family as long as they are 'p' similar and relate them with suffix pairs, where 'p' stands for the number of similar sequenced characters between derived forms. This is assuming suffix pairs from different families don't co-occur. The intuition is implemented using hierarchical agglomerative clustering and minimum/maximum spanning tree graphs respectively, for identifying derivational families and suffixation. There is no evidence if effort was made for sub-clustering of a word's variants; the proportion of any singleton clusters in the result is not reported.

Habash and Dorr [18] developed a large-scale categorical database for English, known as CatVar. It was based on pre-existing data sources and tools: corpora, tree banks, lexicons and stemmer. The clustering of derived and inflected forms is based on three link-ability concepts: natural link-ability (pairs of words whose form doesn't change across categories like zip_V, zip_N), Porter link-ability (words linkable by reduction to a common Porter stem) and CatVar link-ability (link-ability of two words appearing in the same CatVar cluster). It is reported that near to half of CatVar's clusters are singleton entries. Of which, 75% are nouns and one-fifth is adjectives. Unlike this, derivationally related senses/forms in the manually built WordNet[10] consist of two or more POS variants (noun-verb, noun-adjective, verb-adjective; noun-verb-adjective). Unless a cluster has at least two POS variants, the lexicon becomes a simple word list with little purpose.

Inspired by the applicability of CatVar in IR and NLP tasks, Zeller, Šnajder and Pado [46] developed a lemma-based derivational knowledge base, i.e., DERIVBASE, for German using a large German web corpus, pre-existing POS tagger, parser and lemmatizer. The induction of derivational families for nouns, verbs and adjectives was based on rules from text books. The rules capture intra-POS and inter-POS derivations from POS-tagged lemmas and paradigms (zero-derivation[11], prefixes, suffixes, circumfixes and stem changes). Derivation rules are set for POS-pairs as: N-N, N-A, N-V, A-A, A-V, V-V, where N stands for noun, A for adjective and V for verb. The clustering rule is formulated in such a way that a binary derivation relation between two lemma-paradigm pairs is considered valid if the second pair can be derived from the first one. Of the total 239,680 derivational families, 17,799 (around 7.4%) reported to be non-singleton clusters. However, the significant majority (most reported to be compound nouns), i.e., 221,881 (>92%) are singleton clusters. Vodolazsky [42] and Snajder [44] were motivated by the outcome of DERIVBASE and hence used similar methods in developing the derivation lexicons for Croatian and Russian Languages, respectively.

In general, singleton clusters are the major drawback of both CatVar and DERIVBASE. This important problem calls for incorporating innovative heuristics rather than relying only on the link-ability concepts of CatVar or a single intuition as is the case in DERIVBASE or French's derivational families. Considering multiple—possibly hierarchical—heuristics including linguistic ones can reduce the problem.

4.3   Semitic Languages

Our effort to review the literature on derivation lexicons for Semitic Languages reveals that such resources are not yet in place. However, we found some efforts on derivation as a research plus several others which used generation for specific purposes. These exercises imply that derivation is an important approach for resource building.

In this sub-section we look at these efforts. The generation-based methods (including the analysis-based generation) help us to learn about achievements and gaps on derivation lexicon development. Our discussion excludes any manually-developed resources including the lexicons of BAMA[12] and SAMA[13].

---

[10] https://wordnet.princeton.edu/download/current-version, last accessed 2021/06/24.

[11] Zero-derivation results in POS variants of identical forms (e.g., the farm = > to farm;).

[12] Buckwalter Arabic Morphological Analyzer (https://catalog.ldc.upenn.edu/LDC2004L02, accesed on 21/07/07).

[13] Standard Arabic Morphological Analyzer (https://catalog.ldc.upenn.edu/LDC2010L01, accessed on 2021/07/07).

Aqel et al. [3] used rules to capture input word from the user and analyze to its stem and inflectional components. These components then go through generation. Similarly, Attia et al. [4], Habash [17], Neme [34] and Shaalan et al. [39] relied on preprocessing tools to reduce words from corpora to inflection forms and affixation components and then use rules to regenerate various lexicons for different purposes.

Instead of relying on preprocessing tools and corpora, the researches discussed hence forth are based on synthesizing morphological components as input. For instance Wedekind [45] synthesized words alternatively from Amharic roots, perfect or infinitive forms with the goal of determining which one predicts the two others best. Morphology rules, applied to the 42 Amharic verb-classes of Bender and Fulass [6], along with the 1280 Amharic roots from the same source were implemented in BASIC. Kibur [25] developed a rule-based synthesizer-implemented in Visual BASIC 6.0- for Amharic perfective verbs from manually compiled 145 tri-literal roots. The report recommended a comprehensive research that considers other verb types and uses the result in machine translation, spell checking, lexicon compilation, POS-tagging and sentence construction, among others. Halcomb [19] derived words for twenty simple present tense Amharic verbs that begin only with consonants. It is based on the theory of network morphology, implemented using the partially object-oriented tool, DATR. The twenty verbal templates followed four stem patterns such as CVCCVCV, CVCVCV, CV and CVCVCVCV.

Saba and Gibbon [38] developed an XFST-based generator/analyzer for Amharic nouns (loan and native nouns included), verbs and adjectives. The generation component accepts roots (from bi- to quad-radicals) and produces the graphemes. Sisay and Haller [40] developed a similar synthesizer to produce Amharic verb-lexicon for use in a machine translation experiment. The report shows the generation of main verbal-forms from three-to-five radical roots but doesn't indicate the derivation of nouns and adjectives. Both Saba and Gibbon [38] and Sisay and Haller [40] indicate neither the size and source of roots and rules nor the volume of records created.

Gasser [14] developed a python-based FST tool named Horn Morph for the analysis and generation of Amharic, Tigrigna and Oromo (a Cushitic language) words. The input for Amharic included 1851 verb roots from dictionary and 6471 noun stems. However, only 602 verbal roots are used for Tigrigna.

Intending to semi-automatically extend AWN (Arabic WordNet), Rodriguez et al. [37] used lexical rules, as regular expressions, to produce derived forms (nouns, verbs and adjectives) from the roots of 2296 verbs in Arabic WordNet. To filter out over-generated forms, decision tree classifiers in Weka toolbox were used. The learning was based on Arabic Gigaword corpus (to get relative frequency of each inflected form), Arabic NMSU (New Mexico State University) dictionary entries (to check presence of base form and its POS tag) and positive/negative examples.

In a PhD research, Martinez [29] used a rule-based model, to synthesize Arabic verbal lemmas and inflected forms from roots and templates in an effort to develop a morphological analyzer and generator. An input lexicon of 15452 verb lemmas-for 3706 roots-was used to generate a lexicon of more than 1.68 million verbal inflected forms.

Assessments of the research reviewed on Semitic languages have important lessons to learn from. Particularly, it is apparent that the synthesis of words from roots and rules is an established research exercise. Wedekind's [45] use of the Amharic derivation rule set and pre-existing root corpora from Bender and Fulass [6] to derive various verbal forms; and Gasser's [14]'s effort in developing an FST for both analysis and generation of Amharic and Tigrigna is an encouraging input for Amharic lexicon development research. Kibur's [25] attempt to synthesize Amharic verbal forms from roots and rules, though limited, and the outlook towards suggesting for a broader research to develop full-fledged synthesizer for use, for instance, in Amharic lexicon compilation, among others, is an important point. Furthermore, Saba and Gibbon's [38] use of finite state methods to generate Amharic POS variants (nouns, verbs and adjectives) as well as Sisay and Haller's [40]'s derivation of verbs from roots and rules further justifies the viability of root-based derivation in Amharic and an important input to resource development.

From among the papers on Arabic language synthesis-based derivation, the ones by Martinez [29] and Rodriguez [37] have important ideas to consider particularly in their use of organized rule-set and roots to generate verbs, nouns and adjectives. Moreover, Rodriguez's [37] noise filtering approach is also reported to be effective and hence is encouraging. However, most Arabic generation research reviewed (see e.g., [3, 4, 17, 34, 39]) focused on inflection than generation using existing tools and resources.

In general, it is important to note that the efforts on Ethio-Semitic morphological analysis and generation—including those not reviewed here due to space—are at an experimental stage at large. They are not to the level of developing lexicon of derived forms as a resource to be accessible even for research let alone for public use.

Finally, other than generating surface forms for specific uses or as a research in its own right, none of the attempts discussed on Semitic languages utilized rule and root-based generation to produce organized lexical resource similar to CatVar or DERIV-BASE. Thus, no plan or effort is reported in linking (clustering) POS variants (nouns, adjectives, verbs) of a root into meaningful categories. The main component of research in derivation lexicon development is the clustering of POS variants using various methods like machine learning [15], link-ability [18] and rule-based [46].

5 Proposed Approach

We recall that Semitic languages' research in the generation of lexical resources hasn't yet given any attention to derivation lexicon development. Our focus is, then, to advance the existing Semitic derivation morphology research a step further. It is to design a generic approach that synthesizes words from roots using rules, cluster POS variants and POS-homogeneous forms of a root; note that POS homogenous clustering is the main organizing principle of WordNet's synsets[14]; synsets are from the same lexical category.

Generally our approach is novel in that it is the reverse of the lexicon development approaches used in resource-rich languages. For instance, in CatVar or DERIVBASE, the idea is analysis-based generation mainly relying on pre-existing resources and tools. This limits the accuracy of results due to cascading of preexisting resources limitations

---

[14] https://en.wikipedia.org/wiki/WordNet, accessed on 2021/07/07.

into the generated lexicons. Moreover, the use of limited clustering rules/heuristics has resulted in lexicons dominated with singleton members. To overcome this, the intent is to use multiple clustering rules/heuristics and language features.

For instance, POS variant clustering can be achieved using multiple, hierarchical rules/heuristic insights. As a minimum, integrating root signature for each derived-form produces at least one macro-cluster with multiple elements, representing all forms of a root. Given this macro-cluster, further integrating alternative—possibly multiple—heuristics can result in more coherent sub-clusters. One of the heuristics can be setting the threshold for sub-cluster members to be a minimum of two; otherwise, leave the candidates to remain as members of the macro-cluster.

Unlike POS-variants, POS-homogenous clustering is mostly achievable with linguistic rules and hence, it is anticipated to be handled as such. Features for both POS-variant and POS-homogenous clustering can be captured at the time of derivation. Our proposed design consists of five step architecture, as represented in (Fig. 1).

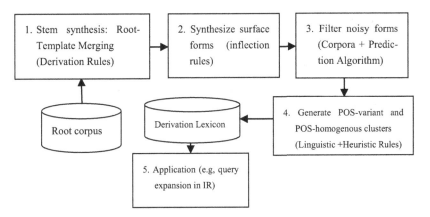

Fig. 1. High-level architecture to design derivation lexicon for Semitic languages

We now illustrate our design highlighting on important points. Implementation of the approach is based on Amharic, the second widely spoken Semitic language. Our objective is to perform rule-based synthesis. Rules from the text books [5, 6] and the root corpora (around 1280) of Bender and Fulass [6] are considered.

Our design excludes simple nouns (e.g., semay: 'sky'), adjectives (qey: 'red") and all adverbs-which are not productive [5]. Instead, it focuses on verbs, de-verbal nouns and adjectives which take up the lion share of these languages' vocabularies.

Rule implementation both for step 1 (derivation) and step 2 (inflection) is based on regular expressions or finite states in general. Noise filtering (step 3) considers the use of corpora[15] and prediction technique. The clustering step has two components: cluster POS-variants and POS-homogenous forms.

---

[15] Accessible organized Amharic corpora will be used, e.g., 342,625 word Amharic corpora: https://www.cs.ru.nl/~biniam/geez/crawl.php, accessed on 2021/07/05.

Given the labeling of each POS variant for a root with multiple features (e.g., type of verb, noun and adjective) at the derivation phase, it is possible to have a more effective POS-variant clustering approach. For instance, one clustering parameter can be to consider the extent to which the noun and adjective forms of a root are semantically linked with the respective verb form. Table 1 shows that cluster 1 is about someone, while cluster 2 is about an 'object'.

On the other hand, POS-homogenous clustering (see Table 2) allows having intra-POS clusters for nouns, verbs and adjectives of a root. This can be handled using rules from Baye [5]. This illustration is based on examples from the Amharic[16] language.

Table 1. POS-variant cluster example of the root 's-b-r', referring to "break"

Cluster	Verb	Noun	Adjective
1	sebber-e: 'broke, broke-in'	sebar-i: 'one who breaks'	sebber: 'defiant'
2	te-sebber-e: 'was broken'	sIbbar-i: 'fragment'	te-sebbar-i: 'fragile', sebar-a: 'broken'

Table 2. POS-homogenous cluster examples (nouns)

Process: Cluster-1	Object: Cluster-2	State/condition: Cluster-3
seber-a: 'act of breaking'	sebar-a: 'broken piece'	sIbbIrat: 'fracture'
sIbr-iya: 'process of breaking'	sIbbar-i: 'fragment'	sIbr: 'feeling of strain/hunger'

6   Conclusion and Future Work

In this paper attempt is made to thoroughly survey the literature from which we arrive at important conclusions. Firstly, the morphology of Semitic languages is quite different from Indo-European languages. While the derivation and inflection morphology in the later is concatenative, the former has predominantly non-concatenative derivational and inflectional morphology. This is a challenge to utilize or adapt available NLP tools and algorithms for Indo-European languages to Semitic languages. Secondly, most Semitic languages suffer from the lack of accessible and well-functioning resources and tools for language processing. Thirdly, most of the research in language processing focuses on morphological analysis or analysis-based synthesis. However, we recall that there are few efforts, particularly for Semitic languages, which focused on synthesis-based resource development. This warrants that morphological synthesis —as an important approach in resource development—is of an interest on its own. Moreover, synthesis involves less preprocessing language tools making it more appropriate for most Semitic languages.

---

[16] The morphological rules are from Baye [5] and English glosses are mainly from Amsalu [1] and Kane [23] Amharic-English Dictionaries.

The thorough literature review justifies the need for a novel approach to design derivation lexicon for Semitic languages for which we have presented illustrated architecture. Moreover, important concepts would be integrated in our architecture. In this context, the concept of FSA in its various forms are relevant in realizing the very early stages of our approach such as in generating forms from roots, patterns, vocalism/vowels and rules. We also benefit by using noise filtering strategy. Finally, we also anticipate to experiment on using a small seed data based word prediction algorithm. However, the later stages such as forming POS-variant derivational clusters and the POS-homogenous clusters require solutions, amounting to important new contributions to the NLP and IR research. The major contribution of this paper is a thorough survey of the literature and an illustrated architecture. It is our future research direction to design and conduct an extensive experiment to validate our approach.

References

1. Aklilu, A.: Amharic-English Dictionary. Kuraz Publishing Agency, Addis Ababa (1987)
2. Angelelli, P., Valeria, C., Burani, C.: The Effect of morphology on spelling and reading accuracy: a study on Italian Children. Front. Psychol. **5**, 1373 (2014)
3. Aqel, A., Alwadei, S., Dahab, M.Y.: Building an Arabic word generator. Int. J. Comput. Appl. **112**(14), 36–41 (2015)
4. Attia, M., Pecina, P., Toral, A., Tounsi, L., Genabith, J.V.: An open-source finite state morphological transducer for modern standard Arabic. In: Proceedings of the 9th International Workshop on Finite State Methods and Natural Language Processing, pp. 125–133. Association for Computational Linguistics, Blois (2011)
5. Baye, Y.: የአማርኛ ስዋሰው:የተሻሻለ ሶስተኛ እትም. 3rd edn. Addis Ababa University Business Enterprise Printing Press Addis Ababa (2009 E.C (E.C. stands for Ethiopian Calendar, which is 7 years (September to Decem-ber)/8 years (January to August) behind from the Gregorian calendar.))
6. Bender, L., Fullass, H.: Amharic verb morphology: a generative approach. African Studies Center, Michigan State University, Michigan 48824, USA (1978)
7. Berant, J., Dagan, I., Goldberger, J.: Learning entailment relations by global graph structure optimization. Comput. Linguist. **38**(1), 73–111 (2012)
8. Bertram, R., Laine, M., Vikkala, M.M.: The role of derivational morphology in vocabulary acquisition: get by with a little help from my morpheme friends. Scand. J. Psychol. **41**(4), 287–296 (2000)
9. Bezza, A.: The Submorphemic Structure of Amharic: Toward a Phono-Semantic Analysis. University of Illinois, USA (2013)
10. Boudelaa, S., Marslen-Wilson, W.D.: Structure, form, and meaning in the mental lexicon: evidence from Arabic. Lang. Cogn. Neurosci. **30**(4), 955–992 (2015)
11. Cohen-Sygal, Y., Wintner, S.: Finite-state registered automata for non-concatenative morphology. Comput. Linguist. **32**(1), 49–82 (2006)
12. Diab, M., Marton, Y.: Semantic processing of semitic languages. In: Zitouni, I. (ed.) Natural Language Processing of Semitic Languages. TANLP, pp. 129–159. Springer, Heidelberg (2014). https://doi.org/10.1007/978-3-642-45358-8_4
13. Freynik, S., Gor, K., O'Rourke, P.: L2 Processing of arabic derivational morphology. Mental Lexicon **12**(1), 21–50 (2017)

14. Gasser, M.: HornMorpho: a system for morphological processing of amharic, oromo, and tigrignya. In: Conference on Human Language Technology for Development, Alexanderia, Egypt, pp. 94–99 (2011)
15. Gaussier, É.: Unsupervised learning of derivational morphology from inflectional lexicons. In: ACL'99 Workshop Proceedings on Unsupervised Learning in Natural Language Processing, College Park, Maryland, USA, pp. 24–30 (1999)
16. Habash, N., Rambow, O., Kiraz, G.: Morphological analysis and generation for arabic dialects. In: Proceedings of the ACL Workshop on Computational Approaches to Semitic Languages, pp. 17–24. Association for Computational Linguistics, Ann Arbor (2005)
17. Habash, N.: Large scale lexeme based arabic morphological generation. In: JEP-TALN 2004, Session Traitement Automatique de l'Arabe, Fès, Morocco (2004)
18. Habash, N., Dorr, B.: A categorical variation database for English. In: Proceedings of the Annual Meeting of the North American Association for Computational Linguistics, Edmonton, Canada, pp. 96–102 (2003)
19. Halcomb, T.M.W.: Generating Amharic Present Tense Verbs: A Network Morphology & DATR Account. College of Arts and Sciences, University of Kentucky, MA, USA (2017)
20. Hulden, M.: Foma: a finite-state compiler and library. In: Proceedings of the Demonstration Session at EACL 2009, pp. 29–32. Association for Computational Linguistics, Athens (2009a)
21. Hulden, M.: Revisiting multi-tape automata for semitic morphological analysis and generation. In: Proceedings of the EACL 2009 Workshop on Computational Approaches to Semitic Languages, pp. 19–26. Association for Computational Linguistics, Athens (2009b)
22. Jurafsky, D., Martin, J.H.: Speech and Language Processing: An Introduction to Natural Language Processing, Computational Linguistics and Speech Recognition. 3rd ed. (draft) (2020). https://web.stanford.edu/~jurafsky/slp3/, Accessed 03 Dec 2021
23. Kane, T.L.: Amharic- English Dictionary of Kane. Volume I. Otto Harrassowitz-Wiesbaden (1990)
24. Kay, M.: Nonconcatenative finite-state morphology. In: 3rd Conference of the European Chapter of the Association for Computational Linguistics, pp. 2–10. Association for Computational Linguistics, Copenhagen, Denmark (1987)
25. Kibur, L.W.: Design and Development of Automatic Morphological Synthesizer for Amharic Perfective Verbs. School of Information Studies for Africa, Addis Ababa University, Addis Ababa (2002)
26. Kiraz, G.A.: Multitiered nonlinear morphology using multitape finite automata: a case study on Syriac and Arabic. Comput. Linguist. 26(1), 77–105 (2000)
27. Koskenniemi, K.: Two-level morphology: A General Computational Model for Word-form Recognition and Production. Department of General Linguistics, University of Helsinki, Hesinki (1983)
28. Levie, R., et al.: The route to the derivational verb family in hebrew: a psycholinguistic study of acquisition and development. Morphology 30, 1–60 (2020)
29. Martinez, A.G.: A Computational Model of Modern Standard Arabic Verbal Morphology based on Generation. Laboratorio, de Linguistica Informatica LLI-UAM, Department de Linguistica, Facultad de Filosofia Letras, Universidad Autonoma de Madrid, Spain (2012)
30. McCarthy, J.: A prosodic theory of non-concatenative morphology. Linguist. Inq. 12(3), 373–417 (1981)
31. Meyers, A., et al.: Annotating noun argument structure for NomBank. In: 4th International Conference on Language Resources and Evaluation on Proceedings of LREC 2004, pp. 803–806. European Language Resources Association (ELRA), Lisbon (2004)

32. Mohamed, M., Oussalah, M.: A hybrid approach for paraphrase identification based on knowledge-enriched semantic heuristics. Lang. Res. Eval. **54**, 457–485 (2020)

33. Moreau, F., Claveau, V., Sébillot, P.: Automatic morphological query expansion using analogy-based machine learning. In: Amati, G., Carpineto, C., Romano, G. (eds.) ECIR 2007. LNCS, vol. 4425, pp. 222–233. Springer, Heidelberg (2007). https://doi.org/10.1007/978-3-540-71496-5_22

34. Neme, A.A.: A lexicon of Arabic verbs constructed on the basis of Semitic taxonomy and using Finite-State Transducers. In: EESSLLI International Workshop on Lexical Resources. WoLeR 2011, Ljubliana, Slovenia (2011)

35. Pado, S., Snajder, J, Zeller, B.: Derivational smoothing for syntactic distributional semantics. In: Proceedings of the 51st Annual Meeting of the Association for Computational Linguistics, pp. 731–735. Association for Computational Linguistics, Sofia (2013)

36. Ravid, D.: Word-level morphology: a psycholinguistic perspective on linear formation in hebrew nominals. Morphology **16**, 127–148 (2006)

37. Rodriguez, H., et al.: Arabic WordNet: current state and future extensions. In: Tanács, A., Csendes, D., Vincze, V., Fellbaum, C., Vossen, P. (Eds.) Proceedings of the Fourth International GlobalWordNet Conference (GWC 2008), pp. 387–405. Department of Informatics, University of Szeged, Szeged (2008)

38. Amsalu, S., Gibbon, D.: A complete FS model for amharic morphographemics. In: Yli-Jyrä, A., Karttunen, L., Karhumäki, J. (eds.) FSMNLP 2005. LNCS (LNAI), vol. 4002, pp. 283–284. Springer, Heidelberg (2006). https://doi.org/10.1007/11780885_27

39. Shaalan, K., Monem, A.A., Rafea, A.: Arabic morphological generation from interlingua. In: Shi, Z., Shimohara, K., Feng, D. (eds.) IIP 2006. IIFIP, vol. 228, pp. 441–451. Springer, Boston, MA (2006). https://doi.org/10.1007/978-0-387-44641-7_46

40. Sisay F., Haller, J.: Amharic verb lexicon in the context of machine translation. In: TALN 2003, Batz-sur-Mer (2003)

41. Shimron, J.: Semitic languages: are they really root-based? In: Shimron, J. (ed.) Language processing and acquisition in languages of Semitic, root-based, morphology, vol. 28, pp. 1–28. John Benjamins Publish Company, Amsterdam (2003)

42. Snajder, J.: DERIVBASE.HR: a high-coverage derivational morphology resource for Croatian. In: Proceedings of the 9th International Conference on Language Resources and Evaluation (LREC'14), pp. 3371–3377. European Language Resources Association (ELRA), Reykjavik (2014)

43. Tayler, A., Nagy, W.E.: The role of derivational suffixes in sentence comprehension. Technical Report No. 357. Bolt Beranek and Newman Inc, Cambridge, Massachusetts, Boston, USA (1985)

44. Vodolazsky, D.: DeriveBase.Ru: a derivational morphology resource for Russian. In: Proceedings of the 12th Conference on Language Resources and Evaluation (LREC 2020), pp. 3937–3943. European Language Resources Association (ELRA), Marseille (2020)

45. Wedekind, K.: Which form predict all other best? variation on the amharic verb "theme." J. Ethiopian Stud. **25**, 73–92 (1992)

46. Zeller, B., Šnajder, J., Pado, S.: DERIVEBASE: inducing and evaluating a derivational morphology resource for German. In: Proceedings of the 51st Annual Meeting of the Association for Computational Linguistics, pp. 1201–1211. Association for Computational Linguistics, Sofia (2013)

47. Borkow, G.: Preface. In: Borkow, G. (ed.) Use of Biocidal Surfaces for Reduction of Healthcare Acquired Infections, pp. 1–6. Springer, Cham (2014). https://doi.org/10.1007/978-3-319-08057-4_1

A Branching Spatio-Spectral Dimensional Reduction Model for Hyperspectral Image Classification and Change Detection

Menilk Sahlu Bayeh[1]([✉])(iD), Anteneh Tilaye Bogale[2],
Yunkoo Chung[2], Kirubel Abebe Senbeto[3],
and Fetlewerk Kedir Abdu[2]

[1] Saint Mary's University, Addis Ababa, Ethiopia
[2] Adama Science and Technology University, Adama, Ethiopia
[3] Woldia University, Woldia, Ethiopia

Abstract. In this paper, a branching convolutional encoder (BCE)-based spatio-spectral hyperspectral image dimensionality reduction model is presented. The architecture consists of a pointwise separable convolution to extract spectral features, and a two-dimensional convolution network to filter spatial features. Later, these two features are fused and fed into a decoder network which attempts to reconstruct the original image. This network is trained in a similar fashion to autoencoders, using a loss function to track the similarity between the original and the reconstructed image. Classification and change detection are important applications of hyperspectral images. The branching convolutional encoder is used together with classification and change detection models to demonstrate its feature representation performance – since the raw image has redundant features and poor interclass separability. The performance of the proposed dimensionality reduction model is compared with a spatial convolutional encoder and a densely-connected encoder. Classification accuracy reaches over 90% on all the datasets which out-performs the comparative methods. Moreover, the branching encoder's representation power is observed with the change detection model as the rate of accuracy reaches over 99% for the Hermiston City-data. This research demonstrably presents the success of a branching convolutional dimensionality encoder for classification and change detection applications.

Keywords: Dimensionality reduction · Autoencoder · Hyperspectral images

1 Introduction

Multiclass classification and change detection are important applications of hyperspectral images used to track changes in a specified geographic location [1, 2]. Multitemporal hyperspectral images are used to track changes in precision agriculture, mineral mining and exploration, security surveillance for military applications, monitoring environment for hazard and natural disasters, etc. [3–5]. Considering the hundreds of bands and redundant information available in HSIs, it is quite evident that these images are useful for spectral analysis to track changes in a desired area in more

© ICST Institute for Computer Sciences, Social Informatics and Telecommunications Engineering 2022
Published by Springer Nature Switzerland AG 2022. All Rights Reserved
M. L. Berihun (Ed.): ICAST 2021, LNICST 411, pp. 532–549, 2022.
https://doi.org/10.1007/978-3-030-93709-6_36

detail. However, this advantage also introduces computational and algorithmic complexity. Performing computation on high dimensional data is resource intensive and takes a long time. This complexity introduced by high dimensional data is called "the curse of dimensionality" [6–9].

This problem has been researched for several decades years now with different techniques ranging from complex feature extractors and change detection algorithms, going through machine learning algorithms in the 2000s and most recently with deep learning architectures. Feature extraction and selection algorithms were employed to reduce the dimension of the original hyperspectral data making the output easy to manipulate for further applications [10]. However, most feature extraction algorithms do not consider both the spatial and spectral information available in HSIs when forming a feature representation.

In this research efficient ways of autoencoder based dimensionality reduction (DR) techniques were explored that involve a deep spatio-spectral feature extractor that creates an efficient latent feature representation for classification and change detection applications. The efficiency of the feature extractor is tested via different classification algorithms. After this has been demonstrated the feature extractor is used with the change detection algorithm. These two are trained in a coupled manner and the effectiveness of the entire framework is tested by different performance metrics. Finally, the framework's performance is compared with existing algorithms to prove its effectiveness of existing techniques.

The rest of the paper is organized as follows. Section 2 introduces previous dimensionality reductions approaches used and the most recent deep learning-based feature extraction techniques for the classification and change detection application. Section 3 presents the detailed of the branching convolutional encoder model architecture along with the classifier and change detection models used to test the DR module's effectiveness. Section 4 includes the details of data preparation and training. It also consists of training results and comparison with other comparative methods. Section 5 concludes the paper and makes recommendations for future works.

2 Dimensionality Reduction for Hyperspectral Images

Dimensionality reduction is the change of information from a high-dimensional space into a low-dimensional space with the goal that the low-dimensional portrayal holds some important properties of the first content, preferably near its natural measurement. Popular dimensionality reduction techniques are commonly divided into linear and nonlinear approaches. Approaches can also be divided into feature selection and feature extraction based on how features are treated. Dimensionality reduction can be utilized for noise reduction, information perception, bunch investigation, or as a transitional step to facilitate different tasks [6, 7].

Lloyd Windrim et al. propose a stacked autoencoder based unsupervised feature learning for Dimensionality reduction [11]. The feature learning algorithm projects feature representation in to a latent space so as to reduce the dimension of the original data to be used for classification application. Moreover, they integrated an information theoretic measure based spectral information divergence metric to make the reconstructed output spectrally similar with the original input. Also, they used Cosine Angle Similarity (CSA) measure to train the autoencoder's latent representation efficient. However, their method does not consider the spatial aspect of the representation as they used a one-dimensional (1D) stacked autoencoder which learns to reconstruct the original spectra.

Ayma et al. propose an orthogonal autoencoder dimensionality reduction approach for classification of hyperspectral images [12]. They introduce an orthogonal reconstruction error which is defined as the sum of mean squared error between the original and reconstructed output, and the mean squared error between the latent variable product and an identity matrix I. The orthogonality between components in the latent space is ensured by the loss function and the training optimizer so that the orthogonality of latent components improves classification performance. They tested their models on the Pavia University, Kennedy Space Center, and Botwana hyperspectral images. However, one obvious draw back in this method is that it does not consider spatial and spatial components during the feature representation.

Filtering approach by using 1D pooling has been proposed by Paul and Chaki to reduce/select important spectral features while reducing the dimension of the original image [13]. The one benefit of this method is that it clearly reduces the computation time taken while reducing the dimension and is less complex in its computation. However, this technique is also in line with the 1D techniques that focus on spectral information primarily, and require reshaping the original input to two-dimensional (2D) pixel vector array which jumbles spatial information along the process.

The alternative candidates to 1D autoencoders are convolutional autoencoder that capture spatial information from the hundreds of channels present in the image [14]. Mei et al. propose a three-dimensional (3D) convolutional autoencoder spatial-spectral feature learning for hyperspectral image classification application [15]. Elementwise 3D convolutions, 3D pooling and batch normalization have been included in this work. The encoder is trained together with a decoder counter-part that attempts to reconstruct the original input from the spatial-spectral feature representation. They tested the model's performance on a support vector machine (SVM) classifier to test the feature representation performance allowing the components to be easily classified.

There is a clear progression from 1D multilayer perceptron autoencoder techniques to higher dimensional convolutional autoencoder to train encoder to create latent representation learning either from hundreds of bands spatially, or from both the spatial and spectral representation. However, separate treatment of the spatial and spectral components is yet to be seen as spectral relationships, spatial relationships and spatio-spectral relationships need to successively considered when designing feature extractor-based dimensionality reduction techniques. BCE aims to overcome this shortage by incorporating a spatio-spectral dimensionality reduction framework.

3   Branching Convolutional Autoencoder

The numerous literatures surveyed in the previous chapter show that most techniques do not effectively combine spatial-spectral representation for dimensionality reduction. This requires a combined dimensionality reduction architecture that integrates both the spatial-spectral features. Branching Convolutional Encoder aims to alleviate this problem by designing to separate convolutional encoder to represent the spatial and spectral information from the original hyperspectral cube. The spectral encoder consists of a point wise convolution that performs 1D convolutions with the pixel vectors which correspond to the values present at a single pixel slice having hundreds of spectral bands.

Since the original cube is in reflectance value corresponding to each and every spectrum, the pixel values need to undergo normalization to avoid gradient explosion during training. After normalization, patches of the original cube will be taken to make the dataset required to train the network. These patches will be later fed in to the encoder section of the autoencoder. The encoder section of branching autoencoder performs separate convolutions on the patches through a spectral and a spatial encoders sub-section.

Later, the output of these encoders is fused together to form the spatial-spectral representation. The output of these feature space is fed into a convolutional decoder that attempts to reconstruct the original input. This output will be compared on with the original patch to compare whether the reconstructed output is similar to the original or not. Training of the autoencoder took place until the reconstruction closely resembled the original. Finally, the encoder section was taken out and used as a feature extractor for classification and change detection application.

The 1D convolution operation convolves a kernel k having dimensions $(1 \times B)$, where B is the number of channels/bands. This kernel is convolved with each and every pixel vector (slice) of the hyperspectral cube give a 2D output of shape $(M \times N)$ where M and N the number of row and column pixel count. 2D-convolution (Conv2D) layer of the Keras library initializes numerous kernels of different initializations where after each 1D kernel has been convolved with the input the output shape becomes (M, N, K). K adjusts the output dimension of the convolution without affecting M and N.

Moving on to the spatial encoder section, 2D convolution is performed to capture spatial information and reduce the size of the output whose depth is determined by the number of kernels present. One convolution operation with a single kernel amongst the total count K' gives output shape specified by the number of strides, zero padding and kernel size. Differing kernel size are used to effectively capture the spatial features present on different neighborhood size. Stacking up these convolutions also stacks up the feature representations where at a certain point the output of the last layers contains some information about each and every pixel vector before it. This enhances spatial feature representation on an integrated 2D level (Fig. 1).

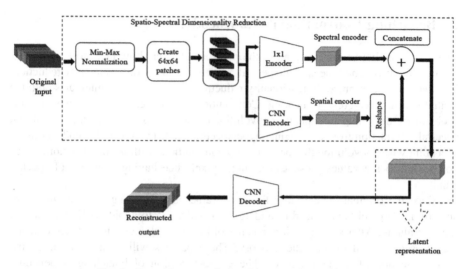

Fig. 1. Branching convolutional autoencoder architecture

The third step is fusing the spatial and spectral representation via a concatenation step. The concatenated output contains both the spectral and spatial features without any significant omission. This concatenated spatio-spectral representation goes to the decoder which consists of deconvolutions (transposed convolution) and up sampling steps that attempt to reconstruct the original dimensions input the encoder network. The spatial dimensions are controlled by the kernel size, stride, and zero paddings, while the depth is maintained by the number of pixels in each ConvTranspose2D layer. Using 1D and 2D convolution will reduce the number of operations done in 3D densely connected models. Training of the encoder-decoder architecture is controlled by a loss function that computes error between the original and the reconstructed output.

$$
\begin{bmatrix}
X_{11} & X_{12} & X_{13} & \cdots & X_{1N} \\
X_{21} & X_{22} & X_{23} & \cdots & X_{2N} \\
X_{31} & X_{32} & X_{33} & \cdots & X_{3N} \\
\vdots & \vdots & \vdots & \vdots & \vdots \\
X_{M1} & X_{M2} & X_{M3} & \cdots & X_{MN}
\end{bmatrix}_{M \times N}
\tag{1}
$$

Unfolding of the matrix above reveals the vectorized representation and the pixel elements on the B bands available in the image. Equation (1) gives the flattened representation of the input where each and every element in the above matrix is expanded to reveal the corresponding pixel elements.

$$\begin{cases} X_{11} = \begin{bmatrix} X_{11}^1 & X_{11}^2 & X_{11}^3 & \cdots & X_{11}^B \end{bmatrix}_{I \times B} \\ X_{12} = \begin{bmatrix} X_{12}^1 & X_{12}^2 & X_{12}^3 & \cdots & X_{12}^B \end{bmatrix}_{I \times B} \\ \vdots \\ X_{MN} = \begin{bmatrix} X_{MN}^1 & X_{MN}^2 & X_{MN}^3 & \cdots & X_{MN}^B \end{bmatrix}_{1 \times B} \end{cases} \qquad (2)$$

Pointwise convolution between the elements and kernel gives the out where each point in the matrix is the convolution between the kernel and the pixel vectors at the corresponding points. The kernel width has to be set equal to the number of the bands as in Eq. (3) for the first step so that the output of the convolution becomes a single matrix as shown in Eq. 4.

$$K_1 = \begin{bmatrix} K_1^1 & K_1^2 & K_1^3 & \cdots & K_1^B \end{bmatrix}_{(I \times B)} \qquad (3)$$

Equation (4) demonstrates the convolution between the kernel vectors and the pixel vectors.

$$K_1 * X = \begin{bmatrix} k_1 * X_{11}^T \\ k_1 * X_{12}^T \\ \vdots \\ k_1 * X_{MN}^T \end{bmatrix} \qquad (4)$$

Where, the convolution between the several kernels and the input becomes:

$$K_1 * X_{11}^T = \begin{bmatrix} k_1^1 \times X_{11}^T + k_1^2 \times X_{11}^2 + \cdots + k_1^B \times X_{11}^B \end{bmatrix} \times \frac{1}{B} \qquad (5)$$

The final depth of the convolution step is determined by the number of kernels specified which successively drops in equal number of steps. Therefore, the output has the same shape as the input show in Eq. (6) but different depth. Later the convolution outputs will be multiplied by weights and added with the biases specified.

$$C_1 = \begin{bmatrix} k_1 * X_{11} & k_1 * X_{12} & k_1 * X_{13} & \cdots & k_1 * X_{1N} \\ k_1 * X_{21} & k_1 * X_{22} & k_1 * X_{23} & \cdots & k_1 * X_{2N} \\ k_1 * X_{31} & k_1 * X_{32} & k_1 * X_{33} & \cdots & k_1 * X_{3N} \\ \vdots & \vdots & \vdots & \vdots & \vdots \\ k_1 * X_{M1} & k_1 * X_{M2} & k_1 * X_{M3} & \cdots & k_1 * X_{MN} \end{bmatrix} \qquad (6)$$

3.1 Densely-Connected Classifier

The conventional setup of classifiers used in image classification networks has been used to design the classifier scheme. Once the dimensionality reduction model has been trained on the available data it will be integrated with the densely connected layers that consist of SoftMax layer that outputs class probabilities on the given it input classifying it to the number of classes available for that dataset. Cross categorical entropy has been used to train this model and update the weights of the network. This model will be used to test performance of BCE and the comparative dimensionality reduction techniques (Densely connected network and a 2D convolutional autoencoder). The diagrammatic representation of the architecture of this network is given below.

3.2   Adapted Convolutional LSTM-Based Change Detection Architecture

The convolutional Long Short-term Memory (LSTM) architecture proposed by Ahram Song et al. is used for determining changes between two multitemporal hyperspectral images [16]. This architecture is trained using paired patches from two multitemporal images and the resulting output is fed in to a densely connected multiclass classification network to plot the multiclass change detection map that not only gives the changed areas but also the classes to which each changed pixel belongs to. A conventional Convolutional LSTM (ConvLSTM) block is used here extract temporal information between the bitemporal images. The cascaded ConvLSTM layers extract information from a time distributed that simultaneously applies a 2D convolutional operation and extracts features which might give information about changes in the bitemporal images. Several components make up the ConvLSTM block such as sigmoid activation represented by σ, tanh activation block, h-blocks that represent hidden layer input from previous slices, forget gates represented by f, pointwise addition and multiplication denoted by circled plus and asterisk sign, etc. (Fig. 2).

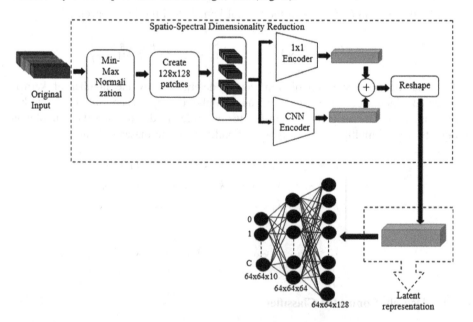

Fig. 2. Branching Convolutional Encoder concatenated with a densely connected classifier (e.g., for the Pavia University dataset)

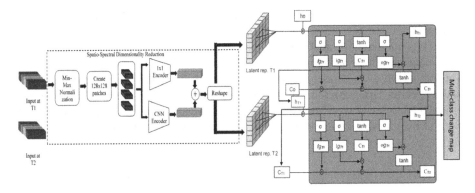

Fig. 3. BCE concatenated with a change detection model

The architecture given on Fig. 3 is integrated with the dimensionality reduction module given above and trained in an end-to-end manner to generate the multiclass change detection map for each patch. Two images from the same spatial slice will be fed in to the dimensionality reduction model and fed to the change detection model, so that change detection model learns from the feature representations of the change detection model. Finally, the densely connected layer at the end of the ConvLSTM model outputs a feature classification map that contains pixels where changes took place and what kind of images took place in those pixels.

4 Implementation Details and Results

In this section the datasets used, the details of implementation step, and the results of the training are provided.

4.1 Branching Convolutional Autoencoder Implementation Details

First the Branching Convolutional Autoencoder (BCAE) is implemented with branching encoders whose outputs are reshaped to match each other and fused together to form the latent representation. Figure 4 below shows the implementation level view of the BCAE model. The decoder consists of an ascending combination of filter size as it is the convention to use varying kernel size in most papers that use convolutional neural network architecture. Moreover, the exact detail showing how the two encoders are implemented in TensorFlow 2.x is described on Table 1 and Table 2 respectively. Table 1 shows that the spectral encoder is composed of convolution layers performing point-wise convolutions on the input. While the spatial encoder has the regular 2D convolution of descending kernel sizes.

4.2 Datasets

Four popular datasets were used first for training the autoencoder for each corresponding dataset, and then used later for the classification task since they have a multiclass annotation available. Pavia Center Scene dataset[1] has 102 spectral bands, and each raster is composed of 1096 * 715 pixels. Pavia Center Scene dataset has nine classes with one extra class consisting of unclassified pixels. This image is used for demonstrating the representation power of the hyperspectral images and later for the classification task. The Pavia University dataset is closely related to the Pavia Center dataset as they were both collected during the same flight. Compared with the Pavia center it has a smaller spatial dimension (610 × 340) but has one extra channel than the Pavia Center dataset. Both of them have the same number of classes and class descriptions.

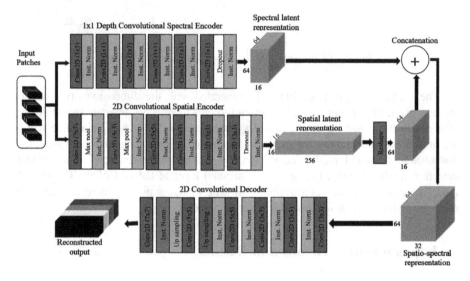

Fig. 4. Implementation-level view of BCAE model (for the PaviaC dataset)

The Salinas Valley scene consists of 16 classes plus one extra unclassified class labelled as zero. The surface reflectance values are available over a grid of 517 × 217 pixels. This dataset is used for testing the feature representation power of the dimensionality reduction models and for testing classification performance. This Kennedy Space Center (KSC) image was captured in the year 1996. The KSC scene image band has been reduced to 176 bands after the removal of water absorption bands. The hyperspectral cube's image is dark and hard to see due to the nature of the conditions when the image was taken – this makes the reconstruction task challenging as the contrast difference between the pixels is not sparse enough to differentiate. The Hermiston city bitemporal images has 242 spectral channels each of which have a 390 × 200 dimension monochromatic images. The represents crop transition of different classes in Hermiston city where center pivot irrigation creates the circular patterns in the image due to water supply.

---

[1] PaviaU, PaviaC, KSC, and Salinas Scene datasets will be found at http://www.ehu.eus/ccwintco/index.php/Hyperspectral_Remote_Sensing_Scenes.

Table 1. TensorFlow implementation level summary for spectral encoder

Convolution operation	Filter size	No. of filters	Padding size	Stride size	Input size	Output size
Conv2D	$(1 \times 1 \times 102)$	85	Zero Pad	$(1, 1)$	$64 \times 64 \times 102$	$64 \times 64 \times 85$
Conv2D	$(1 \times 1 \times 85)$	68	Zero Pad	$(1, 1)$	$64 \times 64 \times 85$	$64 \times 64 \times 68$
Conv2D	$(1 \times 1 \times 68)$	51	Zero Pad	$(1, 1)$	$64 \times 64 \times 68$	$64 \times 64 \times 51$
Conv2D	$(1 \times 1 \times 51)$	34	Zero Pad	$(1, 1)$	$64 \times 64 \times 51$	$64 \times 64 \times 34$
Conv2D	$(1 \times 1 \times 34)$	16	Zero Pad	$(1, 1)$	$64 \times 64 \times 34$	$64 \times 64 \times 16$

Table 2. TensorFlow implementation level summary of the spatial encoder

Operation	Filter size	No. of filters	Padding size	Stride size	Input size	Output size
Conv2D	$(7 \times 7 \times 102)$	16	Same	$(1, 1)$	$64 \times 64 \times 102$	$64 \times 64 \times 16$
MaxPool2D	(2×2)	–	Same	$(1, 1)$	$64 \times 64 \times 16$	$32 \times 32 \times 16$
Conv2D	$(5 \times 5 \times 16)$	64	Same	$(1, 1)$	$32 \times 32 \times 16$	$32 \times 32 \times 64$
MaxPool2D	(2×2)	–	Same	$(1, 1)$	$32 \times 32 \times 64$	$16 \times 16 \times 64$
Conv2D	$(5 \times 5 \times 64)$	112	Same	$(1, 1)$	$16 \times 16 \times 64$	$16 \times 16 \times 112$
Conv2D	$(3 \times 3 \times 112)$	160	Same	$(1, 1)$	$16 \times 16 \times 112$	$16 \times 16 \times 160$
Conv2D	$(3 \times 3 \times 160)$	208	Same	$(1, 1)$	$16 \times 16 \times 160$	$16 \times 16 \times 208$
Conv2D	$(3 \times 3 \times 208)$	256	Same	$(1, 1)$	$16 \times 16 \times 208$	$16 \times 16 \times 256$

4.3   Comparative Models

The encoder sections of the following two comparative autoencoder models were taken as a feature extractor and used for classification and change detection. Their performance was recorded and included below for comparison purpose.

4.3.1   Densely Connected Autoencoder

A densely connected autoencoder was designed and implemented as an autoencoder. The input to the autoencoder is not flattened as with stacked autoencoders, but is the raw patched hyperspectral image (e.g., $64 \times 64 \times 102$ for the PaviaC Image). Later the autoencoder outputs the reconstructed output at the end. In a manner similar to BCAE the dimension at the feature space is consistent so that there is not any discrepancy (e.g., $64 \times 64 \times 32$ for the PaviaC image).

4.3.2   Convolutional Autoencoder

This is a plain convolutional autoencoder where the encoder section consists of max pooling to reduce the size of the image, while the output has a series of interleaved up-sampling layers combined with convolution layers. The dimension of the data at the feature space is the same with the BCAE.

4.4   Implementation Details

In order to use the encoder section of the three autoencoder models including the BCAE the autoencoders first had to be trained until the loss between the original and the reconstructed patches became very small. For the four images mentioned above the original images were normalized and patched to form a dataset that can be used to train the networks. Out of the four datasets 85% of the data was used to train the models and 15% to test the model performance. Once the autoencoders were trained their encoders were sectioned out and integrated with the classification and change detection models. The classification and change detection models were trained after being integrated with the dimensionality reduction model (feature extractor). Optimal hyperparameters for the BCAE and the other networks was determined using grid search. All the models were trained on a computer having NVIDIA RTX 2070 Ti installed.

4.5   Evaluation Metrics

There are three clearly distinct tasks in this paper namely training the autoencoder models for via reconstruction, training the classifier, and training the change detection model. For the first task similarity metrics L1 and L2 losses were used to measure whether the reconstructed image is similar to the original or not. Also, spectral similarity measures Spectral Angle (SA) and Cosine of Spectral Angle (CSA) were used to measure whether the reconstructed images are spectral consistent with their original counter parts. Since the classification and the change detection models have a multiclass map as their output Accuracy, Recall, Precision, and F1-Score are used to measure their performance.

4.6   Experimental Results

Here the results of the three experiments mentioned above are provided with the necessary visualizations.

4.6.1   Autoencoders Reconstruction Results

Each of the autoencoder models BCAE, Densely Connected Autoencoder (DCAE), and Convolutional Autoencoder (CAE) were trained on the four datasets. Finally, they were tested for their reconstruction ability on the four datasets using the similarity evaluation metrics. Out the three models the BCAE has the smallest number of additional artifacts on the reconstructed image, visually resembles the original input. Some significant results to note are the densely connected autoencoder (DCAE) performs the worst on the KSC dataset because of the narrow contrast in the image. Since the DCAE simply performs linear activation and does not have any significant feature transformation, its performance is the lowest. As for the CAE it has a good performance compared to the DCAE, but there are noticeable additional artifacts (grid like and some blurring lines) on the reconstructed image especially on the KSC dataset. The BCAE also has noticeable artifacts on the KSC dataset, but has a better visual similarity to the original than the other two (Fig. 5).

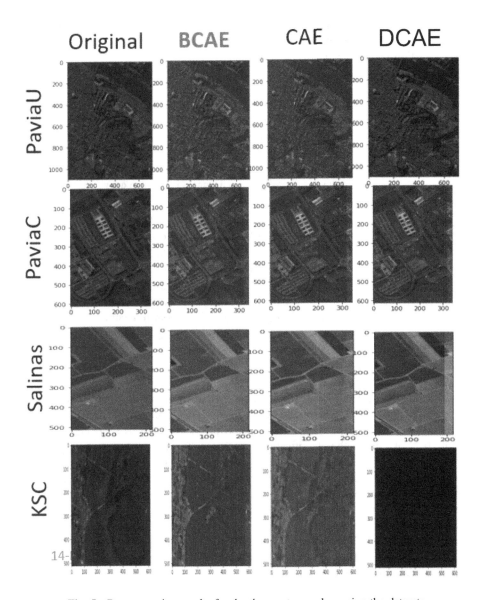

Fig. 5. Reconstruction results for the three autoencoders using the datasets

Taking a closer look at the reconstruction task via the performance evaluation metrics the BCAE reconstruction outputs have the overall small spatial (L1 and L2) and spectral (SA and CSA) losses. However, there are cases where the BCAE losses are not the smallest. This, nonetheless is better understood further by the classification and change detection metrics. The smallest results for each dataset are given in bold. With the exception of two instances BCAE outperforms the others. Table 1 summarizes the reconstruction results (Table 3).

Table 3. Reconstruction performance evaluation for the three autoencoders

Dataset	DR model	Evaluation metrics			
		L1-metric	L2-metric	SA	CSA
KSC	CAE	**0.00223**	0.04434	1.56569	0.9949
	DCAE	0.00274	**0.04333**	1.56571	0.9949
	BCAE	0.00224	**0.04433**	**1.56562**	**0.9948**
PaviaC	CAE	0.01549	0.02418	1.56113	0.9904
	DCAE	0.01191	0.01817	1.56111	0.9904
	BCAE	**0.01083**	**0.01667**	**1.56107**	0.9903
PaviaU	CAE	0.01687	0.03106	1.56112	0.9903
	DCAE	0.02116	0.03250	1.56113	**0.9902**
	BCAE	**0.01083**	**0.01667**	**1.56107**	0.9903
Salinas	CAE	0.01010	0.02351	1.56591	**0.9951**
	DCAE	0.01245	0.03090	**1.56590**	**0.9951**
	BCAE	**0.00549**	**0.01008**	1.56591	**0.9951**

4.6.2 Classification Results

Once the autoencoders finished their training, their encoders (Branching Convolutional Encoder (BCE), Densely Connected Autoencoder (DCE), and Convolutional Encoder (CE)) were sectioned out and used together with the classifier as a feature extractor. Figure 6 below shows the classification map output for three datasets along with the original ground truth map comparison. It can be seen from the image that the number of artifacts present in BCE are smaller compared with DCE and CE. DCE results in the lowest performance out of the three as it's feature representation performance is the lowest. Tabular summary given on Table 4 shows the overall performance of the classifier network with respect to accuracy, recall, precision, and F1-score. With one exception for the Salinas dataset where the CAE has the highest recall, BCAE out-performs the rest with significant margin – which is a clear testament to its feature representation power.

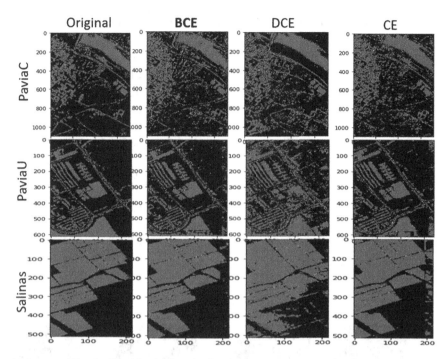

Fig. 6. Classification results for the three encoders on the datasets

4.6.3   Change Detection Results

The three encoders were concatenated with the change detection network and their-change detection map was compared for visual similarity and with the appropriate performance metrics (accuracy, recall, precision, and F1-score). Figure 7 show the bitemporal change detection map for the Hermiston city dataset and the results show that BCE has the smallest extra artifacts and CE having the lowest performance in this case. To get a better view a multiclass change detection map of the test patches is given on Fig. 8. There it can be clearly seen that BCE is almost identical with the original change map, while the others have some minor extra artifacts. BCE's feature representation is able to better represent the between class separability information in the feature space.

Table 4. Classification results summary via performance metrics

Data sets	Performance evaluation metric	Dimensionality reduction models		
		CE	DCE	BCE
PaviaC (10 classes)	Accuracy	0.36	0.88	**0.93**
	Recall	0.66	0.44	**0.69**
	Precision	0.67	0.45	**0.75**
	F1-score	0.63	**0.70**	**0.70**
PaviaU (10 classes)	Accuracy	0.92	0.83	**0.94**
	Recall	0.82	0.59	**0.87**
	Precision	0.80	0.69	**0.88**
	F1-score	0.81	0.57	**0.88**
Salinas (17 classes)	Accuracy	0.94	0.65	**0.96**
	Recall	**0.96**	0.76	0.94
	Precision	0.91	0.77	**0.94**
	F1-score	0.93	0.70	**0.94**

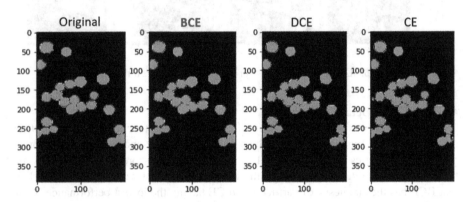

Fig. 7. Change detection shape map for Hermiston city dataset

A numerical analysis of the change detection performance is given on Table and Figure. Also, a confusion matrix is given for the three models to better visuality the rate of classification and misclassification. Table 5 summary shows that BCE significantly outperforms the others on all measure with the exception of F1-Score where it ranks close to the DCE.

Table 5. Change detection results via performance evaluation metrics

Dataset	Models		
	CE	DCE	BCE
Hermiston City (Accuracy)	0.96804	0.98626	**0.99372**
Hermiston City (Recall)	0.61131	0.76273	**0.87152**
Hermiston City (Precision)	0.70575	0.78573	**0.96203**
Hermiston City (F1-Score)	0.79516	**0.93854**	0.88978

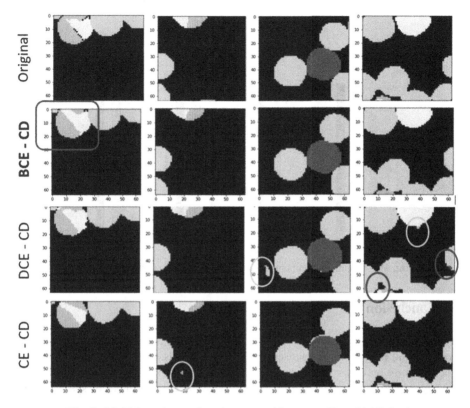

Fig. 8. Multiclass change detection map with extra artifacts highlighted

A graphical representation on Fig. 10 also shows a better visual comparison of the performance metrics (Fig. 9).

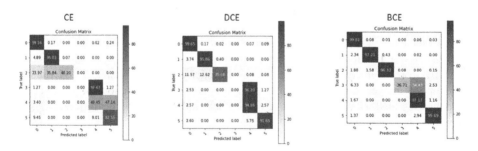

Fig. 9. Confusion matrix for the multiclass change detection map

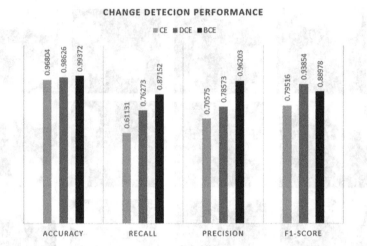

Fig. 10. Graphical summary of the change detection performance metrics

5 Conclusion

Hyperspectral image classification and change detection are important applications of hyperspectral images for remote sensing and other fields. One of the main challenges when performing either classification or change detection on hyperspectral images is the high dimensional nature of the images due to the large number of spectral bands present. Overall, the research was designed to explore other autoencoder techniques for the reduction of hyperspectral images. Namely a convolutional autoencoder and a densely connected autoencoder network have been selected as a comparative technique to compare the proposed techniques performance.

The branching autoencoder network has a better reconstruction capacity as demonstrated by the visual appearance of the reconstructed images and reconstruction loss being the smallest out of the three. For the classification task the dimensionality reduction models were integrated with a classifier to be trained in and to end manner. Out of the three models the classification result using the BCE section had better visual consistency and performance with different metrics (overall accuracy, precision, recall, and F1-score). Finally, the change detection model was trained using the Hermiston bitemporal images in supervised manner. The change map prediction showed that the model integrated with the BCE has fewer artifacts and overlaps on the different classes that the other two models.

References

1. Graña, M., Veganzons, M., Ayerdi, B.: Hyperspectral Remote Sensing Scenes. http://www.ehu.eus/ccwintco/index.php/Hyperspectral_Remote_Sensing_Scenes
2. Manolakis, D.G., Lockwood, R.B., Cooley, T.W.: Hyperspectral Imaging Remote Sensing: Physics, Sensors, and Algorithms. Cambridge University Press, Cambridge (2016)

3. Asokan, A., Anitha, J.: Change detection techniques for remote sensing applications: a survey. Earth Sci. Inf. **12**(2), 143–160 (2019). https://doi.org/10.1007/s12145-019-00380-5
4. Shukla, A., Kot, R.: An overview of hyperspectral remote sensing and its applications in various disciplines. IRA-Int. J. Appl. Sci. (ISSN 2455-4499) **5**(2), 85 (2016). https://doi.org/10.21013/jas.v5.n2.p4
5. Liu, S., Marinelli, D., Bruzzone, L., Bovolo, F.: A review of change detection in multitemporal hyperspectral images: current techniques, applications, and challenges. IEEE Geosci. Remote Sens. Mag. **7**(2), 140–158 (2019). https://doi.org/10.1109/MGRS.2019.2898520
6. Sorzano, C.O.S., Vargas, J., Pascual-Montano, A.: A survey of dimensionality reduction techniques (2014)
7. Nguyen, L., Holmes, S.: Ten quick tips for effective dimensionality reduction. PLOS Comput. Biol. **15**(6), e1006907 (2019). https://doi.org/10.1371/journal.pcbi.1006907
8. Theodoridis, S., Koutroumbas, K.: Feature generation I: data transformation and dimensionality reduction. In: Pattern Recognition. Elsevier (2009)
9. Xie, H., Li, J., Xue, H.: A survey of dimensionality reduction techniques based on random projection (2017). http://arxiv.org/abs/1706.04371
10. Meyer-Baese, A., Schmid, V.: Feature selection and extraction. In: Pattern Recognition and Signal Analysis in Medical Imaging. Elsevier (2014)
11. Windrim, L., Ramakrishnan, R., Melkumyan, A., Murphy, R., Chlingaryan, A.: Unsupervised feature-learning for hyperspectral data with autoencoders. Remote Sens. **11**(7), 864 (2019). https://doi.org/10.3390/rs11070864
12. Ayma, V.H., Ayma, V.A., Gutierrez, J.: Dimensionality reduction via an orthogonal autoencoder approach for hyperspectral image classification. Int. Arch. the Photogram. Remote Sens. Spat. Inf. Sci. **XLIII-B3-2020**, 357–362 (2020). https://doi.org/10.5194/isprs-archives-XLIII-B3-2020-357-2020
13. Paul, A., Chaki, N.: Dimensionality reduction of hyperspectral images using pooling. Pattern Recogn. Image Anal. **29**(1), 72–78 (2019). https://doi.org/10.1134/S1054661819010085
14. Madhumitha Ramamurthy, Y., Harold Robinson, S., Vimal, A.: Auto encoder based dimensionality reduction and classification using convolutional neural networks for hyperspectral images. Microprocess. Microsyst. **79**, 103280 (2020). https://doi.org/10.1016/j.micpro.2020.103280
15. Mei, S., Ji, J., Geng, Y., Zhang, Z., Li, X., Du, Q.: Unsupervised spatial-spectral feature learning by 3D convolutional autoencoder for hyperspectral classification. IEEE Trans. Geosci. Remote Sens. **57**(9), 6808–6820 (2019). https://doi.org/10.1109/TGRS.2019.2908756
16. Song, A., Choi, J., Han, Y., Kim, Y.: Change detection in hyperspectral images using recurrent 3D fully convolutional networks. Remote Sens. **10**(11), 2018 (1827). https://doi.org/10.3390/rs10111827

Shared Syllables for Amharic Tigrigna Text to Speech Synthesis

Lemlem Hagos[1(✉)], Million Meshesha[1], Solomon Atnafu[2],
and Solomon Teferra[1]

[1] School of Information Science, Addis Ababa University,
Addis Ababa, Ethiopia
{lemlem.hagos,million.meshesha,
solomon.tefera}@aau.edu.et
[2] Department of Computer Science, Addis Ababa University,
Addis Ababa, Ethiopia
solomon.atnafu@aau.edu.et

Abstract. In this study, an experiment is conducted to explore and exploit shared Amharic and Tigrigna syllables in the development of Amharic Tigrigna bilingual text to speech synthesizer. Both Amharic and Tigrigna are under resourced languages, yet these two languages share the Geez writing system with large portion of phone sets and syllables. This study therefore shows the possibility of constructing Amharic-Tigrigna bilingual text to speech synthesizer based on the shared syllables to optimize linguistic resources. The dataset for training and testing is composed of consonant-vowel syllables in both languages. Festival speech synthesis framework is used for the experiment. The result shows mean opinion score of 3.09 and 2.08 for intelligibility and naturalness, respectively. Epenthesis vowel insertion and possibility geminates which are not predictable from the text at surface level in both languages greatly affect naturalness of the synthetic speech. Another factor that affects the naturalness is the fact that we used an already existing multilingual speech synthesis framework that has foreign accent. Even though the naturalness is below average because of the aforementioned reasons, the possibility of exploiting shared features to develop multilingual speech synthesis for under resourced languages is encouraging. We have learned that to enhance the performance of the bilingual synthesizer, there is a need to integrate language specific features.

Keywords: Bilingual text to speech · Festival · Syllable · Amharic-Tigrigna

1 Introduction

With the advancement in speech synthesis technology, researchers are aiming to achieve more natural sounding and intelligible speech output. Text to speech synthesis enables computers to convert arbitrary text into audible speech [1]. Text to speech synthesis undergoes the process of text analysis and speech generation [2].

The text analysis is responsible for determining the underlying structure of the sentence and the phonemic composition of each word. This is because of the fact that strings of phonemes form larger units such as syllables; which in turn form words,

M. L. Berihun (Ed.): ICAST 2021, LNICST 411, pp. 550–558, 2022.
https://doi.org/10.1007/978-3-030-93709-6_37

constituting phrases and sentences. These structures need to be indicated in the underlying representations for an utterance, because aspects of how a sentence is pronounced depends on the locations of these types of boundaries showing pronunciation of each word, syntactic structure for the sentence and semantic focus to resolve ambiguity [1].

Speech generation part of text to speech synthesizer transforms the abstract linguistic representation into speech waveform. It is responsible for phonetic realization of each phoneme [1]. The speech synthesis part is also concerned with the selection and concatenation of appropriate concatenative speech units given the phoneme string as well as a speech waveform [2].

Nowadays, text to speech research has been pursued for the various languages in the world, such as English, most European and Asian languages [3, 4]. However, text to speech synthesis is at its infancy stage for under resourced languages including Ethiopian Languages. Having limited resources both data and tools, the aim of this study is to explore the possibility of designing a bilingual text to speech synthesizer for Amharic and Tigrigna, which are the two leading Semitic languages in Ethiopia as a medium of communication.

In the following sections, we present related works, features of Amharic and Tigrigna languages, experimentation, discussion of synthesis results and concluding remarks.

2   Related Research Works

There are studies that attempt to construct a model for Amharic as well as Tigrigna text to speech synthesis. Most of the research works are for Amharic and few are for Tigrigna.

Laine [5] initiated the first text to speech synthesis for Amharic language using diphone based concatenative technique in 1999. Tools used were Pascal and MATLAB programming languages, and the user acceptance evaluation is reported as good. Furthermore, Laine proposed the need for smoothing techniques to improve the performance of the synthesizer.

Henock [6] then applied TD-PSOLA technique for smoothing the concatenative speech units for Amharic. Tools and techniques used include PRAAT for spectrographic analysis and Delphi as well as MATLAB for developing Amharic synthesizer. It is reported that the evaluation of the models using ORT (Open Rhyme Test), and MOS (Mean Opinion Score), is promising and suggested consideration of prosodic elements for further investigation.

Tesfay [7] attempted the first text to speech for Tigrigna language using diphone based concatenative approach in 2004. MATLAB is used for implementation. The performance of the synthesizer is reported as MOS of 3.05. Inclusions of acronym converter to the text processing module and prosody control are issues noted by Tesfay as a way forward to enhance the performance of Tigrigna text to speech synthesis.

Nadew [8] applied formant-based speech synthesis for Amharic vowels using MATLAB. The focus was on vowels since vowels play a big role in changing pronunciation of a word in different contexts. Result indicated intelligibility of 88.85% for isolated vowels. Nadew recommended refinement of the work including consonant consideration, and preparation of standard speech corpus for training and testing.

Bereket [9] modeled an HMM based speech synthesizer with the objective of developing unlimited domain speech synthesizer for Amharic language that can generate a natural sounding and intelligible synthetic speech with less resource requirement. Out of 11,670 sentences 500 of them were used to train the HTS, and 20 sentences were used for testing. The performance result shows MOS of 4.12 and 3.6 for intelligibility and naturalness, respectively. As a future work, Bereket recommended inclusion of prosodic information to identify dialects and word meanings.

Experiment by Alula [10] explored the possibility of including non-standard words (NSWs) in Amharic text to speech synthesis. Alula used diphone based concatenative synthesis and RELP (Residual Excited Linear Predictive) coding. Performance of the synthesizer shows MOS of 3.0 for intelligibility and MOS of 2.83 for naturalness. Alula suggested the need for consideration of all types of NSWs and incorporation of part of speech (POS) tagged corpus for prosody control as a future work.

Each of the research attempts so far are focused on designing mono-lingual text to speech for Amharic and Tigrigna languages. However, with the existence of more than 80 under resourced languages in Ethiopia there is a need to study and exploit the common characteristics of related language family so as to develop a multilingual text to speech synthesis. To begin with, in this paper Amharic-Tigrigna bilingual text to speech synthesizer is reported based on their consonant-vowel (CV) syllable overlap, as per the way forward presented in [11]. The research output can be enhanced by applying transfer learning from resourced languages [12] and [13].

3 Features of Amharic and Tigrigna Languages

Ethiopian Semitic language is a sub family of south-Semitic which in turn is a sub family of West Semitic language under the Semitic language of the Afro-Asiatic super family. It includes Geez, Tigrigna, Tigre, Amharic and Argoba [14]. Amharic and Tigrigna are the second and the third most spoken Semitic languages in the world, next to Arabic [15].

Tigrigna has 29 consonantal phonemes and seven vowels [16]. According to Girmay [16], the plosive labiovelars, ጕ [gw], ኰ [kw], ቈ [k'w], as well as the fricative labiovelars, ዃ [xw] and ቍ [xw] are derivable from their respective core consonantal segments. Furthermore, Girmay notes that the fricative velars, ኽ [x] and ቕ [x'], are allophones of ክ [k] and ቅ [k'] respectively. Thus, these are not included in the consonantal chart of Tigrigna. According to Tsehaye [17] and Daniel [18], however, aforementioned derivable and allophone segments as well as the phoneme ⷂ [V] are included in the consonant chart of Tigrigna. As a result, the number of consonants in

Tigrigna would be 37, which is composed of 32 core consonants and 5 labialized composite segments. The seven vowels are attached to the core consonants to create Tigrigna characters, which are CV syllables. Each of the five labialized segments provide five variants of characters.

Similarly, Amharic contains seven vowels and debatable number of consonants. Baye [19] argues that Amharic has 30 consonants, whereas Mulugeta [20] reduces them to 21 underlying consonants and 6 derivable palatal consonants. For the purpose of our experiment we took Baye's recommendation, with more consonants for Amharic. The character set in Amharic is made up of the 30 consonants by the seven vowels matrix together with 13 incomplete segments which are composed of a consonant followed by short w and the vowel a, as in ሟ/mwa/, ሷ/swa/ and ሯ/rwa/.

Amharic and Tigrigna share about 30 consonants in addition to the seven vowels. The majority of the character set in both Amharic and Tigrigna is composed of CV syllable. Furthermore, syllable structure of Amharic and Tigrigna shows some overlap. According to Baye [19], syllable structure of Amharic is V, VC, VCC, CV, CVC, and CVCC, where V stands for vowel, and C for consonant. On the other hand, Tsehaye [17] and Tesfay [21] noted that syllabic structure of Tigrigna is CV and CVC. Hence, both Amharic and Tigrigna share the CV and CVC syllable structure. The most common shared syllable across Amharic and Tigrigna is CV as both use character set that translate into CV syllable.

4 Experimentation

This study explores the syllable overlap between Amharic and Tigrigna languages. Accordingly, an experiment is conducted towards designing a bilingual text to speech synthesis based on the most frequent CV syllables selected from both Amharic and Tigrigna text. To undertake the experiment, festival text to speech synthesis framework is used since it is an open source multilingual text to speech synthesis framework.

4.1 Dataset Preparation

A dataset of 2000 sentences was purposefully selected from newspapers covering a wide range of issues including socioeconomic and politics among others. The prepared dataset is composed of 1000 sentences from each of Amharic and Tigrigna texts in order to gain good coverage of the character sets in both languages. An increase in the number of sentences used for the purpose of training and testing provides better coverage of the CV dataset.

Phonetic transcription is done using a mapping table that translates each Ethiopic character into its phonetic equivalent, which is usually a consonant-vowel (CV) combination. There are instances however where a consonant is transcribed into the same consonant followed by a short vowel or epenthesis vowel. It is observed that Amharic makes use of less epenthesis than Tigrigna. Accordingly, we tried to transcribe the sixth order character in Amharic as a consonant, while that in Tigrigna is transcribed with the epenthesis vowel following the consonant.

After the transcription of the text, there was insertion of epenthesis vowel in times where there is a cluster of more than two consonants in Amharic, as well as deletion of inserted epenthesis for Tigrigna, especially at word final position.

4.2 Identifying Syllable Overlap

Once the dataset is prepared, we then explore syllable overlap that exists between Amharic and Tigrigna languages. Consonant-vowel (CV) syllables are then counted using python programming language. Tigrigna character set is composed of 32 consonants by 7vowels plus 5 derivable labialized segments each having 5 variants, which makes up 249 characters. We found out that the Tigrigna dataset is composed of 195 distinct characters. Thus, the Tigrigna character set coverage is 78.63%.

Similarly, Amharic character set consists of 30 consonants by 7 vowels plus 13 incomplete characters such as ኳ/kwa/ which are derivable from core consonants followed by short w and then the vowel a. This makes the required number of characters in Amharic to 223. The prepared Amharic dataset is composed of 211 unique characters. The coverage of the character set in Amharic dataset is therefore, 94.61%. Even though the dataset is composed of 1000 sentences for each Amharic and Tigrigna languages, the sentence length in these languages is different as the texts are collected from different sources with different authors. Hence, Amharic sentences are longer compared to Tigrigna sentences. As a result, we found more character coverage in Amharic dataset than in Tigrigna.

Amharic and Tigrigna text is analyzed for the consonant-vowel syllable overlap and found to be 70.51%. This shows that the CV level overlap is a little bit below the actual overlap because of lower coverage of the characters for Tigrigna dataset, which in turn is attributed to the shorter sentences in Tigrigna text.

The most frequent and shared syllables are identified and words that contain these shared syllables are used as an input for the synthesizer. Words that contain the most frequent CV syllables are selected from the aforementioned dataset and used as an input to the synthesizer.

Syllables are sensible to the human ear when their context in a word is understood. Words are also more sensible when embedded in a sentence. In both Amharic and Tigrigna, a syllable can assume a word initial, word medial or word final position. These are the contexts that are considered in this experiment. Accordingly, the words shown in Table 1 below are selected with the intention of including these contexts.

In order for the Festival speech synthesis system to recognize the Amharic and Tigrigna text input, SERA algorithm is applied so as to convert the Ethiopic orthography into its equivalent ASCII representation.

Table 1. Data set for experiment

sylla-ble	Tigrigna			Amharic		
	Word Initial	Word Medial	Word Final	Word Initial	Word Medial	Word Final
ን n/nɨ	ንምህዘ nimihzo	መንጎ məngo	ተግባርን təgbarrin	ንግግር nigigir	ድንቅ dink'	ስኬትን siketin
ብ b/bɨ	ብሞያ bimoja	መብርሒ məbrihi	ሰብ səb	ብርሃን birhan	አዳብራ ʔadabra	ሃሰብ Hasab
ት t/tɨ	ትግራይ tigraj	ፍትሒ fithi	ከባቢታት kəbabitat	ትጋቱ tigatu	ማትረፍ matrəf	ሻልማት ʃillimat
ም m/m(ɨ)	ምኽንያት mixnijat	ተምቤን təmben	አክሱም ʔaksum	ምህረት mihrət	በማምረት bəmamrət	ሰላም səlam
በ/bə	በለ bələ	ማሕበራዊ mahbərawi	ግንዘበ ginizabə	በዘርፉ bəzərfu	ለበርካታ ləbərkata	ያልታሰበ jaltasəbə
ለ/lə	ለአኩለ ləʔakula	መለለጅ mələləj	ጉጅለ gujilə	ለማዘጋጀት ləmazəgajət	በለሙያ baləmuja	በተፋለ bətəʃalə
ተ/tə	ተወሊዱ təwəlidu	እተን ʔitən	ክሊተ kilitə	ተከታታይ təkətatj	በተገቢው bətəgəbiw	እየከፈተ ʔijəkəfətə
መ/mə	መኒነት məninət	ዝተመስረተ zitəməsrətə	ደጋጊመ dəgagimə	መዘጋጀት məzəgajət	በመፍጠር bəməft'ər	እየታተመ ʔijətatəmə
ረ/rə	ረብሓ rəbħa	አረምኩ ʔarəmku	ዝነበረ zinəbərə	ረዳት rəddat	ደረጃ dərəjja	ከጀመረ kəjəmmərə
ዝ/zə	ዝምድብ zimidəb	ብዝርኣይ bizir?aj	እትጉዓዝ ʔitiguʕaz	ዝርዝር zirzir	አቢዝተው ʔaβzitəw	አልማዝ ʔalmaz
የ/jə	የራእኪ jəra?i	አከየዱ ʔakajedu	ሰኒየ sənijə	የያዘው jəjazəw	አየለ ʔajələ	ተለየ tələjə

5 Discussions of Synthesis Results

The extent to which each syllable is clearly heard in the context of the word it embeds is judged by bilingual speakers. The evaluation is based on the five scale mean opinion score (MOS). For evaluation, words that contain the syllable to be evaluated in three different contexts (word initial, word medial, and word final) for the two languages are considered. Thus, the evaluator first looks at each of the six words for every one of the eleven selected syllables. Then he/she is presented with the synthetic speech and asked to specify the level of comprehensibility of each syllable with the scale ranging from poor to excellent. The same 66 words are used to evaluate naturalness, the extent to which the synthetic speech that contains the eleven syllables are pleasant or tolerable or annoying to the human ear.

The evaluation result shows that the synthesizer registers a mean opinion score of 3.09 for intelligibility and 2.08 for naturalness. The intelligibility of the synthesizer is at acceptable level of producing understandable synthetic speech. The decrease in natu- ralness of the synthetic speech is on the other hand related to the fact that some of the characters with unique sound, found in both Amharic and Tigrigna such as families of ቐ, ቝ, ኸ, ጐ, and ዐ, are missing from the festival speech synthesis engine. Even though few characters such as members of ቝ and ኸ are allophones of ቐ and ህ respectively [16], they have their own unique signal spectrograph and there is a need for investigating the signal level relationship among allophones to identify the base signal and the factor to generate the derivable signals. Furthermore, epenthesis vowel and geminates greatly affect naturalness of the synthetic speech as they are expecting the integration of a well-crafted rules during post processing.

Furthermore, variation in intelligibility and naturalness of the same syllable is observed according to the context of the syllable which appears at a word initial, word medial or word final position, as shown in Table 2. Analysis of the context of the syllables, shows that, the average intelligibility and naturalness get the best result at the word initial position of the syllable. Average result is low at the word medial context. This is because of the influence of the surrounding syllables which induce co-articulation effect.

Table 2. Mean opinion score

	Word initial	Word medial	Word final	Average
Intelligibility	3.23	3	3.05	3.09
Naturalness	2.18	2	2.05	2.08

In addition, since the syllables are synthesized on a generic multilingual synthesizer, festival, the naturalness of the synthesized speech is greatly affected as compared to intelligibility of the synthesis result. This is because the generic synthesizer lacks to map the inherent sounds represented in the syllables. This requires integration of the unique Ethiopic sounds observed in Amharic and Tigrigna speech and we are working towards this direction as our future work.

6 Concluding Remarks

In this research, we have explored the consonant vowel syllables that are common for Amharic and Tigrigna to build a bilingual text to speech synthesizer. Amharic and Tigrigna share the same Geez writing system as well as a large portion of their phone sets and syllables. We selected purposefully 2000 sentences of Amharic and Tigrigna texts from newspapers and analyzed consonant vowel syllables across the two languages.

Once the CV overlap between the two languages is analyzed, the most frequent and common consonant vowel syllables are selected to implement a bilingual text to speech synthesizer for these languages. Words containing frequent syllables are selected from the prepared dataset so that the syllables assume three different contexts according to their position in a word, word initial, word medial and word final. Festival speech synthesis framework is used for the experiment.

The performance of the bilingual synthesizer is evaluated for its intelligibility and naturalness by bilingual speakers of the languages. The average performance of the synthesizer, taking into account all three possible contexts of the syllables, is MOS of 3.09 and 2.08 for intelligibility and naturalness, respectively. The result shows that there is a variation of performance in relation to the position of the syllable, where better performance in both intelligibility and naturalness is attained at word initial context; and the least performance at the word medial context. The decrease in intelligibility and naturalness of the word medial syllables is attributed to the effect of the surrounding syllables.

In general, the evaluation result indicates that intelligibility of the synthetic speech is at acceptable level and naturalness needs to be improved further by investigating signal level mappings for the unique sounds in Amharic and Tigrigna, which is our next research direction.

References

1. Taylor, P.: Text to Speech Synthesis. Cambridge University Press, New York (2009)
2. Strout, R., Olive, J.: Text to speech synthesis. In: Vijay, D.B.W., Madisetti, K. (ed.) Digital Signal Processing Handbook, pp. 976–986. CRC Press, Lonndon (1999)
3. Lemmetty, S.: Review of Speech Synthesis Technologies. Helsinki University of Technology, Helsinki (1999)
4. Sagisak, Y.: Spoken output technologies. In: Survey of the State of the Art in Human Language Technology, pp. 165–197. Cambidge University Press, Cambidge (1997)
5. Laine, B.: Text to Speech Synthesis for Amharic Language. Addis Ababa University, Addis Ababa (1999)
6. Henock, L.: Concatenative Text to Speech Synthesis for Amharic language. Addis Ababa Univerity, Addis Ababa (2003)
7. Tesfay, Y.: Diphone Based Text to Speech Synthesis for Tigrigna language. Addis Ababa University, Addis Ababa (2004)
8. Nadew, T.: Formant Based Synthesis for Amharic Vowels. Addis Ababa University, Addis Ababa (2008)
9. Bereket, K.: Developing a Speech Synthesizer for Amharic using Hidden Markov Model. Addis Ababa University, Addis Ababa (2008)
10. Alula, T.: A Generalized Approach to Amharic Text to Speech (TTS) Synthesis System. Addis Ababa University, Addis Ababa (2010)
11. Lemlem, H., Million, M.: Text to speech synthesis for ethiopian semitic languages: issues and the way forward. In: 12th IEEE Africon International Conference, Addis Ababa (2015)
12. Chen, Y.-J., Tu, T., Yeh, C.-C., Lee, H.-Y.: End-to-end text-to-speech for low-resource languages by cross-lingual transfer learning. arXiv e-print arXiv:1904.06508v2 (2019)
13. Lee, Y., Shon, S., Kim, T.: Learning pronunciation from a foreign language in speech synthesis networks. arXiv e-prints: arXiv.1811.09364v4 (2020)
14. Bender, L., Hailu, F.: Amharic Verb Morphology: A Generative Approach, Michiga Michiga State University (1978)
15. Ethnologue Homepage. https://www.ethnologue.com. Accessed 15 June 2017
16. Girmay, B.: The Phonology of Tigrigna: Generative Approach. Addis Ababa University, Addis Ababa (1983)

17. Tsehaye, T.: Reference Grammar of Tigrigna. Georgetown University, Washignton DC (1979)
18. Daniel, T.: Modern Tigrigna Grammar. Biranna Press, Addis Ababa (2008)
19. Baye, Y.: Amharic Grammar. Elleni Press, Addis Ababa (2007)
20. Mulugeta, S.: The Syllable Structure and Syllabification in Amharic. Norwegian University of Science and Technology, Oslo (2001)
21. Tesfay, T.: A Modern Grammar of Tigrigna, Tipografia U. Detti, Rom (2002)

OCR System for the Recognition of Ethiopic Real-Life Documents

Hagos Tesfahun Gebremichael[1(✉)],
Tesfahunegn Minwuyelet Mengistu[1] , Million Mesheha Beyene[2],
and Fikreselam Gared Mengistu[1]

[1] Bahir Dar University, Bahir Dar, Ethiopia
[2] Addis Ababa University, Addis Ababa, Ethiopia

Abstract. A bulk of real-life documents contain vital information and knowledge about history, culture, economy, politics, religion, and science that are written in Ethiopic script. This knowledge has to be shared and the advancement of technology like Optical Character Recognition (OCR) brings the need to digitize documents and make them available for public use. OCR is a process that allows printed, typewritten, and handwritten text to be recognized optically and converted into a machine-readable format that can be accepted by a computer for further processing. Nowadays, effective OCR systems have been developed for languages, like English that has wider use internationally. Researches in the area of Amharic OCR are ongoing since 1997. Attempts were made in adopting recognition algorithms to develop Amharic OCR. This study is, thus, an attempt made to develop an OCR system for real-life documents written in Ethiopic characters. In this study we propose a novel feature extraction schema using Gabor Filter and Principal Component Analysis (PCA), followed by a Genetic Algorithm (GA) based on supported vector machine classifier (SVM). The prototype was tested on real-life Ethiopic documents such as books, newspapers, and magazines, in which an average accuracy of 98.33% for Ethiopic characters is registered.

Keywords: Ethiopic scripts · OCR system · Gabor filter · PCA · GA · SVM

1 Introduction

Over the centuries, paper documents have been the principal instrument to make the progress of humankind permanent [1]. A large number of real-life documents written in Ethiopic script provide essential information and knowledge about history, society, business, politics, religion, and science. Huge collections of documents are archived, written in Ethiopic script in formats such as handwritten, typewritten, or computer printouts [2], which must be translated into electronic form for easy searching and retrieval based on users' information needs or queries. It is sufficient to highlight the massive number of documents in the form of correspondence letters, periodicals, newspapers, pamphlets, and books that are piled up in information centers, libraries, and offices [3]. These documents contain information related to religion, history,

© ICST Institute for Computer Sciences, Social Informatics and Telecommunications Engineering 2022
Published by Springer Nature Switzerland AG 2022. All Rights Reserved
M. L. Berihun (Ed.): ICAST 2021, LNICST 411, pp. 559–574, 2022.
https://doi.org/10.1007/978-3-030-93709-6_38

literature, politics, economics, philosophy, tradition, culture, nature, and other essential shreds of evidence of different nations, nationalities, and people of Ethiopia. Revealing and retrieving the knowledge preserved using Ethiopic script will have a positive impact on social and historical studies. Digitizing this information and allowing public access to these documents will decrease the problems of manual searching and retrieval, and provide vital importance for researchers, historians, tourists, and in general to build a good image about the country and the people. OCR strategies, algorithms, techniques, and tools can be used for this purpose.

Ethiopia is one of the world's ancient countries. It has a well-defined history of more than three thousand years, an ancient and well-developed educational system, philosophy, and writings that are uniquely attributed to it. Furthermore, the country has its language with its alphabets and numerical system, manuscripts, arts, calendars, and hymns which make it unique from all African countries. Most of such identities of the country are found being written in Geez language that is the ancestor of modern Ethion-Semitic languages like Tigrinya and Amharic [2, 3]. Most Ethiopic languages have their own indigenous or native scripts. As a result, libraries, information centers, museums, and businesses have a large number of printed papers. Also, there are plenty of texts which have been circulating among governmental, non-governmental, and private sectors. The digitization of these texts allows existing language technologies to be used to local information demands and advances. The processes by which documents that are created digitally are prepared for electronic access and further research fundamentally from the preservation, searching, and accessing of paper-based texts. Having these types of texts integrated into our digital lives has made OCR such an important technology over the past few years. Due to the trend of IT, and the reasons mentioned earlier, converting Ethiopic documents into electronic format is needed. To convert the text on these documents the conventional way is typing through the keyboard, which is not only time consuming, error-prone, and tedious but also impossible because of the magnitude of documents [4, 5]. The problem of typing into computers is even worse for Ethiopic characters were typing each character needs two keystrokes on average. This emphasizes the importance and tremendous need for developing an OCR system that is capable of recognizing Ethiopic characters. Thus, if automation of documents is needed an OCR software is the preferred means for converting existing documents into machine-readable form.

OCR is a type of document image analysis where a scanned digital image that contains either machine printed or typewritten or handwritten script is input into an OCR software engine and translating into an editable machine-readable digital text format (like ASCII or UNICODE text) [6, 7]. To do this, the OCR system goes through a series of steps, including image acquisition, preprocessing, segmentation, feature extraction, classification, and post-processing, before returning the recognized text documents [8, 9]. By transforming large amounts of printed or handwritten documents into electronic form for subsequent processing, OCR systems make it easier to use computers in everyday life.

2   Related Work

In the 1950s, research and development on automatic character recognition began. Since then, numerous studies on the recognition of various scripts have been conducted, including Latin, Arabic, Chinese, Hindu, Swedish, Russian, Tibetan, Japanese English, Devanagari, Bangla, Farsi, and Kannada, among others. Totally, the complete method is carried out in three phase preprocessing, feature extraction and recognition. In this paper, only Amharic scripture has been studied, which is spoken in countries such as the United States, Israel, Eritrea, Somalia, and Djibouti. Ethiopia is also the only African country with its own indigenous alphabets and writing systems, which is the Geez or Amharic alphabet, while the majority of African countries use English and Arabic scripts or alphabets. [4, 10, 11].

The technique for recognizing Ethiopic characters, on the other hand, is still in its infancy, with the first published study arriving very lately [12]. Furthermore, classifiers face extra challenges due to the structural complexity and interclass similarity of Ethiopic characters. Studies in the application of OCR techniques to Amharic characters have been started in 1997 by Worku et al. [13]. Worku et al. researched the application of OCR techniques to the Amharic characters. His character recognition took into consideration the normal typestyle of WashRa font with a 12-point font size. Under Worku's recommendation, Ermias et al. (1998) conducted more study on the recognition of structured Amharic text as a continuation of Worku's efforts. The goal of this study was to add pre-processing techniques to previously used recognition algorithms so that they could recognize formatted Amharic texts. Ermias used pre-processing techniques for thinning italicized style and underline identification and removal because papers written in Amharic characters occur in diverse font sizes, underline style, and contain italics feature. He incorporated the thinning and underline removal algorithms with the previously adopted recognition algorithm to test the performance of the system [14]. Dereje also attempted to further study in the field in 1999, with the goal of improving Amharic OCR so that it can recognize typewritten Amharic text. Based on his findings, Dereje primarily proposed that in order to improve the Amharic OCR system's recognition accuracy, recognition algorithms that are less sensitive to the peculiarities of character writing styles be used [15].

In the year 2000, Million et al. conducted research in this field with the goal of investigating and extracting the properties of Amharic characters in order to generalize the previously used recognition algorithm to handle diverse Amharic character typefaces [16]. By the same year, Negussie et al. had investigated the recognition of handwritten Amharic legal amounts of bank checks, the purpose of which is to investigate the application of OCR system approaches employed for other characters [17]. In 2002, Yaregal et al. conducted his research in continuation of the research activities done so far to explore the Amharic OCR development approaches, techniques, and methodologies and to come up with a versatile algorithm that is independent of the font size and other quantitative parameters of Amharic characters [4].

Another study by Million et al. was titled Optical Character Recognition of Amharic Documents and was published in 2007. This paper presents an OCR system for converting digitized documents in local languages [18]. Yaregal et al. investigated Hmm-based handwritten Amharic word recognition using feature concatenation in 2009. For offline handwritten text, this paper proposes writer-independent HMM-based Amharic word recognition [19].

Most of the previously done OCR system algorithms for Amharic scripts are based on specific font type, sizes and styles such as Washra, Power Geez, and Visual Geez etc. As this research is a continuous of the previous works, this study focuses on developing generic algorithm and independent of font types, sizes and styles for the recognition of Ethiopic real-life documents using SVM classifier. The contribution of this research is to develop a generic algorithm for Ethiopic real-life documents, to prepare training and testing datasets, we use Gabor Filter for feature extraction and Genetic Algorithm, which has never been used by previous researchers, for selecting the best features of the Ethiopic Characters, to study the experimental result using different kernel functions and analyze which kernel function has scored better result.

3 Ethiopic Character and Proposed OCR System

Ethiopic languages are written from left to right, with no distinction between capital and lowercase letters [16, 17]. As a fundamental character, the Ethiopic writing system consists of 35 characters (named "Fidel"/ "ፊደል"). The thirty-five fundamental characters are organized into seven groups, each of which represents a syllable with a consonant and a vowel after it. Non-basic forms are descended from basic forms through a series of more or less regular alterations. There are also symbols for labialization, numbers, and punctuation signs accessible. With these additions, the script now contains 328 different alphabets, including 245 basic characters, 54 labialize characters, 9 punctuation signs, and 20 numbers [20] (Tables 1, 2 and 3).

The proposed architecture for the OCR System is shown in Fig. 1. Given the digitalized document images of Ethiopic scripts, they are first preprocessed for removing noise, apply binarization, skewness detection, and slant correction. After the image is preprocessed, the next step is segmenting the image into three components: lines, words, and characters. After this stage, the segmented characters are delivered into the feature extraction stage. Under the feature extraction stage, features of the segmented characters are extracted using the Gabor filter. And then the dimensions of the extracted features are reduced using PCA technique. After that, the best features are selected using a GA. Then the best features, selected by GA, are delivered to the classification stage to classify the characters into the correct class using SVM.

Table 1. Ethiopic characters

	Ge'ez	Ka'eb	Salis	Rab'e	Hamis	Sadis	Sab'e
	a	u	i	a	e	h	o
h	ሀ	ሁ	ሂ	ሃ	ሄ	ህ	ሆ
l	ለ	ሉ	ሊ	ላ	ሌ	ል	ሎ
h	ሐ	ሑ	ሒ	ሓ	ሔ	ሕ	ሖ
m	መ	ሙ	ሚ	ማ	ሜ	ም	ሞ
s	ሠ	ሡ	ሢ	ሣ	ሤ	ሥ	ሦ
r	ረ	ሩ	ሪ	ራ	ሬ	ር	ሮ
s	ሰ	ሱ	ሲ	ሳ	ሴ	ስ	ሶ
sh	ሸ	ሹ	ሺ	ሻ	ሼ	ሽ	ሾ
q	ቀ	ቁ	ቂ	ቃ	ቄ	ቅ	ቆ
q	ቐ	ቑ	ቒ	ቓ	ቔ	ቕ	ቖ
b	በ	ቡ	ቢ	ባ	ቤ	ብ	ቦ
t	ተ	ቱ	ቲ	ታ	ቴ	ት	ቶ
ch	ቸ	ቹ	ቺ	ቻ	ቼ	ች	ቾ
h	ኀ	ኁ	ኂ	ኃ	ኄ	ኅ	ኆ
n	ነ	ኑ	ኒ	ና	ኔ	ን	ኖ
gn	ኘ	ኙ	ኚ	ኛ	ኜ	ኝ	ኞ
x	አ	ኡ	ኢ	ኣ	ኤ	እ	ኦ
w	ወ	ዉ	ዊ	ዋ	ዌ	ው	ዎ
x	ዐ	ዑ	ዒ	ዓ	ዔ	ዕ	ዖ
k	ከ	ኩ	ኪ	ካ	ኬ	ክ	ኮ
h	ኸ	ኹ	ኺ	ኻ	ኼ	ኽ	ኾ
z	ዘ	ዙ	ዚ	ዛ	ዜ	ዝ	ዞ
z	ዠ	ዡ	ዢ	ዣ	ዤ	ዥ	ዦ
y	የ	ዩ	ዪ	ያ	ዬ	ይ	ዮ
g	ገ	ጉ	ጊ	ጋ	ጌ	ግ	ጎ
d	ደ	ዱ	ዲ	ዳ	ዴ	ድ	ዶ
j	ጀ	ጁ	ጂ	ጃ	ጄ	ጅ	ጆ
t	ጠ	ጡ	ጢ	ጣ	ጤ	ጥ	ጦ
ch	ጨ	ጩ	ጪ	ጫ	ጬ	ጭ	ጮ
ts	ጸ	ጹ	ጺ	ጻ	ጼ	ጽ	ጾ
ts	ፀ	ፁ	ፂ	ፃ	ፄ	ፅ	ፆ
p	ጰ	ጱ	ጲ	ጳ	ጴ	ጵ	ጶ
f	ፈ	ፉ	ፊ	ፋ	ፌ	ፍ	ፎ
p	ፐ	ፑ	ፒ	ፓ	ፔ	ፕ	ፖ
v	ቨ	ቩ	ቪ	ቫ	ቬ	ቭ	ቮ

Table 2. Labialization characters

ኈ	ኊ	ኍ	ኋ	ኌ
ኈ	ኊ	ኍ	ኋ	ኌ
ጐ	ጒ	ጕ	ጓ	ጔ
ቈ	ቊ	ቍ	ቋ	ቌ
ቘ	ቚ	ቝ	ቛ	ቜ
ኈ	ኊ	ኍ	ኋ	ኌ
ሏ	ሗ	ሟ	ሧ	ሯ
ሷ	ሿ	ቇ	ቧ	ቷ
ቿ	ኇ	ኗ	ኟ	ዟ
ዧ	ዷ	ጇ	ጧ	ጯ
ጿ	ፇ	ፗ	፟	

Table 3. Ethiopic numerals

Ethio- pic Num- bers	Arabic Numbers	Ethio- pic Num- bers	Ara- bic Num- bers
፩	1	፳	20
፪	2	፴	30
፫	3	፵	40
፬	4	፶	50
፭	5	፷	60
፮	6	፸	70
፯	7	፹	80
፰	8	፺	90
፱	9	፻	100
፲	10	፼	1000

An SVM classifier uses a well-known algorithm to determine membership in a given class, based on training data. The classifier has two basic functions: training and classification. The process of generating a classifier based on content that is known to belong to specific classes is referred to as training. Classification is the process of using a classifier constructed with such a training content set to assess if unknown infor- mation belongs in a specific class.

An SVM training algorithm creates a model that allocates fresh samples to one of two categories given a series of training examples, each tagged as belonging to one. An SVM model is a representation of the examples as points in space, mapped so that the examples of the different categories are separated by a large distance. New examples are then mapped into the same space and classified according to which side of the gap they fall on. Finally, the recognized text documents are obtained.

3.1 Preprocessing Ethiopic Real-Life Documents

The accuracy of the recognition step in OCR systems highly depends on the effec- tiveness of their preprocessing steps. From the standpoint of this study, the purpose of preprocessing processes is to remove noise and unwanted artifacts from picture data to an acceptable level and provide a refined image for subsequent tasks in character recognition. Thresholding (the task of converting a gray scale image into a binary (black-white) image), noise removal (filtering out background non-textural matters, interfering strokes, shades, and dots introduced by input devices), and skew detection and correction (aligning the paper document with the coordinate system of the scanner) are some of the necessary analyses to perform before recognizing scanned images.

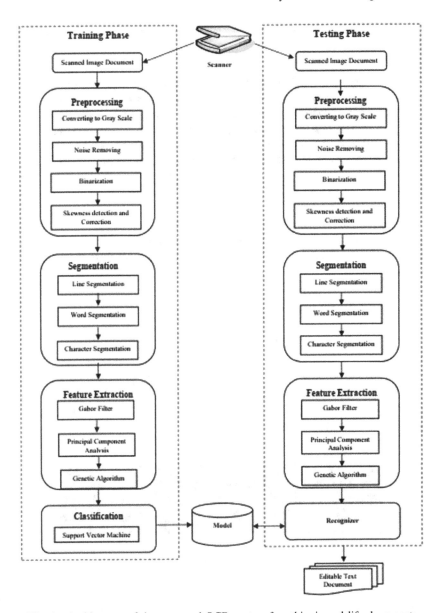

Fig. 1. Architecture of the proposed OCR system for ethiopic real-life documents

Image Segmentation

Line segmentation, word segmentation, and character segmentation are all layers of binary picture segmentation [21].

Line Segmentation: The row histogram was constructed by scanning the input image horizontally and counting the frequency of black pixels in each row to detect text lines.

A boundary between two successive lines is defined as the point where the number of pixels in a row is zero (Fig. 2).

Fig. 2. Line segmentation

Word Segmentation: Following the detection of a line, each line is scanned vertically for word segmentation. A column histogram is made up of the number of black pixels in each column. The section of a line with continuous black pixels is characterized as a word in a line (Fig. 3).

Fig. 3. Word segmentation

Character Segmentation: Each word is scanned vertically for character segmentation once it has been segmented. A column histogram is made up of the number of black pixels in each column. A character in a word is defined as the section of the word with continuous black pixels (Fig. 4).

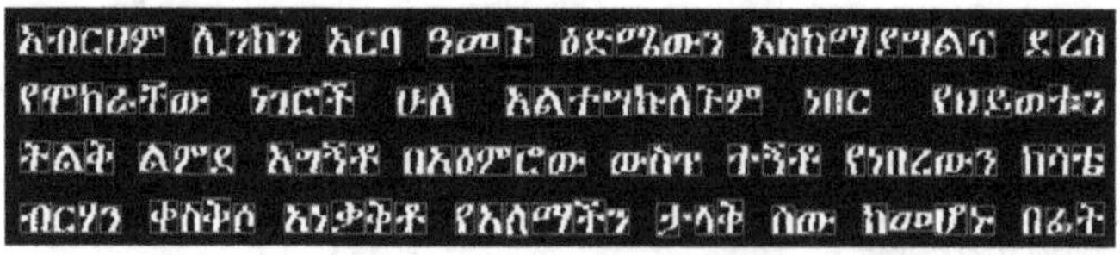

Fig. 4. Character segmentation

3.2   Feature Extraction Steps

The extraction of features is an important aspect of any recognition system. Feature extraction seeks to find patterns with the fewest number of features that are useful in classifying patterns [22]. The performance of the recognition system greatly depends on the features that are being extracted. Using the retrieved features, each character should be able to be classified separately [23]. The Gabor filter was employed to extract features in this study.

1. Gabor Filter

This research presents a new and robust feature extraction method based on Gabor filters for character recognition. Because of their exceptional qualities, Gabor filters are commonly used in image processing and texture analysis: Gabor filters are good for texture representation and discrimination because their frequency and orientation representations are close to those of the human visual system [24].

Gabor wavelets filters have frequency and orientation representations that are close to those of the human visual system, making them suitable for texture representation and discrimination. Gabor filters are widely used in pattern analysis [25]. Gabor filters' most major advantage is its invariance to light, rotation, scaling, and translation. They can also endure photometric disturbances like as variations in illumination and picture noise. A two-dimensional Gabor filter is a Gaussian kernel function modulated by a complex sinusoidal plane wave in the spatial domain, defined as:

$$G(x, y) = \frac{f^2}{\pi \gamma \eta} exp\left(\frac{-x^2 + \gamma^2 y^2}{2\sigma^2}\right) exp(j2\pi f x' + \phi)$$
$$x' = x\cos\theta + y\sin\theta \tag{1}$$
$$y' = -x\sin\theta + y\cos\theta$$

where f is the sinusoidal factor's frequency, θ denotes the orientation of a Gabor function's normal to the parallel stripes, ϕ is the phase offset, σ is the Gaussian envelope's standard deviation, and γ is the spatial aspect ratio, which specifies the ellipticity of the Gabor function's support.

As shown in Fig. 5, our proposed algorithm uses forty Gabor filters in five scales and eight orientations to recognize characters, as well as the real parts of the outcome images after applying Gabor filters to the character image. Given the significant correlation between neighboring pixels in the image, we may reduce the information redundancy by down sampling the feature images produced by Gabor filters [24].

Gabor filters extract the character's variations at different frequencies and orientations. The size of the output feature vector is calculated by multiplying the image size (20 × 20) by the number of scales and orientations (5 × 8) divided by the row and column down sampling factors (2 × 2), resulting in a total of 20 × 20 × 5 × 8/ (2 × 2) = 4000. Even after down-sampling, the feature vector is still quite huge.

As a result, we'll need to employ dimensionality reduction techniques [26]. PCA was used to reduce dimensionality.

Fig. 5. Gabor filter in five scales and eight orientations.

2. Principal of Component Analysis (PCA)

PCA is one of the methods used for dimensionality reduction. Such a method reduces the data down into its basic components, stripping away any unnecessary parts. This should be done without losing valuable information. Reducing dimensions helps to simplify the data and makes it easier to visualize. For PCA to work, we must subtract the mean from each of the data dimensions. The mean is subtracted from the average of all dimensions. As a result, X' (mean values of all data points) is removed from all X values, and Y' is subtracted from all Y values. This results in a data collection with a mean of zero. Following that, the data's covariance matrix must be calculated. The eigenvector and eigenvalues are computed using this covariance matrix. The eigenvectors and eigenvalues for this matrix can then be calculated. These are critical because they offer us with critical data information. Eigenvectors and eigenvalues are always found in pairs: each eigenvector has an eigenvalue. A direction of the principal component is called an eigenvector. An eigenvalue is a number that indicates the amount of volatility in the data in that direction. The eigenvector with the highest eigenvalue is thus the major component.

3. Genetic Algorithm (GA)

The Gabor filter was used to extract the feature, which was then reduced in dimensionality using PCA before being applied to the Genetic Algorithm (GA) to provide the optimum features for optimal accuracy. GA is a set of population-based and algorithmic search heuristics that replicate the natural evolution process [2, 27]. A population of individual solutions is repeatedly modified by the genetic algorithm. At each phase, the genetic algorithm chooses parents at random from the current population and uses them to produce the following generation's children. Over successive generation the population evolves towards an optimal solution. Based on this the surviving chromosome for GA is the string best chromosome = {1 1 0 1 1 1 1 1 0 0 0 1 0 1 1 1 1 0 1 1 1 1 1 0 1 1 0 0 0 1 1 1 0 1 1 1 1 1 0 0 0 0 0 1 1 0 1 1 1 0 1 0 0 1 0 1 1 1 0 0 0 1 1 1 1 0 1 0 1 1 0 1 0 0 1 0 1 1 1 0 0 0 1 0 1 1 0 0 0 1 1 0 0 0 0 0 0 0 0 0}. The positional indices of "1s" in this string are {1 2 4 5 6 7 8 12 14 15 16 17 19 20 21 22 23 25 26 30 31 31 34 35 36 37 38 44 45 47 48 49 51 54 56 57 58 62 63 64 65 67 69 70 72 75 77 78 79 83 85 86 90 91}. The corresponding features from this string are those features positions {1 2 4 5 6 7 8 12 14 15 16 17 19 20 21 22 23 25 26 30 31 31 34 35 36 37 38 44 45 47 48 49 51 54 56 57 58 62 63 64 65 67 69 70 72 75 77 78 79 83 85 86 90 91}, which is 54 features. Equation 2 shows the fitness function which is used in our experiment.

$$F = \frac{\alpha}{Nf} + \exp\left(-\frac{1}{Nf}\right)$$ (2)

Where, F, α, and Nf are fitness function, KNN-Based classification error, and Cardinality of the selected features respectively. The algebraic structure of Eq. 2 ensures the learning of the GA, error minimization, and reduced number of features selected.

In GA, we start with the original population and then apply three operators: the first is a selection, which selects the strings, the second is a crossover, which recombines those selected strings, and the third is a mutation, which alters the shape of strings of

0's and 1's. Now we apply the condition and see if the optimization conditions are met. If they are, we choose the best string, which is our solution, and if they are not, we send it to the initial population, as shown in Fig. 6 (Fig. 7).

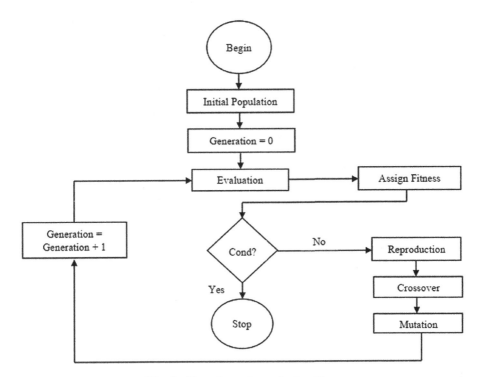

Fig. 6. Flow chart of genetic algorithm.

Genetic Algorithm

Initialization [population];
Evaluation [population];
Generation: = 0;
-do
Selected-parents: = selection[population];
Created-offspring: = recombination[selected-parents];
Mutation [created-offspring];
Population: = created-offspring;
Evaluation [population];
Generation: = geaeration+1;
UNTIL stop-criterion;

Fig. 7. Pseudocode genetic algorithm

4   Result and Discussions

Once the system is developed, an experiment is conducted to evaluate its performance in the recognition of Ethiopic characters. To this end, two experiments are conducted. The first experiment is done using PCA without applying GA and the second experiment is done by applying GA on the reduced feature vectors using PCA. In each experiment, the four kernel functions, such as linear, polynomial, radial basis, and sigmoid of SVM are used to select the best kernel function for the recognition (Fig. 8).

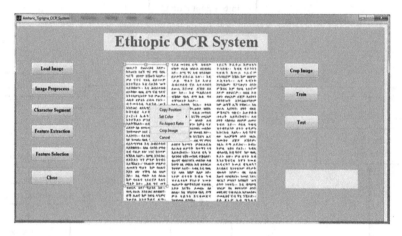

Fig. 8. System prototype interface

4.1   Experiment 1: Performance Analysis Using PCA

In this experiment, first, we extracted 10540×4000 features using the Gabor filter from the segmented characters, and then PCA is applied to reduce the extracted features to 10540×100 feature spaces. The main reason that we reduced the feature space is that to minimize high memory storage consumption and processor computational time during classification process. In addition to this, as the number of features of characters increase, the similarity of the features among characters should also increase. Hence, this leads to increase misclassification errors during recognition. So, that is why we need to reduce the feature spaces from 4000 to 100 using PCA. After we have reduced the dimensional space of the feature vectors of the datasets into 100 feature spaces, then SVM has been trained with 4540 training data and tested with 6000 testing data. Table 4 shows the performance of the OCR system after applying PCA for feature space reduction.

Table 4. The result of the experiment conducted at 100 features reduced using PCA

Training phase			Testing phase		
Training data	Kernel function	Parameter value	Document type	Testing data	Accuracy (%)
4540	Linear	C = 8	Book	2000	87.8
			Magazine	2000	94.2
			Newspaper	2000	96.8
Average					**92.93**
4540	polynomial	C = 4, γ = 0.25	Book	2000	87.5
			Magazine	2000	95
			Newspaper	2000	96.6
Average					**93.6**
4540	Sigmoid	C = 8, γ = 0.0625	Book	2000	76.2
			Magazine	2000	83.7
			Newspaper	2000	83.6
Average					**81.17**
4540	RBF	C = 8, γ = 0.5	Book	2000	89.4
			Magazine	2000	94.8
			Newspaper	2000	96.7
Average					**93.63**

As can be seen from Table 5, the RBF kernel function registered a better result than the other kernel functions with an average accuracy of 93.63% for Ethiopic characters. From the experimental result, we observed that there is a performance difference among books, magazines, and newspapers. The main reason for performance difference is due to printing variations, character similarity, and document degradation. Document recognition happens because of artifacts such as cuts, merges, ink blobs, etc. that are commonly observed in printed document images scanned from books, magazines, and newspapers. Degradations due to cuts break character components into two or more, and ink-blobs join disjoint characters as one connected component.

4.2   Experiment 2: Performance Analysis Using GA

In this experiment, we extracted 54 features from the character dataset. Thus, the dimensionality of the dataset is reduced to 10540 × 54. Pattern or image recognition systems may be threatened by high-dimensional feature sets. In other words, having too many features can impair the identification system's classification accuracy because some of them are redundant and non-informative. To attain the best combination of features, several combinatorial sets of features should be obtained. As a result, to limit the number of features used by the SVM Classifier in this study, a GA-based feature selection (a subspace or manifold projection technique) will be applied. A Feature Subset Selection (FSS) is a mapping from an m-dimensional feature space (input space) to an n-dimensional feature space (output space) using the Fs operator:

$$Fs : R^{rm} \rightarrow R^{rxn} \qquad (3)$$

where m $\geq$ n and m, n $\in$ Z+, Rr $\times$ m is any database or matrix holding the original feature set with r instances or observations, Rr $\times$ n is the reduced feature set including r observations in the subset selection. After selecting the optimal features using GA, the SVM classifier has been trained using these features and the result obtained after applying the GA is shown in Table 5.

Table 5. The result of the experiment conducted at 54 features reduced using GA

Training phase			Testing phase		
Training data	Kernel function	Parameter value	Document type	Testing data	Accuracy (%)
4540	Linear	C = 8	Book	2000	95.7
			Magazine	2000	97.3
			Newspaper	2000	98
Average					**97**
4540	polynomial	C = 8, γ = 2	Book	2000	96.1
			Magazine	2000	97.2
			Newspaper	2000	98.2
Average					**97.17**
4540	Sigmoid	C = 8, γ = 0.0625	Book	2000	84.6
			Magazine	2000	87.4
			Newspaper	2000	88.7
Average					**86.9**
4540	RBF	C = 8, γ = 0.5	Book	2000	97.7
			Magazine	2000	97.9
			Newspaper	2000	98.5
Average					**98.33**

As can be seen from Table 5, the RBF kernel function registered a better result than the other kernel functions. Based on this reason we selected the performance registered by RBF kernel function as accuracy registered by the system. As a result, the system has completed classifying the features of the input characters with an accuracy of 98.33% for Ethiopic characters on average. This shows that an average of 1.67% of Ethiopic characters is wrongly recognized. From this result, we concluded that the accuracy of GA-based dimensionality reduction for feature selection is better than the accuracy of PCA-based dimensionality reduction. The reason why experiment two outperforms better than experiment one is that GA reduces the features of the characters by selecting the most discriminant features that enable the system to recognize correctly some of the similar Ethiopic characters. In this experiment, the performance difference was observed among books, magazines, and newspapers because of printing variations and low document quality. The recognizer correctly classified 97.7% of 2000 characters from books, 97.9% of 2000 characters from magazines, 98.5% of 2000 characters from Newspapers.

In this study, we have used the Support Vector Machine (SVM) for the classification task. The performance of the system is sufficiently promising. Because GA effectively identifies the best properties of a character, the GA-selected features enhanced the classifier's accuracy from 93.63% percent to 98.33% for Ethiopic documents.

The errors encountered in the test result of the developed recognition system can be seen in two broad views: segmentation error and classification/recognition error. Segmentation error is an error that occurred due to the segmentation algorithm. On the other hand, classification/recognition errors occurred in evaluating the performance of the system. The recognition error is an error that occurred due to structurally similarity between the input characters and its recognition result. For example, ለ is recognized as ሰ.

5 Conclusion

The purpose of this study was to design an OCR system for real-life documents written in Ethiopic languages. The developed system has seven phases: Text digitalization, Preprocessing, Segmentation, Feature extraction, Classification model, Recognizer engine, and finally recognized documents. Finally, the performance of the system has been tested with 6000 unknown instances which are collected from Ethiopic Real-Life documents. The average performance of the correctly classified characters for Ethiopic scripts is 98.33%, which is obtained using GA. The majority of the misclassification errors are attributed to the challenges faced by the segmentation and noise removal techniques from poor quality Ethiopic document images.

One of the major challenges in real-life documents is degradation. So, to enhance the performance of the system there is a need to integrate preprocessing techniques such as advanced noise removal algorithms and also image restoration techniques for blurred images. And also, to improve the performance of the system, an advanced segmentation technique that dynamically adjusts the threshold value according to the document under consideration should be developed.

References

1. Marinai, S., et al.: Introduction to document analysis and recognition. IEEE Trans. PAMI **27**(1), 23–43 (2006)
2. Encyclopedia Britannica, Ethiopia: Encyclopaedia Britannica Ultimate Reference Suite. Encyclopaedia Britannica, Chicago (2010)
3. Meshesha, M., Jawahar, C.V.: Matching word images for content-based retrieval from printed document images. Int. J. Doc. Anal. Recogn. **11**(1), 29–38 (2008)
4. Assabie, Y., et al.: Optical character recognition of Amharic text: an integrated approach (Master thesis). School of Information Studies for Africa, Addis Ababa University, Addis Ababa, Ethiopia (2002)
5. Belay, B., Habtegebrial, T., Meshesha, M., Liwicki, M., Belay, G., Stricker, D.: Amharic OCR: an end-to-end learning. Appl. Sci. **10**(3), 1117 (2020). https://doi.org/10.3390/app10031117

6. Eikvil, L., et al.: OCR - Optical Character Recognition, pp. 317–326 (December 1993). Norsk Regnesentral, P.B. 114 Blindern, N-0314 Oslo
7. Getu, S., et al.: Ancient Ethiopic Manuscripts Character Recognition, vol. 38 (July 2020)
8. Tanner, S., et al.: Deciding whether optical character recognition is feasible. King's Digital Consultancy Service (December 2004)
9. Ahmed, M., Abidi, A.: Review on optical character recognition. IRJET **06**, 3666–3669 (2019)
10. Cowell, J., Hussain, F.: Amharic character recognition using a fast signature based algorithm. In: Proceedings of the 7th International Conference on Information Visualization, pp. 384–389 (2003)
11. Belay, B., Habtegebrial, T., Belay, G., Meshesha, M.: Learning by injection : attention embedded recurrent neural network for Amharic text-image recognition (October 2020)
12. Alemu, W., et al.: The application of OCR techniques to the Amharic script (Master thesis). School of Information Studies for Africa, Addis Ababa University, Addis Ababa, Ethiopia (1997)
13. Demilew, F.A., Sekeroglu, B.: Ancient Geez script recognition using deep learning. SN Appl. Sci. **1**(11), 1–7 (2019). https://doi.org/10.1007/s42452-019-1340-4
14. Abebe, E., et al.: Recognition of formatted Amharic text using optical character recognition (Master thesis). School of Information Studies for Africa, Addis Ababa University, Addis Ababa, Ethiopia (1998)
15. Teferi, D., et al.: Optical character recognition of typewritten Amharic text (Master thesis). School of Information Studies for Africa, Addis Ababa University, Addis Ababa, Ethiopia (1999)
16. Meshesha, M.: A generalized approach to optical character recognition of Amharic texts (Master thesis). School of Information studies for Africa, Addis Ababa University, Addis Ababa, Ethiopia (2000)
17. Taddesse, N., et al.: Handwritten Amharic text recognition applied to the processing of bank cheques (Master thesis). School of Information Studies for Africa, Addis Ababa University, Addis Ababa, Ethiopia (2000)
18. Meshesha, M., Jawahar, C.: Optical character recognition of Amharic documents. Afr. J. Inf. Commun. Technol. **3**(2) (2007)
19. Yaregal, A., Josef, B.: HMM-based handwritten Amharic word recognition with feature concatenation. In: Proceedings of the International Conference on Document Analysis and Recognition, Barcelona, Spain, 26–29 July 2009, pp. 961–965 (2009)
20. Trier, O.D., Jain, A.K.: Goal-directed evaluation of binarization methods. IEEE Trans. Pattern Anal. Mach. Intel. **17**(12), 1191–1201 (1995). https://doi.org/10.1109/34.476511
21. Asnake, B., et al.: Retrieval from real-life Amharic document images (Master Thesis). School of Information Science, Addis Ababa University, Addis Ababa, Ethiopia (June 2012)
22. Meshesha, M., et al.: Recognition and retrieval from document image collections. Ph.D. Dissertation, International Institute of Information Technology, India (2008)
23. Mori, M., et al.: Character Recognition. Sciyo (2010). ISBN 978-953-307-105-3
24. Asht, S., Dass, R.: Pattern recognition techniques: a review. Int. J. Comput. Sci. Telecommun. **3**(8), 25–29 (2012)
25. Zhang, D., Lu, G.: A comparative study on shape retrieval using Fourier descriptors with different shape signatures. In: Proceedings of the IEEE International Conference on Multimedia and Expo, Tokyo, Japan, pp. 1139–1142 (2001)
26. Haghighi, M., et al.: Identification using encrypted biometrics. Department of Electrical and Computer Engineering, University of Miami, pp. 440-448 (2013)
27. Akram, S., Dar, M.-U.-D., Quyoum, A.: Document image processing - a review. Int. J. Comput. Appl. **10**(5), 35–40 (2010)

Efficient Architecture for a High Performance Authenticated Encryption Algorithm on Reconfigurable Computing

Abiy Tadesse Abebe[1]($\boxtimes$), Yalemzewd Negash Shiferaw[1],
and P. G. V. Suresh Kumar[2]

[1] School of Electrical and Computer Engineering,
Addis Ababa Institute of Technology, AAU, Addis Ababa, Ethiopia
{abiy.tadesse,yalemzewdn}@aait.edu.et
[2] Ambo University, Ambo, Ethiopia

Abstract. High performance authenticated encryption algorithms are indispensable and preferable for securing the contemporary high speed wireless networks as they can perform their tasks without affecting overall performance of the network, and can provide data confidentiality, data integrity, and authentication cryptographic services simultaneously. Most of existing FPGA based architectures that have been proposed to enhance performance of such algorithms considered generic FPGA fabrics for implementations. Implementing complex algorithms using only traditional FPGA logic requires large amount of such resources that in turn can affect performance. In this work, an efficient architecture for AEGIS-128 authenticated encryption algorithm is proposed using both FPGAs' embedded hard-cores such as digital signal processing slices and block random access memories that have not been fully exploited for such applications with balanced amount of generic logic. The aim is to reduce performance bottlenecks and enhance performance of AEGIS-128. The implementation results show that the proposed architecture outperforms existing similar approaches found in the literature in terms of throughput, and utilization of reduced amount of resources.

Keywords: AEGIS-128 · AES-128 · BRAMs · DSP slices · Cryptosystem · Embedded hard-cores · FPGA

1 Introduction

High performance cryptographic algorithms are useful to secure the contemporary high speed wireless networks since they can perform their security tasks without affecting the overall performance of the network [1]. Authenticated encryption algorithms are preferable for the contemporary information security since a single algorithm can provide multiple cryptographic security services

© ICST Institute for Computer Sciences, Social Informatics and Telecommunications Engineering 2022
Published by Springer Nature Switzerland AG 2022. All Rights Reserved
M. L. Berihun (Ed.): ICAST 2021, LNICST 411, pp. 575–585, 2022.
https://doi.org/10.1007/978-3-030-93709-6_39

including data confidentiality, data integrity, and data origin authentication, simultaneously [1]. These algorithms can be classified as high performance and lightweight Authenticated Encryption with Associated Data (AEAD). The former has been designed targeting high speed applications. Whereas, the latter is designed mainly by considering the resource and performance limitations of constrained devices. High speed authenticated encryption algorithms are useful to secure high performance applications since they can offer the required high throughput if they are efficiently implemented. There are several Advanced Encryption Standard (AES) based high performance authenticated encryption algorithms [1,2]; and, many researchers have proposed different FPGA based architectures to enhance performance of such high speed authenticated encryption algorithms [3]. However, most of them considered the generic FPGA fabrics to implement their proposed architectures. But, in addition to the traditional FPGA logic elements, modern FPGAs have also incorporated embedded hard-cores that have not been fully exploited for implementation of such algorithms. Implementation of complex algorithms using only the common FPGA logic elements have some limitations such as requirement of large amount of such resources that in turn can impact performance.

The main contributions of this research work are described as follows:

- Efficient architecture for AEGIS-128 authenticated encryption algorithm tailored to the security of high performance applications is proposed synthesized, optimized, and implemented on FPGA achieving high throughput results.
- Improving throughput with reasonable hardware resource utilization are the optimization targets for the proposed architecture. Therefore, a hybrid optimization technique including as parallel-pipelining approach is used to meet the intended optimization targets.
- The potential use of modern FPGA resources such as embedded hard-cores including Digital Signal Processing (DSP) slices and Block Random Access Memories (BRAMs) are exploited to implement the proposed architectures with balanced utilization of the traditional FPGA fabrics. This approach enabled to enhance performance of AEGIS-128 algorithm in terms of throughput and resource utilization.

The paper is organized as follows:
Summary of related works are discussed in Sect. 2. Section 3 briefly describes the core of AEGIS algorithm, the Advanced Encryption Standard (AES) and its FPGA based implementation techniques. Efficient AES architecture for FPGA implementation is presented in Sect. 4. Section 5 briefly highlights the state update procedures of AEGIS-128 algorithm based on AES. Section 6 presents the proposed efficient architecture for AEGIS-128. Implementation approaches for the proposed AEGIS-128 architecture on FPGA and result comparisons are presented in Sect. 7. Finally, Sect. 8 concludes the paper.

2   Summary of Some Existing Related Works

There are some proposed architectures for AEGIS algorithm including both high speed and reduced area implementations on FPGA and ASIC platforms.

In [3], two different FPGA based AEGIS-128L architectures were proposed, one for reduced area and the other for high speed using looping and pipelining methods, respectively. In case of pipelining method, they used BRAMs for storing and loading of keys. However, they used a straightforward pipelining technique, but no any other technique was employed. Moreover, they didn't mention about whether they used full pipelining, inner pipelining or both. ASIC based implementation results of various AEAD algorithms were reported including AEGIS algorithm in [4] using HLS tool, but no specific implementation technique was described. In [5], compact ASIC based AEGIS architecture was proposed for secure FPGA reconfiguration. Since a single AES round consists 16 SubBytes(s-box), a ShiftRows, and four MixColumns operations, to reduce the area, they used only four s-boxes; and then, using only one mix-column step. As a consequence, they achieved $1/4^{th}$ of the area consumed if, otherwise, a full round of AES is used. However, their architecture was not evaluated based on FPGA. In the works presented in [6] and [7], full outer and inner pipelining techniques were employed to achieve high throughput.

3 The Core of AEGIS-128 Algorithm: AES

The core of AEGIS-128 authenticated encryption algorithm [1] is AES [8]. AES is a 128 bit block cipher algorithm with three different key sizes, 128 bit, 192 bit and 256 bit with 10, 12 and 14 round operations, respectively. The AES encryption process performs four basic operations: SubBytes (byte substitution), ShftRows (rows shifting), MixColumns (column mixing) and AddRoundKey (adding round keys) to provide data confidentiality. In the last round, there is no MixColumns transformation. Before starting execution of these four basic operations, the 128 bit block data (plaintext) is arranged in to a 4x4 matrix which is known as a state. Each cell in a state contains elements with 8 bits size and are named as state elements. The state is XORed with the initial round key before the round operations are started. The initialization process is done by adding the first round key (128 bits) with 128 bits plaintext. Then, all the four operations are performed consecutively on the resulting state outputs (after each round step), until the specified round number is reached. The final result of the encryption process provides the ciphertext. For each round operation a separate key is used which is generated by using a key generator function [8].

The decryption process generally involves the inverse steps of the encryption rounds: InverseSubBytes, InverseShiftRows, AddRoundKey (which is the inverse of itself), and InverseMixColumns. Details about the construction of AES can be found in [8], and [9].

3.1 Optimization Techniques for FPGA Based AES Implementation

The standard AES algorithm can be efficiently implemented on FPGA targeting small area or high speed optimization metrics, or else the trade-off between them. Small area optimization refers to utilization of small amount of FPGA resources for compact implementation [10] results specially tailored to constrained environments. An example of small area architecture of AES implementation was presented in [11]. This approach used a single round and iteratively processed it ten times for AES-128. The throughput can be obtained by computing the product of the maximum frequency achieved and the data block size (128), and dividing the result by ten (number of rounds) [11] as shown in Eq. 1:

$$Throughput(Mbps) = \frac{F_{max}(MHz) \times 128}{10} \qquad (1)$$

It is possible to improve the throughput outcome with cost of increased area by using loop unrolling or pipelining architectures. In pipelining architecture [12] registers are placed at each round of AES to construct the pipeline. It is possible to determine the depth of the pipeline that can limit the number of the data blocks to be processed concurrently. If fully pipelining is required so as to achieve higher throughput, the total number of rounds of AES is taken as the depth of the pipeline [12,13]. Generally, pipelining increases the encryption speed by processing multiple blocks of data simultaneously. Similar to pipelining, the sub-pipelining architecture is formed by further putting registers inside of each round function of AES. If each round unit has n stages with equal delay, then a K-round sub-pipelined architecture can achieve approximately n times the speed of a K-round pipelined architecture with some increase of area caused by additional registers and control logic. In loop unrolling architecture, registers inserted for pipelining are removed and all rounds are independently implemented in hardware [12]. In this case, multiple AES rounds are processed in the same clock cycle. The delay of each round is the same which depends on the combinational logic used. Unrolled architectures have a large number of rounds that are independently implemented in hardware, and can increase hardware complexity.

4   The Proposed Architecture for AES on Reconfigurable Computing

Combining existing approaches, a hybrid technique is proposed for FPGA based efficient AES implementation. As shown in Fig. 1, the proposed hybrid technique combines: two AES-128 cores working in parallel for high speed, full outer pipelining that pipeline all the AES rounds, inner parallel round functions with partial sub-pipelining that enable selected groups of round operations to be executed in parallel-pipelining mode. The pre-stored BRAMs are used to provide the plaintext (P_t) in parallel mode. The initial round is first performed by XORing the P_t with the initial round key in both AES cores in parallel. Then, the intermediate rounds are performed similarly by XORing the processed state output of each round with the AddRoundKey of their respective round steps in both AES-cores in parallel. After the processing of intermediate rounds are completed, the last rounds are executed in parallel producing the ciphertext (C_t) for

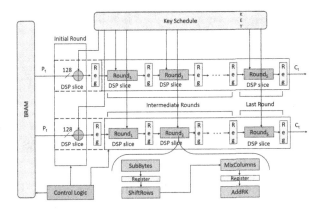

Fig. 1. Structure of the combined AES architecture

both AES-cores. The inner rounds in both paths are partially pipelined and processed in parallel in groups of two in such a way that SubBytes and ShiftRows are processed in parallel with MixColumns and AddRoundKey as shown in Fig. 1, except for the last round that doesn't include MixColumn. The pipelined registers are used to speed up the process. The same round keys are used for both cores. All these operations are performed until all the input message is processed.

The key schedule produces the required keys and stores them in BRAMs, and they are used during execution of the two AES-cores. Key-expansion in AES-128 is the process of generating all Round Keys from the original input key. Ten Round keys are generated with 16 bytes size for the 128 bits key size.

The proposed method differs from existing related architectures in that it combines various techniques to provide an AES-128 architecture based on hybrid approach and implements it using DSP slices and BRAM hard-cores in addition to balanced utilization of the traditional FPGA fabrics, instead of using only one resource type, and excluding the other. This increases flexibility of implementation while exploiting the modern FPGA resources for suitable parts of the algorithm under consideration. The combined effect of the proposed architecture is intended to produce a balanced trade-off between speed and area giving more emphasis to speed.

4.1 Implementation Approaches

For implementation of this architecture, both FPGA generic fabrics and dedicated hard-cores including DSP48E1 and BRAMs are used in order to balance hardware resource utilization and enhance throughput efficiency. The proposed architecture is implemented on Xilinx Virtex-5, Virtex-7, and Zynq FPGA devices. Xilinx Vivado 2018.3 High-level synthesis tool is used to test the proposed architecture's functionality. Figure 2 shows functional verification for encryption part of AES-128. Xilinx Vivado HLS is a modern EDA tool and is state-of-the-art technology which enables to specify the design in software. It

Fig. 2. Functional test of AES-128 using Vivado HLS

can also synthesizes it and produces RTL of the design, and provides flexibility to optimize the design using several optimization directives so as to achieve the desired optimization metrics. The synthesized VHDL code is implemented targeting the specified devices. For older versions of Xilinx FPGA devices that are not supported by Vivado HLS tool, Xilinx ISE 14.5 is used to implement and analyze the performance of the proposed architecture.

Control logic is used to synchronize the parallel operations. And, pipeline registers found in the DSP slices are used for pipelining. Since the proposed architecture is in turn intended to optimize AEGIS-128 algorithm, only encryption part is considered.

Since binary addition operations in hardware are performed using Exclusive-or (XOR) operation, DSP slices are used to perform the XOR operations. The S-box values and constants are pre-stored in BRAMs. Therefore, the BRAMs are read whenever the data and keys are needed for processing the AES states. Cascaded DSP slices are used to perform 128 bit operations.

5   Brief Description of AEGIS-128 Algorithm

AEGIS-128 algorithm [1] is an Advanced Encryption Standard (AES) [8] based algorithm which uses the AES round functions excluding the last round. AEGIS-128 algorithm uses 128 bits key and 128 bits Initialization Vector (IV) to perform authenticated encryption and authenticated decryption processes. It can process less than 2^{64} lengths of plaintext and the associated data. The recommended length of the tag to be used for authentication is 128 bits; though, lesser lengths of tags can also be used [1].

The algorithm uses the AES round functions to update the 640 bits (80 bytes) of state, S_i, with 128 bits (16 bytes) of data blocks, m_i, using its state update function such that: $S_{(i+1)} = StateUpdate128(S_i, m_i)$ as shown in Fig. 3. In Fig. 3, R indicates the AES encryption round function, and w is a temporary 16-byte word [1]. The structure represented in Fig. 3 can also be expressed as follows [1]:

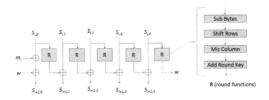

Fig. 3. The state update function of AEGIS-128

$$S_{i+1,0} = AESRound(S_{i,4}, S_{i,0} \oplus m_i);$$

$$S_{i+1,1} = AESRound(S_{i,0}, S_{i,1});$$

$$S_{i+1,2} = AESRound(S_{i,1}, S_{i,2});$$

$$S_{i+1,3} = AESRound(S_{i,2}, S_{i,3});$$

$$S_{i+1,4} = AESRound(S_{i,3}, S_{i,4});$$

AEGIS-128 performs different execution steps including initialization, process of the associated data, encryption, and finalization. The decryption process requires the exact values of key size, IV size, and tag size to perform the verification and decryption tasks [1]. Details about AEGIS AEAD algorithm can be found in [1].

6   Efficient Architecture for AEGIS-128 Algorithm

Since AEGIS-128 algorithm [1] composes advanced encryption standard (AES) algorithm [8] as its central component, optimized architecture of AES in turn optimizes the AEGIS algorithm too. Therefore, the architecture proposed for optimization of AES in Sect. 4 is applied here for optimizing the AEGIS-128 algorithm with some rearrangements based on the specific requirements of AEGIS-128 algorithm. The AES algorithm implemented in Sect. 4 is AES-128. It is selected to fit AEGIS-128 architecture. Though AES-128 consists 10 rounds, AEGIS-128 algorithm uses only five rounds for state update function. Thus, the architecture proposed in Sect. 4 for AES-128 algorithm is modified to use only five rounds; and, the last round is removed as specified in AEGIS algorithm design [1]. Then, two AES-128 cores with only five rounds each, are made to be processed in parallel while maintaining the internal construction of the proposed AES architecture specified in Sect. 4. The structure of the proposed AEGIS-128 architecture is shown in Fig. 4. In addition to the optimized AES architecture, various pipelining stages are constructed to increase the AEGS-128 performance.

As shown in Fig. 4, the two AES-128 cores are executed in parallel each taking 128 bit plaintext independently. In addition, the five AES rounds are fully pipelined in each AES core. Moreover, the round functions in each round are

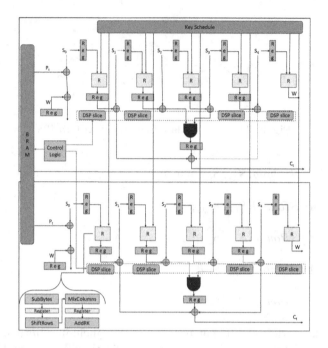

Fig. 4. Structure of the proposed AEGIS-128 architecture

also partially pipelined and are processed in parallel in groups of two similar to the AES architecture presented in Sect. 4.

In Fig. 4, the blocks labeled with R consist the four round operations: *SubBytes*, *ShiftRows*, *MixColumns*, and *AddRoundKey*. Whereas, the blocks indicated by *Reg* represent registers inserted between each round and inter-round for pipelining. The BRAM contains the required inputs values. The Key Schedule provides the required keys for each round operation and stores them in BRAMs to be executed as needed.

In this work, all the five rounds of the AES algorithm are made to process the state of AEGIS-128 concurrently in one clock cycle to update the state and achieve high throughput. The general throughput can be calculated as shown by Eq. 2:

$$Throughput(TP) = Max.Frequency \times 128 \tag{2}$$

The two parallel AES cores, the outer and inner pipelining, and the parallel and pipelined AEGIS-128 constructions, all add to fast processing and throughput increment by four times the throughput that can be achieved based on Eq. 2.

7 Implementation Approaches and Result Comparisons

The proposed AEGIS-128 architecture has been implemented targeting Xilinx Virtex-5 and Virtex-7 FPGA platforms. Xilinx Vivado HLS 2018.3 is used to perform functionality test for both authenticated encryption and authenticated decryption. Figure 5 and Fig. 6 show the functional test results for authenticated encryption and authenticated decryption, respectively. Then, synthesis and implementation of AEGIS-128 have been performed on Virtex-7. The obtained RTL output has also been synthesized and implemented using Xilinx ISE 14.5 tool specifically for Virtex-5 device since it is not supported by Vivado HLS tool directly. As shown in Table 1, for implementation of the proposed architecture on Virtex-5 FPGA device, higher throughput (60.949 Gbps) is achieved compared to existing research results found in the literature. Since the target of optimization for AEGIS-128 is to achieve high throughput, it is achieved with balanced resource utilization.

Fig. 5. Functional test for AEGIS-128 for authenticated encryption

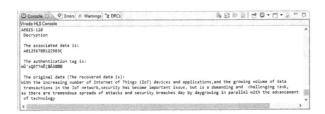

Fig. 6. Functional test for AEGIS-128 for authenticated decryption

Similarly, for implementation of the proposed method on Xilinx Virtex-7 FPGA device, both utilization of smaller slices and higher throughput result are achieved compared to existing research outcomes found in the literature.

The result comparisons are also analyzed graphically as shown in Fig. 7 and Fig. 8 for resource utilization and throughput performance on both Virtex-5 and Virtex-7 platforms, respectively.

Table 1. Comparison the proposed AEGIS-128 implementation results against existing outcomes

Methods	Device	Slices	LUTs	BRAMs	DSPs	Freq. (MHz)	Throughput (Mbps)
[7] pipelined	Virtex-5	5478	–	4	–	324.6	41.55 Gbps
[14] LUT based	Virtex-5	1391	–	–	–	156.5	20.03 Gbps
[6] Pipelined	Virtex-5	5586	–	6	–	348.7	44.6 Gbps
This work: hybrid	Virtex-5	1282	–	8	36	476.168	60.949 Gbps
[3]							
Basic	Virtex-7	9646	–	–	–	–	68121
Looping	Virtex-7	7726	–	–	–	–	64497
Pipelined	Virtex-7	10610	–	–	–	–	88564
[7] Pipelined	Virtex-7	9306	–	–	–	–	89354
This work: hybrid	Virtex-7	1375	–	8	36	–	99412

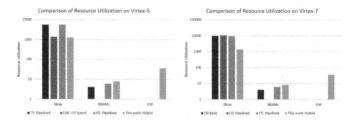

Fig. 7. Comparison of resource utilization

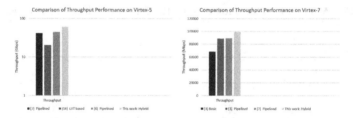

Fig. 8. Comparison of throughput performance

8   Conclusions

Efficient architecture for high performance authenticated encryption algorithm is proposed and implemented on FPGA considering requirements of high speed applications. Improving throughput with balanced hardware resource utilization is the optimization target of this work. Hybrid optimization techniques are employed and FPGAs' hard-cores together with reasonable amount of generic FPGA logic elements are used to enhance performance. Therefore, state-of-the-art optimization tools have been used and better performances are achieved. Therefore, both enhanced throughput and balanced resource utilization optimization targets have been met; and, the required performance metrics have been achieved based on the proposed architectures.

References

1. Wu, H., Preneel, B.: AEGIS: a fast authenticated encryption algorithm (v1. 1). In: Submission to CAESAR (2016)
2. McGrew, D., Viega, J.: The Galois/counter mode of operation (GCM). In: Submission to NIST (2005)
3. Katsaiti, M., Sklavos, N.: Implementation efficiency and alternations, on CAESAR finalists: AEGIS approach. In: 2018 IEEE 16th International Conference on Dependable, Autonomic and Secure Computing, 16th International Conference on Pervasive Intelligence and Computing, 4th International Conference on Big Data Intelligence and Computing and Cyber Science and Technology Congress (DASC/PiCom/DataCom/CyberSciTech), pp. 661–665. IEEE (2018)
4. Kumar, S., Haj-Yihia, J., Khairallah, M., Chattopadhyay, A.: A comprehensive performance analysis of hardware implementations of CAESAR candidates. IACR Cryptol. ePrint Arch., 1261 (2017)
5. Abdellatif, K. M., Chotin-Avot, R., Mehrez, H.: AEGIS-based efficient solution for secure reconfiguration of FPGAs. In: Proceedings of the Third Workshop on Cryptography and Security in Computing Systems, pp. 37–40. ACM (2016)
6. Abebe, A.T., Shiferaw, Y.N., Kumar, P.G.V.S.: Efficient reconfigurable integrated cryptosystems for cybersecurity protection. In: Shandilya, S.K., Wagner, N., Nagar, A.K. (eds.) Advances in Cyber Security Analytics and Decision Systems. EICC, pp. 57–77. Springer, Cham (2020). https://doi.org/10.1007/978-3-030-19353-9_4
7. Tadesse Abebe, A., Negash Shiferaw, Y., Kumar, P.G.V.S.: reconfigurable integrated cryptosystem for secure data exchanges between fog computing and cloud computing platforms. In: Habtu, N.G., Ayele, D.W., Fanta, S.W., Admasu, B.T., Bitew, M.A. (eds.) ICAST 2019. LNICST, vol. 308, pp. 492–501. Springer, Cham (2020). https://doi.org/10.1007/978-3-030-43690-2_35
8. Daemen, J., Rijmen, V.: The design of Rijndael: AES - the advanced encryption standard. Information Security and Cryptography, Springer, Heidelberg (2002). https://doi.org/10.1007/978-3-662-04722-4
9. PUB, NIST FIPS. 197. Specification for the advanced encryption standard (AES) (2001). Accessed 26 Nov 2001, http://csrc.nist.gov/publications/fips/fips197/fips-197.pdf
10. Rajasekar, P., Mangalam, H.: Design and implementation of power and area optimized AES architecture on FPGA for IoT application, Circuit World (2020)
11. Standaert, F.-X., Rouvroy, G., Quisquater, J.-J., Legat, J.-D.: Efficient implementation of Rijndael encryption in reconfigurable hardware: improvements and design tradeoffs. In: Walter, C.D., Koç, Ç.K., Paar, C. (eds.) CHES 2003. LNCS, vol. 2779, pp. 334–350. Springer, Heidelberg (2003). https://doi.org/10.1007/978-3-540-45238-6_27
12. Tadesse, A., Kumar, P.S.: Effective implementations techniques for FPGA based AES algorithm. In: 2016 KICS Korea and Ethiopia ICT International Conference (2016)
13. Zhang, X., Parhi, K.K.: High-speed VLSI architectures for the AES algorithm. IEEE Trans. Very Large Scale Integr. (VLSI) Syst 12(9), 957–967 (2004)
14. Abdellatif, K.M., Chotin-Avot, R., Mehrez, H.: AES-GCM and AEGIS: efficient and high speed hardware implementations. J. Signal Process. Syst. 88(1), 1–12 (2017)

Design and Development of an Autonomous Smart Stick Framework for Assisting Visually Impaired People

Tesfahunegn Minwuyelet Mengistu[1]($\boxtimes$) (iD), Ayalew Belay Habtie[2],
and Fikreselam Gared Mengistu[1]

[1] Bahir Dar University, Bahir Dar, Ethiopia
[2] Addis Ababa University, Addis Ababa, Ethiopia

Abstract. Visually Impaired People (VIP) face numerous obstacles and troubles like physiological, psychological, social, and economic outcomes in their daily life. This work brings an intelligent and comprehensive stick framework aimed to assist VIP and navigate where to go. To increase sensing mechanisms wireless network is used to communicate between system components, enhance battery life. Global Positioning System (GPS) with General Packet Radio Service (GPRS)/Global System for Mobile communication (GSM) plays a vital role to get the location of visually impaired people with a short message service to rescuer them and adding buzzer timer to activate a buzzer in a specific duration with control buttons. It has a high range of obstacle detection, meticulous information conveyed, endowed sensor alert notification, sustainable power supply, short and multimedia messaging service (MMS), face and voice recognition, wireless system component connection, and its foldability gave the smart stick easy to keep and comfort for the VIP when they hold in addition to its robustness.

Keywords: GPS · GPRS · GSM · Navigation · Smart stick · VIP

1 Introduction

Visually Impaired People (VIP) performing many activities by navigation and mobility. To navigate unknown places, VIP brings family members or friends for support. Thus, they are relying on their families for mobility and financial support [1, 2]. Exploiting state-of-the-art technology for improving people's everyday life is always a compelling challenge, especially when the people in question are impaired in some way. In recent years, the rapid evolution of color acquisition devices and computing hardware and their affordability have spawned several solutions to assist blind people in indoor and outdoor mobility. Most of the edge-breaking technologies have been applied to assist or train them. Assistive technology permits people with disabilities to accomplish daily tasks and assists them in communication, education, work, and recreational activities. In general, it helps to attain larger independence and enhance their overall quality of life [3]. From completely different helpful technologies accessible, a special focus was placed on people who enhance the quality of VIP [4] as a result of "Vision is that the

© ICST Institute for Computer Sciences, Social Informatics and Telecommunications Engineering 2022
Published by Springer Nature Switzerland AG 2022. All Rights Reserved
M. L. Berihun (Ed.): ICAST 2021, LNICST 411, pp. 586–602, 2022.
https://doi.org/10.1007/978-3-030-93709-6_40

most significant a part of human physiology as eighty three of data person gets from the atmosphere is via sight" [5]. In 2018, World Health Organization (WHO) estimates that there square measure 1.3 billion individuals within the world with visual impairment, thirty six million of that square measure blind, 188.5 million individuals have a gentle vision impairment, 217 million have moderate to severe vision impairment and 826 million individuals support visual modality impairment however now adays in 2021 this number rise to 2.2 billion [6]. Blindness affects 11.7 million people in South Asia, 6.2 million people in East Asia, 3.5 million people in South East Asia, more than 4% of the population in parts of sub-Saharan Africa and less than 0.5% of the population of Western Europe [7]. Therefore, this study helps the VIP walking confidently guide by the smart stick that communicates with the user through voice alert and vibration [8].

In this research work we proposed a system to provide a smart walking stick to the VIP that enables them to navigate the indoor and outdoor environment, move safely, and passed lots of hurdles which faced in their daily life without any assist of the sighted people. The proposed solution is very cost-effective, user-friendly, ease of use navigational aid, sizeable and comfortable to carry along. Also, it can be used to analyze the surrounding of a person without any human intervention. As a methodology, we applied Design Science Research (DSR) and the system has five main units (i.e., sensing, communication, recognition, alerting, and notification) with controlling button and power supply unit and developed using APL, Prolog, Python, Arduino, SWI-Prolog, PyCharm, and Proteus.

As it has been discussed in the results and discussions section the objective of the work is achieved in a wide range of obstacle detection, by conveyed adequate information of VIP, sensor alert notification, recognition and messaging, system component connection, and in supplying of sustainable power which used to run the integrated circuit and mad the system functions work properly. This is achieved by the aimed combination of several working sub-systems (i.e., water, holes, flame, ponds, staircase, temperature, location…) makes a time demanding system that monitors the environmental scenario of static and dynamic objects and provides necessary feedback forming navigation more precise, safe and secure. We were including some local languages and face recognition system so that several VIP can use this stick to overcome the mobility and navigation problem in daily life and it avail VIP to recognize the person standing in front of him/her and also make it work day and night by using light sensor at the night.

The system has four different output devices which are speech pedagogue, vibrator, buzzer, and torch that area unit accessed assortments relying upon different inputs state. Depending on the distance of the obstacle from the person five zones (i.e., very far (safe) zone, fare zone, middle zone, near zone, very near zone (danger zone) are formed. If obstacles which were small in size and cannot be detected by the Ultrasonic sensor is detected by IR sensor.

If VIP wants to know their current location, they can press the switch assigned for that purpose and audio regarding the current location is heard by the VIP with the help of a speaker. And when VIP is around places like hotels, squares, religious organizations, universities and schools didn't wait until VIP press the button it told automatically where there is current location and also the VIP wants some help during some emergency, the GPS and GSM modules are successfully operated in sending the location of VIP to caregivers via SMS.

If blind people need any help, they can trigger an emergency button which is mounted on the stick and the GSM sends the location information to the predefined contact numbers. A GPS module will offer the period location of static objects in out of doors navigation which will be mapped via satellite. It also can be used in conjunction with voice feedback that might alert the user once the obstacle was found in its path, employing a combination of GPS and also the web. A voice in practicality can be accustomed to input the destination into the stick and also the stick would be able to chart the trail to the destination from the supply exploitation the shortest path for the VIP to follow. Hence voice output is a great benefit to VIP when it comes to independent mobility. This could also be considered a crude way of giving the VIP a sense of vision. Using smart stick is unquestionable because smart stick for blind people is one of the self-operating robots and that minimizes numerous human labors [9].

To use know-how for the well-being of the society, which includes VIP, is the main motivation of this study. This study noticed that normal VIP sticks used by VIP have certain limitations like detecting water, heat, holes, stairs, distant objects, above knee obstacles, etc. At the same time currently, available sensor-equipped sticks are very costly and unaffordable for most people. This study takes a lot of inputs from disable people and comes up with the idea of design and development of an autonomous obstacle-free path indication and navigation framework for assisting VIP via a foldable smart stick which is an economical sensor-equipped stick capable of assisting VIP to navigate easily. The final design of this study is quite cheaper than existing alternatives and warns the person via vibratory and auditory signals. And also make them navigate directions easily.

2   Related Works

Six types of canes are most commonly used. A popular straight vogue cane is created of fiberglass that is ultra-light, provides legion sensory feedback, and bends slightly if it slides below an automobile or similar obstacle. Cane tips are developed for travel in geographical region areas and farms and a large form of cane tips currently give sander operation and additional sturdiness. Every tip has its execs and cons. Generally, a support cane and an inquiring cane area unit designed otherwise and serve terribly completely different functions. Advances in laptop technologies, intelligent sticks, and up to date developments within the field of wireless communications, together with Wi-Fi, Bluetooth, ZigBee, multi-hop wireless computer network, and therefore the international wireless technologies like GPS, GSM, GPRS, 5G, and satellite systems have created a large array of latest potentialities for today's society. Once these technologies began to be employed in conjunction with a stick a new smart stick framework emerged and also because of the improvements in technology the conventional sticks are being replaced with smart blind sticks [10, 11]. Thus, researchers aim to design and implement an intelligent and cheap stick with GPS for visually impaired peoples [1].

In [8] a prototype that can detect objects or obstacles in front of users and feeds warning back in the forms of voice messages and vibration is proposed. In this study, the authors recommended that a power supply meter reading could be installed to monitor its power status. A device can also be incorporated to be used during a scenario of very engorged areas and replace Polyvinyl Chloride (PVC) with steel so it will be additional sturdy and sturdy. Also, a buzzer timer may be added that the buzzer can activate at a particular length.

In [12], the proposed system helps to detect obstacles with the use of infrared, ultrasonic, and water sensors. Also, use GPS modules to give positioning and navigating the stick and GSM modules to give notification when the visually impaired peoples feel a threat. The downside of this planned stick is that it will be troublesome to stay as a result of it absolutely was not designed to be foldaway. Also, running this integrated set of hardware needs another to the battery, A Braille device to administer the visually handicapped person associate degree uncomplicated technique to supply the destination address for navigation.

The proposed device was aimed to help the VIP people to move independently in the unfamiliar environment and to navigate with ease by using advanced technology. Majorly these blind sticks were integrated with the ultrasonic sensor along with temperature, water, dump, label, heat sensor, etc. On sensing obstacles, the sensor passes this data to the Micro Controller (MC). The MC then processes this data and calculates the obstacle is close or far and also if water, heat, the dump is there in the path the microcontroller sends a signal to sound a buzzer, vibrate or voice message. However, hasn't a sustainable power source, nothing to describe stick is it easy to keep or not, doesn't show the finest path by calculating data comes from GPS. This study didn't describe multimedia messaging but using GPRS and doesn't have integration of GPS & GSM module to communicate relative caregiver [13, 14].

Today technology is rising daily in several aspects to produce versatile and safe movement for the VIP who strive to live independently by developing smart stick to give personal independence so that they can move from one place to another easily and safely hence the stick has GPS/GSM modules which help the VIP in navigating even unknown areas independently as the same time if the VIP felt too lost they can communicate with their relative or caregiver by sending short SMS including their location. Almost all papers referenced with [15, 16] number majorly give emphasis on the communication part and faced to such limitation like charge capacity of the device, hadn't flame detector sensor to alert them to escape from the fire accidents, range of sensing mechanism, detecting pits, staircase, holes, label sensor and also easiness of the stick to keep.

3 System Model and Methodology

Based on the research goal, this research has adopted Design Science Research Methodology (DSRM) process model as shown Fig. 1.

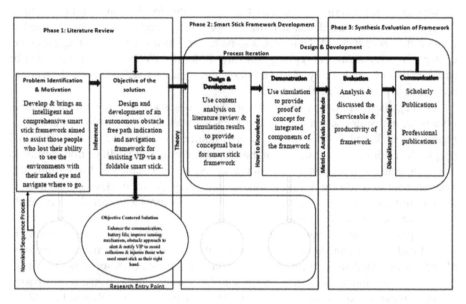

Fig. 1. Research design framework

When an influential person is walking, if any massive obstacles like human, car, animal, tree, and wall appeared ahead of them high-frequency acoustic wave transmitted from ultrasonic sensors, area unit collected across the receiver then theses received waves are going to be sent to the processor in a sort of electrical impulse for the obstacles like holes, stairs or stone that area unit little in size area unit detected exploitation IR detector then the IR detector sends signals to the processor; whereas just in case of the massive obstacle detection passive infrared (PIR) sensor check the motion of the obstacle because human or animal emit heat energy in the form of IR and sending signal to the processor. The processed gives alert the existence of obstacles to VIP using a combination of sound instruction, vibrator or buzzer that helps the VIP to take the right action according to the received notification in order to avoid the possibility of accident or collision occurrences [17]; the overall algorithms of the proposed obstacle detection methodology were illustrated in Fig. 2 and Fig. 3.

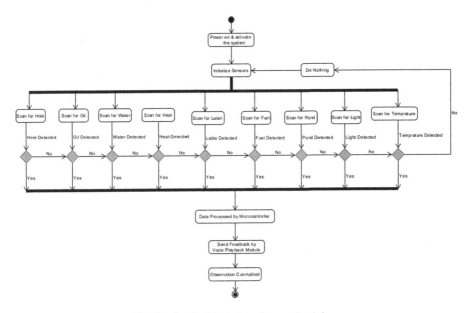

Fig. 2. Small object detection methodology

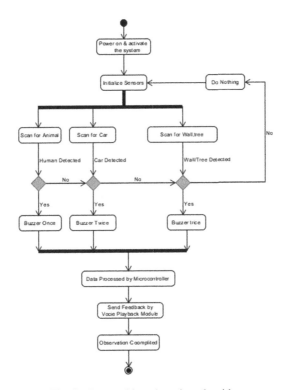

Fig. 3. Large object detection algorithm

The proposed system consists of a camera which is used to capture the face of people around the VIP regularly at an interval of two seconds and send it to the microcontroller. Then the face recognition unit is used to analyze this captured face in the use of morphological analysis. As a producer first chooses a set of training image from any directory under various situations to get the required image whose information is required for training purposes. Secondly the binary images from the original images are found because morphological operations bank solely on the relative ordering of pixel values, not on their numerical values, and particularly suited to the process of binary pictures. Next morphological operations on the training set of images are done to calculate the average intensity value. We also calculate the minimum and maximum values from the set values of the training images. The information is stored for further processing of the face recognition, capture an image of people around VIP then face recognition of the input image are done and newly calculated average intensity value is compared with stored images finally the mostly matched image is used to identify the name of the person [4, 16, 18]. The overall algorithm of the face recognition methodology is illustrated in Fig. 4.

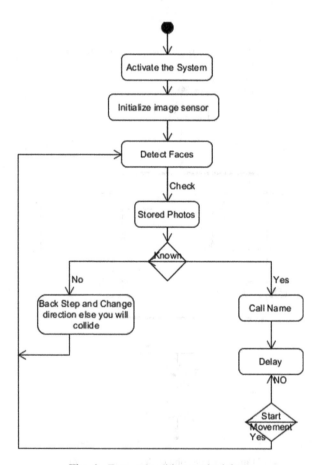

Fig. 4. Face recognition methodology

The GPS tracer is a system that uses the GPS signal to identify the exact location of the vehicle, person, or any other object. It's associated and location information can be sent via a simple text message using GSM/GPRS leading provider of a mobile network. The device offers several advantages some functionalities are the reception of a single location by making a simple phone call to the GPS Tracker which will respond via SMS sending all the information needed to establish its correct localization, latitude, altitude, longitude, speed, degree, satellites, date and time, reception of information about the battery level with the possibility to set/unset the sleep mode (energy saving) and so on. The locator is designed to offer maximum reliability even in extreme conditions, such as high-temperature variation, humidity, moisture and vibration [11]. The GPS module provides a location to the voice module to alert the VIP of his/her destination area. The GPS receiver obtains the data as a whole National Marin Electronics Association

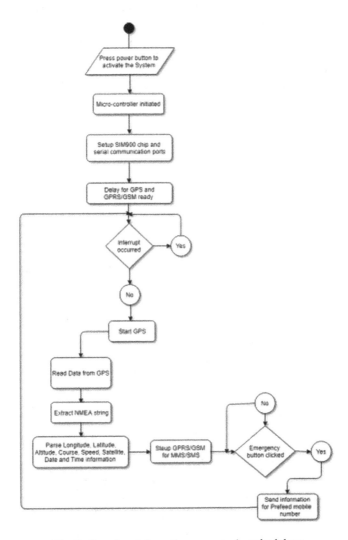

Fig. 5. Location information convoyed methodology

(NMEA) format text here we take latitude, longitude, altitude, degree, speed date, time, and visible satellite using Arduino Tiny GPS library. If the VIP becomes unaware of his/her location, face any difficulties upon pressing the emergency button he/she can send an SMS/MMS to the preferred mobile number [19, 20] as shown in Fig. 5.

3.1 Modeling and Assembly of Foldable Smart Stick

As stated in the above under literature review canes were divide based on purpose into six, foldability into two, and cane tips into four. However, when we came to this designed stick it consists of the most important futures of the canes so it makes it very generic to other canes which were designed. Its length measured 120 cm, the fold-ability joint found in each 40 cm, the system case which used to hold the system was 40 × 20 cm wider which was found at the center of the stick that means 50 cm was left from the bottom and upper of the system case, it had hand grips that give the VIP comfort and support when it holds the stick, also it had a wheel at the bottom of the stick so it will not get stuck on the cracks in the sidewalk and reduce the error which occurred by the ultrasonic sensor due to cane movement because of this the VIP was not miss-lead and made a decision by corrupted information. The foldability of the stick was helping those VIP to keep the stick easily and we use steel not PVC hence it was enough to support the VIP.

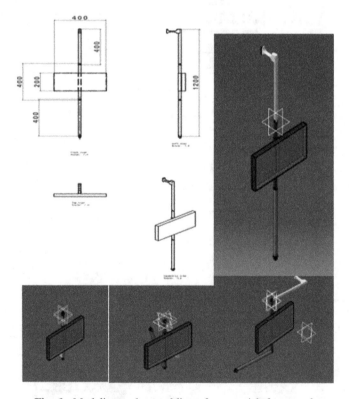

Fig. 6. Modeling and assembling of smart stick framework

4 Autonomous Smart Stick Framework Design

The proposed framework has an Arduino Uno microcontroller which used to control the signals which came from the sensor unit, recognition subsystem, communication unit, control buttons, and also interprets and possessed actions based on the coming signal hence notification sent to the preferred phone number to give information about the current location of the VIP to his/her relatives or caregivers when he/she pressed the emergency button.

The inclusive functions of the system were powered by the rechargeable battery with the solar panel it helps the system to run the integrated circuit properly and works day and night without the failure of power. In order not to spend power the power button used to start when the VIP in need of the Stick else switch off the system it helps to save the power of the rechargeable battery. Via speaker, the system gives the VIP alerts and notifications to warn them not to face obstacles, to take the right path, and to create awareness about his/her environments.

We chose to display time and date from the internet rather than Arduino because the time and date will be incorrect once the Arduino is reset. The date and time have to be compelled to be set once the sketch starts, this may be through a synchronization message from an external time supply like a laptop connected through an interface. While navigation depending on 3G or Wi-Fi to access the intermate and retrieves the map and other information to geographically present your location with the designated route. The general framework is shown in Fig. 7.

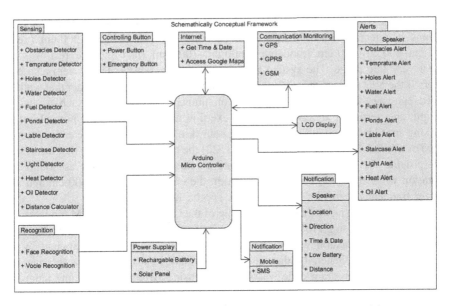

Fig. 7. Schematically representation of an autonomous smart stick

5 Results and Discussions

The experiments had been carried out to evaluate the deliberate Framework. The maximum goal of this looks at turned into to assist VIP to safely-pass amongst obstacles, holes, ponds, and specific hurdles visaged via way of means of them of their existence. The solution evolved is an easy guidance resource for them. The benefit of the gadget lies inside the plain reality that it's going to inspire be a surely inexpensive solution to variation VIP worldwide. The aimed aggregate of many working substructures makes a time-disturbing gadget that video display units the environmental state of affairs of static and dynamic items and gives vital remarks forming navigation a number of precise, safe, and secure [15].

The model of the proposed framework consists of an Arduino Uno board interfaced with sensors which used to sense an obstacle's found in the way of the VIP and that creates a challenge to them also interrupt not to achieve their goal, hence to overcome those problems that VIP faced this system included a lot of sensors which used to detect temperature, holes, water, fuel, ponds, label, staircase, light, heat, oil and distance calculator also GPS, GPRS/GSM was part of the framework mainly which used to outdoor navigation and helps the VIP to aware where he/she existed, hotels, schools, square, religious organizations, universities, bus station, etc. He/She can also send SMS and MMS to their relative or caregiver whose phone number was recorded on the system ample or commensurate information was delivered which include longitude, latitude, altitude, speed, degree and time and date which expressed or used to check when the message was received or sent to those who were responsible for the intended VIP.

The stick was designed in such a way that was used to indoor and outdoor navigations it detects obstacle within 0 cm–50 cm (very near), 50 cm–200 cm (near), 200 cm–400 cm–600 cm (moderate), 600 cm–1000 cm (far) and the rest was put under very fare range. The system was simulated successfully. The system also considers if the VIP walks faster than the standard ranges i.e., despite the fact that walking speed can vary considerably depending on numerous components such as height, weight, age, territory, area, load, culture, exertion and well-being, the normal human walking speed is around 5.0 kilometers per hour (km^2/h) or about 1.4 meters per second (m/s) or about 3.1 miles per hour (mph) [21, 22] the output results show that the system can provide the required output notification (warning) to the user as sound and vibration while detecting the obstacles within the range of 0 cm to 1000 cm and also buzzer frequency increases as the obstacle approaches closely.

The simulation shows that the interfacing of the GPS and GPRS/GSM modules was successfully done using Proteus and finding the finest path and showing the route from source to the destination was successfully done using SWI-Prolong applied by the Dijkstra algorithm. Generally, the system was simulated by using Proteus software and SWI-Prolog. The program code was written by using Arduino programing language, Prolog and Phyton (i.e., which applied in face recognition system which was worked by applying morphological segmentation) furthermore the stick included different buttons like the power button, emergency button, etc. and voice recognizer module which used to control overall function of the system with a stable power supply that helps to run these integrated systems like rechargeable battery integrated with 12 V power supply solar panel.

5.1   Evaluation and Experimentation

The framework was evaluated based on the following criteria which stated below and this framework was excel when we compared with other related works which were done early in terms of obstacle detection range, the information conveyed, sensor alert notification, power supply & foldability, recognition system & foldability, system component connection.

5.1.1   Obstacle Detection Range

Under this section we presented the comparison between this study and other related works based on obstacle detection range as stated in Fig. 8 most of the related works detect obstacles in the maximum range of 4 m; however, this study obstacle detection range exceeds other related works more than twice in detecting obstacles and alerted or gave a notification for those VIP who use the system.

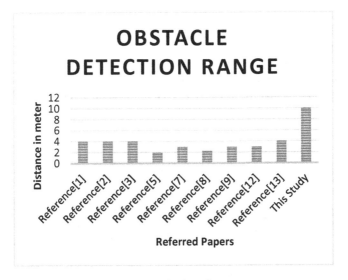

Fig. 8. Obstacle detection range

5.1.2   GPS, GPRS/GSM Information Conveyed

Here in Fig. 9, we were presented with the information conveyed when an accident was occurred the information includes the area of the VIP according to longitude, latitude, and altitude; speed if it was in the moment, date, and time of the message sent to the relative caregiver. Based on this we achieved all these evaluation criteria in comparing other related works which focused or give information only the longitude and latitude and some papers not consider or integrated such modules that helps to conveyed information during an accident and outdoor moment of the VIP.

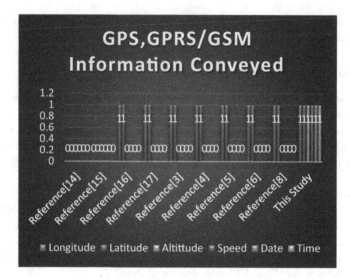

Fig. 9. GPS, GPRS/GSM information conveyed

5.1.3 Sensor Alert Notification

Over here we intended to how this study outshine other studies in case of alerting VIP during their indoor and outdoor moment and navigation as you see in Fig. 10, we took seven evaluation criteria water, fuel, staircase, motion, light, temperature, and hole based on this some related works has not given notification and the rest achieve at max four criteria.

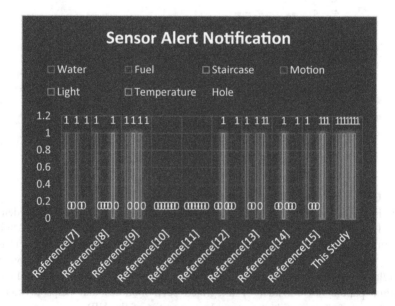

Fig. 10. Sensor alert notifications

5.1.4 Power Supply and Foldability

Under this evaluation criteria we took a look at the backbone of the system which is the power supply and how the stick is smart in accordance with keeping easily this study and other related studies as one can see from Fig. 11 all are not include a solar panel which indicates that they haven't sufficient power supply to run the integrated circuit properly throughout day and night whether in the urban or rural area and aren't foldable so the VIP didn't feel safe when they keep their smart stick; however, in this study, we consider all these things and make the stick more generic following power supply and keeping the stick gives the VIP more comfort than the other smart stick which was made previously.

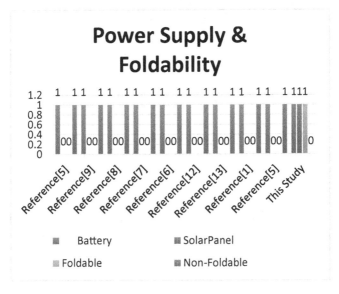

Fig. 11. Power supply and foldability

5.1.5 Recognition System and Messaging

Under Fig. 12, we figured out how the system interacted with VIP through messaging and voice command in addition to recognizing peoples who stand Infront of the VIP and identify who is either known by the VIP or not. Based on this when we evaluated as you see from Fig. 12 some of the related works didn't encompass both of the evaluation criteria that means messaging and recognition system, but some related works include SMS and voice recognition. However, in this study, we include both the messaging and recognition that means voice and face recognition with SMS and MMS hence we use GPRS over GSM which helps to achieve MMS.

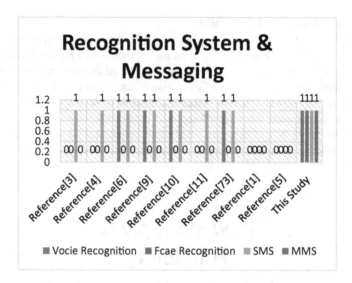

Fig. 12. Recognition system and messaging

5.1.6 System Component Connection

In Fig. 13 evaluated related works and this study based on their component connection did it encompass both wired and wireless connection or not as you see this study possessed both connection types but not the other so using this smart stick is better than the rest which mad previously in different aspects when we connect devices in wirelessly their detection, communication rang also increases and easy to maintain, add or remove components and when we think about foldability using wireless connection became preferred because it didn't oppose in which edge did we bent the stick.

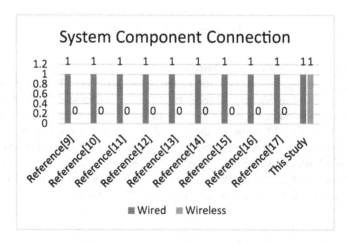

Fig. 13. System component connection

6   Conclusions

Vision is the maximum essential a part of human body structure as 83% of statistics man or women receives from the surroundings is through sight. So, this research work has been done to assist VIP to safely-move among obstacles and hurdles faced by them in their daily life and navigate indoor and outdoor environments without any interface with sighted people. The solution developed is a user-friendly navigational aid for them. The advantage of the system lies in the fact that it can prove to be a very low-cost solution to VIP. The proposed device that monitors the environmental state of affairs of static and dynamic gadgets and presents vital comments forming navigation greater precise, safe, and secure. This could also be considered a crude way of giving the VIP a sense of vision.

References

1. Anwar, A.: A smart stick for assisting blind people. IOSR J. Comput. Eng. **19**(3), 86–90 (2017)
2. Divija, M.V.S., Rohitha, M., Raveendra: Integrated smart shoe for blind people. Int. J. Manage. **8**, 748–752 (2018)
3. Sungheetha, A., Rajesh Sharma, R.: Design of effective smart communication system for impaired people. J. Electr. Eng. Autom. **2**(4), 181–194 (2021)
4. Costa, P., Fernandes, H., Martins, P., Barroso, J., Hadjileontiadis, L.J.: Obstacle detection using stereo imaging to assist the navigation of visually impaired people. Procedia Comput. Sci. **14**, 83–93 (2012). https://doi.org/10.1016/j.procs.2012.10.010
5. Dambhare,S., Sakhare, A.: Smart stick for blind: obstacle detection, artificial visionand real-time assistance via GPS. In: IJCA Proceedings on 2nd National Conference on Information and Communication Technology NCICT, no. 6, pp. 31–33, November 2011
6. Organização Mundial da Saudef: Blindness and vision impairment 2018, vol. 11, no. 2018, pp. 1–5 (2018)
7. Mazumdar, T.: Global blindness set to 'triple by 2050'. BBC, pp. 1–7 (2017)
8. Wahab, M.H.A., et al.: Smart cane: assistive cane for visually-impaired people, vol. 8, no. 4, pp. 21–27 (2011)
9. Sukhija, V., Taksali, S., Jain, M., Kumawat, R.: Smart stick for blind man. Int. J. Electr. Electr. Eng. **7**(6), 631–638 (2014)
10. Aggarwal, R.: Wireless communication: evolution and advance wireless communication. Int. J. Sustain. Dev. Res. **4**(2), 25 (2018)
11. Cimino, M.G.C.A., Celandroni, N., Ferro, E., La Rosa, D., Palumbo, F., Vaglini, G.: Wireless communication, identification and sensing technologies enabling integrated logistics: a study in the harbor environment (2015)
12. Radhika, R., Pai, P.G., Rakshitha, S., Srinath, R.: Implementation of smart stick for obstacle detection and navigation. Int. J. Eng. Sci. Comput. **02**(05), 45–50 (2016)
13. Uppala, S.: Smart Guiding Blind Stick, vol. 6, no. 10, pp. 113–116 (2017)
14. Sathya, D., Nithyaroopa, S., Betty, P., Santhoshini, G., Sabharinath, S., Ahanaa, M.J.: Smart walking stick for blind person. Math. Appl. Sci. Comput. **118**(20), 4531–4536 (2018)
15. Kiruba, G.J.P.J., Kumar, T.C.M., Kavithrashree, S., Kumar, G.A.: Smart electronic walking stick for blind people. Int. J. Adv. Res. Electr. Electron. Instrum. Eng. **7**, 1194–1200 (2018)

16. Swathi, K., Ismitha, E.R., Subhashini, R.: Smart walking stick using IOT. Int. J. Innov. Adv. Comput. Sci. (IJIACS) **6**(11), 124–128 (2017)
17. Gbenga, D.E., Shani, A.I., Adekunle, A.L.: Smart walking stick for visually impaired people using ultrasonic sensors and Arduino. Int. J. Eng. Technol. **9**(5), 3435–3447 (2017)
18. Annas, A.B.T.: Smart cane for visually impaired people (network security), vol. 4, no. 1, pp. 24–28 (2017)
19. Jothi, R., Kayalvizhi, M., Sagadevan, K.: Smart walking stick for visually challenged people. Asian J. Appl. Sci. Technol. **1**(2), 274–276 (2017)
20. Dubey, A.: Smart blind stick. Int. J. Res. Appl. Sci. Eng. Technol. **7**(5), 815–819 (2019)
21. Qamer, M.A.: Fit India : Banega Swasth Bharath India (2020)
22. Schimpl, M., et al.: Association between walking speed and age in healthy, free-living individuals using mobile accelerometry—a cross-sectional study. PLoS ONE **6**(8), e23299 (2011)

Multi-channel Convolutional Neural Network for Hate Speech Detection in Social Media

Zeleke Abebaw[1]([✉]), Andreas Rauber[2], and Solomon Atnafu[3]

[1] IT Doctoral Program, Addis Ababa University, Addis Ababa, Ethiopia
zeleke.abebaw@aastu.edu.et
[2] Institute of Information Systems Engineering, Technical University of Vienna, Vienna, Austria
rauber@ifs.tuwien.ac.at
[3] Department of Computer Science, Addis Ababa University, Addis Ababa, Ethiopia
solomon.atnafu@aau.edu.et

Abstract. As online social media content continues to grow, so does the spread of hate speech. Hate speech has devastating consequences unless it is detected and monitored early. Recently, deep neural network-based hate speech detection models, particularly conventional single-channel Convolutional Neural Network (CNN), have achieved remarkable performance. However, the effectiveness of the models depends on the type of language they are trained on and the training data size. We argue that the effectiveness of the models could further be enhanced if we use multi-channel CNN models even for under-resourced languages that have limited training data size. This is because the single-channel CNN might fail to consider the potential effect of multiple channels to generate better features, which is not well investigated for hate speech detection. Therefore, in this work, we explore the use of multi-channel CNN to extract better features from different channels in an end-to-end manner on top of a word2vec embedding layer. Tested on a new small-scale Amharic hate speech dataset containing 2000 annotated social media comments, the experimental results show that the proposed multi-channel CNN model outperforms the single-channel CNN models but under-perform from the baseline Support Vector Machine (SVM) with an average F-score of 81.3%, 78.2%, and 92.5% respectively. The finding of the study implies that the proposed MC-CNN model can be used as an alternative solution for hate speech detection using a deep learning approach when dataset scarcity is an issue.

Keywords: Social media · Deep learning · Word embedding · Amharic hate speech detection · Single-channel · Multi-channel · Convolutional neural network

1 Introduction

The increasing accessibility of the Internet and social media (e.g., Facebook, Twitter, etc.) has provided people with a plethora of opportunities and advantages including the ability to keep social relationships in the economic, political, and social spheres. As a result, there is an abundance of user-generated online content on social media [1]. The growth of online social media content as a means of free expression has led in changes

© ICST Institute for Computer Sciences, Social Informatics and Telecommunications Engineering 2022
Published by Springer Nature Switzerland AG 2022. All Rights Reserved
M. L. Berihun (Ed.): ICAST 2021, LNICST 411, pp. 603–618, 2022.
https://doi.org/10.1007/978-3-030-93709-6_41

in the economic, political, and social arenas. Despite its democratic nature for free expression, social media has adverse consequences since it is an ideal venue to disseminate hate speech.

Social media users disseminate hate speech against certain social groups, encouraging others to send nasty messages, write harsh critiques, engage in physical assault, and commit hate crimes [2], which has become a global phenomenon. For example, according to the FBI's annual hate crime statistics report[1] for 2019, hate crimes in America increased by 3%, with race-based, religious-based, and gender-based offenses being the most common. Furthermore, during the 2007 Kenyan elections, due to the spread of hate speech, inter-ethnic conflicts and violence 1,300 people were murdered and over 650,000 people were displaced [3].

In recent years, the spread of hate speech and aggressive comments on social media has been observed on Ethiopian related issues, notably during election periods and political unrest [4]. For example, due to the proliferation of hate speech during Ethiopia's 2016 national election, the government was obliged to shut down the Internet and restricted social media sites in order to deescalate tensions among groups [5]. Such acts continue to occur across the country, causing widespread disruption and unrest that impacted the lives of millions, impeded economic activity, closed highways, displaced communities, and even resulted in the deaths of hundreds [6]. Hate speech and hate crimes, in general, poison society by endangering individual rights, human dignity, and equality, increasing social tensions, disrupting public peace and order, and risking peaceful coexistence [7].

Therefore, several actions have been implemented to combat the spread of hate speech on social media. While governments have taken legal action through law enforcement, social media firms have begun to deploy automatic hate speech detection and monitoring systems based on machine learning algorithms. As a result, numerous studies on automatic hate speech detection have been conducted utilizing supervised machine learning techniques with two stages. The first stage is to build features by hand using feature engineering approaches, and the second stage is to choose and apply the best machine learning classifiers available. Handcrafted feature engineering is vital, but it is time consuming and prone to mistakes. Alternatively, methods based on deep learning models have become increasingly popular. This is because, unlike traditional machine learning approaches, deep learning models jointly implement both feature extraction and classification.

Deep neural network models, such as conventional single-channel CNN (SC-CNN), have recently demonstrated good performance in hate speech detection [7–10]. However, a single-channel CNN overlooked the possibility that new features might well be generated through multi-channel techniques. However, this has not been extensively studied for hate speech detection. We observed that utilizing several channels of the CNN model could capture additional features from each channel that would otherwise be overlooked by the max-pooling layer of the single-channel model. Instead, improved features could be generated from the basic CNN model by

---

[1] https://www.splcenter.org/news/2020/11/16/fbi-reports-increase-hate-crimes-2019-hate-based-murders-more-doubled.

initializing distinct channels from the input embedding layer and taking the max-pooling layer from each channel and concatenating them. Therefore, in this paper, we present a multi-channel Convolutional Neural Network (MC-CNN) model built on top of the word2vec word embedding layer that detects hate speech effectively using just a small-scale Amharic hate speech dataset.

We have selected Amharic as a test case because hate speech detection and monitoring algorithms deployed by social media platforms to guarantee compliance with community standards or posting laws have failed miserably in under-resourced local languages like Amharic. This is because the hate speech detection and monitoring algorithms were trained on posts written in resourceful languages such as English. As a result, social media posts written in under-resourced languages could easily evade the monitoring algorithms. For example, on May 29, 2020, we posted hate speech in English (primarily for experimental purposes) to put the monitoring algorithms to the test. During the process, the algorithm identified the post as hate speech, indicating that we had broken the terms of the user agreement, and issued a warning notice *"You cannot publish or comment for 24 h"*[2]. However, the translated version of the post to Amharic simply bypassed the system with no warning notice. Due to lack of hate speech detection tools and benchmark datasets, such under-resourced local languages that are utilized for day-to-day communication by over 30 million speakers in Ethiopia suffer from the spread of hate speech. Furthermore, the propagation of hate speech might be a contributing factor to the present cyber disputes, which could have an impact on social life at both the individual and national levels [11]. As a result, testing models on such under-resourced local languages can help to build a moderate social media ecosystem. Furthermore, the proposed approach is not language-specific and can be used in other languages as well. The key contributions of the paper thus are:

1. We develop a hate speech detection system that is not reliant on time-consuming manual feature engineering techniques.
2. We compare the performance of a multi-channel CNN model to that of a single-channel CNN model in detecting Amharic hate speech.
3. We develop a baseline hate speech detection dataset for Amharic language.

The remainder of the paper is structured as follows. The next section provides a review of current literatures. Sections 3 and 4 cover dataset construction and classification models. Section 5 describes our model's architecture. The experiments and its discussions are presented in Sect. 6 and Sect. 7. Finally, Sect. 8 summarizes the article and suggests further research.

2   Review of Literatures

2.1   Defining Hate Speech

Although there are no universal agreements on the definition of hate speech, academics and social media firms have developed their own to assist in classifying user comments

---

[2] https://www.facebook.com/zeleke.ab.

as hate or non-hate. Hate speech, for example, is defined by [12] as "a statement or expression that denigrates a person or individuals on the basis of (alleged) membership in a social group identifiable by qualities such as color, ethnicity, gender, sexual orientation, religion, age, physical or mental handicap, and others". Furthermore, Facebook[3] defined hate speech as "content that targets individuals on the basis of their real or perceived race, ethnicity, nationality, religion, sex, gender, sexual orientation, disability, or illness". Also, Twitter[4] defined hate speech as "Hateful conduct: You may not encourage violence against or directly attack or threaten other people because of their race, ethnicity, national origin, sexual orientation, gender, gender identity, religious affiliation, age, handicap, or serious disease".

One feature that we can observe and adapt in all of the definitions above is that hate speech is an attack on people's identities. Taking this into account, we developed a working definition of hate speech for this study to offer a common specific boundary for the Amharic hate speech labeling procedure. Hence, we define hate speech as *textual social media comments that promotes discrimination against individuals or groups based on their nationality, ethnic and religious affiliation, gender, or disability.*

2.2   Hate Speech Detection Approaches

Automatic hate speech detection research has increasingly relied on feature engineering techniques and classification algorithms. The effectiveness of the classification algorithms are heavily reliant on the feature engineering technique employed. The two most popular techniques are handcrafted feature engineering in machine learning and automated feature learning in deep learning.

Handcrafted Feature Engineering

Finding the right features to address a problem could be one of the most difficult challenges in machine learning, especially in hate speech detection. In hate speech detection, two types of features have been employed. On the one hand, there are general features that are used in text mining, and on the other hand, there are specific features that we only find in hate speech detection tasks and are intrinsically related to the characteristics of this problem, such as othering languages and stereotypes, which are not proposed in this work. Among the handcrafted feature engineering techniques which were used in several hate speech detection studies include dictionary-based [13], bag-of-words [14], N-gram [15] and [16], TF-IDF [15], Part-of-Speech [17], lexical syntactic features [18], rule-based [19], word sense disambiguation [20], topic modeling [2], and sentiment analysis [21]. Handcrafted feature engineering is vital, but it is time-consuming and error-prone. As a result, the scientific community proposed automated feature learning as an alternative approach.

Automatic Feature Learning

The massive volumes of data available on social media have provided tremendous opportunities for new knowledge discovery through the analysis of patterns of relations

---

[3] https://www.facebook.com/help/135402139904490.

[4] https://www.twitter.com.

that coexist in the data. Learning algorithms can figure out the optimum parameters to use to build the highest performing model. As a result, hate speech detection studies utilizing automated feature learning using deep learning models have demonstrated impressive results [9, 22] and [23].

2.3 Hate Speech Detection Using Deep Learning Approaches

Several researchers developed hate speech detection methods using deep learning approaches particularly CNN models. For example, [8] detected hate speech tweets posted in seven different languages using CNN and character level representation. In terms of accuracy, the highest results were 88.93% for a dataset with five languages and 83% for a dataset with seven languages. Furthermore, [9] used a CNN model with 300 dimensions and pre-trained word embeddings (GloVe and FastText) to detect hate speech against women and immigrants on Twitter in a bilingual environment, including English and Spanish. For English and Spanish, the suggested model received F1 scores of 0.488 and 0.696, respectively. In addition, [10] looked at char n-grams, word Term Frequency Inverse Document Frequency (TF-IDF) values, Bag of Words Vectors (BoWV) over Global Vectors for Word Representation (GloVe), and task-specific embeddings learnt using FastText, CNNs, and LSTMs. The authors obtained an F1-score improvement of 18% using the proposed models. Finally, [11] used the CNN model with word2vec embedding on the Twitter hate speech dataset and compared it to the baseline Logistic Regression with character n-gram. With an F1-score of 78.3%, the CNN model outperformed the Logistic Regression model with an F1-score of 73.9% in a 10-fold cross-validation test.

The above mentioned research provided intriguing techniques for hate speech detection. However, to the best of our knowledge, the integration of multiple channels of the CNN model to generate improved features from each channel for low-resourced language is not widely studied, notably the CNN model. As a result, the primary goal of this research is to investigate how shared features of the multi-channel CNN model on top of the word2vec word embedding layer perform in hate speech detection more efficiently than features generated from a single-channel CNN model on a limited dataset, as in the case of an under-resourced language like Amharic.

3 Dataset Construction

In this work, we build a new hate speech dataset from social media using Amharic language, Ethiopia's national language. We focused on Facebook, which is regarded by Ethiopian and Ethiopian origin diaspora bloggers, politicians, and academics as the most important platform for political and social conversation in Amharic, a phenomenon shared with other countries where Internet penetration is low and "Facebook" is the Internet for many users [23].

3.1   Data Selection and Annotation

Since there is no benchmark dataset for Amharic hate speech detection, we built our own using the Ethiopian Broadcasting Corporation (EBC) Facebook page[5] and some chosen individual Facebook pages[6] that publish hateful comments. We extracted selected comments/posts pertaining to race, religion, and ethnicity using the Facepager API, resulting in a set of 30,000 comments between April 15, 2019 and December 15, 2019. A total of 5,000 comments/posts (1,370 Hate and 3,630 Not-Hate) were chosen at random for annotation, while the remaining 25,000 were not. Three annotators (two candidate PhD. in Linguistics and one MSc. in Law) manually annotated the selected samples as "Hate" or "not-Hate" from which 2,000 (1,600 for training and 400 for testing) examples were chosen according to the label agreement. The average Cohen's Kappa agreement score[7] was 80%, indicating a good agreement. The Ethiopian government's hate speech and misinformation prevention and suppression proclamation[8], as well as our definition of hate speech and the hate speech characterization lists proposed in [24], were provided to the annotators. Accordingly, a speech is labeled as "Hate" when:

- "the speech targets a group or individual as a member of a group (ethnicity, race, religion)"
- "the speech content in the message expresses hatred"
- "the speech causes a harm"
- "the speaker intends harm or bad activity"
- "the speech incites bad actions"
- "the speech is either public and directed at a member of the group"
- "the context makes violent response possible" (Table 1).

Table 1. Sample data from the Amharic hate speech dataset on two classes

No.	Posts/Comments in Amharic	Posts/Comments in English	Label
1	ግም ነሽ ሰው አታቂም ጥንብ እሱ ስለሀገር እንጂ ስለዘር አላወራም ደደብ ነሽ	You are an idiot; he hasn't mentioned race.	Hate
2	ለሀገሩ ክብር ሲል አረፍትና እንቅልፍ ያጣውን መሪ ማድነቅ ብቻ ሳይሆን የአሱን ፈለግ በመከተል ልንደግፈው ይገባል	We must not only admire and respect the tireless and sleepless leader just for sake of his country's greatness, but also follow in his footsteps.	not-Hate
3	በኦሮሚያ በሚኖሩ ትግራዎች ላይ አርምጃ እንወስዳለን በገጀራ አንጋታቸውን እንቆርጣለን	In Oromia, we will take action against the Tigreans and kill them.	Hate

---

[5] https://www.facebook.com/EBCzena.

[6] https://www.facebook.com/604407519910492.

[7] https://www.statisticshowto.com/cohens-kappa-statistic/

[8] https://www.accessnow.org/cms/assets/uploads/2020/05/Hate-Speech-and-Disinformation-Prevention-and-Suppression-Proclamation.pdf.

3.2 Data Preprocessing

In this work, three typical data preprocessing procedures were completed: formatting, cleaning, and sampling. We created text and comma separated value (csv) files throughout the formatting process. We removed Amharic punctuation marks, URLs, unnecessary white spaces, and non-Amharic characters during the data cleaning process. In Amharic, a similar sound can be represented by many characters like Ge'ez, an ancient Ethiopian language. In Ge'ez, each form has its own meaning, but in Amharic there is no clear cut rule that indicates its purpose and usage [35]. Hence, since there are different ways of writing the same Amharic word using different characters/Fidel/, we performed character normalization using a normalization tool[9]. The tool can make a single word out of a range of letters that are used to make multiple versions of the same word, which is crucial for dimension reduction. For instance, the Amharic word ዓለም (world) can have multiple writing styles such as ኣለም (world), ዐለም (world) that can be all converted to አለም (world). However, we did not use stop word removal for dimension reduction in this work. Because, we found that it carries significant meaning in hate speech detection. For example, "ትግሬ ገዳይ ነው" ("Tigrie is killer"). The stop word ነው (is), plays a significant role in labeling the statement as hate speech. We can capture this concept using CNN with n-gram models (3-g).

3.3 Feature Engineering Methods

This step involves extracting key features from the raw text and numerically expressing the retrieved features. We used two distinct feature engineering approaches in this study: n-grams and automated feature learning using word2vec models.

N-gram Based Feature Selection. We utilized the n-gram model as features, feeding the TFIDF (term frequency-inverse document frequency) values to the SVM machine learning model. The occurrence of a word is predicted using an n-gram model based on the occurrence of its $n-1$ preceding word. In this experiment, we put the unigram ($n = 1$) language model to the test as a feature for the SVM classifier.

Word2vec Feature Learning. Given the large amount of textual data accessible, classification models in most resourceful languages (e.g., English) benefit from automated feature learning approaches such as word2vec models. To take advantage of such models, we utilize the continuous-bag-of-words (CBOW) word2vec [25] word embedding model to generate features for our hate speech detection task.

4 Classification Models

4.1 Support Vector Machine (SVM)

This is a training algorithm that optimizes the distance between training patterns and the decision boundary [26]. This is a well-known machine learning approach for

---

[9] https://abe2g.github.io/am-preprocess.html.

classification, regression, and other learning tasks [27]. The Support vector classification (SVC) kernel in LIBSVM [28] is a technique for two-class and multi-class classification. As a baseline, we utilized SVM with linear classifier and TF-IDF features in the experiment.

4.2   Convolutional Neural Network (CNN)

CNN models, which were originally developed for computer vision, have now been proved to be useful for NLP and have produced great results [29]. CNN is intended to learn features automatically and adaptively. CNN is comprised of three main building levels. These are convolution, pooling, and fully connected layers. While the first two, convolution and pooling, extract features, the third, fully connected maps the extracted features into final output such as classification [30, 31].

The model shown in Fig. 2 is a slight variant of the CNN architecture of [30] shown in Fig. 1. Let $x_i \in \mathbb{R}^k$ be the k-dimensional word vector corresponding to the ith word in a sentence. A sentence of length n padded where necessary is presented as:

$$x_1 = x_1 \oplus x_2 \oplus \ldots \oplus x_n. \tag{1}$$

Where $\oplus$ is the concatenation operator, and the convolutional operational consists of a filter $w \in \mathbb{R}^{hk}$, which is applied to a window of h words to produce a new feature. For instance, feature c_i is generated from a window of words $x_{i:i+h-1}$ by:

$$c_i = f(w \cdot x_{i:i+h-1} + b) \tag{2}$$

Where $b \in \mathbb{R}$ a bias is a term and f is a nonlinear function (e.g. rectifier or tanh). This is done for every time step of the input sequence $c\{x_{i:h}, x_{2:h+1}, \ldots, x_{n-h+1:n}\}$ to produce a feature map of:

$$c_i = [c_1, c_2, \ldots, c_{n-h+1}] \tag{3}$$

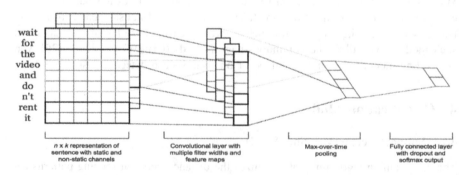

Fig. 1. CNN Architecture for natural language processing taken from [30].

5   Architecture of the Multi-channel CNN Model for Hate Speech Detection

We proposed a multi-channel CNN model for Amharic hate speech detection hoping that the multi-channel architecture would learn better features than the single-channel CNN model as shown in Fig. 2, especially for smaller datasets. The model involves using multiple versions of the standard model [30] with different sized kernels on the dataset. This allows the dataset to be processed at different widths of n-grams (groups of words) at a time, whilst the model learns how to best integrate these interpretations. After several experiments of n-grams (2, 3, 4, 5, 6, 7, 8) with multi-channels (2, 3, 4, 5, 6, 7, 8) we found better results with 4-g and 5-g with two channels. Hence, based on this experimental finding, we defined a multiple input model with two input channels for processing 4-g and 5-g. Each channel is comprised of the following elements:

– Input layer that defines the length of input sequences (Embedding layer set to the size of the vocabulary and 100 dimensional real valued representations).
– One-dimensional convolutional layer with 32 filters and a kernel size set to the number of words to read at once (4-g in one channel, and 5-g in different channel).
– Max-pooling layer to consolidate the output from the convolutional layer.
– Flatten layer to reduce the three dimensional output to two dimensional for concatenation.
– The output from the two channels are concatenated into a single vector and processed by a dense layer and an output layer.

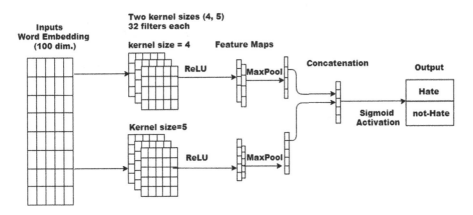

Fig. 2. Architecture of the proposed multi-channel CNN model for hate speech detection.

5.1   Major Component of the Amharic Hate Speech Detection Framework

The following key components make up the overall framework of the Amharic hate speech detection model, as illustrated in Fig. 3.

Data Source: It enable social media users post comments in Amharic, which is the source of data.

Facepager API: It helps collect comments posted by users on Facebook pages.

Preprocessing: It is to prepare textual data prior to training in order to get better classification results.

Word2vec/Input: It produces vector of words in the high dimensional space.

MC-CNN Model: It involves using multiple versions of the standard model with different sized kernels on the dataset as shown in Fig. 2.

Maxpool: It builds the embedding of a whole sentence from word representations. It takes the maximum value for each dimension of the word representations and builds a fixed-length vector by taking the maximum value for each dimension of the word representations. This yields a sentence representation in the same high-dimensional space as the word embedding.

Hate/Not-Hate: It is a differentiable classifier, which inputs the previously constructed sentence representation and outputs the final prediction, which is used to calculate the loss according to the ground truth, and to train the model.

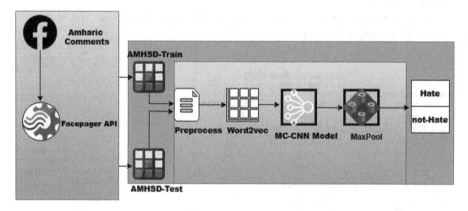

Fig. 3. The general framework of the Amharic hate speech detection (AMHSD) model.

6 Experiments

We did a series of experiments to test the proposed model for Amharic hate speech detection task (SVM, SC-CNN-1, SC-CNN-2, and MC-CNN). In all of these experiments, we used a binary classification task to classify social media comments as Hate speech or not-Hate speech. This section presents the description of the dataset utilized in the experiments, the experimental setups, baseline, and evaluation metrics.

6.1 Datasets

To train the proposed models for Amharic hate speech detection, we utilized the dataset mentioned earlier. The dataset includes 2,000 social media comments labeled as Hate or Not-Hate speech. We partitioned the data in an 80–20 ratio. That is, 1,600 (80%) of the data is used to train classification models to learn classification rules, while 400 (20%) is utilized to test the accuracy of classification models on new datasets.

6.2 Experimental Setups

We built the CNN models utilizing the Keras[10] framework and a TensorFlow[11] backend. The experiments are carried out on Google colab[12], which offers a free Jupiter note-book environment with GPU accelerator. For the CNN classifiers, we used word2vec features. The classifiers' particular settings are as follows:

Single-Channel-CNN-1 (SC-CNN-1): We built the SC-CNN-1 model using an embedding layer and one conv layer. The kernel has a size of 4 and the conv layer contains 32 filters. ReLu (Rectified Linear Unit) is the activation of the conv layer. The output layer is Dense 2 with sigmoid activation function, corresponding to two classes.

Single-Channel-CNN-2 (SC-CNN-2): The second SC-CNN-2 model is built with one embedding layer and one conv layer. The conv layer now contains 32 filters, and kernel size increased to 5 to accommodate more n-gram words. The activation of the conv layer is ReLu. Dense 2 with sigmoid activation function is the output layer, corresponds to two classes.

Multi-channel-CNN (MC-CNN): The MC-CNN model is built with an embedding layer and two conv layers. Each conv layer contains 32 filters, and the kernel sizes are 4 and 5 concatenated. The activation of the conv layer is Relu. Dense 2 with sigmoid activation function is the output layer, which corresponds to two classes.

6.3 Baseline

As a baseline, we used the Support Vector Machine (SVM) classifier, since it demonstrated effective classification performance in previous studies [32] employing keyword-based TFIDF feature engineering techniques. To build the classification model, we used Python's scikitlearn[13] library.

6.4 Model Evaluations

In this subsection, we have presented the assessment of the constructed classifiers to predict the classes of the unlabeled datasets as "Hate" or "not-Hate" speech using the

---

[10] https://keras.io/.

[11] https://www.tensorflow.org/.

[12] https://colab.research.google.com/notebooks/intro.ipynb.

[13] https://scikit-learn.org/stable/.

test dataset. The number of true positives (TP), true negatives (TN), false positives (FP), and false negatives (FN) generated by the classifiers are used to evaluate the performances of the models.

- True Positives (TP) are the number of correctly predicted Hate comments;
- True Negatives (TN) are the number of correctly predicted not-Hate comments;
- False Positives (FP) are the number of incorrectly predicted Hate comments;
- False Negatives (FN) are the number of incorrectly predicted not-Hate comments;

Furthermore, three performance metrics have been used to evaluate the classifiers: recall, precision, and F-measures [33].

Recall: is the proportion of actual positives which are predicted positive.

$$Recall = \frac{TP}{TP + FN} \tag{4}$$

Precision: is positive predicted value. It is the proportion of predicted positives which are actually positive.

$$Precision = \frac{TP}{TP + FP} \tag{5}$$

F-measure: It is the harmonic mean of precision and recall.

$$F - measure = 2 \cdot \frac{Recall \cdot Precision}{Recall + Precision} \tag{6}$$

7   Results and Discussions

7.1   Results

In this section we present the experimental results. Table 2 shows the confusion matrix of all the models (SVM, SC-CNN-1, SC-CNN-2, and MC-CNN). As shown here, out of 200 actual Hate classes, SVM correctly classified 195 comments, SC-CNN-1 correctly classified 142 comments, SC-CNN-2 correctly classified 126 comments, and MC-CNN correctly classified 149 comments. However, SVM incorrectly classified 5 comments, SC-CNN-1 incorrectly classified58 comments, SC-CNN-2 incorrectly classified 74 comments and MC-CNN incorrectly classified 51 comments to the not-Hate class. On the other hand, in detecting the not-Hate class, the performance of the models were as follows. Out of 200 actual not-Hate test datasets, SVM correctly classified 175 comments, SC-CNN-1 correctly classified 186 comments, SC-CNN-2 correctly classified 183 comments, and MC-CNN correctly classified 177 comments. However, SVM incorrectly classified 25 comments, SC-CNN-1 incorrectly classified 14 comments, SC-CNN-2 incorrectly classified 17 comments, and MC-CNN incorrectly classified 23 comments.

Table 2. Confusion matrix of the four models.

	Predicted hate				Predicted not-hate			
	SVM	SC-CNN-1	SC-CNN-2	MC-CNN	SVM	SC-CNN-1	SC-CNN-2	MC-CNN
Actual hate	195	142	126	149	5	58	74	51
Actual not-hate	25	14	17	23	175	186	183	177
Total	220	156	143	172	180	244	257	228

Furthermore, the results of the comparative analysis of SVM, SC-CNN-1, SC-CNN-2, and MC-CNN using precision, recall and F1-score is shown in Table 3. The F1-score is used to evaluate the model performance. In Table 3, SVM and MC-CNN outperformed better than the other models in detecting the hate class. SVM has an F1-score of 92.8%, whereas MC-CNN has an F1-score of 80.2%. The SC-CNN-1 achieved an F1-score of 78.3%, whereas the SC-CNN-2 achieved an F1-score of 74.9%. Similarly, SVM and MC-CNN performed much better than other models in recognizing the not-Hate class, with F1-score detection accuracy of 92.1% and 82.7% respectively. Whereas the SC-CNN-1 performed with an F1-score of 80.0%, the SC-CNN-2 performed with an F1-score of 81.5%. As a result, when the four models were compared, the SVM outperformed than the other convolutional neural network models. When the performance of the convolutional neural network learning models were compared independently, the multi-channel CNN model outperformed than the other two single-channel CNN models.

Table 3. Evaluation of the four models.

Models	Hate			Not hate		
	P	R	F1	P	R	F1
SC-CNN-1	69.5	89.6	78.3	91.5	71.2	80.0
SC-CNN-2	63.5	91.4	74.9	94.0	72.0	81.5
MC-CNN	86.6	74.5	80.2	88.5	77.6	82.7
SVM	88.6	97.5	92.8	97.2	87.5	92.1

7.2 Discussions

In the last row of Table 3, for example, in determining the hate class, the SVM model has a precision of 88.6%, a recall of 97.5%, and an F1-score of 92.8%. These numbers provide important information about the model's classification accuracy when compared to the human annotator. The precision tells us the proportion of properly predicted hate speech comments (True positives) to the total number of predicted hate speech comments (True positives plus False positives). For example, a precision of 88.6% implies that the model can predict that 88.6% of all comments classified as hate speech by a human annotator are indeed hate speech comments. Normally, a high precision number suggests a low rate of false positives. A recall, on the other hand, shows us the proportion of properly predicted hate speech comments to the total number of comments in the actual hate speech class. For example, a recall of 97.5% from the SVM classifier indicates that out of the total number of real hate speech comments (200), the SVM model accurately predicts 97.5% of the hate speech classes. The F1-score, on the other hand, uses the average weights of accuracy and recall to generate a single score.

The experiments proved that the SVM classifier employing n-gram feature engineering techniques and TFIDF value outperformed than the CNN models. Nonetheless, when comparing single-channel CNN models to multi-channel CNN model, the multi-channel CNN model outperformed than the singlechannel CNN models. The theoretical analysis revealed that when comparing the four models, SVM outperformed than the other models in detecting both the Hate and not-Hate classes. Our initial assumption was that deep learning models in a multi-channel environment might surpass traditional techniques. However, this did not work effectively, as SVM with fewer datasets still outperformed the deep learning models. This is due to the fact that SVM is successful at classifying relatively small datasets with low training complexity. When the CNN versions SC-CNN-1, SC-CNN-2, and MC-CNN are compared independently, the MC-CNN outperformed the other single-channel CNN models. This can be due to the influence of shared features created by the mode's multiple channels with varied hyperparameter values. As a result, the proposed MC-CNN model can be viewed as a preferable alternative solution for hate speech detection in a deep learning settings where dataset scarcity is a concern as in the case of the Amharic language.

8   Conclusions and Future Works

In this study, we have presented an effective technique to classify Facebook comments written in the Amharic language as "Hate" or "not-Hate" speech by taking the advantages of the power of deep learning approaches. We have proposed a multi-channel CNN model based on the original CNN model for text classification on-top-of word2vec word embedding. The experiments were carried out using the Amharic hate speech detection dataset. The results of the experiments show the effectiveness of the proposed MC-CNN model compared to the SC-CNN model in a limited dataset. To the best of our knowledge, there is no prior work that used multi-channel features to detect hate speech for the Amharic language. Thus, this work is one additional contribution to the research undertaken for such under-resourced language. To apply the model for other languages, tuning the MC-CNN hyperparameters is fundamental. For the Amharic language, for instance, the model performs well at the 4-g and 5-g of words at two channels (other hyper-parameter settings being equal).

Though the experimental results are promising for a two-class hate speech detection and a monolingual small dataset scenario, further works can be done in the space of improving the model performance by properly considering the potential effect of relatively large datasets, multilingual datasets, and multiple hate speech classes such as hate speech in religion, ethnicity, gender, etc. Hence, a code-mixed dataset both from the resource-rich languages and under-resourced ethnic-based local languages can be tested to alleviate the fundamental problem of hate speech dataset scarcity and improve model performance. Finally, since we were not aware of the availability of a publicly hate speech dataset [35] at the time we didn't test our model on this dataset. Therefore, we will test the developed model on this particular Amharic hate speech dataset and a more standardized English hate speech dataset to test the generalization ability of the model in the next version of our work.

References

1. Plaza-del-Arco, F.M., Molina-González, M.D., Ureña-López, L.A., MartínValdivia, M.T.: Comparing pre-trained language models for Spanish hate speech detection. Exp. Syst. Appl. **166**, 114120 (2021)
2. Alshalan, R., Al-Khalifa, H., Alsaeed, D., Al-Baity, H., Alshalan, S.: Detection of hate speech in COVID-19-related tweets in the Arab region: deep learning and topic modeling approach. J. Med. Internet Res. **22**, e22609256 (2020). https://doi.org/10.2196/22609
3. Rawlence, B.: High stakes: political violence and the 2013 elections in Kenya. United States of America (2013)
4. Mossie, Z., Wang, J.H.: Vulnerable community identification using hate speech detection on social media. Inf. Process. Manage. **57**, 102087 (2020). https://doi.org/10.1016/j.ipm.2019.102087
5. Gagliardone, I., Pohjonen, M., et al.: Mechachal: online debates and elections in Ethiopia-from hate speech to engagement in social media. University of Oxford (2016)
6. Yimam, S.M., Ayele, A.A., Biemann, C.: Analysis of the Ethiopic Twitter dataset for abusive speech in Amharic. arXiv:1912.04419 (2019)
7. Elouali, A., Elberrichi, Z., Elouali, N.: Hate speech detection on multilingual twitter using convolutional neural networks. Rev. d'Intelligence. Artif. **34**, 81–88 (2020)
8. Ribeiro, A., Silva, N.: Convolutional Neural Networks for hate speech detection against women and immigrants on Twitter. Presented at the INF-HatEval at SemEval-2019 Task 5 (2019). https://doi.org/10.18653/v1/s19-2074
9. Badjatiya, P., Gupta, S., Gupta, M., Varma, V.: Deep learning for hate speech detection in tweets. In: 26th International World Wide Web Conference, pp. 759–760 (2017). https://doi.org/10.1145/3041021.3054223
10. Gambäck, B., Sikdar, U.K.: Using convolutional neural networks to classify hate-speech. In: Proceedings of the 1st Workshop on Abusive Language Online, pp. 85–90 (2017). https://doi.org/10.18653/v1/w17-3013
11. Al-Hassan, A., Al-Dossari, H.: Detection of hate speech in social networks: a survey on multilingual corpus. J. Comput. Sci. Inf. Technol. **9**, 83–100 (2019). https://doi.org/10.5121/csit.2019.90208
12. William, M.C.: Hate speech | Britannica. https://www.britannica.com/topic/hate-speech. Accessed 26 Feb 2021
13. Nobata, C., Tetreault, J., Thomas, A., Mehdad, Y., Chang, Y.: Abusive language detection in online user content. In: 25th International World Wide Web Conference, pp. 145–153 (2016). https://doi.org/10.1145/2872427.2883062
14. Pereira-Kohatsu, J.C., Quijano-Sánchez, L., Liberatore, F., Camacho-Collados, M.: Detecting and monitoring hate speech in twitter. Sensors (Switzerland) **19**, 4654 (2019). https://doi.org/10.3390/s19214654
15. Gaydhani, A., Doma, V., Kendre, S., Bhagwat, L.: Detecting hate speech and offensive language on twitter using machine learning: an N-gram and TFIDF based approach. CoRR abs/1809.0 (2018)
16. Waseem, Z., Hovy, D.: Hateful symbols or hateful people? Predictive features for hate speech detection on Twitter. In: Proceedings of the 2016 Conference of the North American Chapter of the Association for Computational Linguistics: Human Language Technologies, San Diego California, USA, pp. 88–93 (2016). https://doi.org/10.18653/v1/n16-2013

17. Djuric, N., Zhou, J., Morris, R., Grbovic, M., Radosavljevic, V., Bhamidipati, N.: Hate speech detection with comment embeddings. In: Proceedings of the 24th International Conference on World Wide Web, WWW 2015 Companion, pp. 29–30 (2015). https://doi.org/10.1145/2740908.2742760

18. Chen, Y., Zhou, Y., Zhu, S., Xu, H.: Detecting offensive language in social media to protect adolescent online safety. In: Proceedings of the 2012 ASE/IEEE International Conference on Privacy, Security, Risk and Trust and 2012 ASE/IEEE International Conference on Social Computing, SocialCom/PASSAT 2012, pp. 71–80 (2012). https://doi.org/10.1109/SocialCom-PASSAT.2012.55

19. Haralambous, Y., Lenca, P.: Text classification using association rules, dependency pruning and hyperonymization. In: CEUR Workshop Proceedings, vol. 1202, pp. 65–80 (2014). https://doi.org/10.6084/m9.figshare.1189289.v1

20. Warner, W., Hirschberg, J.: Detecting hate speech on the world wide web. In: Proceedings of the 2nd Workshop on Language in Social Media, LSM 2012, pp. 19–26 (2012)

21. Davidson, T., Warmsley, D., Macy, M., Weber, I.: Automated hate speech detection and the problem of offensive language. In: Proceedings of the 11th International AAAI Conference on Web and Social Media, ICWSM 2017, pp. 512–515 (2017)

22. Fortuna, P., Bonavita, I., Nunes, S.: Merging datasets for hate speech classification in Italian. In: CEUR Workshop Proceedings, pp. 218–223 (2018). https://doi.org/10.4000/books.aaccademia.4752

23. Gagliardone, I., et al.: Mechachal: Online Debates and Elections in Ethiopia - From Hate Speech to Engagement in Social Media, 1 May 2016. https://doi.org/10.2139/ssrn.2831369

24. Fino, A.: Defining hate speech. J. Int. Crim. Justice 18, 31–57 (2020). https://doi.org/10.1093/jicj/mqaa023

25. Mikolov, T., Le, Q. V., Sutskever, I.: Exploiting similarities among languages for machine translation. arXiv:abs/1309.4 (2013)

26. Boser, B.E., Guyon, I.M., Vapnik, V.N.: Training algorithm for optimal margin classifiers. In: Proceedings of the 5th Annual ACM Workshop on Computational Learning Theory, pp. 144–152 (1992). https://doi.org/10.1145/130385.130401

27. Cortes, C., Vapnik, V.: Support vector networks. Mach. Learn. 20, 273–297 (1995)

28. Chang, C.C., Lin, C.J.: LIBSVM: a library for support vector machines. ACM Trans. Intell. Syst. Technol. 2, 1–27 (2011). https://doi.org/10.1145/1961189.1961199

29. Collobert, R., Weston, J., Bottou, L., Karlen, M., Kavukcuoglu, K., Kuksa, P.: Natural language processing (almost) from scratch. J. Mach. Learn. Res. 12, 2493–2537 (2011)

30. Kim, Y.: Convolutional neural networks for sentence classification. In: Proceedings of Empirical Methods in Natural Language Processing, pp. 1746–1751 (2014). https://doi.org/10.3115/v1/d14-1181

31. Georgakopoulos, S.V., Tasoulis, S.K., Vrahatis, A.G., Plagianakos, V.P.: Convolutional neural networks for toxic comment classification. In: ACM International Conference Proceeding Series 2018, pp. 1–6 (2018). https://doi.org/10.1145/3200947.3208069

32. Kamble, S., Joshi, A.: Hate speech detection from code-mixed Hindi-English tweets using deep learning models (2018)

33. Seliya, N., Khoshgoftaar, T.M., Van Hulse, J.: A study on the relationships of classifier performance metrics. In: Proceedings of the International Conference on Tools with Artificial Intelligence, ICTAI, pp. 59–66 (2009). https://doi.org/10.1109/ICTAI.2009.25

34. Getachew, S.: Amharic Facebook dataset for hate speech detection. https://doi.org/10.17632/ymtmxx385m.1

35. Bender, M.L., Bowen, J.D., Cooper, R.L., Ferguson, C.A.: Language in Ethiopia. Oxford University Press, London (1976)

Automatic Diagnosis of Breast Cancer from Histopathological Images Using Deep Learning Technique

Elbetel Taye Zewde and Gizeaddis Lamesgin Simegn[(✉)] [iD]

Biomedical Imaging Chair, School of Biomedical Engineering,
Jimma Institute of Technology, Jimma University, Jimma, Ethiopia
gizeaddis.lamesgin@ju.edu.et

Abstract. Breast cancer is the primary cause of women cancer death globally. Advancement in screening methods and early diagnosis can increase survival from breast cancer. Clinical breast examination, imaging, and pathological assessment are common techniques of a breast cancer screening. Biopsy test is the standard breast cancer screening method due to its ability to identify types and sub-types of cancer. However, current diagnosis using this method is generally made by visual inspection. The manual technique is time taking, dreary, and subjective, that can also lead to misdiagnosis. The current article proposes an automatic diagnosis system for breast cancer based on the deep learning neural network model. The model was trained and validated on histopathological images obtained from online data sets and local data obtained from Jimma University Medical Center using a digital camera mounted on a microscope. All images were pre-processed and enhanced before being fed into the previously trained ResNet 50 model. The developed technique is able to classify breast cancer into benign and malignant and to their subtypes. The results of our test showed that the proposed technique is 96.75%, 96.7% and 95.78% for the benign subtype and the malignant subtype classification, respectively. The developed technique has a potential to be used as a computer aided diagnosis system for clinicians, particularly in low resources setting, where both resources and experience are limited.

Keywords: Breast cancer · Cancer sub-type · Classification · Grading · ResNet · Transfer learning

1 Introduction

Breast cancer is the number one and most common cause of cancer in women, and it is still the main concern globally [1, 2]. It is an out-of-control growth of cells in breast. It includes both the benign and malignant cancer types. The benign cancer type includes Adenosis, fibro adenoma, phyllodes tumor and tubular adenoma tumor and the malignant cancer types incudes invasive ductal carcinoma, invasive lobular carcinoma, mucinous and papillary [3].

Clinical examination, imaging and pathological test are the methods that are usually used to identify breast cancer type and sub-types [4]. The histopathology is the gold standard for identifying breast cancer type and sub-types [5].

© ICST Institute for Computer Sciences, Social Informatics and Telecommunications Engineering 2022
Published by Springer Nature Switzerland AG 2022. All Rights Reserved
M. L. Berihun (Ed.): ICAST 2021, LNICST 411, pp. 619–634, 2022.
https://doi.org/10.1007/978-3-030-93709-6_42

Because histopathological analysis through biopsy test is done usually through visual inspection, the result is dependent on physician's expertise level and performance. Therefore, breast cancer multi-classification using biopsy test is a complex and the accuracy is dependent on the observer's knowledge and experience. Also, due to the lack of trained pathologists in many of low-income countries, a single pathology expert examines various types of biopsy specimens with different types of cases on a daily basis. The diversity and quantity of microscopic image analyzed by the expert and the intricacy of the histopathological images can lead to wrong diagnosis of the breast cancer. A misdiagnosis can be either an over or under-interpretation. Over-interpretation means that a woman free from cancer could face with potentially harmful treatments and needless expenses. Conversely, under-inaccurate interpretation of the biopsy result could prevent a woman from receiving treatment early, which can lead to the cancer growing in more invasive stages. Furthermore, the decision on the best therapeutic strategy for breast cancer is based on an advanced multi-class classification of cancer type. Precise identification of breast cancer subclasses could help control tumor cell metastasis at an early stage with therapeutic techniques.

Computer aided diagnosis (CAD) techniques has a potential to advance the breast screening method. Intelligent techniques have a potential to boost the screening accuracy of breast cancer, reduce misdiagnosis and decrease the work-load of pathologists [6–8]. However, developing efficient microscopic image analysis, and smart feature-extraction method is a complex task for computer-assisted screening of breast cancer [9].

2 Related Works

Artificial intelligence methods have the potential to enhance image processing and feature extraction techniques by detecting and extracting patterns in the image automatically. Deep learning techniques have been proposed in the literature for classification of breast cancer types from microscopic images [9–13]. To classify the breast tissue microscopic images into normal, benign, or malignant, a convolutional neural network (CNN) based deep patch level voting model and fusion model were proposed and reported to have an accuracy of 87.5% [10]. Similarly, the Deep CNN and Gradient Boosted Tree method have used to classify breast cancer types and an accuracy of 93.8 ± 2.3% and 87.2 ± 2.6% were reported [14]. Support vector machine (SVM) as a classifier and CNN as a feature-extractor were also proposed by Araújo et al. [15] and were implemented for retrieving information from images at various scales, including nuclei and total tissue organization, accuracy of 77.8% for all four classes and 83.3% for carcinoma (in situ and invasive) or non-carcinoma (healthy and benign) were claimed. Inceptionv3 CNN has also been fine-tuned and refined for patch classification and a majority vote was taken into account for the entire slide classification, resulting an accuracy of 85% for all four classes and 93% for non-cancerous type [16]. These studies achieved better precision in classifying breast cancer into 4 main sub-classes. However, precise classification of breast cancer into clinically relevant sub-types is also of particular importance for treatment decisions [17] and the need to classify histological images of breast tissue into more breast cancer subclasses has led many investigators to do more study with machine learning. With this regard, breast cancer classification into their sub-types has been proposed in many literatures [18–22]. However, in many cases, sporadic classes of breast cancers including mucinous-carcinoma were not considered. Moreover, other breast cancer areas, that are different from invasive cancers were wrongly detected as invasive breast cancer [22].

Hence, the techniques proposed in related works to classify breast cancer are either designed for single purpose or computationally expensive and magnification dependent. To determine the appropriate clinical course of treatment and surgical planning, it is essential to have an integrated system for classifying breast cancer using a deep learning technique. This will also help reduce the heavy workload of physicians and reduce errors in diagnosis.

This paper presents an integrated magnification-independent technique for breast cancer classification using a deep-learning technique.

3   Methods

3.1   Dataset

For model training, validation and testing. microscopic histopathological images were collected from Jimma University Medical Center (JUMC) and 'break-his' [23] and 'zenodo repository' [24] online datasets.

The images collected from JUMC were stained using H&E staining technique and were acquired using the Optika-vision camera attached with a simple light-microscope with four magnification powers (40X, 200X, and 400X) and resolution of 2592 × 1936.

Similarly, images collected from the break-his dataset were captured using different magnification factors (40X, 100X, 200X, and 400X) and Nikon digital camera attached to a microscope. The image frames collected were selected from regions aggrieved by tumor growth.

3.2   Image Pre-processing and Enhancement

In the pre-processing stage, image re-sizing and data augmentation were applied to all images. All images were adjusted to 224 × 224 size. To increase the training dataset, all images were also rotated by 90°, 180° and 270°.

For images enhancement contrast limited adaptive histogram equalization (CLAHE) technique was selected and applied to collected data for each RGB channels, separately. RGB to YCbCr color space conversion were also applied to all images to preserve detail information of luminance component [25].

Another enhancement technique applied in this study is histogram matching. Histogram helps reduce color variance in biopsy samples that occur because of variations in scanning conditions and staining protocol. For sample true-color RGB images, each color-channel of the histopathological image was separately matched to the corresponding color-channel of a selected template image. According to the staining protocol, the template image selected was the image where the cytoplasm is presented as pinkish and nuclei are presented as blue.

Data were split after pre-processing stage and images were divided into 80%, 10%, and 10% for training, validation and test, respectively.

3.3 Classification

The accuracy of the classification depends mainly on the properties of the data, difficulty of the problem to be analyzed, and the robustness of the classification algorithm. Accuracy, precision, computation time and memory usage can used to evaluate the robustness of a classification algorithm. Training deep neural networks is challenging due to since the gradient is unstable. Since the gradient propagates back to previous layers through iterative multiplication, the gradient could become extremely small. Due to this, the performance degrades rapidly as a network depth increase [26, 27].

In this paper, ResNet 50 model, initially presented by He et.al (2015) [28] has been used due to its flexibility and efficiency [14, 29–31]. The ResNet50 model uses an identity-shortcut connection to avoid the vanishing gradient problem [28, 32]. Due to this feature, deep neural networks can be trained without gradient instability problem.

The pre-trained ResNet50 model has 3 parts and 4 stages. The parts include the convolutional base, pooling layer (the feature generator) and a classifier that is composed of the fully-connected layers. After an input data is fed to the network, it starts with executing the initial convolution and max-pooling using 7×7 and 3×3 kernel sizes, respectively. First stage of the network has three residual-blocks containing three layers each. 64, 64 and 128 kernel sizes are used for convolution operation in the three layers. In addition, identity-shortcut-connection is used to avoid the vanishing gradient problem by addition the original input to the output of a series of operations [32]. The bottleneck design [28, 33] is also included to increase the efficiency of the ResNet50 model. A 1×1, 3×3 and 1×1 layers are added concurrently in each of the residual function. The network has also Pooling layer at the end, trailed by a fully-connected layer with neurons same as input class numbers.

The model used for this paper was adapted and fine-tuned for BC multiclassification. The model was used as a feature extractor and both its architecture and weight value were adapted. The top layers were frozen, and some parameters including the learning rate, optimizer type, loss function and decay rate, which are used to optimize the model were adjusted. At the end, a soft-max classifier [34] is used to classify each image in their corresponding class. To increase the performance of the system, a set of hyper-parameters such as optimizer, learning rate and activation function were fine-tuned. ADAM [35] optimizer was selected due to its speed convergence and accuracy. A total of 50 number of epochs, with learning rate 0.01–0.001 and Rectified Liner Unit (ReLu) activation function [36] were also set to increase the accuracy of the system. For binary classification a binary cross-entropy loss function and for multi class classification a categorical cross-entropy was selected. The technique used in this paper is demonstrated in Fig. 1.

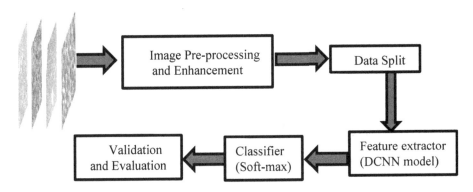

Fig. 1. Overall methodology used for BC classification

The proposed system first categorizes images into two classes: benign or malignant types. Then each of the binary classes are further classified into their sub-classes (benign: adenosis, fibro adenoma, phyllodes and tubular adenoma, Malignant: invasive ductal carcinoma, invasive lobular carcinoma, invasive mucinous carcinoma and papillary carcinoma).

3.4   Performance Evaluation Metrics

For performance evaluation precision, F1-score, recall or sensitivity, specificity and accuracy metrics were selected and calculated from confusion metrices (Eqs. 1–5). Proportions of actual negatives are identified mainly by F1-score and specificity. Accuracy was determined using true positive (TP), false positive (FP), false negative (FN), and true negative (TN) values.

$$\text{Precision} \ = \ \text{TP}/\left(\left(\text{TP}+\text{FP}\right)\right) \tag{1}$$

$$\text{Recall} \ = \ \text{TP}/\left(\left(\text{TP}+\text{FN}\right)\right) \tag{2}$$

$$\text{F1}-\text{Score} \ = \ \left(\left(2*\text{Precision}*\text{Recall}\right)\right)/\left(\left(\text{Precision}\ +\ \text{Recall}\right)\right) \tag{3}$$

$$\text{Specificity} \ = \ \text{TN}/\left(\left(\text{TN}+\text{FP}\right)\right) \tag{4}$$

$$\text{Accuracy} \ = \ \left(\left(\text{TP}+\text{TN}\right)\right)/\left(\left(\text{TP}+\text{TN}+\text{FN}+\text{FP}\right)\right) \tag{5}$$

4   Results

4.1   Image Pre-processing and Enhancement

After image resizing, data augmentation was applied using image transformation (rotation) technique to increase the training dataset. Figure 2 shows sample result of the data augmentation.

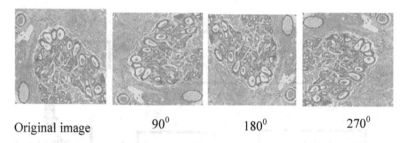

Original image 90^0 180^0 270^0

Fig. 2. Sample images augmented images by applying image transformation operation using 90°, 180° and 270° rotation, respectively

Figure 3 illustrates the original image and CLAHE applied image. The images contrast has been increased after CLAHE is applied. The histogram plots demonstrate an improved histogram distribution. The color differences of the histopathology images were adjusted by applying the histogram matching technique. Figure 4 shows sample result of the effect of histogram matching.

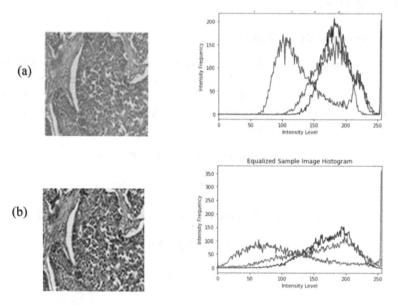

Fig. 3. Result of image enhancement using CLAHE. (a) Original image and its histogram (b) CLAHE applied image and its histogram (Left to Right)

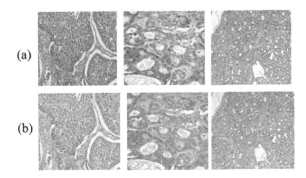

Fig. 4. Effect of histogram matching (a) Original image (b) Histogram matched image

4.2   Classification

Optimal result was achieved at the 37th epoch for the binary classification, yielding a validation loss of 0.1490, training accuracy of 98.58% and validation accuracy of 95.09%. Figure 5 shows the training and validation accuracy and loss plot on epoch versus accuracy and epoch versus loss graph for breast cancer type classification.

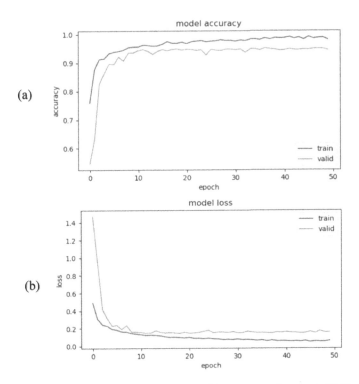

Fig. 5. (a) Training and validation accuracy curve with respect to the epoch (b) Training and validation loss curve with respect to the epoch for breast cancer type classification

Smallest validation loss of 0.1598 was obtained at the 27th epoch for benign sub-type classification resulting 99.14% training accuracy and 94.57% validation accuracy. This is demonstrated in Fig. 6. On the other hand, lowest validation loss of 0.1657 was achieved at the 49th epoch for malignant type classification resulting a 92.15% and 99.67% validation and training accuracy, respectively. Figure 7 shows the results obtained during the training phase for malignant sub-type classification.

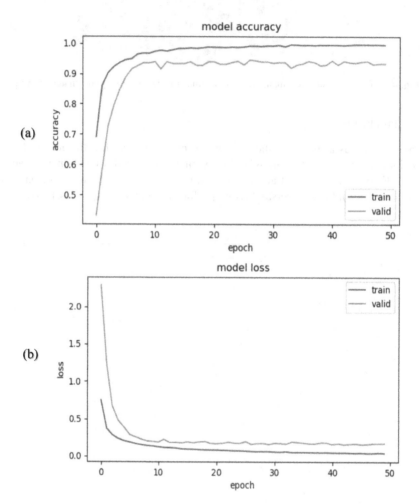

Fig. 6. (a) Training and validation accuracy curve with respect to the Epoch length. (b) Training and validation loss curve with respect to the epoch for benign type classification

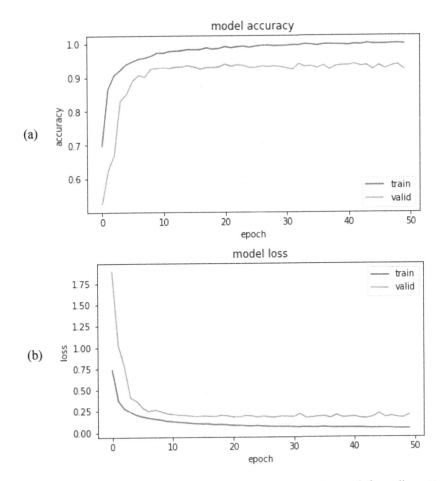

Fig. 7. (a) Training and validation accuracy curve with respect to the epoch for malignant type classification. (b) training and validation loss curve with respect to the epoch for malignant type classification

4.3 Test Results

A total of 708 test images were used for binary classification per class. Table 1 demonstrates the confusion matrix showing the test result of the binary classifier. Among all the malignant class images, a total of 687 images were correctly classified as malignant types, while the rest 21 images were predicted as benign. For the benign class, 683 images were correctly classified as benign tumors, and 25 of the images were wrongly classified in the malignant class.

Table 1. Test result of the binary classifier: malignant ('0') and benign ('1')

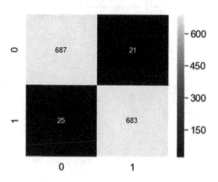

Accordingly, for the test result, an accuracy of 96.75%, precision of 96.755%, recall of 96.75% and specificity of 96.75% were achieved for the benign and malignant type classification as demonstrated in Fig. 8.

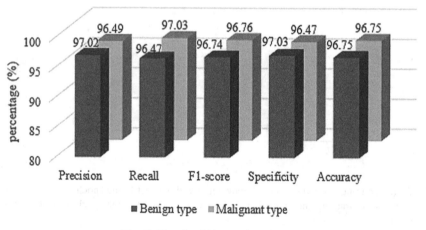

Fig. 8. Result of binary classification

For performance testing of the benign sub-type, 177 images were used per class. The confusion matrix for benign sub-type classification test result is demonstrated in Table 2.

Table 2. Test result of the benign classifier. The benign classes adenosis tumor, fibro adenoma, phyllodes and tubular are labeled as 0, 1, 2 and 3 respectively.

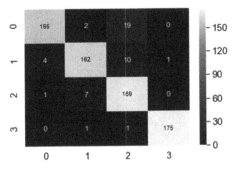

For the malignant sub-type classifier performance testing, a total of 177 images were used per class. The test results are demonstrated in Table 3.

Table 3. Test result of the malignant sub-type classifier with classes of ductal carcinoma, lobular carcinoma cancer, papillary carcinoma cancer and mucinous carcinoma cancer labeled as 0, 1, 2 and 3 respectively

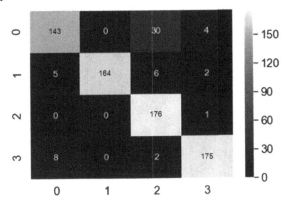

Figure 9 demonstrates the calculated performance metrics for binary, malignant and benign sub-type classifiers. An average accuracy of 96.7%, precision of 93.87%, recall/sensitivity of 93.51% and specificity of 97.8% were achieved for the benign classification. Whereas, an average test accuracy of 95.78%, average precision of 92.49%, an average recall/sensitivity of 91.85% and specificity of 97.17% were obtained for malignant sub-type classification. Figure 10 demonstrates the summary of the model's performance.

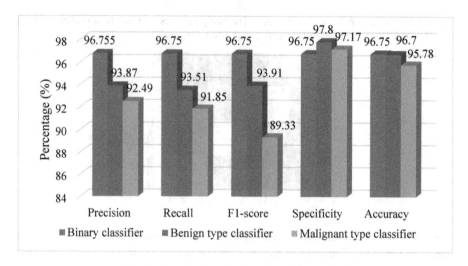

Fig. 9. Result of multi-class classifying model

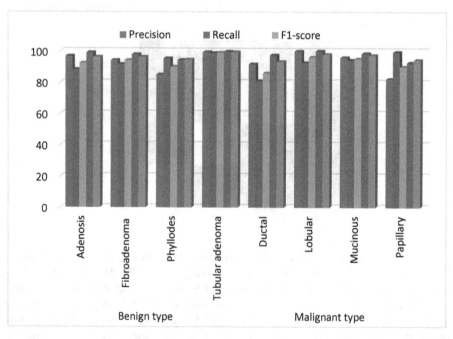

Fig. 10. Performance result summary of the proposed classification technique

5 Discussion

Among the triple assessment techniques, histopathology test is usually assumed as gold standard to identify breast cancer type and subtype prior to conducting a treatment [4]. The lack of trained pathologists and the manual diagnostic process prevent many breast cancer women in most developing countries from being diagnosed at an early stage. Furthermore, due to the subjectivity of the experts and complexity nature of the cancer cells, the manual diagnosis technique may lead to a misdiagnosis [37]. Computer diagnostic systems have a promising potential for early diagnosis of breast cancer by decreasing the rate of misdiagnosis.

This paper presents an automatic classification technique for breast cancer biopsy images using a deep learning technique. For deep model training, validation and testing, histopathological images were obtained from BreakHis online dataset and locally acquired from Jimma University Medical Center. All histopathological images were pre-processed by applying data augmentation, image resizing and normalization and enhancement using contrast limited adaptive histogram equalization and histogram matching techniques prior to model training.

Three ResNet50 model was trained, validated and finetuned. Good results were achieved after model fine-tuning with an ADAM optimizer, a 0.01–0.001 learning rate, 50 number of epochs, ReLu Activation function, 100 batch size, binary cross-entropy loss function (for the binary class classification) categorical cross-entropy (for multi-class classification).

The training evaluation of the model for 50 epochs is demonstrated in learning curves of Figs. 5, 6, 7. The training accuracy and training loss curves were used to observe the model performance and evaluate its classification accuracy. Better results were obtained during accuracy curve increment, loss curve decrement and large epoch size.

For sub-type classification, first a given image has to classified in to its type, either benign or malignant and then its sub-type will be identified. The model's performance for the first classification (binary) was tested using an unseen dataset and promising results were achieved as indicated in Fig. 9. Accordingly, 96.75%, 96.75%, 96.75%, 96.75% and 96.75% average accuracy, precision, Fl-score, recall/sensitivity, and specificity were achieved, respectively. On the other hand, an average accuracy, precision, recall/sensitivity and specify of 96.7%, 93.87%, 93.51% and 97.8% were achieved for the benign type classification. Similarly, for the malignant sub-type classification, an average test accuracy, precision rate, sensitivity/recall, and specificity of 95.78, 92.49%, 91.85% and 97.17% were obtained. The results of these tests show that the proposed method outperforms the recent related studies [21, 23].

In summary, comparing to the results found in related literatures with similar dataset [9, 16, 22, 23, 38], the developed system has a potential of classifying whole slide breast cancer histopathology images with promising classification accuracy. Moreover, the developed system has overcome the gap of further classification of histopathology images in to their sub-types.

6 Conclusion

A transfer learning method has been used to classify histopathological images of breast cancer into cancerous and non-cancerous and further classifies benign class into sub-types (Adenosis, fibro adenoma, phyllodes and tubular adenoma) and malignant in to ductal carcinoma, lobular carcinoma, mucinous carcinoma and papillary carcinoma sub-types. The Resnet50 model was used as a feature extractor and the extracted features were given to a soft-max classifier for classification. As a result, an average accuracy of 96.75%, 96.7%, and 95.78% were obtained for breast cancer type, benign sub-type and malignant sub-type classification, respectively. This developed system can be used as a decision support in the diagnosis of breast cancer and can help pathologists, especially in those resource limited settings.

Acknowledgement. Tools and materials required for this study was supported by the school of Biomedical Engineering, Jimma institute of Technology, Jimma University. We would like to appreciate Jimma University Medical Center (JUMC) for allowing us acquire the data. We would also like to appreciate Dr. Solomon and Dr. Tewodros (staffs of pathology department at JUMC) for their support.

References

1. Li, N., et al.: Global burden of breast cancer and attributable risk factors in 195 countries and territories, from 1990 to 2017: results from the global burden of disease study 2017. J. Hematol. Oncol. **12**(1), 140 (2019)
2. Fitzmaurice, C., et al.: Global, regional, and national cancer incidence, mortality, years of life lost, years lived with disability, and disability-adjusted life-years for 29 cancer groups, 1990 to 2016: a systematic analysis for the global burden of disease study. JAMA Oncol. **4**(11), 1553–1568 (2018)
3. Tsuda, H., et al.: Histological classification of breast tumors in the general rules for clinical and pathological recording of breast cancer (18th edition). Breast Cancer **27**(3), 309–321 (2020). https://doi.org/10.1007/s12282-020-01074-3
4. Zhang, Y.J., et al.: Status quo and development trend of breast biopsy technology. Gland Surg. **2**(1), 15–24 (2013)
5. Rubin, R., Strayer, D.S., Rubin, E.: Rubin's pathology: clinicopathologic foundations of medicine. Lippincott Williams & Wilkins, Philadelphia (2008)
6. Hadjiiski, L., Sahiner, B., Chan, H.P.: Advances in computer-aided diagnosis for breast cancer. Curr. Opin. Obstet. Gynecol. **18**(1), 64–70 (2006)
7. Jalalian, A., et al.: Foundation and methodologies in computer-aided diagnosis systems for breast cancer detection. EXCLI J. **16**, 113–137 (2017)
8. Kaushal, C., et al.: Recent trends in computer assisted diagnosis (CAD) system for breast cancer diagnosis using histopathological images. IRBM **40**(4), 211–227 (2019)
9. Xie, J., et al., Deep learning based analysis of histopathological images of breast cancer. Front. Genet. **10**(80) (2019). https://doi.org/10.3389/fgene.2019.00080
10. Guo Y., Dong H., Song F., Zhu C., Liu J.: Breast cancer histology image classification based on deep neural networks. In: Campilho, A., Karray, F., ter Haar Romeny, B. (eds.) Image Analysis and Recognition. ICIAR 2018. Lecture Notes in Computer Science, vol. 10882, pp. 827–836 Springer, Cham (2018) https://doi.org/10.1007/978-3-319-93000-8_94

11. Nahid, A.-A., Mehrabi, M.A., Kong, Y.: Histopathological breast cancer image classification by deep neural network techniques guided by local clustering. Biomed. Res. Int. **2018**, 2362108 (2018)

12. Nguyen, C.P., Vo, A.H., Nguyen, B.T.: Breast cancer histology image classification using deep learning. In: 2019 19th International Symposium on Communications and Information Technologies (ISCIT) (2019)

13. Zhu, C., et al.: Breast cancer histopathology image classification through assembling multiple compact CNNs. BMC Med. Inform. Decis. Mak. **19**(1), 198 (2019)

14. Rakhlin, A., Shvets, A., Iglovikov, V., Kalinin, A.A.: Deep convolutional neural networks for breast cancer histology image analysis. In: Campilho, A., Karray, F., ter Haar Romeny, B. (eds.) Image Analysis and Recognition. ICIAR 2018. Lecture Notes in Computer Science, vol. 10882, pp. 737–744. Springer, Cham (2018). https://doi.org/10.1007/978-3-319-93000-8_83

15. Araújo, T., et al., Classification of breast cancer histology images using convolutional neural networks. PLoS ONE **12**(6), e0177544 (2017)

16. Golatkar, A., Anand, D., Sethi, A.: Classification of breast cancer histology using deep learning. In: Campilho, A., Karray, F., ter Haar Romeny, B. (eds.) ICIAR 2018. LNCS, vol. 10882, pp. 837–844. Springer, Cham (2018). https://doi.org/10.1007/978-3-319-93000-8_95

17. Dai, X., et al.: Breast cancer intrinsic subtype classification, clinical use and future trends. Am. J. Cancer Res. **5**(10), 2929–2943 (2015)

18. Jiang, Y., et al.: Breast cancer histopathological image classification using convolutional neural networks with small SE-ResNet module. PLoS ONE **14**(3), e0214587–e0214587 (2019)

19. Jaber, M.I., et al.: A deep learning image-based intrinsic molecular subtype classifier of breast tumors reveals tumor heterogeneity that may affect survival. Breast Cancer Res. **22**(1), 12 (2020)

20. Jannesari, M., et al. Breast cancer histopathological image classification: a deep learning approach. In: 2018 IEEE International Conference on Bioinformatics and Biomedicine (BIBM) (2018)

21. Alom, M.Z., et al.: Breast cancer classification from histopathological images with inception recurrent residual convolutional neural network. J. Digit. Imaging **32**(4), 605–617 (2019)

22. Cruz-Roa, A., et al.: Accurate and reproducible invasive breast cancer detection in whole-slide images: a deep learning approach for quantifying tumor extent. Sci. Rep. **7**, 46450 (2017)

23. Spanhol, F.A., et al.: A dataset for breast cancer histopathological image classification. IEEE Trans. Biomed. Eng. **63**(7), 1455–1462 (2015)

24. Dimitropoulos, K., et al., Grading of invasive breast carcinoma through Grassmannian VLAD encoding. PLoS ONE **12**(9), e0185110 (2017)

25. Kang, B., Jeon, C., Han, D.K., Ko, H.: Adaptive height-modified histogram equalization and chroma correction in YCbCr color space for fast backlight image compensation. Image Vis. Comput. **29**(8), 557–568 (2011)

26. Szegedy, C., et al. Going deeper with convolutions. In: Proceedings of the IEEE Conference on Computer Vision and Pattern Recognition (2015)

27. Xie, S., et al. Aggregated residual transformations for deep neural networks. In: Proceedings of the IEEE Conference on Computer Vision and Pattern Recognition (2017)

28. He, K., et al.: Deep residual learning for image recognition. In: 2016 IEEE Conference on Computer Vision and Pattern Recognition (CVPR) (2016)

29. Szegedy, C., et al.: Inception-v4, inception-resnet and the impact of residual connections on learning. arXiv preprint arXiv:1602.07261 (2016)

30. Xiao, T., et al.: Comparison of transferred deep neural networks in ultrasonic breast masses discrimination. Biomed. Res. Int. **2018**, 4605191 (2018)
31. Motlagh, M.H., et al.: Breast Cancer Histopathological Image Classification: A Deep Learning Approach, bioRxiv (2018)
32. He, K., Zhang, X., Ren, S., Sun, J.: Identity mappings in deep residual networks. In: Leibe, B., Matas, J., Sebe, N., Welling, M. (eds.) ECCV 2016. LNCS, vol. 9908, pp. 630–645. Springer, Cham (2016). https://doi.org/10.1007/978-3-319-46493-0_38
33. De Rezende, E.R., et al.: Exposing computer generated images by using deep convolutional neural networks. Sig. Process. Image Commun. **66**, 113–126 (2018)
34. Goodfellow, I., et al.: Deep Learning. vol. 1, MIT Press, Cambridge (2016)
35. Kingma, D.P., Ba, J.: Adam: A method for stochastic optimization. arXiv preprint arXiv: 1412.6980 (2014)
36. Hinton, G.E.: Rectified linear units improve restricted Boltzmann machines vinod nair (2010)
37. Elmore, J.G., et al.: Evaluation of 12 strategies for obtaining second opinions to improve interpretation of breast histopathology: simulation study. BMJ **353**, i3069 (2016)
38. Han, Z., et al.: Breast cancer multi-classification from histopathological images with structured deep learning model. Sci. Rep. **7**(1), 4172 (2017)

Author Index

Abdu, Fetlewerk Kedir   I-532
Abeba, Getasew   I-435
Abebaw, Zeleke   I-603
Abebe, Abiy Tadesse   I-575
Abebe, Metafet Asmare   II-128
Abera, Gemechu Kassaye   I-33
Adem, Kamil Dino   II-443, II-480
Admassu, Bimrew Tamerat   II-492
Admassu, Bimrew Tamrat   II-425
Admasu, Bimrew Tamrat   II-506
Ageze, Mesfin Belayneh   II-565
Agizew, Henok Yared   I-446
Ahmed, Seid Endris   II-128
Alemayehu, Getaneh Firew   I-17
Alemneh, Esubalew   I-435
Ali, Addisu Negash   II-350
Ali, Addisu Negashe   II-339
Amare, Endale   I-17
Amogne, Abayneh Agumass   II-112
Andualem, Amogne   I-424
Andualem, Yenehun Gidyelem   I-73
Anguera, Jaume   I-331
Aredo, Shenko Chura   I-117
Asfaw, Esmael A.   II-195
Assefa, Beakal Gizachew   I-368
Assegie, Addisu Alemayehu   I-17
Atanew, Eshetie Berhan   II-277
Atlabachew, Mulugeta   I-132
Atnafu, Solomon   I-550, I-603
Aure, Temesgen Wondimu   II-15, II-160,
      II-195
Avvari, Muralidhar   II-326
Ayalew, Enchalew Y.   I-517
Ayalew, Hailu Dessalegn   I-173
Ayele, Delele Worku   II-543

Bacha, Ebise Getacho   I-44
Bakare, Fetene Fufa   II-377
Bantelay, Dessie Tarekegn   II-492
Bayeh, Menilk Sahlu   I-532
Bayu, Fitsum Getachew   II-262
Bedru, Tesfaye Kassaw   I-3
Bekele, Ephrem Teshale   I-318
Bekele, Getachew   II-522

Belachew, Aweke Mulu   II-365
Belay, Tewekel Mohammed   I-73
Belayneh, Getamesay   I-368
Belete, Mulugeta Dadi   II-175
Berhan, Eshetie   II-262
Beyene, Asrat Mulatu   I-446
Beyene, Million Mesheha   I-517, I-559
Beyene, Tinsae Tsega   I-73
Bicks, Ashenafi Tesfaye   II-391
Bihonegn, Bayu G.   II-27
Birlie, Melkamu   I-59
Bogale, Anteneh Tilaye   I-532
Borena, Tafesse G.   II-326

Casademont, Jordi   I-132
Chung, Yunkoo   I-532

Damtie, Menwagaw T.   II-68
Danbara, Teshale Tadesse   II-175
Debo, Feyisa   I-117
Dejen, Arebu   I-331
Delele, Mulugeta Ademasu   II-226
Delele, Mulugeta Admasu   I-73
Dessie, Habtamu Melaku   II-3
Devadas, Rajaveerappa   I-117

Ebinger, Frank   II-262
Ejigu, Yohannes Biadgligne   I-500
Enku, Temesgen   II-128
Enyew, Sewale Yasabu   II-350
Eshetie, Daniel G.   II-27
Eshetie, Sisay Mengistie   II-99

Fante, Kinde Anlay   I-304
Fikadu, Abreham   I-117
Forsido, Sirawdink Fikreyesus   I-17

G/Meskel, Tamiru G.   I-256
G/Meskel, Tamiru Getahun   I-215, I-237,
      I-256
G/michael, Dawit M.   I-256
Gabbiye, Nigus   I-87
Gebeyehu, Sisay Geremaw   II-277
Gebeyehu, Sisay Geremew   II-295

Gebremedhen, Hailu Shimels   II-243
Gebremichael, Hagos Tesfahun   I-559
Gebresenbet, Girma   II-492
Gelaw, Tariku Adane   I-401
Gemeda, Mulugeta Tegegn   I-304
Getnet, Aschale   II-233
Getnet, Lamesgin Addisu   II-425
Gizaw, Aregash Mamo   I-73
Goshu, Ayane Lebeta   I-304
Gualu, Alemayehu Golla   II-15, II-160,
   II-195

Habtie, Ayalew Belay   I-586
Habtu, Nigus Gabbiye   I-33, II-543
Hagos, Lemlem   I-550
Hagos, Misgina Tsighe   I-401
Haile, Beneyam B.   I-318
Haile, Dargie   I-87, I-106
Hailu, Sintayehu Alemnew   II-464
Hangarasa, Fikiru Temesgen   I-33
Hassen, Abdulkadir Aman   II-443

Jayasinghe, Jeevani   I-331
Jejaw, Atrsaw   II-233

Kassahun, Metadel   I-59
Kassew, Amare   II-554
Ketema, Abel Fantahun   II-49
Kolhe, Kishor Purushottam   II-295, II-326
Koricho, Ermias Gebrekidan   II-339
Kumar, P. G. V. Suresh   I-575

Lake, Melaku   I-412
Laxia, Tang   II-365
Lemessa, Addis   I-59

Malede, Yosef Birhanu   I-153
Meheretu, Getnet M.   II-554
Mekonnen, Hanna Teshager   I-489
Mekonnen, Tadelle Nigusu   I-73
Mekonnen, Tewodros Walle   II-391
Mengistu, Fikreselam Gared   I-153, I-559,
   I-586
Mengistu, Tesfahunegn Minwuyelet   I-559,
   I-586
Mengistu, Yared   I-59
Meretie, Gedefaye Achamu   II-277
Meselaw, Tewodrose D.   II-144
Meshesha, Beteley Tekola   I-3
Meshesha, Mengistie Abate   II-99

Meshesha, Million   I-550
Mihretie, Tesfaye Wondatir   II-413
Miliket, Temesgen Abriham   II-565
Minale, Temesgen Assefa   II-480
Mohapatra, Sudhir Kumar   I-368
Molla, Sissay Wondmagegn   I-73
Mulugeta, Nigusse   II-413

Nallamothu, Ramesh Babu   II-211
Nebey, Abraham H.   I-184
Nebiyu, Wallelign Mulugeta   II-49
Negash, Yalemzewd   I-117, I-132
Nigatu, Haile Melkamu   I-500
Nuramo, Denamo Addissie   II-3, II-49

Rafie, Nooria   I-382
Rauber, Andreas   I-603
Ridwan, Murad   I-331
Roose, Bart   II-554

Schmitter, Petra   II-27, II-68, II-144
Sefene, Eyob Messele   II-295
Semu, Tamirat   II-82
Senbeto, Kirubel Abebe   I-532
Shanka, Derara Senay   I-343
Shewarega, Fekadu   II-522
Shiferaw, Menberu Zeleke   II-243
Shiferaw, Samuel Demeke   II-160
Shiferaw, Yalemzewd Negash   I-575
Shih, Shao-Ju   II-377
Shimels, Hailu   II-554
Shumi, Lema Deme   I-44
Sileshi, Senay Teshome   II-443
Simegn, Gizeaddis Lamesgin   I-619
Sinta, Rahel S.   I-288
Sisay, Tesfaye B.   I-196
Stranks, Samuel D.   II-554

T/Himanot, Yakob Kiros   I-215
Tadesse, Habtamu A.   II-15
Takele, Dagnew Y.   II-27
Tasew, Ayele Getachew   II-175
Taye, Biniyam Z.   I-184
Teferi, Fetene Teshome   II-295, II-309, II-326
Teferi, Solomon Tesfamariam   II-391
Teferra, Solomon   I-550
Tegegne, Tesfa   I-412, I-424
Teklehaimanot, Tsigab Tekleab   I-44
Tennyson, Elizabeth M.   II-554
Tesfay, Abadi Hadush   II-377

Tesfaye, Daniel G.   I-269
Teshager, Minbale Adimas   I-17
Teshager, Minbale Admas   II-543
Tigabu, Muluken Temesgen   II-506, II-565
Tilahun, Seifu A.   II-27, II-68, II-144, II-554
Tola, Yetenayet B.   I-17
Tonja, Atnafu Lambebo   I-480
Tsegaw, Assefa Asmare   II-309, II-326
Tsegaye, Shewit   II-522

Van Vuure, Aart Willem   II-226
Vieu, Laure   I-517

Wang, Bang   I-382
Wase, Minyamer Gelawe   II-464
Woldeyohannis, Michael Melese   I-468,
    I-480, I-489
Wondie, Yihenew   I-117
Wondimu, Temesgen   II-82
Wood, D. H.   II-506
Workeye, Enderias Alemayehu   I-215

Workeye, Endrias Alemayehu   I-237
Workineh, Tewodros G.   I-184, I-196
Workineh, Zerihun Getahun   II-543
Worku, Ababay Ketema   II-543
Worku, Belay   II-82
Worku, Getachew Biru   II-464
Worku, Menbere Hailu   I-468
Wubetu, Getasew A.   II-554

Yetayew, Tefera Terefe   I-196, I-237, I-256,
    I-269, I-288
Yigezu, Mesay Gemeda   I-480
Yimer, Amare Kassaw   I-153

Zegeye, Amare Demelie   II-226
Zeleke, Marta   II-211
Zeleke, Seifu Girma   I-318
Zelelew, Tibebu Merde   II-339
Zewde, Elbetel Taye   I-619
Zimale, Fasikaw Atanaw   II-27, II-68, II-112,
    II-144

Printed in the United States
by Baker & Taylor Publisher Services